EXCAVATING Q

The History and Setting
of the Sayings Gospel

John S. Kloppenborg Verbin

FORTRESS PRESS
MINNEAPOLIS

EXCAVATING Q
The History and Setting of the Sayings Gospel

Cover photo: K. C. Hanson. Used by permission.
Interior photos: John S. Kloppenborg Verbin. Used by permission.

Library of Congress Cataloging-in-Publication Data

Kloppenborg, John S.
    Excavating Q : the history and setting of the sayings gospel / John S.
Kloppenborg Verbin.
        p.   cm.
    Includes bibliographical references and indexes.
    ISBN 0-8006-2601-8
    1. Q hypothesis (Synoptics criticism)   I. Title.

BS2555.2 .K567   2000
226'.066—dc21   99-046058

The paper used in this publication meets the minimum requirements of American National Standard for Information Sciences—Permanence of paper for Printed Library Materials, ANSI Z329.48–1984.

Manufactured in the U.S.A.   AF 1-2601

04   03   02   01   00   1   2   3   4   5   6   7   8   9   10

Contents

List of Figures

Preface

THIS BOOK EXPLORES two sets of issues crucial to the study of early Christianity: first, the basic methodological issues bearing on the identification and reconstruction of one of the earliest documents of the Jesus movement; and second, how so seemingly abstract and hypothetical a project has belonged and continues to belong to the history of discourse on early Christianity and what importance it has in that discourse. In short, it is a book on *how* one talks about Q, and *why* it matters.

The motivations for this book are several. First, I have been thinking and writing about Q for two decades and have watched it transformed from a documentary source of rather limited interest into a major point of debate in matters of the delineation of the early Jesus movement and in the quest of the historical Jesus. With much work already accomplished, this seems a good juncture at which to review and evaluate what has been done. Second, for the last several years I have also conducted a doctoral seminar on the Synoptic Problem, inviting students to examine seriously, sympathetically, and critically a variety of solutions to the Synoptic Problem—not only the Two Document hypothesis (2DH), but the Two Gospel (Griesbach) hypothesis (2GH), the complex hypotheses of Vaganay, Boismard, and Rolland, the solution of the so-called Jerusalem school, and the Farrer-Goulder hypothesis. Part of my concern has been to ensure that graduate students appreciate both the strengths and weaknesses of various Synoptic solutions, and that they understand the difference between well and poorly constructed hypotheses.

Finally, it is intellectually important for me to live with the consequences of well-constructed hypotheses: the 2DH is one of them. During twenty years of listening to colleagues and students, I have heard a variety of strategies for avoiding those consequences: some declare that the relationship among the Gospels is a "completely open" question, as if two centuries of serious thinking about their origins count for nothing. Others admit to

x   *Preface*

hold Markan priority but doubt the existence of Q, even though they also
affirm the independence of Matthew and Luke. This is simply not a logical
option, for the existence of Q is *required* in the combination of Markan priority and the independence of Matthew and Luke. Others "believe" in Q
but wonder whether one can really say anything about its theology or composition. Sometimes such statements reflect entirely appropriate methodological concerns about reconstructing the theology of a document whose
exact contours are unclear; but just as often these hesitations reflect worries
about what one might find in Q that will run counter to long-held views.
Still others agree that meaningful and responsible conclusions can be drawn
about Q's theology but doubt whether there was ever any social formation
that reflected that theology, as if documents arise in social vacuums. For better or for worse, this book tries to illustrate the consequences of holding
that the 2DH best accounts for the origin of the Synoptics, and to observe
the larger entailments in that hypothesis.

In writing this book I have been helped immeasurably by many colleagues. It is the combination of their evident commitment to academic and
humanistic values and their generosity of spirit that has made it easy to
accept their sometimes searching criticisms and a pleasure to benefit from
their learning. In debates over Gospel origins and the historical Jesus, where
basic civility is so often lacking, it is a delight to have such colleagues as
these.

I wish to express my deep gratitude to William R. Farmer for having read
carefully and critically through the chapters pertaining to the Synoptic
Problem and its implications. Those who know him will also know that he
and I disagree on most matters regarding the Synoptic Problem, most especially the respective viabilities of the Two Document and the Griesbach
(Two Gospel) hypotheses. He has, however, helped me better to understand
what was at stake, both methodologically and theologically, in nineteenth-
and twentieth-century debates about the Synoptic Problem. For his gen-
erosity and frankness I am grateful.

William Baird, Ron Cameron, Zeba Crook, Christoph Heil, Paul Hoffmann, Merrill Miller, James M. Robinson, and Leif E. Vaage read through
the entire manuscript and made numerous suggestions for improvement.
William E. Arnal, Robert Derrenbacker Jr., K. C. Hanson, Douglas E. Oakman, Gerald T. Sheppard, Daniel Smith, Christopher M. Tuckett, and Benedict T. Viviano each read individual chapters and generously shared their
learning, sparing me from various errors and overstatements. In rewriting
and revising, constant conversations with my partner and wife, Hami
Verbin, have forced to clarify many parts of the argument. Without her clarity of thought and intellectual honesty this book would not have been *this*
book. Mordechai Avi'am, F. Gerald Downing, David Dungan, Christoph
Heil, Frans Neirynck, Douglas E. Oakman, David Peabody, Jonathan Reed,

Peter Richardson, and Hans Rollmann kindly supplied me with unpublished or newly published materials. Finally, it is a pleasure to acknowledge how much I have learned from the doctoral students with whom I have been privileged to work, who have helped me sharpen arguments, and whose own work on the Synoptic tradition and Q is variously acknowledged throughout this book: William E. Arnal, Alicia Batten, Willi Braun, Robert Derrenbacker Jr., Kyu Sam Han, Alan Kirk, Daniel Smith, and Kristen Sweder.

The draft of this book was written during a sabbatical leave spent at the Tantur Ecumenical Institute for Advanced Theological Studies in Jerusalem. Thanks are due to its rector, Fr. Thomas Stransky, C.S.P., for inviting me as a visiting scholar for the 1994–95 academic year, to his executive assistant Geneviève Daleh for expediting a variety of matters, to Sr. Marianora and Sahar Hazboun, the librarians at Tantur, and to its excellent staff, in particular Vivi Siniora. Fr. Kevin McCaffrey, O.P., graciously extended to me privileges at the library of the École biblique et archéologique française.

The final editing of the book was completed at the Institute for Antiquity and Christianity, Claremont Graduate University. I am grateful to its co-directors, James M. Robinson and Karen Jo Torjeson, for their generosity in inviting me as a visiting scholar, and especially to the associate director, Jon Ma. Asgeirsson, who in numerous ways made my stay in Claremont most pleasant.

I am grateful to my school, the University of St. Michael's College, for granting a sabbatical leave and to the (then) dean, Michael Fahey, S.J., and to Mrs. Sharon McGhie for numerous kindnesses. My year in Jerusalem was supported by a generous fellowship from the Jack and Roberta Rudin Foundation and by assistance from Sr. Maureena Fritz, N.D.S., the (then) director of English Language Programs at Ratisbonne. Invitations to give lectures at King's College (University of Western Ontario), the William Morris Memorial Lecture at Lakehead University, the Harvard Divinity School, and the Université de Lausanne and the French-speaking Swiss universities gave me the opportunity to try out new ideas and to discuss them with many colleagues. Two doctoral students in Toronto, Richard Ascough (now of Queen's University) and Alicia Batten (now of the College of St. Thomas), kept me supplied with articles unavailable in Jerusalem.

A note on nomenclature and spelling. Throughout I refer to the "Old Testament" as the Tanak (i.e., *Torah, Nevi'îm, weKethuvîm*, Torah, Prophets and Writings), except when the reference is to the first part of the *Christian* Bible. With a few exceptions, I also use Semitic spellings of many place-names (e.g., Kefar Naḥum rather than Capernaum; Gush Ḥalav for Gishala; Yodefat for Jotopata; the Kinneret for the Sea of Galilee). This is a small but deliberate effort at defamiliarization in an attempt to create an intellectual space for reconsideration of more weighty theoretical issues. In the preference for Tanak to Old Testament lies a recognition of the fact that the writings to which the Q people occasionally referred were not yet the *Old* Testament but comprised the civil and criminal code of ancient Israel, accounts of Israel's epic history, and collections of prophetic, didactic, and liturgical texts.

Texts from Q are cited by their *Lukan* versification. For example, Q 6:20b refers to that Q text lying behind Luke 6:20b/Matt 5:3. This convention does not, however, imply that Luke's wording is necessarily closer to Q's than Matthew's wording. Q/Matt is used to designate those (few) texts represented in Matthew but not in Luke but which likely derived from Q, e.g., Q/Matt 5:41.

This book, intended partly to introduce students to the problems of Q and others to the problems in its history, is dedicated with love to two younger students, my sons Stefan and Andreas, who have variously shared, endured, and satirized their father's efforts.

filiis carissimis

Stefan John • Michael Andreas

Introduction

THIS BOOK IS ABOUT Q, a reconstructed document of the Jesus movement, and the difference its existence makes. The possible existence of a sayings collection underlying the Synoptic Gospels has consequences for many aspects of the reconstruction of the early Jesus movement. Simply put, if there was a Q, its existence makes a difference. It does so because by most accounts, Q represents a different type of gospel form. To posit Q amounts to positing "differentness" at the very beginnings of the Jesus movement. Insofar as hypotheses are *our* intellectual constructs to make sense of data, the formulation of, and adherence to, the Two Document hypothesis (2DH), with Q as its corollary, entails the acknowledgment of difference. It demands of us that we provide a historical, social, and theological accounting of Q.

Q was originally hypothesized in order to solve a relatively narrow problem, that of the literary relationships among the Synoptics. It seemed a viable solution to the Synoptic Problem that Matthew and Luke each drew from two sources: the Gospel of Mark and a sayings collection. The particularities of Q, however, were consequential. To hypothesize a sayings source which turns out to focus far more on Jesus' sayings than his wondrous deeds, which mentions the advent of the Son of Man but is silent about a vicarious death or a resurrection, and which appears to reflect and extol a social marginality, had far-reaching and partially unforeseen implications for how we reconstruct the theology, practice, and social location of the early Jesus movement.

It is rather like the case of black holes. In 1916 Karl Schwarzschild's manipulation of gravitational equations suggested the theoretical possibility that stellar bodies existed which emitted no light because they were of sufficient mass to have escape velocities greater than the speed of light. Later it was noticed that such stars as Cygnus X-1 behaved as if they were in proximity to extremely large, yet invisible, gravitational bodies. Schwarzschild's hypothesis appeared to offer an explanation of such phenomena, even though it was by definition impossible ever to observe directly a black hole (or a "Schwarzschild singularity"). The idea of a black hole was, however, of much greater moment than was first imagined. A singularity hidden by the event horizon not only made sense of the odd orbital movements of certain visible stars. It turned out to have much broader theoretical implications for cosmology, cosmic history, and the geometry of space.

In a similar way, the positing of a sayings collection alongside Mark not only "solved" certain source-critical problems; it brought with it the need to rethink the history and character of the early Jesus movement and to redraw its theological, textual, and social map. If Q is a viable literary hypothesis and if modern reconstructions of Q approximate its original shape, the understandings of gospel origins and the nature of the early Jesus movement need to be refined to accommodate this additional complexity. We must take account of an early expression of the Jesus tradition that did not feel the urgency of accounting for his death in soteriological terms. We must take account of a document that drew heavily upon Deuteronomistic theology, visible only incidentally in Mark or 1 Thessalonians. We must take account of a document that privileged sayings rather than wondrous deeds and, in accord with this emphasis, the heavenly Sophia. We must take account of a sector of the Jesus movement rather unlike the urban Pauline churches, characterized by a distinctive—even radical—social practice. And we must take notice of a document that grounded its practice not in a once-and-for-all "Christ event" but in relation to the epic history of Israel.

The existence of documents such as Q runs counter to the rhetoric of unity and concord found in many early Christian writings and renders more difficult the conventional attempts to define a common set of views that characterized all sectors of the Jesus movement, or at least those parts whose views were later to be canonized. The distictiveness—even differentness—of Q also provides an instrument by which to measure how much the intracanonical Gospels have covered their own tracks, making it difficult to glimpse the complex, perhaps fractious, history that contributed to the ultimate formation of those gospels. Q—along with the *Gospel of Thomas*, the epistle of James, and the *Gospel of Peter*—lets us see that the process that led to the formation of the Gospels was incomparably richer, more complex, and more experimental than earlier models have supposed.

It would have been possible to analyze the methodological problems and history of scholarship of almost any New Testament document in order to illustrate how increasingly precise methods and increasingly attentive scrutiny have produced a highly differentiated map of the social and intellectual terrain of antiquity. For example, scholars have identified significant differences between Matthew and Paul, or between the authentic Pauline letters and the Pastorals, or even between early and later Pauline letters. These differences not only require a careful historical accounting but also constitute obstacles to simple theological appropriation. Sharp differences among New Testament documents on matters of Christology and soteriology, for example, pose problems for those engaged in the theological enterprise of constructing a "New Testament theology." How, or in what sense, can one speak of a coherent theology of the Jesus movement? The same differences create problems for the historian in her effort to understand how (or to what extent) the Jesus movement constituted a single movement, or how to imagine social and/or intellectual continuities between, say, Q and Matthew, or between the Pauline and the deutero-Pauline groups.

The Sayings Gospel Q turns out to be an excellent window through which to view the "discovery" of diversity and difference in early Christianity and to examine at close quarters the consequences of using various analytical methods current in New Testament exegesis—why they have been thought useful and the tacit or explicit theoretical assumptions operative in those methods.

The very hypothetical nature of Q, far from being an embarrassment, provides an excellent site for seeing, first, how hypotheses are constructed in order to make sense of data and, second, the larger consequences or entailments that such hypotheses have. Scholarship on Christian origins often suffers from a misplaced positivism that assumes that certain things are known as "facts," either because they are espoused by a large number of scholars or because alternative scenarios have not (yet) been advanced. In a recent article, a noted scholar declares that "Luke's use of Mark is a fact (or generally accepted as one)." He makes this extraordinary statement, presumably, because most contemporary Synoptic scholars assume (or actually argue) that Luke used Mark. As will become clear, however, there are many exceptions. For much of the eighteenth and nineteenth centuries most scholars did not hold this view, and today William Farmer and his colleagues argue precisely the contrary: that Mark used Luke. But even if it were true that most scholars advocated Markan priority, this fact would be irrelevant. No volume of support for a *hypothesis* will ever turn it into a fact. Hypotheses may be good hypotheses insofar as they account for most of the available data; they may be effective hypotheses insofar as they provide explanations of data which assist in addressing a variety of other problems. But they are not facts. They are our ways of configuring and accounting for data in a manner that seems best to respond to the nature and diversity of the data, and in a way that reflects our historiographic or theological interests. Precisely because Q is professedly the product of a hypothesis, scholarship on Q nicely exemplifies the intellectual process of trying to make sense of the diversity and particularity of historical data.

Q turns out to be interesting for other reasons too. Disputes about Q and the Synoptic Problem are found at key junctures in the history of New Testament scholarship. The Synoptic Problem first emerged as an issue amid eighteenth- and nineteenth-century disputes over the relation of Christian dogma to the documents of the New Testament. Although at first blush the

Synoptic Problem seemed to deal with a narrow and rather technical question of the literary relation among the Synoptics, it existed as part of a much larger debate over the relation of the Gospels to the historical Jesus and the place of the Gospels within the history of theology. The energy driving the literary inquiry was not antiquarianism, but a keen interest in the theological utility of the Gospels.

Q itself became an explicit object of attention a century later when scholars realized that they must account for the transmission of the Jesus tradition from its earliest stages to the composition of the Synoptic Gospels. Slowly, the consciousness of profound diversity within the Jesus movement emerged—both a diversity in sources antecedent to the final forms of the Synoptic Gospels and diversity in the forms and functions of early Christian discourse. Q figured importantly on documentary "maps" of the early Jesus tradition. In form-critical discussions, Q exemplified some of the tensions between kerygma and paraenesis: between the eschatological proclamation of the advent of God's dominion and the ethicizing, ecclesial, and domesticating tendencies of the tradition.

After the Second World War, simple diversity modulated into real difference. Q attained special prominence with the collapse of the supposition of a uniform and normative kerygma underlying all early Christian theology. At the time when scholars began to recover many theologically divergent and uncooperative elements of the Jesus tradition preserved in gnostic documents, Jewish Christian gospels, and in the views of the "opponents" lurking behind 1 Corinthians and Galatians, Q came to be seen as a good example of just one such "different" gospel. The Sayings Gospel cannot be treated as an apocryphal or rejected gospel; it is in a real way "innercanonical" in the sense that it is now embedded in the fabric of Matthew and Luke and part of their prehistories. This means that Q's existence poses significant theological questions about diversity and difference at the very foundational stages of the Jesus movement, not just at some secondary, aberrant stage.

More recently, scholarship on Q has occupied a central position in the renewed quest of the historical Jesus and in attempts to describe the social practices of the Jesus movement. Perhaps owing to an explosion of social, historical, and archaeological studies on first-century Galilee (the probable provenance of the Sayings Gospel), Q has become the focal point of efforts to coordinate early Christian discourse about the kingdom, poverty, debt, violence, the Son of Man, judgment, the Temple, and so forth with a variety of social, economic, and political features of Jewish Palestine. As with the case of 1 Corinthians, where social, historical, and archaeological data from Roman Corinth can be coordinated with certain aspects of Paul's letter, Q provides a space where social history can meet and interact with texts of the Jesus movement. The reconceptualizing of the function of early Christian language which this meeting has occasioned not only has ramifications for our thinking about the Jesus movement in the 50s or 60s of the first century, but has aided in a reimaging of the quest of the historical Jesus.

The presentation of this book will be "bifocal." The first part attends to the methods employed in the study of Q, their presuppositions, and a survey of the state of research. This part can be divided into four phrases, corresponding to source-, form-, redaction-, and social-scientific criticisms. Thus, the first part treats Q as a necessary postulate of the Two Document hypothesis (chapter 1); the identification of Q as a Greek document whose arrangement and wording can be reconstructed (chapter 2); the determination of the theological and literary principles by which it was composed (chapter 3); and, in two chapters, the social formations that are reflected by the document (chapter 4) and the place of Q in first-century Galilean society (chapter 5).

The second part of the book revisits the four topics of the Synoptic Problem, Q as a document, the redaction of Q, and its social location, but poses more theological and theoretical questions. Chapter 6 seeks to place the discussion of the Synoptic Problem within the context of the challenge to theological scholarship posed by Reimarus's devastating essay on the purpose of Jesus and his disciples, and traces the way that the predecessors of the 2DH finally emerged as part of an effort to ground theological discourse in a responsible reconstruction of the life of Jesus. In this chapter I am not so much interested in the logical and evidentiary features of the Gospels that support various solutions to the Synoptic Problem, but in the theological and ideological forces which impelled the quest in the first place, and which variously inclined scholars to one or other solution.

During the early part of the twentieth century and in the wake of a flurry of manuscript discoveries (both biblical and nonbiblical) and intense efforts at textual criticism, Q came to be regarded, not merely as an interesting idea for solving the Synoptic Problem, but as a significant *documentary source* for the transmission of the Jesus tradition. As a counterpart to chapter 2 (on the reconstruction of Q), chapter 7 inquires into the theological context in which the task of reconstruction was carried out. The breakdown of confidence in the Markan narrative outline, the rise of form criticism and neo-orthodox "kerygmatic" theology, and, among Catholic exegetes, the 1911–12 decrees of the Pontifical Biblical Commission all had significant influences on the way the reconstructive task was defined and the kinds of questions that reconstructions tried to address.

Parallel to chapter 3, on the composition, redaction, and genre of the Sayings Gospel, chapter 8 inquires into the impact that Q scholarship has had (and ought to have) on key aspects of New Testament theology. Q's lack of an account of Jesus' death and its lack of a resurrection account or indications of an Easter faith raise searching questions about the "place" of Q within the Jesus movement. It is here that the seemingly vexed question of an apocalyptic or sapiential denomination of Q arises, along with the largely unspoken theological assumptions that lurk behind the terms "apocalyptic" and "wisdom."

The final chapter revisits current attempts to situate Q within the social-historical environment of first-century Galilee. Of interest here are not the details or plausibility of specific attempts to specify the social location of Q, but what such attempts signal about the commitments and priorities of scholarship on Christian origins. The opposition to the so-called cynic hypothesis serves as a lens for this inquiry. The opposition to the hypothesis has been mounted with a level of vehemence and disingenuousness that suggest that the cynic hypothesis has touched a deep nerve. This nerve is apparently less connected to historiographic centers than it is to theological and ideological preferences and convictions.

New Testament scholarship, for all its technical vocabulary and specialized conversations, does not now operate, and has never operated, in a vacuum. It does not pose its questions innocently. Its discourse has been embedded in the larger sweep of theological discourse, functioning both to support and to criticize theological enterprises; at the same time, it shares the preoccupations of humanistic scholarship. In North America at least, New Testament scholarship and the study of Q simultaneously belong, as I do, to theological faculties and to the humanistically oriented research university.

PART I

TEXT AND HISTORY

Gush Ḥalav. Third- or fourth-century synagogue (from the southwest).

Text and History

THIS BOOK WAS originally conceived as a basic introduction to the study of Q. Although in the course of writing it escaped these bounds in both depth and scope, the original intent is still visible in the outline of the first five chapters. These chapters ask four basic questions. First, how do scholars arrive at the postulate of a sayings document underlying Matthew and Luke in the first place (chapter 1)? The chapter thus concerns the so called Synoptic Problem—the problem of the literary relationship among the first three Gospels. I shall discuss a few alternate ways of solving the Synoptic Problem; but since this book is on Q, the center of gravity is not on the Synoptic Problem as such, but on the way in which the Two Document hypothesis (and its postulate of a saying source Q) has served as one plausible solution to the problem

The second question, raised in chapter 2, concerns the documentary status of Q, that is, why do we refer to the Two *Document* hypothesis? It is one thing to argue that Matthew and Luke independently used two *sources*, Mark and another set of sayings and stories; it is another matter to conclude that this second source was a document, with reasonably clear contents and sequence. Because one still occasionally encounters statements to the effect that "Q" might be oral or written, it is crucial to be clear about the data and the arguments that have led most specialists on Q to conclude that it was a written document.

Third, if Q indeed is a written source with a particular arrangement of materials, is it possible to ascertain the editorial perspective of its framers (chapter 3)? Did it have a distinct "theology" and how, methodologically, does one go about describing that theology? This line of inquiry extends the agenda of redaction and genre criticism, employed in the study of the Gospels since the 1950s, to Q itself.

And finally, is it possible to determine the social interests and level of those for whom the document was produced (chapter 4), and what place would such persons occupy in the society of Jewish Galilee (chapter 5)? I have addressed this question in two separate chapters fora simple methodological reason. Chapter 4 looks at Q itself and asks whether there are textual signs that point to the social interest and social level of its framers and readers/addressees. Chapter 5 offers a reconstruction of social dynamics of the Galilee in the early Roman period (without looking at Q), and only then asks the question, Is it possible to imagine Q as fitting into that environment?

Hence, the flow of the argument of these chapters is from the general problem of agreements and disagreements among the first three Gospels and the literary puzzle that these raise, to various inquiries into the specific profile of Q, or the Sayings Gospel Q. It will also become clear that the questions raised in chapter 1 (on the Synoptic Problem) have haunted scholars for better than two centuries, while those of chapters 4 and 5 are quite recent, raised only because of new excavations in the Galilee and new ways of interrogating our sources. Thus chapters 1 to 5 move not only from general to particular, but from older to quite contemporary concerns.

Throughout these chapters, my interest is to lay out the basic data and arguments relevant to these four topics—the Synoptic Problem, reconstructing Q, assessing Q's theology and genre, and determining a "place" for Q in the society of Jewish Palestine. Although it will be necessary to discuss the works of a few representative scholars, I have made no attempt to provide an exhaustive treatment of how scholars have treated Q and its setting. The second part of the book will revisit the four questions given above, and will attempt to situate those questions and the answers that have been given within the politics and ideology of biblical scholarship. But it is important for me that the issues of the basic data and arguments not be confused with the issue of how, in the course of the past two centuries, various hypotheses have been seen to reflect or to interfere with broader theological or ideological tendencies within the academy. It is important to assess historical hypotheses on the basis of historical evidence and argument, not, as is so often done, on the basis of the coherence with theological programs.

1

Q *and the Synoptic Problem*

M ODERN SCHOLARSHIP on the Sayings Gospel Q is founded on a hypothesis. It is a venerable one, older than many of the working hypotheses in New Testament scholarship today. It has certainly not gone
unchallenged; the last thirty years of discussion of the Synoptic Problem
have seen challenges in which other solutions which do not invoke Q have
been defended. Yet the hypothesis has withstood criticism. Because it offers
the most economical and plausible accounting of the form and content of
the Synoptic Gospels, it continues to be by far the most widely accepted
solution to the Synoptic Problem. But it remains a hypothesis. Other early
Christian sayings collections have been found, but no papyrus copy of Q
has yet been discovered.

Does this mean that it would be wise not to read any further, since everything that follows is "merely hypothetical"? Hardly. For to do so would be
to misunderstand in a fundamental way the function of hypotheses. The
classical electromagnetic wave theory of light is a hypothesis. It has not been
proven; but neither is it a mere opinion or *thesis*. What makes the wave
theory of light a good *hypothesis* is that many observable data are congru-
ent with the hypothesis; optical and radiotelemetric instruments can be built
using the hypothesis; and a coherent set of measurements can be assembled
by employing the theory. In other words, it is an *effective* hypothesis—one
that has explanatory power. That does not mean that the hypothesis
accounts for everything; indeed, experiments indicate that light is not continuous and infinitely divisible, as the wave theory implies it should be.
Under some conditions light displays the attributes of localized concentra-
tions of energy and momentum—the characteristics of particles rather than
waves. Quantum mechanics and the Schrödinger wave equation provide a
partial reconciliation of the wave-particle paradox for certain types of particles, but only within the limits prescribed by the Heisenberg uncertainty
principle and only at certain optical frequencies. The anomalies and

11

limitations of the wave theory, however, do not disprove it or render it less useful as an explanatory device.

There is very little that can be said of the Gospels that is not sponsored by hypotheses. We do not, for example, know the original wording of any of the Gospels, for the autographs have long since perished. What we possess are about six thousand manuscripts—none from the first century, small fragments from the second, portions of individual NT books from the beginning of the third ($\mathfrak{P}^{45}$, $\mathfrak{P}^{46}$, $\mathfrak{P}^{66}$, $\mathfrak{P}^{75}$), and complete Bibles only after the fourth. There are tens of thousands of points at which readings are in dispute. Text critics, however, have devised hypotheses regarding the transmission of the text of the Gospels and have formulated criteria that allow them to choose among the many variant readings and to reconstruct a hypothetical exemplar which is then published, with an appropriate critical apparatus, as "the Greek New Testament." But the original text of the Greek New Testament, despite the seeming tangibility that the printed page confers, remains at many points just out of reach, ambiguous, and blurred, like the nature of light itself.

We are also far from knowing the concrete social and historical circumstances that gave rise to the writing of the Gospels. None of them can be dated or located precisely in the way that, for example, private letters and administrative documents from Ptolemaic and Roman Egypt can. Nevertheless, models and hypotheses have been formulated which render the rhetoric and structure of each writing intelligible. The large majority of critics accept that Matthew was penned after the First Revolt (66–74 CE) and probably in a locale where there were significant Jewish and Gentile populations and where there were strained relations with a synagogue. On this hypothesis—and it is a working hypothesis—much of the structure and argument of Matthew can be rendered intelligible. This and many other such hypotheses have achieved wide acceptance among NT critics and now shape our view of other matters; but they remain hypothetical, for in most cases we have access to the situation of the writer only via the writing itself, not independently through other documents or reports.

The Two Document Hypothesis

The "Synoptic Problem" or the question of the literary relationships among the Gospels is rather like the nuclear physics of biblical criticism, full of mathematics, charts, and algebraic unknowns. Yet like physics, it remains a fundamental building block of other types of Synoptic analysis. As complex as the Synoptic Problem may seem, it is an indispensable part of the study of the Gospels. The most commonly invoked solution to the Synoptic Problem is the Two Document hypothesis (2DH). Stated succinctly, the Two Document hypothesis proposes that the gospels of Matthew and Luke independently used Mark as a source. Since Matthew and Luke share about 235 verses that they did not get from Mark, the 2DH requires that they had independent access to a second source consisting mainly of sayings of Jesus. This, for want of a better term, is the "Sayings Gospel," or, "Q." Hence:

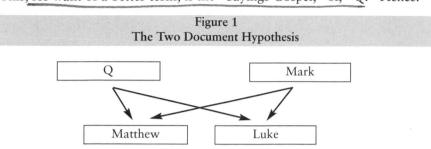

Figure 1
The Two Document Hypothesis

Like other hypotheses, the 2DH is constructed on the basis of various sets of data—patterns of agreements and disagreements among the gospels—and from the inferences permitted by these data. The agreements that exist among the Synoptic Gospels—many of which are extensive—imply that some kind of *literary* relationship exists. Disagreements—where one gospel reads *x* and another reads *y*—raise the question whether one gospel used and modified another, or whether the two drew upon and variously edited a common source.

Before proceeding further, two preliminary remarks are necessary. First, it must be said that what constitutes "the Synoptic data" can be described in different ways. Comparison of the Synoptics is done by means of synopses which align the three (or four) gospels in parallel columns. Synopses can be constructed in various ways and many factors affect how agreements and disagreements are registered. The most basic factor is the choice of text of the Greek New Testament used in a synopsis, for there are small but significant differences among the various available editions of the Greek New Testament published in the last two centuries. Because text critics continue to sift the six thousand or so manuscripts of the NT, and because there is a constant refinement of the criteria for evaluation of those manuscripts, the resultant text of the NT is always in flux. To use the most recent Nestle-Aland[27] edition in a synopsis may, for example, suggest that Matthew and Mark display more verbal agreement in a given pericope than would be indicated if one used Boismard-Lamouille's edition of the NT, or previous Nestle-Aland editions, or the even earlier editions of Tischendorf or Westcott and Hort. At other points, Nestle-Aland[27] may imply greater divergence among the Synoptics than other editions, even its own predecessor, Nestle-Aland[25].[1]

Another important choice concerns the length of pericopae: does one break the text of the gospels into a few long units, even if not everything in

---

1. For a useful discussion of the relationship between text criticism and the Synoptic Problem, see Fee 1980; J. K. Elliott 1990; 1993.

each unit finds a clear parallel in the other gospels? Or is it preferable to have a larger number of very short pericopae? The former choice may conceal the extent of disagreement within pericopae, while the latter may exaggerate the discord or make it more difficult to grasp visually the points of agreement. Furthermore, it is often not a simple matter to decide how to align parallel texts. Take the hypothetical example of two sequences of pericopae, one in Gospel *A* (a b c d e f g) and a second in Gospel *B* (a b d e c f g).

Figure 2
Alignment of Synoptic Parallels

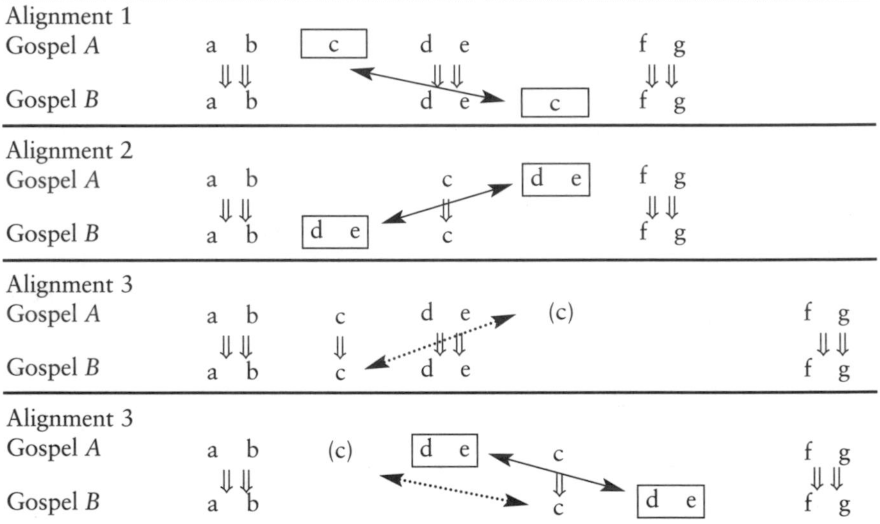

Alignment 1

Gospel *A*   a   b   [c]   d   e   f   g
Gospel *B*   a   b   d   e → [c]   f   g

Alignment 2

Gospel *A*   a   b   c → [d   e]   f   g
Gospel *B*   a   b   [d   e]   c   f   g

Alignment 3

Gospel *A*   a   b   c   d   e → (c)   f   g
Gospel *B*   a   b   c   d   e   f   g

Alignment 3

Gospel *A*   a   b   (c)   [d   e]   c   f   g
Gospel *B*   a   b   c   [d   e]   f   g

Is it preferable to align the elements so as to imply that Gospel *B* transposed *c* to a later point (or that Gospel *A* shifted *c* to an earlier point) (Alignment 1)? Or is Alignment 2 better, which suggests that Gospel *B* has moved *de* earlier (or that Gospel *A* has moved it later)? Each alignment makes assumptions regarding which elements were stable and which were movable, and each alignment implicitly or explicitly invokes more general principles according to which a given alignment is to be preferred.

Finally, it often occurs that one gospel contains two possible parallels to elements in another gospel. Hence the problem arises: which is the primary parallel and which is secondary? For example, is Alignment 3 to be preferred, where the first *c* in Gospel *A* is treated as a primary parallel to *c* in the Gospel *B*? Or should the two gospels be aligned as in Alignment 4, implying that first *c* is the minor parallel or anticipation of the second occurrence of this element?

Careful comparison of Huck's synopsis with those of Tischendorf, Aland, Huck-Greeven, Orchard, and Boismard-Lamouille reveals differing texts and differing arrangements of parallels, each producing a distinctive set of

Synoptic data.[2] The differences are rarely of such an order that a particular solution to the Synoptic Problem is made impossible; but one synopsis may make it easier or more difficult to *see* how a particular solution works.

The second preliminary comment concerns the types of arguments that are constructed from the data. They are of two orders. First, there are *logical* inferences: relationships among the gospels that are logically possible and impossible given the Synoptic data and given some basic assumptions. Assume, for example, that the patterns of agreements and disagreements among three documents, A, B, and C, are such that one suspects that they are related to one another in a literary way. Assume, further, that the three have several elements (*wxy*) in common, but B and C share an element (*z*) not found in A, and that B and C agree in the wording and placement of *z* (between *x* and *y*), so that one must also assume a literary relationship between B and C. To account for these data, various literary relationships could be proposed, including,

(1) $A(w\text{-}x\text{-}y) \longrightarrow B(w\text{-}x\text{-}z\text{-}y) \longrightarrow C(w\text{-}x\text{-}z\text{-}y)$

(2) $B(w\text{-}x\text{-}z\text{-}y) \longrightarrow C(w\text{-}x\text{-}z\text{-}y) \longrightarrow A(w\text{-}x\text{-}y)$ where $P \longrightarrow Q$ means P is the source of Q.

In both instances, C copied B in full, but in the first scenario, B added the *z* element to A; in the second, A took only the *wxy* elements, but omitted the *z* element from C. One relationship, however, is not possible as a *sufficient* explanation:

(3) $B(w\text{-}x\text{-}z\text{-}y) \longrightarrow A(w\text{-}x\text{-}y) \longrightarrow C(w\text{-}x\text{-}z\text{-}y)$

This arrangement cannot account for the presence of *z* in C since there is no direct relationship between B and C. One would have to make the improbable assumption that C by coincidence added the *z* element in exactly the same form and at exactly the same place that it had in B. Although such coincidences cannot be excluded entirely, the possibility is remote indeed. There are of course several other possible pedigrees of these three imaginary documents that could account for the elements; but none is logically defensible that places A as the sole intermediary between B and C.

It is only at this level that one can approach absolute proofs and disproofs. The third option is impossible as it stands. Logical considerations, however, do not help us to determine whether (1) or (2) is to be preferred; both are possible, and several others as well.

The situation is similar with the Synoptic Gospels. There are many ways to arrange three gospels to imply direct or indirect literary relationships. The special characteristics of the Synoptic data (described below) *exclude* some of these arrangements as extremely unlikely. Logical considerations,

2. On the theoretical problems involved in creating a synopsis, and on the problem of their neutrality, see Dungan 1980; 1985; 1990b; J. K. Elliott 1991; Neirynck 1985; 1986; Orchard 1978; 1986; Hieke 1998.

however, do not narrow the field to a single solution. Several arrangements remain possible. Other criteria are needed.

The second type of argument has to do with offering *explanations* of the data that are plausible from a historical or literary perspective. If one can give a plausible historical or editorial account of gospel *B*'s procedures on the assumption *A*(wxy) → *B*(wxzy), but cannot provide an equivalent or analogous explanation for *C*(wxzy) → *A*(wxzy), then *A* → *B* → *C* is the better hypothesis, even though *B* → *C* → *A* might also be logically possible. That is, if one can account for the addition of the *z* element by *B* but not its omission by *A*, then the *B* → *C* → *A* relationship, while possible, is less likely.

Obviously, there is a certain ambiguity lurking in the term "plausible." Plausible for whom? Those acquainted with the history of the Synoptic Problem will know that many contradictory editorial procedures have been thought plausible by one critic or another. Is it plausible that a writer using another document as a source would substantially rewrite the source? Would that writer feel free to insert extra dialogues? or delete whole incidents? or delete long speeches? or rearrange the narrative framework? or completely reverse a narrative outcome? Of course it is impossible to answer such questions in the abstract. Much will depend upon the type of material under discussion. Even when the options are clear, critics are sometimes in disagreement as to which option is more plausible. It is at this point that deeper assumptions and explanatory habits come into play.

Some of the "arguments" adduced in support of some solutions to the Synoptic Problem are not arguments at all; they only rename the problem. One often encounters arguments that take the form: gospel *A* changed or deleted *z* (a word, a pericope, or a larger unit) from gospel *B* (the putative source) because the evangelist did not "like" *z*. Goulder, for example, asserts that Luke knew Matthew's lengthy Sermon on the Mount but reduced it in size because Luke "does not like long units" (1989:346). This is not an argument. It is only the *observation* that Luke's Sermon on the Plain is shorter than Matthew's Sermon on the Mount converted into a statement about Luke's aesthetic preferences with the help of the *presupposition* of Luke's use of Matthew. Since it presupposes precisely what is to be proven, it is not an argument at all. In order to create a plausible argument, one would have to show, for example, that elsewhere in Luke-Acts, the author tends to favor short speeches or that other writers of Luke's caliber preferred short, pithy speeches. Only in this way would it be plausible to claim that if Luke encountered a long speech in a source, he would reduce it in length. Parenthetically, it can be observed that both Luke and Acts have rather long speeches, longer than the twenty-nine verses of Luke's Sermon on the Plain.[3] Thus, at least this line of defense of Luke's procedure fails to

---

3. Goulder 1989:346: "Matthew's Sermon is too long. Who can take in so much spiritual richness in a single gulp?" Against Goulder's assertions, Tuckett (1995:41) appeals precisely to

convince. In order for an explanation to be at all plausible, it must appeal to some data external to the matter under examination.

In some cases it is possible to imagine explanations for mutually contradictory directions of dependence. For example, Griesbach argued that Mark omitted Matthew's and Luke's infancy accounts because he wished to focus on Jesus' role as a teacher (1789–90, ET 1978:103). William R. Farmer suggested that Mark modeled his gospel on the Petrine speeches preserved in Acts, which typically exclude matters pertaining to Jesus' birth, and hence excluded the infancy accounts (1977:287). On theories of Markan priority, Matthew and Luke added the infancy stories because of an interest in correlating Jesus' extraordinary abilities with an extraordinary birth. Both directions of dependence are logically possible and both types of explanations seem possible. Both see the elimination or addition of the infancy accounts as a function of an editorial interest. The challenge is to impose some controls on the subjectivity of the critic.

In his comparative analysis of Greco-Roman biographies, Philip Shuler (1990) observed that infancy accounts typically functioned in order to serve the eventual characterization of the adult life of the hero. Thus there are good reasons for imagining why Matthew and Luke would add them: they were simply conforming their accounts to the typical features of biographies. Shuler noted that some biographies lack infancy and childhood stories. The *Gospel of the Ebionites* and Marcion deliberately omitted infancy stories for theological reasons. In order to make plausible Mark's omission of the infancy accounts, however, it is not sufficient simply to note that some biographies lack these stories. It would be necessary to supply an editorial reason for Mark's omitting the stories. Griesbach's suggestion, however, is no answer: Luke's infancy accounts, which stress Jesus' wisdom and abilities as a teacher at a young age, would reinforce rather than undermine Mark's interest in Jesus as a teacher. One would have to propose other editorial reasons for Mark's omission—for example, that he had come to think of Jesus' kin as opponents or as persons of inferior belief. As I have argued elsewhere, it would also be necessary to suggest a historical or social setting in which such a strategy would be intelligible (Kloppenborg 1992b). None, thus far, has been proposed.

In the limited space available, I do not propose to survey and evaluate all source theories. The point of this chapter is to outline the basis for the 2DH and the existence of Q. In doing this, however, it will be necessary to indicate briefly how other source theories make sense of the same data upon which the 2DH is built.

Lukan preferences in speech length elsewhere in Acts: "When one compares too the lengths of some of the 'pericopes' in Acts (cf. Peter's long Pentecost speech, Stephen's 52-verse oration in Acts 7, the story of Cornelius's conversion in Acts 10), any appeal to the short supply of stamina on the part of Luke's audience/readership becomes even harder to believe." See also Tuckett 1996:26–27.

Three sets of Synoptic data are pertinent: agreements in wording and sequence, patterns of agreements in the triple tradition (Matthew / Mark / Luke), and patterns of agreement in the double tradition (Matthew / Luke).

AGREEMENTS IN WORDING AND SEQUENCE

Among all three Gospels and between any two of them, there is sufficient agreement, both in wording and in the sequential arrangements of pericopae, to warrant the conclusion that some sort of relationship of *literary* dependence exists. Strong verbal agreements are attested between each pair of Gospels and in many instances, there is close agreement among the Gospels in highly variable aspects of Greek grammar. For example:

Matthew—Luke
Matt 12:43-45   Luke 11:24-26
60 words)   (54 words)   50 identical

Matthew—Mark
Matt 21:12-13   Mark 11:15-17
(45 words)   (65 words)   37 identical

Mark—Luke
Mark 13:30-32   Luke 21:32-33
(49 words)   (50 words)   40 identical
                      (See Morgenthaler 1971:239–62.)

Such agreement is hardly explicable except on the supposition that one gospel is literarily dependent upon the other or that the two directly depend on a common source.

There are also striking agreements in the sequence of pericopae. Luke and Mark display a high degree of agreement throughout and while Matthew and Mark disagree in the sequence of their earlier sections, after Mark 6:14 (Matt 14:1) the two concur completely.[4] The significance of these agreements lies in the fact that the relative ordering of most of the Synoptic pericopae is not intrinsically determined by their content. Of course, stories pertaining to Jesus' death naturally come at the end of the gospels and those concerning his birth come at the beginning. But there is no necessary or inevitable reason, for example, that the Call of Levi/Matthew should follow the healing of a paralytic. Yet it does in all three Synoptics and this fact suggests that some form of *literary* relationship exists.

PATTERNS OF AGREEMENTS IN THE TRIPLE TRADITION

Close comparison of Gospels reveals a distinctive pattern of agreements and disagreements in Synoptic pericopae for which Mark has a parallel ("the

4. There are internal changes *within* pericopae in Mark 7:1-23 and 10:2-12 and Matthew compresses Mark 11:11, 15-17 (representing two days) into a single pericope (Matt 21:10-17) (see Figure 3).

triple tradition"). This pattern has two dimensions. (1) In both wording and sequence there are points at which all three gospels agree and a larger number of points where Matthew and Mark are in agreement (against Luke) or where Mark and Luke are in agreement (against Matthew). There are, however, relatively few points at which Matthew and Luke agree *in wording* against Mark (i.e., where Mark is present) and none where Matthew and Luke concur against Mark in the *sequence* of pericopae.[5] Take, for example, the pattern of verbal agreements in Mark 2:14 and its parallels:

Matthew 9:9	Mark 2:14	Luke 5:27
καὶ παράγων	καὶ παράγων	καὶ
ὁ Ἰησοῦς ἐκεῖθεν		μετὰ ταῦτα ἐξῆλθεν καὶ
εἶδεν ἄνθρωπον	εἶδεν Λευὶν τὸν τοῦ Ἁλφαίου	ἐθεάσατο τελώνην ὀνόματι Λευὶν
καθήμενον ἐπὶ τὸ τελώνιον,	καθήμενον ἐπὶ τὸ τελώνιον,	καθήμενον ἐπὶ τὸ τελώνιον,
Μαθθαῖον λεγόμενον,		
καὶ λέγει αὐτῷ, ἀκολούθει μοι.	καὶ λέγει αὐτῷ, ἀκολούθει μοι,	καὶ εἶπεν αὐτῷ, ἀκολούθει μοι.
καὶ	καὶ	καὶ καταλιπὼν πάντα
ἀναστὰς ἠκολούθησεν αὐτῷ.	ἀναστὰς ἠκολούθησεν αὐτῷ.	ἀναστὰς ἠκολούθει αὐτῷ.
And	And	And after this
as Jesus was walking away	as he was walking	he went out and he noticed
he saw someone	he saw	a toll collector
called Matthew	Levi son of Alphaeus,	named Levi
sitting at the toll booth,	sitting at the toll booth,	sitting at the toll booth;
and he says to him, "Follow me"	and he says to him, "Follow me"	and he said to him, "Follow me"
and arising	and arising	and arising (and) leaving everything behind
he followed him.	and followed him.	he was following him.

Words that are *underscored* indicate Matthew–Mark agreements, while those in **bold** signal Mark–Luke agreements. While there are several points where Matthew and Luke agree, Mark is always in agreement too. In other words, Matthew and Luke do not agree *against Mark*. As a generalization, this holds true throughout the whole of the Synoptics: the large majority of agreements are Matthew=Mark=Luke, Matthew=Mark, and Mark=Luke

5. Sanders (1968–69) produced a list comprising 29 instances of Matthew–Luke agreements against Mark in sequence but his list includes 5 instances of pericopae being placed *differently* by all three evangelists, 4 cases of Matthew disagreeing with Mark and Luke omitting the pericope altogether, and 13 cases of Matthew and Luke placing *non-Markan* material (and in all but 4 cases, not the same non-Markan material) in the same place relative to the Markan outline, none of which is relevant to the point here. Moreover, Neirynck (1973; repr. 1974a) has pointed out that Sanders included rearrangements *within* pericopae along with rearrangements of complete pericopae. Closer inspection of the remaining cases indicates that none constitutes a genuine agreement against Mark. Cf. Fuller 1975:65: "Nearly all of Sanders's alleged agreements in order of Matthew-Luke against Mark collapse under examination."

agreements. Only in a minority of instances (usually called "minor agreements") do Matthew and Luke agree against Mark (see the tabulation in Neirynck 1974b).

(2) While in general, Matthew and Luke agree with Mark's order, both register some disagreements. Matthew disagrees with Markan sequence mainly in Matthew 8–9 and makes a few transpositions within Markan pericopae (figure 3). Markan and Lukan orders also diverge at a few points, but these are distributed fairly evenly throughout Luke. In two instances (Luke 4:16-30; 5:1-11), it is not really a matter of Luke transposing a Markan pericope, but of having an alternate version of a Markan episode, which Luke also places differently (figure 4). In comparing these two tables, it is important to note that Luke's disagreements with Mark do not correspond to Matthew's disagreements with Mark.[6] Or, to put it differently, Matthew and Luke never agree *against* Mark in placing an episode that has a parallel in Mark.

The conclusion to be drawn from these two observations is that *Mark is medial*: the relationship between Matthew and Luke is mediated by Mark, at least in sections where Mark has parallels. Mark is either the middle term between Matthew and Luke, or their source, or a conflation of the two. Only in these three ways is it possible to account for the fact that Matthew and Luke rarely agree in wording against Mark and never agree against Mark in sequence. A number of arrangements account for these data (figure 5). The two straight-line arrangements account for the lack of sequential Matthew–Luke agreement against Mark by making Mark the link between Matthew and Luke: gospel "C" knew gospel "A" only via Mark. Triple agreements are easily explained: Mark copies "A" exactly, and "C" copied Mark exactly. The agreements of one gospel with Mark and against the other are also easily explained: Mark changed gospel "A", and "C" copied Mark exactly, or Mark copied "A" exactly, while "C" changed Mark. But it would be impossible for "A" and "C" to agree *against* Mark, except by coincidence. It might indeed be thought odd that whenever Mark altered the sequence of his source (A), the gospel dependent on Mark (C) (almost) always agreed with Mark and only when Mark was *not* altering "A"—which "C" could not know—did "C" feel free to alter the sequence of Mark (see Figures 3 and 4). Since, however, neither the Matthew–Mark nor the Mark–Luke disagreements are very extensive, it is well within the realm of probabilities that only once (Mark 3:13-19) does gospel "C" transpose a pericope that had also been transposed by Mark from gospel "A."

6. See Neirynck 1990b:588. The exception is Mark 3:13-19 (following a summary statement on healings), which Matthew places before Mark 2:23—3:12 (Matt 12:1-16) but also before his mission speech and Baptist material (Matthew 10–11); Luke, by contrast, merely inverts the order of Mark 3:7-12, 13-19. Mark 11:11, 12-14, 15-17 is also sometimes treated as a common transposition of Mark (Sanders 1968–69:255: "perhaps"), but in fact Luke has omitted Mark 11:11-14 completely; only Matthew has rearranged Mark by compressing Mark's two days into one.

Figure 3
Matthew's Disagreements with Markan Order

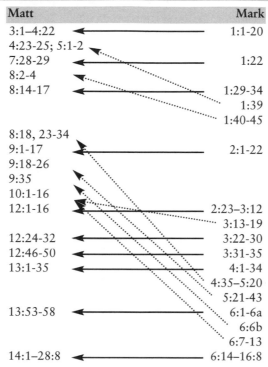

Matt	Mark
3:1–4:22	1:1-20
4:23-25; 5:1-2	
7:28-29	1:22
8:2-4	
8:14-17	1:29-34
	1:39
	1:40-45
8:18, 23-34	
9:1-17	2:1-22
9:18-26	
9:35	
10:1-16	
12:1-16	2:23–3:12
	3:13-19
12:24-32	3:22-30
12:46-50	3:31-35
13:1-35	4:1-34
	4:35–5:20
	5:21-43
13:53-58	6:1-6a
	6:6b
	6:7-13
14:1–28:8	6:14–16:8

Changes within Pericopae in Matt 14:1—28:8

Matt	Mark
15:1-2	7:1-5
	7:6-7
15:3-6	7:8-13
15:7-9	
15:10-20	7:14-23

Matt	Mark
19:3	10:2
	10:3-5
19:4-6	10:6-9
19:7-8	
19:9	1-:10-12

Matt	Mark
21:10-11	11:11a
21:12-13 (14-16)	
21:17	11:11b
	11:12-14
	11:15-17
21:18-19	

Sigla

19:9	←————	Agreement with the order of Mark
19:7-8	←·········	Disagreement with the order of Mark

Figure 4
Luke's Disagreements with Markan Order

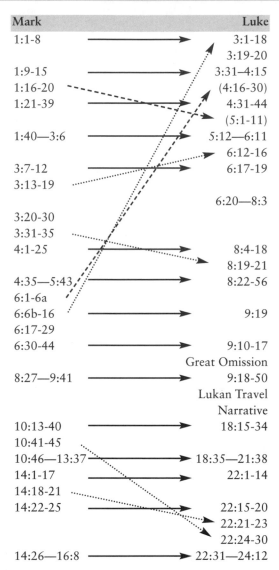

Mark	Luke
1:1-8	3:1-18
	3:19-20
1:9-15	3:31—4:15
1:16-20	(4:16-30)
1:21-39	4:31-44
	(5:1-11)
1:40—3:6	5:12—6:11
	6:12-16
3:7-12	6:17-19
3:13-19	
	6:20—8:3
3:20-30	
3:31-35	
4:1-25	8:4-18
	8:19-21
4:35—5:43	8:22-56
6:1-6a	
6:6b-16	9:19
6:17-29	
6:30-44	9:10-17
	Great Omission
8:27—9:41	9:18-50
	Lukan Travel Narrative
10:13-40	18:15-34
10:41-45	
10:46—13:37	18:35—21:38
14:1-17	22:1-14
14:18-21	
14:22-25	22:15-20
	22:21-23
	22:24-30
14:26—16:8	22:31—24:12

Sigla

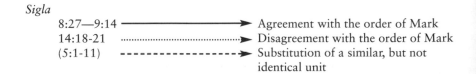

8:27—9:14	Agreement with the order of Mark
14:18-21	Disagreement with the order of Mark
(5:1-11)	Substitution of a similar, but not identical unit

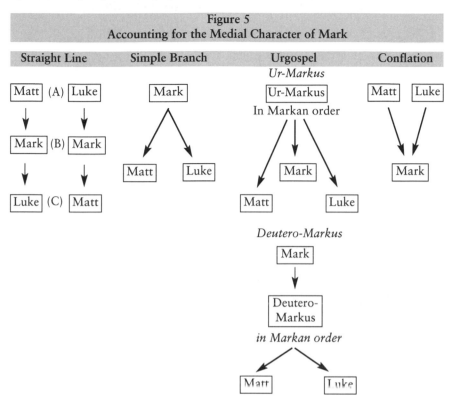

Figure 5
Accounting for the Medial Character of Mark

The simple branch solution also places Mark between Matthew and Luke, but as their common source. The lack of their agreement against Mark is a function of their independence; agreements against Mark could only be coincidental or the result of some other (non-Markan) influences. This applies as much to order as it does to wording: the fact that Matthew and Luke transpose *different* Markan pericopae is precisely what one should expect. And even when they coincidentally move the same pericope (Mark 3:13-19), they transpose it to different locations.

Primitive gospel (*Urgospel*) solutions do not place Mark between Matthew and Luke but instead posit as the common source of the gospels a document agreeing substantially with Mark. That this primitive gospel resembles Mark more than Matthew or Luke is suggested by the fact that in any disagreement in order, Mark always "votes" with the majority. Hence, the *Urgospel* version of the Call of Levi/Matthew (above) would have to be almost identical in wording to Mark 2:14 and the *Urgospel* would have to agree closely with Mark's sequence. There are in fact two variations of this type of solution, one that posits an earlier version of Mark (*Ur-Markus*) and another that posits a later version of Mark (*Deutero-Markus*). These types of solutions, however, are necessary only if there are other reasonable grounds for distinguishing Mark from the *Urgospel*—for example, if one

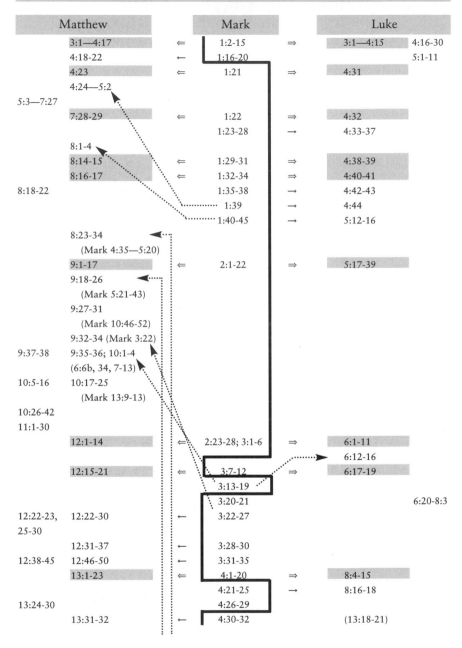

Figure 6*
Matthaean and Lukan Support of Markan Sequence

Matthew		Mark		Luke	
3:1—4:17	⇐	1:2-15	⇒	3:1—4:15	4:16-30
4:18-22	←	1:16-20			5:1-11
4:23	⇐	1:21	⇒	4:31	
4:24—5:2					
5:3—7:27					
7:28-29	⇐	1:22	⇒	4:32	
		1:23-28	→	4:33-37	
8:1-4					
8:14-15	⇐	1:29-31	⇒	4:38-39	
8:16-17	⇐	1:32-34	⇒	4:40-41	
8:18-22		1:35-38	→	4:42-43	
		1:39	→	4:44	
		1:40-45	→	5:12-16	
8:23-34					
(Mark 4:35—5:20)					
9:1-17	⇐	2:1-22	⇒	5:17-39	
9:18-26					
(Mark 5:21-43)					
9:27-31					
(Mark 10:46-52)					
9:32-34 (Mark 3:22)					
9:37-38	9:35-36; 10:1-4				
	(6:6b, 34, 7-13)				
10:5-16	10:17-25				
	(Mark 13:9-13)				
10:26-42					
11:1-30					
12:1-14	⇐	2:23-28; 3:1-6	⇒	6:1-11	
				6:12-16	
12:15-21	⇐	3:7-12	⇒	6:17-19	
		3:13-19			
		3:20-21			6:20-8:3
12:22-23,	12:22-30	←	3:22-27		
25-30					
	12:31-37	←	3:28-30		
12:38-45	12:46-50	←	3:31-35		
13:1-23	⇐	4:1-20	⇒	8:4-15	
		4:21-25	→	8:16-18	
13:24-30		4:26-29			
	13:31-32	←	4:30-32		(13:18-21)

---

*This table uses the alignments of Huck (1935; [10]1950), except for the placement of the Sermon on the Mount, where Neirynck's (1976) position is accepted. Compare the table in Griesbach 1789–90, ET 1978, 108–10. Note that in Griesbach's synopsis (1776; [2]1797) Griesbach aligned Mark 1:40-45; 4:35—5:21; 5:22-43; 6:7-13 with Matthew.

Figure 6, continued

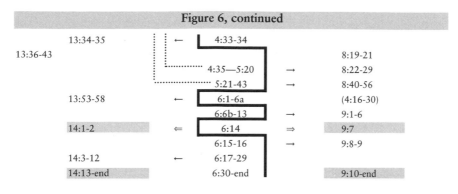

Sigla

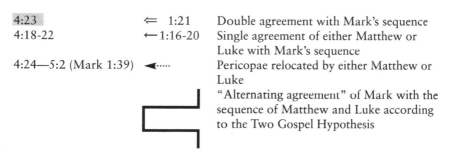

somehow knew that Mark was later than Matthew and/or Luke or if Mark contained other material whose omission by the others was hardly imaginable. In the absence of such grounds, these solutions reduce to the simple branch solution.

The fourth arrangement (conflation) accounts for the lack of agreement of Matthew and Luke against Mark by seeing Mark as a harmonization or conflation of the other two. Whenever Mark saw that Matthew and Luke agreed, he reproduced that agreement, always in the case of sequence and almost always in wording. When they disagreed, he chose between Matthew's and Luke's wording. Only occasionally did he formulate his own wording. In matters of sequence, however, he disagreed with Matthew and Luke only once. This arrangement implies that Mark in general is quite conservative, normally following his sources and adding only six pericopae of his own (Mark 3:20-21; 4:26-29; 7:32-36; 8:22-28; 13:33-37; 14:51-52).

Proponents of the conflation theory have also suggested that Mark evidences a pattern of alternating agreement such that whenever Mark departs from Matthew, he agrees with Luke and vice versa. Mark, when confronted with a disagreement between his sources, had no other basis for ordering his material and so chose between the sources. Hence, on the conflation hypothesis, Mark zigzags between Matthew and Luke, alternatively supporting one, then the other.[7] This also accounts for Mark's omission of the two great sermons: since Mark shifted from Matthew to Luke at Mark 1:21, he passed over Matthew 5–7 (which occurs between Mark 1:21 and 1:22), and by the time he got to Luke 6:20-49 (and 7:1-50) he had moved over to follow Matthew's sequence. This is illustrated by the heavy snaking (━) line on figure 6, which compares the Synoptics in the pericopae parallel to Mark 1:1—6:30, where most sequential disagreements occur.

The fact that Matthew and Luke fail to agree against Mark in the sequence of pericopae forms the basis for the key argument in the Synoptic Problem, the so-called argument from order (Neville 1994). Although historically this argument has been employed in support of several solutions—conflation,[8] an *Urgospel* hypothesis,[9] simple branches,[10] and straight-line solutions[11]—it must be emphasized that the argument from order is inconclusive in itself: it allows *any* arrangement in which Mark (or a document with Markan order) is medial.[12] It can be narrowed to support one view against the others only by invoking additional assumptions or by overstating the evidence. For example, Johann Jakob Griesbach, who first used the argument from order (along with compositional arguments) to support his conflation hypothesis (the Griesbach hypothesis [GH]), did so only by also

7. Griesbach 1789–90, ET 1978:108–10. The clearest presentation of this phenomenon is given by Meijboom 1866, ET 1991:152–53. Longstaff (1977) argued that in the wording of Mark, the same phenomenon may be observed, with Mark copying blocks of Matthew and then switching to Luke at points where Matthew and Luke were in agreement. With close examination of these alleged conflations, however, it is very difficult to see such a clear pattern, much less posit reasons for Mark's allegedly switching from one gospel to another in the middle of a pericope, when nothing substantial is accomplished thereby. See further, Dewey 1987–88 and responses by Longstaff 1987–88 and Walker 1987–88.

8. Griesbach 1789–90, ET 1978:108–10.

9. Lachmann 1835, ET Palmer 1966–67.

10. Weisse 1838, 1:72-73: "In those portions that all three Synoptics have in common, the agreement between the two others is always mediated by Mark. This means that in these portions the other two agree—both in regard to overall order as well as particular wording—only insofar as they also agree with Mark. Whenever they depart from Mark, they also—leaving aside a few insignificant omissions in which their agreement must be regarded as accidental—always depart from each other."

11. Butler (1951b) advocated the "Augustinian hypothesis" (Matthew→Mark→Luke, with Luke using both Matt and Mark).

12. A number of more complex variations of the four solutions outlined above are also logically possible, although seldom, if ever, proposed. For example, the straight-line and simple branch solutions could be modified thus:

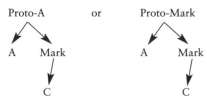

assuming (without argument) that Matthew was the first gospel to be written. Thus his only real decision was between a conflation hypothesis and a straight line in which Luke was last. Karl Lachmann invoked a form of the argument from order in favor of the *Urgospel* solution,[13] but only after dismissing, also without argument, the possibility that Matthew and Luke used Mark directly. Likewise, F. H. Woods used the argument to support Markan priority after dismissing on other grounds Griesbach's solution (1886–90, 2:66–67). Ironically, Butler, who is often credited with having first noted the inconclusive nature of the argument from order,[14] favored the "Augustinian" hypothesis (Mark knew Matthew, and Luke knew both), but did not even consider Griesbach's to be among the possible solutions.[15]

The argument from order has also been narrowed to support a single source solution by restating the phenomenon of order. Farmer has argued:

> Mark's order shows no independence of Matthew and Luke (excepting the single case of his ordering of the cleansing of the temple). This seems explicable only by a conscious effort of Mark to follow the order of Matthew and Luke. Neither Matthew nor Luke could have achieved this alone. They would have to conspire with one another or find some other way to contrive this chronological neutering of Mark, i.e., robbing his chronological independence. Mark on this view can only be third and must have known Matthew and Luke. There seems to be no other satisfactory solution. Such an extraordinary state of affairs is made possible when the author of one narrative document has followed and preserved much of the order of the events given in the other. Only someone writing later who was attempting to combine the two narrative documents has the possibility of preserving what order the second preserved from the first and then, wherever the second departed from the first, following the order of either one or the other. (Farmer 1977:293–94)[16]

---

13. Lachmann 1835:576–77; ET Palmer 1966–67:372: "It used to be said that Matthew must have put back into correct temporal order the events at which he had been present. No scholars, I suppose, would now hold this view; for recent learned controversy can hardly have left anyone supposing the gospel attributed to Matthew to be either more accurate than the others chronologically, or to have been written by an apostle. Even more implausible (since it makes less sense of the necessity which I mentioned) is the view of Mark as a bungling dilettante, unsure of his way, borne hither and thither between Matthew's and Luke's gospels by boredom, desire, carelessness, folly or design. Adherents of this view must have been taken in by a certain discussion of Griesbach's which, though it looks clever and subtle, is really not ingenious at all, but an absolute frost." Note the misprint of this in the reprint by Bellinzoni 1985:125: "Even more *plausible*. . . ."

14. Erroneously, as Neirynck (1982a:113) has pointed out: a century before Butler, the logical ambiguity of the argument was already recognized by Schwarz (1844:307) and A. Maier (1848:35–36). Chapman (1937:4) more clearly than Butler recognized the options listed above (apart from the *Urgospel* hypothesis) but dismissed conflation as "extremely improbable" and the sequence Luke→Mark→Matthew as "almost absurd."

15. Butler 1951b:62–71. Elsewhere in his book there are references to the Griesbach hypothesis, which he dismisses as "the absurd theory" (171) and "a surrender of critical principles" (5).

16. Farmer (1964:213) first formulated this argument as a corrective to Streeter's assertion that "[t]he relative order of incidents and sections in Mark is in general supported by both

This statement of the data requires correction. The kind of phenomenon in which Farmer's observations would convincingly apply is, as Burton has described:

> [i]f two of the documents, say *b* and *c*, are so entirely distinct from one another as to suggest no interdependence, while the third, *a*, is a combination of elements drawn from *b* and *c*, such evidence will clearly point to [a conflation hypothesis] as against any of the other hypotheses enumerated. (1904:8)

In such a case, it would be plainly illogical to suppose that *b* and *c* were derived from *a*, for in that case, one would have to suppose just the kind of "independent collaboration" in their use of *a* that Farmer describes. With the Synoptic Gospels, however, documents *b* and *c* (that is, Matthew and Luke) are not dissimilar. As Figure 6 exemplifies, they agree substantially in sequence. Mark does not "alternate" between Matthew and Luke. On the contrary, in many cases *both* Matthew and Luke support Markan order (note the shaded texts and the double arrows [⇐, ⇒]). Hence it is tendentious to assert that Mark is following only one. Even in the instances of sequential disagreement (←, →) where, e.g., Luke supports Mark and Matthew transposes the pericope, there are significant agreements between Matthew and Mark against Luke *in wording*.[17] Hence, it would be necessary to imagine Mark consulting the wording of Matthew's transposed pericope even when allegedly following Luke.[18] This is, of course, logically possible, but hardly preferable in any obvious way to the simple branch solution or to other solutions where Mark is medial.

Matthew and Luke; where either of them deserts Mark, the other is usually found supporting him" (1924:151). Focusing only on the second half of Streeter's statement, Farmer correctly argues that alternating agreement with Mark constitutes a problem, not a support for Markan priority, since one would have to explain how Matthew could (nearly) always agree with Mark when Luke disagreed and vice versa. Farmer (1964:214) also argued that alternating agreement with Mark posed problems for Lachmann's *Urgospel* hypothesis, since one would have to explain why there are not more instances of both Matthew and Luke departing from the *Urgospel* (=Markan) order.

A less cautious form of this argument is found in Stoldt (1980:136, 141), who refers to the "shifting parallels between Mark on the one hand and Matthew and Luke on the other—sometimes with one, sometimes with the other" (141). This is a serious misstatement of the phenomenon of order.

17. E.g., in Matt 8:1-4 (Mark 1:40-45/Luke 5:12-16) Matt and Mark agree against Luke in ἐκαθαρίσθη, καὶ λέγει αὐτῷ ὅρα μηδενὶ . . . εἴπῃς, ὕπαγε, σεαυτὸν δεῖξον, and ἃ/ὃ προσέταξεν Μωυσῆς. Similarly, Neirynck 1982a:118: "To conclude, since the 'Lucan' sections in Mark show more elements in common with Matthew than Griesbach's table may suggest, the examination of the relative order—together with the phenomenon of conflation—tends to mitigate the statement on alternation."

18. Moreover, at 2:1-22 Mark would, on a conflation theory, be following both Matt 8:1-17 and Luke 5:17-39 (moving between the wording of his sources for reasons that are far from clear), but then without explanation would have passed over Matt 9:18—11:30, containing, for example, the more dramatic version of the raising of the daughter of the synagogue president, the mission speech, and the words about John the Baptist. See also Neirynck 1982a:118.

PATTERNS OF AGREEMENTS IN THE DOUBLE TRADITION

The third significant set of Synoptic data is the considerable bulk of material found in Matthew and Luke but not in Mark—the "double tradition." This consists mainly of sayings or brief stories which feature sayings and amounts to about 4,500 words, approximately the size of 2 Corinthians.[19] Examples of these Matthew–Luke materials are the makarisms (Matt 5:3-4, 6, 11-12 / Luke 6:20b-23), woes against three Galilean towns (Matt 11:20-24 / Luke 10:13-15), the saying about serving two masters (Matt 6:24 / Luke 16:13), and the healing of the centurion's serving boy (Matt 8:5-10, 13 / Luke 7:1b-10). As with the triple tradition, the level of verbal agreement in much of the double tradition is such that one must posit some sort of *literary* relationship between Matthew and Luke; the degree of agreement is too high to be due to independent use of oral tradition (see chapter 2, p. 63).

The double tradition exhibits two important and seemingly contradictory features. First, while there is often a high degree of verbal agreement between Matthew and Luke within these sections, there is practically *no agreement* in the placement of these sayings *relative to Mark*. Matthew's makarisms follow either the call of the four fishermen (Matt 4:18-22 / Mark 1:16-20, 21) or the description of Jesus' preaching tour through the Galilee (Matt 4:23 / Mark 1:39), depending upon how Synoptic tables are aligned (see Neirynck 1976; 1982c). In Luke, however, the makarisms follow the healing of the man with the withered hand (Luke 6:6-11 / Mark 3:1-6) and the naming of the Twelve (Luke 6:12-16 / Mark 3:13-19). In Matthew the woes against the Galilean towns are part of Jesus' attack on "this generation's" rejection of John the Baptist and Jesus (Matt 11:2-30), while in Luke they form part of the commissioning speech directed to the seventy-two disciples (Luke 10:1-16). Similarly, the saying on serving two masters appears in the middle of Matthew's Sermon on the Mount, while in Luke it appears toward the end of the gospel after the parable of the Unjust Steward and various sayings concerning money and greed. There is, in other words, little to suggest that Matthew was influenced by Luke's placement of the double tradition or vice versa.

Second, if one does not measure sequential agreement of these Matthew–Luke materials relative to Mark, but relative to each other, approximately one-third of the pericopae, accounting for almost one-half of the word count, are in the same relative order. That is, in spite of the fact that Matthew and Luke place double tradition materials differently *relative to*

19. Kloppenborg 1988a:209. According to my 1988 count, the *verbatim* agreement between Matthew and Luke amounts to 2,414 Matthaean or 2,400 Lukan words (the disparity deriving from the fact that in a few instances, Matthew or Luke has a doublet [e.g. Matt 9:32-34 / 12:22-24 / Luke 11:14-15]). The total word count for Matthew–Q and Luke–Q pericopae is respectively 4,464 and 4,652 words. Hence the degree of verbatim agreement is 54 percent (of Matthew–Q) or 51.6 percent (of Luke–Q).

Mark, they nonetheless agree in using many of the sayings and stories in the same order relative to each other. For example, the double tradition materials in Matt 3:3, 7-10, 11-12; 4:1-11, 13; 5:3-6, 11-12, 39-42, 45-47, 48; 7:1-2, 3-5, 16-20, 21, 24-27; 8:5-10, 13; 11:2-11, 16-19, 20-24, 25-27; 12:22-30, 38-42; 13:31-32; 18:12-14, 15-22; 24:26-28, 37-41; 25:14-30 agree in sequence with those in Luke 3:3, 7-9, 16b-17; 4:1-13, 16a; 6:20b-23, 29-30, 32-35, 36, 37-38, 41-44, 46-49; 7:1-10, 18-28, 31-35; 10:13-15, 21-22; 11:14-23, 29-32; 13:18-21; 15:4-7; 17:3b-4, 23-37; 19:12-26.[20] This implies that even if Matthew and Luke are not in direct contact with one another, something has influenced them in the overall order of the double tradition.

If we return to the four basic options given above (p. 23) and integrate the observations from the double tradition, it is immediately clear that none of the options is viable by itself. The level of agreement between Matthew and Luke in the double tradition indicates that some sort of relationship, direct or indirect, exists in the absence of Mark. None of the options given above explains how Matthew and Luke can agree where Mark is not present. What is needed is a line connecting Luke with Matthew, either directly or indirectly, but without involving Mark or Markan material. Moreover, a model is needed that accounts both for Matthew's and Luke's basic agreement in the relative sequence of the double tradition (independent of Mark) and for their nearly complete disagreement in the way in which these materials are combined with the Markan framework and with Markan stories and sayings.

Hence, we need to draw a line that connects Matthew and Luke that does not go through Mark *and* that does not connect Matthew and Luke directly. For if Luke used Matthew (or vice versa), it would be difficult to account for the fact that Luke's placement of the double tradition differs almost entirely from that of Matthew.[21] The simplest solution is to posit an

---

20. See Kloppenborg 1987a:72–80 and below, chap. 2 (figure 14).

21. McNicol (1996:14–21 and passim) attempts to account for the disagreements in placement of the double tradition material by arguing the Luke scanned Matthew several times, lifting out and placing Matthaean material in new contexts. In Luke 3:1—10:22, for example, Luke allegedly scanned Matthew five times, lifting out materials *in Matthaean order* and deploying them in five slightly overlapping blocks. McNicol also requires Luke to have scanned the long Matthaean discourses separately, extracting sayings material in Matthaean order and reassembling them in the Lukan Travel Narrative. In order to maintain the appearance of agreement with Matthew's sequence, McNicol requires many "passes" (two in order to construct Luke 10:1-42, and twenty-five to construct the entire Travel Narrative). As will be noted in chapter 2, Vincent Taylor proposed the same model of multiple "scans" in order to explain the composition of Matthew's sermons from Q. For Taylor, Matthew was collecting thematically related materials into discourses. The 2GH must assume opposite interests, for Luke *distributes* Matthew's thematically grouped sayings throughout his rather heterogeneous Travel Narrative. The scenario proposed by McNicol is logically possible, but there seems no convincing editorial reason for Luke to have done this. On the issue of the plausiblity of McNicol's explanations, see Derrenbacker 1998.

unknown document that will serve as the source of Matthew's and Luke's double tradition. In this way, both Matthew and Luke can use the unknown document, independently combining it with Mark to arrive at two different fusions. This is what the Two Document hypothesis suggests:[22]

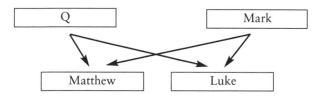

Figure 7
The Two Document Hypothesis

The 2DH accounts for the data outlined above in a satisfactory manner. The hypothesis accounts for the fact that Matthew and Luke tend not to agree *against Mark* in sequence because both have used Mark independently. Hence, they sometimes take over from Mark the same wording and sequence (resulting in triple agreements); sometimes Matthew reproduces Mark and Luke chooses another order or wording; sometimes the reverse. But when Matthew and Luke both alter Mark, they rarely alter Mark's wording *in the same way* and *never* agree in sequence against Mark. Even though both Matthew and Luke rearranged Mark, they transpose *different* Markan pericopae and the only pericope which both transpose (Mark 3:13-19) is not transposed in the same way. This is precisely what one ought to expect if Matthew and Luke used Mark independently.

Likewise, Matthew and Luke independently used a non-Markan source (Q). Sometimes they copied Q exactly, resulting in the verbatim agreement between Matthew and Luke (e.g., Matt 3:7-10 / Luke 3:7-9). Of course, if even one of them altered the wording of Q, a verbal disagreement between Matthew and Luke would result. Since neither Matthew nor Luke had seen the other's work, they could not be expected to agree in placing the non-Markan material relative to the Markan material. Matthew, for example, locates the Sermon on the Mount, drawn largely from Q, at a point corre-

22. There are, of course, several other solutions that are *logically* possible but which would require incredible assumptions. For example,

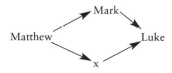

would account for the fact that Luke has combined the 'x' material with Mark differently than it was in Matthew, but one would also need to account for why Matthew would be broken down into two more or less discrete subcollections, and why, if Luke knew these two sub-Matthaean collections, he did not know and use Matthew's gospel directly.

sponding to Mark 1:21, where Mark first mentions Jesus' teaching[23] (or possibly at Mark 1:39); but Luke places Q's Sermon, which seems to have mentioned the disciples (Q 6:20), after the naming of the Twelve (Mark 3:13-19 / Luke 6:12-16). Nevertheless, since the Q material had a fixed order, both Matthew and Luke were influenced by that order and hence agree in many instances in *relative* sequence, even if they have fused it with Mark differently.

The only exception to this "rule" of Matthew's and Luke's failure to attach double tradition material to the *same* Markan context is rather easily explicable. Matthew and Luke agree only in the first few verses of Mark (see figure 8, p. 33).

In all three cases (Q 3:3, 7b-9; 3:16-17; 4:1-13), the Q material that was combined with Mark partially overlapped Mark in content. Q 3:3, 7-9 contained an introduction to John's oracle (3:3, 7a) that overlapped Mark 1:2-6; both Mark and Q contained a version of the prediction of the Coming/Stronger One, although Q's version (3:16-17) was longer than Mark's; and both Q and Mark had a testing story, Mark's being only two verses long (1:12-13), while Q had an elaborate three-part test (Q 4:1-13). Naturally, Matthew and Luke attached the Q saying regarding John's preaching to the same Markan pericope (Mark 1:2-6) because there Mark is also describing John's preaching. Similarly, Mark's version of John's prediction of the "Stronger One" (Mark 1:7-8) was the obvious point at which to use Q's longer prediction of the Coming One and his eschatological activities (Q 3:16-17). Finally, Mark's short account of Jesus' temptation (Mark 1:12-13) is virtually the only place at which Matthew and Luke could have used Q's longer and more elaborate temptation account (Q 4:1-13). After this point in Mark, Matthew and Luke are consistent in not placing Q material in the same place relative to Mark.

It would be misleading to leave the impression that the 2DH can account equally well for all of the Synoptic data. I have already alluded to a set of agreements of Matthew and Luke against Mark in Markan contexts—normally called "the minor agreements." These seemingly violate the principle that Matthew and Luke do not agree in wording against Mark. Some of these agreements are common omissions of Markan pericopae, phrases, or words; some are common additions to or elaborations of Mark (but normally not the *same* addition or elaboration); some are agreements against Mark in word order or inflectional form; and some are more substantial verbal agreements against Mark.

How these minor agreements are counted and evaluated is itself a matter of dispute. Some scholars lump all of the minor agreements together and claim that their sheer number constitutes too long a list of "exceptions" to be accommodated by the 2DH. But are the common omissions of Markan

23. Thus Neirynck 1990b:589–90.

Figure 8
Matthew–Luke Agreements in Placing the Double Tradition

Q	Matthew	Mark	Luke	Q
3:3 ⇒ John in the Wilderness	3:1-6 (Q+Mk)	⇐ 1:2-6 ⇒ John in the Wilderness	3:1-7a (Q+Mk)	⇐ 3:3 John in the Wilderness
	3:7a			
3:7b-9 ⇒ Preaching of Repentance	3:7b-10 (Q)		3:7b-9 (Q)	⇐ 3:7b-9 Preaching of Repentance
3:16 ⇒ Announcement of the Coming One	3:11 (Q+Mk)	⇐ 1:7-8 ⇒ Announcement of the Coming One	3:16 (Q+Mk)	⇐ 3:16 Announcement of the Coming One
3:17 ⇒	3:12 (Q)		3:17 (Q)	⇐ 3:17
	3:13-17	⇐ 1:9-11 ⇒ Jesus' Baptism	3:21-22	
4:1-2 ⇒ The Testing of Jesus (setting)	4:1-2 (Q+Mk)	⇐ 1:12-13a ⇒ The Testing of Jesus	4:1-2 (Q+Mk)	⇐ 4:1-2 The Testing of Jesus (setting)
4:3-13 ⇒ 3 Challenges by the Devil	4:3-11a (Q)		4:3-13 (Q)	⇐ 4:3-13 3 Challenges by the Devil
	4:11b	⇐ 1:13b Conclusion: The angels appear		

Sigla

3:7b-10 Agreement of Matt and Luke in placing double tradition material at the same point relative to Mark

3:1-6 Overlap of Mark and Q

3:10-15 Special material or editorial additions

pericopae, phrases, or words to be evaluated in the same way as positive agreements against Mark in the use of a particular word or phrase? In most cases, common omissions do not require the supposition of collaboration between Matthew and Luke but arise instead from similar responses to the text of Mark. For example, in Mark 1:1-6, Matthew and Luke both omit Mark 1:2b (=Mal 3:1), a quotation that Mark erroneously ascribed to Isaiah, perhaps because of Mark's error or because Matthew and Luke had the Malachi quotation on Jesus' lips in Q (Q 7:27). The omission of Mark 1:2b, however, must be seen in the fuller context of the treatment of Mark by Matthew and Luke: Matthew also omits Mark's "baptism of repentance for the forgiveness of sins" (which Luke retains). Luke omits the description of John's dress and food (which Matthew retains). In other words, to focus only on Matthew's and Luke's joint omission of Mark 1:2b is to distort the evidence. It is not a case of Matthew and Luke always agreeing in omitting the same Markan material; here, both omit various materials from Mark and they coincide in *one* of those omissions.

There are of course common omissions of entire Markan pericopae. Both Matthew and Luke omit Mark 3:20-21 and 8:22-26. This, however, is not surprising given the content of these two pericopae: a report that Jesus' kin thought him insane and a miracle account in which complete restoration required two healing gestures. The first casts Jesus' family in a bad light and thus conflicts with the glowingly positive portrayals of his family in the widely divergent Matthaean and the Lukan infancy accounts. In the case of Mark 8:22-26, this is part of a long block of Markan material omitted by Luke (Mark 6:45—8:26), whereas Matthew omitted only Mark 8:22-26. There is something peculiar about the story, however, for it easily raises awkward questions about the effectiveness of Jesus' miracle-working power and thus conflicts with the elevated sense of Jesus' powers in Matthew and Luke. In other words, seemingly identical editing of Mark by Matthew and Luke does not necessarily signal literary dependence; it arises quite naturally from the later evangelists' respective theologies of Jesus' family and his capacity for wondrous deeds.

At other points, Matthew's apparent agreement with Luke against Mark arises from a concern that is completely different from Luke's concern. For example, the common omission of "Nazareth" from Mark's baptismal pericope is linked to two quite different editorial procedures on the part of Matthew and Luke. It is not an indication of direct contact between Matthew and Luke.[24]

---

24. Matthew's deletion of Nazareth is a function of his geographical schematism, which follows the principal domiciles of Jesus from Bethlehem (2:1, 11), Egypt (2:14), Nazareth (2:23), and Kefar Naḥum [Capernaum] (4:13), each connected with a fulfillment citation (2:6, 15, 23b; 4:15-16). In 3:13 Jesus is not leaving Nazareth but only coming from the Galilee for baptism and a brief stay in the wilderness. Nazareth is not mentioned expressly after 2:3 until 4:13, when Jesus quits Nazareth for Kefar Naḥum. Luke, on the other hand, eliminates entirely the

The majority of positive agreements against Mark are easily explained within the framework of the 2DH on the basis of coincidental editorial activity. A large number of these agreements occur with Markan usages that both Matthew and Luke normally correct and, hence, sometimes correct in the same way. For example, both Matthew and Luke tend to avoid Mark's tedious use of καί ("and") to connect main clauses. They do so by substituting participial constructions, subordinating conjunctions, articular infinitives, and so forth. Sometimes they coincide in altering Mark in the same or similar ways. At other points, one makes the alteration and the other does not, or makes a different alteration (Neirynck 1974b:207–11). As Neirynck has insisted, it is misleading to isolate only one set of evidence (the points where Matthew and Luke agree against Mark), and neglect the fuller profile of Matthew's and Luke's treatment of Markan style. To examine the larger body of data makes the minor agreements much less impressive.

Another sort of potentially problematic data has to do with Mark's double expressions. The classic example is Mark 1:32, "that evening, when the sun was setting," where Matthew (8:16) has reproduced the first part of the phrase and Luke (4:40) the second. This is a phenomenon that Griesbach attributed to Mark's conflation of Matthew and Luke and which some critics of the 2DH have thought fatal to the hypothesis, since it would be unlikely that Matthew and Luke could "independently collaborate" in taking from Mark alternating portions of Mark's double expressions. An analysis of *all* of the 213 Markan double expressions reveals, however, that there is no such independent collaboration. Both Matthew and Luke tend to reduce Mark's double expressions and do so in a way that is perfectly consistent with the supposition of independent use of Mark.[25]

There are, nonetheless, a few instances of more significant agreements against Mark that are not so easily explained.[26] At Mark 4:11, for example,

---

verb "to come" from the baptismal scene and subordinates Jesus' baptism to the descent of the Spirit and the heavenly audition. Both "from Nazareth" and "Galilee" are omitted in the process.

25. On the phenomenon in general, see Neirynck 1972. Tuckett's analysis of the 213 double expressions in Mark indicates that, far from there being a pattern whereby Matthew and Luke routinely take alternate parts of Markan double expressions (which would be exceedingly difficult to explain on the 2DH), the Markan double expressions fall into every conceivable class: Matthew taking one half, Luke the other; Matthew taking one half, Luke both; Matthew taking one half, Luke with no parallel; Luke taking one half, Matthew both; Luke taking one half, Matthew with no parallel; both omitting the same half; both taking both halves; Matthew taking both, Luke with no parallel; Luke taking both halves, Matthew with no parallel; both with no parallel (1983:16–21).

26. Neirynck 1991c:12–28 treats the most difficult of the agreements: Mark 4:11; 5:27; 9:19; and 14:65. Longer lists of "significant" agreements are given in Neirynck 1991d:10–11 (29 significant agreements and 7 slightly less important agreements) and Ennulat 1994:passim (23 agreements which Ennulat thinks points to a post-Markan recension and 33 which less clearly do). Ennulat has a very generous definition of Matthew–Luke agreements, however,

Matthew and Luke have ὑμῖν δέδοται γνῶναι τὰ μυστήρια ("to you is given *to know* the myster*ies*") while Mark has ὑμῖν τὸ μυστήριον δέδοται ("to you the mystery is given")—disagreeing in word order, in the number of μυστήριον, and in the addition/omission of the infinitive γνῶναι. This Matthew–Luke agreement has been treated within the context of the 2DH either by suggesting coincidental redaction by Matthew and Luke (McLoughlin 1967:26; Neirynck 1991c:26–27), the influence of oral tradition (Fusco 1982), textual corruption (Streeter 1924:313), or an earlier (Koester 1983:48) or second recension of Mark (Ennulat 1994:123–28). The fact that there is little agreement on a solution to the handful of such problems is not necessarily a symptom of a flawed hypothesis, as it sometimes alleged by critics of the 2DH. Indeed, the problem is not a lack of solutions, but too many solutions and not knowing which is preferable![27]

The lack of a consensus regarding the minor agreements derives from two factors: (1) it is impossible to reconstruct with absolute precision the Greek text of the any of the gospels; and (2) the transmissional processes by which one gospel came to be used by another evangelist are not known at all. In this situation, critics assume a range of transmissional and editorial models or working hypotheses, each with its own implicit canons of plausibility. To proceed on the twin assumptions that the Nestle-Aland[27] text closely approximates that of the final form of the gospels and that Matthew and Luke knew Mark in the *same* form that we have, implies that the solution to the minor agreements must lie in coincidental editorial modification[28] or the occasional influence of non-Markan tradition.[29] If, however, one assumes a less controlled transmission of texts, either "between" the gospels or in the earliest stages of scribal transmission (or both), the minor agreements might more plausibly be addressed as a recensional[30] or text-critical problem. That is, the version of Mark (II) used by Matthew and/or Luke may have differed slightly from canonical Mark (I). Diagrammatically, the options can be expressed thus:

---

and many on his list are not even included in any category by others. See also Friedrichsen 1991:383–84.

27. Friedrichsen 1989:391 rightly observes, "disagreement amongst Two-Source theorists about explanations of particular minor agreements does not serve as an argument against the hypothesis."

28. E.g., Neirynck 1991c:29: "[I]t is sound methodology among Markan priorists that no alternative for the minor agreements is needed as long as the basic assumption of independent redaction provides a satisfactory solution. The main objection is the difficulty of some individual cases, but, as indicated in Section II [where Neirynck treats Mark 4:11; 5:27; 9:19; and 14:65], the extent of the 'unexplained remainder' is not irreducible."

29. E.g., Bovon (1989:20) holds that "Luke used a form of the gospel of Mark that differed from canonical Mark in only minor respects" and hence explains some of the minor agreements on the basis of influence of oral tradition. See Bovon 1989:245 (Luke 5:17-26); 268 (Mark 2:27); 413 (Luke 8:10) and passim.

30. E.g., Luz 1985–90, 1:30: "In my view Matthew and Luke used a recension of Mark which at many points is secondary to canonical Mark."

Figure 9
Models of Transmission

Redactional Models   **Recensional Models**

Deutero-Markus

Oral Tradition

Q   Mark

Matt   Luke

Q

Mark I
(canonical Mark)

Mark II
(secondary Mark)

Matt   Luke

Ur-Markus

Q

Mark I
(primitive Mark)

Mark II
(secondary Mark)

Matt   Luke

Text-Critical Model

Q   Mark (original)

Matt   Luke

Copyists' Modifications

Matt   Luke   Mark
canonical   canonical   canonical

Sigla

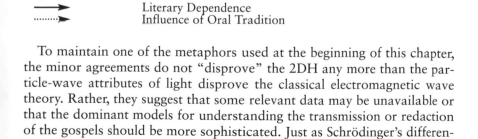

Literary Dependence
Influence of Oral Tradition

To maintain one of the metaphors used at the beginning of this chapter, the minor agreements do not "disprove" the 2DH any more than the particle-wave attributes of light disprove the classical electromagnetic wave theory. Rather, they suggest that some relevant data may be unavailable or that the dominant models for understanding the transmission or redaction of the gospels should be more sophisticated. Just as Schrödinger's differential wave equation resolved some of the seeming anomalies in particle physics without rendering invalid the wave theory, so too further data or refinements of theoretical models are not likely to change the general outlines of the 2DH.

Other Solutions

Griesbach, "Augustine," and Farrer-Goulder

It would be unfair to give the impression that the 2DH is the only possible explanation of the Synoptic data, even if it is the most widely held hypothesis. The Griesbach (Two Gospel) hypothesis also has Mark in a medial position (as a conflation of Matthew and Luke) but posits direct dependence of Luke upon Matthew (Farmer 1990). John Chapman (1937) and B. C. Butler (1951b) sought to defend the "Augustinian" solution,[31] which places Mark in a medial position, between Matthew, the earliest Gospel, and Luke, who used both Matthew and Mark. Austin Farrer and Michael Goulder concur with the supposition of Markan priority, but also suggest that Matthew and Luke used Mark, and that Luke used Matthew (see figure 10).[32]

While a full discussion of the strengths and weaknesses of these competing hypotheses overreaches the bounds of this book,[33] five observations are pertinent.

First, like the 2DH, each has Mark in a medial position: as a conflation of Matthew and Luke (Griesbach); as the common source of Matthew and

31. I use quotation marks around "Augustinian," because it doubtful that Augustine's *De consensu evangelistarum* 1.2.4 implies anything more than a straight-line solution (Matthew→Mark→Luke→John) and probably does not mean to imply literary dependence in the strict sense at all. De Jonge (1992a) notes that since Augustine throughout the work speaks of Matthew omitting material from Mark (2.37.61; 2.46.96, etc.), Mark omitting from Luke (3.25.73), and Matthew adding to what is reported by Mark and Luke (2.80.157), he cannot be using *omittere, praetermittere*, etc. as technical terms for the treatment of sources. Rather, he means "fails to narrate" or "leaves unnoticed." Augustine's intention is apologetic—to defend the evangelists from the charge that they are deficient. Apropos of Augustine's description of Mark as a follower (*pedisquus*) of Matthew, McLoughlin (1963:28) remarks: "Augustine speaks of Mk following Mt, and while in our scientifically-minded age such a suggestion carries causal implications, it is much less certain that it does so for the Platonic-minded Augustine: a second witness, who adds nothing to what the first and principal witness had already said, could well in such a mentality be described as his follower."

The actual view of Augustine nothwithstanding, at least from the sixteenth century (Chemnitz 1593, ²1652:3) it was assumed that Augustine held a conflation hypothesis. See chap. 6, n. 3.

32. Farrer 1957, repr. 1985; Goulder 1989. A slightly modified version of this solution is also defended by Sanders and Davies 1989.

33. The proceedings of the 1984 Jerusalem colloquium (Dungan 1990a) offer defenses and critiques of the 2DH, the 2GH, and the "Multistage" hypothesis of M.-É. Boismard. For contrasting evaluations of the Farrer-Goulder hypothesis, see Goodacre 1996 and Neirynck 1997.

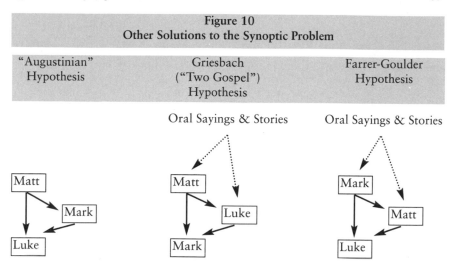

Figure 10
Other Solutions to the Synoptic Problem

Luke (Farrer-Goulder); or as the link between the earliest and the latest gospel ("Augustine").

Second, unlike the 2DH, each posits a *direct* dependence of Luke upon Matthew. It is for this reason that a hypothetical document such as Q is not needed, for what the 2DH ascribes to Q is instead explained as Luke's direct appropriation from Matthew. This supposition is not without its difficulties. For both the "Augustinian" and the Farrer-Goulder hypotheses, a serious question is raised: why, in pericopae where both Matthew and Mark were present, did Luke always choose *Markan* order and never Matthaean order, and why did he overwhelmingly prefer Markan wording even when Matthew offered something different (often in better Greek)? Moreover, all three hypotheses require one to suppose that Luke rather aggressively dislocated sayings from the context in which he found them in Matthew, often transporting them to contexts in which their function and significance is far less clear than it was in Matthew.[34] This may be illustrated by sayings in Matthew's Sermon on the Mount (see figure 11).

Figure 11 indicates (a) the different placements of the Sermon relative to Mark, (b) the agreements between Matthew and Luke in the basic outline of the Sermon (the shaded pericopae), and (c) the substantial expansion of the Sermon by Matthew's relocation of Q material that appears later in Luke. On the 2DH, the core of the Sermon existed in Q (enclosed in the box). Matthew collected and organized into his Sermon sayings scattered throughout Q, while Luke preserved Q's order. On hypotheses suggesting a direct relation between Luke and Matthew, however, Luke would have both changed the location of the Sermon from a position corresponding to Mark 1:21 (or Mark 1:34) to Mark 3:19 for no obvious reason and dislocated

---

34. For a recent attempt to given an account of Luke's procedure, see above, n. 21.

Figure 11
Matthew's Sermon and Luke's Parallels

Mark	Matthew			Luke		Mark
1:16-20	⇔ Matt 4:18-22			6:6:11	⇔	3:1-6
1:39	⇔ Matt 4:23			6:12-16	⇔	3:13-19
1:32, 34	⇔ Matt 4:24—5:1			6:17-19		
	5:2	Introduction	⇔	6:20a	Introduction	
	5:3-12	Beatitudes	⇔	6:20b-23	Beatitudes	
	5:13	Salt				
	5:14-16	Lamp				
	5:17-20	The Law				
	5:21-26	On Settling Disputes				
	5:27-30	On Adultery				
	5:31-32	On Divorce				
	5:33-37	On Swearing				
	5:38-42	On Retaliation	⇔	6:29-30	On Retaliation	
	5:43-48	On Loving Enemies	⇔	6:27-36	On Loving Enemies	
			⇔	6:31	Golden Rule	
	6:1-4	On Almsgiving				
	6:5-8	On Prayer				
	6:9-13	Lord's Prayer				
	6:16-18	On Fasting				
	6:19-21	On Treasures				
	6:22-23	Sound Eye				
	6:24	God and Mammon				
	6:25-34	On Anxiety				
	7:1-3	On Judging	⇔	6:37-39	On Judging	
	7:3-5	Judging a Brother	⇔	6:41-42	Judging a Brother	
	7:6	Pearls before pigs				
	7:7-11	Ask, seek, knock				
	7:12	Golden Rule				
	7:13-14	Two Ways				
	7:15-20	Trees and Fruit	⇔	6:43-44	Trees and Fruit	
	7:21	Lord, Lord	⇔	6:46	Lord, Lord	
	7:22-23	Self-Deception				
	7:24-27	Two Builders	⇔	6:47-49	Two Builders	
1:22	⇔ Matt 7:28-29			7:1—8:3	⇔	4:21-25
				8:4-18	⇔	4:21-25
				11:2-4	Lord's Prayer	
				11:9-13	Ask, seek, knock	
				11:33	Lamp	
				11:34-36	Sound Eye	
				12:22-32	On Anxiety	
				12:33-34	On Treasures	
				12:57-59	Settling Disputes	
				13:23-24	Two Ways	
				13:26-27	Self-Deception	
				14:34-35	Salt	
				16:13	God and Mammon	
				16:17	The Law	
				16:18	On Divorce	

sayings that were already collected and well contextualized in Matthew. Defenders of both the Griesbach and the Farrer-Goulder hypotheses have now begun the painstaking task of attempting a detailed account of Luke's procedures and their rationale.[35] Whether these efforts will succeed in rendering Luke's procedures intelligible remains to be seen. The explanation, in any event, will necessarily take a different form from that of the 2DH. For whereas the 2DH accounts for the disagreements between Matthew and Luke in the ordering of the Q material by an explanation that combines their independence (noncollaboration) in the use of Q with intentional factors (Matthew's penchant to collect and organize sayings), the Matthew → Luke hypotheses must account for Luke's dislocations exclusively in *intentional* terms: Luke deliberately altered Matthew. The sheer scale of Luke's dislocations and modifications makes this a daunting prospect indeed.[36]

Third, it has been observed that Luke fails to reproduce Matthew's "additions" to Mark and fails to adopt the more obvious Matthaeanisms in the first gospel. Or, to put it more neutrally, in Lukan material for which there are Matthaean and Markan parallels, Luke rarely reflects what is distinctive of Matthew when it is compared with Mark. For example, Luke lacks the conversation between John the Baptist and Jesus in Matt 3:14-15 (contrast Mark 1:9-11 / Luke 3:21-22) and Matthew's extension of the quotation of Isa 6:9-10 (contrast Mark 4:12 / Luke 8:10). Neither Mark nor Luke reproduces Matthew's favorite "kingdom of the heavens." Luke's agreements with Matthew, moreover, begin where Mark begins and end where Mark ends: Matthew and Luke both have infancy stories and resurrection stories, but their accounts are completely different. For Luke to have so consistently avoided what Matthew added to Mark (Farrer-Goulder) or the material that Mark eliminated from Matthew ("Augustine") requires an idiosyncratic view of Lukan editorializing;[37] obviously, it is far simpler to conclude that Luke lacks these Matthaeanisms because he has edited Mark independently of Matthew.

Fourth, the Griesbach and "Augustinian" hypotheses must in addition hold that Mark saw relatively good quality Greek in Matthew ("Augustine") or in both Matthew and Luke (Griesbach) and often substituted poorer Greek. This, of course, is not impossible.[38] Nor is it impossible that

---

35. For the Griesbach (Two-Gospel) hypothesis (2GH), see Farmer 1987; 1994; McNicol 1990; Cope, Dungan, et al. 1992; 1993; 1994 (and the response in Kloppenborg 1992a); 1995; McNicol 1996. For the Farrer-Goulder hypothesis, see Goulder 1989.

36. This is true also of the 2GH's view of Mark: Mark's deviations from and combinations of Matthew and Luke must be explained on the basis of authorial or editorial *intention*.

37. This objection obviously does not apply equally to the 2GH.

38. Sanders's (somewhat restricted) analysis of the "tendencies" of the Synoptic tradition concluded that there were few strongly defined tendencies of later documents apart from the tendency to create direct discourse and the use of the first person, and the addition of proper names or the substitution of names for pronouns (1969:274–75). While his analysis included features such as the presence or avoidance of parataxis (the overuse of "and" for connecting

Mark's editing created various awkwardnesses, including, e.g., the transformation of Matt 13:58, "he *did not* do any mighty works there *because*
of their unbelief" to Mark 6:5-6a, "he *could not* do any mighty work there
. . . *and he marveled* at their unbelief." But the reverse direction of development seems the more likely.

More seriously, Mark omitted a great deal of Matthew ("Augustine";
Griesbach) and Luke (Griesbach), including the long sermons of Matthew,
the infancy accounts, and the appearance stories. This objection, while
important, should not be overstated. On any hypothesis, including the
2DH, later documents have omitted materials in an earlier document and
such omissions need to be explained. It is perhaps possible to imagine
scenarios in which the omission of the infancy stories or the long sermons
might be reasonable, although it is hardly satisfactory merely to assert, as
Griesbach did, that Mark wanted to write a short book.[39] Even more problematic for the Griesbach hypothesis is the fact that various scenes that portray Jesus' parents and disciples in a positive light—for example, the infancy
accounts and scenes like Peter's walking on the sea (Matt 14:28-31) or
Jesus' promise of Peter's rehabilitation after the resurrection (Luke 22:31-
32)—are entirely omitted by Mark and replaced with scenes that create a
uniformly negative view of Jesus' kin and a very negative view of his disciples (see Kloppenborg 1992b). While such transformations are *logically*
possible, it is also necessary to posit a historical occasion in which such a
development would be *plausible*. None, so far, has been offered.

Finally, Griesbach and (presumably) "Augustine" have to posit Lukan
access to pre-Matthaean materials in those instances such as the request for
a sign (Luke 11:29-32) or the Lord's Prayer or Luke 17:23-30 where Luke
seems to have a more primitive version of what appears in Matthew.[40] Of

---

clauses and sentences), asyndeton (the lack of connective particles between sentences), and the
historic present, he did not treat features such as the creation of periodic sentences and more
complex features of style, nor the resolution/creation of syntactical, narrative, or theological
difficulties.

39. Griesbach 1789–90, ET 1978:108 n. 17: "Mark . . . forsakes Matthew and passes over
to Luke since he decided to pass over Christ's sermon on the Mount, which follows at this point
[4:22] in Matthew; for, as he meant to write a short book, it seems to him verbose, and besides,
it comprises many things which specially pertain to those persons who heard Christ speaking
on the mountain." Ironically, Griesbach (1978:108 n. 16) explained the omission of the
infancy stories with the claim, "these chapters are entirely omitted, because Mark meant to
narrate only those deeds performed by Christ in his capacity as a public teacher" but does not
notice that Luke's infancy stories in fact prepare precisely for Jesus' role as a teacher.

40. Farmer (1975, 1:46–48 n. 4) acknowledges that Luke 17 does not derive from Matthew
24, in spite of the parallels; hence it is necessary "to hypothecate another source, an apocalyptic source, that Luke had copied." Similarly, McNicol 1990:162, 168–73.

Goulder's appeal to pre-Lukan sources is far more restricted: he argues that Matthew
created the Lord's Prayer and that Luke abbreviated it (1989:496–97); thus he does not have
to posit Lukan access to pre-Lukan or pre-Lukan material. His argument is similar on Luke
11:29-30 (1989:511–12) and 17:23-30 (1989:648–55). Even the special Lukan material Goul-

course, it is necessary in any case to account for Lukan special material which Luke has not obtained from Matthew or Mark ("Augustine"; Farrer-Goulder) or from Matthew (Griesbach), and one might suppose that some of this special material overlapped Matthaean sayings, containing more primitive forms which Luke preferred. Nevertheless, such a solution mitigates the apparent economy of the Matthew ⟶ Luke solutions, whose appeal consists in being able to account for all of the Synoptic data on the basis of extant documents and without having to posit additional relationships and coincidentally overlapping documents or traditions. The more it is necessary to grant Luke special access to pre-Matthaean forms of sayings or stories, the less satisfactory such solutions become, quite apart from their other difficulties.[41]

It is necessary to reiterate that several solutions to the Synoptic Problem are logically possible: those in which Mark is medial. Each of the major hypotheses mentioned above—the 2DH, Griesbach, Farrer-Goulder, and "Augustinian" hypotheses—offer logically possible accountings for the Synoptic data. The real point of disagreement among Synoptic Problem specialists is not what is logically possible, but which hypotheses imply *plausible editorial procedures* on the part of the evangelists. In my view, it is far easier to accommodate the few significant minor agreements against Mark, for which various, if not completely satisfying explanations have been proposed, than it is to accept a Luke who drastically rearranged Matthew, or a Mark who conflated and abbreviated Matthew and Luke and in doing so darkened the portrait of Jesus' family and disciples.[42] Advocates of the other hypotheses, all fair-minded and careful scholars, evidently do not sense these difficulties so acutely and hence the Synoptic Problem remains a problem.

MORE COMPLEX SOLUTIONS

Before leaving this topic, we should mention some of the more complex solutions to the Synoptic Problem that have been advanced, mainly by French Roman Catholic scholars. The reasons for these proposals have partly to do with historical factors that will be discussed in chapters 6 and 7. But in part, they assume that the complex nature of the Synoptic data and the testimony concerning the gospels by patristic writers warrants a com-

---

der is more inclined to derive from Matthew and Mark than from special pre-Lukan traditions, though he does not entirely exclude such tradition (1989:73 138).

41. It should be added, however, that Farrer-Goulder and the 2GH do not need a *document* such as Q, nor do they need to posit Luke's access to pre-Matthaean forms on the scale that the 2DH requires Luke's access to Q material. Most of Luke's "Q" material on the 2GH and the Farrer-Goulder hypothesis is taken directly from Matthew and, as the previous note indicates, Goulder thinks that Luke is responsible for most of the divergences of Luke from Matthew in the "Q" material, and for much of the Lukan special material too.

42. See now the careful evaluation of challenges to the 2DH by Tuckett (1995).

plex solution. The most important of these complex solutions are those of
Léon Vaganay (1954) and Marie-Émile Boismard (1972; 1990).[43]

For Vaganay, patristic statements about the composition of the gospels
constitute important data. Key among these are the statements of Papias (in
Eusebius, *Hist. eccl.* 3.39.16-17), who believed that Matthew composed his
gospel in Aramaic, which was subsequently translated into Greek, and that
Mark's gospel was directly associated with Peter. Vaganay also invokes the
argument from order but with a slightly different twist. He argues that both
Matthew and Luke place the Sermon on the Mount between Mark 3:13-19
and 3:20-21 and that this coincidence indicates that Matthew and Luke are
based not simply on Mark but on an earlier source that had at this position
the Sermon, the healing of the centurion's slave and the sayings about John
the Baptist. Mark also knew this source, but abbreviated it.[44] Thus he posits
an Aramaic *Urgospel* (M) and its Greek translation (Mg) as the source of all
three Synoptics. This was a primitive apostolic catechism used in Jerusalem
and associated with Peter. At the same time Vaganay recognizes that the
phenomenon of order in the triple tradition indicates that Mark's sequence
of pericopae is more original than that of Matthew[45] and accepts both the
dependence of Matthew and Luke on Mark and the independence of the
first and third evangelists (1954:444–45). While Matthew's gospel, apart
from a few transpositions, reflects the structure and content of Mg, Luke
derived the material found in the Travel Narrative (9:51—18:14) from a
second pre-Synoptic source in Aramaic (S) and its Greek translation (Sg),
which may have circulated in several forms (1954:57). The minor agreements are explained easily since Vaganay posits Matthaean and Lukan
access not only to Mark but also to Mg. And Mark's more vivid language
is explained on the assumption that alongside the written Mg, Mark also
drew upon the vivid memories of Peter's Roman catechism (Vaganay
1954:185).

Vaganay's thesis combines an *Urgospel* solution with a simple branch
solution and posits a source like Q (S, Sg) which, however, lacks the Temptation, the Sermon on the Mount/Plain, the healing of the centurion's slave,
and the Baptist material in Luke 3 and 7, since these are ascribed to M and
Mg. The key difference between this solution and those already discussed

43. See also Léon-Dufour 1959; 1972; Gaboury 1970; Rolland 1984.

44. Vaganay 1954:57. His conclusion that Matthew and Luke agree in placing the Sermon
at Mark 3:19 seems to have come from his use of the synopses of either Lagrange and Lavergne
(1926:§§55–56) or Vannutelli (1936:§§34–35), both of whom use this placement against
Huck and Lietzmann (1935:§§18, 73), who place the sermon at Mark 1:39 for Matthew and
at Mark 3:19 for Luke.

45. Vaganay 1954:59: "The majority of sequential arrangements unique to Matthew and
Luke (additions, omissions, transpositions) find a plausible explanation in the hypothesis that
these authors knew an arrangement that approximated that of Mark. . . . Conversely, the order
of Mark cannot be justified if one supposes that he worked on the basis of Matthew or Luke."

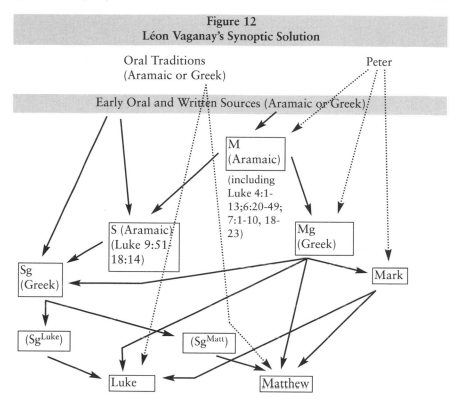

Figure 12
Léon Vaganay's Synoptic Solution

has to do with its logical architecture. Vaganay's starting points are not the internal Synoptic data; they are instead the patristic statements about Matthew and his a priori assumption that if such an Aramaic gospel existed it surely must have been known and used by all other later evangelists (1954:56). Thus before Vaganay comes to the internal data, he has already excluded the solutions listed above that attempt to account for as much of the Synoptic data as possible on the basis of direct utilization of one gospel by another. His only problem is the origin of Luke 9:51—18:14, but this is solved by positing a special source (S, Sg). This, however, must ultimately be related to Mg because it overlaps the contents of Mg (1954:117–26).

For reasons that will be explained in chapter 2, Papias's statement concerning Matthew, Vaganay's starting point, is extremely problematic. Vaganay attempts to secure his second assumption—the use of Mg by all three evangelists—by means of his argument concerning Mark 3:13-19. Matthew's sermon, however, is more probably located at Mark 1:21 or Mark 1:39, not at Mark 3:19.[46] Without this alleged agreement between

---

46. Among the most important synopses of the last century, there is considerable disagreement as to the placement of Matthew's sermon: At *Mark 1:21*: Griesbach 1789–90; Schmid

Matthew and Luke, Vaganay's foundations for Mark's knowledge of Mg
and Mark's alleged omission of Matthew 5–7, 8:5-13, and 11:2-19 crum-
ble. While Vaganay's Mg accounts for the minor agreements though a type
of *Urgospel* hypothesis, he made no attempt to explain them by more direct
means, in particular by the extensive redactional explanations that were
already available to him in the work of Josef Schmid (1930).

The logical difficulty with Vaganay's solution is not that it fails to explain
the Synoptic data. Indeed, it posits so complex a web of relationships that
virtually any conceivable datum can be accounted for. The difficulty is that
the solution is predicated on *possible*, but hardly necessary or even probable, assumptions. Moreover, it ignores much simpler resolutions. It is not
surprising that it has not attracted any significant following.[47]

Another complex solution has been proposed by Marie-Émile Boismard
(see figure 13).[48] Despite the even greater complexity of Boismard's solution, it is in fact less wedded to patristic evidence and based more securely
on internal evidence. He begins with the assumption that the similarities
among the gospels are not to be explained by direct utilization of one gospel
by another, but on the basis of dependence upon hypothetical sources
(1990:231). While this may not appear a very economical solution, he justifies it by arguing that each gospel has aspects which, in comparison with
its parallels in the other gospels, are primitive. For example, Boismard
argues that the report of Herod's opinion of Jesus in Matt 14:1-2 is more
primitive than Mark's complex account (Mark 6:14-16), part of which

---

1953:156–57; Neirynck 1976; at *Mark 1:39*: Griesbach 1776; Huck 1910 (and all subsequent
editions); Schmid 1949; Deiss 1963; Sparks 1964; at *Mark 3:19*: Tischendorf 1851; Huck
1898; Camerlynck and Coppieters 1908; Larfeld 1911; Burton and Goodspeed 1920;
Lagrange and Lavergne 1926; Vannutelli 1936; Aland 1963 (and all subsequent editions);
Benoit and Boismard 1965; Orchard 1983; Boismard and Lamouille 1986. It should be noted
that those arrangements that place Matthew's sermon at Mark 3:19 do so only by printing
Matt 8:1-4; 9:1-19; 12:1-15; 10:1-4 *before* the Sermon and following on Mark 1:39.

47. Among its few adherents, Cerfaux 1954.

48. Boismard 1972:17. A seemingly simplified version is presented in Boismard 1979-80,
where no distinction is made between Mark[int] and final Mark or between proto-Luke and
Luke:

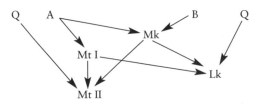

It it clear, however, from his latest book (1994) that he wishes to preserve the distinctions
between Mark[int] (now proto-Mark) and final Mark, and between proto-Luke and final Luke.
Boismard has, however, partially dissolved the distinction between B and Mark[int] (proto-
Mark).

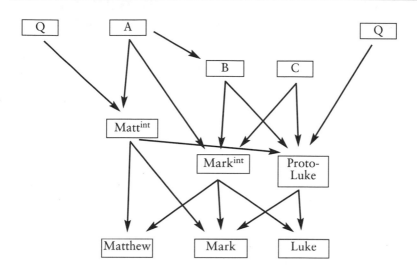

Figure 13a
M.-É. Boismard's (1972) Synoptic Solution

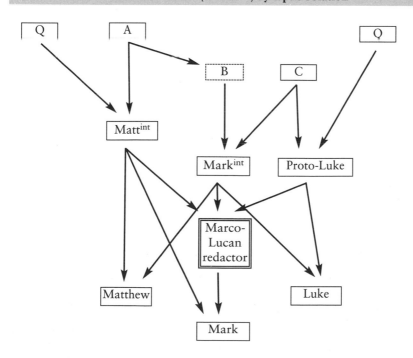

Figure 13b
M.-É. Boismard's (1984/94) Synoptic Solution

reappears in the story of Peter's confession (Mark 8:28).[49] In Matt 13:10-15, however, the agreement between Mark and Luke in placing the saying "to whoever has will more be given" (Mark 4:25 / Luke 8:18; cf. Matt 13:12) indicates that Matthew is secondary to Mark / Luke. Finally, the formula τίνι δὲ ὁμοιώσω . . . ὁμοία ἐστίν ("to what shall I compare . . . it is like"), which Matthew preserves in his gospel only at 11:16, is the more original introduction to the parable of the mustard seed (Matt 13:31 / Luke 13:18), even though there Matthew has dropped the first part of the formula. Hence Luke 13:18 (which has the formula) shows itself to be more primitive than Matthew (1990:239).

In order to account for these features, Boismard rejects any hypothesis that places one of the canonical gospels prior to the others in an absolute sense. The minor agreements, accordingly, are not to be explained by coincidental redaction or textual corruption, but rather as resulting from Mark's modification of intermediate Mark (Mark^{int}) or from Matthew's and Luke's use of intermediate Matt (Matt^{int}).[50] Thus, Boismard proposes a double *Urgospel* hypothesis. On the other hand, Mark's double expressions or "minor doublets" (e.g., 1:32) are explained by a conflation hypothesis: canonical Mark conflated Mark^{int}, proto-Luke, and Matt^{int}.[51]

At this point Boismard invokes a key assumption, that the presence of doublets in any document is the result of conflation. The 2DH better accounts for the "major doublets" in Matthew and Luke than the Griesbach hypothesis insofar as the 2DH traces some of the doublets to the use of Mark and Q.[52] In order to explain the major doublets in Mark, however, Boismard suggests that Mark combined three sources, christened "A," "B," and "C." Thus, for example, Mark has three different passion predictions (A: Mark 9:31; B: Mark 9:12b; C: Mark 14:41c), two multiplications (A: Mark 6; B: Mark 8), and two sendings of the disciples (A: Mark 6:7; B: Mark 3:14-15) (1972:19–20). According to Boismard "A" was Palestinian in origin and served, along with Q, as the principal source for Matt^{int}. "A"

49. Boismard 1990:237-38, esp. 238: "But it is clear that Mark combined two accounts which had different origins. This is indicated by the repetition 'and he heard . . . and hearing' (καὶ ἤκουσεν [v. 14] . . . ἀκούσας δέ [v. 16]). Here too Matthew's account is surely more primitive than that of Mark."

50. Boismard 1972:41: "These agreements are explained, either by the fact that the final editor of Mark abandoned or modified the text of the source common to the three evangelists, or by the fact that Luke depends not on Mark but on intermediate Matthew. More precisely, Luke's alternating agreement with Matthew against Mark, and with Mark against Matthew proves Luke's dependence on two different sources, one Matthaean and one Markan."

51. Boismard 1972:5. Boismard (1990:234) misstates the phenomenon of double expressions: he asks whether one can say "that Mark had a naturally redundant style and that Matthew and Luke simplified Mark, each choosing, as if by coincidence, the part of the formula that the other omitted" and suggests that it is more normal to conclude that Mark is the result of conflation. See, however, Tuckett's tabulation of the double expressions (above, n. 25).

was reinterpreted for Gentile Christian use in "B," which became the main source of Mark[int]. The latter, however, also incorporated parts of "A" and "C," thus accounting for the Markan "major doublets." "C" represented a very archaic independent tradition, probably Palestinian in origin.

Matt[int] was revised completely. In the sections where it paralleled Mark[int], its text was largely replaced by that of Mark[int] and the order of Mark[int] substituted. As indicated above, final Mark derived mainly from Mark[int], but its "minor doublets" reveal the influence of Matt[int] and proto-Luke. Proto-Luke was indebted mostly to Matt[int] and Q (with some influence of "B"), but in the passion narrative it used "C" as its principal source. Final Luke was "a fundamental revision" influenced by Mark[int] from which Luke adopted largely his structure and the literary form. This explains the alternating agreement of Luke, sometimes with Matthew, sometimes with Mark (1972:15–19).

Boismard's solution thus combines the 2DH, acknowledging both the influence of the (pre-)Markan outline on final Matthew and final Luke[53] and the use of a sayings collection (Q) in the Matthaean and Lukan streams,[54] with an *Ur-Markus* hypothesis (to account for the minor agreements), and a conflation hypothesis (to account for the "minor doublets").

It is extremely difficult to provide a succinct evaluation of Boismard's theory, since it is constructed not on the basis of the "gross Synoptic data" of the phenomenon of order and the general patterns of agreements and disagreements, but on the basis of a pericope-by-pericope analysis. His entire theory does not become visible in any one pericope but must be assembled from numerous individual analyses. Nevertheless, a few observations on its architecture are possible.

---

52. Boismard 1972:54: In favor of the hypothesis that the double and triple traditions are of separate origins, "one may also cite the presence in Matthew of numerous doublets, where one form of the doublet is attested by the triple tradition (Matt / Mark, and in many cases also Luke), and the other by the double tradition (Matt / Luke)."

53. Boismard 1972:29: "One must distinguish two different levels in Matthew: intermediate Matthew was completely independent of the Markan tradition; but, at the level of the final redaction of Matthew, his text was largely replaced or supplemented with that of intermediate Mark." 40: "One must distinguish two redactional levels in Luke: a proto-Luke, independent of Mark and whose origin is not completely clear; and a final Lukan redaction in which proto-Luke was supplemented and revised with reference to the gospel of Mark [*sic*]."

54. Note, however, that Boismard's "Q" does not correspond with that of the 2DH. "We have attributed to a unique document Q a large part of the material common to Matthew and Luke but absent from Mark, in order not to make any more complicated a general theory that is already quite complex; the reader is advised that the designation «Q» could in fact stand for several different sources which it is no longer possible to distinguish" (1972:54). He excludes from Q. Luke 3:7-9; 4:1-13 (and parallels), which he ascribes to Matt[int] (which Luke used), and Luke 7:1-10, which he attributes to 'A' as a doublet of B's healing of the Canaanite girl (Mark 7:24-30). He adds to Q Matt 13:44-46 (because of its similarity to Matt 13:31-33 = Luke 13:18-21) and Luke 15:8-10 (because of its similarity to Matt 18:12-14 / Luke 15:4-7) (1972:54–55).

First, Boismard's approach to the phenomenon of doublets ("major doublets")—for example, the two Markan miracles of the loaves—is possible but unnecessarily complex. It implies that the double account in Mark arises from the conflation of "A" (Mark 6) and "B" (Mark 8) by Mark[int], while Matthew's double account results from his use *both* of "A" (via Matt[int]) *and* Mark[int]. If the Matthaean doublet can be explained from Mark([int]) alone, there is no reason to posit an earlier version of Matthew. On Boismard's theory, Matt[int] must have lacked the second account because Luke, who used Matt[int] as his principal source, lacks this. But this hardly solves the problem of Luke's omission, since on his hypothesis proto-Luke also had direct access to "B," which contained the second account, and final Luke had access to Mark[int] which contained both. If one can devise reasons for proto-Luke or final Luke omitting the second account (along with all of Mark 6:45—8:26) in "B" or Mark[int], then it is unnecessary to posit a Matt[int] to account for its omission.

Second, it should be conceded that Boismard's assumption that the differences among the Synoptics derive from their use of hypothetical documents is a priori no less (or more) probable than the assumption of direct utilization. This, however, only pushes back the question, "How did the differences arise?" to a pre-gospel level. It does not solve the problem. To argue that disagreements between overlapping accounts x and y result from their independent use of, respectively, x^i and y^i, is not obviously more economical a solution than to argue that $x \rightarrow y$ or $y \rightarrow x$, since one would still have to account for the differences between x^i and y^i. Neirynck (1984), moreover, has answered Boismard's analysis of Mark 6:32-34 (1979–80), arguing that both Matthew's and Luke's accounts can be derived from Mark, and this being so, there are no grounds for positing Matt[int] (or Matt I).

Third, as noted above (n. 25), the phenomenon of Markan double expressions (Boismard's "minor doublets") is exactly as the 2DH predicts: far from Matthew and Luke regularly taking alternate halves of Mark's double expressions, their treatment of the 213 double expressions reveals every logically possible combination. This is precisely what one should expect if Matthew and Luke worked independently. This observation diminishes (if it does not entirely eliminate) the necessity of positing Matt[int] and Mark[int] which Mark conflated.

Merely a Hypothesis?

Even if Boismard has not succeeded in demonstrating the necessity of his hypothesis, either logically or in terms of literary plausibilities, his efforts illumine several important theoretical issues in Synoptic Problem studies. First, Synoptic hypotheses are simplifications. Hypotheses usually aim at parsimony: simple explanations are more desirable than complex solutions for the reason that the more variables a hypothesis includes, the greater the number of equivalent hypotheses at the same level of complexity, and the more difficult it is to demonstrate the superiority of any one hypothesis. This is precisely the logical difficulty with Boismard's hypothesis: even if it were right it would be impossible to demonstrate its correctness. Parsimony, however, is a virtue of explanatory logic; it is not a feature of historical or literary realities. Brief reflection on human experience should tell us that few events can be reduced to simple causes, and causal chains are rarely unilinear and uncomplicated by other influences.

The currently competing explanations of Synoptic data propose scenarios which are parsimonious in varying degrees, but which are also unlikely to represent precisely or fully the *actual* compositional processes of the gospels. It is extremely unlikely, for example, that Matthew and Luke used the same manuscripts of Mark and Q. The copies of Mark and Q which eventually found their way into the hands of the later evangelists would have been subject at a minimum to copyists' errors and had perhaps undergone more substantial changes. If among the six thousand or so New Testament manuscripts, one cannot find two identical—when many were copied by professional scribes or monks for whom the text was canonical and the work an act of piety—then it is simply incredible that two copies of the pre-canonical Mark or Q, copied by pious but untrained copyists, would agree in all respects! Moreover, we are not even in a position to know the exact wording of any of the canonical gospels. Our earliest (fragmentary) manuscripts date from well over a century after their composition. Thus we cannot be sure that the patterns of agreements and disagreements upon which our understanding of Synoptic relationships is predicated are those of the autographs. Cross-fertilization ("harmonization") of manuscripts by the earliest copyists may have obscured the patterns that would allow a clearer resolution of the Synoptic Problem.

Some of the factors that went into the composition of a gospel might be accessible to the historian, but many fall outside her ken and calculation. History is rarely regular and predictable; freak events, accidents, chance encounters and the like are part of its fabric. Yet it is impossible to factor into our models the many imponderables that may have contributed to the composition of the gospels, for this would have the effect of destroying the explanatory power of the model. Even though the 2DH best accounts for the relationships among the gospels, it should not be confused with a *description* of "what happened." Hypotheses are heuristic models intended to aid comprehension and discovery; they do not replicate reality.

Second, hypotheses tend to focus upon those aspects of the problem that are viewed as key to its understanding and over which the investigator has some control. Few critics nowadays focus much attention on the transformations and developments that doubtless occurred in the oral tradition prior to its inscription in written documents as a means of resolving the Synoptic Problem. This is not because such knowledge would not be quite useful, but because it is simply beyond our reach. Instead, solutions to the Synoptic Problem tend to construe the issues mainly or exclusively in literary terms—the ways in which gospel *x* edited gospel *y* or some common source *z*—for these data are relatively more accessible.

This is probably the reason that the hypotheses of Vaganay and Boismard have not attracted a significant following. To accept either would imply that most of the significant transformations in the Synoptic tradition occurred long before the inscription of our canonical gospels and, for that reason, are beyond reconstruction and discussion. From his point of view, Vaganay considers this to be an advantage: to posit Mg and Sg and further, to suppose that some of the variations in sayings of Jesus should be traced to Jesus' own multiple and varied performances, suggests that the evangelists are very conservative editors. Commenting on Matt 4:23, which he thinks was composed from Mark 1:32b, 34, 28, 38, 39 and 3:7b-8, Vaganay concludes:

> An author who refuses to invent even a small transitional phrase and who searches for elements in the sources at his disposal or in a record that he preserved would not have created out of his own imagination a parable or a saying. It seems that he lacks imagination. At any rate he has too much respect for the materials he used to rely on his own whim and fancy. (1954:243)[55]

On the differences between Matthew and Luke, he suggests:

> It is perhaps surprising that Matthew and Luke should be so different when both drew upon the same sources. But first of all, the written sources were not always identical, in particular Sg which may have had divergent forms, depending on its environment. Next, the contribution of oral tradition enhanced the differences, not only in parallel pericopae but also by transmitting completely new episodes. Finally, and above all, Matthew and Luke were not compilers. They treated their sources in different ways in accordance with their own tendencies. (1954:313)

In spite of his protestations, Vaganay's evangelists are not authors; they merely arranged their oral and written sources. This is also true, though to a more limited degree, of Boismard's evangelists. Boismard can speak of the style of Matthew (or Matt[int]) and can identify some general theological characteristics; but his approach could never generate a sharp profile of Matthew, Mark, or Luke as authors. Much of the variation among the evangelists disappears into the mist of Boismard's primitive and intermediate documents.

In other words, complex solutions lack heuristic utility as far as the final

---

55. Ironically, Vaganay insists that Matthew and Luke were not mere compilers (*compilateurs*) but "true authors" (1954:313). Matthew's authorial role, however, consists only in his choice and arrangement of materials (241: "Matthew invents nothing; but he knows how to make selections, and his choice is inspired"). The peculiarities of Luke, whom Vaganay describes as "an author who was concerned about literary arrangement" (311), are traced to his use of Mark, Mg, Sg, and elements of oral tradition (313).

forms of the gospels are concerned. They distribute the moments of editorial transformation throughout several levels of oral and literary activity and correspondingly reduce the initiative of the evangelists to the simple combining and arranging of preexisting sources and traditions. In this sense these solutions are pre-redaction critical solutions, not because they are unable to identify Matthaean, Markan, and Lukan stylistic or theological features, but insofar as they locate the significant moments of theologizing and innovation not with the evangelists but at rather vaguely defined and inaccessible earlier moments.[56]

By the same token, it should be recognized that the simpler utilization hypotheses, by positing only one or two sources, correspondingly concentrate the creative theologizing on the evangelists themselves. This also obliges the interpreter to propose editorial scenarios and theologies for each evangelist that can compass all of the literary transformations that are implied. To take Matthew as an example: if Matthew used only Mark and Q (2DH) or Mark alone (Farrer-Goulder), then we must be prepared to imagine an editor who was able by himself to effect all of the alterations, rearrangements, and reconfigurations that are required to transform Mark (and Q) into Matthew. This is a far more active and sophisticated editor than Boismard's Matthew. With the maturing of redaction criticism over the last generation, one may now find critical, detailed, and complex expositions of Matthew's theology that can compass both Matthew's seeming prohibition of a Gentile mission (10:5-6) and his endorsement of it (28:16-20), or his variety of statements on the Torah, not all of which, on the face of it, are compatible. The advent of literary criticism, with its focus on the final form of the text, has created an even stronger imperative to reconcile and integrate all of the elements on the textual surface. As much as one may find such explanatory efforts persuasive—for a generation of gospel scholarship has trained us to imagine that early Christian writers were perfectly capable of complicated thinking—it would be naive not to recognize the subtle interplay between the textual data and the explanatory habits of modern New Testament criticism. Simple versions of utilization hypotheses seem

---

56. From the point of view of Synoptic theory Boismard's explanations may seem vague. It should be noted, however, that Boismard's formative work was text-critical, where he noted the fundamentally *unstable* character of the NT textual tradition. Moreover, his insistence on including the Fourth Gospel within the discussion of the origins of the Gospels, signaled also by his careful integration of John into his synopsis (1986), inclines him of necessity toward models that are capable of compassing far more development and variation than classical source criticism, which limits itself to the literary relationship, narrowly conceived, among the three Synoptics. Boismard's model for understanding the development of the tradition is more indebted to text criticism than other Synoptic theories. This indebtedness also explains why Boismard finds incredible Neirynck's tendency to account for Matthew and Luke from the final text of Mark, identified for all practical purposes with the Nestle-Aland[26] edition.

intellectually satisfying because *we* are able to imagine sophisticated evangelists, not because we somehow know that such evangelists ever existed.

Good hypotheses are those that are judged to offer the most economical and most plausible account of the largest number of data. Over the last two hundred years, there have been remarkable shifts in what factors were considered to be key in constructing hypotheses and the ways in which the canons of plausibility were conceived. One sees, for example, in the transition between the eighteenth and nineteenth centuries a shift from reliance upon patristic testimony as the major reliable evidence, to the use of evidence internal to the gospels themselves. Simultaneously, explanations of the gospels which had recourse to the vagaries of oral tradition gave way to literary, documentary explanations. And during the past two centuries of Synoptic criticism there has been quite stunning variation in the range of literary procedures that could "plausibly" be ascribed to a given evangelist. Hypotheses are *our* intellectual constructs which configure the data in accord with our canons of intelligibility and plausibility and in a general framework controlled by what *we* deem to be significant. What was a satisfying explanation of gospel composition a century ago might now seem quaint or downright unlikely. This has much to do with the types of questions that we pose of the texts and with the explanatory habits that we have adopted.

To admit that the 2DH is a hypothesis and qua hypothesis is, on the one hand, unable to render a full and unambiguous account of all Synoptic data and, on the other, that it is not unaffected by the explanatory habits of those who formulated it, is not to encourage the kind of sloppy thinking or worse, intellectual laziness, that causally sweeps aside two centuries of Synoptic criticism with the assertion that "it is all hypothetical." *Hypotheses are all that we have and all we will ever have.* The Synoptic Problem can be addressed *only* at the level of theory and hypothesis.[57] Hypotheses are to be constructed carefully and used critically and self-consciously. They are to be challenged and corrected by careful review of the evidence. When they are ignored with a whimsical dismissal it is time to wonder what nerve has been touched and whose undefended (or indefensible) assumptions have been threatened.

---

57. Cf. Cameron (1996b:352), who has put the matter succinctly, adapting Voltaire: "Although some try to deny the composite character of the Sayings Gospel, frequently through specious appeals to the hypothetical nature of the reconstructed text, such attempts fundamentally misunderstand how theory works, and thus seek—whether consciously or not—to bypass the results of scholarship and the actual evidence of the gospel texts. For if Q did not exist, we would have to reconstruct it. Theory would demand it. Once the synoptic problem is resolved theoretically by the positing of Q and Q is accorded a documentary status, there is no reason not to examine the text for evidence of possible layers of its literary history. It is necessary to be insistent at this point. We do have a text of Q; what we do not have is a manuscript."

2

The Character and Reconstruction of Q

> If Q did not exist, we would have to reconstruct it.
> Theory would demand it.
> —Ron Cameron

CHAPTER ONE OUTLINED the logical basis for the 2DH and for positing a sayings source ("Q").[1] There I suggested that the 2DH provides a more economical and plausible accounting of the Synoptic data than other available solutions. To have concluded this, however, still leaves a host of specific issues in regard to the second Synoptic source, Q. Was Q simply a set of oral traditions or was it written? And if the latter, was it one document or several? What was its original language? Which Synoptic pericopae should be assigned to Q? When Matthew and Luke disagree in the wording or sequence of Q texts, which wording and sequence ought to be preferred? Did Q overlap Mark at points? Are there materials singly attested in Matthew or Luke that should also be ascribed to Q? What kind of document was Q, if indeed it was a document?

Describing the Character of Q

Two sets of problems may be distinguished, the first having to do with the nature of the Q material and the second, with reconstructing Q. To the first set belong the subissues of the documentary status of Q, its original language, and its approximate date. Only once it has been ascertained that Q is a document will it be possible to ask whether the reconstruction of its wording and order is possible (and by what criteria), and the related question of whether multiple recensions of Q existed.

---

1. On the origins of the siglum "Q," see below, chap. 7, p. 330.

Q AS A WRITTEN DOCUMENT

The majority of students of the Synoptic Gospels have held that Q was written. This follows from three observations: (1) the near-verbatim agreement between Matthew and Luke in certain double tradition pericopae; (2) the significant amount of sequential agreement between Matthew and Luke in some portions of the double tradition;[2] and (3) the use by Matthew and Luke of the same unusual phrases or words.

1. The degree of verbal agreement between Matthew and Luke in Q material ranges from nearly 100 percent to about 10 percent, but is extremely high, for example, in Matt 6:24 / Luke 16:13 (98 percent),[3] Matt 12:43-45 / Luke 11:24-26 (93 percent), Matt 11:20-24 / Luke 10:13-15 (90 percent), Matt 3:12 / Luke 3:17 (88 percent), Matt 12:27-32 / Luke 11:19-23 (88 percent), Matt 23:37-39 / Luke 13:34-35 (85 percent), Matt 3:7-10 / Luke 3:7-9 (85 percent), among others (Morgenthaler 1971:258-61). Take, for example, the last-named pericope (non-agreements are italicized):

Matt 3:7-10	Luke 3:7-9
7 *But when he saw many Pharisees and Sadducees coming for* his *baptism, he said to them,*	7 *John said to the crowds that came out to be baptized by* him,
"You brood of vipers! Who warned you to flee from the wrath to come? 8 Bear *fruit* (καρπόν) worthy (ἄξιον) of repentance. 9 Do not *presume* to say to yourselves, 'We have Abraham as our ancestor'; for I tell you, God is able from these stones to raise up children to Abraham. 10 Even now (ἤδη δέ) the ax is lying at the root of the trees; every tree therefore that does not bear good fruit is cut down and thrown into the fire."	"You brood of vipers! Who warned you to flee from the wrath to come? 8 Bear *fruits* (καρπούς) worthy (ἀξίους) of repentance. Do not *begin* to say to yourselves, 'We have Abraham as our ancestor'; for I tell you, God is able from these stones to raise up children to Abraham. 9 Even now (ἤδη δὲ καὶ) the ax is lying at the root of the trees; every tree therefore that does not bear good fruit is cut down and thrown into the fire."
76 words in Greek: 61 (80 percent) identical with Luke; 63 (83 percent) if καρπόν and ἄξιον are included as agreements.	72 words in Greek: 61 (85 percent) identical with Matthew; 63 (87.5 percent) if καρπούς and ἀξίους are included as agreements.

2. The presence of doublets in the Synoptic tradition has been used to argue not only for the existence of Q, but also for its documentary status: Fitzmyer 1970:152–53; Vielhauer 1975:312; Kümmel 1975:66–67; Devisch 1972:72. This is not in itself a strong argument, for not all doublets in Matthew and Luke need be explained by recourse to two discrete sources, still less two discrete *documents*. However, doublets function as an instructive subset of the argument from order. Matthew, for example, has two requests of a sign, one in Matt 12:38-42 (par. Luke 11:29-32) and one in 16:1-4 (par. Mark 8:11-12). The first occurs in a predominantly Q context (following the Beelzebul accusation) and the latter in a Markan context. If Matthew were using Mark and oral tradition, one might more reasonably expect him to fuse the two. Instead, he uses the story twice, once in Markan sequence (16:1-4) and once in the same context in which Luke (independently) has it.

3. The figures are based on the number of common words divided by the total number of Lukan words. Slightly different percentages would obtain if the Matthaean word total were used.

What is striking about this type of agreement is that it includes not only the choice of vocabulary—in the speech portion, Matthew and Luke only disagree over *"presume* to say"/*"begin* to say" and Luke's additional καί in 3:9—but extends to the inflection of words, word order, and the use of particles, the most variable aspects of Greek syntax. This type of agreement can be explained only on the supposition that Matthew and Luke used a written source. Hypotheses that have tried to trace the double tradition material exclusively to oral tradition have either ignored or minimized these agreements or have made romantic, but quite unrealistic, assumptions about the nature and faithfulness of oral tradition.[4]

A few have challenged this conclusion.[5] Theodore Rosché (1960) analyzed the extent of agreement among the Synoptics, comparing the Matthew–Mark and Mark–Luke agreements in Markan sections with Matthew–Luke agreements in the double traditions. Finding the latter to be less than the agreements with Mark, he concluded that Q must be oral. Rosché's procedure was fallacious, however, as Carlston and Norlin pointed out. Instead of comparing Mark *individually* with Matthew and Luke in Markan sections, he should have compared the degree of agreement between Matthew and Luke in *both* the Markan and the non-Markan sections. When Carlston and Norlin made this comparison, they discovered that, on average, Matthew and Luke display a slightly *higher* degree of verbal agreement in the double tradition than they do in the triple (Markan)

---

4. See Kloppenborg 1987a:42–46. Bailey 1991 distinguishes three forms of oral transmission: "formal controlled" (e.g., rabbinic tradition, transmitted by trained persons); "informal uncontrolled" (where free variation occurs); and "informal controlled." He attempts to defend (anecdotally) the faithfulness of "informal controlled" transmission, which he supposes to represent the form of transmission of Jesus' sayings. He acknowledges, however, the pervasive presence of uncontrolled forms of transmission in the Levant and concedes that in "informal controlled" transmission what is most likely to remain stable are proverbs, poems (where there are metrical constraints) and the punch lines in stories and parables, rather than the entire speech or narrative portions (1991:90–92). One should note, however, that even aphorisms (as contrasted with proverbs) are subject to performance variations: compare, e.g., Q 16:13 with *GThom* 47a.

5. Jeremias (1930) argued from the fact that double tradition sayings in Matthew and Luke sometimes have different catchword connections with their respective contexts that Q was oral rather than written. This conclusion in no way follows: it assumes wrongly that catchword association is an oral rather than a literary phenomenon (and hence, differing catchword associations implies differing oral contexts). As an analysis of ancient sayings collections reveals (Kloppenborg 1987a:chap. 7), catchword association is a regular compositional technique. The fact that Matthew, for example, has a different catchword association than Luke may only mean that Matthew moved a saying to a new context. It indicates nothing as to whether Q was originally oral or written.

tradition.[6] This suggests that Matthew and Luke were slightly *more* conservative in reproducing Q than they were when using Mark.[7]

2. That Q was written is also suggested by the fact that Matthew and Luke concur in the relative sequence of more than 30 percent of the double tradition pericopae (see figure 14 below). This agreement exists despite the fact that Matthew and Luke combined Q and Mark differently. Such independent agreement in the sequence of Q's sayings finds its best—perhaps only—reasonable explanation in the supposition that Matthew and Luke used a document and were thus influenced by its arrangement of sayings.[8]

There are also two other types of sequential agreements between Matthew and Luke. First is the agreement in the relative order of individual sayings even in clusters which Matthew and Luke place quite differently

6. Carlston and Norlin (1971:71) distinguish between narrative, words of Jesus, and other words. Their findings (expressed as a percentage of the total word count) are:

	Triple Matt	Luke	Avg.	Double Matt	Luke	Avg.
Narrative	50.2	46.9	48.5	55.7	51.8	53.7
Words of Jesus	63.5	68.3	65.8	69.5	73.6	71.5
Misc. words	56.7	60.6	58.5	87.5	80.9	84.1
Average	56.0	56.0	56.0	69.8	72.2	71.0

7. The method employed by Carlston and Norlin has been analyzed by Mattila (1994), who notes (a) the small and uneven distribution of sayings in Carlston and Norlin's "miscellaneous words" category, (b) the sizable differential between the double and triple traditions in the number of words of Jesus, and (c) their elimination of unparalleled (single tradition) materials and redactional framing and the inclusion of synonyms as agreements in both the double and triple traditions. This accounts for a rather wide disagreement between their statistics and those of Honoré (1968), whose criterion for registering agreements required not only lexical but grammatical identity; hence Honoré arrived at very low figures for both the triple and the double tradition. My own statistical results (which do not include the triple tradition and do not distinguish types of materials within Q) are lower than those of Carlston and Norlin: 54.08 percent agreement (2414/4,464) in Matthaean Q pericopae, and 51.59 percent (2,400/4,652) in Luke Q pericopae (1988:209). The higher overall word count and the lower percentage agreement for Luke result from the fact that more Lukan than Matthaean *Sondergut* is included as "probably in Q." On the other hand, I have not counted synonyms as agreements, but have excluded some redactional introductions from both Matthew and Luke. Interestingly, Mattila's analysis of Honoré's statistics still confirms that Matthew's and Luke's agreement in the double tradition is significantly higher than their agreement in the triple tradition (39.1 percent compared with 30.7 percent) (1994:319). Unfortunately, Mattila's argument is not based on an independent analysis and fails to use the comprehensive statistical tables by Morgenthaler (1971). A new study of the problem is desirable but preliminary examinations (see the table on p. 63 below) indicate that while the statistics would change, the overall result would not. See now Carlston's answer to Mattila (Carlston and Norlin 1999).

8. By contrast, attempts to suggest a *documentary* relationship between Q and, for example, the *Gospel of Thomas* founder precisely on the issue of the sequence of sayings, for there is practically no agreement between the putative order of Q and that of Thomas. In order to maintain a thesis of documentary dependence of Thomas on Q or vice versa, one would also have to assume an aggressive program of dislocation of sayings by one of the authors; but such a supposition would mean that the second author did not treat the source *as a document* and this solution would then become indistinguishable from the thesis of common dependence on oral tradition.

relative to Mark and to other Q material. For example, the several sayings on John the Baptist (Q 7:18-23, 24-26, 27, 28, 31-35) appear in the same order in Matthew and Luke even though they are differently placed in the overall outlines of the respective gospels; the parables of the householder (Q 12:39-40) and the faithful servant (Q 12:42b-46) appear in the same sequence despite the fact that Matthew uses them in his apocalyptic discourse and Luke includes them in his Travel Narrative. And Matthew, who connects the parables of the mustard (Q 13:18-19) and the leaven (Q 13:20-21) with the Markan parables discourse (Mark 4 = Matt 13), presents the parables in the same order as Luke, who includes them in his travel section.

Second, Matthew has clusters of double tradition materials that in Luke are scattered, but nonetheless, Matthew presents the sayings *in Lukan order*, as if he had scanned Q, lifting out and collecting sayings as he found them in Q.[9] For example:

Matt 10:24-25	Luke 6:40
Matt 10:26-33	Luke 12:2-9
Matt 10:34-36	Luke 12:51-53
Matt 10:37-38	Luke 14:26-27
Matt 10:39	Luke 17:33[10]

Such agreements in sequence are explicable only on the assumption of reliance on a common document, for it would be extraordinarily unlikely that two authors, drawing on a pool of oral sayings, would display so high a degree of sequential agreement, especially if nothing in the sayings requires a particular ordering relative to other sayings.

3. Finally, as Hawkins noted eighty years ago, Matthew and Luke agree in reproducing various peculiar or unusual words and grammatical constructions such as "of those born of women" (ἐν γεννητοῖς γυναικῶν, Q 7:28), "worthy that" (ἵκανος ἵνα, Q 7:6), "say with a word" (εἰπὲ λόγῳ, Q 7:7), "fear" + "from" (φοβεῖσθε ἀπό, Q 12:4), and "confess" + dative (ὁμολογεῖν ἐν, Q 12:8) (Hawkins 1911:99). One might add several other words: "clothe" (ἀμφιέννυμι, Q 7:25), "cut in two" (διχοτομέω, Q 12:46), and "sweep clean" (σαρόω, Q 11:25). These are either rare or completely unattested in the Septuagint and in the rest of the New Testament. It is highly improbable that two independent oral renditions of the same tradition would concur in using such unusual words and constructions. These agreements, however, are explained without difficulty by the supposition of a written Q.

To conclude that Q was written rather than oral should not, however,

9. For similar arguments, see Streeter 1911b; Solages 1973:153–82; and V. Taylor 1953; 1959 (all discussed in Kloppenborg 1987:66–72).

10. See Kloppenborg 1987b:78. Subsequently, I have discovered that this agreement had already partly been noted by Castor (1912 [1918]:122), who noted the correspondence between Matthew and Luke in the sequence of Q 10:1-12; 12:2-9, 51-53; 14:26-27.

encourage the conclusion that its transmission and character are explicable solely in literary terms, as if once committed to writing, prior oral traditions simply died out. In fact, it is mistaken to conceive of the relationship between oral and written "stages" as sequential and unidirectional. Ancient documents were written *scripta continua*—with no word breaks or punctuations. Under these circumstances, it was practically impossible to read a document silently (or very quickly). Since literacy levels were very low, most persons would know the contents of documents only through their oral recitation by readers who were capable of "performing" them. Reading itself was an act of interpretation insofar as the reader prepared in advance for performance, deciding how to break the continuous string of letters into words and sentences, where to place "paragraph breaks," and which portions to emphasize. This implies that the written text was never a separate and discrete entity but always existed in the context of oral performance, functioning more like a musical script than a modern book. The literary inscription of Q accounts for the elements of relative fixity that have been noted above. This fixity, however, could never be absolute. Each oral performance of Q could be varied, depending on the occasion. Subsequent copyings of Q could not be isolated from the influence of such performances.[11]

A SINGLE DOCUMENT?

The argument that Q was a written document rather than merely a set of oral traditions focused primarily on agreements in wording and order between Matthew and Luke. These two evangelists, however, display a rather broad range of levels of agreement in reproducing Q materials, from over 90 percent, in the pericopae listed above, to barely 20 percent in pericopae such as the Parable of the Entrusted Money (Q 19:12-27 [22 percent]), to less than 20 percent in the Parable of the Great Supper (Q 14:16-24 [14 percent]) and the saying on divisions (Q 12:51-53 [11 percent]).

A few scholars have noted these disparities (Hawkins 1911:110–11), but most have considered them in relation to the reconstruction of Q rather than its fundamental definition. That is, the fact that a pericope exhibits low Matthew–Luke agreement has sometimes provoked the question of whether such a pericope belongs to Q in the first place. Such considerations are regularly raised apropos of the Parables of the Entrusted Money (Q 19:12-27) or the Great Supper (Q 14:16-24), or the sayings on salt (Q 14:35) or on reconciliation (Q 17:4); ought they be included in Q? In these pericopae the degree of verbal agreement is low enough to cast doubt on whether Matthew and Luke were drawing on a common source; they may simply

---

11. On the nature of the relationship between oral performance and written text, see Gamble 1995 and Robbins 1995.

have been using similar oral and/or written traditions (see the compilation of opinions in Kloppenborg 1988a).

Others have gone further. Paul Ewald (1890) divided the double tradition into three categories based on whether Matthew and Luke displayed (I) a high or (II) a low degree of verbal agreement or (III) only agreement in general content. While the materials from category I belonged to Q, those from II and III, including most of the Sermon on the Mount, did not. Wilhelm Bussmann thought that the disparities in verbal agreement could be accounted for by positing two documents, "R" [for *Redequelle,* "the discourse source"], an Aramaic document which had been independently translated into Greek by the evangelists (and hence a lower degree of verbal agreement), and "T" [for *Täufer,* Baptist], a Greek document compiled by a former Baptist disciple and used directly by the evangelists (1929:155–56). In support of his thesis, he listed no fewer than 122 "translation variants" in the "R" material (1929:151–55). Moreover, he distinguished the two documents on both lexical and theological grounds: each document had a distinctive vocabulary, and while "T" displayed an imminent or present eschatology, "R" was futuristic.

Bussmann's thesis found little acceptance.[12] His attempt to isolate collections with discrete lexical and theological profiles was accomplished only by ascribing some high-agreement pericopae to "R" and some low-agreement passages to "T," thus violating his original criteria. His conclusion, moreover, that the variations between Matthew and Luke in reproducing the double tradition rendered a single-document hypothesis unlikely, rested on the assumption that each evangelist would always treat his sources in a uniform way. Such an assumption is belied by an examination of the ways in which Matthew and Luke have treated Mark. Furthermore, most of Bussmann's "translation variants" are simply synonyms. One hardly needs to posit an Aramaic source to account for Luke 11:43 using ἀγαπάω ("love") where Matthew has φιλέω ("love") (see Kloppenborg 1987a:55–56).

C. K. Barrett (1943) also noted discrepancies between Matthew and Luke in wording and order and concluded that only when there was strong agreement in wording can the double tradition safely be ascribed to Q. Elsewhere, Matthew and Luke drew on various traditions that sometimes overlapped in content but which did not form a single document. W. L. Knox (1957:3) doubted that the double tradition could be compassed by a single document, not because of the disparities in verbal agreement, but because he admitted difficulty in imagining why such a document (without a passion narrative) would have been compiled in the first place. He was also impressed by the fact that much of the non-Markan material in Luke (including the double tradition) is found in short groups of sayings,

---

12. Bammel 1965:199 n. 1 declares that "Q is to be split into two sources" but this statement is never justified. For a criticism of Bussmann, see Kloppenborg 1984b:36.

thematically related or connected by catchwords. This, he suggested, might mean that 'Q' was in fact a series of short tracts that Matthew and Luke variously combined with Mark (1957:46–47). C. J. A. Hickling (1982) observed that much of the double tradition that is reproduced verbatim by Matthew and Luke also shares the polemical theme of opposition to "this generation." This material, he suggested, might be ascribed to one document, but the remainder of the double tradition should be ascribed to at least one other document which the evangelists felt freer to modify, and to oral traditions.

The most ambitious recent attempt to address this problem is in the Hamburg dissertation of Thomas Bergemann (1993).[13] Taking the degree of verbal agreement between Matthew and Luke as the principal criterion for assigning pericopae to Q, Bergemann argues that most of the sayings in Luke 6:20b-49, where, he suggests, the agreement averages only about 30 percent, were not part of Q. This conclusion is reinforced by a detailed analysis of the redactional tendencies of Matthew and Luke in which Bergemann argues that in most of the instances where Matthew and Luke differ in wording, the data do not permit one to conclude that either Matthew or Luke altered the source. He suggests, nevertheless, that the sayings in Luke 6:20-49 derived from a discrete document, not Q, but a *Grundrede* ("foundational discourse") written originally in Aramaic and available to Matthew and Luke in divergent recensions. The divergences between Matthew and Luke were due partially to translation variants (1993:54–56) and partially to the lengthy transmissional process lying behind the inscribing of the two discourses in Matthew and Luke (1993:236).

What Bergemann proposes is conceivable, of course, but hardly required by the evidence. There is, moreover, a logical problem with his argument. It has to do with his premise that verbal agreement is the only significant ground for assigning a pericope to Q and that, consequently, low verbatim agreement provides a reason to deny a pericope to Q. Assuming that Matthew and Luke were independent in their use of a common source,

13. See now a critical discussion of Bergemann's thesis in Denaux 1995. An earlier version of this thesis was espoused by Burton (1904:esp. 34–53), who rejected the simple form of the 2DH on the grounds that it did not account for the entirely independent infancy narratives and it could not explain the disagreements in wording and order of the common Matthew–Luke material (34–35). In place of Q, Burton posited (a) a "Peraean" document, containing the common Matthew–Luke material in Luke 9:51—18:14; 19:1-28 (in Lukan order); and (b) a "Galilean" document containing Luke 3:7-15, 17-18; 4:2b-13 (14-15), 16-30; 5:1-11; 6:20-49; 7:1–8:3. In addition, Matthew used a Matthaean document, identified with Papias's *logia*, containing the special Matthaean sayings in Matthew 3–26. See also Burton 1912. Burton's division of Q into two subdocuments rests on the assumption that Matthew and Luke would have treated each source document more or less uniformly and, hence, that variations in the degree of verbal agreement between Matthew and Luke are attributable not to differing usages but to the use of different documents—this in spite of the fact that Burton also admits that neither evangelist hesitated to modify his sources (1912:98).

random probability would predict that the two evangelists would agree on only 25 percent of the words of Q, since either Matthew or Luke could choose to retain the wording of the source or to vary it. Alteration by either Matthew or Luke (or both) would create a disagreement; only when both chose to retain Q's wording would there be an agreement. Of course, neither editor worked randomly; considerations of content and style, among other things, would have influenced editorial choices. Surely one of the factors that would have influenced their reproduction of Q was that Q was largely sayings of Jesus; but neither Matthew nor Luke displays a consistent or absolute fidelity to the formulation of sayings of Jesus in Mark; hence, there is no a priori reason to think that their reproduction of Q would be significantly better or worse.

This is in fact what one finds in the double tradition. The following table, drawing on Morgenthaler's statistics, displays the range of verbatim agreement between Matthew and Luke. The first column divides the double tradition into five ranges based on the degree of verbatim agreement (from greater than 80 percent to less than 20 percent). The second and third columns indicate the number of pericopae and the percentage of Q (using Lukan word totals) represented in each range. The fourth and fifth columns give the average Matthaean and Lukan agreement in each range.

Variations in Agreement in the Double Tradition

Range	No. of pericopae	% of total words	Average Agreement Luke	Matt
98–80%	11	13.2%	86.7%	82.8%
60–79%	15	27.8%	68.9%	66.3%
40–59%	15	24.8%	46.4%	44.4%
20–39%	14	25.9%	28.5%	26.9%
0–19%	8	8.2%	12.4%	10.9%
	63	100%	50.6%	47.9%

As one ought to expect, there is a range of verbatim agreement, from a significant minority of extremely high-agreement pericopae (11 pericopae or 13.2 percent of the bulk of Q), to a larger number of pericopae displaying lesser agreement.[14] It is worth noting that the average verbatim agreement of approximately 50 percent is significantly higher than what random probability would predict. This is presumably a function of the fact that the double tradition is largely sayings of Jesus and John. It is also worth noting that there are relatively few pericopae that display extremely low agreement—less than 10 percent of the bulk of the double tradition.

14. Morgenthaler (1971:261) includes Luke 14:5b in his statistics (used above), which is doubtfully ascribed to Q.

The fact that some pericopae display lower agreement does not mean that they are automatically to be excluded from Q; it only means that, as expected, sometimes either Matthew or Luke (or both) chose to vary the wording of their sources. What is important for the evaluation of Bergemann's proposal is that the sayings found in Luke 6:20-49 do not in fact fall at the bottom of the scale, but squarely in the middle. Luke's double tradition in Luke 6:20-49 has 526 words compared with Matthew's 570 and the two agree in 261 (Luke) or 277 (Matt) words or 49.6 percent for Luke and 48.6 percent for Matthew.[15]

There is an obvious control which few, including Bergemann, have chosen to employ. Comparison of Matthew and Luke, first in non-Markan and then in Markan sections, indicates that there is as wide a disparity in verbal agreement in the Markan pericopae as there is in "Q" pericopae. For example, the agreement between Matthew and Luke is 80 percent in Mark 8:34-37; 70 percent in Mark 13:28-32 and 32 percent in Mark 12:1-11, but barely 12 percent in Mark 15:33-39—to take only pericopae containing a large proportion of speech material. A priori this is precisely what one should expect of two authors independently reproducing Mark. This is no reason to believe that Mark was really two or three documents; it only means that Matthew and/or Luke sometimes intervened substantially in their sources and at other times did not. The same applies, mutatis mutandis, to Q.[16]

What the above implies is not that Bergemann's thesis is impossible; only that the principle upon which he founds his investigation needs complete revision. If, for example, it turned out that many of the low-agreement pericopae appeared in the same context in a particular gospel and if they differed significantly in content, form, style, rhetorical stance, or theology from the more probable Q pericopae, one might have the beginnings of a case for positing an independent *Grundrede*. The prologue of the Fourth Gospel, for example, is usually thought to embody a pre-Johannine hymn

15. The statistics are based on my own count. They exclude Luke 6:20a, 24-26 and Matt 5:39a; 7:15, 19; 12:34; 10:25b as redactional but include Luke 6:34-35a, 37b-38a, 39a; Matt 5:41, some of which may be redactional. Matthew has two parallels for Luke 6:43-44, one in 7:15-20 and a second in 12:33, which accounts both for Matthew's higher overall word count and for the extra agreements.

16. Denaux 1995:118–20 offers a similar criticism, also using Morgenthaler's *Statistische Synopse* (1971) (which Bergemann seems not to know). He notes that in sayings of Jesus, the agreement of Matthew with Mark ranges from 0 percent (3 instances) to 100 percent (6 instances); the agreement of Mark with Luke ranges from 0 percent (1 instance) to 100 percent (1 instance). He concludes: "These lists show a line as continuously smooth as the list of Bergemann with respect to the Mt/Lk pericopes; and here also it is true that when the percentages are placed in the Mt- or Lk-sequence, they appear randomly arranged. . . . In short, the phenomenon of unequal treatment of the same source, which Bergemann demonstrates in the Double Tradition, is not so unusual: Matthew and Luke proceed in a similar manner with the words of Jesus which they read in Mark" (1995:119–20).

(John 1:1-5, 9-11, 14, 16) because these verses distinguish themselves from the rest of the Gospel (and from other sources John may have used): in their use of poetic or semirhythmic prose, in the use of several key terms (λόγος, χάρις, πλήρωμα) not found elsewhere in the Gospel, and in their awkward fit with the narrative structure of the Gospel. Such, however, is not the case with Q 6:20-49. The double tradition sayings in the Lukan Sermon are not noticeably different in their profile of agreement from the rest of the double tradition. Agreements with Matthew range from 83.5 percent (Q 6:41-42), 71 percent (Q 6:40) and 66 percent (Q 6:43-45), to 24 percent (6:47-49), with the average falling only fractionally beneath the overall average for Q.[17] Moreover, the Sermon, while of course having its own distinctive features, coheres with the other portions of Q in content as well as in style and form—admonitions with buttressing illustrations drawn from nature (arboriculture) or from ordinary human transactions (village conflict, house building). In short, it does not seem as though the sayings in the Lukan Sermon display characteristics significantly different from the rest of Q to warrant the suspicion of a separate source.

Bergemann also confuses the issue of reconstruction with that of the assignment of a pericope to Q. That we cannot know with certainty the wording of a particular Q pericope is not grounds in itself for asserting that the pericope did not not belong to Q at all. Legitimate doubts have been raised as to whether some double tradition pericopae—the saying about salt (Matt 5:13 / Luke 14:34-35), for example—belong to Q. This is not simply because the degree of verbal agreement is very low but also because Matthew and Luke do not agree in placing the parable in the same position relative to other Q material. The same can be said of the Parable of the Great Supper, which Matthew and Luke located differently. In the case of the Sermon, however, Matthew and Luke agree in placing this block of material in the same place relative to Q 3:7-9, 16-17; 4:1-13 and 7:1-10 in spite of the fact that they disagree in its placement relative to Mark. This suggests that both evangelists are influenced by the structure of a source document; they are not independently fusing Q with some other document.[18]

17. Q 6:41-42 and 6:43-45, in fact, prove embarrassments to Bergemann because they seem not to fit his definition of the *Grundrede* material. In the latter case, he posits *two* versions of tradition, one from Q (containing the sayings about trees and fruit, the warning against false prophets, and the saying about treasures) and one in the *Grundrede* (containing only the first two components). Luke interpolated the Q version into the *Grundrede* while Matthew used the shorter *Grundrede* version in Matthew 7 and a shortened version of Q in Matthew 12. Similarly, he must suggest that Q 6:41-42 was found in both sources and that Matthew and Luke coincidentally preferred Q to the *Grundrede* version and coincidentally interpolated it at the same point in the *Grundrede*. See Bergemann 1993:236–48.

18. There are also some questionable features of Bergemann's use of statistics to demonstrate that neither Matthew nor Luke would have reason to alter the source. He is rightly cautious in using word frequencies to support claims of redactional tendencies. But his view of

To conclude that Bergemann (and his predecessors) have not made their case for the partitioning of Q does not of course mean by default that Q was a single document. On the contrary, an argument must be made. I have already alluded to the outlines of this argument. The controlling logical principle for all Synoptic Problem–related investigations is the principle of parsimony or Ockham's razor: *causae non sunt multiplicandae praeter necessitatem,* "causes should not be multiplied except by necessity." In the case of the 2DH itself, necessity—dictated by the medial position of Mark in Synoptic relationships and the unlikelihood of a direct literary relationship between Matthew and Luke—requires the positing of Q as one of the two "causes" of Matthew and Luke. In the present context, the principle of parsimony requires that unless compelling reasons can be adduced to warrant treating the double tradition as multiple and varied in nature, it should be treated as a single "cause" or document.

A plausible case for the unity of Q may be made on two grounds, the first having to do with the content of Q, and the second, with the order of the double tradition.

1. It is true that the double tradition contains sayings of varied character and rhetorical form. John the Baptist's opening words (Q 3:7-9, 16-17) comprise a threat of fiery destruction, while Jesus' saying in Q 12:22-31 offers consolation and the promise of divine surveillance to the faithful. The double tradition contains two miracle stories—both focusing on sayings of Jesus (Q 7:1-10; 11:14-15, 17-20)—many proverbs and admonitions, several *paradeigmata* (illustrative narratives), a testing narrative (Q 4:1-13) and the quotation of an oracle of heavenly Wisdom (Q 11:49-51). Yet Arland Jacobson has shown that several common themes run through the double tradition and that despite the diversity of its sayings-types, Q has a distinctive profile when compared with Mark: Q has forms that are otherwise uncommon in Mark (makarisms, woes, correlatives, and prophetic threats), and the forms that Q shares with Mark (miracle stories, parables) are used in a noticeably different manner (Jacobson 1982a = 1994; 1992b:61–76).

In addition, several elements in the double tradition contribute to produce overarching unities. John the Baptist announces the imminent appearance of a "Coming One" in Q 3:16; his disciples ask Jesus whether he is that

---

redaction is extremely narrow: it assumes that the evangelists' redaction and our ability to detect redaction are based on the frequency of lexemes rather than on their grammatical function, semantic effect, or the wordfield to which these lexemes belong. For example, Bergemann argues that πατέρες ("fathers") in Luke 6:23 (Matt 2x; Luke 7x) provides "no basis for a redactional preference or avoidance" (1993:98). He fails to note (a) that Luke displays a tendency to specify subjects, and (b) frequently uses the phrase "your/their fathers" in contexts having to do with the rejection of God's envoys. It may be that such arguments are less quantifiable than sheer statistics, but they provide a far more meaningful representation of actual redactional procedures.

figure (Q 7:18-23); and in the Sophia oracle of Q 13:34-35 the title returns as Jesus' title both in his current appearance and in his imminent reappearance. The motif of judgment also appears at strategic points, in John's description of the Coming One, in Jesus' castigation of Bethsaida and Khorazin (Q 10:13-15), and in the role promised to Jesus' followers (Q 22:28-30) (see further, Kloppenborg 1987a:92–95).

Two key pericopae in the double tradition serve to relate some of the more disparate elements within Q to one another. The illustration of the quarrelsome children (Q 7:31-32) is furnished with two sayings that reflect on the rather different roles of John the Baptist and Jesus—one, an ascetic, the other at home in convivial settings—and assert that these differences notwithstanding, both are children of Heavenly Wisdom or Sophia (Q 7:35). This serves to relate the severe image of John as a desert-dwelling preacher that emerges from Q 3:(3),[19] 7-9, 16-17, and 7:24-26 to that of Jesus, whom Q represents as engaged, or talking about engagement, with everyday social interaction (Q 6:27-35, 36-38, 41-42; 17:3-4). Similarly, Q 6:39-40; 10:16, and 22:28-30 reflect on the relationship between Jesus and his followers in respect to both the hortatory sayings and the prophetic judgments.

In other words, the double tradition not only exhibits thematic and formal coherence, but also contains sayings and organizational features that expressly attempt to lend to the collection unity and structure. No one would claim that Q (or any other early Christian document for that matter) is perfectly homogeneous or that all parts fit equally well. That is not the point. It is rather that in spite of Q's varied contents, there are signs of unity and of attempts to negotiate its variety. In the face of these unities—unities that extend over large sections of the double tradition—it becomes difficult to argue that the double tradition in fact represents two or more smaller, independent collections. On the contrary, it is preferable to assume that it represents a single document.

2. The second set of data that suggests the unity of the double tradition is the common agreement between Matthew and Luke in placing the double tradition. The following table (see figure 14) illustrates the facts, alluded to several times before, that (a) after the initial four or five pericopae, Matthew and Luke fail to agree in placing the double tradition in the same Markan location; and that (b) in spite of this, Matthew and Luke concur in placing a significant proportion of Q pericopae (27 out of 67) in the same *relative* sequence.

While the order of the first few pericopae agrees with Mark's order—given the content, it is hard to imagine how they could be placed otherwise—Matthew and Luke then diverge completely, with Luke placing most of his double tradition materials at two points: between Mark 3:19 and

---

19. The parentheses indicate a text which cannot be ascribed to Q with certainty.

Figure 14
The Double Tradition in Matthew and Luke:
Order Relative to, and Independent of, Mark

Sigla

3:7-9	Agreements between Matthew and Luke in the sequence of the double tradition
1:2-6 ↔	Major "attachment points" of Matthew and Luke to Markan materials
1:2-6⇔3:1-6	Major "attachment points" of Q to Markan materials
(11:33)	Pericopae out of canonical sequence
omit	omission of Markan text from Matthew or Luke

Mark	Matthew	Q	Luke	Mark
1:2-6 ⇔	3:1-6	*(3:3)*	3:1-6 ⇔	1:2-6
	3:7-10	*3:7-9*	3:7-9	
1:7-8 ⇔	3:11-12	*3:16b-17*	3:16-17 ⇔	1:7-8
1:9-11 ↔	3:13-17		3:21-22 ↔	1:9-11
1:12-13 ⇔	4:1-11	*4:1-13*	4:1-13 ⇔	1:12-13
1:14-15 ↔	4:12, 17		4:14-15 ↔	1:14-15
	4:13	*4:16a*	4:16a	
1:16-20 ↔	4:18-22		4:31-44 ↔	1:21-39
1:21 (1:39) ⇔	4:23		/////////	/////////
	4:24-25		6:12-16	
			6:17-19 ↔	3:7-12
				3:13-19
	5:3—7:27		6:20—7:35 ⇔	
	5:1-2	*<6:20a>*	6:20a	
	5:3-10	*6:20b-23*	6:20b-23	
	5:13		(14:34-35)	
	5:14-16		(11:33)	
	5:18		(16:17)	
	5:25-26		(12:58-59)	
	5:32		(16:18)	
	5:38-48	*6:27-36*	6:27-36	
	6:9-13		(11:2-4)	
	6:19-21		(12:33-34)	
	6:22-23		(11:34-36)	
	6:24		(16:13)	
	6:25-34		(12:22-31)	
	7:1-2	*6:37-38*	6:37-38	
	(15:14)	*6:39*	6:39	
	(10:24-25)	*6:40*	6:40	
	7:3-5	*6:41-42*	6:41-42	
	7:7-11		(11:9-13)	
	7:12		(6:31)	
	7:13-14		(13:23-24)	
	7:15-20	*6:43-44*	6:43-44	

Mark	Matthew	Q	Luke	Mark
	(12:33-35)	6:44-45	6:44-45	
	7:21	6:46	6:46	
	7:22-23		(13:26-27)	
	7:24-27	6:47-49	6:47-49	
1:22	↔ 7:28-29			
1:23-28	⇔ omit			
(1:40-45)	8:1-4			
	8:5-10, 13	7:1-10	7:1-10	
	8:11-12		(13:28-29)	
			7:11-17	
1:29-34	⇔ 8:14-17			
1:35-38	omit			
1:40-45				
	8:18-22		(9:57-62)	
(4:35-41)	8:23-27			
(5:1-20)	8:28-34			
2:1-22	↔ 9:1-17			
(5:21-43)	9:18-26)			
(10:46-52)	9:27-31			
	9:32-34		(11:14-15)	
(6:6b, 34)	9:35-36			
	9:37-38		(10:2-3)	
(3:13-19)	10:1-4, 5-6			
	10:7-16		(10:4-12)	
(13:9-13)	10:17-23		(12:11-12)	
	10:24-25		(6:40)	
	10:26-33		(12:2-9)	
	10:34-36		(12:51-53)	
	10:37-38		(14:26-27)	
	10:39		(17:33)	
	10:40		(10:16)	
(9:41)	10:41—11:1			
	11:2-11	7:18-28	7:18-28	
	(21:31-32)		7:29-30	
11:12-15				
	11:16-19	7:31-35	7:31-35	
			7:36—8:3 ⇔	3:31-35
			8:4-18 ↔	4:1-25
			8:19-21	(3:31-35)
			8:22—9:17 ↔	4:35—6:44
			omit	6:45—8:26
			9:18-50 ↔	8:27—9:41

Mark	Matthew	Q	Luke	Mark
			9:51 ⇔	10:1
	(8:18-22)	9:57-60 (61-62)	9:57-60, 61-62	
	(10:7-16)	10:2-12	10:2-12	
	11:20-24	*10:13-15*	10:13-15	
	(10:40)	10:16	10:16	
	11:25-27	*10:21-22*	10:21-22	
	(13:16-17)	10:23-24	10:23-24	
			10:25-28	(12:28-34)
	(6:9-13)	11:2-4	11:1-4	
	(7:7-11)	11:9-13	11:9-13	
2:23—3:12 ↔	12:1-21			
3:13-19				
3:22-27 ↔	12:22-30	*11:14-23*	11:14-23	
3:28-30 ↔	12:31-32		(12:10)	
	12:33-37		(6:44-45)	
		11:24-26	11:24-26	
		(11:27-28)	11:27-28	
	12:38-42	*11:29-32*	11:29-32	
	12:43-45			
3:31-35 ↔	12:46-50			
	(5:14-16)	11:33	11:33	
	(6:22-23)	11:34-35 (36)	11:34-36	
	(23:1-39)	11:39-44, 46-52	11:37-54	
	(10:26-33)	12:2-9	12:1-9	
	(12:31-32)	12:10	12:10	
	(10:19-20)	12:11-12	12:11-12	
	(6:25-34)	12:22-31	12:22-31	
	(6:19-21)	12:33-34	12:33-34	
	(24:43-51)	12:39-40, 42-46	12:39-46	
	(10:34-36)	12:51-53	12:51-53	
	(16:2-3)	12:54-56	12:54-56	
	(5:25-26)	12:58-59	12:58-59	
4:1-29 ↔	13:1-30			
4:30-23 ⇔	13:31-32	*13:18-19*	13:18-19	
	13:33	*13:20-21*	13:20-21	
4:33-34 ↔	13:34-35			
6:1-6a ↔	13:53-58			
6:6b-13 ↔	(9:35—10:14)			
	(7:13-14)	13:24	13:23-24	
	(7:22-23)	13:(25), 26-27	13:25, 26-27	
	(8:11-12)	13:28-29	13:28-29	
	(19:30)	13:30	13:30	
	(23:39)	13:34-35	13:34-35	
	(23:13)	14:11/18:14	14:11	

Mark	Matthew	Q	Luke	Mark
	(22:1-10)	14:16-24	14:16-24	
	(10:37-38)	14:26-27	14:26-27	
	(10:39)	17:33	17:33	
	(5:31)	14:34-35	14:34-35	
6:14—7:31 ↔	14:1—15:31			
7:32-37	omit			
8:1-21 ↔	15:32—16:12			
8:22-26	omit			
8:27—9:28 ↔	16:13—17:20a			
9:29 ⇔	17:20b		(17:6)	
9:30-37 ↔	17:22—18:5			
9:38-41	omit			
9:42-48 ⇔	18:6-9		(17:1-2)	
	18:10-14	*15:4-7*	15:4-7	
	(6:24)	16:13	16:13	
	(11:12-13)	16:16	16:16	
	(5:10)	16:17	16:17	
	(5:31-32)	16:18	16:18	
	(18:6-7)	17:1b-2	17:1b-2	
	18:15-22	*17:3b-4*	17:3b-4	
	(17:20b)	17:6b	17:6b	
10:1-22 ↔	19:1-22			
10:23-31 ⇔	19:23-27, 29-30			
10:29 ⇔	19:28		(22:28-30)	
10:32—12:12 ↔	20:1—21:46			
		22:1-10	(14:16-24)	
12:13-37a ↔	22:15-46			
12:37b-40 ⇔	23:1-36		(11:39-52)	
	23:37-39		(13:34-35)	
13:1-20 ↔	24:1-22			
13:21-23 ⇔	24:23-25			
	24:26-28	*17:23-24, 37*	17:23-24, 37	
13:24-32 ⇔	24:29-36			
	24:37-41	*17:26-27, 34-35*	17:26-30, 34-35	
13:33 ⇔	24:42			
	24:43-51		(12:39-46)	
			18:15-43 ⇔	10:13-52
			19:1-10	
	25:14-30	*19:12-13, 15-26*	19:12-27	
			19:28—20:40 ↔	11:1—12:27
			20:41—22:23 ⇔	12:35—14:25
			22:24-27	
	(19:28)	22:28-30	22:28-30	
14:1—16:8 ↔	26:1—28:8		22:31—24:9 ↔	14:26—16:8

3:31[20] and between Mark 9:41 and 10:13.[21] Matthew, by contrast, attaches
Q sayings to a wider selection of Markan contexts and gathers other sayings
into his long discourses in Matthew 5–7, 10, 13, 18, and 23–25.[22] Nevertheless, there are important agreements in the relative placement of the initial Baptist material, the temptation, inaugural sermon, healing of the
centurion's slave, a second block of Baptist material, the Beelzebul accusation and request for a sign, the sayings about the Day of the Son of Man and
judgment.[23] Such agreements are fatal to Bergemann's thesis and would be
difficult to account for on the other theses outlined above.

It is of course possible that one or more sayings that are used very differently by Matthew and Luke (e.g., Matt 5:13 / Luke 14:34-35) were not
derived from Q. But this does not gainsay the data and arguments that suggest that, taken as a whole, the double tradition is best explained as deriving from a single document.

THE LANGUAGE OF Q

One of the most oddly persistent debates regarding Q has to do with its
original language. It is fair to say that without Papias's statement about

20. Instead of Mark's Beelzebul accusation (Mark 3:20-21, 22-30), Luke uses Q's longer
version, placing it in the "Q order" (i.e., before the request for a sign, Q 11:29-32).

21. Luke omits Mark 9:42-48 (cf. Luke 17:1-2 [Q]); 9:49-50 (cf. Luke 14:34-35 [Q]); and
10:1-12 (cf. Luke 16:18 [Q]), in each case because he has already included a saying from Q
that treats the substance of the Markan pericope.

22. Matthew used Mark 1:21, the first mention of Jesus' teaching, as the occasion for the
Sermon on the Mount, in which he also collects numerous Q and special Matthaean (M) sayings; then he used Mark's description of the reaction to Jesus' teaching (1:22) to conclude the
Sermon. Since Matthew placed the Sermon outside Kefar Naḥum (unlike Mark), he then uses
a series of stories describing Jesus' return to Kefar Naḥum (8:1-4 [Mark 1:40-45] outside the
town; 8:5-13 [Q] entering it; 8:14-17 [Mark 1:29-32] in Kefar Naḥum), followed by another
cycle of departure stories (8:18-22 [Q]; 8:23-27 [Mark 4:35-41]; 8:28-34 [Mark 5:1-20]),
before returning to Kefar Naḥum and Markan sequence (9:1-22 = Mark 2:1-17). John's question from prison (Matt 11:2-6 [Q]) seems to have served a major role in the organization of
Matthew's gospel as well, for Matthew maneuvered stories that correspond to (and hence
anticipate) each of the items mentioned in Jesus' response to John (11:5): sight to the blind
(9:27-31 [Mark 10:46-52]), mobility to the lame (9:1-8 [Mark 2:1-12]), cleaning of lepers (8:1-
4 [Mark 1:40-45]), speech and hearing restored (9:32-34 [Q]), the dead raised (9:18-26 [Mark
5:21-43]), and the evangelization of the poor (9:35-10:42 [Q + Mark 6:34]). After the sayings
regarding John (11:2-19) and the woes against the Galilean towns and the thanksgiving
(11:20-24, 25-27), Matthew used Mark 3:22-30 as the attachment point for the Beelzebul
accusation and request for a sign. Q's parables of the mustard and leaven are fused with the
Markan parables discourse (Mark 4:1-34) and miscellaneous Q sayings are connected with
Mark 9:29, 9:42-48, and 10:29. The final two large sections of Q are fused with Mark 12:37b-
40 (against the Pharisees) and 13:1-33.

23. In the latter part of table 14, agreements between Matthew and Luke could be designated in several ways, for example, designating Q 14:16-24 rather than 15:4-7 and 17:3b-4 as
"in order." This would not, however, significantly affect the overall bulk of Q material upon
which Matthew and Luke agree in relative sequence. For slightly different tabulations of
sequential agreements, see Patton 1915:251–52; Castor 1918:120–21.

Matthew and Schleiermacher's comments on Papias, this debate would probably never have started. Curiously, even though Papias's testimony is no longer treated as credible in respect to Q, the cause of an Aramaic Q continues to find champions who adduce a handful of points at which Matthew or Luke may have mistranslated Aramaic words.[24]

Several preliminary distinctions are necessary. Few would contest the fact that Q, like much of the Synoptic materials, reflects Semitic features. These may be seen at the level of syntax (e.g., the preference for καί over δέ for linking independent clauses), style (e.g., the use of synonymous and antithetic parallelism and *qal weḥomer* arguments [from the lesser to the greater]), and idiom (e.g., using "debt" to mean "sin") (Bussby 1954). Such features, however, imply only that the author(s) was (were) influenced by Semitic (or Septuagintal) syntax and style; they do not show that the document was penned in a Semitic language. Mark contains similar features, but no one nowadays thinks that Mark was translated from Aramaic (Maloney 1981). In order to demonstrate composition in Hebrew or Aramaic, one would have to show both (a) that Q contains features that may be explained only by appeal to an Aramaic document; and (b) that Q's Greek is most easily explicable as translation Greek. The former requires that we identify differences in wording between Matthew and Luke that can be explained only by positing an Aramaic word or idiom which the two evangelists choose to render differently or, ideally, an Aramaic word that could be mistranslated because of an optical confusion, i.e., the mistaking of one letter for another. The latter requires identifying syntactical features that are either common in Semitic languages but rare or generally avoided in Greek and features that are possible only in Greek, and then showing that Q consistently tends toward semitizing constructions and avoids exclusively Greek forms.

The matter is complicated by the fact that, as the previous discussions have shown, Q must be seen as a single document. Moreover, it is clear that Matthew and Luke have consulted Q in Greek; otherwise their near-verbatim agreement in pericopae such as Q 3:7b-9; 10:13-15; 11:24-26; 11:31-32, and 13:20-21 would be inexplicable. This means one of two things. Either Q was translated from Aramaic into Greek before Matthew and Luke used it (figure 15A); but in that case, it would be impossible to find instances of translation variants or translation mistakes that would

---

24. D. Allison (1997:47–49) agrees that the final form of Q was Greek but pleads for an Aramaic version of its earliest stratum (see chap. 3, p. 117 for a discussion of Allison's stratigraphy). His case that the final form of Q is Greek is based on the observation that Q's citations of the Tanak are all Septuagintal (though he misses the fact that Q 7:27 is non-Septuagintal). His case for asserting that Q 9:57—11:13; 12:2-12, 22-31 [32] was a collection of "Aramaic traditions" is based on the presence of "translation Greek." Ironically, his authority for this, R. Martin (1987:100–101), considers both 9:57-60 and 12:22-31 to fall outside translation Greek frequencies. On the latter, see below n. 33.

demonstrate the existence of the Aramaic original. Or one would have to assume that in addition to the Greek copy of Q, both Matthew and Luke also had an Aramaic version that they occasionally consulted and used to modify the Greek version (Castor 1918:17; figure 15B); or that in the course of transmission in Greek Q was itself "corrected" against the Aramaic original and thus developed into two recensions (Wellhausen 1911:60; figure 15C); or that there were two translations of Q from Aramaic, in most respects identical, but occasionally exhibiting the disagreements traceable to translation variants or mistakes (Patton 1915:123–24 [apparently]; figure 15D). None of these assumptions make for a very tidy solution; the thesis of an Aramaic Q threatens to collapse under the weight of its own ingenuity.

Julius Wellhausen's commentaries on the Synoptics (1904a; 1904b) provided the backbone for the thesis of an Aramaic Q. Wellhausen noted various instances, including several Q texts, in which variations between Synoptic accounts might be traced to varying translations of specific Aramaic words.[25] Castor (1918:17, 208) and Patton (1915:123–25) quickly saw that these texts could be used to argue that Q was composed in Aramaic, against such critics as Wernle (1899:229), who thought that Q was composed exclusively in Greek. In his influential book, *An Aramaic Approach to the Gospels and Acts* (1967), Matthew Black reviewed and supplemented Wellhausen's list. He concluded nonetheless: "it is doubtful if we are justified in describing Q, without qualification, as a translation of Aramaic. . . . [I]t is the Greek literary factor which has had the final word with the shaping of the Q tradition" (1967:191 [emphasis original]). Black's instances were reviewed by the present writer (1987a:54–59), who argued that none offers compelling evidence of an Aramaic original. In a rejoinder, Black (1990) rehearsed three pieces of evidence, which I shall use here to illustrate the debate.[26]

1. Wellhausen suggested that the difference between Matt 23:26, καθάρισον, "cleanse," and Luke 11:41, δότε ἐλεημοσύνην, "give alms," could be explained by positing the Aramaic original as דכי, "cleanse," which Luke misread as זכי, "give alms" (1904a:61; 1911:27). The suggestion was attractive, since orthographically, the two words were so simlar. C. F. D. Moule, however, objected, arguing three points: (a) that זכי could mean both "give

---

25. Q 6:22 (Wellhausen 1904a:24; 1905:36; Black 1967:135); Q 6:23 (Wellhausen 1904a:24; 1905:36; Black 1967:191–92); Q 6:46 (Wellhausen 1911:27; Black 1967:193); Q 10:5 (Wellhausen 1904b:45; 1905:36; 1911:27; Black 1967:193); Q 11:41 (Wellhausen 1904a:61; 1905:36–37; 1911:27; Black 1967:2).

26. The complete list of alleged translation variants is not long: Luke 6:22; 6:23; 6:46; 10:5; 11:3, 4; 11:41, 42, 48; 12:10; 14:27 and parallels. See Kloppenborg 1987a:54–59 for a discussion.

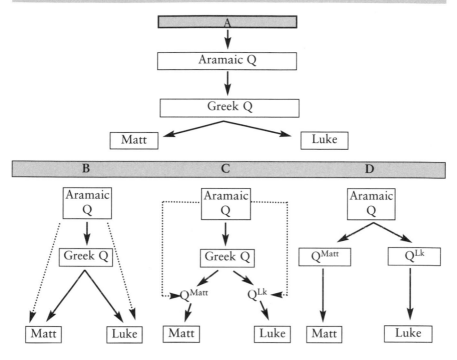

Figure 15
An Aramaic *Vorlage* for Q?

alms" and "cleanse"; (b) that זכי meant exclusively moral purity and hence would never have been confused with דכי used with reference to the purification of cups; and (c) that "the evidence for the currency of the word [זכי] in Palestinian Aramaic seemed precarious" (Moule 1959:186). The third of Moule's objections might be reassessed in view of the occurrences of the word in Palestinian targumim.[27] Moule's second point is better suited as an objection against a thesis that זכי was original and Matthew (not Luke) confused it with דכי; his first point, however, stands.

Wellhausen's conjecture seems plausible until one looks at the larger context. First, since both Matthew and Luke have καθαρίζετε ("cleanse") in Matt 23:25 / Luke 11:39b, one would have to suppose that Luke (or some pre-Lukan translator of Q) saw דכי the first time and translated it correctly, but then confused it for זכי, which cannot refer to physical purity. Hence the translator of Luke 11:41 had to eliminate the reference to the cup (Matt 23:26). This of course also assumes that Luke knew Aramaic, for which the

---

27. Black (1990) cites Dalman's list of vocabulary of the Palestinian Talmud (1930:71), which is, of course, rather late. Jastrow 1985:399 lists no occurrences of the word in the Mishnah, Tosephta, or early midrashim. The word does appear, however, in the Fragment Targum and in Targum Neophyti I (Gen 24:41; Deut 24:5; 25:1; 32:4), always with a moral sense. See Sokoloff 1990:177.

evidence is rather scant.[28] Second, it is clear that Luke has not simply mis-translated one word; the entire sentence is different:

<table>
<tr><td align="center">Matt 23:25-26</td><td align="center">Luke 11:39b-41</td></tr>
<tr><td></td><td>Νῦν ὑμεῖς οἱ Φαρισαῖοι τὸ ἔξωθεν τοῦ</td></tr>
<tr><td>25 . . . καθαρίζετε τὸ ἔξωθεν τοῦ ποτηρίου</td><td>ποτηρίου καὶ τοῦ πίνακος καθαρίζετε, τὸ δὲ</td></tr>
<tr><td>καὶ τῆς παροψίδος, ἔσωθεν δὲ γέμουσιν ἐξ</td><td>ἔσωθεν ὑμῶν γέμει ἁρπαγῆς καὶ πονηρίας.</td></tr>
<tr><td>ἁρπαγῆς καὶ ἀκρασίας.</td><td></td></tr>
<tr><td>26 Φαρισαῖε τυφλέ,</td><td>40 ἄφρονες, οὐχ ὁ ποιήσας τὸ ἔξωθεν καὶ</td></tr>
<tr><td></td><td>τὸ ἔσωθεν ἐποίησεν;</td></tr>
<tr><td>καθάρισον πρῶτον τὸ ἐντὸς τοῦ ποτηρίου,</td><td>41 πλὴν τὰ ἐνόντα δότε ἐλεημοσύνην, καὶ</td></tr>
<tr><td>ἵνα γένηται καὶ τὸ ἐκτὸς αὐτοῦ καθαρόν.</td><td>ἰδοὺ πάντα καθαρὰ ὑμῖν ἐστιν.</td></tr>
<tr><td></td><td></td></tr>
<tr><td></td><td>Now, you Pharisees:</td></tr>
<tr><td>. . . you cleanse the outside of the cup and</td><td>you cleanse the outside of the cup and the</td></tr>
<tr><td>the dish, but inside they are full of extortion</td><td>plate, but your inside is full of extortion</td></tr>
<tr><td>and rapacity. Blind Pharisee!</td><td>and evil. Fools! Did not the one who made</td></tr>
<tr><td>Cleanse first the inside of the cup so that its</td><td>the outside also make the inside? But give</td></tr>
<tr><td>outside might also be pure.</td><td>as alms what is inside, and behold, every-</td></tr>
<tr><td></td><td>thing is clean for you.</td></tr>
</table>

Matthew's woe focuses on the contradiction between outer and inner, between clean exteriors and fouled interiors, a contrast that pervades his redaction of the woes (Matt 23:1-39). For Luke, the vice of the Pharisees and lawyers is not so much hypocrisy as bad leadership—leadership that neglects redistribution of resources. Regardless of which version better approximates Q,[29] the variations cannot be accounted for by a theory of two translations—even interpretive translations—of an Aramaic original. On the contrary, both Matthew's focus on hypocrisy and Luke's interest in almsgiving are part of larger redactional strategies visible in their respective editings of Mark's Greek text and, presumably, in their editing of Q.[30] To appeal to a mistranslation of an Aramaic word in Q 11:41 not only begs the question of Luke's knowledge of Aramaic; it is neither necessary, since Lukan editorial habits explain the alteration equally well,[31] nor sufficient,

28. It is clear that Luke knows the Septuagint and has been influenced by its style (Fitzmyer 1981:109–16). Fitzmyer (117) cites four instances of Lukan phrases (all from 1:32-35) that have parallels in 4Q246, five phrases (one from Q 10:21!) with parallels in other Qumran Aramaic texts, and four usages (εὕρωσιν = "be able"; ὤφθη = "he appeared"; ὀφειλέται = "sinners"; and ἀπὸ μιᾶς = "at once") that may reflect Aramaic. None of these, however, indicates that Luke translated anything from Aramaic.

29. The IQP (J. M. Robinson 1992a:504) was undecided on the reconstruction of Q 11:41 because signs of Matthaean and Lukan redaction were equally in evidence.

30. Note that Luke uses "give alms" in a redactional introduction to 12:33 (/ Matt 6:19-21). Luke's interest in almsgiving is also obvious in his editing of Mark 2:14; 10:21, in his special material (Luke 19:1-10), and from Acts 3:2, 3, 10; 9:36; 10:2, 4, 31; 24:17.

31. Similarly Tuckett 1996:88: "Thus there is no need to look any further than Luke's redaction interests to account for Luke's difference from Matthew and any theory of an Aramaic Vorlage seems unnecessary."

since no Aramaic phrase can account for the wide variation between Matthew and Luke in this woe.

2. Black suggests that Luke's σκιρτήσατε ("leap," 6:23) and Matthew's ἀγαλλιᾶσθε ("rejoice," 5:11) come from the Aramaic or Syriac verb *dwṣ*, which Matthew rendered correctly and Luke interpretively (1967:193). While this explanation is possible, it is hardly necessary.[32] Luke shows an inclination to use vivid, highly visual language, for example, "leaping" (1:44), "the Spirit descended upon him *in bodily form* like a dove" (3:22); "lest she beat me black and blue" (ὑπωπιάζω, 18:5), and "a sound like the rush of wind . . . and tongues of fire" (Acts 2:2-3). Black objects: "*Parallelismus verborum* in both Gospels, however, demands the meaning 'rejoice'; to suggest that this was redactionally modified by Luke to become 'leap' is straining credulity" (1990:37). But "leap" is precisely what σκιρτήσατε means, regardless of how it came to be in Luke's gospel! Black's argument is a non sequitur: Luke could not have changed Q's ἀγαλλιᾶσθε ("rejoice") into σκιρτήσατε ("leap") because of its parallel with χάρητε ("rejoice"); therefore, Luke must have (mis)translated *dwṣ* as σκιρτήσατε (and thus violated the parallelism)!

3. Black's third example is ὀφειλήματα ("debts") in Matt 6:12, which Luke renders as ἁμαρτίας ("sins," [11:4]; 1967:140; 1990:37). It is correct that the use of "debt" to mean "sin" is an Aramaism (from *ḥub;* Jastrow 1985:140). The issue, however, is not whether Q's term is an Aramaism; the issue is whether one needs to posit an Aramaic document to account for Luke's "sins." The answer, clearly, is no. As Luke 13:2-4 and 7:41-50 make plain, Luke knows very well that "debt" can be used as a metaphor for "sin." That he chooses "sin" in the Lord's Prayer probably only means that Luke is also aware that in Koine Greek ὀφείλημα normally refers to monetary debts, not moral failings. Thus he avoids potential misunderstanding of the petition by substituting "sins." This substitution allows him to preserve ὀφείλοντι (Matt: ὀφειλέταις) in the second part of the petition: "as we ourselves forgive everyone who is *indebted* to us." He uses precisely the same technique in 7:41-50 and 13:2-4: the Semitism "debt" is used, but only when the context makes it clear that it in fact serves as a metaphor for sin rather than a statement about monetary debt.

Let me be clear on the point. The issue is not whether Q contains Aramaisms—it does, as Wellhausen and Black have ably demonstrated. The issue is not whether Q was formulated in an environment in which Aramaic speech patterns could influence its language.[33] The issue is whether Q was *written* in Aramaic and then translated into Greek. For this, the evidence is

---

32. Thus also Gundry 1982:74; Davies and Allison 1988:464.

33. Raymond A. Martin has kindly shared with me part of a manuscript that has appeared in the meantime (1995) in which he argues that most of Q's syntax falls within the ranges expected for translation Greek or in the ambiguous zone shared by *both* translation and orig-

scant, hardly sufficient to make a coherent case, especially since each instance admits of other explanations.

One can, however, fully agree with Black's statement that "Greek literary factor . . . has had the final word with the shaping of the Q tradition." As Nigel Turner (1968–69) and the present writer (1987:59–64) have noted, Q's Greek as measured with several indices—the use of postpositive particles, the relative frequencies of καί to δέ, the position of the verb in independent clauses, and the separation of an article from its substantive (hyperbaton)—is notably different from the profile of Septuagint books that are known to have been translated from Hebrew or Aramaic (see also Vassiliadis 1978:55–57). Moreover, there are phrases in Q—εἰ υἱὸς εἶ τοῦ θεοῦ (4:3), or οἱ ἐν ἱματισμῷ ἐνδόξῳ καὶ τρυφῇ ὑπάρχοντες (7:25), for example—that are impossible in a Semitic language and cannot be direct translations.

The other mainstay of the thesis of an Aramaic Q, Papias's testimony, has now been discredited. Indeed, the celebrated statement that enlivened Schleiermacher's imagination, "Matthew arranged (συνετάξατο) the *logia* in the Hebrew language, and everyone interpreted (ἡρμήνευσε) them as he was able" (Eusebius, *Hist. eccl.* 3.39.16), is as complex as Q itself. For the statement is Eusebius's citation of Papias, who in turn claims to be quoting an otherwise unknown "John the Elder." Two issues are distinguishable: what were Eusebius, Papias, and the elder describing by the term *logia*, and why was this particular term used?

Schleiermacher thought that Papias must have meant a collection of sayings rather than a narrative gospel, since the basic meaning of the term *logia* is "oracles." It is clear from the context, however, that Eusebius himself understood Papias to be referring to the canonical gospel of Matthew (Sellew 1992:124–25). There is also no doubt that Papias thought the same and that his quotation of the Elder in the preceding paragraph (*Hist. eccl.* 3.39.16) in respect to Mark was formulated with other gospels in view; the statement is intent on apologizing for Mark's lack of "order" (τάξις), something that could only be said if canonical Matthew, Luke, and/or John were available for comparison.[34] Moreover, neither the title of Papias's book, from which Eusebius took the citations, nor the Elder's own usage of the term *logia* provides support for Schleiermacher's contention that *logia* cannot be a description of canonical Matthew, which contains narratives. Papias's book, Λογίων κυριακῶν ἐξήγησις, "Exposition of the Dominical

---

inal Greek. Only one pericope (Q 12:22-31) "has clear original Greek frequencies" (1995:136). Nevertheless, Martin does not conclude that Q as a whole was translated from Aramaic, but rather that "all, or nearly all, of the Q material had an Aramaic background before it made its appearance in Greek" (1995:138). Indeed, the presence of exclusively Greek syntactical devices (the absolute genitive, hyperbata) and quotations from the Septuagint (Q 4:1-13; 7:22) prohibits the conclusion that Q was in toto a translation document.

34. See Kürzinger 1983:11; Cameron 1984:100–12; Kloppenborg 1987a:52–53; Merkel 1990:570.

Logia," clearly includes much more than simply "sayings" or "oracles."[35] Similarly, the Elder refers to the contents of Mark as τὰ κυριακὰ λόγια in his statements on Mark.

Dieter Lührmann has recently provided a helpful resolution of the second problem, why *logia* was used in the first place. He notes that it is in Papias's fragments that *logia* first occurs as a description of sayings of Jesus. The earlier and more usual term was *logoi,* "sayings." Papias admits to being suspicious of written traditions and much preferred reliance on oral reports that he received from his elders. Lührmann suggests that Papias's description of both Mark and Matthew—Mark lacking "order" and Matthew being a collection that had been variously interpreted—indicates that Papias saw both gospels as deficient.

> Papias was the first to understand the sayings of Jesus as oracles preserved from antiquity, but down to his own time found only poor or even false translations and/or interpretations of such oracles, and wished himself to supply the interpretation, which with oracles is always necessary. He knew the gospels of Mark and Matthew, but for various reasons considered them unsatisfactory. He wanted to set his own work in their place. He offered a new collection of his own of the Λόγια, which was founded on the written versions and also upon oral tradition. (Lührmann 1995:111)

This implies even more strongly that one cannot rely at all on his use of *logia,* since it is *Papias's* coinage to solve a particular problem he saw in the written gospels. It is utterly irrelevant to Q.

On the other hand, Matthew Black devised an ingenious way to rescue Papias's testimony as evidence of Q. He concedes to Kürzinger and this author that Papias was speaking of canonical Matthew but suggests that *Papias's informant* was speaking of Matthew's source (1989:33). This is accomplished only by arguing that the juxtaposition of the statements on Mark and Matthew—and hence their apologetic tone—was Eusebius's doing, not Papias's or the Elder's. This in turn allows Black to claim that the statement about Matthew was perhaps not from the Elder at all but from some other informant, since only the statement about Mark is explicitly ascribed to the Elder. Black thus separates the statements on Mark, where *logia* is used imprecisely, from those concerning Matthew where, he suggests, *logia* ought to be understood in its precise meaning of "saying" or "oracle" and hence cannot apply to canonical Matthew.

All this fails to persuade, for Eusebius, who quotes Papias's remarks on the gospels dismissively and without further comment (Sellew 1992:125), had no reason to construct the apologetic for Mark. This being so, there are no grounds for separating the statement on Matthew from that on Mark or for interpreting the two statements differently, either in the case of the Elder or in that of Papias. Both had the canonical gospels in view and hence the

---

35. Kürzinger 1983:24–26, 33; Körtner 1983:154–56.

statement on Matthew is without value for reconstructing Q. Black's argument would also now have to respond to Lührmann's thesis, that *logia* is Papias's own term, coined for his own theological purposes.[36]

The thesis of an Aramaic original of Q is extraordinarily weak. The origin of the speculation, Papias's statement about Matthew, is legendary at best. The linguistic data employed to demonstrate an Aramaic original is scant and what little there is admits of more economical explanations that avoid having to posit yet another document. Finally, the dazzlingly improbable logistics needed to account for Matthew's *and* Luke's occasional revision of their Greek Q by recourse to a *written* Aramaic version that *both* had (and could read!) reduce the likelihood of demonstrating an Aramaic Q to near zero.

THE DATE OF Q

The dating of the documents of the New Testament is notoriously difficult. In the case of some of Paul's letters (Galatians; 1–2 Corinthians; Romans) where Paul's previous and expected travels are mentioned, it is possible to ascertain at least the relative sequence of the letters. One can even reconstruct an absolute chronology, provided that one or two points can be fixed with reference to other datable events (e.g., Paul's escape from Damascus). In the case of the gospels there are few fixed markers. The 2DH obviously implies a relative chronology for the four documents it involves, but insofar as Matthew and Luke tend to be dated rather vaguely from the 80s or 90s and Mark about 70, this leaves a wide scope for Q.

If it could be shown that Mark used Q, then Q could safely be placed at least a few years before 70. But scholars are very much divided on the question of whether Mark knows the final form of Q or merely shares some tradition with Q.[37] That latter view seems preferable, for Mark does not show any signs of knowing what is distinctive of Q's redaction. The matter is complicated even more by the fact that, as will be argued in the next chapter, Q shows evidence of having at least two, and more probably three, stages of development.

Kirsopp Lake provided one of the first serious treatments of the problem (1909). Beginning from Q's almost certain lack of passion and resurrection narratives and the paucity of sayings concerning Jesus' fate,[38] he asked:

36. This section of the present chapter was sent to Professor Black, who had on earlier occasions kindly offered me corrections and criticisms. It reached him only a few days before his death on October 2, 1994, when biblical scholarship lost a generous and erudite colleague.

37. In favor of Mark's dependence on Q: Fleddermann 1981; 1995; Lambrecht 1982; 1992; Catchpole 1992; Mack 1991b; 1993:177–80, 227–28. In favor of independence: Laufen 1980; Schüling 1991; Tuckett 1993; Dunderberg 1995; Neirynck 1995a.

38. Lake thought that Luke 17:25 was from Q but noted its rather vague description of Jesus' fate (1909:497). Q 14:27 presupposed Jesus' crucifixion and glorification, but only in

Under what conditions would such a silence be intelligible? His answer was a brilliant conjecture based on Paul's letters. Since in real letters (as distinct from literary epistles), one normally does not discuss matters of common knowledge but only issues that are new or under dispute, it is likely that Paul's use of Christ's resurrection as an analogy for the resurrection of the believer in 1 Corinthians 15 was a "new" issue in the 50s. An earlier stage of belief is reflected in 1 Thessalonians 4, when believers were not concerned about their own resurrections because they imagined that the Day of the Lord would arrive during their own lifetimes. Only after the reality of the deaths of believers had become a theological issue was it necessary to reflect expressly upon the resurrection of Jesus as an event having personal significance for the believer. Hence, Lake suggested that the *terminus ad quem* for Q was ca. 50 CE; every year after that, Q's silence about Jesus' resurrection would be increasingly difficult to explain.

There is a methodological problem with Lake's argument. He assumes a uniform theological development throughout the Jesus groups of the Mediterranean such that what was perceived as a problem for Aegean Christians in the Pauline orbit would in the Palestinian Jesus movement have likewise seemed a problem requiring reflection on the resurrection of Jesus. The Gospel of John, obviously composed after 50 CE, does not employ Jesus' resurrection in the way Paul did, even though the followers of Christ—including the so-called Beloved Disciple—had died by that time. Instead, John employs a doctrine of the Spirit along with a strongly realized eschatology. Indeed, the fact that Q's "successor," Matthew, coordinates the resurrection of Jesus with that of the "saints" (Matt 27:52-53) may suggest that the Pauline rather than the Johannine solution influenced the Synoptic tradition. But it is simply impossible to gauge at what chronological point this type of solution would have become necessary or inevitable.

One of the usual ways in which to set a *terminus a quo* for any document is to find an allusion to the First Revolt.[39] Such allusions are clear in Matthew (22:8) and Luke (21:20-23). Wellhausen thought that he would find a similar allusion in Q. He did this by ascribing to Q Matthew's version of Q 11:49-51, which mentions the murder of Zechariah ben Barachiah which occurred in 67 or 68 (Josephus, *War* 4.335; Wellhausen 1911:118–20). Unfortunately, the reference to Zechariah ben Barachiah is probably Matthaean; Luke (and probably Q) names Zechariah without a

---

passing. Few today ascribe Luke 17:25 to Q since it fits too well with Lukan redactional interests and vocabulary.

39. Catchpole (1992:39), citing Q 17:23-24, argues that Q must be dated sometime after 45 CE, since it was during the procuratorship of Cuspius Fadus (44–48 CE) that various "signs prophets" became active. D. Allison (1997:50) rightly observes that Josephus notes that the Samaritan prophet was active in 36 CE (*Ant.* 18.85-87).

patronym but probably refers to the murder of Zechariah ben Jehoiada in 2 Chron 24:20-22 who was killed in the sanctuary.[40]

A much earlier date has been proposed by Gerd Theissen (1989, ET 1991). Beginning with the Temptation story (Q 4:1-13), which he acknowledges to be one of the latest additions to Q, Theissen argues that its three key elements—prostration (*proskynēsis*) before the world ruler, the power to bestow kingdoms, and the direct offense against the worship of a single God—combine to suggest that the account was a response to Gaius Caligula's attack on Jewish monotheism in 40 CE (1991:206-21). *Proskynēsis*, known since the time of Alexander, was not practiced in Roman circles until Caligula. Despite his brief principate, Caligula established six kings in the East, including the gift of Antipas's tetrarchy to Agrippa I in 39 (enlarged by Claudius in 41 to include Judaea). Finally, the challenge to monotheism implied in the third temptation (Q 4:4-8) evokes the infamous incident of Caligula's attempt to have a statue of himself erected in the Jerusalem temple and worshiped.

Theissen supplements this case by adducing two other indications of an early date: First are several indications that Q was involved in an "Israel mission" that antedated the Jerusalem council (Galatians 2; Acts 15). These include Q's expectation that the Twelve will rule or judge Israel (22:28-30), the conservative attitude Q takes toward the Torah (Q 11:42c; 16:17), and the limitation of the "mission" to Israel implied by Matt 10:5-6, 23.[41] Second, he notes similarities between Q and Paul: the common use of Deuteronomistic theology (1 Thess 2:14-16; Rom 11:3; Q 6:22-23; 11:49-51; 13:34-35); Paul's notion that Gentiles will make Israel "jealous" (Rom 11:11) and Q's penchant for using exemplary Gentiles to shame Israel; and the common expectation of a Gentile pilgrimage (Q 13:28-29; Rom 11:25) and the reconciliation of Israel (Q 13:35; Rom 11:26) (1991:224). A centurion, in fact, is depicted in a surprisingly positive light, which Theissen suggests may reflect the positive role that another Gentile, Petronius, had taken in the Caligula crisis (1991:226). It is worth noting that Philo claims that Petronius had acquired "rudiments of Jewish philosophy and piety," either because of his zeal for *paideia* or through contact with Jews (*Legatio* 245). Josephus reports speech strikingly like that ascribed to the centurion in Q 7:8: "For I too must obey the law of my master . . . for I too, like you, am under orders (καὶ γὰρ αὐτός, ὥσπερ ὑμεῖς, ἐπιτάσσομαι)" (*War* 2.195).[42]

---

40. The death of Zechariah ben Jehoiada was not only important for Q but, since his was the last murder to be reported in the Hebrew canon, assumed considerable importance in rabbinic literature. On this, see S. Blank 1937–38.

41. Theissen 1991:222–24. Theissen is aware that very few reconstructions of Q ascribe Matt 10:5-6 or 10:23 to Q, but nonetheless asserts that "they are important for an assessment of the document" and introduces (without any literary analysis) the supposition that these sayings may belong to a second redactional level of Q.

42. Theissen (1991:227) does not suggest that Q 7:1-10 derives from the Petronius story,

In a detailed reassessment of Theissen's thesis, Myllykoski (1996) has pointed out several difficulties. First, none of the references to *proskynēsis* adduced by Theissen[43] indicates that Caligula introduced prostration— Philo in fact states that *others* had introduced this "barbaric custom" (*Legatio* 116). Nor was prostration associated with investiture.[44] Second, there is no evidence of any connection between the investiture of Agrippa and Caligula's plans to erect a statue in Jerusalem. In other words, it is very doubtful that the devil's offer of kingship in exchange for *proskynēsis* in the third temptation[45] would be recognized as an allusion to Caligula's activities. In fact, the first clear reference of *proskynēsis* associated with investiture comes from the time of Nero (63 CE).[46] Third, Myllykoski rightly notes that while Q 22:28-30 speaks of the twelve tribes, it is not at all clear that it referred to twelve thrones;[47] hence the saying does not obviously privilege the Twelve. Besides, even if this text did refer to the Twelve, that would not be a sign of an early date: the three Synoptics feature the Twelve even more prominently and Matthew can adapt Q's Thrones saying (Matt 19:28; Q 22:28-30) even though he writes long after the First Revolt. Finally, the signs of Torah observance are not evidence of an early date. Myllykoski points out that

> [t]he obedience to the law (11:39, 42) and the strict affirmation of its validity (Q 16:17) might be taken as evidence of the early origins of Q, if we did not find these ideas in an intensified form in Matthew (Matt 5:17-20; 7:12; 12:5-7; 19:17; 22:40). The Matthaean theology of the law demonstrates the actuality of Jewish-Christian practice after the Jewish War. (1996:168)

Theissen makes much of Josephus's account of the execution of James in 62 at the instigation of the Sadducean high priest Ananus (Josephus, *Ant.* 20.200-201) and the criticism that this evoked from the Pharisees. From this episode he concludes that the hostile depiction of the Pharisees in Q 11 cannot come from the 60s, but better reflects the more antagonistic relations of Pharisees and Palestinian Christians from the late 30s and the time of Agrippa I, when Stephen and James the son of Zebedee were killed, and when Paul the Pharisee was persecuting Jewish Christians. 1 Thess 2:14-16 also refers to persecution of Jewish Christians in Judaea, presumably during

---

only that the positive depiction of a Gentile officer in a document that is otherwise critical of Roman rule is intelligible after the Caligula crisis and Petronius's role in it.

43. See Suetonius, *Vitellius* 2; Philo, *Legatio* 116-17, 352; Cassius Dio 59.24.4; 59.27.1.

44. Myllykoski 1996:160–62, citing Bilde 1978.

45. On the order of the three temptations, see below, p. 91.

46. In a reference noted by Theissen himself, Tiridates of Armenia prostrated himself and laid his crown before Nero. According to Cassius Dio (63.5.3) Nero explained to confused onlookers that this act demonstrated his power to take away and bestow kingdoms (ὅτι καὶ ἀφαιρεῖσθαι βασιλείας καὶ δωρεῖσθαι δύναμαι).

47. See Moreland and Robinson 1995:485.

the 40s, which, like Q, Paul connects with the Deuteronomistic motif of the persecution of the prophets.[48]

Yet 1 Thess 2:14-16 identifies the persecutors simply as "Judaeans" (Ἰουδαῖοι) rather than Pharisees and it is far from clear that "persecution," either in 1 Thessalonians or in Q, was anything more than slander and social pressure.[49] Moreover, it is not clear that the woe in Q 11:47-51 against killing the prophets was directed at Pharisees: while Matthew consistently addresses the woes to the "scribes and Pharisees" (23:2, 23, 25, 27, 29), Luke addresses the first four woes (11:39, 42, 43, 44) to the Pharisees, and the last three (11:46, 47, 52) to "lawyers" (*nomikoi*). Since these latter woes (on imposing heavy burdens on people, building tombs, and "locking the kingdom") presuppose that their addressees have effective political and judicial power, Luke's designation of the addressees as *nomikoi* (probably the equivalent of "scribes") makes more sense than Matthew's inclusion of "Pharisees."[50] Prior to the First Revolt the Pharisees, while seeking political and social influence, were generally not in positions that enabled them to do the things that Q's last three woes presuppose.[51] But if Q 11:47-51 is addressed to lawyers or scribes, the connections which Theissen seeks to establish between Pharisees, persecutors, and the addressees of Q 11:47-51 dissolve.

In default of datable internal references that provide a *terminus a quo*, one must rely on rather general arguments from the state of Q's theological development. Such arguments are of course notorious for their impressionistic nature,[52] but they are all that are available. Lührmann, for example, placed the date of Q in the 50s or 60s (1969:85–89; ET 1994:60–63). He argued that Jesus had already been identified with the Son of Man prior to

48. Theissen 1991:230–31. On the authenticity of 1 Thess 2:14-16, see Pearson 1971 (arguing for a post-Pauline interpolation) and Hurd 1986 (arguing its integrity).

49. Myllykoski 1996:174 cites Menoud 1964:181: "If we had only the testimony of the Apostle, we would not hesitate to admit that these attacks against the church must have been fundamentally theological. A Pharisee is an exegete; he was neither a policeman nor an executioner."

50. The IQP general editors have included Luke's νομικοί in Q 11:46 and 11:52 at a level of {C}.

51. See Saldarini 1988a:132–33. Contrast the scribes (ibid., 266–68) who occupied a wide range of social position, extending to senior officials associated with the Temple and the Sanhedrin.

52. D. Allison (1997:49–54) asserts that his earliest stratum of Q (9:57—11:13; 12:2-12, 22-32) was written in the 30s. He cites the presence of dominical sayings, the absence of a developed Christology and hints of a Gentile mission, and its concentration of itinerant missionaries. None of this is very convincing: the presence of dominical sayings is hardly an indication of an early date. Allison's arguments concerning Christology and participation in the Gentile mission unnecessarily assume a uniform theological development. He argues, further, that 1 Thess 2:14 may know the final form of Q, which would set a *terminus ad quem* of ca. 50 CE. The similarities between Q 11:47-51 and 1 Thess 2:14, however, are hardly sufficient to indicate literary dependence.

the final redaction of Q, that whatever rivalries existed between the followers of John and Jesus have now been settled, and that Q may have been involved in a Gentile mission. Each of these seems to presuppose a long period of theological development.

Paul Hoffmann, by contrast, suggests that the integration of the Son of Man concept into Q should be seen precisely in the context of the final stages of the First Revolt (1992, ET 1995). Hoffmann does not hold that Q redaction is responsible for the creation of Son of Man sayings; only that the Son of Man concept "gained special significance for Christian circles during this late phase in the transmission of Q" (1995:193). He sees this thesis confirmed by a parallel development in Mark: the reception of Danielic Son of Man imagery in Mark 13 also reflects the period of the First Revolt.[53] Q 13:34-35 provides Hoffmann with a key text for deciphering the historical context of Q's threats of coming judgment. The announcement of the abandonment of the Temple (ἰδοὺ ἀφίεται ὑμῖν ὁ οἶκος ὑμῶν) coupled with the redactional addition of the reference to the speaker's return "for the ruin of the Jerusalemites" (13:35b)[54] fits well the context of the final stages of the Revolt.[55] The intensification of End-expectation visible in Q 3:7b-9, 16-17; 6:47-49; 12:39-40, 42-46, and 19:11-27 also fits with what may be assumed to be the situation during the final phase of the First Revolt.

Tuckett raises two important objections to such a dating. First, he argues that neither 11:49-51 nor 13:34-35 should be read as "a fatalist reflection on Israel's final and definitive rejection" but as "a desperate plea to the Jewish people to change their ways before it is too late." This, for Tuckett, excludes a date just after the First Revolt. Second, the fact that the warnings

---

53. Hoffmann (1995:193–94) notes also the appearance of the Son of Man in the *Similitudes of Enoch*, which arguably belong to the first century CE, and "a similar process of the combination of the deuteronomistic tradition with messianic tradition characterized by the [Son of Man] concept in the thirteenth chapter of *4 Ezra*, the author of which is trying to work through the catastrophe of the year 70 theologically."

54. Hoffmann 1995:191. On the redactional nature of Q 13:35b, see below, chap. 3, p. 148 n. 66.

55. Steck 1967:237–38 drew attention to the account in Josephus (*War* 6.299-300) of nocturnal voices heard just before the destruction of the Temple: when "the priests came into the inner court of the temple, by night . . . they would have heard, as they say, first a commotion and a din, and after that a voice of a host, 'We are departing hence' (μεταβαίνομεν ἐντεῦθεν)." Tacitus (*Hist.* 5.13) has a similar report: "Contending hosts were seen meeting in the skies, arms flashed, and suddenly the temple was illumined with fire from the clouds. Suddenly the doors of the shrine opened and a superhuman voice cried: 'The gods are departing' (*deos excedere*): at the same moment the mighty stir of their going was heard." *2 Apoc. Bar.* (8.1-2), ostensibly speaking of the Babylonian siege of Jerusalem (but writing from the perspective of ca. 100 CE) has: "Then the angels did as he had commanded them; and when they had broken up the corners of the walls, a voice was heard from the interior of the temple, after the wall had fallen, saying, 'Enter you enemies of Jerusalem, and let her adversaries come in; For he who kept the house had abandoned it.'"

in Q 17:23-37 depict the end coming, not in the midst of ever-worsening conditions, but in the midst of the perfectly normal activities of eating, drinking, and marrying, seems to exclude a setting in the period immediately prior to the First Revolt.[56] Myllykoski agrees with this reading of Q 17 but not with Tuckett's conclusion. In his view the peculiar combination of Q's warnings against false prophets (Q 17:23) with the assertion of the utter normalcy of conditions at the time of the judgment (Q 17:26-30, 34-35) recommend a date after the war.[57] He disagrees entirely with Tuckett's first point: the sayings about the Temple (11:49-51; 13:34-35) presuppose its destruction (Myllykoski 1996:198).

Such arguments are difficult to assess. Hoffmann's observations about 13:34-35 depend on the assumption that what to us seems the obvious trigger for predictions of the Temple's abandonment and heightened expectations of judgment were what triggered the writers of Q. The assumption is not very secure, since observation of minority groups has taught us that factors all but unnoticed by the external observer might serve as triggers for apocalyptic predictions. Tuckett's counterproposal, that Q 13:34-35a is a severe warning to which is appended an "optimistic" hope for a "bright future" (1996:204–7) and hence excludes a date either just after or just before the Revolt, rests on a strained reading of Q 13:35b. The immediate *literary* context of Q 13:34-35—describing Gentiles sitting with the Patriarchs and "you" being cast out (13:28-29), and a spurned dinner host being "enraged" and inviting others (14:16-24)—casts grave doubt on Tuckett's reading. Moreover, the two closest redactional analogies to 13:35b—10:12; 11:51b[58]—both place the emphasis on the negative, not the positive, outcome of judgment. Tuckett's other observation, regarding the *lack* of crisis conditions in Q 17:23-37, is more weighty, for it makes difficult a date between 66 and 70 CE, and just as improbable, Myllykoski's date of just after 70. It is difficult to imagine a setting in Palestine where life went on in a way untouched by the Revolt and its aftermath.

Yet Hoffmann's conjecture is perhaps not far off. Josephus reports the

<hr style="width:40%" />

56. Tuckett 1996:362. On this feature of Q 17, see Kloppenborg 1987b:301–2; 1995b:298–99.

57. Myllykoski 1996:192. Cf. Jacobson 1992b:238: "[T]he problem presumed in the son of man sayings [in Q 17] is not enthusiasm but its absence. Neither can we say that there has been a shift in eschatological outlook. The rejection of signs, of apocalyptic watching, that we find in Q 17:23, 37b, and elsewhere in Q is only made clearer in the son of man additions. Thus no apocalypticizing of the tradition seems to have occurred, even though new (son of man) language is used. We can observe a shift in context: the level of messianic excitment has subsided, even disappeared. Such waxing and waning of messianic enthusiasm is not an improbable scenario, even within short periods of time." Jacobson, however, does not try to situate these features of Q with respect to the Revolt, although he notes that the Q apocalypse is "relatively late."

58. See Kloppenborg 1996c:19–21 and below, chap. 3, p. 148 n. 66.

activities of Jesus ben Ananias, who began announcing the ruin of the people and of the Temple beginning at *Sukkôt* of 62 CE, "during a time of profound peace and prosperity."[59] This at least provides an analogy for two key elements in Q: announcement of the Temple's ruin or abandonment and the relative absence of overt signs of imminent war. Whether similar conditions obtained in the Galilee in the late 50s or early 60s is unclear. By 66–67 CE, however, the presence of Legio X Fretensis, V Macedonia, and XV Apollinaris in the Galilee would make Q's relative absence of signs of overt conflict curious to say the least. I will argue in the next chapter that 13:34-35 and most of the other texts used by Hoffmann belong to a second redaction of Q that accounts for the bulk of the document. A date in the late 50s or very early 60s is certainly possible. But since the temptation story (Q 4:1-13) and two glosses (11:43c; 16:17) are probably later additions, it would mean that Q did not achieve its final form until slightly after the events of 70 CE, even if the bulk of Q was redacted just before the First Revolt.

Reconstructing Q

The conclusions of the foregoing discussion, that Q is a written document and that it was composed in Greek, are now largely taken for granted, at least by Synoptic specialists. What commands more attention in recent discussion is the actual reconstruction of Q—its order, wording, and extent. Obviously, in an introductory book such as this, it is impossible to provide a full reconstruction of each Q text and a discussion of its original position in Q. Rather, I shall indicate the principles used in the process of reconstruction, and refer the reader to the specialized synopses for Q,[60] to the existing reconstructions,[61] and especially to the collaborative reconstruction being produced by the International Q Project.[62]

---

59. Josephus (*War* 6.300-301): "Four years before the war, when the city was enjoying profound peace and prosperity, there came a feast at which it is the custom of all Jews to erect tabernacles to God, one Jesus ben Ananias, a rude peasant, who, standing in the temple, suddenly began to cry out, 'A voice from the east, a voice from the west, a voice from the four winds; a voice against Jerusalem and the sanctuary, a voice against the bridegroom and the bride, a voice against all the people.'" Josephus (*War* 6.303-9) reports that the magistrates handed him over to Albinus, who scourged him but then released him, supposing him to be mad. He continued his prophetic activities throughout the siege and was eventually killed by a catapult stone from the *ballista*.

60. Kloppenborg 1988a; Neirynck 1988.

61. Harnack 1907, ET 1908; Polag 1979, ET 1986; Schenk 1981.

62. J. M. Robinson 1990; 1991a; 1992a; Moreland and Robinson 1993; 1994; 1995. The IQP's Critical Edition will be available in 2000 and the database has already begun to appear: Carruth and Garsky 1996; Carruth and Robinson 1996; Garsky and Heil 1997; Hoffmann and Amon 1997.

THE ORIGINAL ORDER OF Q

There is near unanimity that Luke best preserved the sequence of Q sayings. This was not always so, especially in the nineteenth century when, under the spell of Papias, it was assumed that Matthew's order replicated Q. Lachmann (1835), for example, assumed without argument that Matthew's order of sayings represented that of Schleiermacher's *logia* and that canonical Matthew had rearranged portions of Mark to fit the sequence of his other source. Both Godet and Barnes thought that Matthew's fivefold division of speech material derived from a fivefold division of Q's sayings.[63] Ewald (1890:27–33) argued that the organized form of Matthew's sayings was more appropriate to apostolic authorship than was Luke's more aphoristic presentation, while Burney (1925:7) thought that Matthew better preserved the poetic format of Q. None of these views was, however, founded on an examination of the double tradition itself. Instead, each took its cue from assumptions that in retrospect are dubious at best.

As early as Holtzmann (1863:142–43) voices were raised that preferred Lukan order; and by the first decades of the twentieth century the evidentiary and argumentative basis for this conclusion had been secured.[64] Working independently, G. D. Castor in the United States (1912 [1918]:120–39)[65] and B. H. Streeter in Britain (1911b) noted the fact that Matthew and Luke already agreed in the relative order of much of the double tradition (also Solages 1973:153–82). In instances of disagreement, two factors created a presumption in favor of Luke: Luke, with minor exceptions, preserves the order of Mark as it stood and hence might be presumed to have done the same with Q; and Matthew quite clearly not only conflates Mark with other sources but also rearranges and recombines portions of Mark (similarly, Patton 1915:249–54). Moreover, the reasons for Matthew to have rearranged Q are patent, normally having to do with a desire to produce thematically related groupings (e.g., in Matthew 5–7; 10:1-42; 13:1-53; 18:1-35; 24–25). By contrast Luke's motives for dislocating sayings from their Matthaean setting are quite opaque. Indeed, Harnack, who generally preferred Matthew's order, confessed he could not discover Luke's reasons for the putative transpositions (Harnack 1907, ET 1908:180) and described Luke's method as "highly capricious" (1908:181).

To these arguments, Castor (1912:122), V. Taylor (1953; 1959), and the

63. Godet 1893–1899, 2/1:199–200, 217–20; Barnes 1905.
64. See also B. Weiss 1886, ET 1887–88, 2:220; Wernle 1899:228; J. Weiss 1907:36; Wellhausen 1905:67; 1911:58–59; Bussmann 1929:109; Manson 1949:15, 30.
65. Castor's book was originally his dissertation, submitted in 1907 to the University of Chicago. Although it was published (by Shirley Jackson Case) only in 1918, the manuscript was finished and ready for production at the time of Castor's accidental death in 1912. The latest citation is 1909, probably indicating that the manuscript was completed not much later than 1909 or 1910, a year before Streeter's essay.

present author (1987a:78) added another. In several instances, Matthew has small collections of sayings that are dispersed in Luke. Nevertheless, Matthew reproduces the sayings *in Lukan order*, as if he had scanned Q, collecting sayings that he thought were related and might fit together well. The clearest instance of this is found in Matt 10:24-39, comprising ten Q sayings:

Matt 10:24-25	Disciples and teachers	Luke 6:40
Matt 10:26	Revelation of the hidden	Luke 12:2
Matt 10:27	What is said in the dark	Luke 12:3
Matt 10:28-31	Do not fear	Luke 12:4-7
Matt 10:32-33	Confessing Jesus	Luke 12:8-9
Matt 10:34	Casting fire on the earth	Luke 12:49
Matt 10:35-36	Families divided	Luke 12:51-53
Matt 10:37	Hating one's parents	Luke 14:26
Matt 10:38	Carrying the cross	Luke 14:27
Matt 10:39	Saving/losing one's life	Luke 17:33

Although Luke may have moved 17:33 to follow his illustration of the fate of Sodom (17:31 [from Mark], 32), it would be exceedingly difficult in the other instances to assert that Luke saw in Q a topically ordered set of sayings and scattered them throughout Q. This problem is particularly acute in the case of Luke 6:40, which, as many critics have observed, seems to interrupt the connection between 6:39 and 6:41-42. It should be obvious that it is much simpler to suppose that Matthew collected and organized sayings than to think that Luke broke up originally unified clusters and used the debris in such a counterproductive manner.

A survey of the history of scholarship shows that Lukan order for Q is often defended on the basis of an argument from general probability: since Matthew has rearranged and recombined Markan passages, it is likely that he has done the same with Q, and since Luke has in general preserved Mark's order, he probably preserved Q's order. As useful as this argument might seem, it is precarious to build a case on so general an observation. We should not assume a priori, for example, that Luke would automatically treat a document lacking a clearly narrative structure in the same way that he treated a narrative document like Mark.

The case for Lukan order, however, can be founded much more securely (Kloppenborg 1987a:72–80). By beginning with (a) the twenty-seven pericopae that Matthew and Luke already have in the same order (see above figure 14), and adding (b) those pericopae that Matthew conflated with a Markan passage,[66] (c) those that have been inserted into a Markan

---

66. Q 6:40 (Matt 15:14 → Mark 7:1-23); Q 10:23-24 (Matt 13:16-17 → Mark 4:12); Q 11:39-44, 46-52 (Matt 23:4, 6-7, 13, 23, 25-31, 34-36 → Mark 12:37b-40); Q 12:10 (Matt 12:32 → Mark 3:28-30); Q 12:11-12 (Matt 10:19-20 → Mark 13:11); Q 13:18-19 (Matt 13:31-33 → Mark 4:30-32); Q 13:30 (Matt 19:30 → Mark 10:31); Q 17:1-2 (Matt 18:7 →

sequence,[67] and (d) the ten sayings in Matt 10:24-39 mentioned above, one has already accounted for approximately 85 percent of Q. In the pericopae listed under (b), (c), and (d), we are *certain* that Matthew's location of the text does not represent Q, since these pericopae are made to function in a *Markan* context, i.e., in a context that they could not have had in Q. All but two (Q 6:39 and 6:40) are found in the Lukan Travel Narrative (Luke 9:51—18:14), whose organization is rather loose and has in fact defied attempts to specify an overarching structuring principle. If Luke *also* rearranged the sayings, his reasons for doing so are far from clear; his only obvious interventions seem to have been to intersperse some of his special material and to add a few transitional expressions such as Luke 10:23a ("turning to the disciples by themselves, he said"), 11:29 ("as the crowds were increasing, he said"; cf. 12:1), and 12:54 ("he said to the crowds"). In other words, given the certainty that Matthew's location is secondary and a corresponding lack of reason to suspect that Luke has rearranged the sayings, it is only reasonable to conclude that Luke preserves Q's order.

There remains only a handful of sayings, almost all of them found in Matthew's Sermon on the Mount.[68] Given Matthew's organizational predelictions and given the complete unlikelihood that Luke would have disassembled sayings had he seen them in their Matthaean location, it is again *probable* that Luke's location is more original, especially since some of Luke's juxtapositions produce relatively awkward results (e.g., Luke 16:16, 17, 18).[69] The critical principle operative might be called *complexio*

Mark 9:42); Q 17:6 (Matt 17:20 → Mark 9:29); Q 22:28-30 (Matt 19:28 → Mark 10:29-31).

67. Q 9:57-60 (Matt 8:18-22 → Mark 1:29-34); Q 10:2-12 (Matt 10:7-16 → Mark 6:6-11); Q 12:39-40, 42-46 (Matt 24:43-51 → Mark 13:37).

68. Q 6:31 (Matt 7:12); Q 11:2-4 (Matt 6:9-13); Q 11:9-13 (Matt 7:7-11); Q 11:33 (Matt 5:15); Q 11:34-36 (Matt 6:22-23); Q 12:22-31 (Matt 6:25-33); Q 12:33-34 (Matt 6:19-21); Q 13:24 (Matt 7:13-14); Q 13:25-27 (Matt 7:22-23); Q 14:34-35 (Matt 5:13); Q 16:13 (Matt 6:24); Q 16:17 (Matt 5:18); Q 16:18 (Matt 5:32).

69. Burton (1912:108) observed, additionally, that the materials in the Sermon on the Mount parallel to Luke 9:51—19:28 are not especially well integrated into the Sermon and "constitute a digression from the theme of the basal discourse." Burton also used this as an indication that Luke's order for these sayings was original, since they were even less well organized in Luke and since Matthew's use of them betrayed signs of secondary insertion. Burton assumed that the double tradition in the Sermon on the Mount derived from a "Galilean document" that had already been fused with the Matthaean *logia* (for Burton, not Q, but the 'M' sayings), before the Peraean materials found in Luke 9:51—19:28 were interpolated. This theory resembles in some respect a newer theory by Betz (1985b; 1991), although Betz sidesteps in a very unsatisfactory manner the relation of the Sermon on the Mount to the Q material in Luke 9:51—19:28: "The most probable solution, in my view, is that both sermons were conceived independently from Q, and that they were inserted into Q at a later stage of its development, so that the Sermon on the Mount was taken up into QMatt and the Sermon on the Mount [sic] into QLuke. This solution raises other questions, but they can all be answered without bending the evidence or denying difficulties" (1991:76). More recently, however, Betz seems to have shifted to a more conventional view: "[T]he conclusion is most likely that

difficilior potior: the more difficult or awkward position is the earlier, and the smoother, less problematic one secondary.

In only a few instances is there a consensus that Luke has reordered Q, and in most instances, it concerns rearrangement of components *within* a Q pericope. Luke probably inverted the second and third temptations (Luke 4:5-8, 9-13) so as to have the temptation in Jerusalem as the climactic test; the saying about losing one's life (Luke 17:33 / Matt 10:37) was probably moved into Luke's eschatological discourse to function as a warning related to his example of Lot's wife;[70] the first two woes against the Pharisees (Luke 11:39b-41, 42) were probably inverted so that the woe pertaining to meals (11:39b-42) would appear first and follow naturally from the meal setting that Luke provided (11:37-39a); and Luke probably reversed the order of clauses in Luke 13:28-29 (see Kloppenborg 1988a:ad loc.).

THE ORIGINAL EXTENT OF Q

One of the most potentially important problems current in the study of Q has to do with determining its original extent. The nineteenth century offered quite divergent assessments of the scope of Q. Holtzmann ascribed the material behind Luke 3:7-9, 17; 4:1-13; 6:20-49, and 7:1-10 to *Ur-Markus* ("A") with the consequence that his Q (Λ) began only at Luke 7:18-23. By contrast, Bernhard Weiss included much Markan material in Q. With the gradual abandoning of the *Ur-Markus* hypothesis in the twentieth century, there was a stabilization of what was deemed to be in Q: Q was roughly coextensive with the double tradition of Matthew and Luke.

"Roughly coextensive with the double tradition," however, leaves plenty of room for disagreement, both because "roughly" admits of exceptions and because the exact extent of the "double tradition" is open to debate. One version of Q would emerge if we should determine that Q was to be identified only with those materials in which Matthew and Luke agree, either in wording or in substance, in the absence of any Markan parallel. This might exclude the Parable of the Great Supper (Matt 22:1-10 / Luke 14:16-24), where doubts have even been raised as to whether Matthew and Luke in fact have parallel stories. It would exclude portions of the Beelzebul accusation (Q 11:14-23), which has a partial Markan parallel (Mark 3:22-27). If one were to include in Q some materials that have Markan parallels, another form of Q would be produced. This would, of course, raise different questions. It is relatively certain, for example, that the temptation story (Q 4:1-13), the Beelzebul accusation (Q 11:14-23), and the parable of the

---

Matthew as well as Luke found the S[ermon on the] M[ount] and the S[ermon on the] P[lain], respectively, in their recension of Q (Q^Matt and Q^Luke)" (1995:44; but he also says [1995:42] that his earlier view is "pursued in this commentary as well").

70. Neirynck 1982b:49–51 and several others (see Kloppenborg 1988a:170) doubt that 17:33 is from Q at all, and instead derive it from Mark 8:35 and Luke 9:24.

mustard seed (Q 13:18-21) existed in both Mark and Q, for there are significant Matthew–Luke agreements against Mark, and in each instance, Matthew and Luke have a much longer version than the Markan account. But what is one to do with the baptism of Jesus, where there are only a few agreements against Mark, or the question about the Great Command (Mark 12:28-34), where again there are a few agreements against Mark, but where Mark's version is *longer* than the account in Matthew and Luke? Finally, it is clearly possible that just as both Matthew and Luke have occasionally omitted portions of Mark, these two evangelists omitted sayings from Q. This would mean that singly attested Matthaean (e.g., 5:41) or Lukan (11:27-28; 15:8-10) *Sondergut* might derive from Q.

The issue of the original extent of Q potentially is of great significance. The most obvious theological challenge is presented by Q's lack of a passion narrative (see below, chapter 8). This seeming anomaly, of course, could be alleviated by arguing with Bundy (1955:481, 499–502) that elements of a passion narrative were present in Q. Such a view, however, finds virtually no textual support and it is not surprising that few scholars have followed Bundy. The assessment of Q might be affected in more modest ways by somewhat more likely reconstructions. If, for example, the baptism of Jesus were to be included, the opening sequences in Q 3-4 would begin to look very much like Mark's introduction and hence, more like a biography rather than a sayings collection. Parenthetically, it might be added that the more Q comes to look like the opening of Mark, the more likely is the conclusion that either Mark knew Q or vice versa. Finally, the inclusion of certain disputed pericopae would introduce new theological dimensions into Q's repertoire: to include Luke 10:25-28 and Luke 14:1-6 in Q, as some scholars have argued, would be to introduce controversy chriae on the Torah and the Sabbath, topics that are otherwise unattested in the document.

Most recent reconstructions of Q include both (a) the double tradition and (b) items triply attested where the degree of agreement against Mark is substantial and where the agreements are not likely to be merely coincidental, that is, the result of the independent editorial improvements of Mark by Matthew and Luke. On this definition, Q contains the following (by Lukan versification):

> Q 3:7b-9, 16b-17; 4:1-13; 6:20b-23, 27-33, 35c, 36-37b, 38c, 39-49; 7:1b-2, 6b-10, 18-19, 22-23, 24-28, 31-35; 9:57-60; 10:2-16, 21-22, 23b-24; 11:2-4, 9-13, 14-20, 23, 24-26, 29-35, 39-44, 46-52; 12:2-12, 22b-31, 33-34, 39-40, 42b-46, 51-53, 54b-56, 58-59; 13:18-19, 20-21, 24, 26-27, 28-30, 34-35; 14:11/18:14; 14:16-24, 26-27; 14:34-35; 15:4-7; 16:13, 16, 17, 18; 17:1b-2, 3b-4, 6b, 23-24, 26-27, 30, 17:33; 34-35, 37b; 19:12-13, 15b-26; 22:28-30.[71]

---

71. See Kloppenborg 1988a; Neirynck 1988. Neirynck does not consider 13:30, 17:2, or 17:33 to be part of Q, but adds 14:5 to this list. For a defense of latter, see Neirynck 1991b.

A few expansions have been proposed that involve materials attested also in Mark.[72] Since it is not possible to examine each in detail, two examples will have to suffice. While virtually all ascribe Matt 3:7b-10, 11-12 par. Luke 3:7b-9, 16b-17 to Q, there is much less agreement on the preceding and following materials, for example.

(a) The account of Jesus' baptism is attested in all three Gospels and hence not part of the double tradition. Some scholars, however, have observed a number of points at which Matthew and Luke agree against Mark, agreements that may signal the presence of a Q version of the baptism.[73] They argue that Q requires an account in which Jesus is acclaimed as Son of God in order for the devil's address in Q 4:1-13 to be meaningful.[74] Such arguments have failed to persuade others, who note that none of the minor agreements between Matthew and Luke requires the positing of a Q version, since each is explicable on the basis of Matthaean and Lukan editorial habits.[75] Moreover, the argument that Q requires a narrative in which Jesus is identified as the Son of God is unconvincing; this is no more required than is a narrative accounting for the titles "Son of Man"—none of the gospels has such an account—or "Christ" or "Son." For these reasons, many Q scholars exclude a baptismal account from Q.[76]

72. Luke 3:2-4 (see below); Luke 3:21-22 (see below); Luke 4:16-30 (Tuckett 1982); Luke 10:25-28 (D. Zeller 1984:70; Lambrecht 1995; against this, see Neirynck 1994; Kiilunen 1989); Luke 12:1b (Davies and Allison 1991:589); Luke 17:2 (Schlosser 1983); Luke 17:31 (Lambrecht 1966). Neirynck (1995b) has argued in each case that Matthaean and Lukan redaction of Mark is a more parsimonious solution.

73. In contrast to Mark, Matthew and Luke use (a) a participial form of "baptize"; (b) ἀνοίγω, "open" instead of σχίζω, "tear"; (c) ἐπ᾽ αὐτόν, "upon him" rather than εἰς αὐτόν, "to him"; and (d) both place "descend" before "as a dove." The following have argued that some form of the baptismal story was in Q: Harnack 1908:310–14; Streeter 1924:188; Vassiliadis 1978:73; Polag 1979:30–31 (with hesitation); Schürmann 1969:197; D. Zeller 1984:23; Sato 1988:25; Jacobson 1992b:85–86; J. M. Robinson 1992b. The IQP initially included the baptism in Q, but only with the lowest degree of probability {D}, meaning that no actual Greek words are printed: Moreland and Robinson 1993:502. Subsequently, the grade has been raised to {C}. On the IQP grading system, see below, p. 101.

74. Thus Schmithals 1980:54; Schürmann 1969:197, 218; Sato 1988:25; J. M. Robinson 1992b:383–86. Jacobson (1992b:86), however, describes this argument as "circumstantial."

75. Fitzmyer 1981:479; Kloppenborg 1987a:84–85. See now Neirynck 1995b:67: "There is no need to repeat here the demonstration that these agreements [between Matt and Luke] are easily explained as redactional changes of Mark."

76. See the tabulation in Kloppenborg 1988a:§5. Further, Neirynck 1988; 1995b; Mack 1993; Vaage 1994:8–9; Arnal 1997b. Catchpole (1993:62–63) makes the excellent point that in other instances where a challenge occurs ("if you are the son of God . . ."), the text has already introduced the title: Wis 2:16, 18; Matt 26:64; 27:40, 43. The latter example does not quite illustrate the point, for in Matt 26:64, the title to which Jesus accedes is "Son of Man," and in 27:40 it is the bystanders, not the witnesses to the trial, who first introduce the taunt with "Son of God," which is then echoed by the "scribes and elders" (27:43). J. M. Robinson (1992b:384) points out that while christological epithets are normally simply presumed and used as commonly known and accepted, Q 4:1-13 "is built primarily (in two of the three temp-

(b) Matt 3:2-6 par. Luke 3:2-4 offer a more complex case. Again, there is a Markan parallel (Mark 1:2-6) and Matthew and Luke display a relatively high degree of verbal agreement with Mark. Most of the agreements between Matthew and Luke—"John," "preaching," "in the wilderness," and the quotation of Isa 40:3—are due to Mark. Nevertheless, Matthew and Luke concur against Mark in the use of a rather unusual phrase, πᾶσα(ν) ἡ (τὴν) περίχωρος(ν) τοῦ Ἰορδάνου, "all the circuit of the Jordan." This might be taken as a coincidence were it not for the fact that this phrase (or περίοικος τοῦ Ἰορδάνου) has a technical meaning, referring to the ʿArava, the southern Jordan rift valley from the Dead Sea to Zarethan. Moreover, the phrase appears almost exclusively in connection with the story of Lot (7x in Gen 13:10-12; 19:17, 25, 28).[77] It is doubtful that Matthew and Luke coincidentally added the phrase, for neither uses the phrase in its technical sense: Matthew confuses the area with the "wilderness of Judaea" (Matt 3:1), which does not include the ʿArava, and Luke shows no specific knowledge of Judaean geography at all.[78] The Lot story, with which the phrase is associated, plays no role in Matthew's or Luke's interpretation of John's ministry, for both, under Mark's influence, immediately associate it with the motif of restoration and repentance taken from Isaiah 40.

In Q, however, the evocation of Genesis 19 coheres extremely well with what follows. John's preaching refers to "fleeing from the wrath to come," appeals to a kinship with Abraham, destructive fire, and the transformation of "stones into progeny of Abraham" (cf. the opposite fate of Lot's wife). Moreover, as I have argued elsewhere, Q has several other references and allusions to the Lot story (10:12; 17:28-29, 34-35), allusions which neither Matthew nor Luke develops (Kloppenborg 1990a:151–52).

Besides the verbal agreement between Matthew and Luke that cannot be easily explained as coincidental, and the degree of coherence that the phrase from the Lot story exhibits with other elements of Q, there is an argument from "necessity." Q cannot have simply begun, "You brood of vipers."

---

tations) around defining and defending the title. . . . But if there were no baptismal scene with the φωνὴ ἐξ οὐρανοῦ announcing συ εἶ / οὗτός ἐστιν ὁ υἱός μου, the putting of the question of the title by the devil would be uncalled for." This presumes that the narrative functions to *define or defend* the title. It does not, but instead demonstrates that Jesus remains true to a set of expectations of fidelity inherent in the title, which are already presumed by the audience.

77. Tannehill (1991:190) disputes the connection between περίχωρος τοῦ Ἰορδάνου and the Lot story by citing the *one* instance of the eight biblical occurrences that does not make this connection (2 Chron 4:17; cf. 1 Kings 7:46).

78. See McCown 1940:117. Neirynck (1995b:69) takes the view (which I had earlier espoused in 1988a ad loc.) that Matthew and Luke's περίχωρος could be explained as independent developments of Mark's χώρα (1:5). While this is possible, the fact that Matthew and Luke independently arrive at the formulation πᾶσα(ν) ἡ (τὴν) περίχωρος(ν) τοῦ Ἰορδάνου (contrast Mark's πᾶσα ἡ Ἰουδαία χώρα) makes it more difficult to agree with Neirynck's view, especially given the technical nature of the phrase.

Neither Matthew nor Luke identifies the speaker in Matt 3:7a/Luke 3:7a even though it is clear that both attribute the speech to John. This means at the very least that John must have been indicated as the speaker in Q and, given the vituperative tone of the speech, there must have been some indication of audience and setting. Recollection of the Lot story would fit this admirably.[79] For these reasons, the present author and the International Q Project have included portions of Luke 3:3 in Q, albeit in a highly lacunary form: "John . . . all the circuit of the Jordan. . . ."[80]

A problem of a different sort for determining the extent of Q has to do with pericopae that are attested in only one gospel. Matthew or Luke may occasionally have omitted pericopae from Q, just as they omitted materials from Mark. As in the two instances cited above, the key problem has to do with criteria: Under what circumstances is it reasonable to suppose that a single tradition pericope (*Sondergut*) belonged to Q? Petros Vassiliadis advanced the following criteria: a singly attested pericope could be assigned to Q if (1) it was a component of texts already assigned to Q on other grounds; (2) it accorded theologically with other Q texts; (3) it does not show any sign of the editorial activity of the evangelists; (4) good reasons could be adduced for its omission by the other evangelist; (5) it exhibited the language of "country life"; and (6) it is found in Luke's Travel Narrative (9:51—18:14) (1978:67, slightly rearranged).

Some adjustments to these criteria are needed. The criterion of coherence (2) should be reframed, giving priority to stylistic coherence (which is less subjective), even though theological (or better, material) criteria may still be relevant. The third criterion (3) should be revised, for there are signs of Matthaean and Lukan editorial activity in many pericopae that quite clearly belonged to Q. More pertinent is the question whether Matthew or Luke would have reason to *create* the pericope or saying to fulfill some editorial function (as Matthew has done, e.g., at 3:15) and, conversely, whether there is any evidence of a prior independent existence. Two good indications that the evangelist has not formulated the pericope are that there are signs that it was incorporated into the gospel only with some difficulty and that an independent version of the pericope exists in Mark or the *Gospel of Thomas*.[81] In practice, language of "country life" (5) is not an especially

---

79. Catchpole (1993:60–78) likewise argues that elements from Luke 3:3-4 derived from Q (including the Isa 40:3 quotation), but encumbers this thesis with the further complication that Mark derived his beginning from Q. Similarly Lambrecht 1992.

80. Kloppenborg 1990a; contrast 1988a:§2; J. M. Robinson 1992b:501. It is impossible to know what verbs might have been associated with the phrase, or even whether John was the subject or object of the verb. Neirynck (1995b:65–72; 1996:62–70) is not convinced of the presence of Q 3:3. His alternative is to argue that both Matthew and Luke independently changed Mark's χώρα into περίχωρος τοῦ Ἰορδάνου, which is of course possible, but is not obviously a more parsimonious solution than positing Q.

81. The issue of whether and to what extent the *Gospel of Thomas* represents tradition

helpful criterion[82] since the entire economy of the Mediterranean was agriculturally based and hence, agricultural language and metaphors can be found practically everywhere. Vassiliadis's final criterion (6) (which of course applies only to Lukan _Sondergut_) is founded on the observation that most of Luke's Q material is found in the Travel Narrative, but this is neither a necessary nor a sufficient reason for attribution to Q.

Again, it is impossible to treat all of the _Sondergut_ pericopae that have been ascribed to Q by one critic or another.[83] Let me illustrate the issue with one example, Luke 15:8-10, the Parable of the Lost Drachma.

(1) In Luke this parable forms a pair with the Q Parable of the Lost Sheep (Luke 15:4-7 / Matt 18:12-14). Thus while the second parable is not a "component" of the first, it is found closely associated with a Q context.

(2) The issue of stylistic coherence is complicated, for it begs the question of the reconstruction of the Parable of the Lost Sheep. Both Lukan parables, for example, begin τίς ἄνθρωπος/γυνὴ (ἐξ ὑμῶν) ἔχων/ἔχουσα, "what man/woman (among you) who has . . ." and use the verb ἀπόλλυμι for "lost," whereas Matthew begins, τί ὑμῖν δοκεῖ; ἐὰν γένηταί τινι ἀνθρώπῳ, "what do you think? If a man should have . . ." and uses πλανάω for "lost." Matthew's opening question is probably editorial, since the same formula in 17:25[S]; 21:28[S]; 22:17[R], 42[R]; 26:66[R] is either in _Sondergut_ ([S]) or in Matthew's redaction of Mark([R]). Luke's formula, by contrast, is securely attested in Q 11:11; 12:25 (also in Luke 11:5[S]; 17:7[S]), and is the preferred introduction to Q 15:4.[84] Luke's verb ("lost") is also to be preferred, for Matthew's choice has been influenced by the context of chapter 18, which deals with offending and misleading "little ones"—Matthew's term for church members. In that context, "to lead astray" (πλανάω) was the more appropriate verb than ἀπόλλυμι, although in 18:14 Matthew betrays knowledge of that verb.[85]

While other aspects of Luke's two parables betray his hand (see Dupont 1968:273–79), the basic structure of his Lost Drachma is parallel to the Lost Sheep in Q: "What woman, having ten drachmae, and should lose one, will not . . . seek until she finds it . . . rejoices. . . ." This brings us to the important stylistic feature of paired, male-female illustrations. It is well known that Luke's gospel pays attention to women in a way that the other synoptists do not, and that there are several gender-paired illustrations:

independent of the Synoptics is discussed by Chilton 1984; Fallon and Cameron 1988; Fieger 1991; and S. Patterson 1992a.

82. Vassiliadis appears to have derived this from Crum 1927, whose fourth chapter is entitled "Q and Country Life."

83. For the most widely discussed passages, see Kloppenborg 1987a:passim.

84. Thus Schmid 1930:308; Lührmann 1969:115; Schulz 1972:387; Polag 1979:72; Schenk 1981:113; Jacobson 1992b:225 n. 99; Catchpole 1993:194.

85. See Trilling 1964:112; Dupont 1968:275; Polag 1979:72; Jacobson 1992b:225; Catchpole 1993:192; in support of Matthew: Schulz 1972:387; Schenk 1981:113.

Luke 2:25-38 (Simeon; Anna); 4:25-27 (Elijah and the widow; Elisha and Naaman); 7:1-17 (Jesus heals a centurion's slave, then raises a widow's son); 18:1-14 (the widow and the judge; two men praying).[86] The same, however, is true of Q, which has a number of double illustrations[87] and at least four gender pairs: 11:31-32 (the Queen of the South; Jonah); 12:24-28 (those who farm; those who spin); 13:18-21 (a man sowing; a woman making bread); 17:34-35 (two men in bed; two women grinding).[88] It might even be argued that Luke got the idea to use paired illustrations from Q. In any event, the feature is as consistent with Q as it is with Luke.

(3) A few scholars have asserted that the Parable of the Lost Drachma, while not from Q, is pre-Lukan (from "L").[89] The suggestion is extremely unlikely, for it would be incredible that Q and some completely independent source would contain two parables that were almost identical in form. The only viable options are that the parable is from Q, or that it is a Lukan creation, patterned on 15:4-7. While various scholars have asserted the latter, little justification is forthcoming. Bultmann's observation, that the two parables cannot be a unitary composition since both, not just the second, have been furnished with an application (vv. 7, 10) (Bultmann 1968:171), only indicates that at some point the second parable was added to the first. It does not show that this was a Lukan innovation (nor does Bultmann claim this, despite Conzelmann's comments [1960:111]).[90] Although Bultmann could not have known it when he wrote *History of the Synoptic Tradition*, the Parable of the Lost Sheep, but not the Lost Drachma, appears in the *Gospel of Thomas* (107), thus confirming his basic insight.

The reasons Luke would have had to compose 15:8-10 remain obscure. Luke has three exempla in chapter 15—the Lost Sheep, the Lost Drachma, and the Lost Son—each featuring a celebration and the proclamation that "what was lost has been found" (15:6, 9, 24, 32). Both motifs constitute a redactional refrain that answers the Pharisaic and scribal complaint about Jesus' dining with sinners with which Luke frames the three exempla. The most effective of these exempla is the third, since it features a human who sins and returns; the least effective is the lost drachma, an inanimate object. It is, of course, conceivable that Luke composed the Lost Drachma out of a commitment to gender balance; but in view of Q's penchant for paired male-female illustrations, the case is just as strong for derivation from Q. Stronger, in fact, for without Luke's emphasis on repentance and his apologetic for Jesus' dining habits, the economics of the two parables comes

---

86. Cadbury 1961:234; Tannehill 1986:132–39; Jacobson 1992:227.

87. Q 6:44 (figs; grapes); 10:13-15 (Khorazin/Bethsaida; Kefar Naḥum); 11:11-12 (stone for bread; snake for a fish); 12:24-28 (ravens; lilies).

88. See Batten 1994:47–49 and Arnal 1997a.

89. Manson 1949:283; Grundmann 1961:306; Fitzmyer 1985:1073.

90. Bultmann (1968:326) does suggest that Luke 15:7, 10 might be Lukan, but concedes that this is not even certain.

better into focus: a shepherd with one hundred sheep, who must care for
them himself, is poor, as is a woman with ten drachmae. Both are quite
unlike a man with servants, robes, shoes, rings, and fatted calves or a mer-
chant with a manager, and to whom is owed large sums (16:1-8; Kloppenborg 1989a). In other words, the first two exempla cohere with the poor
village or small-town environment otherwise thought to reflect the situation
of Q.[91]

(4) The final question is key, having to do with Matthew's omission of the
Lost Drachma. For both Müller (1908:21) and Fitzmyer (1985:1073), the
difficulty in explaining Matthew's omission was decisive in the case against
its belonging to Q. Yet the reasons for Matthew's omission are plain, as
Dupont has noted: "Matthew put the parable of the lost sheep at the service
of a pastoral exhortation which invites one to follow the example of the
shepherd's conduct; it would have been tactless to add the example of a
woman searching for a drachma."[92]

The evidence inclines in favor of Luke 15:8-10 deriving from Q. It
appears in a Q context and is stylistically consistent with Q; indeed it displays Q's characteristic doubling of illustrations and the use of gender-
paired illustrations. The reasons for Luke to have created the illustration are
unclear, given the redactional themes present in Luke 15. On the other
hand, Matthew cannot have preserved the parable in the context in which
he uses the Lost Sheep. These arguments, taken together, constitute a moderately strong case for inclusion.[93]

These three pericopae illustrate the methodological problems that attend
reconstruction. If one were to adopt a minimalist approach to Q, none of
these pericopae would be included, since in the first two, the degree of
Matthew–Luke agreement against Mark is not very high, and in the third,
a Matthaean parallel is lacking. This is the simplest approach, but not the
most reasonable. For it implicitly denies what a priori is likely: that Mark
and Q occasionally overlapped and that where a Markan version was pres-

91. B. Weiss 1907:247 notes that "in fact the basic idea of the two parables [15:4-7, 8-10]
differs completely from that of the parable of the Lost Son; for they depict the love of God that
searches for sinners, while (in the latter) nothing is said of the efforts of the father to recover
his lost son."

92. Dupont 1975:337 = 1985:615. Similarly, Lambrecht 1981:38; Davies and Allison
1991:769; Catchpole 1993:191.

93. Thus Holtzmann 1863:155; Loisy 1907–8, 2:138; Easton 1926:236; Schmid
1930:305–6; Dupont 1958:248; Schneider 1977–78:324–25; Weder 1978:170; Lambrecht
1981:38–41; Koester 1990:148; Catchpole 1993:190–94. The IQP has included the pericope
with a {C} rating. In favor of Lukan redaction or L: Manson 1949:238; Conzelmann 1960:111;
Fitzmyer 1985:1073; Sato 1988:60. Some exclude the pericope without comment: Harnack
1908:143–44; Streeter 1924:291; Hoffmann 1972; Schulz 1972; Schenk 1981; D. Zeller 1984.

ent, both Matthew and Luke were strongly influenced by it.[94] And it implicitly rejects the possibility that on occasion Matthew or Luke chose not to include a Q pericope, even when this is plainly the case with Mark.

It should be stressed, on the other hand, that I am not proposing an inordinate expansion of Q, either by Markan material or by *Sondergut*.[95] The judicious and rigorous application of the principles mentioned above would allow for a very modest expansion of Q from 235 to 264 verses, only 29 additional verses. On this view, Q would include the pericopae listed in figure 16 (with the additional verses included in parentheses and verses sometimes, but doubtfully, ascribed to Q in angle brackets).

There is of course room for disagreement among experts. Some like Frans Neirynck prefer a minimal Q, others such as Polag, Tuckett, Hoffmann, Catchpole, J. M. Robinson, and the present author are prepared to entertain very modest expansions, although of course, not all would agree on which texts are to be included.[96] From the point of view of the character and theology of Q, little is affected if, for example, the Lost Drachma is included or not. Even if Q 3:3 is included in Q, the character of Q would not be much affected, although the allusions to the Lot story might more clearly stand out as a redactional theme. On the other hand, if the quotation of Isaiah in Luke 3:4 / Matt 3:3 and especially the Baptism of Jesus with its heavenly voice were included, it would be virtually impossible to avoid the conclusion that Mark was literarily dependent upon Q, since it would be almost incredible that two completely independent documents could both begin with the sequence of a quotation of Isa 40:3, John's message of the Coming One, the Baptism of Jesus, and the Temptation. Precisely this line of depen-

---

94. Compare, for example, Mark 4:30-32 and Matt 13:31-33 / Luke 13:18-21. Where Mark has a parallel (in his Parable of the Mustard Seed), there are some Matthew–Luke agreements against Mark (ὁμοία ἐστὶν ἡ βασιλεία, ὃν λαβὼν ἄνθρωπος, δένδρον, ἐν τοῖς κλάδοις), but also many points where Matthew (especially) agrees with Mark or has conflated Mark and Q. As soon, however, as Mark is no longer a factor, in the following Parable of the Leaven, Matthew and Luke exhibit extremely strong agreements. This phenomenon may be similar to that found in Mark 1:2-6 and Matt 3:1-10 / Luke 3:2-9: where Mark is present, there is considerable "interference" from Mark and hence, difficulty in reconstructing Q. But where Mark is no longer a factor (Matt 3:7-10 / Luke 3:7-9) the degree of agreement increases sharply.

95. Schürmann (1968:111–25) has proposed a long list of additional pericopae but no one, to my knowledge, has followed Schürmann in this.

96. Another possibility exists, that some of these extra texts belong to pre-Matthaean and pre-Lukan expansions of Q, a solution adopted by Sato 1988; Kosch 1989a; 1989b; and Sato's teacher, Luz 1983. While this is obviously a logical possibility, it should, in my view, be invoked only in the case of a pericope that is contiguous with doubly attested Q material and in which there are (a) strong considerations against its being in Q (on grounds of vocabulary, style, or content), and (b) no evidence of redactional creation by the evangelist who preserves it, and (c) strong grounds for supposing that the other evangelist would have preserved it had he seen it.

Figure 16
The Contents of Q

Sigla
3:7b-9   Highly Probable
3:(3)   Probable
<3:21-22>   Doubtful

3:(3)	Setting of John's Preaching	12:(13-14,	Divider; Rich Fool
3:7b-9	John's Preaching of Repentance	16-21)	
		12:22b-31,	On Anxiety over Life
3:16b-17	The Coming One	33-34	
<3:21-22>	<The Baptism of Jesus>	12:<35-38>,	<Watch for the Son of Man>
4:1-13	The Temptations	39-40	
4:(16a)	Reference to Nazara	12:42b-46	Faithful and Unfaithful
6:20a	Introduction to the Sermon		Servants
6:20b-23	Beatitudes	12:49, 51-53	On Divisions
6:(24-26)	Woes	12:54-56	Weather Signs/Signs of the
6:27-33	On Retaliation; Generous Giving; Golden Rule		Times
		12:58-59	Settle with a Creditor
(Q/Matt 5:41)	Go the Second Mile	13:18-19,	Parables of the Mustard
6:(34-35b), 35c	Conclusion	20-21	Seed and the Leaven
6:36-37b, 38c	On Mercy and Judging	13:24, (25),	The Two Ways; Closed
6:39-45	On Self-Correction	26-27	Door
6:46	Why Do You Call Me Lord?	13:28-29, 30	Many Will Come from East
6:46-49	The Two House Builders		and West
7:1b-2, 6b-10	The Centurion at Kefar Naḥum	13:34-35	Lament over Jerusalem
		14:<5>	<A Sheep Who Falls into a
7:18-19, 22-23	John's Question		Pit on the Sabbath>
7:24-28	Jesus' Eulogy of John	14:11/18:14	Exalting the Humble
7:(29-30)	John, Tax Collectors, and Prostitutes	14:16-24	The Feast
		14:26-27;	Three Discipleship Sayings
7:31-35	Children in the Agora	17:33	
9:57-60,	Two (Three?) Volunteers	14:34-35	Savorless Salt
(61-62)		15:4-7	The Lost Sheep
10:2-16	Mission Instructions	15:(8-10)	The Lost Drachma
10:21-22	Thanksgiving for Revelation	16:13	God and Mammon
10:23b-24	Commendation of Disciples	16:16	The Kingdom Suffers Violence
<Matt 10:5b-	<Limiting the Mission to		
6, 23>	Israel>	16:17-18	The Torah; Divorce
<10:25-28>	<The Great Command>	17:1b-2	On Scandals
11:2-4, <5-8>	The Lord's Prayer, <Midnight Friend>	17:3b-4	Forgiveness
		17:6b	Faith like a Mustard Seed
11:9-13	Sayings on Prayer	17:<7-10>	<Unprofitable Servants>
11:14-20	The Beelzebul Controversy	17:(20-21)	(The Kingdom and Signs)
11:(21-22)	Binding the Strong Man	17:23-24, 37b	The Coming of the Son of
11:23	Whoever Is Not against Me		Man
11:24-26	Return of the Evil Spirit	17:26-27	The Days of Noah
11:(27-28)	A Woman in the Crowd	17:(28-29), 30	The Days of Lot
11:29-32	Request for a Sign	17:34-35	Two in a Field; Two at the
11:33-35 (36)	Lamp; Sayings on Light		Grindstone
11:39-44,	Woes against Pharisees and	19:12-13,	The Entrusted Money
46-52	Lawyers	15b-26	
12:2-12	Fearless Confession	22:28-30	Judging the Twelve Tribes

dence has been asserted by some.[97] Others have argued, persuasively in my view, that elsewhere the verbal similarities between Mark and Q are not such as to suggest direct dependence of Mark on Q.[98]

RECONSTRUCTING THE WORDING OF Q

The reconstruction of the wording of Q can be discussed only briefly. The principles for reconstructing Q have not changed substantially since the time of Harnack, even if today they may be applied with greater rigor and with a fuller knowledge of the editorial practices of Matthew and Luke. Simply put, where Matthew and Luke disagree in wording, the version which appears to be less likely the product of redaction is more likely to be the wording of Q.[99] The results of reconstruction can only be stated as probabilities—more and less likely—never as absolutes, and there are instances where both versions betray the editorial interests of the evangelists and hence, the original wording of Q may be irrecoverable.

The International Q Project, sponsored by the Society of Biblical Literature, has taken as a task the assembling of a database of all significant arguments used in the reconstruction of Q since the time of Holtzmann (1863) and the preparation of a collaborative reconstruction of Q.[100] Arguments are analyzed carefully and sorted into the categories, "Luke=Q, pro," "Luke=Q, con," "Matthew=Q, pro," and "Matthew=Q, con," in recognition of the fact that the presence of editorializing in Mathew, for example, is not a sufficient reason to suppose that Luke represents Q, since there may also be factors weighing against Luke. Once the database is complete, arguments are weighed and a reconstruction is proposed and rated as to its probability ({A} to {D}, that is, from high to low probability), in imitation of the United Bible Societies' system for grading textual variants.

The strongest cases are those in which one version, say Matthew's,

---

97. Lambrecht 1982; 1992; Catchpole 1991; 1992; Fleddermann 1981; 1995; Mack 1991b.

98. Laufen 1980; Schüling 1991; Dunderberg 1995. The most sophisticated argument, however, has been mounted by Tuckett 1993, who makes a strong case that in Q–Mark overlaps, elements that may be plausibly ascribed to Q redaction as distinct from pre-redactional stages, are missing from Mark. This implies that the contacts between Q and Mark are not at the level of the final redaction of Q.

99. Contrast Goulder's misstatement: "The reconstruction of Q is based on its vocabulary being *unlike* that of Matthew and Luke" (1996:671, emphasis original). Given the fact that the reconstruction of Q begins from the vocabulary and syntax of Matthew and Luke, Q's vocabulary and syntax will inevitably resemble either or both of the later gospels. Faced with a disagreement between Matthew and Luke, the decision, as it is in text criticism, is a matter of determining the redactional tendencies of each evangelist (using their treatment of Mark as a control) and then assessing the likelihood that one (or both) has intervened editorially in Q.

100. See above, n. 62.

exhibits well-attested redactional features that are also congenial to Luke (Matthew=Q, con) while Luke's version is free of obvious Lukanisms—i.e., there are no "Luke=Q, con" considerations—and Luke's version coheres with other features of the minimal Q text (Luke=Q, pro). Thus, it can be argued, on the one side there is both positive evidence of Matthaean redactional habits and the further indication that Matthew is unlikely to represent Q, for in that case Luke surely would have adopted Matthew's wording. On the other side, there is no indication of Lukan intervention, but coherence with Q's style attested elsewhere. For example, at Q 11:29, Matt 12:39 has "an evil and adulterous generation seeks (ἐπιζητεῖ) a sign" while Luke 11:29 uses ζητεῖ for "seek." Three arguments favor the thesis that Matthew introduced the compound and Luke preserved Q. First, Matthew converts Mark's simple verbs to compounds at various points (e.g., 8:16; 9:2, 14, 20; 19:15; 21:12; 27:46); second, Luke has a very strong preference for compound verbs over simple ones and hence would have no reason to change ἐπιζητεῖ to ζητεῖ; and third, the minimal Q text has the simple verb at 11:9, 10; 11:24; and 12:31 (and the compound only at 12:30). Analogous situations obtain at Q 6:44 and 10:22 where Luke has simple verbs and Matthew compounds of the same root.

Of course, there are many instances where the evidence is not so clear and where, for example, there are some grounds to suspect Luke, but nothing either in favor of, or against Matthew, or where some factors favor Matthew and others Luke. The IQP procedure, modeled on the evaluative procedures used in the reconstruction of the UBS *Greek New Testament*, allows for varying levels of probability, depending on how many or how few different factors support a particular reconstruction.

The task of reconstructing the "text" of Q must be kept in a realistic perspective; it trades in probabilities rather than certainties. On the other hand, it must also be kept in mind that there is already in the double tradition approximately 50 percent verbal agreement even if it is still sometimes necessary to decide the syntax of the sentence. For example, in Q 15:4 there is much verbal agreement: of the 27 Matthaean and 28 Lukan words, there is absolute agreement (indicated by underscoring) in 11 words, with only a minor disagreement in the order of the phrase ἓν ἐξ αὐτῶν, and a further three words where Matthew and Luke disagree only in inflection or form (ἄνθρωπος, οὐ(χί), and πορεύεσθαι).[101]

101. Depending on how the parallels are aligned, τί and τίς might be treated as an agreement (so Kloppenborg 1988:174). Whether they are or not, it remains that Matthew and Luke present the parable as a rhetorical question to be answered, "Everyone, of course."

Matt 18:12	Luke 15:4
Τί ὑμῖν δοκεῖ;	Τίς ἄνθρωπος
ἐὰν γένηταί τινι <u>ἀνθρώπῳ</u>	ἐξ ὑμῶν ἔχων
ἑκατὸν πρόβατα καὶ πλανηθῇ	ἑκατὸν πρόβατα καὶ ἀπολέσας
ἓν ἐξ αὐτῶν,	ἐξ αὐτῶν ἓν
οὐχι ἀφήσει τὰ ἐνενήκοντα ἐννέα	οὐ καταλείπει τὰ ἐνενήκοντα ἐννέα
ἐπὶ τὰ ὄρη <u>καὶ πορευθεὶς</u>	ἐν τῇ ἐρήμῳ <u>καὶ πορεύεται</u>
ζητεῖ	
<u>τὸ</u> πλανώμενον	ἐπὶ <u>τὸ</u> ἀπολωλὸς
	ἕως εὕρῃ αὐτὸ;

What do you think?	
If a *person* has *100 sheep and one of them* wandered away, will he *not* leave *the 99* on the hills and *going, search for the one that* wandered away?	What *person* among you, having *100 sheep and* having lost *one of them*, does *not* leave *the 99* in the wilderness and *go* after *the one that* is lost, until he should find it?

This text is typical. It illustrates the fact that disagreements in vocabulary notwithstanding, the general sense of the Q text is clear. Either Matthew or Luke (or both) have adapted the text redactionally. Some of these redactional interventions are patent. I have already noted that Matthew's introductory question is attested in redactional contexts elsewhere, while Luke's introductory formula is securely attested in Q (above, p. 96). On other points, there is less certainty. Matthew's "wander away" suits the ecclesial setting of Matthew 18, which concerns community members who are enjoined to "receive" the little ones (18:1-5), not offend them (18:6-9), discipline errant members (18:15-18), and forgive them (18:21-22, 23-35). In such a context it is more appropriate to speak of "searching" for a sheep that has "wandered away" than of "losing" a sheep. On the other hand, Luke's verb ἀπόλλυμι ("lose") appears as one of the common threads of Luke 15 (vv. 4, 6, 8, 9, 17, 24, 32) and hence must be regarded either as redactional or as the catchword that Luke used to unite the three Parables of the Lost Sheep, Lost Drachma, and Lost Son. A survey of the past 130 years of reconstructions of Q indicates that few have defended the originality of Matthew and most have suspected it of being redactional. Most have favored Luke, although the repetition of "lost" throughout chapter 15 is enough in the view of the IQP to reduce the rating from {A} or {B} to {C}.[102]

It should be emphasized that, as in the case of the thousands of variations in the text of the New Testament, many of the variants are rather easily decided using the principles of *lectio difficilior* ("the more difficult reading") and the reading that explains the others. So too with the reconstruction of Q. While there are many variation points between Matthew and

---

102. The IQP database and evaluation was written by Stanley D. Anderson, with responses by Albrecht Garsky and Leif E. Vaage. Q 15:4-7 was discussed at the summer 1994 working session of the IQP in Rattenbach, Bavaria, Germany, and again in Bamberg in summer 1999.

Luke, many are relatively easily decided in favor of Matthew or Luke on the basis of the observation of the evangelists' redaction of Mark. Just as in the manuscript tradition of the New Testament, there are a number of intractable problems where evidence and arguments are balanced on both sides. The reconstitution of Q is likewise a matter of probabilities. This fact does not make the resultant text any less usable than the text of the New Testament, nor, by the same token, any less subject to the cautions that should attend the use of the reconstructed text of the Greek New Testament.

MULTIPLE RECENSIONS OF Q?

A slightly different way of posing the issue of the reconstruction of Q is to ask whether the version of Q used by Matthew was the same as that used by Luke. This question can be put in two ways, first from the point of view of what is intrinsically probable with respect to Q, and then from the point of view of our ability to know or reconstruct Q. Is it likely that Q would have remained sufficiently stable in form to arrive in the hands of Matthew and Luke in the same form? And can the efforts to reconstruct Q hope at anything more than the reconstruction of the versions of Q available to Matthew and Luke?

The possibility of multiple recensions of Q was first raised by Paul Wernle, who invoked this explanation in order to account for certain differences between Matthew and Luke.[103] Wernle suggested that strongly nomistic sayings such as Matt 5:17-48; 10:5-6; and 23:3 derived from a "Judaized" version of Q (Q^J) which represented a development of the original Q.[104]

More recently, some have appealed to slightly divergent versions of Q (Q^{Matt}, Q^{Luke}) as a convenient way to handle instances where the differences between the respective wordings of Matthew and Luke (seemingly) cannot be solved by arguing that one of the two versions is due to redaction. Luz, for example, accounts for some of the variation between the Matthaean and

---

103. The possibility was already entertained by Weizsäcker 1864: "If it can be shown that the insertion of Luke [9:51—18:15] contains the same basic stock of discourses that Matthew has and, further, that the discourses in both (Matthew and Luke) display basic similarities in the grouping (of sayings), then no other assumption is possible than that both depend upon one and the same document, even if this may have been available to them in divergent forms."

104. Wernle 1899:229–31, esp. 231: "There probably were several copies of approximately the same length. Between the original Q and the collections available to Matthew (Q^{Matt}) and Luke (Q^{Luke}) stood Q^1, Q^2, Q^3; but it would be a waste of our time to try to distinguish these. A particular stage in this development is marked by the Jewish form (Q^J)." Wellhausen (1911:60) suggested that some of the verbal disagreements between Matthew and Luke may go back to two slightly divergent Greek recensions of Q which arose from "subsequent corrections, partly on the basis of the Aramaic original [of Q]."

Lukan makarisms as the result of redaction, but traces some of the disagreements to two versions of Q:[105]

Q^{Matt}	Q^{Luke}

Q^{Matt}

6:20b Blessed are the poor [πτωχοί] ((in spirit)), for theirs is the kingdom (of God).
6:21b ((Blessed are those who mourn [πενθοῦντες], for they shall be consoled. [παρακληθήσονται]))
Q/Matt 5:5 (Blessed are the meek [πραεῖς] for they shall inherit the land.)
6:21a Blessed are those who are hungry [πεινῶντες],
for they shall be filled.

Q/Matt 5:7 (Blessed are the merciful, for they will receive mercy.)
Q/Matt 5:8 (Blessed are the pure in heart, for they shall see God.)
Q/Matt 5:9 (Blessed are the peacemakers, for they shall be called the children of God.)
6:22 Blessed are you when they reproach and ((hate)) you

and say ((all manner of)) evil against you on account (of the Son of Man).
6:23 Rejoice   (and be glad)
for your reward is great in heaven; for thus ((they did)) to the prophets (before you).

Q^{Luke}

6:20b Blessed are the poor, for yours is the kingdom of God.

6:21a Blessed are you who are hungry ((now))
for you shall be filled.
6:21b Blessed are you who weep ((now)) for you shall laugh.

6:22 Blessed are you when they hate you (and when they exclude and reproach you)
and ((cast out your name as evil)) on account of the Son of Man.
6:23 Rejoice ((on that day)) ((and leap)) ((for)) your reward is great in heaven; for thus they did to the prophets ((before you)).
Q/Luke 6:24 (But woe to you rich, for you have your consolation [παράκλησις].)
Q/Luke 6:25 (Woe to you who are filled ((now)), for you shall hunger.)
(Woe to you who laugh ((now)), for you shall mourn [πενθήσετε] and weep.)
Q/Luke 6:25 (Woe to you when they ((all)) speak well of you; ((for thus)) they did to the false prophets.)

Luz agrees with the consensus of scholarship that Matt 5:10 and the phrases "the Kingdom of the heavens" and "[thirst after] righteousness" are due to

---

105. Luz 1983. Luz's sigla: ( ) wording supported by only one evangelist but which probably represents Q; (( )) wording supported by only one evangelist; the reconstruction of Q is "fully hypothetical." Luz's 1983 article suggests that Matthew's third person formulation of the makarisms was original; Luz 1985-90, 1:201 (ET 1989:227) argues that the second person was original in Q (and presumably, Q^{Luke}) but was adjusted by Q^{Matt} to the third person. The following synopsis, taken from Luz 1983, has been adapted in accordance with Luz's later comments.

Matthew's redaction. He is more hesitant to assign the additional Matthaean makarisms to redaction, preferring the alternative that they were added to Q in a later recension (Q^{Matt}). If this is so, then the first four Q^{Matt} makarisms displayed alliteration, with each keyword beginning with π.[106] It was this during this expansion that the original second person address of the first three (Lukan=Q) makarisms was changed to a third person form. At this stage too, the third (Lukan) makarism was reformulated, assimilating it to the language of Isaiah 61 (using "mourn" rather than "weep") and moved to second position in the list. Since, however, the Lukan woes, which Luz ascribes to the Q^{Luke} expansion of Q, reflect some of these Isaian elements in the Q^{Matt} version of Q 6:21b (παράκλησις, πενθήσετε), he posits the influence of Q^{Matt} on Q^{Luke}, via oral tradition.[107]

The fact that Luz places Matthew's "in spirit" and Luke's "now" in double parentheses indicates that these might also be, respectively, pre-Matthaean and pre-Lukan rather than redactional. Moreover, while he is certain that Matthew's "persecute" (5:11, 12), "all manner of" (5:11), "falsely" (5:11), and "on my account" (5:11)[108] are redactional, it is less sure that "exclude" and "reproach" were in Q^{Luke} and even less sure that "hate" was in Q^{Matt}.

Luz's appeal to two recensions of Q is not merely a way to remain agnostic on the reconstruction of Q, for Luz does decide between Matthew and Luke on several points and is able to suggest a reconstruction of the Q that lies behind his two intermediate recensions (indicated in bold). At the same time, however, the model of two recensions of Q means that Luz is not required to ascribe every difference between Matthew and Luke to the evangelists' editing.[109] His model is can be represented visually by the diagram of his student Migaku Sato (see figure 17a).

---

106. Luz (1989:228) here draws on the suggestion of Michaelis 1968, who also tries to find alliteration in an alleged Aramaic original: עניים (= πτωχοί), ענוים (= πραύς), אבלים (= πενθοῦντες), and רעבים (= πεινῶντες). "The first pair are the עניים [poor] and the ענוים [meek] which, irrespective of their differences in meaning, are very closely related semantically; the second pair is אבלים [mourners], and רעבים [hungry]. At first sight, this pair does not seem especially alike, but with respect to alliteration, one must recognize that the alliteration of א and ע was common and that in Aramaic the distinction between them was disappearing" (1968:158).

107. Luz 1989:228: "[W]e have to reckon not with a unilinear development of the text but with a juxtaposition of written and oral transmission in Greek. In this phase of transmission, the Beatitudes were formulated in the light of Isa. 61 and various psalms." Similarly, Sato 1988:48.

108. Luz 1989:229: "Matthew probably replaced the title Son of Man by ἕνεκεν ἐμοῦ. . . . The generalizing πᾶν (πονηρόν) is probably Matthaean. The hapax legomenon ψευδόμενοι, which makes it more precise, is probably secondary but does not permit further definition. . . . It is particularly noticeable how pointedly Matthew speaks of persecution. . . ."

109. Betz's (1995) views are similar with regard to the Sermon on the Mount/Sermon on the Plain. Matthew and Luke have used two divergent forms of the sermon in Q^{Matt} and Q^{Luke} and hence, not all of the differences may be attributed to Matthaean or Lukan redaction.

Figure 17
Q^Matt and Q^Luke

17a: Q^Matt and Q^Luke and the Q Beatitudes
From: Migaku Sato, *Q und Prophetie* (WUNT 2/29; Tübingen: J. C. B. Mohr [Paul Siebeck], 1988) 49.

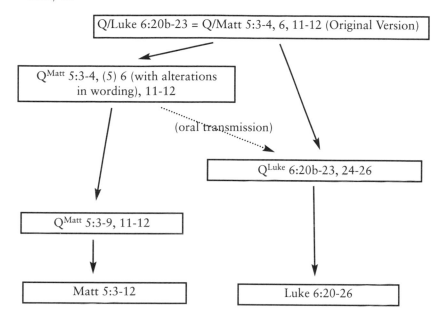

17b: Explaining Divergences by Appeal to 2 Recensions of Q (and Mark)
From: Daniel Kosch, "Q: Rekonstruktion und Interpretation," *Freiburger Zeitschrift für Philosophie und Theologie* 36 (1989) 414.

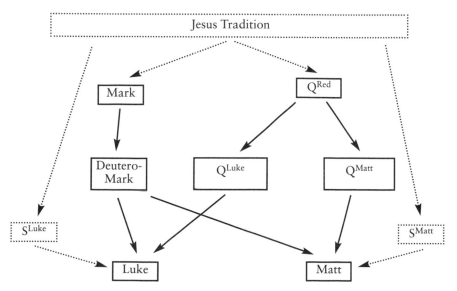

Appeal to two recensions of Q functions on a somewhat more ambitious level in Sato's own work. Sato treats much Matthaean and Lukan special material as deriving from two expanded recensions of Q.[110] In fact he also considers double tradition sayings that occur between Luke 14:16 and 17:6 as possibly deriving from two later recensions.[111] Indeed, he ascribes to Q[Luke] many sayings that others include in Q itself: Q 14:16-24, 26-27, 34-35; 15:4-7; 16:16-18; 17:1, 3-4, 6, 33; 19:12-27 (1988:53). Daniel Kosch has also endorsed Luz's recensional theory of Q 6:20b-23 (1989a:242–46) and Sato's overall view of Q as an expanding quantity:

> Q is a growing structure which never reached a finished form and therefore always remained relatively open to expansions and modifications. . . . The origin of divergent recensions of Q can therefore be understood as the extension of the growth- and compositional process of Q beyond the redaction of Q. (Kosch 1989b:413–14)

Kosch is more modest than Sato in what he ascribes to later recensions of Q, mentioning only Luke 3:10-14; 6:24-26, 27c-28a; 7:3-6a; 9:61-62; 11:5-8; 11:41; 12:16-21; 16:19-26; and perhaps even 1:51-53 (1989b:417–20). Sato accounted for the divergences in wording in the double tradition sayings in Luke 14–17 by positing a continuing oral interaction between Q[Matt] and Q[Luke], whereby additional sayings from one stream eventually found their way into the parallel stream, albeit in a modified form. Kosch, by contrast, attributes most of these sayings to Q itself,[112] and explains their divergences with the suggestion that Q also exerted an influence on special

110. Sato (1988:18–19, 20–28, 47–62) ascribes the following to Q[Luke] (with "uncertain texts" in parentheses): Luke 3:10-14; (4:16-30); 6:24-26, 37b-38b; 7:3-6a, 29-30; 9:61-62; 10:18-19; 11:5-8, 36; 12:16-21, 32, 35-38, 47-48, (54-56); (13:1-5, 6-9); (14:16-24, 26-27, 34-35); (15:4-7); (16:16-18); 17:(1, 3-4, 6), 28-29; (18:2-8); (19:12-27). Sato's Q[Matt] includes Matt 5:5, 7-9, (13, 18-19, 32); 6:34; 7:(2a), 6; (10:5b-6, 23, 37-38); 11:(12-13), 28-30; (17:20); (18:7, 12-14, 15, 21-22); (22:1-13); (23:15-19, 24); 25:1-12, (14-30).

111. Sato 1988:53: "Oral tradition offers one explanatory model: these sayings might represent orally transmitted materials of Q which were incorporated literarily only later in divergent ways in Q[Matt] and Q[Luke]. Another possibility is that after the bifurcation [of Q] into Q[Matt] and Q[Luke]—as occurred with Matt 5:4 and Luke 6:24-26—there continued to be an interrelation between the two at the level of oral tradition. Then it would be conceivable that dubious sayings, which originally belonged to only one part of the Q-group (e.g., Q[Matt]), eventually came into the possession of the other group (e.g., Q[Luke]) by means of this relationship and [were] inscribed in a different way."

112. Kosch includes in Q 6:37b-38b (1989a:248: "an assured Q text"); 14:5 (1989a:200–206); 14:26 (1989a:353); 16:16-18 (1989a:423). In response to Sato's suggestion, Kosch replies: "Especially between Luke 14 and 17 one finds a set of isolated sayings which have parallels in Matthew. Unless one wishes to presuppose that Luke used a different compositional technique in this section, it is likely that here we have a pre-Lukan conflation of Q with the so-called special Lukan material. This would also explain the considerable disparity in wording [between Matthew and Luke]" (1989b:415).

Lukan material (S^{Luke}), producing alternate forms of Q sayings which were then conflated with Q by the author of Luke (see figure 17b).

There is nothing a priori unlikely either in the modest appeal to divergent versions of Q as a way of explaining minor verbal disagreements between Matthew and Luke or even in the more elaborate suggestions of Sato or Kosch. At a minimum, it should be conceded that the copies of Q used by Matthew and Luke differed in at least some minor respects. After all, among the thousands of manuscripts of the New Testament there are hardly two that agree in all respects, despite the fact that those who copied these works held them to be sacred Scripture and that many of the manuscripts were copied by professional scribes. That Q, which was neither "scriptural" nor copied by professionals, could have been preserved in identical forms in two or more copies simply strains credulity. Not only slight differences in wording but even the occasional variation in the placement of sayings might be explained through scribal adaptation.[113]

Nor is it even necessary to lay the responsibility for variations at the doorstep of copyists. As noted above, the nature of the "reading" and "performance" of ancient documents always held the potential for transformations, subtle or more substantial. Examination of other literature indicates that *authors themselves* were sometimes responsible for multiple recensions of their works. There are at least seven recensions of Basil of Caesarea's *Ascetikon*, five of which arose from Basil's *own* rewritings and rearrangements of the questions and answers that make up this work.[114] In *Adversus Marcionem* (1.1) Tertullian refers to a first edition of the work which he had published and then subsequently withdrawn after it had been copied selectively and published in a way that Tertullian had not approved. This required him to produce a third edition to replace the previous two, both of which were still in limited circulation.[115] Hence, the suggestion of two (or more!) recensions of Q has good historical analogies.

Some, on the other hand, resist such possibilities, preferring to ascribe differences between Matthew and Luke to redaction. Neirynck wonders whether "the need for positing an intermediate stage is . . . not a logical con-

113. Compare the fragmentary Greek version of the *Gospel of Thomas* with the later Coptic version, which shows variations in most of the sayings for which two versions exist. There is even some variation in order: saying 77b (Coptic) is found in the Greek fragments as the conclusion of saying 30. On this see Attridge 1979.

114. I am indebted for this reference to my colleague Paul J. Fedwick. On Basil's *Moralia*, see the brief discussion in Quasten 1966, 3:211–14.

115. Multiple versions of some homilies were available. Socrates (*Hist. eccl.* 6.4) reports that two groups of John Chrysostom's sermons could be distinguished, those written by Chrysostom himself (presumably as sermon notes) and the stenographic copies produced by secretaries present at the sermons.

sequence of [a] too restrictive notion of Matthean and Lukan redaction?"[116]
Indeed, the problem is analogous to that raised in regard to the so-called
complex solutions to the Synoptic Problem discussed in chapter 1. Complex
models distribute the transformation of the Jesus tradition over several
stages, making each stage less dramatic, while simple models localize significant transformations at a few points but require each transformative
moment to be more complex, subtle, and creative.

It is impossible in the abstract to decide which model is preferable. Each
has a degree of plausibility and historical analogies for each can be adduced.
In practice, the choice of one model over another is a function of its heuristic value in solving a particular problem. Recensional models have special
heuristic value insofar as they imply a highly differentiated view of the
redaction of the canonical Gospels. Luz's model of the makarisms, for
example, allows him to distribute the large number of diverse transformations required between Q and Matthew among several stages, so that the
influence of Isaiah 61 and the Psalms belongs to a different level than the
addition of distinctively Matthaean vocabulary. In Sato's case, as will be
seen in chapter 3, the appeal to Q^{Matt} and Q^{Luke} functions as a way to handle
material that does not easily fit into his compositional theory for Q. Tuckett, on the other hand, admits the possibility of divergent recensions of Q,
but his view of the theology of Q can compass most or all of the double
tradition. Since his interest lies with Q rather than with its "post-history,"
theories of multiple recensions are simply irrelevant (1996:100).[117]

On the other hand, simpler models impose an obligation upon the interpreter of Q to decide each point of disagreement between Matthew and
Luke and to reconstruct a text with clear contours. A particular pericope is
either in Q or not; a particular word is either from Q or it is redactional.
This is implicitly the model at work in the International Q Project. Like the
United Bible Societies' *Greek New Testament*, the IQP allows gradations of
certainty, but in theory it aims to reconstruct a single "text" that explains
all subsequent texts. Given what has been said about the constant interaction between oral performance and written scripts and the possibility of
authors revising their own works, the notion of a single "text" lying behind
all others is an abstraction. *Which* text is being reconstructed? Nonetheless,
the notion of a "text" is a useful abstraction, functioning precisely in the
same way that the idea of the "text" of the New Testament has functioned
for modern exegesis.

---

116. Neirynck 1990a:390. Neirynck points out that both Fitzmyer (1981) and Bovon
(1989) can account for items such as the Lukan woes and Luke 6:37b-38b without appealing
to intermediate recensions between Q and Luke.

117. Some critics invoke the possibility of multiple recensions in a rather frivolous way, to
sidestep the issue of the reconstruction of Q and to minimize Q's importance.

It is sometimes said that the reconstruction of Q amounts to a hypothesis built upon a hypothesis. It is of course correct that inferences about the date of Q and decisions regarding the wording of particular pericopae are logically posterior to the positing of Q and are based on data that are separate from the "Synoptic data"—patterns of agreements and disagreements—on which the 2DH is built. Other issues of reconstruction treated in this chapter are, however, much more integrally related to decisions regarding the Synoptic Problem itself. For example, the conclusions that Q was a document rather than a set of oral traditions, that Matthew and Luke consulted this document in Greek rather than Aramaic, and that its order more closely conformed to Lukan order of the double tradition than Matthaean order are based on the *same* data and many of the same logical deductions that are used in the defense of the 2DH in the first place. The twin sets of data, that after Luke 4:13 Matthew and Luke never agree in the placement of the double tradition relative to Mark, and that they display significant agreement in its sequence relative to each other, are most easily explicable, on the one hand, on a hypothesis that Matthew and Luke have independently employed a common source, and, on the other, that this source was written rather than oral. The instances of near-verbatim agreement between Matthew and Luke and the instances of sequential agreement in the double tradition which, from the perspective of the Synoptic Problem, require a hypothesis of literary dependence, are precisely the same data that require that Q be a Greek document. And the logical considerations adduced against the supposition that Luke used Matthew directly and deconstructed Matthew's well-ordered speeches and dis-integrated double and triple tradition materials are, from the standpoint of the reconstruction of Q, the same principles invoked in support of Luke's order better representing the original order of Q.

The conclusions that Q was a Greek document and that it conformed generally to Luke's sequence are not further hypotheses added onto the 2DH, but are entailed in the 2DH by the very nature of the Synoptic data themselves. To embrace the 2DH and what it implies about the various relationships among the Gospels does not allow one then to evade the imperative to reconstruct Q and, ultimately, to face the literary and theological implications of reconstruction.

3

The Composition and Genre of the Sayings Gospel Q

PRIOR TO THE SECOND WORLD WAR Synoptic scholars, working under the prevailing model of form criticism, tended to view the Gospels as compilations of individual units of traditions. The literary features of the Gospels were largely ignored and the evangelists were viewed as weak figures, merely arranging existing traditions. The issue of the literary genre of the Gospels hardly even arose, since as sedimentations of oral tradition, the Gospels were supposed to be sui generis and uninfluenced by classical literary genres.

In the 1950s redaction criticism began to reassess these assumptions. Analysis of the Gospels provided reasons to suppose that they were deliberate compositions, each with a distinctive theological and stylistic profile. One could now speak of the "theology of Mark," for example, and contrast it with the "theology of Matthew." Once the genuinely literary dimension of the Gospels came into view, it was possible to ask whether and to what extent early Christian writings shared the generic conventions of late antiquity and how the Gospels would have been viewed by other persons living in the ancient Mediterranean world.

These recognitions brought with them a methodological challenge: how, and with what tools, can the critic describe the editorial perspective of the compiler or writer of the Gospels and Q? Neither the Gospels nor Q were created ex nihilo. On the contrary, they represented the complex interplay of traditional sayings and stories inherited by the evangelists and in use in the evangelists' communities, on the one hand, and the editorial interests of the writers themselves, on the other. It was now important to identify the overriding interests of the writer and to see how these interests were at work in the editing and arrangement of individuals pericopae.

As the literary dimension of the Gospels and Q came into focus, the question of genre arose: Was it really the case that the Gospels (and Q) were unique? What would it mean for these writings to be completely unparalleled as literary products? And if they were not without parallels, how does one go about determining which literary genres provide the most helpful analogies to the Gospels and Q?

The Redaction of Q

REDACTION CRITICISM

What method is appropriate to determine the compositional or redactional intent of Q? The earliest forms of redaction criticism made a sharp distinction between "tradition" and "redaction." The theology of the evangelist was to be constructed in the first instance from redactional elements. Much of the pioneering work had been done on Matthew and Luke where one of the sources (Mark) was available. It was a relatively simple matter to compare Mark with Matthew and Luke and to determine the ways Matthew and Luke edited Mark. Mark was the "tradition" that the later evangelists redacted. Since the original working and order of Q could be inferred, it was also possible to see how Matthew and Luke inscribed Q differently in their gospels. From these observations, scholars drew conclusions about the stylistic preferences and theological inclinations of the later evangelists. Because this form of redaction criticism conceived editing as a process of transformation through time, it could be called "diachronic."

Redaction criticism emerged as a scholarly tool precisely at a point in the evolution of Western theology when it was important to be able to trace theological developments, to understand their antecedents, and to situate later developments within a historical framework. Conceived as "redaction history" (*Redaktionsgeschichte* in German), this form of compositional analysis was an apt expression of the confidence that the theological history of the Gospels could be written.

The diachronic form of redaction criticism suffered from important defects. It privileged the distinction between tradition and redaction and hence ran the double risk of undervaluing elements in a gospel that have been taken over more or less unchanged from a source, and of overvaluing elements that had been added or newly created by the editor. Moreover, diachronic redaction criticism also tended to discuss redaction in terms of authorial intent, as if one were able to peer into the mind of the ancient editor. In an effort to redress these difficulties other critics developed "synchronic" approaches. These downplay or even ignore authorial intent, convinced that the author's intentions are at least irrecoverable and possibly even irrelevant to the meaning of the work. They also refuse to privilege portions of the gospels merely because they were created by the evangelists, arguing that an evaluation of the text must be based on the complete configuration of textual elements, irrespective of their history or origin. Thus, synchronic approaches do not try to look "behind" the text, either to the author behind the text or to the traditions used by the author, but base their analysis on the arrangement and disposition of textual elements on the surface of the Gospel.

Despite their differing approaches, diachronic and synchronic approaches are not opposed but complementary. They serve to corroborate, supplement, and correct each other, since, after all, both seek to understand the construction and intent of the gospels, merely from different perspectives. Most actual analyses of gospel literature will involve both forms of analysis.

METHOD IN THE ANALYSIS OF Q

In the case of Mark, where we do not have independent access to Mark's sources, diachronic analysis is not as easily accomplished as it is with Matthew and Luke. Synchronic analysis is the logical starting point. It begins with the narrative structure of the Gospel, in particular the repetitive elements that dominate Mark's architecture: two disclosures of Jesus' identity (1:11; 9:7); two climactic confessions (8:29; 15:39); a threefold iteration of Jesus' approaching death and resurrection (8:31; 9:31; 10:32-34); the double multiplication of the loaves and discourse summarizing the significance of the loaves (8:14-21); several apparently successful attempts to prevent demons from revealing Jesus' identity; several unsuccessful attempts of Jesus to silence persons whom he has healed; repeated misunderstandings on the part of the disciples; and various inclusions ("tear" [σχίζω] in 1:10 and 15:38; "Son of God" in 1:1 and 15:39).

Another important clue to Markan intent lies in the "seams" (e.g., Mark 1:21-22; 2:13) and "summary statements" (e.g., Mark 3:7-12). It is by means of these that the evangelist achieved a smooth narrative.[1] And it is here that the editor's voice is the clearest. Here too we find repeated Mark's interest in Jesus as a teacher "with authority" and as an exorcist whose identity the demons know. From the analysis of the repetitive structuring elements and these bits of "narrative glue" a coherent view of Mark's theology begins to emerge.

In approaching Q we are faced with analogous though not identical problems. In Mark the plot is key to a redactional analysis, for it determines the sequence and disposition of individual episodes, crucial to a synchronic analysis. The exigencies of continuous narration account for the creation of seams and summaries, the starting point of diachronic analysis. Obviously, with a document such as Q which contains narratives but lacks a continuous narrative frame, one cannot simply apply the redactional techniques that prove effective for Mark. Nor is it simple to identify instances of "pure Q redaction," since Q has relatively few joining devices. Even where two stories or sayings have obviously been joined editorially—for example,

1. Stein 1969; 1970; 1971; cf. Hedrick 1984.

John's question about Jesus (7:18-23) and Jesus' eulogy of John (7:24-28)—
it is not clear whether this joining is the work of the "final" editor of Q or
some earlier stage.

After nearly thirty years of redaction critical analysis of Q there is general
agreement that redactional intent can be perceived primarily in the arrangement and ordering principles of Q's component sayings, and secondarily in
interpretive additions and glosses made on individual sayings and longer
clusters.[2] Three kinds of observations are key.

First are repetitive elements—recurring motifs, formulas, and words—
that give shape to the collection as a whole. No less than in Mark, repeated
formulas, recurring motifs, and strategically placed echoes are the features
that cause the reader or hearer to construe the entire contents in a particular way. It must be assumed that such elements are the product of deliberate editorial arrangement.

A second key observation concerns the way in which a series of textual
elements stretching over several blocks of sayings taken together form an
"argument."[3] In the case of narrative texts where the reader or hearer is led
from one disclosure to another, it is relatively simple to trace the steps in an
argumentative progression. In Mark, for example, one of the key "arguments" consists of the progressive revelation of the identity of Jesus to his
disciples—an identity that includes both a wonder-working Son of God and
a suffering and dying Son of Man. Despite the fact that Q lacks a continuous narrative framework, it too contains various argumentative progressions that involve long blocks, in some cases compassing the whole of Q. It
is precisely because these have to do with extensive sections of Q and not
merely individual sayings that they provide access to the intent of the edi-
tor(s) responsible for the framing of Q.

A third type of observation concerns the structure and intent of the several subcollections that make up Q.[4] Synchronic analysis examines how

2. See the essays by Jacobson 1982b, D. Zeller 1982, Sato 1988 (all reprinted in Kloppenborg 1994b) and Jacobson 1987; Kloppenborg and Vaage 1991b. For a survey of earlier
approaches, see Kloppenborg 1984b.

3. By "argument" I do not mean only logical and syllogistic proof. Persuasion in antiquity
used several types of "proofs": logical, based on inductive or deductive logic; ethical—appeals
to the character to the speaker; and pathetical, or appeals to the self-interest of the audience.
Proofs took a variety of forms, including maxims and proverbs, examples from history,
invented proofs (fables, etc.), as well as deductive proofs (*enthymemes*).

4. While slightly differing divisions of Q have been proposed, I will assume the presence of
14 subcollections: (*1*) 3:3, 7-9, 16-17; (*2*) 4:1-13, (16); (*3*) 6:20b-23, (24-26), 27-33, (Q/Matt
5:41), (34-35b), 35c, 36-37b, 38c, 39-45, 46-49; (*4*) 7:1b-2, 6b-10, 18-19, 21-23, 24-28, 31-
35; (*5*) 9:57-60, (61-62); 10:2-16, 21-24; (*6*) 11:2-4, 9-13; (*7*) 11:14-20, (21-22), 23-26, (27-
28), 29-35, 39-44, 46-52; (*8*) 12:2-12; (*9*) 12:(13-14, 16-21), 22-31, 33-34; (*10*) 12:39-40,
42b-46, 49, 51-53, 54-56, 58-59; (*11*) 13:18-21; (*12*) 13:24, 26-30, 34-35; 14:11/18:14;
14:16-24, 26-27; 17:33; 14:34-35; (*13*) 15:4-7, (8-10); 16:13, 16-18; 17:1b-2, 3b-4, 6b; (*14*)
17:23-24, 37b, 26-27, (28-29), 30, 34-35; 19:12-13, 15b-26; 22:28-30.

individual sayings have been purposefully juxtaposed and framed within a subcollection and how the positioning of these subcollections contributes to a "meaning effect" in Q as a whole. Not all of the subcollections of Q appear to be organized from the perspective of the major framing redaction. This raises the question whether to regard such subcomponents as the seeds of earlier collections in Q, or as evidence of an antecedent stratum of the document, or even as foreign bodies that later found their way into the collection.

In stating the principles for isolating Q's redaction in this way, two key methodological insights are operative. First is the importance of establishing the order of Q's sayings as a necessary prerequisite to the discussion of redaction.[5] This follows naturally from seeking redaction in the purposeful juxtaposition of originally independent sayings. Of course, one may speak about the compositional effect of a particular sequence only where the original order of Q is reasonably certain and only where the context in which a particular saying occurred in Q is reasonably well known. For example, the sequence of the sayings in Q 7:18-28, 31-35, all having to do with John the Baptist, is not seriously in doubt, for Matthew and Luke agree on the order of virtually all elements. Redaction criticism therefore can ask how the arrangement of elements in 7:18-28, 31-35 creates a particular construal of its component parts, from which a view of John emerges. How does the particular arrangement of individual sayings and stories affect the way each story is read? Which parts are emphasized? Where does the center of gravity lie?

In the case of the saying on God and Mammon (16:13) where Matthew and Luke disagree on its placement, compositional analysis is more difficult. Even if, as is usually argued, the Lukan placement (roughly speaking, after 15:4-7, [8-10] and before 16:16-18) is original, it is by no means clear that Q 14:34-35; 15:4-7, (8-10); 16:13, 16-18 was conceived as a single unit in which the component sayings were purposefully connected. In other words, some portions of Q more than others are susceptible to a compositional analysis based on the combination of sayings than others.

A second methodological principle is that redactional analysis is to be accomplished *backwards* or *downwards*—beginning with the document in its "final form" and discerning its organizing principles and themes. Only once this has been done is it possible to determine whether there are subcollections organized along significantly different lines. Only once the lines of the main redaction have been determined is it possible to ascertain the

5. The principle is implicit in the work of Lührmann (1969), Schürmann 1975 (ET 1994); 1991; D. Zeller 1982 (ET 1994); and D. Allison 1997 and explicit in Jacobson 1978; 1992b; Kloppenborg 1984b; 1987a; Kloppenborg and Vaage 1991b; Kosch 1989a; Piper 1989; Sato 1988:30 (ET 1994:162); Sevenich-Bax 1993; Tuckett 1993; and Uro 1987.

presence of later glosses or insertions.[6] The alternative procedure, to begin with the individual components of Q and to determine how they were assembled into a whole, despite its seeming appropriateness, has a serious flaw. In a collection such as Q, comprising many originally isolated sayings, how could one determine where to start? The arbitrary choice of one saying over another as the starting point will necessarily determine the outcome. To choose the mission instructions (9:57—10:16) as the starting point implicitly (and arbitrarily) privileges this unit and will incline the interpreter to try to relate all other sayings to this starting point. But on what basis could one know that 9:57—10:16 is the best starting point and not, for example, the first three makarisms (6:20b-21) or the Beelzebul Accusation?[7] The only way that a measure of control can be placed on the critic's imagination is to work in the *reverse direction* that the collection was originally composed and, as it were, to "peel back the layers."

Although the term "stratigraphy" is frequently used (and will be used) in this context, the analogy of archaeology is not completely apposite. To be sure, the archaeologist discerns the history of the tell by proceeding from the top down, reconstructing the history of the tell from its most recent stages of occupation to its most ancient, rather than working upwards from its earliest to its latest strata. Yet with literary documents we are not dealing with physically discrete layers but rather with the incorporation of smaller literary units or stages into larger ones. Archaeology does provide at least one helpful analogy. In many instances, a site contains several different building structures superimposed upon one another on a single horizontal plane. An earlier small building may have had its walls broken and extended as it was incorporated into a larger structure; its doors or other orienting

---

6. The principle of proceeding backwards is seen in the organization of Kloppenborg 1987a (chap. 3: Q as a whole; chap. 4: the major redactional phase; chap. 5: preredactional collections); 1989; Kloppenborg and Vaage 1991b. The same principle is acknowledged by Vaage 1991:104-5 and Jacobson 1992b:46. By contrast, D. Zeller 1982 ET 1994; Sato 1988; and various essays by Schürmann 1975; 1982; 1986; 1991; 1992 proceed from the smaller form-critical units, observing how these are formed into more complex units.

7. Despite many interesting observations, D. Allison's compositional history suffers from this fundamental problem (1997:30–40). He rightly observes that 9:57—11:13; 12:2-12, 22-32 is seemingly interrupted by 11:14-52 but then designates 9:57—11:13; 12:2-12, 22-32 as the earliest stratum of Q (Q[1]) on the grounds that it is addressed to itinerant missionaries. He then asserts that 12:33—22:30 was added as the next stage (Q[2]), and finally supplemented by 3:7—7:35 and 11:14-52 (Q[3]). He provides no grounds for his assertion that 12:33—22:30 was added second or for 3:7—7:35 being added third, and no grounds for his initial choice of 9:57—11:13 as the starting point. It is not even clear that 11:2-4, 9-13, or 12:2-12 or 12:22-31 were addressed to itinerants. On the contrary, these materials speak of "debts" (11:3) and parental relations (11:11-13), neither of which are relevant to homeless "missionaries." His many worthwhile observations on the internal connections between pericopae and the thematic coherence of some subsections are thus vitiated by an arbitrary construction of his compositional theory.

features may have been moved to serve new functions. The excavations on the Temple Mount in Jerusalem, for example, have revealed both Hasmonean and Herodian ashlars (cut stones) at the same vertical level, as well as various structures from the Byzantine, Early Arab, Crusader, and Mamluk periods that either break or use these earlier structures. By examining the building techniques, architectural continuities, and the ways in which one structure has broken the integrity of earlier structures, a history of building phases can be deduced—how earlier structures were incorporated into later structures without either burying or completely destroying the earlier stages.

With these principles in mind, let us turn to the larger structuring features of Q.

Major Redactional Structures in Q

Recurring Motifs

(a) Coming Judgment. A survey of the contents of Q quickly reveals that the motif of a coming judgment runs throughout. Q begins with John's warning of an impending and fiery judgment and an injunction to repent (Q 3:7-9). On its heels follows a description in similarly fiery terms of the "Coming One" (Q 3:16-17). Specific towns (Bethsaida, Khorazin, Kefar Naḥum [Capernaum]) are threatened with a more severe judgment than Sodom or the Gentile cities of Tyre and Sidon (Q 10:12-15); and Jerusalem, its Temple, and (presumably) its elite are pronounced "desolate" (Q 13:34-35). At points the threat of judgment is directed more vaguely at "this generation" (Q 11:31-32, 49-51) or "you" (pl.), identified only by contrast with the "many who will come from East and West" to sit at table with the Patriarchs (Q 13:28-29). This judgment will come suddenly and without warning (Q 12:39-40; 17:23-34) and its results will be fearful (Q 12:42-46; 19:12-27). Since the theme of judgment is found in the sayings that frame the entire collection (Q 3:7-9, 16-17; 17:23-34; 19:12-27; 22:28-30) and at various points throughout, it is a reasonable supposition that the threat of judgment is a major editorial theme of Q.[8]

(b) *The Story of Lot.* A more specific embodiment of the judgment theme appears at three strategic points in Q. As noted in chapter 2 (pp. 94–95), it is probable that the opening of Q placed John "in the circuit of the Jordan" (πᾶσαν ἡ [τὴν] περίχωρος[ν] τοῦ Ἰορδάνου), a phrase that occurs in the

---

8. Thus, with slightly differing emphases: Lührmann 1969; Jacobson 1978; 1982b; 1982a (=1994); 1992b:37–40; Schönle 1982:96–97; D. Zeller 1982 (ET 1994:129); 1984:93–96; Crossan 1983:137–39; Sellew 1986:48; Kloppenborg 1987a:102–70; Uro 1987:4–5; Vaage 1987:19; Sato 1988:44–46; Kosch 1989a:422–23; Piper 1989:166–70; Koester 1990:135 n. 2, 150; Attridge 1991; J. M. Robinson 1991b; 1993:14; Tuckett 1991; 1993:157; 1996:107–207; Hoffmann 1992; 1995; Mack 1993; and others.

Tanak principally in connection with the story of Lot (Gen 13:10-12; 19:17, 25, 28).[9] This might be taken as insignificant were it not for the fact that the oracle of John that follows speaks of "fleeing" the coming wrath, warns against reliance on kinship to Abraham, threatens a fiery destruction, and inverts the story of Lot's wife by declaring God's ability to fashion people out of stones or pillars.[10] Further allusions to the Lot cycle occur in Q's threat against inhospitable towns: "I tell you, it will go easier for Sodom on that day than for such a town" (Q 10:12). The Lot story is invoked a final time near the end of Q, explicitly in 17:28-30[11] and implicitly in 17:34-35. In Q 17:28-30 the destruction of Sodom in the midst of normal everyday activities is used as a figure of the unanticipated character of the "day of the Son of Man"; in 17:34–35 Q continues this motif by raising the specter of kin or coworkers torn apart, one being "swept away" (παραλαμβάνεται) and the other "spared" (ἀφίεται). The same pair of verbs appears in Gen 18:26 and 19:17 to describe the destruction of the wicked and the sparing of Lot's family.

Lot is significant for Q in two respects. First, the Lot story already had a long history of exegetical use in the Tanak and the literature of Second Temple Judaism, being employed as the archetype of a divine judgment that was total, sudden, and enduring, and which occurred without human instrumentality.[12] Although English readers often focus on the sexual nature of the Sodomites' sins, the dominant Hebrew exegetical tradition identifies arrogance and inhospitality as their gravest sins. Ezekiel 16 accuses Sodom

9. While the current inclination is to identify the region of Sodom and Gomorrah in the southern ʿArava, south of the Dead Sea, the Tanak appears to locate it north of the Dead Sea. See 2 Chron 4:17 ("in the circuit of the Jordan between Sukkoth and Zerathan") and Deut 32:49; 34:3, where Moses atop Mount Nebo, was able to see "the plain (ככר), that is, the valley of Jericho the city of palm trees, as far as Zoar." Genesis 13:3, 10 pictures Lot surveying the ʿArava from between Bethel and Ai and choosing the Jordan valley because it was "well watered" and selecting Sodom as his home. Because of the salt haze that rises from the surface of the Dead Sea, the region south of the Dead Sea cannot be seen from Bethel or Ai. Byzantine pilgrims were shown various sites along the western edge of the Dead Sea. Recent archaeology associates the Sodom and Gomorrah traditions with two Early Bronze Age (*EB* III) sites south of the Dead Sea, near the modern site of Sdom. On this see Rast 1987.

10. Tannehill 1991:190 objects: Q should have to have read "we have Abraham as an uncle" if the Lot story were in view. Of course, such a statement would be absurd and the objection reveals a wooden understanding of literary allusion. It is true, as Tannehill points out, that the aphorism in Q 3:9 comes from the agricultural practice of uprooting and burning nonproductive trees (from which observation he concludes that 3:7-9 does not allude to Lot). But it is equally true that the first part of the oracle does not recall agricultural practice at all, but rather flight before destruction. In other words, Q is rather nimble in its use of allusion.

11. This saying, which stands in parallel with Q 17:26-27, is attested only in Luke. For a summary of arguments for its inclusion in Q, see Kloppenborg 1988a:194. The IQP includes the two verses in Q with a {D} rating.

12. See Fields 1992:188–224, who notes the use of these aspects of the Sodom tradition in Lam 4:6; Deut 29:22; 32:32, 35; Isa 1:7-10; 13:19-22; 30:33; Jer 20:16; 49:18; 50:40; Amos 4:11; Hos 11:8; Zeph 2:9; Job 18:15; Ezek 38:22; Ps 11:6; 1QpHab 10.5; *Jub.* 16.5.

of pride and failing to share its excess of food with the poor and needy (16:49), while Isa 3:9-17 accuses Jerusalemites of imitating Sodom by oppressing the poor and doing so with unbridled arrogance. This is strong language indeed, for the Sodomites are regularly remembered as the worst of sinners, occupying the lowest reaches of the abyss (*T. Isaac* 5.27). When Q threatens the "children of Abraham" with Sodom's judgment it continues the tradition of Isaiah and when it suggests that Sodom will fare better in the judgment, it elaborates the exegetical tradition of Ezekiel 16:

> This was the guilt of your [Jerusalem's] sister Sodom: she and her daughters had pride, excess of food, and prosperous ease, but did not aid the poor and needy. They were haughty and did abominable things before me; therefore I removed them when I saw it. Samaria has not committed half your sins; you [Jerusalem] have committed more abominations than they and have made your sisters appear righteous by all the abominations that you have committed. Bear your disgrace, you also, for you have brought about for your sisters a more favorable judgment; because of your sins in which you acted more abominably than they, they are more in the right than you. So be ashamed, you also, and bear your disgrace, for you have made your sisters appear righteous. (Ezek 16:49-52)

Of course, Q's talk of judgment is not founded exclusively on the Lot story. Nevertheless the peculiar dynamics of the Lot story as it had been developed in biblical and postbiblical tradition are especially congenial with the overall theme of judgment in Q. For Q dwells upon the finality of judgment that is faced by "this generation" (Q 11:49-51) and its suddenness (17:23-35). Moreover, like Ezekiel, Q freely engages in a shaming technique: Sodom, deserving of the furthest extremity of punishment, will fare better than inhospitable Israelite towns (10:12); the notorious Gentile cities of Tyre and Sidon will fare better than the Galilean towns of Bethsaida and Khorazin, which had better reasons for repenting; Gentiles will condemn "this generation" in the judgment (11:31-32); they will sit at table with the Patriarchs while Israelites will be thrust out, weeping and gnashing their teeth (13:28-29); and a Roman soldier displays greater faith than "Israel" in his approach to Jesus (7:1-10). Like Ezekiel, Q threatens Jerusalem and its elite with judgment and desolation (13:34-35) (see Kloppenborg 1990a). Sodom provided a spectacular and geographically proximate—and therefore concrete—instance of the finality and terror of judgment in a way that other occasions of judgment recorded in the Tanak did not. It was this finality and terror that eloquently served a variety of Israelite writers—including those responsible for Q—in their endeavor to create a compelling rhetoric that could serve various hortatory or polemical ends.

Second, it is important to note *where* these allusions to the Lot cycle appear: in the framework of Q—at the beginning and at the end—and, significantly, in 10:12, which is almost certainly the creation of the redactor who joined Q 10:2-12, 16 with 10:13-15 (see below, p. 148). This implies that the allusions to the Lot cycle are not simply an accident of the hetero-geneous traditions absorbed in the collection but derive from purposeful editing at a stage near the main redaction of Q.

(c) *Deuteronomistic Theology.* Arland Jacobson (1982a) has drawn attention to the pervasive presence of Deuteronomistic theology. According to this theology, the history of Israel is depicted as a repetitive cycle of sin-fulness, prophetic calls to repentance (which are ignored), punishment by God, and renewed calls to repentance with threats of judgment. Common in this schema is the motif of the rejection of the prophets and even of their murder, in spite of the fact that the Tanak itself records no instance of the murder of a named prophet. While the Tanak depicts prophets as critics of the monarchy and as advocates of social reforms, in Deuteronomistic theology the prophets are represented primarily as preachers of repentance and, generally speaking, as rejected preachers.[13]

This reading of history appears at various points in Q. Q 6:23c; 11:47-51; and 13:34-35 recall the persistent rejection, persecution, and even mur-der of the prophets. Q associates Jesus' followers with those prophets and their fate (6:22-23). John is interpreted primarily as a repentance preacher (3:7-9) and he, along with Jesus, is rejected by "this generation" (7:31-35). Although highly varied sayings are attributed to Jesus, his role too is implic-itly characterized as having to do with repentance in 10:13-15 and 11:29-32. Q's Parable of the Great Supper (14:16-24), appearing just after a threat that Israelites will be expelled (13:28-29) and the woe over Jerusalem (13:34-35), functions as commentary on the rejection of God's envoys by Israel, the first invitees, and their eventual reception by others.

It is again especially significant where these occur: at the beginning of Q (3:7-9) and in at least two points that on other grounds can be identified as redactional insertions into earlier materials: 6:23c and 11:47-51.[14] This suggests that the appeal to Deuteronomistic theology is a function of redac-tion rather than tradition. Its location in Q indicates that it belongs to a principal moment of editing.

These three interrelated complexes—judgment, appeals to the Lot cycle, and the Deuteronomistic view of the prophets—lend Q a thematic unity,

---

13. The basic study of the Deuteronomistic view of history and of prophecy is Steck 1967. In the Hebrew Bible, see Deut 4:25-31; 28:45-68 + 30:1-10; 1 Kings 8:46-53; Jer 7:25-34; 25:4-14; 29:17-20; 35:15-17; 44:2-14; Lam 3:42-47; Dan 9:4b-19; Zech 1:2-6; 7:4-14; 2 Chron 30:6-9; 29:5-11; 15:1-7; Ezra 9:6-15; Neh 1:5-11; 9:5-37. In the literature of Second Temple Judaism: Bar 1:15—3:8; 3:9—4:4; 4:5—5:9; Tob 3:1-6; 13:3-6; *T. Levi* 10.2-5; 14; 15.1-4; 16.1-5; *T. Jud.* 23.1-5; *T. Iss.* 6.1-4; *T. Zeb.* 9.5-9; *T. Dan* 5.4-9; *T. Naph.* 4.1-5; *T. Asher* 7.2-7; *1 Enoch* 93.1-10 + 91.12-17; 85—90; 91—104; *Jub.* 1.7-26; CDC 20.28-30; 1.3-13a; 4QDibHam 1.8—7.2; *Pss. Sol.* 2:9; 8:2; 17:17; *4 Ezra* 14.27-35; 3.4-25, 27; 7.129-130; Ps.-Philo, *Bib. Ant.* 2; *2 Apoc. Bar.* 1:1-5; 4:1-6; 31:1—32:7; 44:1—46:7; 77:1-17; 78—87.

14. See below, p. 149 (on Q 6:23c) and p. 148 n. 66 (on 11:51b).

appearing at the beginning and the end and at various strategic points throughout.

Argumentative Progressions

In addition to the thematic unity imposed on Q by various repeated elements, there are several discursive progressions which further enhance the impression of unity. By a "progression" I mean a set of episodes (sayings, anecdotes, stories) which together form a sequence constituting an argument. To borrow the terminology of Kenneth Burke, "logical progression" is "the form of a perfectly conducted argument advancing step by step," as in the case of a prediction followed by its fulfillment. "Qualitative progression" represents a sequence in which "the presence of one quality prepares us for the introduction of another" (Robbins 1984:9; cf. Burke 1968:123–83).

Q 3–7 provides an instance of both types of progressions. Q opens with John's prediction of the imminent appearance of the "Coming One" (ὁ ἐρχόμενος), thereby raising the expectation of the fulfillment. This expectation is engaged at 7:18-23, where John's envoys ask Jesus whether he is this figure. Jesus' response, though oblique, is evidently affirmative. He adduces a string of evidences of God's reversal of the fortune of the disadvantaged and the poor that recalls elements from Psalms (146) and Isaiah (29:18; 35:5; 42:7; 49:1-2; 61:1-2). The title appears a third time, now on Jesus' lips, at Q 13:35b in the lament over Jerusalem. Here an identification of Jesus and the Coming One is presupposed: "I tell you, you will not see me until you say: 'Blessed is the one who comes (ὁ ἐρχόμενος) in the name of the Lord.'" Even without Q having a narrative framework, the arrangement of elements that are distributed across a large portion of Q contributes to a logical progression in which expectations about a Coming One are raised and then resolved.

Qualitative progression is present too, forming an argument that John and Jesus, despite their very different appearances, are colleagues rather than rivals. In Q John is a repentance preacher who announces the imminent coming of a fiery judge and who dwells in the Jordan rift valley (3:3). One must "go out" in order to see him (7:24). John's portrait of what is to come recalls Malachi's "coming day" (Mal 3:19), when Elijah will appear to bring repentance (Mal 3:22-23)[15] and a figure associated with Elijah—either God or an angelic figure—will "come to his temple" and "purify" (καθαρίζω, cf. Q 3:17 διακαθαρίζω) the sons of Levi with fire, burning up evildoers like stubble, "leaving neither root nor branch" (Mal 3:19).

At first blush, there is little in Q's first characterizations of Jesus that coheres with this: despite his brief sojourn in the wilderness (4:1-13), Q

---

15. Cf. Sir 48:10, where Elijah is destined to "calm the wrath of God before it breaks out in fury, to turn the hearts of parents to their children and to restore the tribes of Jacob."

does not depict Jesus as active there. On the contrary, 7:1–10, 18-28, 31-35 place him in the well-watered area near Kefar Naḥum. Nor does the Sermon (Q 6:20b-49) give any reason to suppose that Jesus is either a fiery repentance preacher or, still less, the divine judge predicted in Q 3:16-17. Thus when John asks, "Are you the Coming One?" one might be tempted to wonder why the question would arise in the first place. But Q has anticipated this problem. The answer Jesus gives in Q 7:22 also evokes expectations associated with an Elijah-like figure, but focuses instead on Elijah's miracles. A recently published text from Qumran (4Q521) provides part of the missing link. Dating from the first century, 4Q521 lists deeds of the messiah (חישמ), deeds that turn out to bear a remarkable resemblance to those of Q 7:22.[16] This messiah, though associated with the restoration of justice, is neither a fiery judge nor a *Davidic* messiah (J. Collins 1994). His activities, particularly that of raising the dead, have strong affinities with Elijah. In Q the association with Elijah is stronger still, for Jesus' activities in 7:22 include the cleansing of lepers *and* the raising of the dead,[17] deeds which recall the Elijah/Elisha cycle.

Q seems aware of the fact that Jesus does not fit John's description of the "Coming One," but wishes nonetheless to affirm the equation. Hence the conclusion, "Blessed is the one who takes no offense in me" (7:23). A few verses later, Q asserts that John himself is Elijah (7:27) and the concluding pericope in this unit (7:31-35) places John beside Jesus, acknowledging their very different appearances and activities, but nonetheless affirming that both are "children of Sophia" (7:35).

The "progression" or argument that Q makes is based on the introduction of qualities that Malachi 3–4 associated with Elijah. These qualities are applied both to John, as one who brings about repentance (Q 3:7-9), and to the Coming One who effects judgment (Q 3:16-17). Once the Elijianic expectations are engaged, the question of Q 7:19-20 and its answer in 7:22 are less unnatural, since 7:22 also invokes qualities associated with Elijah. When Q mentions the Coming One in 13:34-35, he is described in terms that recall Mal 3:1-2: he will "come" with judgment to Jerusalem and its Temple. The interplay between various expectations associated with Elijah

16. See Puech 1992. Q 7:22 refers to the blind seeing, the lame walking, lepers being cleansed, the deaf hearing, the dead rising, and the poor being evangelized (7:22). 4Q521 (frag. 2 ii + 4) reads: "(1) . . . for heaven and earth will obey his (?) messiah. . . . (5) For the Lord will take care for the pious and the righteous he will call by their name; (6) upon the poor his spirit shall rest, and he will renew the faithful by his strength. (7) For he will honour the pious upon a throne of an eternal kingdom, (8) freeing captives, *restoring sight to the blind*, and raising up those who are bowed down . . . (12) for he will heal the wounded, *the dead he shall revive*, and the *humble he shall evangelize;* (13) he shall satisfy the poor and shall invite the starving to a banquet (?) . . . ." (emphasis added).

17. Neither the cleansing of lepers (cf. Elisha in 1 Kings 5:1-19) nor raising of the dead (mentioned also in 4Q521 of the "messiah") is mentioned in Psalm 146 or any of the Isaianic texts which seem otherwise to have informed both 4Q521 and Q 7:22.

allows Q to distribute these qualities between John and Jesus and thus to negotiate the relationship between the two figures. John proclaims repentance and is the Elijianic messenger; Jesus is the Coming one who emulates Elijah's restorative ministry; both are children of Sophia.

Once the respective roles of John and Jesus are sorted, Q places judgment oracles on Jesus' lips. As John threatened those who came out to him, Jesus threatens three Galilean towns (10:13-15) and later "this generation" (11:31-32) for failing to repent. The key vocabulary of John's opening oracle is assimilated but it is also subtly transformed: "repentance" is not simply a matter of preparation for judgment by moral reform, but more specifically, the recognition and welcoming of Q's "workers" (10:10-12) and the recognition of "that which is greater than Solomon and Jonah" (11:31-32). At issue is not the recognition of the person of Jesus but rather grasping the significance of the time as the dawning of God's kingdom. The language of judgment returns at the end of Q, where Jesus' followers are promised a share in the judicial powers (22:28-30). Hence, one sees a qualitative progression according to which Jesus absorbs and transforms John's judicial language and Jesus' followers (i.e., Q's immediate addressees) are then allowed to participate in the ultimate judgment of Israel.

 It seems plain that at one level of editing, the motifs of impending judgment, the threat of sudden destruction, and the Deuteronomistic interpretations of Israel's history and of the role of the prophets played a formative role in Q's architecture. Much energy, moreover, is devoted to characterization: characterization of John and Jesus by means of their activities, and characterization of a contrasting set of persons, including unresponsive Galilean towns and Jerusalem and others, vaguely called "this generation." John and Jesus, despite their different activities, are placed under the same rubric of "children of Sophia," and the immediate addressees of Q are treated as successors to the prophets (6:23) and as inheritors or participants in a kingly rule that is envisaged for the future (22:28-30). Insofar as elements belonging to this complex appear with some density at the beginning and the end of Q, and insofar as elements related to the Lot cycle and the Deuteronomistic view of the prophets appear in redactional creations, it is likely that this set of redactional interests represents that of the major framing redaction of Q.

Analysis of the Subcollections: Purposeful Juxtaposition

The most important way in which redaction is observed at the level of its smaller collections is in the juxtaposition of sayings and stories which do not necessarily or inevitably belong together. A variety of methods of juxtaposition can be observed:[18]

18. See the discussion by D. Zeller 1982 (ET 1994), whose typology is adapted in what follows.

1. Some sayings are united by a set of catchwords, an editorial method observed in many proverb collections. For example, the Lord's Prayer (Q 11:2-4) shares with the following pericope on prayer (11:9-13) the words "father," "bread," and "give," even though these words are used with somewhat different connotations. Q does not simply offer a miscellany on prayer, however. Instead it makes an argument—one that is related to other "arguments" found in Q. Ronald Piper demonstrated that 11:9-13 displays a four-part argumentative pattern, attested in a number of smaller collections in Q, characterized by (a) an admonition which is almost embarrassing in scope (11:9), followed by (b) a supporting maxim (11:10), (c) a rhetorical question (11:11-12), and concluding with (d) a saying that applies the entire complex to a particular issue confronting the earliest Christians "in which persuasion would have been of critical importance."[19]

When attached to 11:2-4, Q 11:9-13 highlights and develops several points in the prayer. First, it underscores the centrality of the filial relationship that is implied in the vocative "father" of 11:2 but left aside in the remainder of the prayer. Second, the implied characterization of God in the prayer as a generous provider of the necessities of life is reinforced by the illustration of parent-child relationships in Q 11:11–12 and the *qal wehomer* argument of 11:13. Third, the juxtaposition underscores the basis for confidence in such a God by means of the staccato assurances of 11:9-10. Finally, even though the other items mentioned in the prayer—the thematic "Reign of God," debt/sin forgiveness, and preservation from testing—are left undeveloped, the characterization of God that 11:9-13 provides and its appeal to confidence create a rhetorical situation in which these expectations also become believable. If the divine Father provides food more abundantly than human fathers, this God will surely also forgive debts and preserve his own, thus bringing about his Reign.

In fact, elsewhere in Q the topics left aside in 11:9-13 are the express focus of argument: debt forgiveness and sin forgiveness (6:30-35; 17:4); God's providential care and the seeking of the kingdom (12:22-31); and divine surveillance in the midst of threats to life (12:2-7, 11-12). In other words, the association of the prayer in 11:2-4 with 11:9-13 is not due to a mechanical clustering of similar sayings, but shows signs of the attempt to form an argument for confidence in the ethos expressed in the Lord's Prayer. The argumentative or rhetorical articulation of one cluster of Q sayings finds resonances in other clusters located elsewhere in the collection. Hence, it is not only the judgment and Deuteronomistic motifs that unify discrete sub-collections in Q; other subcollections are unified by their common appeal to a provident and generous God whose character serves as model of ideal human relationships.

---

19. Piper 1982:416. See Piper's fuller elaboration of this in Piper 1989.

While catchword composition often leads to the grouping of sayings with thematically compatible perspectives, the rather mechanical nature of the procedure can also produce less coherent arrangements. Sayings in 7:18-28, 31-35 are connected in part on the basis of the mention of "John." This unit compasses a variety of views of John, juxtaposing Jesus' high praise for John (7:24-27) with an apparent denigration of John (7:28), and finally with 7:31-35, which seems to treat John and Jesus equally as "children of Sophia."[20] Here too, an argument can be discerned and the sequence of sayings is far from arbitrary. While there are tensions between the depiction of John as an uncertain questioner in 7:18-23 and Jesus' high praise of this wilderness figure as "more than a prophet" (7:24-26), these are resolved, at least in part, by three sayings that interpret John's role vis-à-vis (a) the history of salvation (7:27; cf. Mal 3:1; Exod 23:20), (b) members of the Q group (7:28), and finally, (c) Jesus, on the one hand, and Q's opponents ("this generation") on the other (7:31-35). In the end, the differences between John and Jesus are admitted, but their roles are nonetheless subsumed under the Heavenly Sophia (7:35). In other words, while sayings are set side by side because of a common topic or catchword, their ordering is a matter of reflection and creates an "argument." To have ended the collection with 7:18-23 or 7:28 would have produced an entirely different effect.

Catchword composition can on occasion produce highly artificial connections. A dramatic case of this awkwardness produced by composition is Q 12:33-34 + 12:39-40, joined on the basis of the words "dig through" (διορύσσω) and "thief" (κλέπτης). What makes the connection so jarring is that 12:33-34 concerns the acquisition of "treasures" which *in principle* a thief cannot steal, while 12:39 speaks of measures taken to prevent an actual theft. In 12:33-34 the thief is an enemy to be thwarted; in 12:39 the thief is the Son of man who cannot be thwarted. That is, while the two units employ the same key terms, they are used in completely divergent ways.

2. Units which have a common structure or which display common formal elements can be grouped together. For example, Q 6:20b-23 juxtaposes three makarisms taking the form "honorable are the . . . for . . ." (μακάριοι οἱ . . . , ὅτι) and appends to this a fourth makarism with the form "honorable are you when . . ." (μακάριοί ἐστε . . . ὅταν). Elsewhere in Q one may find associations of chriae (Q 9:57-58, 59-60, [61-62]), parables (13:18-19, 20-21; 15:4-7, [8-10]), and prophetic sayings (17:34, 35). With such groupings, it may be a matter of an editor connecting two or more sayings that were originally independent; or an editor may have created additional sayings on the analogy of the first.

---

20. See Cameron 1990.

3. Thematic groupings are attested throughout Q. For example, Q 6:36-
45 consists of a cluster of sayings that concerns counsel, (self-)correction
and judicious speech. This does not mean, of course, that all component
sayings originally had to do with self-correction. Q 6:38c is probably a
maxim originally having to do with the repayment of agricultural loans, and
Q 6:43-44 is a bit of wisdom from arboriculture and viticulture. When used
in 6:36-45, however, these maxims assume the function of "proofs" (by
analogy) in an exhortation to practice self-correction. As Mark 4:24 shows,
the "measure for measure" saying (Q 6:38c) could function in a quite different thematic context.

4. Originally independent sayings or chriae are sometimes joined by syntactical devices to create a subordination, a sequence, or an inference. For
example, John's question to Jesus (Q 7:18-23) is joined to the following
chria (7:24b-28) by means of a genitive absolute, "Now when the messengers of John had departed" (7:24a). This not only imputes a temporal
sequence to the two episodes but creates a two-panel elaboration of the
issue of the identities of John and Jesus: the first panel treats the relation of
Jesus to John's "Coming One" and the second, John's place in the history of
Israel and his relation to Jesus. Or again, Q's warning to be prepared for the
coming of the Son of Man (12:40) is joined by means of the illative particle
ἄρα ("then, therefore") to the following parable of the faithful and unfaith-
ful slave (or steward; 12:42-45), such that the parable becomes an elaboration of the consequences of the day of the Lord (see Kloppenborg 1995b).

5. Even more complex rhetorical units appear in Q. One of the longest is
Q 6:20b-49, consisting of several topical arguments (6:27-35, 36-42, 43-
45) enclosed by a series of makarisms (6:20b-23) and a warning, using the
figure of the ruined house (6:47-49).[21] As noted above, Piper has discerned
in several clusters of Q sayings a four-part rhetorical pattern involving
admonitions with buttressing maxims, rhetorical questions, and a concluding maxim or question (1982; 1989).[22]

---

21. This structure (programmatic opening; imperatives; concluding warning) is paralleled
in the structure of several of the wisdom instructions in Proverbs 1–9; see B. Lang 1972:29–34,
100; Kirk 1998:93–104. On rhetorical figures in the Sermon, see Sellew (1990) and essays by
Carruth (1995) and Douglas (1995).

22. Sevenich-Bax (1993) recently argued that Q 3—7 displays an elaborate concentric structure. She divides Q 3–7 into five episodes, the first and last subdivided into two parts (3:[3-6],
7-9, 16-17 and 3:21-22; 7:18-23 and 7:24-35) and the middle three consisting of the temptation (4:1-13), the Sermon (6:[12a.17] 20-49) and the healing of the centurion's servant (7:1-
10). This division, according to Sevenich-Bax, reveals several symmetries: in both the first
(3:3:[3-6], 7-9, 16-17 and 3:21-22) and last (7:18-23 and 7:24-35) episodes, John and Jesus
are placed in opposition to a larger public; the term "the Coming One" appears in the first and
final episodes; and the second and fourth episodes are both narratives that depict ideal figures—the ideal (and obedient) Son and the Gentile as an ideal (and obedient) Israel (1993:265–
66). The Sermon occupies the central position in this structure.
The Sermon itself, which falls easily into the class of sapiential speech, is flanked by the

6. Finally, the framers of Q have employed devices that confer a pragmatic unity on disparate units of tradition by constituting them as the same communicative event. For example, the phrase "in that hour Jesus said" (Q 10:21a) not only points forward to Q 10:21b-22, 23-24, but backward to 9:57-60, (61-62); 10:2-16. Q thus creates a complex but coherent episode filled with contrasting panels. It begins with persons who volunteer to follow Jesus but are rebuffed or admonished about the gravity of their offer. Then follows Jesus' instructions to the "workers" (10:4-11), prefaced and concluded by Jesus' own legitimating commentary (10:2-3, 16). The unit concludes with contrasting prophetic pronouncements on those who reject the preaching of the kingdom (10:12-15) and those who receive it (10:21-22) and a final commendation of the disciples (10:23-24). Similarly, a pragmatic unity is constructed in Q 7 by various elements: Jesus' entry into Kefar Naḥum (7:1b), John's hearing about Jesus and "sending" disciples to inquire of Jesus, and Jesus' various sayings upon the departure of these envoys (7:24-28, 31-35). The first episode, the healing of the centurion's serving boy, does not have anything thematically to do with John the Baptist; but the series of pragmatic connections which Q makes construes this healing as the beginning of a larger communicative event that apparently occurred in Kefar Naḥum.

From Redaction Criticism to Compositional History

From the preceding examples of redaction at least three important observations can be made.

First, the pericopae in which the unifying motifs of the coming judgment, allusions to the Lot cycle, and the Deuteronomistic view of the prophets appear comprise a rather small set: Q 3:3, 7-9, 16-17; 6:23c; 7:18-35; 10:12, 13-15; 11:31-32, 49-51; 12:39-40, 42-46; 13:28-29, 34-35; 14:16-24; 17:23-37; 19:12-27; 22:28-30. Several blocks of Q sayings are untouched by these concerns but do evince other, mainly didactic and hortatory, concerns.

Second, compositional techniques vary among the subcollections, and between the subcollections and the document as a whole. The subcollections employ a variety of compositional and rhetorical techniques. Some

---

temptation story and the healing of the centurion's son. Both of these "underscore a paraenetic understanding of the sermon and in particular stress for the addressees its soteriological significance as the eschatological Torah of the Son of Man" (463). Hence the Sermon, which consists mainly of the "older" forms of wisdom (464), is enclosed within materials that underscore the importance of obedience to both Torah and Jesus' teachings, which are in turn framed with materials that evoke the "newer" wisdom materials, with the myth of Sophia's rejection by humankind. A synchronic analysis of the whole of Q has now been attempted by Kirk (1996; 1998), who argues that the genre of the instructional speech controls the construction of Q.

have a strong topical focus (e.g., 3:3, 7-9, 16-17; 11:2-4, 9-13; 12:13-14, 16-21, 22-31, 33-34; 17:23-37 + 19:12-27 + 22:28-30). The Sermon (6:20b-49) seems to have been the result of particularly careful composition: it contains several topically-organized collections (6:27-35, 36-45) furnished with an anaphoric introduction (6:20-23) and a concluding warning (6:46, 47-49). Other subcollections, while showing signs of planning, are more loosely integrated (e.g., 7:1-10, 18-28, 31-35; 12:39-59); others still are quite miscellaneous (13:24—14:35). The means by which one large block of material is associated with another is often a catchword. Q 12:22b-31, 33-34 is connected with the following block (12:39-40, 42b-46, 49, 51-53, 54-56, 57-59) by the catchwords "dig through" (12:33, 39) and "thief" (12:33, 39), even though there is a glaring inconsistency in the way the metaphors of theft are employed (see above). Similar connections may be observed throughout Q.[23] The rather artificial nature of this particular use of catchword composition makes it difficult to discern larger argumentative strategies emerging in the juxtaposition of one large block with the next.

Finally, the subcollections differ quite markedly in their apparent func tions, implied addressees, and modes of rhetoric. Q 6:20b-49; Q 11:2-4, 9-13 and Q 12:2-7, (8-9), 11-12; 12:22b-31, 33-34, for example, are generally hortatory and deliberative, directed at adherents of the Jesus movement. They attempt to inculcate and legitimize a particular ethos in the adherents of the Q group by a variety of means, including appeals to agricultural and domestic metaphors. There is no defense of that ethos or of Jesus himself. The sayings on prayer (11:2-4, 9-13) discussed above, for example, simply take for granted the intrinsic appeal of an ethos characterized by dependence upon the providential care of God and by debt forgiveness. They do not attempt an argument in defense of Jesus as a reliable teacher.

In striking contrast to these are the openly polemical units in Q 3:7-9, 16-17; 7:1-10, 31-35; 11:14-26, and 11:39-52 or the counterbalancing praise of Jesus, John, and their disciples found in 7:18-28, 31-35; 10:21-24. In these portions of Q, the rhetoric is epideictic—the rhetoric of praise and blame—and the intent seems to be to defend the ethos (character) of Jesus and that of the Jesus group. This is done both indirectly, by attacking an "out-group," most often referred to as "this generation," and directly, by defending a portrait of Jesus (and John) as reliable.

These observations do not in themselves suggest a particular compositional history for Q. It is quite possible to imagine an author combining didactic, deliberative, and epideictic materials side by side, as occurs in

23. There are other such catchword connections between larger blocks of Q material: (a) 3:(3), 7-9, 16-17 / 4:1-13 connected by "spirit" (3:16; 4:1); (b) 4:1-13 / 6:20b-49 connected by "kingdom(s) of the world/kingdom of God; (c) 6:20b-49 / 7:1-10, 18-28, 31-35 connected by "Lord" (6:46; 7:6), "word" (6:46, 47, 49; 7:7), "do" (6:46, 47, 49; 7:8), and "wind" (Matt 7:27; Q 7:24) or "shake" (6:48; 7:24); (d) 7:31-35 / 9:57-60, (61-62); 10:2-16, 21-24 connected by "Son of Man"; and (e) 10:2-16, 21-24 / 11:2-4, 9-13 connected by "father."

some of the *Testaments of the Twelve Patriarchs* or *1 Enoch*. It is equally
imaginable that a framing redaction compassed earlier materials with different theological proclivities, as has occurred, for example, with the appropriation of a Jewish "Two Ways" document in the *Didache*. Nothing can be
decided in the abstract; careful analysis of the actual text of Q is needed.
What these observations do suggest is that the final redaction of Q is distinct from the editing of *some* of the component collections in terms of its
literary method and intention. It suggests as well that the subcollections
themselves were organized by varying means and for varying purposes. Two
decades of close analysis of Q has convinced most specialists that a fairly
complex compositional history preceded the "final text."[24] Whether it is
possible to ascertain what that history was, however, is another matter.

THREE ANALOGIES

To illustrate the issues faced with the composition of Q, it may be useful to
summarize some of the results of the compositional analysis of three other
nonnarrative documents: the biblical book of Proverbs, the *Didache* (or
"Teaching of the Twelve Apostles"), and the *Manual of Discipline* (1QS)
from Qumran Cave 1.[25] These models are depicted graphically in figure 18.

Proverbs

While Proverbs might at first glance appear homogeneous, variations in
the compositional features of the book prohibit the conclusion that it was
composed in a single stroke. The first nine chapters are not individual

24. Even though scholars speak as if there were a "final text" of Q, this should be seen as a
covenient heuristic concept rather than as a description of an actual literary stage. Like other
biblical literature, the "text" was subject from its earliest stages to glosses and copyists' errors
and corrections. In the case of Q, it is entirely conceivable that it developed in two forms that
eventually could be described as Q[Matt] and Q[Luke], containing some of the extra materials
included by Matthew and Luke, respectively. Sato (1988, ET 1994) uses the analogy of a loose-
leaf book that could have pages continually inserted into it (see also Kosch 1989b). To speak
of the "final text" of Q is to posit and privilege, somewhat arbitrarily, a stage of development
that satisfactorily accounts for the contents of *both* Matthew and Luke. See the discussion of
this problem in chapter 2, above.

25. Another example from Qumran might be added: Torleif Elgvin (1995b) has recently
suggested that 4QSapiential Work[A] (4Q415; 4Q416; 4Q417; 4Q418a; 4Q418b; 4Q423) is a
composite work that adapted "pre-sectarian" sapiential admonitions, adding other materials
more distinctive of the Qumran community. "It would then be this second literary layer which
deals with God's mysteries and revelation as well as eschatology" (1995b:433; cf. Elgvin
1995a:562). Elgvin added: "Such a combination of sectarian and non-sectarian wisdom material has a parallel in 4Q420/421 (4QWays of Righteousness): the first part of this work deals
with the organisation of the *yaḥad* and the inclusion of new members into the community. The
second part consists of proverbial sentences about the righteous man, and towards the end of
the scroll comes a section dealing with temple issues" (1995b:433). On the latter text, see
Elgvin 1996.

Figure 18
Stratigraphy in Composition

a. Proverbs

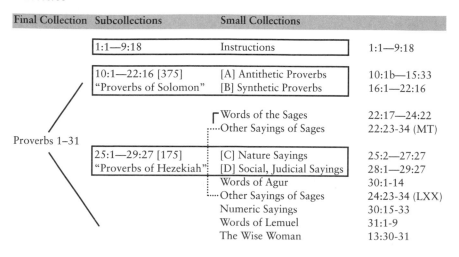

Final Collection	Subcollections	Small Collections	
	1:1—9:18	Instructions	1:1—9:18
	10:1—22:16 [375] "Proverbs of Solomon"	[A] Antithetic Proverbs [B] Synthetic Proverbs	10:1b—15:33 16:1—22:16
Proverbs 1–31		⌐Words of the Sages ·····Other Sayings of Sages	22:17—24:22 22:23-34 (MT)
	25:1—29:27 [175] "Proverbs of Hezekiah"	[C] Nature Sayings [D] Social, Judicial Sayings Words of Agur ·····Other Sayings of Sages Numeric Sayings Words of Lemuel The Wise Woman	25:2—27:27 28:1—29:27 30:1-14 24:23-34 (LXX) 30:15-33 31:1-9 13:30-31

b. Manual of Discipline (1QS)

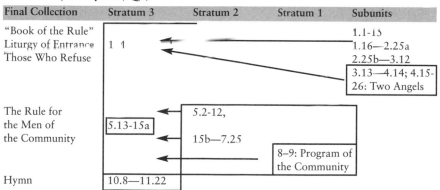

Final Collection	Stratum 3	Stratum 2	Stratum 1	Subunits
"Book of the Rule" Liturgy of Entrance Those Who Refuse	1 1			1.1-15 1.16—2.25a 2.25b—3.12 3.13—4.14; 4.15-26: Two Angels
The Rule for the Men of the Community	5.13-15a	5.2-12, 15b—7.25	8–9: Program of the Community	
Hymn	10.8—11.22			

c. The Didache

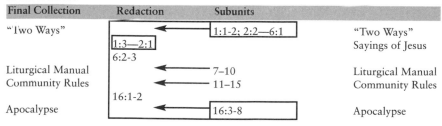

Final Collection	Redaction	Subunits	
"Two Ways"	1:3—2:1 6:2-3	1:1-2; 2:2—6:1	"Two Ways" Sayings of Jesus
Liturgical Manual Community Rules		7-10 11-15	Liturgical Manual Community Rules
Apocalypse	16:1-2	16:3-8	Apocalypse

proverbs at all but sapiential "instructions," organized by theme.[26] At least one of these instructions also uses a numeric schema: Prov 2:1-22 is a twenty-two-line poem patterned after the number of letters of the Hebrew alphabet. By contrast, Prov 10:1—22:16 consists mainly of strings of proverbs, some connected by catchwords (e.g, 15:2-4 ["tongue"]; 15:16-17 ["better"]), some by common theme, and others more loosely juxtaposed. Yet even within this block, important variations can be observed. The proverbs in 10:1—15:33 (collection "A") are dominated by antithetic parallelism, while those in 16:1—22:16 (collection "B") display synthetic parallelism. Proverbs 22:17—24:22, introduced as "The Words of the Sages,"[27] is an instruction appended to these collections. Structurally, it has more in common with Proverbs 1–9 and the Egyptian "Instructions of Amenenope" than with Prov 10:1—22:16.[28] The same can be said of another collection of "Words of the Sages" which appears in Prov 24:23-34 (placed by the LXX after 30:1-14). Two genuine proverb collections, Proverbs 25–27 [C] and 28–29 [D], can be distinguished as originally separate collections.[29] Prov 30:1-14 is called the "Words of Agur"; Prov 30:15-33 is a string of mainly numerical sayings; Prov 31:1-9 is called the "Words of Lemuel" while Prov 31:10-31 is a twenty-two-line alphabetic acrostic on the virtues of a good wife.

It would be extraordinarily difficult to imagine all of this diversity compassed in a single compositional effort and few scholars would try. The consensus holds that Proverbs was composed in stages from several subcollections. The precise sequence of composition is more difficult to ascertain, since one block is simply appended to the next. If it could be assumed, as many have done, that Proverbs 1–9 was postexilic, one could at least conclude that this section was added after the formation of the main body of proverbs and that the author of Proverbs 1–9 was perhaps even the editor of the entire book (thus Skehan 1971:15–26). This supposition has been disputed, however: Kayatz (1966) and B. Lang (1972), for example, have argued that Proverbs 1–9 is considerably older than usually thought, thus rendering the tradition-historical grounds for a compositional history insecure.

26. I use "instruction" in a specific and technical sense, denoting a distinct Near Eastern wisdom genre. The hallmark of the instruction is the exhortation and admonition with motive clauses, serialized with related admonitions or furnished with proverbs, questions, comparisons, etc. to enforce the point under discussion. See B. Lang (1972), who distinguishes ten instructions (1:1-19; 2:1-22; 3:1-12; 3:21-35; 4:1-9; 4:10-19; 4:20-27; 5:1-23; 6:20-35; 7:1-27) and three speeches of Wisdom (1:20-33; 8:1-36; 9:1-6). Slightly differing divisions are dicussed by Whybray 1965, McKane 1970, and Murphy 1981. On the instruction in general, see Brunner 1970; Kitchen 1979.

27. *Dibrê ḥakamîm* is the restoration of *BHK*.

28. See Kloppenborg 1987a:276–78 and the literature cited there.

29. Skladny's (1962:46–67) division of Proverbs 25–29 is now widely accepted. See the excellent study of Proverbs 25–27 by Van Leeuwen (1988).

There are, nonetheless, some clues. While originally two separate collections, Prov 10:1–22:16 [A+B] contains a total of 375 proverbs, the numerical equivalent of the name *ŠLMH* (Solomon) who appears in the superscription (10:1). Similarly, Proverbs 25–29, also representing two subcollections [C+D], has 140 sayings, the equivalent of the name *YHZQYH* (Hezekiah; 25:1).[30] These facts suggest a purposeful editing of collections A+B and C+D.[31] Since the two double collections employ the *same* numeric technique of coordinating the number of proverbs with the numerical equivalents of the names in the superscriptions (10:1; 25:1), it is a reasonable supposition that the same editor was responsible for the combination (though not necessarily the composition) of the two collections (A+B, C+D).[32] The second collection of "Words of the Sages" (24:23-34), given the superscription "these *also* are [words] of the sages" (24:23: גם־אלה לחכמים), must have been added with 22:14—24:22 in view, whether or not it was inserted after 22:17—24:22, where it appears in the MT, or after 30:1-14 as in the LXX. In other words, even if one cannot describe the entire compositional history of Proverbs, at least some stages may be discerned with some probability.

The Manual of Discipline

Literary analysis of the *Manual of Discipline* (1QS) from Qumran has likewise shown it to be a composite document in which several literary strata can be discerned.[33] The "Two Angels" section in 1QS 3.13—4.26 has long been recognized as separable from its current context and as an originally independent composition.[34] From a literary point of view, however, it does not seem to have been the formative unit. On the contrary, a combination of literary and tradition-historical observations has led to the identification of the material in columns 8–9 as the nucleus of the document.[35] To

---

30. Skehan 1971:15–26; Murphy 1981:50. Hezekiah is spelled with an initial *yodh* in 2 Chron 32:23, 27; Hos 1:1; and Mic 1:1, giving a numerical equivalent of 140.

31. The proverbs at the end of Collection "B" (16:12-16) revert to an antithetic form, suggesting that the editor of Collections A+B added a few proverbs to bring the number to 375. This conclusion seems more dubious.

32. Skehan 1971:23–26, 43–45 suggests that the total number of lines in Proverbs (932) is sufficiently close to the numeric equivalents of the three names in Prov 1:1 (Solomon, David, Israel = 930) to make probable the conclusion that the general editor of Proverbs used this numeric schema too. This conclusion seems more dubious.

33. Knibb 1987:77 notes as evidence of a complex compositional process the existence of (a) headings which distinguish separate sections of 1QS; (b) duplicate passages (three statements of the aims of the community [1QS 1.1-15; 5.1-7a; 8.1-4c]; two rules for admission [5.20b-23; 6.13b-23]; two lists of punishments [6.24—7.25; 8.16b—9.2]); and (c) various contradictory statements about leadership (9.7; 5.2b-3a).

34. See D. Allison 1980; Murphy-O'Connor 1969:541–42. Allison argues on grounds of vocabulary and structure that 1QS 4.15-26 was a later addition to 3.13—4.14.

35. Murphy-O'Connor 1969 isolates two strata within 8.1—10.8a, the nucleus (8.1-16a + 9.3—10.8a), and an addition 8.16b-19 + 8.20—9.2 (2d stage). Working independently, Pouilly

this core was added 5.1—7.25, which begins with a new superscription. These two stages have in turn been bracketed by two other blocks. 1QS 1–4, in spite of its superscription ("the book of the rule of the community" [*SPR SRK HYḤD*]),[36] is a miscellaneous block containing a statement of general requirements (1.1-15) followed by the extract of a liturgy of entrance (1.16—2.25a), an admonition concerning those who incompletely submit to the rule (2.25b—3.12) and the "Two Angels" tract (3.13—4.14 + 4.15–26). The closing bracket is a hymn in the first person singular (1QS 10.8—11.22). Murphy-O'Connor identifies 5.13b-15 as a small interpolation into 5.1–7.25. This is because of the abrupt change from third person plural to third person singular address and the fact that 5.13b–15 can be omitted without any loss of sense.[37] He assigns this interpolation to the final redactional stage on the basis of material consistency: like 2.25b—3.12 it is concerned with those who enter the community without fully subscribing to its discipline.[38]

The Didache

The *Didache*, an early second-century Christian composition, is also clearly composite, consisting of a "Two Ways" section (chaps. 1–6), a liturgical manual (7–10), instructions on the reception of traveling prophets (11–15), and a brief apocalypse (16).[39] Marked divergences in style and content as well as the presence of doublets and obvious interpolations make plain the fact that the *Didache* was not cut from whole cloth. The dominant view today is that the document was composed on the basis of several independent, preredactional units which were assembled by either one or two redactors (Niederwimmer 1989:64–70, ET 1998:42–52). Comparison of the "Two Ways" section with several other "Two Ways" documents suggests that *Didache* 1–6 is itself the result of multistage editing. The document began with rather haphazard organization (cf. *Barnabas* 18–20), but was reorganized in a source common to the *Didache*, the *Doctrina apostolorum,* and the *Apostolic Church Order* and supplemented by a sapiential meditation on minor and major transgressions (3.1-6) (Kloppenborg

---

(1976) agreed with only slight modifications. Puech (1979) argues that columns 8–10 form the nucleus, but thinks that the grounds for discerning prior stages of redaction are insufficient. Cf. Knibb 1987:77.

36. The title is missing in the MS. from Cave 1 but available from one of the Cave 4 fragments (4QS*a*).

37. Murphy-O'Connor 1969:546–47. Pouilly (1976:45–50) argues that the whole of 5.13b—6.8a is an interpolation. Puech 1979:107–8 recognizes that 5.13b—6.8a seems to be a doublet but hesitates to see this as an interpolation into 5.1—7.25 (his stage 2).

38. Murphy-O'Connor 1969:546–47; similarly Pouilly 1976:82–83. Murphy-O'Connor does not use the metaphor of stratigraphy for his compositional model, but orally indicated to me that he regards this term as entirely appropriate.

39. See in general, Audet 1958; Giet 1970; Rordorf and Tuilier 1978; Wengst 1984; Niederwimmer 1989 (ET 1998); Jefford 1989; 1995.

1995c). In addition to this "Two Ways" section it is also possible to discern the presence of a mini-apocalypse related to some of the materials that eventually found their way into Matthew 24–25 (Kloppenborg 1979).

The most obvious insertion in the *Didache* is a catena of sayings of Jesus (1.3-6) which interrupts the continuity between 1.1-2 and 2.2. The same hand that added 1.3b-6 (and the transitional phrase in 2.1) appears also to be responsible for a transition in 6.2-3 and for the introduction to the apocalypse (16.1-2), which like 1.3b—2.1 Christianizes the earlier documents by affixing sayings designed to evoke the sayings of Jesus.[40] It seems clear, then, that the composition history of the *Didache* involves at least two originally independent documents (*Did.* 1.1-2; 2.2—6.1; and *Did.* 16.3-8) which were combined with other materials by an editor into a church manual, and "Christianized" by the interpolation of sayings of Jesus.

These documents illustrate three rather different styles of editing. The redactor of Proverbs has left few tracks in the collection itself, contenting himself with juxtaposing originally discrete collections, but without supplying an overarching framework or unifying devices. The editor of 1QS is more intrusive, providing both a framework for the two earlier strata and inserting materials into the middle of those earlier collections. The final editor of the *Didache* is less energetic: his efforts are restricted to the interpolation of 1.3-6 and the creation of transitional phrases in 2.1; 6.1-2; and 16.1-2. He is less an editor than an interpolator.

A Diachronic Approach to the Redaction of Q

Turning to Q, there is now wide agreement on two fundamental and seemingly divergent points. First, at the level of Q as a whole we can speak of Q as a "literary unity" held together by the themes of the announcement of judgment and appeals to the Deuteronomistic view of history and of the fates of the prophets.[41] Second, Q is not homogeneous when taken at the level of its components: a fairly wide variety of forms is represented, various subcollections are present, and these subcollections are organized by a variety of editorial techniques.[42]

The key phenomenon with which diachronic approaches to Q must wrestle is the fact that differing types of organization and rhetoric subsist in the same document. In this respect Q is no different than Proverbs, the Manual

---

40. Niederwimmer (1989:66–70, 256; ET 1998:42–46, 126) assigns 1.3b-2.1; 6.2-3; 12-15 and 16.1-2 to the principal redactor.

41. See above, n. 8.

42. This conclusion was already defended by Bultmann in his only essay on Q (1913, ET 1994). He did not, however, propose an editorial model in which this diversity could be resolved, instead regarding it as a reflection of the varied forces that shaped early Christian tradition.

of Discipline, and the *Didache*. In the past decade several models have been proposed for understanding the relationship among the various parts in Q. In the present context it is not possible to provide a survey of all of the models.[43] Rather, I would like to consider two analyses which illustrate both the important points of consensus as far as methodology is concerned and the key divergences in the application of methods and the final characterization of the nature and genre of Q: Migaku Sato's *Q und Prophetie* (Q and prophecy), completed as a dissertation in 1984 and published in 1988; and the present author's 1984 dissertation (1984a), published in 1987 (=1987a). I select these not because I regard either as definitive but rather because they both represent the convergences and typify the divergences in the modern assessment of Q. Both treat Q as composite and attempt to specify some aspects of its composition history. Sato concludes that Q's organization is ultimately controlled by the model of a prophetic book, while I have argued that it originated as set of instructions that were later expanded.

There are many points of agreement between these authors concerning individual units in Q but, more important, both of these models are fundamentally *literary*: they begin from literary observations concerning the effect of juxtaposing one saying with another or one cluster with another rather than with tradition-historical assumptions regarding the putative age or authenticity of sayings in Q. For both, the final arrangement and order of Q's sayings is the starting point.

Migaku Sato: Q as a Prophetic Book

Sato cites with approval Lührmann's statement that Q stands at "the end of long process of tradition"[44] and hence resists a simple model for the composition of Q that would entail only a single redactional moment. He is doubtful that one can speak of a final redaction at all. On the contrary,

> [t]he document Q was not fixed redactionally all at once but came into existence through a long process of collection, addition, redaction and editing. Q is characterized by *successive reworkings*. (1988:46, ET 1994:177; emphasis original)

Sato begins his analysis with the assumption that the material extending from Q 3:(2-4?), 7-9, 16-17, (21-22) to Q 7:24-28 was redacted as a unit. It is framed by the mention of the Baptist (3:1-6, 7-9, 16-17; 7:18-28) and by the references to the Coming One (3:16; 7:19) and the wilderness around the Jordan (3:3; 7:24). Jesus' initial and final words concern the kingdom (6:20b; 7:28) and the poor (6:20b; 7:22). Q 6:20b-23, 27-35 serve to explicate John's call to repentance in 3:8; and the response of a non-Israelite to

43. See Kloppenborg 1996c for a fuller survey of the history of compositional models.
44. Sato 1988:28 (ET 1994:162) citing Lührmann 1969:84.

Jesus in 7:1-10 resumes themes introduced in John's warning (3:8b) and anticipates the warning in 7:23. The entire unit may have been apophtheg-matized—that is, given a concrete setting—by the addition of Q 4:16 and 6:20a.[45] Sato concludes that "it is therefore probable that the finished complex represents a consciously composed literary unity which has in view the relationship of Jesus to the Baptist in particular" (1988:35, ET 1994:167). He calls this document "Redaction A."

Redaction A contains a few secondary additions, however. Sato excludes 7:31-35 despite the fact that it concerns the relation of John to Jesus. He does so because it introduces the new theme of "this generation" and shifts its address from the sympathetic public to the unbelieving masses. The temptation story and Q 7:27 are both excluded from Redaction "A" as later interpolations, the former because it has no obvious links with John, because it expressly quotes the LXX, and because it employs the title "Son of God," and the latter because it likewise introduces a biblical quotation with "it is written" (γέγραπται) and associates John with Elijah (1988:34–36, ET 1994:166–68).[46]

Sato also identifies earlier collections (*Spruchsammlungen*) embraced by Redaction A, most notably 3:7-9, 16-17, and 6:20b-49, the latter containing in turn several smaller sayings clusters. Q 6:39-40 and perhaps 6:43-45, however, are more recent additions than Redaction A (1988:36, 45, ET 1994:166, 176).

A second early constituent document is Redaction B. This begins with one chria (Q 9:57-58) and concludes with another one (10:21-24). The introductory phrase of 10:21 ("at that time") refers back to the first chria, hence, constituted the entire unit as a pragmatic unity and bracketing the intervening material. The unit depicts Jesus as twice testing the disciples, then commissioning them, and finally giving thanks to God for the revelation of eschatological salvation (10:21; cf. 10:5-6, 9). A makarism introduced by λέγω ὑμῖν ("I tell you," 10:23-24) signals the end of the unit (1988:37, ET 1994:169). Sato holds that this too was an originally independent source which was secondarily joined to Redaction A by means of 7:31-35, which was attracted to the preceding material by mention of John and to the following by the catchword "Son of Man" (7:34; 9:58).

Like Redaction A, Redaction B has undergone secondary glossing. Q

45. This is the view taken in the 1984 dissertation (40). In the 1988 version, Sato maintains that "one should take note of the strong apophthegmatizing of the entire complex [3:2–7:28]" (1988:35, ET 167) but omits the references to 4:16 and 6:20a. He includes these two items in Q "with greater caution" (1988:24–25).

46. Sato 1988:36 seems to suggest that Q 4:1-2a (par. Mark 1:12-13) may have belonged to Redaction "A" and that this was later expanded. This point is made more clearly in the typescript of 1984 (1984:41), where he also expresses some hesitation about 3:21-22. That the entire paragraph is dropped in 1988 suggests that he now includes 3:21-22 in Q and in Redaction "A."

10:12, 13-15 interrupts the connection between Q 10:10-11 and Q 10:16.[47]
Sato also regards Q 10:22 as an interpolation, since it employs the title
"Son" and like 4:3, 9 seems to presuppose the baptismal theophany of Q
3:21-22. Like Redaction A, Redaction B comprises smaller collections,
notably 10:3-11 to which Q 10:2 and Q 10:16 were added at the time of the
assembling of that source (1988:38, ET 1994:169–70).

The Beelzebul controversy and the Request for a Sign provide Sato with
his key to a main compositional stage of Q. Since these two pericopae refer
to the Heavenly Sophia (11:31), the Son of Man (11:30), and opposition to
"this generation" (11:29-32), they must be related to Q 7:31-35, where
these terms also appear. Since Q 7:31-35 is the redactional clasp which connects Redaction A with Redaction B, Q 11:14-32 must also belong to this
secondary compositional stratum. Sato christens this Redaction C. This
stage is not quite comparable with the two preceding redactions, since it
does not form a continuous unit. Instead it brings together the two preceding strata by framing them with materials critical of "this generation." Sato
also assigns the woes against the Pharisees (11:39-52) to Redaction C. The
woes seem to have been a smaller sayings collection (*Spruchsammlung*) that
was glossed with 11:49-51, which mentions both Sophia and "this generation," two of the key terms in Redaction C (Sato 1988:40–41, ET
1994:172). Another cluster of sayings (13:23-24, 25-27, 28-29, 34-35) is
unified by the motifs of judgment and condemnation. Although this cluster
lacks the phrase "this generation," the tone of 13:23-35 agrees with other
materials from Redaction C, and 13:34-35 in particular bears the marks of
a saying of Sophia (1988:42–43, ET 1994:173–74). To Redaction C also
belongs Q 17:23-37, which employs the Son of Man title and emphasizes
the universality of judgment. Sato explains the lack of the motifs of Sophia,
"this generation," and a specific judgment of Israel by the supposition that
17:23-37 was an early collection that was incorporated into Redaction C en
bloc.[48]

Several clusters of sayings present Sato with difficulties. He acknowledges
that Q 11:2-4, 9-13 was a fixed cluster on prayer and that its position—
before Q 11:14-26, 29-32—is relatively certain. Yet he describes its location
in Q as "completely unmotivated." Likewise, 11:33-35 seems to fit with
neither 11:14-32 nor 11:39-52 (1988:39–40, ET 1994:171). A further small
collection that does not fit is Q 12:2-12, 22-31, 33-34, formed around a
core of 12:4-12 and subsequently augmented by 12:2-3 and 12:22-31.
Q 12:39-46 and 12:49–13:21 are also smaller clusters, but in both instances,
the connection with 11:39-52 or 13:23-35 is difficult to fathom.

This causes a dilemma. Would Redaction C have interposed 12:2-12, 22-

---

47. Sato 1988:45 (ET 1994:176) suggests that 10:12, 13-15 are added by Redaction C.
48. Q 19:12-27 and 22:28-30, according to Sato, are only doubtfully ascribed to Q and cannot be assigned to any redactional stratum.

34, and 12:39–13:21 between 11:39-52 and 13:23-35 when the former had so little material connection with the main themes of Redaction C? Sato considers two possibilities: either Redaction C incorporated this material "without a compositional plan" or, more likely, the lack of clear organization is due not to Redaction C at all, but to various "unsystematic interpolations and additions" *subsequent* to Redaction C (1988:43, ET 1994:174).[49] Further, he is doubtful whether the double tradition material that falls between 13:35 and 17:23 (i.e., 14:16-24, 26, 27, 34-35; 15:4-7; 16:16-18; 17:1, 3-4, 6) or Q 19:12-27 and 22:28-30 can be ascribed to Q at all. In any event, he sees no way to integrate these sayings into one of his redactional strata.[50] This process of successive and sometimes "unsystematic" expansions becomes logistically possible for Sato if Q is visualized as a notebook or loose-leaf book (*Ringbuch*) into which additional sheets might easily be inserted (1988:62–65, ET 1994:178).

The principal difficulty with the scenario proposed by Sato is that a large amount of Q is relegated to the status of "unmotivated" or "unsystematic" accretions. Indeed, the scale on which these unmotivated additions occurs creates a stark contrast with the very deliberate character of Sato's three principal redactions. That half of a document is the result of controlled editorial activity and half is the result of unsystematic accretion is, of course, possible, but surely not a happy scenario. Moreover, Sato is unable to decide whether substantial blocks such as 12:2-12, 22-34, and 12:39—13:21 are early or late relative to Redaction C. Much of his argument depends on the plausibility of the suggestion that Q was constructed like a *Ringbuch*. While Sato offers evidence of the existence of notebooks, he provides no evidence that literary works were ever composed using a "loose-leaf" model.[51]

A secondary problem is created by Sato's suggestion that Redaction A was compiled to deal with the issue of the relation between John and Jesus. The amount of material in this putative redaction is such that it cannot have been simply an oral cluster; it is far too long for this and must have been a document. It may be doubted, however, whether debate with the Baptist disciples would provide a sufficient motivation for the composition and transmission of this unit. Much of the content of Redaction A has nothing to do

49. In a footnote Sato (1988:43 n. 99, ET 1994:174 n. 34) considers the possibility that 12:2-34 was incorporated prior to Redaction C.

50. Sato (1988:23, 43 + n. 101) is convinced that 16:13 belonged to Q and that 16:16-18 constituted a "chain" of sayings, although he cannot place either in any redactional stratum.

51. That the notebook (Lat. *caudex*), consisting of one to ten thin wooden leaves, either whitened or covered with wax and strung together with thongs, was in use in the first century is clear from literary references, material remains, and artistic representations (e.g., a fresco from Pompeii depicting a woman with four tablets [*pugillares*] joined as a notebook in the Museo Archeologico Nazionale, Naples). Sometime in the first century small parchment codices were developed (probably in Rome; Quintilian 10.3.31-32). While both wax tablets and parchment leaves could be erased, there is no evidence of Sato's proposed procedure of adding leaves to an existing notebook. On notebooks, see Gamble 1995:49–59.

with the Baptist. Sato makes no suggestion regarding the original function of his Redaction B, which is much shorter than Redaction A. But the *Sitz im Leben* of Redaction B cannot be restricted to the envoys sent out, since, as Sato (rightly) observes, Q 10:2 (and 10:21, 23-24) are directed at a wider audience. Nevertheless, while Q 9:57—10:24 is extensive enough to require literary rather than oral transmission, it is scarcely comparable in length to other known church rules.

The Genre of Q. Sato's monograph not only presents a compositional analysis of Q but argues the case that Q was modeled on a prophetic book. The analogy of prophetic books is appealing insofar as both the prophetic books of the Tanak and Q were formed through an extended process of growth. This point, of course, is scarcely probative. For even if Sato were right about the process of the composition of Q, nonprophetic books—for example, Proverbs, *1 Enoch,* and the *Didache*—are also the results of extended compositional processes.

The heart of Sato's case is built on a comparison of Q and prophetic books on the level of major structural features. Three features are fundamental to prophetic books. First is the claim to an immediate divine origin of the sayings contained in the book, expressed in formulas such as "thus says the Lord" (τάδε λέγει ὁ κύριος) and "the Word which came from the Lord to NN son of NN." Second, Sato observes that the naming of the human tradent of the divine sayings is a constant feature; there are no anonymous prophetic books. Finally, prophetic books typically contain a variety of prophetic micro-genres, including call narratives, visions, proclamations of salvation or condemnation, oracles of doom, woes and makarisms, and admonitions. Conversely, they lack parables and miracle stories, and they never provide an account of the death of the prophet.

Each of these characteristics, Sato argues, is evidenced in Q. The claim to a divine origin of the sayings is found in Q 10:16 ("Whoever receives you receives me, and whoever receives me receives the one who sent me") and 10:22 ("All things are given me by my Father"). Q 11:49 has Jesus quoting an oracle of the "Wisdom of God" and confirming it with his own authority (11:51b: "Yes, I tell you . . ."). Q differs from prophetic books only insofar as it is prepared to make exclusive claims on behalf of Jesus' mediation of divine revelation that prophetic books do not.

Even though the incipit of Q cannot be reconstructed with certainty, there is little doubt that Q identified Jesus as the speaker of most of its sayings. Sato notes that no prophetic book presents *two* prophets simultaneously;[52] yet it is undeniable that Q also represented John as a prophet (Q 7:26) and attributes to him prophetic sayings (3:7-9, 16-17). Sato argues, however, that John has no independent significance in Q. He is subordinated to Jesus

---

52. In Jer 26:18 an oracle of Micah is recalled; but Micah was not a contemporary of Jeremiah (Sato 1988:79).

or juxtaposed to him because both suffered the same fate of rejection (Q 7:33-35).

In both what Q contains and what it lacks, Sato sees indications of a prophetic genre. The baptismal account (Luke 3:21-22), which he ascribes to Q, affords an analogy for both the prophetic call story and perhaps even a prophetic vision (although Sato hesitates because the reconstruction of Q is here in doubt). In addition, Q contains a variety of prophetic speech forms: prophetic announcements, oracles of salvation and doom, invectives, woes, admonitions, makarisms, and "eschatological correlatives,"[53] and at each of Sato's compositional levels.

Like prophetic books, Q also has few parables and similitudes and those it does relate (7:31-32; 12:39, 42-46; 13:18-21) do not function as teaching devices. Instead they are used as polemical sayings against "this generation." It is at this point that the consequences of his compositional analysis become clear, for Sato excludes from Q the parabolic materials in Luke 14–19, which include the Parables of the Great Supper, the Lost Sheep (and Lost Drachma), and the Entrusted Money. Like prophetic books, Q shows no interest in miracle stories as such but transforms both 7:1-10 and 11:14-15 into chriae. Finally, Q's lack of a passion story makes it comparable with prophetic books, which typically do not narrate the prophets' death.

Sato is of course correct in noting the substantial contribution of prophetic speech patterns to Q and in arguing that any discussion of the genre of Q must take these into account. In this respect Sato is right in noting the deficiencies in the characterization of Q as a whole as sapiential. His compositional analysis establishes a literary unity in Q, however, only by truncating the materials in Luke 14:16—17:6; 19:12-27; 22:28-30 and by characterizing significant blocks as "unmotivated" additions. All things are possible, but this is surely not a very "clean" solution.

More important, Q lacks the principal generic markers of a prophetic book. As Sato rightly insists, prophetic books make explicit the claim that the words of the book represent divine speech. But it is important to note *how* this is established. In Isaiah, for example, the book opens by reporting a vision (1:1) in which the Lord speaks. Variations on this formula appear repeatedly (1:2, 10, 11, 18, 24). The book is peppered by references to visions and oracles which Isaiah received (2:1; 6:1; 7:3; 8:1, 11; 13:1; 14:28; etc.). Similarly, Jeremiah begins with the formula "The word of YWHH first came to [Jeremiah] in the days of Josiah, son of Amon, king of Judah, in the thirteenth year of his reign" (1:2). Such formulas as "This word of YHWH came to me . . ." appear throughout. These framing devices leave no doubt as to the nature of the speech.

When one turns to Q, such generic markers are not nearly so clear. If one could reconstruct the beginning of Q with Luke 3:1-2, "In the fifteenth year of Tiberius . . . the word of the Lord came to John son of Zechariah in the

---

53. More accurately termed prophetic comparisons: see D. Schmidt 1977.

wilderness," one might have the beginnings of an argument, at least for the presentation of *John* as a prophet. Such a reconstruction finds no support, however. The use of synchronicities is Lukan (cf. 1:5; Acts 12:1); only Luke reports the name of John's father; and the depiction of John as a prophet is strongly embedded in Lukan theology.[54] While the baptism of Jesus obviously serves a legitimating function, it does not obviously imitate prophetic call stories. As I have suggested in chapter 2, the grounds for attributing it to Q are dubious at best. More important, when Jesus is first introduced in 6:20, there are no indications at all of prophetic speech formulas. As Shawn Carruth (1995) has observed, Q's sermon lacks any appeal to external authority, including God. Ronald Piper's study of several other Q subcollections has shown the same: the argumentative strategy of Q is not to command but to persuade via appeals to experience and nature.[55] The λέγω ὑμῖν ("I tell you") and τίς ἐξ ὑμῶν ("who among you") formulas that Schulz (1972:57–61) and others once labeled as "prophetic"—equivalents to "Thus says the Lord"—are hardly so. "Who among you" normally introduces wisdom statements expecting the answer "everybody, of course" or "nobody." There is no indication at all that "I tell you" makes a claim equivalent to "Thus says the Lord."

To make matters worse, Q offers a sharp contrast with prophetic books: *In Q God never speaks.* John speaks; Jesus speaks; Jesus and the devil quote the Hebrew Bible; and once (or perhaps twice: 11:49-51a; 13:34-35) Jesus *quotes* an oracle of Sophia. But God's voice is never heard directly. This does not mean that Q represents Jesus' speech as debatable or nondefinitive: on the contrary, faithful adherence to Jesus' words is a fundamental criterion for Q (6:46-49) and Q is careful to establish that Jesus' words via the disciples have the authority of divine speech (10:16). But none of this employs the specific generic markers of prophetic books. Again, we must be clear: Q contains forms that also appear in prophetic books, as Sato has recently reiterated (1995); but Q is not *framed* as a prophetic book.

Sato's other fundamental characteristic of prophecy—that it is invariably ascribed to a named figure—is just as invariably a characteristic of sapiential collections, as the present author has shown in an extensive survey of Near Eastern and Greek wisdom collections.[56]

Finally, in the attempt to characterize Q's subforms as dominantly prophetic, Sato classifies many clusters of sayings (6:27-35, 36-37a, 38c; 12:2-7, 22-31) and a large group of sapiential admonitions as "prophetic"

---

54. See especially Schürmann 1969–84, 1:152, who points out Luke's imitation, here and elsewhere, of Jer 1:1, 11; Gen 15:1, 4; Ezek 1:3; Hos 1:1; and Zech 1:1.

55. Piper (1989) detects a consistent structural pattern in Q 6:37-42; 6:43-45; 11:9-13; 12:2-9; 12:22-31, and extends his analysis to related clusters in 6:27-28, 31-36; 6:29-30; 12:33b-34; 12:58-59; 13:23-24; and 17:3b-4.

56. Kloppenborg 1987a:263–316. Virtually all known sapiential instructions and proverb collections are attributed to a named sage when an incipit is extant.

simply because (a) they use the second person plural, (b) they envisage a relatively narrowly defined audience, (c) they contain "specifically prophetic [!] speech elements" such as "fear not" (Q 12:4-6, 7b), and (d) they reflect the conviction that the eschaton is come (1988:225). None of this is convincing. In a later article (1995) Sato appears to retreat from this claim, arguing instead that originally nonprophetic sayings were indirectly "prophetized" and directed toward Q's eschatological expectations through incorporation into Q. This is a very different type of argument, for it shifts from formal and generic considerations to content and theology. This topic will occupy us in chapter 8, but for now what is important to note is that it is illegitimate to conclude from the fact that (some of) the sayings in Q have an eschatological orientation that the book *as a whole* is framed as a prophetic book. No one would seriously argue that the Wisdom of Solomon, which has similar eschatological interests, is prophetic; it contains none of the formal markers of prophecy. Nor does Q. One cannot confuse theological characterization with formal or generic description. Both are important, but they are not the same thing.[57]

J. S. Kloppenborg: Q as an Expanded Instruction

Rather than beginning with putative subcollections or "redactions" and proceeding, as it were, chronologically from simplest unit to the most complex, I worked backwards from the macrostructural features of Q to its constituent sayings complexes and sayings clusters. As has been noted above (pp. 188–22), Q appears to have been framed by the motifs of judgment, polemic against "this generation," and Deuteronomistic understanding of history. I would now add that allusions to the story of Lot also belong to this redaction (above, pp. 119–21). Not only do these motifs appear at the beginning and end of Q; they are found as the organizing principles in four, and perhaps five, blocks throughout the collection:

1. Q 3:(2-3),[58] 7-9, 16b-17, containing allusions to the story of Lot; John's announcement of coming judgment; a call to repentance; and a

---

57. A useful analogy is provided by B. Scott (1993), who argues that Matthew 24–25 is a "sapiential performance of an apocalyptic discourse." Matthew offers a "scribal reading" of Mark's apocalypse shifting many of its futuristic statements into the present. Even though apocalyptic is itself a scribal phenomenon (Smith 1975b; repr. in Smith 1978:67–87), Matthew's reading of Mark 13 represents "the final deconstruction of the apocalyptic form—the seer not only does not know the hour, but having given the sign of the Son of man, the seer plants doubts about one's certainty of its application" (B. Scott 1993:262). Analogously, Q may use prophetic language at points, but that does not make it prophecy.

58. Although in 1987a (and 1988a) I did not consider elements in 3:3 as deriving from Q, more recently I have argued that Q began with an allusion to the Lot story of Genesis 19, and that this served fittingly as an introduction to the other materials in the framing redaction, in particular, 3:7-9; 10:12, 13-15; and 17:28-30. See Kloppenborg 1990a and chap. 2 above (pp. 94–95).

challenge to the security of Israelite identity;

2. Q 7:1-10, 18-28, 31-35, using a Gentile to shame Israel; and describing the rejection of John and Jesus as prophets and envoys of Sophia;

3. Q 11:14-15, 16, 17-26, (27-28), 29-32, 33-36, 39b-44, 46-52, containing several instances of the nonrecognition of Jesus; announcements of judgment; representing the prophets as envoys of Sophia; calls to recognition and repentance; and the use of Gentiles to shame Israel; and

4. Q 17:23-24, 37b, 26-30, 34-35; 19:12-27; 22:28-30 with allusions to the story of Lot; the announcement of coming judgment; a challenge to prevailing apocalyptic scenarios; and the judgment of Israel.

To this might be added

5. Q 12:39-40, 42b-46, 49, 50-53, 54-59, containing an announcement of coming judgment; admonitions to preparedness; and a call to recognition (and repentance?) (see Kloppenborg 1986:450; 1987:102–70).

As was noted above, what suggests that this set of redactional themes represents the perspective of the main redaction of Q is not just that they are distributed throughout the document, but the specific locations of their occurrence: at the beginning of the document and at its end, and at the beginning and endings of subcollections such as Q 3:2–17 (passim); 7:1-35 (esp. 7:1-10, 31-35); 11:14-52 (esp. 11:14-23, 49-51); 12:39-59 (esp. 12:39-40, 42-46; 12:57-59); 17:23–22:28 (esp. 17:28-30; 22:28-30). The point here is that both in terms of the structuring of these subcollections and of Q as a whole, the themes of judgment, Lot, and the Deuteronomistic view of history and of the prophets are determinative.

This set of themes is not distributed evenly throughout Q, but tends to cluster in several subcollections. Other clusters of sayings are untouched or minimally influenced by such themes: Q 6:20b-49; 9:57—10:24; 11:2-4, 9-13 and 12:2-7, (8-9), 11-12; and 12:22b-31, 33-34. What unites these subcollections is not only that they lack features of the main redaction; they also evince an interlocking set of concerns which have to do with the legitimation of a somewhat adventuresome social practice—including debt forgiveness, the eschewing of vengeance, and the embracing of an exposed and marginal lifestyle. This legitimation is accomplished by reference to a God who is generous to enemies and friends alike, who is superabundantly provident, and whose activities are best perceived not in the aspects of "high culture" and wealth but in nature and the simplest of human transaction.

Two other features are noteworthy. First, as Piper has shown, these clusters share a common rhetoric—the rhetoric of persuasion, rather than that of prophetic pronouncement or declamation. This rhetoric focuses not on defending the ethos (character) of Jesus or those associated with him or on attacking opponents; that is the rhetorical strategy of the main redaction.

Instead, these subcollections are deliberative, enjoining a particular way of life. There is no defense or legitimation of the ethos of Jesus; it is simply taken for granted that Jesus is a reliable and authoritative teacher. Second, these subcollections display a common structure, beginning with program-matic sayings (6:20b-23; 9:57-60; 11:2-4; 12:2-3; 13:24), continuing with second person imperatives, and concluding with a saying that underscores the importance of the instructions (6:47-49; 10:16, 23-24; 12:33-34; 14:34-35). In other words, in terms of thematic organization, rhetorical posture, and structure, the six above-mentioned clusters show themselves to cohere as a group and, in all likelihood, as a discrete redactional stratum.

The key question is, what is the relationship between these two sets of Q materials, which for convenience I shall call (anticipating my conclusion) Q^1 or "the formative stratum" and Q^2, "the main redaction"? Do they coexist at the same compositional level? Or do they represent successive layers, and if so, what is the sequence? Are clusters like 11:2-4, 9-13, and 12:22-34 later "unsystematic" additions, as Sato suggests? Or do they belong at an earlier compositional stage?

Analogies from other documents—for example, *1 Enoch*—indicate that there are no a priori grounds for thinking that deliberative or hortatory materials cannot subsist in the same document with other materials. Of course, at the level of the final form of Q, they do. The examples of *1 Enoch*,[59] along with Proverbs, the *Manual of Discipline*, and the *Didache*, underscore the problem at hand, for each is clearly composite or stratified, even if some level of redaction could compass the diverse elements repre-sented.[60] The composition history of Q, however, cannot be settled by merely adducing parallels, since parallels can be cited on all sides of the debate.[61] There are two questions that are germane: does the actual deploy-

---

59. In fact *1 Enoch* is itself clearly composite, even the Book of Watchers (*1 Enoch* 1–36), whose author according to Milik (1976:25) incorporated an earlier written source (*1 Enoch* 6–19) virtually unchanged, rewriting chapters 20–25, and contributing chapters 1–5, 26–36 himself. Hartman's study of chapters 1–5 (1979:138–45) notes that while there are thematic and semantic continuities between 1–5 and 6–36, the two sections evince significantly differ-ent assumptions on the nature of evil, nature's orderliness, and covenental categories.

60. Ironically, in his efforts to refute stratigraphic analyses of Q, Horsley (1991a:207–9) adduces the analogy of the organization of the *Didache*—a document whose composite and stratified nature is beyond doubt!

61. As J. Collins (1993) attempts to do. He devotes an article to showing, ostensibly against my analysis (1987a), that "there is no generic incompatibility . . . between [wisdom] speeches and an apocalyptic worldview. . . . [W]e should beware of imposing our ideals of generic purity" (1993:185). He suggests further that apologetic interests are at work in my suggestion that Q does not evince a full-blown apocalypticism (though he never explains what those apologetic interests might be).

This is a straw-man argument since I did not argue that wisdom was incompatible with apocalyptic or prophecy and expressly rejected "generic purity" arguments. The argument for

ment of these materials in Q suggest *from a literary point of view* that they were created or at least edited from a unitary perspective? If not, are there "stratigraphic markers"—literary features—that indicate the direction or vector of the relationship of one set of materials to the other?

The first question is best answered in the negative. The elements of Q that are most obviously related to the main redaction described above are unevenly distributed in Q and do not control the composition of all of the subsections. Some of the subcollections such as 6:20b-49; 11:2-4, 9-11; 12:22-31, 33-34 are wholly (or almost wholly) untouched by the features of the main redaction, but do evince a common structure, rhetorical posture, and a set of rhetorical concerns of their own. In this respect Sato's compositional scenario is unnecessarily complex. He treats 6:20b-49 as early (from a compositional viewpoint) but relegates similarly structured materials in 11:2-4, 9-11 and 12:22-31, 33-34 to later unsystematic additions. It would seem preferable to consider all related materials together, and to posit two strata, "the formative stratum" (Q^1) and "the main redaction" (Q^2).

What I suggest is that one level of Q can be discerned, consisting of several clusters of sayings that are not united by the themes typical of the main redaction, but by paraenetic, hortatory, and instructional concerns:

1. Q 6:20b-23b, 27-35, 36-45, 46-49
2. Q 9:57-60, (61-62); 10:2-11, 16, (23-24?)
3. Q 11:2-4, 9-13
4. Q 12:2-7, 11-12
5. Q 12:22b-31, 33-34 (13:18-19, 20-21?) and probably
6. Q 13:24; 14:26-27; 17:33; 14:34-35.[62]

This brings us to the second question, that of the vector or direction of the relation of one set to another. On what basis are these subcollections designated as "formative" and the other materials as "redaction"? It is at this point that stratigraphic markers are critical. In the case of Proverbs it was difficult to trace the compositional history precisely because one collection is laid alongside another; there are few points where the redactional

---

the stratification of Q does not rest on presumptions about the (in)compatibility of wisdom and apocalyptic, much less on any assumptions about the character of Jesus' preaching; it proceeds from an analysis of the *actual literary deployment* of Q sayings, noting aporia, abrupt disjunction, changes in rhetorical and argumentative mode. In other words, it depends on *literary* not theological factors. The question is not whether wisdom and apocalyptic, or wisdom and prophecy, can subsist in the same document; of course they can and do in various documents. The question is, when diverse elements subsist in a document, how does one understand the *literary* and *generic* relationship among the various elements? Collins's misunderstanding is tediously repeated by others: Horsley 1994:736; Witherington 1994:216; D. Allison 1997:4–5.

62. Kloppenborg 1986b (repr. 1994a); 1987a:171–245. More recently, I also suggested that Q 13:18-21 was perhaps attached to Q 12:22b-31, 33-34 (1995b:311) and that Q 15:4-7, 8-10; 16:13, 16, 18; 17:1-2, 3-4, 6 belong to the earliest level of Q (1995b:314–15).

concerns of one collection have intruded into those of another. In the case of the *Didache* and 1QS, by contrast, literary features provide a key to composition history.

The clearest instance of an interpolation is Q 10:12, 13-15. Q 9:57—10:24 treats the activities of those whom Q calls "workers" (10:2, 7), who are evidently to travel without provisions and rely upon the hospitality of the villages they visit. The bulk of the unit concerns the ethos of those workers: they are to emulate the homelessness of Jesus and to consider former ties as nonbinding (9:57-60, [61-62?]); they are to travel in a vulnerable and exposed manner (10:3, 4-7a), relying on hospitality (10:8) and offering benefits in exchange (10:9). This unit also provides the justification for the activity of these workers: they are engaged in a "harvest" in which the Q group cooperates with God (10:2); they are treated as workers who deserve payment (food and lodging, 10:7b); and their activities are part of a divine sending (10:3, 16) which represents a culmination of history (10:23-24).[63]

The most obvious distraction in this unit is Q 10:12, 13-15. The woes against the Galilean towns not only represent an abrupt shift of rhetorical stance, from instruction to prophetic woe, but break an original connection between 10:10-11 and 10:16 based on the term "welcome" (δέχομαι).[64]

> 10 Whenever you enter a town and they do not *welcome* (δέχωνται) you, go outside the town and (11) shake off the dust from your feet.
> 12 I tell you that *it will be more tolerable* for Sodom on that day *than* for *that* town.
> 13 Woe to you, Khorazin; woe to you Bethsaida! For if the wonders that had been done among you had occurred in Tyre and Sidon, they would have repented long ago, sitting in sackcloth and ashes. 14 Indeed at the judgment *it will be more tolerable* for Tyre and Sidon *than* for you. 15 And you, Kefar Naḥum, will you be exalted to heaven? No, you will be brought down to Hades.
> 16 Whoever *welcomes* (δεχόμενος) you welcomes (δέχεται) me, and whoever welcomes (δεχόμενος) me welcomes (δέχεται) the one who who sent me.

The process by which Q 10:13-15 was added can be reconstructed: Q 10:10-11 raised the possibility of the nonreception of the "laborers" and the

63. In Kloppenborg 1987:201–3, I treated 10:23-24 as part of the secondary redaction of Q (along with 10:21-22). Q 10:21-22, because of several anomalous features, has proved difficult to place in the composition history of Q, though most tend to put it relatively late. Q 10:23-24, however, is less problematic. Since it does not obviously evince the themes typically associated with the major redaction of Q, it may be taken as the positive counterpart to 9:57-60, (61-62) and located accordingly in the redaction history of Q. Kirk (1998:310–12), however, considers 10:23-24 to be the beginning of the next unit of Q rather than the conclusion of Q 9:57—10:22.

64. The IQP reconstructs Q 10:10, 16 as [[εἰς ἣν δ´]] ἂν [[πόλιν εἰσέλθητε καὶ]] μὴ δέχωνται ὑμᾶς, ἐξερχόμενοι [[ἔξω]] [[τῆς πόλεως ἐκείν]]ης· . . . 16 ὁ δεχόμενος ὑμᾶς ἐμὲ δέχεται, [[καὶ]] ὁ ἐμὲ δεχόμενος δέχεται τὸν ἀποστείλαντά με. At Q 10:10 Matthew and Luke agree in using δέχομαι; at Q 10:16 the IQP favors Matthew's δέχομαι over Luke's ἀκούω.

issue of inhospitality in turn triggered the reference to Sodom and its fate (10:12). Q 10:13-15, which deals not with inhospitality but impenitence and hybris, is connected to the preceding on the basis of the repeated formula "it will be more tolerable" and the logic of comparing a notorious city to an Israelite town or village. The shift in perspective is dramatic, for 10:13-15 looks back on impenitence and unresponsiveness as an accomplished fact, not as something that is to be anticipated. Moreover, the direct address to Kefar Naḥum in 10:15 relates back to 7:1 (belonging to the main redactional stratum), where Jesus marvels at a Gentile's faith as he enters the town. Catchpole rightly notes that "the secondariness of Q 10:13-15 in their present (Luke/Q) context is beyond doubt" (Catchpole 1991:162; cf. Kloppenborg 1996c:18–19).

Not only is 10:13-15 an editorial intrusion; 10:12 is one of the best candidates for a saying *created* by the editor of Q.[65] The phrase "for that town" in 10:12 points backward to and depends on "town" in v. 10. For this reason, v. 12 cannot have existed independently of 10:10-11. The parallel between 10:12 and 10:14 suggests that v. 12 was patterned on v. 14. So long as 10:2-11, (16) and 10:13-15 circulated independently, v. 12 would hardly be needed. Only when the woe oracle was appended to the mission instruction was a transitional phrase necessary. Since 10:12 concerns judgment and evokes the Lot cycle, it is a prime candidate for Q^{Red}.[66]

To return to the issue of the composition of Q: since the woes against the Galilean towns—which call for repentance, pronounce doom, and engage in the same "shaming" technique that is seen in Q 3:7-9; 7:1-10; 11:19, 31-32—cohere with other elements of the main redaction of Q, and since 10:12 reflects the very specific redactional interest in the fate of Sodom, Q 10:12, 13-15 should be assigned to that redactional phrase too. It would be difficult to argue that the "mission speech" as a whole was assembled from or con-

---

65. Thus Lührmann 1969:62–63; Hoffmann 1972:288, 303; Jacobson 1978:192; 1978b:421, 422; 1982b:421; 1992b:145; Kloppenborg 1986b:452; 1987a:195–96, 199; Laufen 1980:274–75; Neirynck 1982b:65, 69; Sato 1988:38 (ET 1994:170); Schenk 1981:55; Schmithals 1980:123; Uro 1987:100, 168; Vaage 1987:274–75; 1994:108, 112; D. Zeller 1982:404 [ET 1994:125].

66. Neirynck observes the structural similarity between 11:51b; 13:35b; and 10:12: in each case a λέγω ὑμῖν ("I tell you") formula introduces a threat of judgment for those who rejected Jesus' envoys and a condemnation of those who rejected Jesus' ministry (1982:66–67). Since all three evince themes characteristic of the main redaction of Q, he concludes that all three are most likely due Q^{Red}. With this judgment I concur. See Kloppenborg 1996c:19–21.

The principal dissenters from the view that 10:12 is redactional are Schulz (1972:409 + n. 40, 418 n. 102), who thinks that 10:12 is an integral part of 10:2-12, and D. Zeller (1994:125; cf. 1984:46–47) who holds that v. 12 is secondary, but was part of the preceding unit (10:4-12) because it was this verse that occasioned the addition of Q 10:13-15. This, of course, ignores the parallel between 10:12 and 10:14 which is too striking to be coincidental. Catchpole (1991:163–64) is hesitant: he notes the striking parallels with 10:13-15, which are normally viewed as additions to 10:2-11, but observes that v. 12 is a smooth and uncomplicated continuation of v. 11a, consistent with the topic of (refusal of) hospitality.

trolled by this perspective.[67] On the contrary, the woe oracle, while not unrelated to the content of 10:2-11, 16, has every appearance of a later insertion. Its foreign nature no doubt explains why Matthew could so easily dislocate it and move it (along with Q 10:21-22) to the second part of Matthew 11, where he commences a sustained attack on a series of opponents.

There are at least two other instances of intrusive sayings interpolated into the midst of clusters that do not otherwise evince the themes of the main redaction: Q 6:23c ("for thus they did to the prophets before you") is widely regarded as intrusive[68] on literary grounds—it is redundant after 6:23b—and it expresses the deuteronomistic motif of the killing of the prophets. Moreover, this phrase is unattested in the parallel versions of the persecution makarism found in the *Gos.Thom.* 68, 69a; 1 Pet 3:14; 4:13-14; and Clement of Alexandria, *Strom.* 4.6.41.2. Since it is thematically related to other Q sayings such as 11:49-51 and 13:34-35, and more broadly, to the efforts to relate Jesus and his activities to the epic history of Israel (3:7-9; 10:13-15; 11:30-32; 13:28-29), this phrase is most plausibly associated with the redactional stratum in which those pericopae appear.

Similarly, Q 12:8-9, 10 rather abruptly shifts the theme of the discourse (12:2-7, 11-12) from encouragement to proclaim the disclosure of kingdom to confession of Jesus (12:8-9) and blasphemy of Jesus and the Spirit (12:10). Q 12:8-10, moreover, interrupts the logical and semantic connection between 12:4-7 and 12:11-12 based on the admonitions, "fear not" (μὴ φοβεῖσθε) and "do not be anxious" (μὴ μεριμνήσητε).[69] The discourse as a whole encourages a distinctive comportment on the part of the addressees in the face of hostility (12:4-7, 11-12) and physical deprivation (12:22-31, 33-34), and does so by adducing the power (12:4-5) and loving surveillance of God (12:6-7, 24-31), and the ineluctable disclosure of the kingdom and its benefits (12:2, 31). With 12:8-10, the qualifications of the speaker (Jesus) and the issue of "name-calling" (i.e., blasphemy) enter the horizon in a way that they are not present before or after. Since the concern to defend the unique qualifications of Jesus as an envoy of God is a preoccu-

---

67. Jacobson (1992b:147–48) agrees that the "mission speech" was not originally assembled from the perspective of the Deuteronomistic redaction. Thus, 9:59-60; 10:3, 4-11, 16 existed as a unit, and 9:57-58; 10:2; and 10:12, 13-15 were added in the Deuteronomistic redaction. Jacobson's connection of 9:57-58 with the redactional stratum is based on its use of the "Son of Man" title and its alleged theme of rejection. He also argues that 10:2 expresses the theme of coming judgment. Neither of these is convincing: Q 9:57-58 concerns homelessness rather than rejection, and the use of "harvest" in 10:2 is not obviously an evocation of the motif of judgment. In a fundamentally agricultural economy, harvest is more directly a metaphor of fulfillment, reward (hence the mention of the "payment" of the workers in Q 10:7b), and consummation.

68. See especially Steck 1967:259–60; Kloppenborg 1986a; Sato 1988:259; Jacobson 1992b:100; Tuckett 1996:180.

69. For details, see Kloppenborg 1986b:452–55 (=1994a:146–49); 1987a:190, 199–200, 211–16, 243–44.

pation of Q², and since it is there that the motif of the threat of judgment is
especially prominent, it seems best to regard 12:8-10 as deriving from that
redactional stratum.

The importance of 6:23c; 10:12, 13-15; 12:8-10 is that they are "stratigraphic markers." This is not because the theme of judgment or persecution
of the prophets or some other theme is arbitrarily assumed to be later than
other themes, but because of the *interruptive character* of the sayings which
bear these themes, and because of their obvious relation to the main redaction. The conclusion about the stratigraphy of Q is thus not based on a
priori decisions about what themes in Q are early and late, but rather on *literary* observations about the way various subcollections are related to one
another.[70]

It is necessary to be insistent on what is being argued. The argument of
The Formation of Q has been misconstrued by some who suppose that the
delineation of two strata in Q was based on a thematic or form-critical
analysis and, in particular, a (false) presumption that "prophetic" or "apocalyptic" sayings are incompatible with "sapiential" sayings.[71] This is a seri-

70. Sato (1995) has examined the deployment of "sapiential" and "prophetic" sayings in
Q, suggesting that the sapiential sayings have been "prophetized," and notes that in the
Tanak's prophetic books also employ wisdom sayings. The latter point, while perfectly correct,
misses the point of literary-critical analysis. While wisdom sayings can be used by prophets
(e.g., Isa 5:1-7) and prophetic tropes by wisdom writers (Prov 1:20-33), the *compositional*
issue is how these materials are *framed*. No one would confuse Isaiah with wisdom or Proverbs
with prophecy. Since Sato treats the Q sayings as isolated units, he also misses the way literary
composition affects the construal of sayings. He also seems to equate prophecy with eschatological sayings and wisdom with noneschatological sayings, so that any sayings that display
either "future eschatology" (Q 6:47-49[!]; 7:31-32[!]) or "present eschatology" (10:2; 11:21-
22, 23, 33; 12:2; 13:18-19, 20-21, etc.) are "functionally quite close to prophetic speech." This
seems simply to confuse literary-critical and generic observations with theological ones.

71. See J. Collins (above n. 61). Horsley (1989b:109–10) rejects the conclusions of *The Formation of Q* on this basis, but without noticing that the argument was literary-critical, not
thematic or form-critical. What he quotes (and rejects) are not the *criteria* used for the delineation of literary strata in Q but the *description* of the contents and character of the strata once
they had been delineated. That is, Horsley confuses conclusions with criteria. This confusion
is persistent, reappearing in Horsley 1989a:186–95 (despite the rejoinder in Kloppenborg
1989b:204–11); 1991b:196–200; 1994:740–48 and 1996:102. Horsley (1991:200a) also mis-
understands the point of the method when he claims that "Kloppenborg and others have relied
on Koester's analysis of the Gospel of Thomas as the basis for the claim that 'as far as *Gat-
tungsgeschichte* is concerned, the *Gos. Thomas* reflects a stage antecedent to the final form of
Q'" (quoting Kloppenborg 1987a:33). He fails to note that the quotation is immediately qualified and its methodological assumptions inverted: "Koester's procedure must be revised and
turned on its head: one must first determine the principles of composition of Q and the portions of it which were formative *from a literary critical perspective*. Only then is it possible to
compare Q with antique genres and determine the extent to which Q shares or fails to share
the characteristics and tendencies of those genres. It must be shown on *redactional grounds*
that certain elements . . . belong to a secondary compositional level and that compositionally
and literarily the wisdom sayings, and the wisdom-genre format, are foundational and formative for the document. *Such a conclusion can be obtained in the first place only from an analy-*

ous misreading not only of the method employed in *The Formation of Q* but also of that used in the mainstream of Q studies since Lührmann, which implicitly or explicitly rejects thematic or tradition-historical analysis as an adequate basis for describing literary history.

The tracing of a compositional history of Q is not a matter of placing its sayings into two or more "piles," sorted by form or by supposed theological orientation. Still less it is accomplished by smuggling a social or theological history into the analysis.[72] Nor is there any assumption that hortatory materials are necessarily early, or authentic, or that the Jesus movement was originally "sapiential" or "apocalyptic" or "prophetic." It should also be noted that in the foregoing analysis, the terms "sapiential" and "apocalyptic" rarely even occur and are not used *at all* as the basis for the delineation of strata in Q. The argument has been strictly literary, not theological.

The sole reason for positing two strata in Q is the particular configuration of literary data encountered in Q: the contents divide roughly into two types of material, each with a distinctive literary organization and rhetorical posture. Where the two are juxtaposed (e.g., in Q 10), the results are rather jarring *from a literary point of view*. Stratigraphical analysis has nothing to do with the presumed age or provenance of either set of materials, or their claim to authenticity. It is sheerly a literary issue and qualitatively no different than the literary problem posed by diverse organizational strategies encountered in the book of Proverbs, 1QS or the *Didache*. To imagine that stratigraphical analysis is driven by a priori judgments about "wisdom" and "apocalyptic" is simply nonsense.

---

sis of Q itself, not by comparative analysis" (1987a:38–39, emphasis added). Only in 1994:738 does Horsley note the qualification, but then states: "because [the last two decades of Q studies] assumed that Q was basically a collection of sayings, the procedure for determining the genre of the document or its component strata has usually been to determine the type or category (form) of the individual sayings (even though most of the immediate sayings are not particularly intelligible apart from their immediate or larger literary context in Q)" (1994:735) and pleading that Q be treated not as a "collection of sayings but a series of discourses or speeches" (1994:737). This can only be regarded as a stunning misreading of the mainstream of Q scholarship since Lührmann (1969). Since Q scholarship has precisely *not* treated Q simply as a sayings collection, it has avoided form criticism and preferred composition criticism (Jacobson's term) as the key to the analysis of Q. For more than two decades (Schürmann 1975) Q has been treated not as a concatenation of sayings, but as a thematically organized set of discourses or speeches.

72. Because Horsley reads Q and the early Jesus movement through the lens of a homogeneous construct of social history, he is disinclined to conceive of a *document* that is not organized in accordance with that social history. See Kirk 1998:48–49: "Horsley derives his characterization of Q from an *a priori* definition of its rustic milieu of origin. The logic should move in the opposite direction: the clues to Q's creation *as a text* are to be found in an analysis of its modes of composition. . . . For Horsley the social function of the text fills the text-generative role left vacant by his explusion of genre considerations, but it is not at all clear that social function alone suffices as a centripetal formative force with regard to texts."

Before leaving the composition history of Q, it is important to add that along with Jacobson and D. Zeller, I regard the temptation account as one of the latest additions to Q, probably subsequent to the main (Q²) redaction (Kloppenborg 1987a:246–62). Q 11:42c and 16:17 are two other such additions. In each instance, the grounds for suspecting interpolation are literary: each fits poorly with its immediate context and displays anomalous characteristics when viewed in the context of Q as a whole. The temptation account (4:1-13) has long struck critics as anomalous and some even excluded it from Q altogether.[73] It is now usually put relatively late in Q's composition history,[74] though sometimes on rather insubstantial grounds.[75] The most obvious anomaly of the temptation account is its direct citation of the Hebrew Scriptures introduced with a citation formula ("it is written"). A citation formula occurs also in Q 7:27, but only in 4:1-13 are the Scriptures cited in the context of a debate.[76] The rhetorical stance of the temptation story is also striking, for only here and in 11:42c and 16:17 is it assumed that the Torah is a self-evidently appropriate basis for argument; elsewhere, Q shows no concern to anchor Jesus' behavior by appeals to the Torah.[77] Moreover, the apparently positive reference to Jerusalem and the Temple in the second (Matthaean) temptation is in striking contrast to the negative depictions of Jerusalem elsewhere in Q (11:49-51; 13:34-35). This does not mean that the temptation is a foreign object in Q. On the contrary, the themes of the temptation—reliance upon God, the rejection of demonstrative signs and of worldly wealth and power—can be seen as consonant with topics discussed elsewhere in Q,[78] and, as I have argued elsewhere (1987a:325–27), it is not uncommon in sayings collections to begin with a "qualifying test" undergone by the speaker, which serves to demonstrate his or her reliability. Nevertheless, the idiom and rhetorical form of the story, and the assumptions it makes about the Torah, stand in contrast to the rest of Q.[79]

---

73. See Lührmann 1969:56 (but his later synopsis [1985] includes 4:1-13). Suspicions that the temptation account did not belong to Q go back to Weisse 1856:156–57. Argyle's argument (1952–53) against the presence of the temptations in Q was based on the assumption that the rest of Q was a translation of an Aramaic original and therefore the temptations, based on the LXX, could not derive from Q.

74. See Luz 1985:160 (ET 1989:183–84); Mahnke 1978:183–87; Schenk 1981:22.

75. Bultmann (1931:354; ET 1968:328) and D. Zeller (1982:62; 1984:22–23) include 4:1-13 along with 7:1-10 and 10:21-22 and assign them to a (Jewish-)Hellenistic stratum. Schulz includes it in his Hellenistic Jewish-Christian stratum (Q²), which in fact comprises the bulk of Q (1972:177–90, esp. 185). See the excellent analysis of the arguments by Tuckett 1992.

76. Tuckett 1992:485 notes the unusual character of a controversy dialogue that focuses on the Torah, but tries to mitigate this by arguing that Luke 10:25-28 was also in Q (1983:125–33; cf. Kertelge 1985; Fuller 1978b). The latter, however, is seldom included in Q and was excluded with a {D} by the IQP.

77. See Kloppenborg 1990c; Kosch (1989a:60, 236–37, 451) also points out that both formally and materially, Q 4:1-13 fits poorly in the unit 3:7—7:35.

78. See Kloppenborg 1987:246–62 and Tuckett 1992.

79. See also Jacobson 1978:36–46, 93, who mentions the use of the Hellenistic title "son of

Even more obviously intrusive are 11:42c,[80] which actually interferes with the logic of the woes,[81] and Q 16:17, which appears specially formulated to obviate any inference from 16:16 that the Torah had been abrogated.[82] Since all three units, 4:1-13; 11:42c; and 16:17, share a common perspective on the centrality of the Torah, they are best treated together. Within the larger compositional units of Q there is no evidence of a nomistic piety, and indeed, no special interest in the Torah at all. Only with the temptation narrative does Torah-obedience become an issue and only in 11:42c and 16:17 is there an explicit statement embracing the validity of the Torah. It is logical to locate all the Torah-centered glosses at one redactional stage. Since each fits uncomfortably in its current setting, and is either positioned to function with regard to the entire collection—as is the case with 4:1-13— or to correct or qualify sayings from the main redaction (11:42c; 16:17), this stage must be a very late one. This stage, which might be called Q^3, does not really represent a full redactional phrase in the way that the editing of the hortatory instructions (Q^1) or the editing and insertion of the Deuteronomistic materials (Q^2) did. Instead, it is a matter of minor glossing, in two instances, "correcting" possible readings that might arise from Q 11:39-41, 42 and 16:16, 18.

God," the scribal character of 4:1-13, its use of the LXX and of explicit quotation formulas, the "apparently late literary form," and the use of (διάβολος) for Satan as indices of the lateness of the unit. Kloppenborg 1987:247–48 adds that the understanding of the miraculous as deeds of Jesus differs from the rest of Q, where miracles are events pointing to the presence of the kingdom.

80. The absence of 11:42c in Codex Bezae and Marcion suggested to several critics that 11:42c did not belong to Luke or Q at all, but was a textual interpolation from Matthew. Thus Harnack 1908:101; Wellhausen 1904a:61; Manson 1949:98.

81. See Kloppenborg 1990c:40–43 and Vaage 1988; 1994:75–78. The woe itself (11:42ab) takes the form of a lampoon, representing as Pharisaic a tithing practice that corresponds to no known rabbi or school. Yet the concluding phrase shifts abruptly from lampoon to admonition and implies a tacit approval of practices which were just burlesqued: "it is necessary to observe these things [justice and the love of God] but not neglect the others [i.e., tithing]." Sato (1988:197) calls the phrase "a secondary mitigation [of the woe] that is bound to the Law," observing that its ostensible addressees are no longer the Pharisees but the Q group itself. More recently, Jolliffe 1990:128, 170–71 argues for the same view: "With the primary exception of Q 11:42d [i.e., 11:42c], apparently added during the final redactional stage of Q, legal discussion is hardly a factor in the evolution of the woe-discourse. At no level is there evidence of argument or discussion concerning the validity of Torah" (1990:171). Similarly, Tuckett 1992:487, who treats 11:42c as "Q redaction."

82. Merklein 1981:92–93. Kosch 1989a:434–35, 443 regards 16:17 as a "Jewish-Christian commentary-word"—that is, an originally independent saying—which is nonetheless *compositionally* secondary to 16:16, the "base-saying." He concludes that the saying does not derive from Q redaction, which shows no interest in the issue of Jesus' view of the Torah; instead, it coheres with 11:42c and because it too comments upon a "base saying" rather than on a larger composition, it must derive from a relatively early compositional stage. See also Broer 1980:44 n. 89. Tuckett 1992:487: "Q 16,17 may well be an editorial attempt to ensure that the verse which (probably) precedes it in Q, Q 16,16, is not to be interpreted in an antinomian way."

The Genre of Q

To inquire about the genre of Q is not simply an idle exercise in taxonomy but is of fundamental importance in evaluating *what kind* of discourse Q represents. This is key to the topic that will concern me in chapter 4, that of the social location of Q and the persons represented by the document, for the selection of genre provides important clues to the interests and self-identity of both its framers and its addressees.[83] Indeed, the connection between genre and social history is explicit in the work of Migaku Sato, who infers from his genre designation for Q that the framers of Q were former wandering prophets who had become local leaders (1988:380–81). The relationship of genre to social location is also fundamental to my own work and that of F. Gerald Downing, who has also worked out a detailed proposal for the genre of Q. In each case, the determination of the genre of Q is understood as a necessary preliminary to the determination of the social location of Q.[84]

My proposal, worked out in *The Formation of Q*, is based on the compositional analysis of Q outlined above. The formative stratum of Q comprises six subcollections of hortatory sayings, topically organized and characterized in particular by second person imperatives with buttressing sayings (maxims or rhetorical questions). Some of these collections are prefaced with programmatic pronouncements and conclude with sanctions or

83. See Kirk 1998:68–69: "A text, like any other communicative activity, arises and is enacted within an interactive social situation encompassing the producer of the text and its recipients. A text constitutes a specific response to and hence is shaped by the exigencies of a given social situation, with the text itself influencing perceptions of the situation. A text comes into existence because its producer wants to achieve a certain goal—has a communicative intention—with respect to influencing a set of recipients similarly enmeshed in the social situation. . . . Genres are patterns for structuring communicative acts—and hence generative templates for executing communicative, rhetorical strategies—which have achieved conventional status because of the recurrent and diverse nature of various communication tasks, occurring within various social settings, addressed within a particular society. As socially and culturally inculcated linguistic conventions, genres form part of the cognitive apparatus of text recipients as well as producers, though here an important distinction exists between 'active' and 'passive' genre competence."

84. Rather than vice versa, as is the case with Horsley 1991a, who (as suggested above) reads his social construct into his analysis of Q. See above n. 72. Similarly, Horsley 1994:741, where he declares, apropos of stratigraphic analyses, that "[c]ritical assessment of how wide a range of comparative material is appropriate for interpretation of Q depends in turn on one's picture of the social location and cultural situation in which Q was produced. . . ." In the end, he rejects (what he wrongly supposes to be the basis of) the stratigraphic division of Q into "sapiential" and "apocalyptic" layers by arguing that both wisdom and apocalyptic literatures came from the same scribal circles (1994:748–49, echoing 1989a:191: "A distinction between two separate [!] traditions surely makes little sense sociologically"). The point is both correct and trivial: of course, literature came from scribal circles, but that hardly means that all scribes had the same social interests, any more than that all professors have the same social (theological, cultural) interests.

warnings or other such sayings that underscore the gravity of the discourse. A good example is the opening "sermon," which contains three topical clusters flanked by an introduction and a conclusion:

Introduction
Four programmatic makarisms   6:20-23
    ("How honorable are . . . for . . .")[85]
Imperative [2pl.] + motive clause   6:23
    ("rejoice . . . for your reward is great. . . .")

1. Programmatic imperatives
    "love [2pl.] your enemies, [do good . . . bless] . . .
        pray . . ."   6:27-28
    "turn [2sg.] your cheek . . . do not withhold"   6:29
    ". . . go [2sg.] with him two miles . . ."   Q/Matt 5:41
    "As you wish others to do to you, do [2pl.] also to them"   6:31

Rhetorical questions + appeals to common observation
    ("for if you love . . . what reward do you have? Do
    not tax collectors do the same? . . .")   6:32-33, (34ab?)
Summarizing imperatives ("love [2pl.]. . . do good . . . lend. . .")   6:35a
    Motive clause ("for your reward is great.")   6:35b
Concluding generalization + rationale ("You will be children
    of the Most High, for he raises his sun on the evil and the good
    and sends rain . . .")   6:35c

2. Programmatic imperative ("Be merciful [2pl.] . . .")   6:36
Imperative [2pl.] + motive clause (agricultural aphorism)
    ("judge not . . . for by the measure you measure it will be
    measured back")[86]   6:37-38
Gnomic question ("Can a blind person lead a blind
    person? . . .")   6:39
Gnomic saying ("A disciple is not above his teacher . . .")   6:40
Gnomic question ("Why do you [2sg.] see the speck in your
    brother's eye? . . .")   6:41-42a
Concluding admonition ("Hypocrite! First remove [2sg.] the
    log from your own eye . . .")   6:42b

3. Maxim about arboriculture ("No sound tree bears bad
    fruit . . .")   6:43a

---

85. For a discussion of the translation of μακάριος as "how honorable," rather than as a blessing, see Hanson 1994.

86. Q 6:38b ("for by the measure you measure it will be measured back") is not simply an abstract statement of reciprocity, but is drawn from the actual practice of making agricultural loans. In a lending system where general standards of weights and measures were lacking, it was customary to measure the returned grain by the same grain scoop or "measure" that was used in the initial loan.

Gnomic explanation ("for by its fruit the tree is known")	6:43b
Rhetorical question: ("Do they gather figs from thorns? . . .")	6:44

Correlative maxim on human character ("A good person brings
    forth good things from the good storeroom . . .")   6:45a
Gnomic conclusion ("for from the abundance of the heart
    the mouth speaks")   6:45b

Conclusion
Closing admonition to listen and obey ("Why do you [2pl.]
    call me 'Lord', and not do what I say?")   6:46
Exemplum of the two builders   6:47-49

The structure of this unit is not wooden or repetitive and the three central units employ somewhat differing argumentative strategies and a range of grammatical forms. While Q 11:2-4, 9-13 (on prayer), Q 12:2-7, 11-12 (on anxiety in the face of opposition), and Q 12:22-31, 33-34 (on anxiety over subsistence) focus on a fairly narrow range of concerns, Q 6:20b-49 treats at least three topics. The first arises from the mention of enmity and conflict in the final makarism, but deals not only with enmity but with a variety of human interactions (hostility, insult, robbery [or lawsuits], beggary, lending, and borrowing). The second unit concerns the mitigation of conflict within the Q group, and the third, which shifts from admonitions to maxims, represents a meditation on the relation of speech to moral character. A variety of forms and tropes is employed, and there is even alternation between the second person plural [2pl.] and the second person singular [2sg.] in the admonitions. These variations are perhaps a function of the fact that the Sermon was not invented out of thin air by the framers of Q, but rather from a repertoire of sayings of Jesus originally spoken in other contexts.

    This is not the place to provide an exposition of the rhetoric of the Sermon.[87] What is pertinent to the discussion of the genre of Q[1] is to notice, first, the repertoire of forms present: makarisms; imperatives with buttressing maxims; rhetorical questions; gnomic sayings and comparisons; exempla drawn from common experience. Second, the nature of Q's argumentation is noteworthy: it represents a mode of persuasion that proceeds by invoking common experience (6:32-33, 39, 40, 43, 44) and by establishing analogical relationships between natural and human phenomena (6:43-44, 45), or by grounding the recommended behavior in what can be deduced about God's character from the ordinary observation of rain or sun (6:35c). The appeals are to the observation of nature (weather; arboriculture), ordinary social transactions (teacher–pupil relations; agricultural loans), and ordinary human activities (house building).

    Third, and related to the mode of rhetoric, is the nature of the speaker's "voice." Q 6:20b-49 proposes a rather adventuresome social practice, one

---

87. See Carruth 1992 and Kirk 1998:152–76.

that is justified by appeal to the divine ethos. This in turn presupposes a claim to special insight on the part of the speaker. That the speaker claims special insight is already clear from the formulation of the first three makarisms, which reverse common observations. The first instructional unit also makes a claim as to what constitutes filiation with God (6:35c). Nevertheless, the speaker does not adopt the postures of either the oracular mouthpiece or the seer. He is neither a prophet, conveying the voice of God, nor a visionary, communicating secrets disclosed in dreams or tours of heaven or by visiting angels. Instead, the ethic of Q is proposed by means of skillful manipulation of *words*: maxims, which typically display hermeneutical openness, are generalized, narrowed, or applied to different semantic fields; admonitions are elaborated by the skillful adducing of arguments from common wisdom or observation.

Finally, Q 6:20b-49 employs a range of tropes: mild rebuke ("Hypocrite!" 6:42; "Why do you call me 'Lord'?" 6:46);[88] eyesight as a metaphor for insight; and housebuilding as a metaphor of the acquisition of knowledge. The speech itself deals with the topics of the relation of teachers to students (6:39-40, 46-49); interpersonal relations (6:27-35); correction (6:41-42); good speech (6:45); pragmatic relations with superiors (Q/Matt 5:41); and conflict avoidance (6:29).

This pattern conforms very closely to a widely attested genre in Near Eastern literature, the "instruction," examples of which are found in Proverbs 1-9; Sirach; 4Q185;[89] 4QSapiential Work[C] [4Q424]; *Amenemope* [hieroglyphic]; *Ankhsheshonq* [Demotic]; *Shubi-awilum* [Akkadian]; and the *Teachings of Silvanus* and the *Instructions of Apa Antonius* [Coptic] (see Kloppenborg 1987a:329–36). The basic building block of the instruction is the admonition—an imperative with a motive clause[90]—and what follows attempts to command assent and conviction by adding additional gnomic sayings, rhetorical questions, maxims, examples, promises, and threats.[91] Prov 6:20-35 provides a good example of the genre:

88. Carruth 1995:101 has shown that, far from intrusions into this hortatory speech, such rebukes (formulated as direct address) are instances of *licentia* (παρρησία) which demonstrate that the speaker is "friendly both to the hearers and to the truth" (citing *Rhetorica ad Herennium* 4.37.49; cf. Dio Chrysostom 32.11).

89. See Tobin 1990, who argues that 4Q185 is probably not a sectarian composition, since it lacks distinctive sectarian vocabulary and has characteristics otherwise unattested at Qumran. See also 4QSapiential Work[A] (above n. 25).

90. See McKane 1970:3; B. Lang 1972:31–36; Kloppenborg 1987a:267–68.

91. Kirk 1998:149: "The signals of the genre [instruction] are as follows: (1) the *programmatic admonition*, positive, prohibitive, or both, which inaugurates the speech and strikes its programmatic theme; (2) a more or less extended *course of argumentation* which seeks to persuade of the wisdom (reasonableness) of the programmatic admonition and, accordingly, motivate obedience to it, using additional gnomic sayings, additional or reiterative admonitions, maxims, rhetorical questions, comparisons, examples, promises of present or future makarism of various sorts, or any combination of these and other small wisdom forms." Especially typical are the programmatic maxim and the threat of divine sanction.

General admonition: "My child, keep your father's commandment
    and do not forsake your mother's teaching."   6:20
Exposition: "Bind them upon your heart always; tie them around
    your neck . . ."   6:21
Motive clause: "When you walk they will lead you; when you
    lie down they will watch over you."   6:22

Topical maxim (on adultery)
"For the commandment is a lamp and the teaching a light . . .
    to preserve you from the wife of another, and from the
    smooth tongue of the adulteress."   6:23-24
Admonitions / Comparisons
"Do not desire her beauty . . . ; for a prostitute's fee is only a loaf
    of bread, but the wife of another stalks a man's very life."   6:25-26
Rhetorical question: "Can fire be carried in the bosom without
    burning one's clothes, or can one walk on hot coals without
    scorching the feet? So is he who sleeps with his neighbor's wife;
    no one who touches her will go unpunished."   6:27-29
Gnomic comparisons: "Thieves are not despised who steal only
    to satisfy their appetite when they are hungry. Yet if they are
    caught they will pay sevenfold; they will forfeit all the goods of
    their house. But he who commits adultery has no sense; he who
    does it destroys himself. He will get wounds and dishonor and
    his disgrace will not be wiped away."   6:30-33
Motive: "For jealousy arouses a husband's fury, and he shows no
    restraint when he takes revenge. He will accept no compensation
    and refuses a bribe no matter how great."   6:34-35

The basic intent of this instruction is a prohibition of adultery. It attempts
to win assent to this imperative by means of a variety of appeals: by the initial linking of the instruction with parental values and general promises
about results of obedience; by comparisons; by appeal to common experience and the application of such experience to the situation of adultery
(6:27-28); and by explicit and implicit threats. Other instructions employ in
varying arrangements a comparable set of forms and make comparable
appeals. Topics range from the pursuit of wisdom and piety to a host of specific issues such as behavior before superiors, dealings with the public, attitudes toward teachers and pupils, hearing and adjudicating disputes,
marriage, domestic life, the rearing of children, public speaking, study, table
etiquette, etc. In longer instructions topic organization was common, even
if there are a few one-topic instructions and some that are quite miscellaneous in organization.
    Q of course exhibits some peculiarities: it does not employ the fiction of

having the author speak in the role of parent as many instructions do,[92] even if it does invoke the fiction of a school setting (6:39-40). Whereas many of these are the products of conservative scribal schools, Q promotes a less conventional ethic. These two features are related: it would be difficult for a collection that relativized family bonds (Q 9:59-60; 14:26-27) to depend on the fiction of parental instruction. The dominance of instructions from scribal schools is only to be expected: such schools used instructions as exercises for copying and some of the examples we have are from schoolboys' notebooks. It is clear, however, that the instruction could be and was used in more sectarian environments, as 4Q185, 4QSapiential Work[C], the *Instructions of Apa Antonius,* and the *Teachings of Silvanus* show. Moreover, as will be shown in chapter 8, one of the tendencies operative in later wisdom works was a relativization of the importance formerly ascribed to the family.

Again it is important to be clear on what is being claimed. To argue that Q[1] conforms to the genre of an "instruction" is to assert a "family resemblance" between Q and other documents typically designated "instructions."[93] This is asserted in the first place on the basis of Q[1]'s dominant grammatical forms, then the nature of argumentation (its warrants and methods), then the nature of the authorial "voice," and finally, its typical idioms and tropes. The designation "instruction" does not rest on a subjective judgment about its theological orientation—that is, that it is "sapiential" rather than "prophetic" or "apocalyptic." Still less does it imply that Q conforms precisely to any other instruction or that there is nothing distinctive in Q: that would be to misunderstand completely what "genre" is.[94]

92. There are other exceptions: The *Counsels of Amenotes* (Wilken 1897); the *Counsels of Piety of Sansnos* (Bernand 1969: no. 165).

93. The Wittgensteinian notion of "family resemblance" (Wittgenstein 1958:65–68) employed by Burridge (1992:38–54) as applied to genre does not require that all members of a genre share a set of common characteristics; rather, the representatives of a genre can be grouped together by a series of overlapping similiarities, even if no single feature runs through the whole set.

94. Some have argued that Q's lack of the address "my son," found in many (though not all) instructions, and its less than conservative comportment disqualify the analogy of instruction out of court, or invoke theological criteria to rule all comparisons out of court. D. Zeller (1992:391), for example, argues that Q[1] cannot be a "sapiential instruction" because it contains prophetic forms (Q 6:46 [!]) and because the "rules for missionaries in 10:2-16 do not have a proverbial character and are completely controlled from the point of view of content by the knowledge of the in-breaking eschaton." This represents a basic confusion about the nature of genre, which is not in the first place a function of theological orientation. Zeller surveys gnomologia, categorizing them into four main types (1992:393–401). Although he admits that Q resembles some aspects of gnomologia (topical organization; dominance of imperatives; the use of exordia and conclusions), he argues that it does not exactly correspond to any instance. He observes, moreover, that while Q prefers the second person plural (though not exclusively), Greek gnomologia prefer the singular. Apart from the fact that the main comparative materials for Q[1] were drawn from Near Eastern instructions such as Proverbs 1–9; 22:17—24:22,

The supplementation of the Q^1 instructions by the Q^2 material introduced a new element into Q: narrative framing. Q 3:3 situates John's sayings geographically and 3:7a provides the occasion for John's prophetic warning. Q 7:1 has Jesus entering Kefar Naḥum and implicitly associates the subsequent actions mentioned in Q 7:18 (John's messengers approaching Jesus) and Q 7:24 (Jesus speaking with the crowds) with that town. Q 9:57, 59 (probably already part of Q^1) and Q 10:21a provide a setting for the intervening materials, including the woes pronounced on Kefar Naḥum and the other two Galilean towns. Q 11:14, 16, 29 provide a brief setting for Jesus' rebuttals of opponents' challenges and questions.

The furnishing of sayings with a brief setting is the characteristic of the *chria*, a well-known didactic and rhetorical form in the ancient Mediterranean world.[95] The isolated chria is encountered in a variety of contexts and takes the form:

> Pittacus of Mitylene, being asked if anyone escapes the notice of the gods in committing some sinful act, said: "No, not even in contemplating it." (Theon, *Progymnasmata* 56-58; Hock and O'Neil 1986:84–85)

Chriae could be framed as simple assertions ("NN used to say: . . ."), as comments on particular circumstances ("Seeing *x*, NN said: . . ."), as responses to questions either requiring a simple response or an explanation ("Being asked about *x*, NN said: . . ."), or as responses to a comment or challenge.[96]

While often encountered in isolation, chriae were also collected and serialized, forming either anthologies of sayings by several sages on particular topics or proto-biographies—the collected chriae of one sage.[97] The rabbinic tractate *m. 'Abot* offers an instance of an anthological collection of sayings of various sages (Fischel 1968). Diogenes Laertius's *Lives of Eminent Philosophers* preserves a number of chriae collections concerning Anti-

---

and Sirach (and, it could be added, 4Q185; 4Q525) where the second person plural is used, it should be obvious that Zeller's approach to "comparison" is preprogrammed to rule out all analogies. Hence it hardly comes as a surprise when Zeller declares Q to be a "Unicum" (1992:401). It should also be obvious that the preference for the second person singular in gnomologia is a function of the fictive setting of most instructions: of a father to a son. As soon as the fictional setting is shifted, as it is in many Near Eastern instructions, the singular shifts to a plural, as it does in Q.

95. On chriae in general, see Colson 1921; R. Taylor 1946; Hock and O'Neil 1986; Robbins 1988; 1989; Mack and Robbins 1989; Mack 1990b.

96. Theon ("On the Chreia," *Progymnasmata* 29–123) divides chriae into sayings chriae, action chriae (i.e., where an action serves as the response), and mixed chriae (where sayings and actions function as the response). He subdivides sayings chriae into (a) simple responses (ἀποφαντικαί), (b) circumstantial (κατὰ περίστασιν), (c) and responsive (ἀποκριτικαί), the latter further divided into responses requiring (i) a simple affirmation or negation, (ii) a simple answer, (iii) an answer with an explanation, and finally, (iv) a response to a remark.

97. On the biographical capacity of chriae collections, see Momigliano 1971:72–73.

sthenes, Bion, Crates, and Diogenes of Sinope. Lucian's *Demonax* is largely
a collection of chriae, as is *Secundus the Silent Philosopher*. There are, in
addition, several fragmentary papyrus chriae collections, representing short
bioi of Diogenes of Sinope, Simonides, and Socrates (see Kloppenborg
1987a:340–41).

Q does not represent as homogeneous a document as, for example, the
Diogenes chriae of *P. Mich.* inv. 41, which comprises a collection of two- or
three-line chriae, each beginning with "Diogenes the philosopher. . . ." Nor
is Q like the chriae of *P. Bouriant* 1, which begins each chria with "When
he saw . . ." (ἰδὼν δέ).[98] Other chriae collections, however, are more varied
in their contents: the Socrates chriae of *P. Hibeh* 182 combine chriae with
extended sayings. Lucian's *Demonax* (12-67) contains chriae of varying
types and lengths, saving Demonax's remarks about his death until the end
(62-67). Q is even less homogeneous, combining chriae such as Q 11:14-20
or 11:16, 29-30 (and perhaps 11:27-28 and 12:13-15) with longer discourses such as 6:20b-49 or 10:2-16.

Even though I have suggested that the temptation account is a late addition to Q, from the standpoint of genre it does not represent a foreign body.
Both in instructions and in chriae collections, it is common to begin with a
story of an ordeal or test suffered by the sage, an ordeal that demonstrates
the sage's reliability. Thus *Ankhsheshonq* and *Ahikar*, both instructions,
begin with an ordeal story. In the *Sentences of Secundus* (a chriae collection), Secundus is put through a test to determine whether his "Pythago-
rean" vow of silence is genuine. Testing and wisdom are, of course,
intimately linked. Sirach 2:1, 4-5 puts it thus: "My son, if you come forward
to serve the Lord, prepare yourself for temptation. . . . Accept whatever is
brought upon you and in changes that humble you be patient. For gold is
tested in fire and acceptable men in the furnace of humiliation."

Prescinding from speculations about the composition history of Q, F.
Gerald Downing has mounted the most comprehensive argument for seeing
Q as a *bios* analogous to *Demonax*. Following Richard Burridge's analysis
of the genre of the gospels (1992), Downing notes several other features in
Q that strongly resemble *bios* literature:

(1) First, Q shows a strong focus on one person, reflected in the fact that
Jesus is the subject of the majority of the verbs of speaking (33 verbs; 26 for
others) and is the "utterer of between 630 and 700 verbs; others of only
around 60" (Downing 1994:7). By contrast, most of the features of a *bios*
are wanting in prophetic books: "the prophets quite specifically do not
announce their teaching in their own name: they proclaim, 'So says Yahweh'
rather than 'I tell you'" (1994:8).

98. *P. Mich.* inv. 14 (published: Gallo 1975–80, 2:235–40); *P. Bouriant* 1 (published:
Jouguet and Perdizet 1906:148–61).

There are other noteworthy similarities to *bioi*.

(2) In the allocation of space, "most space is given to 'many stories and anecdotes, each leading up to a pronouncement of a saying of the sage.'"[99]

(3) *Bioi* often lack a continuous narrative but have varying degrees of topical organization.

(4) "Lives" range from 3,000 words (*Demonax*) to 82,000 words (Philostratus's *Life of Apollonios*); the size of Q (about 4,500 words [Downing estimates only 3,500 words]) is thus comparable to *Demonax* or Diogenes Laertius's *Diogenes* (of Sinope).

(5) Philosophical "lives" tend to be limited in scope to the deeds, sayings, and character of the subject, although a few treat briefly the hero's relationship to predecessors or teachers. The focus of Q is obviously on Jesus, though John serves as both a forerunner and a figure for comparison.

(6) Almost all philosophical "lives" "are formed from a similar range of units of stories and anecdotes, sayings and speeches, with some being rather carefully composed while others are more a loose connection of units" (Burridge 1992:173). By this standard, Q conforms to a *bios* well and displays relatively impressive organization in at least some of its speeches.

(7) Downing also notes that characterization typically occurs by means of the sage's words or deeds without further commentary, often by means of comparison (1994:13). Indeed, the use of comparison is pervasive in Q: John and Jesus are compared and contrasted (7:31-35); John compares himself with the Coming One; Jesus is compared with the devil, with those who challenge him (11:14-32), and with Pharisees (11:39-52); God is compared with humans (6:35; 11:2-4, 13); good and bad disciples are compared; and "this generation" and unsympathetic hearers are characterized through comparison with Jesus, Jewish exorcists (11:19), figures from Israel's epic history (11:31-32; 13:28-29), and even Gentiles (7:1-10; 11:31-32; 13:28-29).

Downing contends that to contemporary Greek ears Q would have sounded like the *bios* of a teacher—indeed, a Cynic teacher. Whether Q indeed is best characterized as "Cynic" is a topic to be considered in the final chapter. For the moment, it can be observed that while chriae are indeed common in Cynic lives and may even have originated in Cynic circles, the chria was by the early Roman period not the exclusive property of Cynics: it was widely used in elementary rhetorical education in schools and in various non-Cynic literary contexts. The chriae collection was not exclusively Cynic, as *m. 'Abot* and the *Sentences of Secundus* clearly

---

99. Downing 1994:9, quoting Burridge 1992:166–67. Downing notes (against Burridge) that not all philosophical *bioi* narrate the birth or death of the sage: Demonax's death is mentioned by Lucian, but it is lacking in most of lives of Diogenes Laertrius and Philostratus.

demonstrate. Hence, it is rather odd that Tuckett (1989)[100] and D. Zeller (1992) reject the contention that the final form of Q resembles a chriae collection by arguing that Q was not Cynic.[101] This confuses genre with content. The genre of chriae collection was quite adaptable to various sorts of contents.[102]

Conclusion

The inquiries into both the compositional principles and the genre of Q are efforts to perceive the document in the terms and according to the principles that its original framers employed. Redaction criticism attempts to fathom the means by which diverse materials are framed and ordered to present a coherent message. Genre criticism attempts, first, to discern the formal principles by which Q is organized and then to situate Q's particular form of discourse within the range of available ancient genres.

There is a very broad consensus among specialists in regard to the character of what I have called the main redaction of Q: it is marked thematically by repetitive elements—the announcement of judgment and the employment of a Deuteronomistic view of history. I would add that the main redaction evokes the story of Lot and the destruction of Sodom. What is especially significant from the standpoint of the Synoptic Problem is that

---

100. Tuckett 1989:360 rightly observes in a footnote (n. 38) that I consider Cynic lives to be only a subset of the more inclusive genre of chriae collections and acknowledges that I have resisted the identification of Q as "Cynic." But he then states: "whether or not the individual units in Q can appropriately be called chreiai or not, there is still the issue of how far the Cynic Lives provide a genuine *generic* parallel to Q *as a whole*" (1989:361, emphasis original); and again, "in terms of audience reaction, Q and the Cynic Lives do not seem close enough for contemporary hearers/readers to have been immediately struck by their *literary* similarities" (1989:363).

101. More recently, Tuckett (1996:379–83) has been careful to distinguish the argument made in *The Formation of Q* (on the basis of the *formal* similarity of Q to *chriae* collections) from the arguments of Vaage and Downing, based on the allegedly Cynic *content* of Q. Nevertheless, I fear he still misconstrues my observations to the effect that Q exhibits a somewhat more sophisticated internal structure than most chriae collections, arguing (curiously) that "Kloppenborg gives no real examples of organizing principles in the material about Diogenes or Demonax which come near the (at times) tightly structured arrangement in Q" (1996:381). This is, in fact, *precisely* the point: while a few chriae collections (e.g., *P. Bouriant* 1) display some elementary topical or syntactical groupings, none approaches the sophistication of Q. Similarly, I argued that Q comes "closer in *level* of organisation (though not in type of organisation)" to *m. 'Abot* (1987:381), to which Tuckett retorts: "Nor is there much comparable [in structure] in *m. 'Abot*." Tuckett oddly misses the point: I did not argue (as the parenthesis clearly indicates) that Q used the same *type* of organization as *m. 'Abot*—for example, the transmissional sorites in 1.1-15. I did argue that a comparable or better *level* of organization of sayings was present in Q.

102. Insofar as the *Gospel of Thomas*—certainly not "Cynic"—frames most of its sayings with "Jesus said," it is arguably a collection of (mostly *apophantic*) chriae.

the "double tradition," once extracted from Matthew and Luke, displays a strong thematic coherence and organization that do not derive from the main redactional themes of either Matthew or Luke. To return to the architectural metaphor invoked at the beginning of the chapter, it is as if, once having bracketed out the Byzantine and Mamluk additions and modifications to a particular building complex, the early Roman structure stands out in its distinctiveness. To be sure, this does not constitute a "proof" of the 2DH; but it is precisely the sort of outcome that indicates the workability of the hypothesis—that the document posited by logic of the 2DH indeed *looks* like a document, with a distinctive theological organization and genre.

As to the attempts to discern beneath the surface of Q a compositional history, it can be said that there is also agreement that Q represents a complex document, whether or not a composition history can be described convincingly. I have outlined two such attempts to do so, attempts which both illustrate the consensus in method that exists and which epitomize the differing ways of treating the diverse materials present in Q. The disagreements between Sato and myself—and other stations between these two "poles" could easily be added—make clear that the composition of Q is not a simple issue that can be solved with facile solutions. Precisely because of its complexity, the study of Q becomes a fertile ground for probing inquiry into the method of redaction and genre criticism, and the theological assumptions at work in that method.

The disagreements evident in the assessment of the genre of Q—is it a prophetic book or a proto-biography that incorporates a didactic collection?—are in part refractions of the prior disagreements about composition history and in part differing estimations of how genre is to be determined. I have argued that in discussing the compositional history of Q and its genre, theological considerations, and especially subjective assessments of what is "sapiential," "prophetic," and "apocalyptic," should not be allowed to take precedence over more neutral literary-critical indicators of composition, or over controlled generic comparisons.

Determining Q's theological outlook and genre has considerable importance. From the standpoint of drawing the map of the theological landscape of the Jesus movement, it is clear that Q represents an important and distinctive moment in early Christian theologizing—in particular, because there is no evidence that Q had developed a view that found particular salvific meaning in the death of Jesus himself. In its appeal to the Deuteronomistic view of the prophets—as ignored, persecuted, and even killed—one can see an instance of one set of Jesus' followers availing themselves of resources from the tradition in order to render intelligible their own experience and their memory of their hero. This theology, so fundamental to the redaction of Q, finds only echoes in other documents—Mark 12:1-9; Acts 7:52; 1 Thess 2:13-16; and James 5:10—and was eventually supplanted by more elaborate meditations on Jesus' death and its special significance. Q's theology, however, remains an early monument to this deuteronomistic theology.

Reflections on the genre and scope of Q also provide the best clues in the efforts to ascertain the social location of its framers and first-intended audience. This is no different from the case of the canonical gospels, where the forms of argumentative appeals and what is unspoken in those arguments reveal the kind of audience that those gospels have in view. As with the case of the canonical gospels, conclusions about the social location of the addressees of the document derive from literary observations of the document, not vice versa, as if a predetermined social history can be allowed to control the reading of the document.

In all of these investigations the hypothetical status of the endeavor must be kept in view. Here I do not use "hypothetical" as a way of rendering fundamentally dubious and peripheral the tasks of constructing a redactional portrait of Q or of situating Q on the theological landscape of the Jesus movement and social landscape of the Lower Galilee. On the contrary, hypotheses that are critically assembled and which show themselves to have explanatory force represent the *constructive tools* for the task of theological and social history, indeed, the only tools we have.

4

The Q Document and the Q People

A PART FROM PERSONAL LETTERS, contracts, receipts, and the like, ancient documents were seldom composed merely for private use. They were intended instead for performance before various publics, whose likely reactions had to be anticipated in the very act of composition. That public might be a large, diverse, even rowdy crowd at an oration in a public assembly, or a more select group, as in the case of lectures given in a private hall or school, or an intimate gathering at a symposium convoked for the recitation of a new work. Whatever the forum, the author had to take the audience into account by appealing to what it already knew or believed, evoking shared convictions, capitalizing on the common ground, anticipating points of resistance, and overcoming that resistance through an appropriate disposition or arrangement of arguments. Composition was thus a social act in which the audience was not an incidental "consumer" of the literary work but was present in the act of composition from the beginning.

In spite of the increasing use of writing from the time of Plato, ancient Mediterranean culture was still fundamentally oral. William Harris estimates that during most of the Hellenistic and Roman periods, the rate of literacy was probably 10 percent and certainly no greater than 15 percent (1989:22, 328).[1] This 10–15 percent, moreover, was unevenly distributed. More males could read than females and more elite than nonelite. Slaves attached to wealthy families might be trained to read so that they could function as teachers or secretaries (Booth 1979); but other domestic slaves and most agricultural and industrial slaves were illiterate. Some craftsper-

---

1. Bar-Ilan's sophisticated 1992 study of literacy found inverse correlations between literacy and the dependence of a society on agriculture and direct correlations with urbanization, population growth and life expectancy. On the basis of these coordinates, he argues that the total literacy rate—he means reading literacy—was less than 3 percent in the first century, up from 1.5 percent in the second century BCE. He suggests that literacy ranged from 0 percent in rural areas, 1–5 percent in the urban population, and 10 percent in large urban centers. Baines 1983 estimates literacy in ancient Egypt at 0.5 percent.

sons were literate, but very few soldiers. It would be a rare peasant who could read or write. Thus, if one visualizes ancient society as a pyramid, with large numbers of (mostly rural) poor at the bottom, tiny numbers of "well-born" persons at the top, and their retainers, craftspersons, and the like just below them, the literate sector would appear as slice along the edge of the pyramid, reduced to nothing at the base and slowly increasing in width toward the apex.

To make matters more complex, "literacy" itself admits of various levels: signature-literacy; the ability to read simple contracts, invoices and receipts; full reading literacy; the ability to take dictation; and scribal literacy—the ability to compose.[2] Only a small number of persons would be able to read with ease and an even smaller percentage would have had the ability to compose documents longer than private letters. The pervasive refrain in contracts and receipts, "NN [a scribe] wrote this because s/he [one of the principals] is illiterate," evidences the general lack of writing literacy, even if some of these documents bear the scrawls of the principals' signatures (see Youtie 1975b).

One of the impediments to reading lay in the fact that ancient documents and inscriptions were written in *scripta continua*—lacking word spaces and punctuation. For any text of significant length, reading was a laborious effort and almost always entailed the vocalization of what was being read. Only the well-trained reader—one who had passed through both primary and secondary education—could recite a text publicly. Performance required prior preparation and particular skill in delivery.[3]

It is unlikely that Christians of the first century enjoyed any greater rate of literacy than the population as a whole. Of course some Christians were literate. Some of the Corinthian Christians named by Paul (e.g., Gaius, Crispus, Stephanus, Cloe) were probably among the elite. The bulk of the membership, however, was nonelite, as 1 Cor 1:26 indicates. Many of the elite and some nonelite such as craftspersons and educated slaves might have been able to read but the majority of the Corinthian Christians would have had to rely on others to inform them of the contents of Paul's letters. Harry Gamble is probably correct in his estimate that no more than 10 percent of

---

2. Cf. Cribiore 1996:10, who distinguishes within writing literacy, "(1) writing as handwriting, the physical act of tracing characters or words; (2) writing as copying, as taking dictation, the recording of others' words; (3) writing as crafting lexical, syntactical, and rhetorical units of discourse into meaningful patterns; (4) writing as authoring, or producing an independent and original text for a specific audience and purpose."

3. Preparation of a text for reading required decisions regarding punctuation, accentuation, and expression, the three aspects of recitation treated by the grammarian Dionysius Thrax (II/I BCE), whose grammar was widely influential. Marrou (1956:165–66) notes that "expressive reading" was not taught until the secondary level of schooling. Some papyri bear stokes that the student added in order to separate lines, words and syllables so as to make reading easier (e.g., *P. Berol.* 13839; Schubart 1918:plate III,3).

any Christian group would have had the ability to read (1995:5). Fewer still would have the capacity to compose literary or technical works such as the gospels or Q.

Low rates of literacy meant that if the documents of a group were to be known at all, they had to be performed. A written text functioned less as a discrete artifact than as the "script" for oral recitation. As Kenneth Quinn observes, apropos of literary works:

> [T]he written text played very much the same role which the printed score of a musical composition plays today. It recorded the final text as passed for publication by the author. But you acquired a copy with the intention of having it performed for you by a professional reader, or as a record of a performance which you had heard by the author. It was not in itself a substitute for performance. (1982:90)

The other side of this symbiosis between text and performance is that the writer had to compose with the sensibilities and expectations of the intended audience in view. Philo (*De Iosepho* 35) claims that these expectations might at times weigh so heavily that the orator effectively became a slave to his audience. Behind the hyperbole lies a truth that applied to orators and authors alike: an effective work had to engage and reflect audience expectations and values. As F. Gerald Downing points out:

> Even when you were attempting to move your audience in some fresh direction, most of what you said had to be familiar, commonplace, echoing the present ideas and opinions of those listening. And that this betokens more than a simple awareness of the need to use understandable language is shown by the frequent warnings of the ease of a descent into flattery, of being a captive to your audience. The audience's anticipated and expressed expectations would seem to have a powerful effect in social composition, and the effect would for the most part have been "conservative" in the sense of largely conserving their preconceptions and prejudices. (1996:32–33)

The audience was imaginatively present in the act of composition. Real audiences, too, might be present prior to the final stage of composition. Downing cites instances of authors holding preliminary recitations of a work before select audiences with the goal of trying out new ideas and gathering criticisms so as to be able to insert corrections in the final version.[4] His conclusion is apt: "Word processing in the ancient Mediterranean world will have been consistently oral *and collaborative*" (1996:37, emphasis original).

The implications for deducing something of the social location of the intended addressees of Q should be obvious. Composition was essentially "conservative"—conservative, not in relation to societal values as a whole

---

4. Downing 1996:33, citing Cicero, *Atticus* 2.1.1-2; Pliny, *Epistulae* 7.17. See also Rajak 1983:63.

but in relation to the specific audience in view. Ancient rhetorical practice itself ensured a strong correlation between the values and interests of the audience and the shape of the text. In order to construct an effective speech, a writer had to consider carefully both the "issue" (*stasis, quaestio*) and the "rhetorical situation."[5] Determination of the *stasis* controlled the kinds of proofs suitable to that issue, while knowledge of the rhetorical situation allowed the writer to anticipate the points of resistance in the audience and to employ the kinds of appeals that would likely succeed in effecting persuasion. If one assumes that Q's discourse was effective, it follows that its very architecture and fabric reflect the interests and values of its intended audience.

It is of course possible that some compositions failed, either because their authors misjudged the rhetorical situation and *stasis* or because they advocated views that simply were bound to be rejected. In the case of Q, however, this seems unlikely. The fact that it survived long enough to be copied at least twice and thus fall into the hands of Matthew and Luke, and the likelihood that it underwent periodic revision and expansion, suggest that it had been received and used by a group or set of groups for some significant span of time.

Numerous grammatical and rhetorical features signal the "presence" of an intended audience. At a grammatical level can be observed the pervasive nature of second person plural address and the use of vocatives ("hypocrite," 6:42) and direct address ("Why do you call me Lord, Lord?" 6:46). From the standpoint of rhetoric, the instructional portions of Q are largely deliberative, advocating and buttressing a counterstructural lifestyle. The Deuteronomistic elements, on the other hand, appear to be directed to apologetic and epideictic ends, defending the portrait of Jesus and John (and by extension, the Q people) and attacking imagined opponents. The instructional components aim to promote an ethos for the audience and the epideictic portions seek to define communal boundaries and to defend Q's proposed social practice against challenges. Neither strategy would be meaningful without a real audience in view.

From Text to Social History

How does one go about determining what sort of audience(s) might have been addressed by Q? On what basis could one suggest a geographical

---

5. On *stasis* theory, see Nadeau 1964. Hermogenes, a second-century CE rhetor, defines four *staseis* or "issues," each requiring a different form of proof: conjecture (*stochasmos*), i.e., whether an act took place; definition (*horos*), i.e., the essential qualities of a thing; quality (*poiotems*), i.e., nonessential qualities of a thing; and objection (*metalempsis*), i.e., technical matters such as jurisdiction and procedure. On the notion of "rhetorical situation," see Bitzer 1968.

provenance for the document? And how does one determine *what else* the
Q people knew? Three preliminary comments are in order.

"Q COMMUNITY" OR "Q PEOPLE"?

An earlier generation of scholarship could refer almost unself-consciously
to the "Q community" (*die Q-Gemeinde*) in the same way that it was accustomed to speak of "Matthew's church" or "the community of the Beloved
disciple." The categories of form criticism were invoked to produce a
description of this "community," mapping the contents of the document
onto various ecclesial functions: catechesis, exhortation, discipleship, mission, polity and discipline, instruction on last things, and so forth. Thus the
characterization of the Q people tended to be predominantly ecclesial and
theological. Paul Meyer's description of the "Q community" (1967), for
example, focused on Q's missionary activities and the theological contents
of its preaching. The Q group, a "non-Hellenistic Jewish Christian community," embraced a fully futuristic eschatology, proclaimed the coming judgment to fellow Jews, and was Torah-observant even if it did not accept
"rabbinic traditions" (1967:86–88). Similarly, Siegfried Schulz's monumen-
tal commentary on Q (1972) distinguished two layers within Q, an older
Palestinian Jewish-Christian layer and a later (Syrian) Hellenistic Jewish-
Christian one. He described the later Syrian community (*Gemeinde*) as
engaged in an eschatological mission to Israel, conceived as a continuation
of Jesus' own preaching of the kingdom. The Q community considered itself
to be faithful to the Torah, a faithfulness grounded in the charismatic and
apocalyptic radicalism of Jesus' own Torah interpretation. Conflict with the
Pharisees was not over the interpretation of the Torah as such, but over the
relative weighting of the "ceremonial Torah" vis-à-vis the "ethical Torah"
(1973:61). Apocalyptic expectation led to a radicalized form of discipleship, including the call for a total renunciation of property, homelessness,
and rejection of family ties (1973:65).

   This type of approach focused in particular on the theological characterization of Q's audience. Little attention was paid either to the social location of the addressees or to the relation between Q's theological orientation
and its social location. Moreover, the earlier efforts to describe the "Q community" adopted too easily the models and terminology of "community,"
"catechesis," "discipleship," "mission," and "discipline"—terminology
that had been borrowed from *urban* groups of the Pauline sphere. That the
term can be applied meaningfully to the largely rural environment of (presumably) first-century Galilee is doubtful. The term "community"
(*Gemeinde*) is problematic insofar as it is used to refer to a discrete and
bounded "church" with a clear membership, identity rituals, and the means

by which to distinguish its members from other persons residing in the same locale.[6] The existence of such "churches" is scarcely conceivable in a village (which typically consists of 80–100 nuclear families representing 2–4 clans) and barely possible in a large town.[7] One might just as easily imagine the audience of Q to be a network of villages sympathetic to Jesus' kingdom message or a subculture or counterculture within the larger towns and cities of the Lower Galilee. In what follows, therefore, the terms "Q group" or "Q people" will be employed very broadly to refer to the intended audience of Q, pending a closer determination of the kind of group that audience might represent.

GEOGRAPHICAL PROVENANCE

Determining the provenance of the documents of primitive Christianity is notoriously difficult, except in those rather rare instances such as 1 Corinthians or Romans where internal references and a general knowledge of Paul's itinerary combine to allow fairly secure conjectures concerning the place of writing. In the case of the Gospels, most of the suggestions that have been advanced—Antioch or Sepphoris for Matthew, for example—are guesses. These guesses are often based on some hard evidence such as the early attestation of Gospel traditions at a given locale and the perfectly reasonable assumption that the type of audience presupposed by the author of a given Gospel was indeed found at that location. Given the highly fragmentary nature of our knowledge of the distribution of Christian groups in the early empire and our equally fragmentary knowledge of the character of population centers in the Mediterranean region, however, it is impossible to build a very compelling case for any conjectured location or to exclude other candidates.

In most recent analyses of Q it has been assumed that the document derives from the Galilee or southern Syria. This conclusion is sometimes justified on the grounds that Q mentions by name three towns on the north and northwest side of the Kinneret: Kefar Naḥum (Capernaum), Khorazin, and Bethsaida.[8] Such an argument is admittedly not very convincing. These

---

6. Hoffmann 1972:10 was the first to reject the term *Gemeinde* ("church" or "community"), preferring *Q-Gruppe* ("Q group"). Hoffmann's reason for avoiding *Gemeinde* derived from his not wanting to imply that the theology of the Q group was the "only witness to early Christian theology."

7. For a discussion of the size and population of settlements, see chapter 5, pp. 214–15.

8. Thus Harnack 1908:168; Streeter 1911a:213–16; Havener 1987:42–45; Sato 1988:387; Horsley 1995d:42; Tuckett 1996:102. Schenk (1993:489) argues that Tiberias was the place of composition on the basis of the order the place names in Q 10:13-15. Khorazin—Bethsaida—Kefar Naḥum describe an arc from the northeast to the northwest if one were looking across the Kinneret from Tiberias. This seems a rather insubstantial basis for identifying Tiberias as the place of composition. Moreover, Schenk must propose an unusual identification for Khorazin: not Khirbet Keraze (3 km northwest of Kefar Naḥum), the usual identification, and the

place-names occur in only two Q pericopae (Q 7:1-10; 10:13-15). Mark also mentions Kefar Naḥum, Bethsaida, and other sites around the Kinneret, but few would place the composition in Mark in Galilee, because Mark seems in other respects to be unclear about Galilean geography. Moreover, the towns of Kefar Naḥum, Khorazin, and Bethsaida also appear in Matthew and Luke, who took the names over from Q. Although a few argue that Matthew is Galilean, almost no one would suggest that Luke was.

The facts that Q was used by Matthew, whose provenance may be Syrian, and that it bears some relationship to the *Gospel of Thomas*, which may also have come from Syria (Koester 1971a:127–28; Arnal 1995), might invite the conclusion that Q was composed in an area at least adjacent to Syria. This type of argument, however, depends on the rather dubious assumption that Q, composed (say) in the 50s or 60s, did not circulate much beyond Palestine and Syria in the thirty years prior to the compositions of Matthew and of the *Gospel of Thomas*. As Tuckett observes, the same logic ought to imply that Luke was composed in Syria too (1996:102–3)—a conclusion that few nowadays would venture.

A more sophisticated approach to the provenance of Q appears in the 1995 study by Jonathan Reed on the social map of Q. Drawing on the insight of contemporary theorists of geography that social values are at work in the perception of place, Reed observes that the nine place names mentioned in Q describe three concentric circles. Kefar Naḥum is at the center of the circles, appearing alongside Khorazin and Bethsaida (both

---

site of a thriving town at least in the second century CE, but with Kursi (=Gerasa, Mark 5:1), on the Wadi es-Samak on the eastern side of Kinneret.

In 1911a Streeter based his case for a Palestinian provenance for Q on the supposition that Q's lack of mention of Jesus' death was due to the fact that such knowledge could be assumed "in every bazaar in Palestine" (1911a:215). By 1924 Streeter argued that Q's Greek form meant that it was circulated "with the backing of the Church of some important Greek city," naming Antioch as the most likely sponsor (1924:232). Nevertheless, he suggests that it may originally have "emanated" from the Galilee, citing the mention of Capernaum (233). An Antiochene provenance was accepted by Manson (1949:20) and Grant (1957:51). Schulz (1972:481; 1973), on the basis of tradition-historical assumptions, located the earliest layers of Q in the "Palestinian-Syrian region" and the final redaction in an "hellenistic Jewish-Christian community" in the Transjordan or the Decapolis.

Fowler (1924) proposed a Jerusalem provenance on the basis of Q's marked theological differences from Paul (evidently assuming that anything that was non-Pauline derived from Jerusalem); Crum (1927) also advocated Jerusalem on the grounds that it represented "Judaistic" Christianity (and on this assumption attributes to Q much special Matthaean material). L. Johnson (1995:119–20) declares that "there is no positive reason for locating the development of Q materials in Galilee rather than in Jerusalem," citing as support the "remarkably percipient" essay by "H. T. Thatcher" (read: H. Thatcher Fowler [1924]). He seems unaware that Fowler did not even consider the possibility of a Galilean provenance, much less refute it. Similarly, Johnson seems unaware of the contents of the article by "Kloppenburg [*sic*] 1992." (i.e., Kloppenborg 1991) that he cites (n. 304), or the various essays of Reed (1994b; 1995) defending a Galilean provenance for Q.

within an easy walk of Kefar Naḥum). "These three places distinguish themselves from the other six places in Q by the vehemence of their condemnation and by their otherwise anonymity in antiquity" (Reed 1995:21). Q 4:16 provides a fourth Galilean place-name, "Nazara." Reed suggests that a further geographical reference is implicit in the mention of Jonah (11:32), who came from Gath-Hepher, 3 km from Nazareth (Reed 1996; cf Jeremias 1958:24–28). All five, of course, are towns of the Lower Galilee.

Three cities form a second circle, Jerusalem in the south and Tyre and Sidon to the north. It might at first be doubted whether these cities have any significance for determining Q's provenance. Tyre and Sidon might simply be stereotyped literary allusions to Israel's traditional enemies. Tyre and Sidon are, after all, mentioned in Israelite prophecy, although not as frequently as Babylon, Assyria, or Egypt. Reed, however, argues that the two cities were not merely relics of the epic imagination; recent numismatic analysis has made clear that Tyre was one of the main influences on the economy of first-century Galilee.[9]

> The choice of Tyre and Sidon as a contrast to Khorazin and Bethsaida is not an arbitrary selection from the Hebrew prophets. These twin cities are precisely what one would expect a lower Galilean group to select: they are the closest gentile cities that are part of their past epic traditions and that are still part of their present social and economic situations. (Reed 1992:22)

To the south, Jerusalem also belongs to Israel's epic tradition; but no less than Tyre, Jerusalem was a real influence on Galilean economy and society. Q's attitude toward Jerusalem, according to Reed, rules out the possibility that Q was penned in Jerusalem or that Jerusalem was at the center of Q's narrative map. The criticism of Jerusalem is strident: it is a pretentious city which kills the prophets, and whose sanctuary is barren (Reed 1995:23).

The third concentric circle touches cities of the mythic and epic past, Nineveh (11:32) to the north and Sodom (10:12; 17:28-30) to the south. Neither was a living city at the time of Q's composition. Nevertheless Q invokes these peripheral cities in order to threaten and shame the center: the specter of Sodom is employed to threaten nonreceptive Galilean towns (10:12). Its destruction looms up from the south to threaten those who "come out"

---

9. The coinage of Tyre appears with a special frequency in the Upper Galilee, at Meiron (Meyers, Strange, and Meyers 1981:260–272; Raynor and Meshorer 1988), Khirbet Shemaʿ (Meyers, Kraabel, and Strange 1976:148–50 and plate 6.1), and Gush Ḥalav (R. Hanson 1980:51–54). For the first century CE, Tyrian coins account for almost one-half of the total supply at Meiron and 62.5 percent of the supply in the second century (R. Hanson 1980:53). Tyrian coinage is also frequent in the eastern Lower Galilee: at Magdala/Tarichaeae (Meshorer 1976); Khorazin (Meshorer 1973); Sepphoris and Bethsaida (Arav and Meier 1995:61). Of the 23 pre-Byzantine coins found in connection with the first-century Kinneret boat, 2 are from Sidon, 3 from Akko-Ptolemais, and 4 from Tyre (one is Hasmonean and one from Herod Philip). See Gitler 1990.

(3:7a; 7:24) to hear him (Kloppenborg 1990a). In the other direction, Gentile Nineveh and its repentance stand as witnesses against unrepentant Israelites.

Reed suggests that this "map" draws attention to a Galilean center, with Kefar Naḥum situated at the hub. This map is not merely the accidental consequence of the historical Jesus' activity in the Galilee. All of Q's place references belong to its redactional stage (Q²) and thus reflect the imaginative map of the framers of Q. He notes, moreover, that Q uses the term "Israel" (7:9; 22:30) but never "Judaea" or "Judaeans" (*Ioudaioi*), perhaps because "Israel" was a preferable identifier for a Galilean audience.[10]

It is perhaps rather speculative to identify Kefar Naḥum as the center of Q's map on the basis of concentric constructions, especially when Q does not draw specific attention to its map (as happens, for example, in Act 1:8). Q 10:12-15 juxtaposes the "real" cities of Tyre and Sidon (Reed's second circle) with Sodom (the third circle) without seemingly making any distinction between them. Nonetheless, there is a particular focus on Kefar Naḥum in the final form of Q insofar as Q's geographical markers move from the "circuit of the Jordan" (3:3), to the wilderness [of Judaea?] (4:1), to Nazara (4:16), and then focuses on Kefar Naḥum from 7:1 to at least 10:15, where the town is addressed directly (καὶ σύ). After 10:15, Q has only one geographical reference in the address to Jerusalem (13:34), but Reed is no doubt correct that Q's view of Jerusalem makes that city an unlikely provenance.

Care must be exercised when applying literary-critical observations to conclusions about geographical provenance. Luke's gospel, after all, which has a well-known geographical focus on Jerusalem, was hardly written there or even in Jewish Palestine. In spite of Luke's geographical idealization of Jerusalem, he seems to have a rather poor knowledge of Palestinian geography.

Another set of considerations favors a Palestinian provenance, but one at some remove from Judaea. Q's complaints against the Pharisees and lawyers, especially those concerning tithing and the washing of cups (11:39-41, 42), presume quite specific local knowledge of the practices of Pharisees on the part of the audience. I have argued elsewhere that Q's woes function as burlesque. Q's description of Pharisaic practices is just close enough to the truth to be biting and just exaggerated enough to be effective as ridicule (Kloppenborg 1990c). For such rhetoric to be effective, the hearer must recognize both the truth and the exaggeration. Q knows that some Pharisees made distinctions between the inside and outside surfaces of cups and that some discussed the susceptibility of certain herbs to tithing. Q is far better

---

10. Cohen (1979:206–7) notes that in *Vita*, Josephus only once refers to inhabitants of the Galilee as Ἰουδαῖοι, and this in a context where the contrast is with Gentiles. Elsewhere, Ἰουδαῖοι refers to Judaeans, and Γαλιλαῖοι to Galileans. On this, see below, chap. 5, p. 230.

informed about the Pharisees than is Mark, whose vague generalizations and sometimes erroneous statements about Pharisees indicate a non-Palestinian location for that Gospel. As Neusner (1976) has pointed out, moreover, Q's woe about cups presumes a *Shammaite* distinction that was dominant prior to the First Revolt but supplanted by a Hillelite position thereafter.

Q's woes as a whole presuppose that Pharisees and lawyers may be encountered in the marketplaces and in assemblies (Q 11:43). Its rhetoric also appears to suppose that the burlesquing of Pharisaic practices could weaken their influence or even render them inconsequential. That is, Q knows that the Pharisees and lawyers are formidable enough to require an energetic attack, but imagines that burlesque can dislodge them from their position of influence or respect.

The rhetoric of Q accords well with the situation that must be assumed for the Lower Galilee prior to the First Revolt. Freyne (1980) and Saldarini (1988a) argue that Pharisees represented an intermittent presence, but restricted to the larger cities of the Galilee (i.e., Tiberias and Sepphoris). Their emphasis on tithing and their adaptation of a priestly model of piety made them good representatives of the hierocracy in Jerusalem, who wished to collect taxes and to exert influence in regions that lay outside their direct political control (Saldarini 1988a:35–49). Freyne notes further that there is evidence of pockets of Shammaite Pharisees in the Galilee (Freyne 1980:311–18). Under such conditions, Q's woes may be seen as local resistance to Pharisaic presence in the Galilee. The otherwise curious linkage that occurs in the woes between the Pharisees and lawyers—who historically had nothing to do with killing the prophets—and the killing of Zechariah *in Jerusalem* (Q 11:49-51) is likewise intelligible if they were perceived to represent the interests of the hierocracy in Jerusalem.

The unlikelihood of a Jerusalem provenance for Q, combined with the focus of Q's map on the Lower Galilee and the local knowledge that Q assumes on the part of its addressees form the best basis for the assumption of a Galilean provenance for Q. Other locales might theoretically be possible; but the farther one moves from centers where the actual presence of Pharisees can be assumed prior to the First Revolt, and the more difficult it will be to account for Q's local knowledge. And the farther from Kefar Nahum one goes, the more difficult it is to explain the apparent focus of Q's 'map' on this otherwise insignificant town.[11]

11. The geography of Luke-Acts privileges Jerusalem (where his Gospel begins and ends) but sees the progressive extension of the gospel from Jerusalem to the "outermost parts of the earth" (Acts 1:8). Matthew, written after the First Revolt, betrays real contact with Pharisees (or their successors) and thus presupposes a locale where they are present (Saldarini 1992). The dispersion of the scribal schools following the First Revolt makes a number of locations possible, but most of the relocation seems to have been within Palestine (notably, Yavneh). Overman (1990:158–59) favors Sepphoris (or possibly Tiberias), because of Matthew's "unusual

SOCIAL LOCATION

In asking about the people behind the document, I am not simply asking about the geographical provenance of Q. In fact, even if one could determine with certainty that Q was composed, for example, in Kefar Naḥum or Khorazin, this would not necessarily be of great help in interpreting Q, since we do not otherwise know much about either town. Geographical location is in some respects less important than *social location* or the position(s) that the Q people occupied within the matrix of Galilean society. To inquire into their social location is to ask, for example, whether the Q people represent peasants, smallholders, craftspersons, or elite (priestly or nonpriestly?), or some mixture of these. Are they associated with one of the administrative centers of the Lower Galilee (Tiberias, Sepphoris, Tarichaeae, Gabara);[12] or one of the towns where priestly elite may have been present (Sepphoris, and later Meiron in the Upper Galilee);[13] or one of the larger towns; or the perioicic villages under the control of one of the toparchic centers?

To inquire into the social location of Q is to ask about the social conditions assumed by the framers of the document. How is the social and symbolic "world" of Q constructed? What is its attitude toward the ruling Herodian elites? toward the priestly elite? toward Gentiles? toward the Temple and Jerusalem? toward Tyre, the principal economic influence to the north?

It is of course too much to expect that one could obtain a complete picture of the social world of the Q people from so short a document. Q does not offer a catalogue of the group's views, much less a complete profile of its social, economic, and political postures. To complicate matters, our knowledge of the culture and social organization of Roman Palestine is fragmentary at best and some of the available data are open to a variety of construals. The effort to reconstruct a plausible social location of Q and its addressees is a matter, then, of attempting to coordinate Q's incomplete textual signs with an incomplete picture of Roman Palestine. Under the circumstances, the investigation must proceed with relatively modest expectations of results.

Despite the uncertainties attending the reconstruction of the social location of the Q people, the exercise is both necessary and feasible. Necessary, because without a controlled and informed view of the social world of the persons whom Q addressed, the interpreter almost inevitably resorts unconsciously to uncontrolled and casual assumptions about the audience, nor-

---

concentration on Galilee," because his imagery suggests an urban setting, and because his description of Jesus' opponents appears to have Galilean Pharisees (who were present in Sepphoris) in view. Others more vaguely suggest a locale in Syria or Coele-Syria (Saldarini 1994:26).

12. On the toparchic centers of the Galilee, see Schürer 1973:195 n. 43.

13. On the relocation of the priestly *mishmarôt* (courses) in Galilee, see below (chap. 5, pp. 242–45).

mally constructed on the basis of twentieth-century European or North American experience. Stated positively, the text, if it is to be understood adequately, must be situated in the system of cultural and social signs for which it was originally framed.

The project is also feasible. Just as the architecture of Q betrays a particular geographical imagination, so its arrangement of other textual elements reflects the sensibilities and argumentative habits of its framers and its addressees. The presupposition of any effective rhetoric is a knowledge of the audience to be persuaded. Commenting on modern rhetoric, Perelman and Olbrechts-Tyteca point out that "every social circle or milieu is distinguishable in terms of its dominant opinions and unquestioned beliefs, of the premises that it takes for granted without hesitation: these views form an integral part of its culture, and an orator wishing to persuade a particular audience must of necessity adapt himself to it" (1969:20–21). Each piece of rhetoric "constructs" an audience in the way it presents its argument, invokes shared insights, and presupposes shared attitudes. If the rhetoric is to be effective, the "constructed audience" must approximate the real audience. For if there are too many gaps that the real audience cannot fill in or argumentative maneuvers that the real audience cannot follow, the rhetoric fails. The awareness of the intended audience's beliefs, suppositions, expectations, and points of resistance was arguably even more acute in antiquity, given the mechanics of composition outlined at the beginning of this chapter. Thus elements of a text such as genre, argumentative strategies, and the repertoire of appeals provide clues to the social location of the audience as must as to the author(s).

It should be added immediately that the reconstruction of the audience of Q is not a matter of naively reading the text as if it offers a simple description of the audience. Still less is it the kind of "mirror reading" that was once employed in the reconstruction of the views of Paul's opponents, where any positive claim was taken to indicate that the audience (or opponents) held the opposite. Rather, reconstructing Q's audience involves a careful analysis of what Q's rhetoric takes for granted—both in the way it argues and what it can presuppose without argument—and therefore what likely belongs to the symbolic world of the audience.

John H. Elliott has provided a set of nine questions to ask of a text in order to specify more closely its social location:

1. Who are mentioned (or implied) as the addressees? What is their geographical location and social composition? What is their relationship to the author(s)? To what social networks might they belong and what is their social location in general? What social and cultural scripts, plausibility structures, and particular traditions and beliefs does the document presuppose on the part of its audience?

2. What is expressly mentioned or implied about the author-sender of the document?

3. How is the social situation of the addressees described? What information is mentioned expressly, what is repeated (and what is assumed)?

4. How does the author diagnose the situation, and what is singled out for praise or condemnation? What beliefs, values, norms, and sanctions are invoked in this evaluation?

5. How is the strategy of the text evident in its genre, content, and organization?

6. What response does the author(s) seek from the targeted audience?

7. How does the author(s) attempt to motivate or persuade the audience? To what shared goals, norms, sanctions and traditions is appeal made? Are any dominant "root metaphors" used to characterize the collective identity and action of the audience?

8. What is the nature of the situation of the text as seen from a social-scientific perspective, with the aid of comparative social-scientific research? Are there comparable groups in comparable situations? What social issues are at stake (identity, organization, order, cohesion, roles and statuses, internal and external interaction)?

9. What are the self-interests and/or group interests that motivate the author(s)? What ideology is discernible in the document and how is it related to the interests of the author and the group the author represents? (1993:72–74, abbreviated and partly paraphrased)

Efforts to describe the social world of the Q people so far have not attempted to address the full set of questions proposed by Elliott. Nevertheless, some initial steps have been taken toward a description of the world assumed by the text. These may be divided into two main types: those that focus on one or more specific textual sites and attempt to infer details of Q's social situation, and those that proceed on the basis of the document as a whole, its expressed and implied logics, and its construction of a "story world." I will designate the former "microtextual," and the latter "sociorhetorical" approaches.[14] These do not correspond neatly to Elliott's categories, although the microtextual approaches tend to focus on the data embedded in the text (Elliott's points 1 and 3) while sociorhetorical approaches pay as much attention to issues of genre (5), argumentative form (7), mode of description (4), and what these imply about the author (2). These approaches ought not be seen as contradictory and both must be coordinated carefully with data derived from historical, anthropological, and archaeological findings.

14. The term "sociorhetorical criticism" is, I believe, the coinage of Vernon K. Robbins. See Robbins 1984; 1996a; 1996b.

[handwritten note at top: Think about Frankfurt School — Critchley & the Marxist school one]

Microtextual Approaches

RADICALISM AND ITINERANCY: THE MISSION SPEECH

In the past twenty-five years several textual sites have been proposed as potentially important for establishing Q's social location. The most obvious of these is the mission speech (Q 9:57—10:16) with its apparent allusions to itinerancy. The characterization of the Son of Man as one who has "no place to lay his head" (Q 9:58) and the so-called equipment instruction (Q 10:4) appear to privilege a homeless or itinerant lifestyle.

Paul Hoffmann's *Studies on the Theology of Q* (1972) stressed the apocalyptic tone of Q and described its tradents as charismatics. The ethos of the envoys described in Q 10 was close to that of the entire Q group. "Homelessness, a radical separation from family and possessions, and renunciation of anxiety regarding subsistence and clothing—all typical of Jesus—are also characteristic of the Q group" (1972:329). Hoffmann's attention was also drawn to the reference to the "child of peace" in Q 10:6 and to the temptation account. The temptations appeared to reject specific aspects of Zealot messianism: reenactment of the manna miracle, demonstrations of power at the Temple, and the ideal of world rule (also Hoffmann 1969). Thus he suggested that the Q group found itself embroiled in the conflict that arose from the Roman occupation of Palestine, with the Q group adopting an antizealot stance (1969:214). The Q people were a relatively short-lived and small group of wandering charismatics whose functions were defined by the interests of a mission, which had antizealot aspects (1972:330, 333). In a subsequent essay he adjusted this view somewhat: while the wandering preachers might have been responsible for the transmission of the Q material, Q nonetheless addressed a broader group of underprivileged persons (1984:74–75; but see 1989:126–27).

The thesis that significant portions of the Jesus movement included wandering charismatics was popularized in Gerd Theissen's essay "Itinerant Radicalism" (1973, ET 1992b) and his subsequent book-length treatment of the sociology of the Jesus movement (1977, ET 1978). Although he did not treat Q as such, Theissen acknowledged many of Hoffmann's conclusions. Q sayings (Q 9:59-60; 10:2-12; 12:22-31, 33-34, 51-53; 14:26) play a key part in his conclusion that the ethical radicalism of the Synoptic tradition could only be sustained and transmitted by homeless charismatics (1992b:40).

In the face of the severe political, economic, and social pressures facing first-century Galilee, the Jesus movement functioned in several ways. It represented on the one hand "the peace party" which set the reign of God over against both Roman rule and the priestly theocracy. At the same time it rejected the violent solutions of revolutionaries. On the other, it was an experiment "with a vision of love and reconciliation" that aimed at the overall reduction of tension within society. The combination of ethical radicalism, the call to repentance, and the ethic of love served as compensation for the aggression that inevitably results from grinding poverty. Compensation was achieved though internalization, transference, and transformation of that aggression.

Ironically, the same tensions that gave rise to the Jesus movement ensured that it would not succeed. According to Theissen, rising tension between Jews and Gentiles and the nationalist retrenchment that such tension produced proved uncongenial soil for anyone who put Jewish identity into question and, in particular, any group that fraternized with Gentiles. Only in cities of the empire did the Jesus movement succeed. But in the context of urban life, patronage by wealthy Christians, and the conservative political stances that these encouraged, wandering charismatics and their radical theocratic ideals had little currency (Theissen 1978:98, 112–19).

The implications of his study and Hoffmann's for Q were quickly grasped by Luise Schottroff (1978, ET 1986), who argued that the people responsible for Q were "wandering preachers of the proximate end of the world" (1986:38). Even more recently she has spoken of "Wanderprophetinnen"— wandering women prophets among the Q people (1991b, ET 1991a). While Theissen insisted that "poverty was not only a fate, but a calling" (1978:13), Schottroff argued the opposite: itinerancy, defenselessness, and poverty were not voluntary, demonstrative acts in the face of zealot messianism, but simply reflected the straitened economic situation of the majority of the Palestinian population. The Jesus movement offered a utopian vision whose purpose was not "to depict a future, other world of God, but to help realize the reign of God as God's absolute claim over human beings in their present life, and thus to help them live a human life that is something 'more' than can be destroyed by hunger and death" (Schottroff 1986:52).

When Theissen revisited the topic of the social history of Q (1989, ET 1991), he appealed less to functionalist and psychological categories and paid greater attention to the conflicts between the Q people and the ruling elite. Q reflected the crisis sparked by Caligula's order to set up a statue of himself in the Temple.[15] Theissen still regarded the Q material as transmitted principally by itinerant charismatics and hence did not need to identify Q with any specific locale in Palestine. But rather than dwelling on the ultimate failure of these itinerants, Theissen spoke of their "pride in the overcoming of the Caligula crisis, viewed as a great satanic temptation" (1991:233). They represented a prophetic renewal movement within Judaism—though Theissen is not very clear on what this renewal entailed— which came into conflict with the Pharisees, despite their own Torahobservant stance (1991:221–34).

There are a number of interesting common denominators to these views

---

15. Above, chap. 2, pp. 82–85.

as well as important disagreements. Perhaps most prominent is the fact that the analyses of Hoffmann, Theissen, and Schottroff in particular pioneered a shift in attention from the "theological" aspects of Q to its social and political postures—an interest that continues in virtually all recent studies of Q. Yet theological categories remain, since each of these authors understands the Q people to be engaged in a "mission" of renewal, whether or not it was successful.

There is also an important commonality in method. Each treats Q without regard to its compositional history. It is true that Hoffmann was one of the first to distinguish between tradition and redaction in Q; but in practice he stressed continuities rather than discontinuities, with the result that the "redaction" of Q does not emerge as distinct from other material (1972:3). Similarly, while Theissen in his later work is aware of compositional studies of Q, he dismisses them (1991:205; similarly, Schottroff 1992). While Theissen accepts the view that redactional interests can be determined by noting the ordering and arrangement of Q sayings and even that the temptation story is a "late" addition to Q, these observations practically have no influence on his analysis. The sidestepping of compositional questions allows a few pericopae to determine the way in which the entire document is read. For those who see itinerancy as dominant, Q 10:3-12, 16 is given pride of place, and other sayings (Q 9:57-58, 59-60; 12:22-31; 14:26-27) are read in the light of this.

The Role of the "Sympathizers"

To reconstruct the social setting of Q largely from the mission instructions raises an issue with both practical and theoretical aspects. What was the relationship between the itinerants (or Q people) and others? Theissen popularized the distinction between itinerants and "sympathizers," the latter being groups and persons (not "communities") upon whom the charismatics relied for support. Although he spoke of a complementarity between the two groups, the itinerants were the virtuosi: they were the "decisive spiritual authorities in the local communities" (Theissen 1978:7). The "sympathizers," whose norms for behavior were considerably less radical, did not represent the heart of the Jesus movement, either organizationally or ideologically. "From the point of view of organization, these groups of sympathizers remained within the framework of Judaism. They were less obviously the embodiment of the new element which had emerged with earliest Christianity . . ." (1978:8).

This formulation is unfortunate on several counts. First, there is no evidence from Q 10 that the itinerants were supposed to be authorities. There is no hint of the "workers" founding or leading groups; rather, they visit villages (which either welcome or reject them) and perform wonders in exchange for hospitality. Their designation as "workers"—the ordinary term for agricultural day laborers—rather than more statused titles such as "apostle" or "prophet"—gives no indication that they are leaders.

Second, Theissen's characterization of the itinerants as "Christian" smuggles a theological distinction—and one of very dubious merit—into the task of social description. It reifies itinerancy and identifies it arbitrarily with what is "Christian." This is probably a function of Theissen's collateral description of the itinerants as "charismatics"—a term that Theissen employs in a psychological manner, implying some sort of personal endowment. Crossan is rightly critical of this use, arguing that "charisma" is more properly a *relational* term, referring to the reciprocal relations between persons and groups, not the characteristics of individuals (1997:8).[16]

Finally, the depiction of Q's itinerants as individual virtuosi, rather incidentally supported by "sympathizers," neglects the structure of Q's own description of the two groups. Q 10:2-16 is framed from the point of view of the group that prays for workers to be "sent out" (Q 10:2: δεήθητε . . . ὅπως ἐργάτας ἐκβάλῃ), sends them out, and warrants that they be paid as workers (Q 10:7b). Itinerancy exists for Q in a social symbiosis in which itinerancy is legitimized and supported by local groups. The apparent function of these itinerants is not to found or lead new groups, much less to convert persons to a homeless lifestyle, but rather to announce the advent of the kingdom. In the rural society of Jewish Palestine, the act of receiving such persons into a town or village would have amounted to a declaration of agreement with Q's social, political, and theological postures. That is, Q's itinerants should not be reified and viewed apart from the groups which legitimated their roles in the first place, and the towns and villages which welcomed them, thus signaling consent with the kingdom they represented. Without such support and acceptance, the itinerants would simply starve.

Anthony Blasi stressed an ambivalence in role structures: on the one hand, the Q people had a disruptive function, recruiting members from relatively stable households; but on the other, they looked to households for support and functioned as religious workers, encouraging reconciliation, prayer, and ethical achievements in those households (Blasi 1986:246; 1989:115). In responding to Blasi, L. Michael White made the key observation: the fact that the Q traditions were set down in written form points to a retrospective view of those traditions. "The Q stratum bearers are already localized leaders (the *pater familias*?), who look *back* to the earlier itinerant missionaries as their 'source' for the words of Jesus."[17] It is in fact

---

16. Crossan cites Bryan Wilson (1973:499): "*Charisma* is a sociological, and not a psychological concept. . . . [I]t expresses the balance of claim and acceptance—it is not a dynamic, causally explanatory, concept; it relates to an established state of affairs, when the leader is already accepted, not to the power of one man to cause events to move in a particular direction."

17. White 1986:256 (emphasis original); cf. Schmeller 1989:94.

attention to the documentary character of Q and to its compositional features that has called for a major reevaluation of the itinerancy hypothesis of Hoffmann, Theissen, and Schottroff.

A key literary observation was made by Dieter Zeller, who noted the tension between Q 10:2 ("beg the Lord of the harvest to send out workers into his harvest") and 10:3 ("behold, I send you as sheep among wolves"). While Q 10:3 was arguably directed at itinerants, the saying that frames and introduces Q's mission speech is addressed to those responsible for commissioning the "workers."[18] This means that while Q may contain some materials directed to itinerants, in the present form it is the product of a settled group or groups. D. Zeller in fact thinks that itinerants founded communities, which in turn framed and transmitted the Q materials, adding further paraenetic and polemical sayings.[19]

Risto Uro made a similar proposal. An early "mission code," consisting of Q 10:4-11a, was transmitted by "wandering missionaries." This was later incorporated into Q by a redactor in a community in which itinerants may have been present, but whose interests were no longer controlling factors (1987:242–43). What D. Zeller had observed with regard to Q 10:2-3 applied equally to other materials that frame the "mission code" (e.g., Q 10:21-22, 23-24; 11:2-13). For Uro, by the time of the final redaction of Q ecclesial formation had begun to occur and autonomous itinerants had become "representatives of their home church" (1987:205; see also Kim 1990).

Migaku Sato also coordinated conclusions from literary analysis with social history. Q 9:57—10:24, which he identified as a distinct redaction (his Redaction B), was framed not from the perspective of the wandering missionaries but by the sedentary communities which constituted the reserve from which new missionaries were recruited and from which those missionaries were commissioned (1988:380). Other segments of Q (Redaction A) and the framing redaction (Redaction C) likewise required the scribal work of a settled community. Nonetheless, as the title of his book (*Q und Prophetie*) indicates, Sato wishes to stress the prophetic character of the entirety of Q and suggests that the final redactors of Q might, like those mentioned in *Did.* 13.1-2, have been former wandering prophets who had become local leaders (1988:380–81).

Hence, an alternative image of the Q people emerges, one which acknowledges the activities of the itinerant workers, but which implicitly restricts their activities to the early stages of group formation. Itinerants may still have been present when Q was edited, but they no longer exerted

18. D. Zeller 1982:404; ET 1993; similarly Kloppenborg 1987a:193; Uro 1987:113, 204.
19. D. Zeller 1977:93; 1994:128–29. In 1987 I accepted this scenario (1987a:239), but am more dubious about it now.

a controlling influence on the formation of the document. Nor did their interests dominate those of the entire group.

THE Q PEOPLE AS CYNICS

At least since Hoffmann's seminal study, the lifestyle of Greek and Roman Cynics has been considered as a possible analogy to the homeless and vagrant life of Q's "missionaries" (Hoffmann 1972:318; cf. Theissen 1973:255–56). Yet as Leif E. Vaage pointed out in his 1987 Claremont dissertation, the analogy was never taken very seriously (1987:27–59). This may be due partially to a pervasive assumption that first-century Galilee was insulated from the culture of Hellenism, despite evidence to the contrary (Meyers 1979). And it may have to do with an a priori conviction that early Christians were up to something so fundamentally different from any other Mediterranean persons that any analogy is bound to fail (Smith 1990).

Beginning with Q's mission speech (Q 10:2-16) and extending his analysis throughout the formative stratum of Q, Vaage argued that for virtually all of the component sayings, the closest analogies were to be found in the realm of Cynicism (cf. also Downing 1984; 1988a; 1988c). The Q people, like contemporary Cynics, "enjoy a constitutive poverty . . . they beg for sustenance. They have learned to survive rejection well . . . they demonstrate their discontent and condemnation by a symbolical act. They understand themselves to be sent" (1987:386).

According to Vaage, Q did not offer a utopian alternative or a program of renewal, restoration, or reform. Instead, it was satisfied with an attack on the current order of things. The "kingdom of God" in Q does not serve as a utopian symbol but rather as an instrument of sociopolitical destabilization. To pronounce an impoverished way of life to be honorable (Q 6:20b), to compare the kingdom of God to a weed like mustard (13:18-19), is to "imagine and construct an alternate reality to the dominant social institutions of [Q's] immediate context and its prevalent moral values" (1994:56). The cynic-like deportment of the Q people appears especially in the woes against the Pharisees (11:39-44, 46-52). Q's criticism, rather than being a debate about exegetical norms or the hermeneutics of Torah, focused on the gap between appearance and reality, between the pretense of virtue and reality, between the ostensible basis of behavior and the silliness of its appearance.[20] Vaage concludes that

[l]ike the Cynics, the "Galilean upstarts" whom Q's formative stratum represents conducted in word and deed a form of "popular" resistance to the offi-

---

20. Similarly, Downing 1992:136: "The controversy with Pharisees in Q is phrased in terms of the Stoic but also Cynic contrast between inner reality and 'mere' externals."

cial truths and virtues of their day. Registered in their unorthodox ethos, ethics, ideology, and ad hoc social critique as well as the sparse but vivid memory they maintained of certain "anti-heroes" of the recent past (John and Jesus) was both a decisive "no" to the typical habits and aspirations of their immediate cultural context, as well as a curious confidence in their own peculiar ability here and now. . . . (1994:106)

Burton Mack's work on Q (1993) continues and develops this view. Mack argues that the Q people—at least those represented at Q's formative stages—were comparable to Cynics, engaging in social critique and countercultural behavior.

> The aphoristic style of Q^1 was very close to the Cynic's way of making pointed comment on human behavior, and the logic involved in recommending extravagant behavior in Q was very close to the rhetoric of a Cynic's repartee when challenged about his own behavior. The forthrightness with which social critique was registered in Q was exactly like that of the Cynics' attitude called *parresia* or bold, outspoken manner. (1993:46)

Mack's reading of the social history of Q embraces virtually all of the document but does so by distinguishing five successive stages. Beginning with the aphoristic core antecedent to the Q^1 speeches (stage 1),[21] Mack detects a consistent perspective that exposes claims to "superior status based on such things as wealth, learning, possessions, secrets, ranks and power" as hollow (1993:111). The elaboration of these aphorisms into the larger blocks of Q^1 (stage 2) preserved this critique of conventional values. The aim of the Q people as reflected in Q^1 was not, argues Mack, social reform. It was social critique. Mack finds Q replete with cynic-like themes: an exhortation to a natural and simple lifestyle; voluntary poverty; renunciation of needs; rejection of family ties; fearlessness; troublesome public behavior; and a critique of wealth, pretension, and hypocrisy (1993:64, 115). Yet, itinerancy itself is not characteristic of the Q people nor is it proper to speak of a Q "mission." The instructions in Q 10, while formulated as "guidance for a movement that had spread throughout Galilee," are much less programmatic than Theissen or Hoffmann had thought. The movement spread almost casually, "in the normal course of contact and travel wherever talk about God's rule caught the attention of persons willing to listen" (Mack 1993:130; cf. 1988a:623).

Although Mack emphasizes the cynic-like character of Q's sayings, he also notes elements of social formation that distinguish Q from Cynicism, even at the earliest stage. Evidence of a rudimentary social formation can be detected in the shift from aphorisms to maxim-like generalizations ("Where your treasure is, there is your heart," Q 12:34), the high incidence of imperatives, the use of the second person to address readers, and a heightened

---

21. Mack 1993:110–11: Q 6:20b, 27-28, 38c, 39, 40, 43; 9:58; 10:2; 11:10; 12:2, 7, 23, 33; 14:11; 17:33; 14:34-35.

interest in human relations and in egalitarian social roles. At the literary stage of Q¹, the aphoristic core is transformed into a set of community rules and instructions. Mack also sees the beginnings of an effort to legitimate the group's ethos in three elements: references to the rule of God, appeals to nature as a manifestation of the divine, and the invocation of Israel's history in the person of Solomon (Q 12:27) (1993:122). The rule of God in Q¹ was not an apocalyptic fantasy but rather stood for "something that can be accomplished, something that contrasts with the conventional, meriting a change of attitude or behavior worthy of a new vision" (1993:124).[22] The appeals both to nature and to an ancient and ideal king should be seen in the context of Hellenistic discussions and critiques of the present order. "The past was plumbed for golden ages, the natural order was imagined as being governed by laws, the cosmos was viewed as the eternal city in which all human beings lived as 'cosmopolitans,' and hope for better times was sustained by projections of the ideal kingdom into the future" (1993:125–26). The Jesus movement as represented by Q¹ had not yet located the kingdom of God in the social formation of the movement, but there was an "overlap of the rule of God as an alternate realm or way of life everywhere available to daring individuals" and the ethos of the Q group (1993:127).

At the level of Q² many changes are evident. In place of aphoristic imperatives, one finds prophetic warnings, examples from the epic tradition, controversy stories, and apocalyptic announcements. Mack thinks that even before the inscribing of Q² more attention was paid to the role of Jesus as a founder and to matters of loyalty to the Jesus movement.[23] Conflict with the Pharisees appears at this stage (stage 3) and this conflict led to an effort to read biblical epic in such a way that it would ground the identity of the Q people. Thus Jesus is associated with the Heavenly Sophia, with John the Baptist, with a string of figures of Israel's epic history, and is fitted into a scenario of apocalyptic judgment.

Thus at the level of the second redaction (Q², stage 4), mythmaking was in full swing. Jesus was recast as a prophet and related to the Deuteronomistic themes of the rejection of the prophets and Sophia's sending of the prophets to Israel. The Jesus movement located itself with reference to the "foundations of the world" (Q 11:50) and the day of the Son of Man (17:26-28), and to many intervening points in epic history. Q² appropriated the two mythological figures of Sophia and the Son of Man:

22. Downing (1995a) has noted the broad currency of protological and eschatological expectations of the golden age or "life under Cronos" that functioned both to undergird countercultural behaviors and as criticism of the prevailing cultural arrangements. Koester (1992:10–13) points out that the language of divine kingship in Second Temple Judaism should be seen in relation to imperial propaganda of a new age of peace and prosperity realized in Augustus's reign. In this context, the invocation of God's rule, especially when associated with various countercultural imperatives, amounted to a confrontation with that propaganda.

23. Mack 1993:138–39, citing Q 6:22-23; 7:23; 10:16, 23; 11:20, 23; 12:8-9; 14:26-27.

[I]n order to join these two mythological figures exactly where they had to be joined, the people of Q reimagined Jesus as the child of wisdom and as the seer who knew what the son of man would say at the end of time. Each of these mythological developments deserves some discussion, for taken together they put us in touch with an amazing accomplishment. The people of Q created a myth of broad horizon by elaborating the unlikely genre of the sayings of a sage. (1993:147)

Q³ (stage 5) represents an even more advanced stage of mythmaking.[24] Here Mack locates a shift from describing Jesus as a child of Wisdom to Son of God (4:1-13) and an attendant shift from viewing Jesus as a sage to an otherworldly being, the sole mediator of revelation (10:21-22) and the heir to the kingdom (22:28-30). Both the Temple and the Torah figure at this stage (13:34-35; 16:17), and both indicate the extent to which the Q people had come to regard themselves as a distinct social formation. Earlier debates with the Pharisees were retracted and the Torah was recovered and affirmed. Mack thinks that Q³ comes from a period just after the First Revolt, and thus the Q people look back on the Temple and its destruction, not with any satisfaction but with the conviction that Sophia, who had failed to find a place in Second Temple society, was now to be located in the Q group (1993:175).

At least three aspects of the work of Vaage and Mack are noteworthy. First, both have paid attention to Q *as a document* in a way that their predecessors did not. This has two consequences. On the one hand, both try to construct a social history, not on the basis of the somewhat arbitrary selection of one or two clusters of sayings, but by tracing the successive literary elaboration of Q and what changing rhetorical postures imply about the social location of its tradents. Thus, the discussion of social history is strictly coordinated with literary history. Vaage, of course, treats only the formative stratum, but in doing so attempts to incorporate most of its component parts.[25] This procedure is in sharp contrast to the essentially form-critical approach of Theissen and Schottroff (and Horsley), which privileges

24. Mack 1993:173–73 includes in Q³ not only Q 4:1-13; 16:17 (11:42c) (so Kloppenborg 1990c) but Q 10:21-22; 11:27-28; 12:4; 13:34-35; and 22:28-30. The grounds for such an allocation appear to be more tradition-historical and thematic than literary-critical. For a critique, see J. M. Robinson 1996.

25. Vaage's formative stage in fact differs slightly from Kloppenborg's and includes Q 6:20b-21, 27-49; 7:24-26, 28a, 33-34; 9:57-60; 10:3-6, 9-11, 16; 11:2-4, 9-13, 14-20, 24-26, 33-36, 39b-48, 52; 12:2-7, 22-31, 33-34; 13:18-21, 24; 14:26-27; and 17:33 (1996:10, 107-20). Thus he includes Q 7:24-26, 28a (on John the Baptist), 33-34 (comparing John and Jesus); 11:14-20, 24-26 (Beelzebul accusation), 33-36 (sayings on Light), 39b-48, 52 (the woes against the Pharisees). The ascription of 7:24-26, 28a, 33-34 to Q¹ in my view is not adequately defended, for Vaage does not show on literary grounds why these should be regarded as antecedent literarily to what surrounds them, nor how literarily they would cohere with the rest of the formative stratum. For a similar criticism, see J. M. Robinson 1994a:260–61 (on Mack); 1994b (on Vaage); Tuckett 1996:369–72.

one set of sayings without asking whether the way in which sayings were framed and arranged in Q discloses anything important about those for whom the text was created. Vaage and Mack, by contrast, employ *literary* signals to direct their social-historical interpretations.

Second, and perhaps surprisingly, itinerancy does not figure very prominently in either Vaage's or Mack's reconstruction of Q's ethos. Despite the title of his dissertation, "Q: The Ethos and Ethics of an Itinerant Intelligence," Vaage only occasionally refers to Q people as "wandering philosophers" (1987:495; 1996:38, 103). Both he and Mack are more concerned to establish the ethos of Q with its abrasive posture toward its surrounding culture and institutions. It is not itinerancy as such, but Q's critical and rootless posture that bespeaks its cynic-like character.

Because of the way in which the ethos of Q is articulated, a third common feature emerges. While both Vaage and Mack assume that the Q people were in some sense active in promoting their views, this should not be construed as a clearly defined program of a mission to Israel (or anyone else). Even if one supposes that Cynics or the Q people would recognize themselves in Epictetus's characterization of the Cynic as a messenger of the gods (*Diss.* 3.22.23-25), the kind of "mission" entailed is a far cry from what Hoffmann and others supposed regarding the "mission" of the Q people.

Since Vaage deals only with the formative stratum of Q, it is unclear how he would imagine the transformation of a cynic-like Q[1] into the final version of Q, with its appeal to Israel's epic history, Deuteronomistic theology, fellowship with the Patriarchs, and continuity with the prophets. Mack's reconstruction tries to account for these transformations and it is noteworthy that, accordingly, his view of the Q people explicitly acknowledges more group formation, even at the earliest stages, than Vaage's. Downing has criticized reconstructions of the social history of Q that imagine too radical a discontinuity between one literary stage and another on the grounds that an editor (of Q[2]) would not have been able to "get away with" testing a drastically revised version of the document on an audience that had become accustomed to the earlier edition.[26] I think that it is fair to say that Mack is not in fact as susceptible to this criticism as Downing thinks, for Mack is quite careful to draw lines of continuities between his five stages.[27]

26. Downing 1996:42. Tuckett (1991:214) directs a similar criticism against my stratigraphy: "If too much of a disjunction between layers is postulated, or if total rejection of the earlier tradition by the later editor is proposed, the question arises why the earlier tradition was ever used at all by the later editor." The second part of Tuckett's conditional is quite irrelevant, since neither I nor Mack imagines a "total rejection of the earlier tradition," and *The Formation of Q*, at least, has stressed the *continuities* between Q[1] and Q[2] (pp. 317–28).

27. Downing's insistence on continuity is also exaggerated, for his rather glib assumption that an audience would resist significant alterations simply ignores the fact that Matthew, for example, has completely reversed certain Markan characterizations (e.g., the disciples' reaction to the walking on the sea, Matt 14:33). One must either assume that the Matthaean audience

PROPHETS OF LOCAL RENEWAL AND RESISTANCE

The most vigorous opponent of both the notions of itinerants and of a cynic-like Q is Richard Horsley. In his *Sociology and the Jesus Movement* (1989b) Horsley launched a full-scale attack on Theissen's reconstruction, arguing that the texts regularly adduced to support the existence of wandering charismatics either (a) do not imply the abandoning of home and family (Q 10:4) or (b) were intended in a figurative way (Q 9:59-60; 14:26-27) or (c) do not point *only* to itinerants (Q 6:20-23; 12:11-12, 22-31, 33-34; 16:13) (1989b:43–46). Far from advocating a social radicalism, the Q people were engaged in the "revitalization of local community life" (1989b:117).

Horsley's argument with Vaage and Mack is twofold. First, he challenges the parallels to Q 10 that Vaage adduced and suggests the text is virtually *anti-Cynic*: the prohibition of a wallet (πήρα) and a staff (both typical pieces of Cynic equipment) and the admonition not to greet anyone along the way (10:4) distinguish the Q people from Cynics (1989:117; cf. Tuckett 1989:367–68). At this level, the debate appears to be whether the Q people *were* Cynics or not. As will be seen below (chap. 9), this completely misses what is at stake for Vaage and Mack. For the point is not one of *identity* or homology but of *analogy*: to *compare* the Q people with Cynics allows one to see in Q a critical posture, a rootlessness, experimentation, and playfulness. It is not an argument about "influence" or genealogy.

Horsley's other disagreement with Vaage and Mack concerns the general posture of the Q group and its relationship to Israelite tradition. Because Vaage's analysis is concentrated on Q[1], which notably lacks appeals to Israel's epic tradition, there is little occasion for him to elaborate on this aspect of Q. Mack, of course, spends considerable space on Q[2]'s use of epic materials. For Mack, however, the figures from Israel's past are invoked in a secondary (mythmaking) reflex; they do not function to provide foundational metaphors of group identity. Since Horsley rejects the stratigraphical analysis of Q upon which Mack and Vaage depend, he can treat all of the Q materials as evidence of a single moment of early Christian social history rather than distinguishing two or more historically and rhetorically identifiable moments.

From one point of view this disagreement might seem inconsequential, since Horsley's rejection of stratigraphy only means that his "Q" is virtually coextensive with what Mack and Kloppenborg describe when they treat Q[2].[28] Yet the role of the stratigraphic model of composition invoked by

---

was completely unfamiliar with Mark (and so had no occasion to resist Matthew's rewriting) or that it rejected Mark's characterizations and so embraced Matthew's. Neither assumption is very likely.

28. The temptation account (Q 4:1-13) and the other two Q[3] texts (11:42c; 16:17) do not figure specifically in Horsley's analyses (1991c; 1995d).

Mack and Kloppenborg has important consequences. It means that later stages must be understood in their historical and rhetorical relationship to prior stages—as developments, rationalizations, or, in Mack's terms, myth-making. None of this is necessary for Horsley. Since he offers no concrete model for the composition of Q beyond calling it "sayings of prophets" (1991a), and since he in practice does not attend to the (literary) framing features of the collection,[29] he is not obliged to begin, as Mack and Kloppenborg are, either with the overall framing of Q(²) or with the dynamisms at work in the earlier stages of Q.

Horsley's starting point in fact is not the document at all, but a recon-struction of the social history of Palestinian society set out in earlier publi-cations (1987; 1989b). Basic to this analysis is the assumption that "the fundamental social divide . . . [was] between the rulers and the ruling insti-tutions in Jerusalem and the people in village communities, with the scribes and Pharisees representing the former to the latter" (1991c:57; similarly, 1995d:42). Here Horsley draws upon the important study of the Pharisees by Saldarini, who argued that Pharisees functioned in the Galilee as "retain-ers" of interests in Jerusalem.[30] The opposition of the Q people to the rulers and their retainers is seen in Q's "prophetic" sayings: in the woes against the Pharisees (Q 11:39-52), in the lament over Jerusalem (13:34-35), and espe-cially in the concluding saying of Q (22:28-30), which Horsley insists should be seen as a promise that the Q people will "rule" (or "liberate") Israel, rather than "judge" it (1989b:123; 1991c:59; 1995d:44–51).

Among the villagers themselves, Q encouraged local cooperation: gen-erosity (Q 6:29-30); debt cancellation (11:2-4); and measures to reduce tension—love of "enemies" (6:27-28), forgiveness (17:3-4), and dispute set-tlement (12:58-59). Thus the Q people promoted a vision of the kingdom of God understood as the renewal of village life, the most basic unit of "Israel," and the development of egalitarian family relationships (1989b:123; 1995d:43–44).

The dominant model operative in Horsley's reconstruction of the Q peo-ple is one of a prophetic opposition to the ruling elite and a prophetic advo-cacy of local renewal. This, it should be noted, does not follow from a literary analysis of the document—that is, from an analysis such as Sato's attempt to characterize Q as a prophetic book *in literary terms*. Nor does it flow from the identification of smaller clusters of sayings in Q as sharing specifically prophetic genres.[31] Rather, it follows simply from the privileg-

---

29. Horsley (1995d:41) argues that Q is not a "collection of sayings" like the *Gospel of Thomas* but a "series of sayings-clusters or discourses" and that accordingly it must be approached "discourse by discourse." Thus he avoids dealing with the overall framing of the collection and to the features that govern the reading of Q as a whole.

30. Saldarini 1988a; 1988b; 1988c, drawing on the typology of Lenski 1966:214–96.

31. The one exception to this is Horsley's assertion that Q 13:28-29, 34-35; 14:16-24 represents a "prophetic discourse" ostensibly directed against the Jerusalem rulers (1995d:46).

ing of individual prophetic sayings in Q. Horsley repeatedly characterizes these admonitions as "covenantal exhortations" (1995d:43, 44, 48), in spite of the fact that Q contains no obviously convenantal language.

From this description it is clear why he should find so problematic Mack's comparison of the Q people with Cynics. Even though Mack himself suggests that the Cynics functioned as "the Greek analogue to the Hebrew prophets" in their role as critics of conventional values and oppressive forms of government (1993:114), the Cynics provide no analogy for what Horsley evidently thinks essential about the Q people: that they functioned as advocates for a local renewal based on covenantal values. Horsley, however, is unable to provide either evidence of covenantal language in Q or a demonstration that the framers of Q represented themselves or Jesus as prophets. None of the standard indicators of prophetic literature is present in Q.

Horsley's prophetic paradigm also accounts for his resistance to certain literary conclusions, in particular the understanding of "this generation" and "to judge" (κρίνειν). Horsley insists that Q's term "this generation" (Q 7:31-35; 11:29, 31, 32, 49-51) does not refer to "Israel" and might better be rendered as "this type" or "this evil breed" (1991b:191–92). He is concerned lest a portrait of Q emerge that depicts the Q group as having already abandoned any mission to other Israelites and embraced a purely Gentile mission, since this would rather obviously undermine his understanding of Q as prophetic renewal. For the same reason Horsley insists that κρίνειν in Q 22:28-30 should be rendered "rule" (the twelve tribes of Israel) rather than "judge" (1987:199–208; 1991b:196; 1995d:38).

While Horsley has allowed his assumptions about social history to determine his reading of the document rather than vice versa, his approach has occasioned a needed clarification in literary analysis of Q. Lührmann had argued from the construction of Q's speeches and the intensity of its polemic against "this generation" that "a repentance by Israel is no longer anticipated in this preaching of judgment; there remains only the judgment."[32] Against Steck, who had earlier suggested that Q was engaged in a "revival of Israel" (1967:286), Lührmann noted both the positive view of the Gentiles expressed in Q and the lack of any notion of "revival" (1969:87–88, ET 1994:61–62). The combination of judgment sayings directed against "Israel" or "this generation" and sayings that treat Gentiles favorably has suggested to some that the Q people were either engaged in a "Gentile mission"[33] or at least knew of it and were sympathetic.[34]

Even here, Horsley adduces no comparative materials and engages in no formal analysis of the construction of the unit.

32. Lührmann 1969:47; similarly, Kloppenborg 1987:148.

33. Manson 1949:20; Lührmann 1969:58, 87–88; D. Zeller 1972:93; 1984:96; Laufen 1980:192–94; Uro 1987:210–23.

34. P. Meyer 1970; Jacobson 1992b:110, 256.

Both a Gentile mission and a negative view of Israel are inimical to Horsley's reconstruction, since he assumes that the text directly reflects a social reality. Hence he is obliged to deny the obvious force of Q 13:28-29, which describes "many" coming from "east and west" to recline at table with the Patriarchs in the kingdom of God while "you" are excluded. Horsley pleads that these "many" who are to be seated with the Patriarchs are not Gentiles but the Jewish Diaspora (1995d:38). Such a reading, however, leaves unexplained why the Patriarchs are mentioned here. There is nothing extraordinary about the claim that Diaspora Jews should be identified with the Patriarchs; they already belong to Israel. What is striking is the structure of the saying, which claims that the addressees—clearly Israelites—will be disestablished (IQP: ἐκβληθήσ<εσθε>), while others will enjoy the company of the Patriarchs. These others can only be Gentiles. There is nothing at all in Q to suggest that its framers were interested in Diaspora Judaism. Against Horsley's insistence that κρίνειν in Q 22:30 means "rule" (the twelve tribes of Israel), Dupont's observation stands: the New Testament furnishes no examples of this verb meant in the Semitic sense of "to govern" (1964:372), and all of the other occurrences of κρίνειν and its cognates in Q (6:37; 12:57; 11:31-32) quite clearly mean "judge."

Literary analysis demands that the exegete pay attention not merely to isolated sayings or even small clusters of sayings, but to the larger compositional strategies at work in the document. Horsley ignores the plain sense of the construction of Q 7:1-10, 18-35. This unit is bracketed by two pericopae which express criticism of the response of Israel to Jesus and John. In Q 7:1-10 the obvious interest of the redactor is in the saying of Jesus, "I tell you, not in Israel have I found such faith" (Q 7:9b). The rhetorical strategy at work is shaming. In an agonistic culture such as that of ancient Palestine, to point out the exemplary faith of a non-Israelite is a way of shaming Israelites. The closing pericope in this complex, Q 7:31-35, likewise criticizes the responses of "this generation" to Sophia's children, John and Jesus (and, one supposes, to the Q people who no doubt see themselves as continuing the activities of John and Jesus). If Q 7:31-32 were once a free-floating saying, it is conceivable that the term "this generation" might have had different valences. But once 7:31-32 became part of the complex of Q 7:1-10, 18-28, 31-35, it is impossible *not* to read "this generation" alongside "Israel." When these units in turn are read alongside such sayings as Q 10:12, 13-15 and 11:31-32, which deliberately use Gentile figures to shame "this generation," or alongside Q 11:49-51 and 13:34-35, which describe the unhappy history of God's attempt to send envoys to Jerusalem, or alongside threats of exclusion directed against Jesus' contemporaries (13:26-27) and the counterbalancing announcement of a Gentile pilgrimage (13:28-29), or, finally, alongside the promise to Jesus' followers that they will "judge the twelve tribes of Israel" (22:30), it is virtually impossible to avoid the conclusion that for rhetorical purposes, Q is underscoring an opposition between "Israel"/"this generation" and non-Israelites.

This is rhetoric, however, not social description. One cannot immediately conclude from the apparent criticisms of "this generation" that the Q people have begun a Gentile mission. At the same time, however, it is illegitimate to rewrite the text or ignore its rhetorical force because it seems to not cooperate with prior assumptions about Q's social world. Rather, a more sophisticated understanding of the relation of text, rhetoric, and social world is needed,[35] one that does not simply project individual textual features onto a putative social world.

As an instrument of social communication a text encodes a set of values (opinions, wishes, beliefs, expectations, judgments) of its framers and intended audience. These values appear not only in the explicit statements of the text, but also more subtly in the genre and argumentative strategies employed and in the repertoire of textual elements used in the construction of explicit statements and arguments. What is absent from this repertoire is potentially as great in significance as what is present. Rather than concluding that Gentiles in the text stand for Gentiles in the Q group, or that "this generation" in the text stands for the ruling elite in Q's social world, it is necessary to describe *how* Gentiles, "this generation," and a lengthy list of other textual items are deployed in the imaginative world of the text, then to ask what argumentative strategy is at work in this arrangement of textual items, and then to inquire into the social locations in which such a strategy might be effective and intelligible. This is a movement from the inner texture of the text to the imaginative world of the text, to its place within a "real" world, and not a preemptive importation of an assumed social world into the text.

This should not be taken to imply that Horsley's construction of the social world is wrong. As will be seen below, I am much in agreement with his description of the basic social and economic dynamics of first-century Galilee and the possible ways in which the Jesus movement might be seen in this milieu. But his social history of Q is constructed backwards. The essentially form-critical (rather than literary-critical and rhetorical) approach allows the text to be short-circuited and, for example, treated as the product of "prophets" despite the fact that none of the standard signs of prophetic speech is present.

SUSPICION OF LOCAL ADMINISTRATIVE INSTITUTIONS

Without offering a full description of the social location of the Q people, Ronald Piper (1995b) supplied important details about the Q people by

---

35. See now the exemplary discussion of method in sociorhetorical criticism by Robbins 1996a; 1996b.

looking at Q's aphoristic sayings (6:22-23, 27-36, 37-38; 11:2-4, 9-13; 12:2-3, 4-7, 11-12, 22-31, 58-59). Beginning with Q 6:27-36 (+Q/Matt 5:41), Piper observed that each of its component parts concerns institution-alized or ongoing violence and exploitation. Q 6:29a ("to whoever slaps you on the right cheek, turn the other") is not a matter of casual, sporadic violence but a deliberate insult where one's honor is threatened. Q 6:29b ("If anyone wants to sue you and take your cloak [ἱμάτιον], let him have your shirt [χιτων] as well")[36] raises the specter of a person so poor that he has only his cloak to give as collateral. The law in Deut 24:10-13, 17 would theoretically protect such a person from this seizure by requiring that the cloak be restored before sunset. According to Piper, however, the saying advises against an appeal to the courts and reliance on the rights supposedly offered by Deuteronomy 24. Similarly, in both Q/Matt 5:41 (on corvée) and Q 6:30 (on borrowing), Q's advice in the face of exploitation or default of loans is not to insist on the "rights" one theoretically enjoyed.

What is common to these sayings is not the advice to suffer in silence but rather to avoid the courts at all costs:

> Give away even more, voluntarily, rather than appeal to secular institutions of justice in cases of being physically abused or sued or even in pursuing a debtor or defaulter. In one sense, this might be seen simply as general sapiential teach-ing. What sage would not be wary of litigation? Yet its extreme nature seems more likely to reflect at least a profound lack of confidence among the Q peo-ple regarding the social and judicial institutions active in their sphere. (Piper 1995b:60)

This distrust of judicial mechanisms continues in the next Q saying, Q 6:37-38, "Judge not and you will not be judged." Even more indicative of Q's suspicions of the courts is Q 12:58-59, which counsels settlement with cred-itors *before* getting to court. Piper adduces parallel instances of persons of the lower social orders involved in litigation (Llewelyn 1992:90–92). Even more to the point is the evidence from Egypt assembled by Roger Bagnall (1989) and Deborah Hobson (1993). These data indicate clearly that among the lower orders, petitions to the courts were a last, not a first resort and normally presupposed preliminary stages of arbitration, mediation, negotiation, and coercion (Hobson 1993:199). The scenario evoked by Q 12:58-59, thus, is not an initial attempt of a lender to extract a debt but a late stage in a long process. Noteworthy is Q's pessimism. Whether the cred-itor's claim is just or not seems irrelevant; the verdict is a foregone conclu-sion. Peasants and tenant farmers knew that when they came to the court they had entered a foreign territory where their interests would not be pro-tected, especially if plaintiffs of the higher orders were involved (see

---

36. Piper (1995:56) dissents from the IQP reconstruction, which followed the Lukan ver-sion (which appears to have robbery rather than a lawsuit in mind).

Garnsey 1970). Any kind of informal settlement, however unjust, would be preferable to a judicial remedy.

On two occasions, Q juxtaposes sayings about judicial proceedings with concerns about subsistence. Q 12:4-7, 11-12 begins with assurances to those who are dragged into the courts and immediately turns to sayings concerning daily economic anxieties (Q 12:22-31). The same juxtaposition of subsistence ("daily bread") and "trials" is found in the Lord's Prayer and its appended sayings (Q 11:2-4, 9-13). In both 12:22-31 and 11:9-13, Piper suggests, Q attempts to counter anxieties raised by governing and judicial procedures by appealing to a provident and generous God who can be counted upon to supply subsistence.

Piper adopted my suggestion that the social location reflected in Q's aphoristic sayings was the lower scribal sector of towns and villages—precisely those persons who daily wrote loan, rental, marriage and divorce agreements and who daily came into contact with both poverty and the exploitation of judicial procedures (Kloppenborg 1991:86–89). Piper writes:

> Indeed this sector stands at the interface between local, village social concerns about indebtedness and the administrative structures for dealing judicially with such business and social relations, which inevitably would refer back to the cities. The evidence for lack of confidence in the judicial system, specific fears about "authorities," and a concern to suffer loss rather than seek redress would suggest a clear suspicion about the benefits to be won under higher administrative procedures. This concern may not have been *directly* aimed at Rome, particularly in Galilee, but neither were the structures governing life in Galilee viewed as objects of trust. . . . The suspicion about the institutions of power seems to have been sufficiently strong to make voluntary surrender the preferred option. (Piper 1995b:63, emphasis original)

Piper thus follows a consistent thread of suspicion directed at the official mechanisms of control, and discerns a contrasting strain of hope in God's renewal of society, a renewal in which the poor would acquire honor and dignity (Q 6:20b-21). He doubts that those responsible for the framing of Q still functioned as village scribes; they seem to have become disenchanted with the legal system. But neither were they itinerants. Q 16:13, "you cannot serve both God and Mammon," was virtually their motto: it is impossible "to declare God's renewal of society providing new honor and dignity for the poor or oppressed, and yet to use the present institutions of society to pursue one's own material claims and affirm conventional codes of honour" (Piper 1995b:66).

The significance of Piper's observations lies not simply in the fact that he identified a common concern about institutionalized violence running through a series of Q sayings, but that he had earlier shown *on purely literary and rhetorical grounds* that these same sayings display a common set of argumentative features and assumptions and must therefore belong to the same compositional moment (Piper 1989).[37] In other words, his prior observations about a rhetorically distinct subset of Q's clusters provided the *literary* basis for his social-historical analysis. The textual control that is so noticeably lacking in Horsley's analysis (to say nothing of those of Theissen or Schottroff), the movement from the text and its rhetoric to social history, is fully present in Piper's work.

Sociorhetorical Approaches

Whereas the above approaches to social history focus on one or more specific textual sites (with varying degrees of literary control), another approach inquires into the ways in which the text as a whole is constructed so as to commend itself to its hearers and readers.

In the scheme outlined above (pp. 177–78) sociorhetorical approaches ask what the genre of the text and its method of organization imply about its intended audience; how the author diagnoses the situation addressed; and how arguments are constructed so as to be persuasive. It is not only the explicit arguments that are important, but the way they are constructed—their selection of metaphors, their choice of evidence, and the conduct of their arguments.

Elsewhere I have argued, following Schutz and Luckmann, that foundational documents of a group bear a homological relationship to the symbolic world of the group, such that the "truth" of the documents is rendered self-evident by their correspondence to the structure of the social world. Conversely, the group's manner of knowing the world is buttressed by the way its literature represents and explains the nature and processes of knowing. Insights that were once subjective are condensed into symbols that can be shared; they are objectified and generalized and rendered self-evidently true.[38]

The Formative Stratum and its Social World

Genre and Rhetoric

The genre selected by the framers of Q provides an important clue to the social identity of the framers and their audience. Sato, who understands the genre of Q to be that of a "prophet-book," argues analogously that its framers were former wandering prophets who had become local leaders (1988:380–81). If indeed it could be shown that Q consciously imitated tra-

---

37. In 1989 Piper did not speak of strata in Q, though his discovery in fact pointed in that direction. In later works he speaks of the "more sapiential stratum (or clusters) of Q" (1995:54).

38. Kloppenborg 1991:79–80; cf. Schutz and Luckmann 1973:284.

ditional prophetic genres and that its argumentative appeals and metaphors mirrored the appeals and metaphors of classical prophecy, it would be a reasonable conclusion that Q's framers wished to represent themselves in relation to Israelite prophets. The difficulty that I have with Sato's proposal is not its logic but its initial assumption: that Q is framed as a prophetic book. Q lacks virtually all of the key indicators of prophetic genres and its argumentative appeals are not based on oracular pronouncements. The only oracular pronouncement in Q (11:49-51a) is in fact a *quotation* rather than direct speech.

The alternative reading of Q's social location I proposed derives, like Sato's, from a consideration of Q's genre and style of argumentation.[39] It begins from a characterization of Q's formative stratum as an instruction, a well-attested genre of Near Eastern sapiential literature. Again, it must be emphasized that this classification is not in the first place based on theological or material criteria, but upon formal considerations. Nor does it have anything to do with a particular understanding of the historical Jesus. It is only about the *literary* choices of the framers of Q and the implications of these choices for the social location of those framers.

The instructional genre was remarkably stable, attested from the third millennium BCE (*Ptaḥḥotep*) to the tenth century of the common era (the monastic *Instructions of Apa Antonius*) (Kloppenborg 1987a:329–36). Originally associated with scribal schools, it was eventually adopted for the transmission of popular instructions (*P. Insinger*, *P. Louvre D. 2414*), sectarian wisdom (*Teachings of Silvanus*), and monastic instructions. As a genre of sapiential discourse, the instruction serves to transmit wisdom from a competent teacher to dependents or students (often, though not exclusively using the fiction of parental instruction). It thereby seeks to cultivate and purvey a particular ethos.

Because they are formulated within groups that are intentional about education, instructions regularly contain reflections on the nature of the educative process itself. Human learning is valorized, the process of handing on tradition is celebrated, and there are reflections on the origin, nature, and means by which wisdom is acquired. Even a superficial reading of Proverbs 1–9 will show quickly that alongside admonitions advising or dissuading certain behaviors are numerous sayings that describe the process of learning itself, underscoring its importance, and meditating on its heavenly origins. These metareflections on the *process* of instruction embody the self-interests of those responsible for the genre: scribes who transmit learning but who also reflect on its warrants and functions.

Q[1] provides a good example of instructional literature, offering topically organized instructions on several themes. Like instructions, Q also contains sayings reflecting on various key parts of the instructional process: on the

39. For a fuller treatment of what follows, see Kloppenborg 1991.

relationship of masters and students (6:40, 46-49; 10:16; 14:26-27); and on the importance of good guidance (6:40, 41-42), good speech (6:43-45), and good examples (17:1-2). God and Jesus are held up as mimetic ideals (6:35, 36; 9:58; 11:13; 12:3; 14:26-27). Q 12:2 (on the revelation of things hidden) is not only a wisdom saying, but reflects a characteristic sapiential interest in what is hidden as an object of research; it conceives the process of disclosure to be grounded in the relationship of God to the world (cf. Sir 39:1-11).

The literary organization of Q^1 is a relatively simple topical one and in this regard falls handily within the organizational strategies typical of instructions. To the extent that Q^1 uses and maintains topical organization throughout,[40] it represents one of the better organized instructions, since in many instructions, the topical organization is not sustained throughout.[41] Q, however, does not display the sophisticated and learned types of organization based on devices such as repeated formula, sorites, chiasms, alphabetic acrostics, or numeric patterns seen, for example, in Prov 31:10-31 or *Papyrus Insinger*. This suggests that the framers of Q^1, while not without skill, do not come from the upper reaches of the scribal establishment.

As Piper's analysis indicates, many of the sayings in Q^1 reflect a degree of disenfranchisement with local judicial mechanisms. The bulk of Q^1 is in fact concerned with quite local matters: managing conflict (6:27-28, 29; 12:2-7, 11-12; 17:3-4); lending and borrowing (6:30); corvée (Q/Matt 5:41); maintaining subsistence (11:2-4, 9-13; 12:22-31); divorce (16:18); solidarity and reconciliation (15:4-7, 8-10; 17:1-2, 3-4); attitudes toward wealth (12:33-34; 16:13); and the conduct and support of the "workers" (9:57-62; 10:2-11, 16). The social level presupposed in these sayings is relatively low; the evident concern for subsistence and the assumption of Q/Matt 5:41 that the addressees are susceptible to forced labor indicate that the addressees include smallholders or handworkers. Q 6:30 also implies that the addressees might *make* loans too. When money is mentioned, however, the denominations are small: Q 12:6 refers to a Roman *assarion* (a copper coin equivalent to 1/16 of a denarius); and the Parable of the Lost Drachma seems to concern the lifesavings of a woman, amounting to only 10 denarii or less that one-half of a year's supply of grain for one person. The Parable of the Lost Sheep describes a man with a medium-sized flock but certainly

---

40. The topical organization of most of the Q^1 blocks is reasonably clear: the section containing Q 13:24; 14:26-27; 17:33; 14:34-35 is somewhat miscellaneous, although all of the sayings deal in general with the demands of discipleship; Q 15:4-7, 8-10; 16:13, 16, 18; 17:1-2, 3-4, 6, if it is an organized block, concerns broadly reconciliation and peacemaking (see Kloppenborg 1995b:314–15).

41. See Kloppenborg 1987a:chap. 7. Some instructions are quite miscellaneous in their organization; some connect individual sayings only on the basis of catchword or formal analogy; others that begin topically dissolve into a miscellany at the end; a few sustain topical organization throughout, and a smaller number use special devices (acrostics, numeric patterns, etc.) for organization.

not wealthy (Jeremias 1972:132-33). Those with conspicuous wealth are held up as negative examples (12:16-21) or at least as persons whose splendor nature can outdo (12:27).

Another important clue to the social location of the framers and their addressees is found in the construction of Q's arguments. Observations drawn from nature and quite ordinary human transactions form the basis for Q's proofs: these include the coming of rain (6:35); the cultivation of figs and grapes (6:44); housebuilding (6:47-49); parents' provision for their children (11:9-13); small purchases (12:6-7); the survival of birds (12:22-24), field flowers (12:26-27) and grass (12:28); shepherds (15:4-7) and poor widows (?) (15:8-10); and simple planting and bread making (13:18-21). Noticeable by their absence are appeals to "higher" forms of culture: major political and public institutions, kings and their retinues, palaces, the agora, the gymnasium, the theater, and the assembly. Q¹'s rhetoric appeals not to the sophisticated constructs of higher culture but to "nature" (however much the idea of nature is itself socially constructed) and the simplest of human transactions.

Beyond the appeal to Solomon's proverbial wealth (12:27) there is no allusion to Israel's epic history. Nonetheless, the environment of Q¹ is largely Israelite—indicated by the fact that Q can rather casually cite Gentiles as examples of persons from whom one does not expect exemplary behavior (6:33-34; 12:30).

What is absent from Q's repertoire of arguments is as telling as what is present. The basis of an argumentative appeal is not the priesthood, or the Temple, or purity distinctions, or the Torah (or writings) (see Kosch 1989a; Kloppenborg 1990c). This is surprising, since at a number of points Q might have invoked the Torah or examples of Israel's epic history in support of its arguments. If Piper is correct that Q 6:29 alludes to the law in Deut 24:10-13, 17, which requires that a poor man's cloak (ἱμάτιον) be returned before sundown, it is equally telling that Q's argument makes no use of this law. Instead it assumes that such an appeal would either be ineffectual, given actual judicial practice, or otherwise beside the point.

Q¹ also lacks oracular appeals; the voice of God is not heard nor does Jesus speak as a prophet. Persuasion is not effected by command or an oracular disclosure of divine will; instead, the dominant argumentative mode of the document is persuasion through rhetorical questions, examples, and comparisons based on ordinary experience or on nature. The inferences—that loving enemies and lending without expectation of return make one a "child of God" (6:35)—might be striking and extraordinary, but that does not make them "prophetic." Q¹ is full of confidence in divine providence, in God's loving surveillance, and the possibility of transformed human relationships; but there is no indication whatsoever that this is mediated by Torah or the Temple or the priestly hierarchy, or that it is based on oracular disclosures or commands.

Social Location

If one asks, who would be in a position to frame the Sayings Gospel as it has been framed, the answer would appear to be village and town notaries and scribes.[42] These were the local embodiment of literary technology, and it was they who in the life of the village were most keenly aware of many of the matters that preoccupy Q—debt (Q 6:30; 11:4; 12:58-59), divorce (Q 16:18), lawsuits (6:29); for it was they who wrote loans contracts, petitions, and bills of divorce. The fact that Q[1] is framed as an instruction—a typically scribal genre—and reflects the interest of scribes in the *process* as well as the content of learning is also best explained on the supposition that Q[1] is the product of scribes.

These scribes should not be placed too high on the professional ladder. This is indicated by Q's general lack of compositional affectations, by the generally mundane topics it addresses, and by the unpretentious nature of its rhetorical appeals. It was evidently formulated to address persons living at or near a subsistence level, who experienced the conflict endemic in town and village life as well as occasional pressures brought on by corvée, the courts, and other exactions.

Horsley has objected to this portrait, declaring that Q "offers virtually no indications of scribal activity" (1991c:58). By this he seems to mean that Q does not evince the level of biblical learning and quotation found, for example, in Matthew. The point is both true and irrelevant. Horsley's declaration betrays a monolithic conception of scribes as belonging by definition to the "retainer" class and therefore as inimical to the interests of Q.[43] Such a view is mistaken on several counts. First, it should be self-evident that insofar as Q represents a written document, it is the product of scribal technology;

---

42. On such notaries, see, e.g., Youtie 1975a; 1975b; Saldarini 1988a:261–64. The village scribe (κωμογραμματεύς), at least in Egypt, was responsible for tax and census records and might be regarded as a "retainer" (see Preisigke 1903; Oertel 1917:157–60). This is probably the level of minor village official that Josephus has in mind when he records the threat of Herod's sons Aristobulus and Alexander to reduce their other brothers to the status of "village scribes" (κωμῶν γραμματεῖς, *War* 1.479; κωμογραμματεῖς, *Ant.* 16.203). If the pattern from Egypt applies in Roman Palestine, towns and villages also had other scribes, with varying educational levels, prepared to assist the illiterate majority (see Lewis 1983:82–83).

43. Earlier, Horsley (1989a:191) declared: "In a traditional agrarian society such as ancient Judea in the second Temple period the principal people who were literate and capable of or inclined to produce literature were those who worked in some capacity as scholarly 'retainers' for governing groups." Yet later he is forced to concede that Q was produced by scribes (1989a:201); but, since this evidently conflicts with his notion of scribalism, he resorts to the suggestion that they merely "shaped blocks of sayings . . . for purposes other than for more controlled communication of those sayings among the general membership of the movement, where oral communication surely still prevailed." I have criticized this schematic view of scribalism, citing evidence from Auranitis, where there is ample evidence of petty scribal and administrative structures at the level of village and town (Kloppenborg 1989b:211–13; cf. Jones 1931; Harper 1928; MacAdam 1983; Dentzer 1985; Villeneuve 1985).

who besides scribes had the ability to compose it this way and who would have chosen a typically scribal genre? Second, Q does in fact betray a number of features characteristic of scribes, as has been indicated above: interest in the process of as well as the content of instruction. Finally, scribes did not uniformly serve the interests of the ruling elite. There is ample evidence from Egypt to indicate the presence of a variety of scribes, of varying educational levels, in towns and villages, some serving in the apparatus of the provincial administration and others functioning as freelance professionals. The κωμογραμματεύς (village scribe) was concerned with tax and census matters. But the writing of loan and lease agreements presupposed the existence of private professionals prepared to assist in these transactions (see above, n. 42). There is no reason at all to suppose that this sector was uniformly aligned with the ruling classes against the poor or that this sector functioned exclusively as retainers of the elite. Q^1 reflects the technology and interests of these private professionals.

THE MAIN REDACTION OF Q

Genre and Rhetoric

With the main redaction of Q (Q^2) there is a noticeable shift in the formal characteristics of the collection as well as the types of rhetorical appeals. Despite these shifts, there is no strong reason to suppose a radically different social setting, much less to suppose that a different set of persons is being addressed. The changes are more likely due to a new rhetorical situation—the need to defend the practice of Q^1 and the character of Jesus in the face of challenges—than they are the result of a change of audience. An altered rhetorical situation required alterations in rhetorical posture.

The most obvious formal shift from Q^1 to Q^2 has to do with the increased density of chriae—that is, sayings furnished with a brief setting.[44] This setting could be as simple as "Jesus said" (as occurs in the *Gospel of Thomas*). More often the setting provides some indication of the occasion upon which a statement was made or the comment or question that elicited a particular response (e.g., Q 3:7a; 7:18-19, 24a; 10:21a; 11:14-15, 16, etc.). One of the main functions of the chria was characterization of the speaker or of the speaker's interlocutors. Fittingly, it is at this stratum that we first encounter allusion to the prophets and Sophia and Israel's epic history, both in connection with the positive characterization of Jesus and John, and in connection with the Deuteronomistic theme of the killing of the prophets, an instrument of polemic and reproach. It is here that the "this generation" appears in the rhetoric of Q, denoting a group or type of persons opposed to the Q group.

44. On chriae, see R. Taylor 1946; Butts 1986; Hock and O'Neil 1986; Mack and O'Neil 1986; Robbins 1988; Mack and Robbins 1989; Mack 1990b; Cameron 1990b.

Whereas at the formative stratum the dominant grammatical form was the hortatory imperative buttressed with a variety of programmatic statements, motive clauses, and concluding warnings, the main redaction contains woes, warnings of judgment, and prophetic correlatives.[45] It also includes chriae occasioned by a healing (7:1-10), a question from John the Baptist (7:18-23, 24-28, 31-35), and two challenges to Jesus (11:14-23, 29-32). The presence of prophetic sayings does not, however, turn Q into *chresmologoi*—an oracle collection. For although prophetic forms are present and the examples of prophets are invoked (6:22-23; 7:26; 10:23-24; 11:32, 49-51; 13:34-35), and while an Elijah-like figure is described in 3:16-17; 7:22, most of the sayings of Q[2] are framed as chriae rather than as direct oracles. Q employs the technique of extending or elaborating an initial chria by appending additional chriae, or by attaching further sayings to the initial chria.[46] It is for this reason that Downing sees in Q the beginnings of a *bios*, for this technique creates a series of pragmatic unities which constitute disparate units of tradition as part of the same communicative event.

The development from an instruction to a *bios* is not unusual.[47] At least part of the impetus for the introduction of biographical elements—a narrative introduction, for example—had to do with the inherent requirement of the instructional genre for legitimation for the sage's words. The sayings of a well-known sage like Solomon might not require any special introduction; but in the cases of lesser-known sages (e.g., Ankhsheshonq) or sages whose legitimacy was subject to challenge, special narratives might be added. One of the most usual strategies of legitimation was to supply narratives that underscore the reliable character of the sage. Testing or ordeal stories, which displayed the constancy and integrity of the sage's character, were ideal for this purpose.

In rhetoric, persuasion is effected not only by the logical plausibility of arguments (*logos*), but also by appeal to the audience's self-interest (*pathos*) and the speaker's character (*ethos*). Chriae are in fact ideally suited to the display of ethos, for they place the speaker in situations requiring decisive pronouncements and clever repartee. In Q Jesus is depicted as able to defeat critics with a few well-chosen sayings (7:31-35; 11:14-23, 29-32). He is quick to commend others (7:1-10, 24-28; 10:21-22, 23-24) or to correct misplaced praise (11:27-28). Some of the pronouncements are designed to

45. Examples of the prophetic correlative are Q 11:30; 17:24, 26, 30. On the form, see D. Schmidt 1977.

46. This is the case for the main blocks of Q[2] sayings: (1) Q 3:3, 7-9, 16-17 (1 extended chria); (2) Q 7:1-10, 18-28, 31-35 (3 chriae with elaborations) (see Cameron 1990b); (3) 11:14-26, 27-28, 29-36 (3 chriae with elaborations); (4) 11:39-44, 46-52 (1 extended chria, beginning ὁ δὲ [[εἶπεν]]; (5) 14:16-26 (a chria beginning καὶ εἶπεν [[αὐτοῖς]]); and (6) 17:23-24, 26-30, 34-37; 19:12-27; 22:28-30 (an extended chria). The block of Q[2] sayings in 12:39-59 is simply attached to 12:33-34 by catchwords.

47. Kloppenborg 1987:279, 326. See also Momigliano 1971.

underscore the inferior character of opponents (7:31-35; 10:12-15; 11:39-52) or to warn others of potential dangers (3:7-9, 16-17; 12:39-49, 51-59; 17:23-37; 19:12-27). Others implicitly connect Jesus with the Elijah-like "Coming One" (7:18-23; cf. 3:16-17; 13:34-35) and Heavenly Wisdom (11:49-51); still others are quite explicit in asserting divine authorization, both for Jesus (7:35; 10:21-22) and for John (7:26, 27; 7:35).

The density of forms that display the ethos of Jesus and John and the contrasting ethos of their competitors suggests that at this stage of Q, the rhetorical situation demanded a defense or legitimation of the Q people's existence. This was accomplished both by attacking opponents and by associating Jesus and John with Sophia and prophetic figures, and by aligning Jesus and John with characters in Israel's epic history. This stratum of Q draws a sacred map of "Israel" (Q 7:9; 22:30), expressly naming Abel (11:51), Abraham (3:8; 13:28), Noah (17:26-27), Lot (17:28-29; cf. 3:3; 10:12), Isaac (13:28), Jacob (13:28), Solomon (11:31), Jonah (11:32), Zechariah (11:51), and the prophets (6:22-23; 11:49-51; 13:34-35). The framers of Q clearly situated themselves in this company over against their opponents, who are described as persecutors and killers of the prophets (6:22-23; 11:49-51; 13:34-35). Using a strategy of shaming, Q asserts that Gentiles have responded (or would respond) more adequately to Solomon or Jonah and the Patriarchs than their opponents and that the notoriously evil cities of Sodom, Tyre, and Sidon will fare better at the judgment than Israelite towns that reject the Jesus movement. It is perhaps significant that neither Moses nor David—associated with Torah learning and kingship—appears in Q's list of heroes. Solomon appears, but as a sage rather than as a king (11:31).

Is there a location where such a posture would make sense? Reed suggests that Q² was associated with a larger population center such as Kefar Nahum. In support, he cites the frequency of urban images and metaphors. The term *polis* itself occurs at least three times (10:8, 10 [*bis*]) and there is mention of palaces (7:25), *agorai* (7:31; 11:43), plazas (10:10; 13:26; 14:21), a collection of rooftops (12:3), judges and prisons (12:58-59), a city gate (13:24), banquets (14:16-24), and banks (19:23) (1995:26-27). In the mission speech God is said to send *out* (ἐκβάλλειν) workers to the harvest fields (10:2). When describing agricultural practices, Q uses the impersonal plural: "*they* do not gather figs from thorns" (6:44); "if salt becomes insipid . . . , *they* throw it away" (14:35). This stands in contrast to Q's use of the second person when describing other practices (e.g., "why do *you* see the speck in your brother's eye?" 6:41; "why do *you* call me Lord, Lord?" 6:46). This, according to Reed, implies that the framers of Q have no first-hand experience of agricultural practices.

Reed also notes, however, that almost all of the urban imagery used by Q has a negative cast. Kings and their palaces are contrasted with John the Baptist's rude dress and desert locale. The *agora* is a place where one can expect rejection and abuse, or Pharisees expecting to be greeted. A banquet initially intended for urban elite becomes a metaphor of salvation only when the servant goes outside the city to invite guests, after the first invitees have declined. Reed concludes that "although Q betrays an awareness of the city, the Q community does not seem to have scaled the social hierarchy of the city very high" (1995:28).

Without endorsing Reed's suggestion of Kefar Naḥum, it is appropriate to conclude with Reed that the Q people are associated with towns sufficiently large to have markets and a small scribal sector, and sufficiently proximate to the larger centers of Tiberias and Sepphoris to come into periodic contact with Pharisees and other representatives of the Judaean hierocracy. Q's cultural allegiances, however, are with the Galilean countryside and against the city, which is regarded with distrust and suspicion. In defense of the Jesus movement, the framers of Q construct a notion of Israel and its epic heroes which stands in opposition to Jerusalem, the Herodian dynasty, the Pharisees and lawyers, and the unbelief that is encountered in the marketplaces.

What is at issue in Q²'s defensive and apologetic posture? The most prominent features of Q's rhetoric are complaints about nonrepentance (Q 3:8; 10:13; 11:32) and attendant threats of judgment. Repentance does not seem to connote a change in one's interior disposition; rather it has to do with the adoption of certain patterns of behavior and group allegiance, cast in the metaphor of "returning" (שׁוּב). In Q's usage repentance is paired with welcoming Q's workers (10:10-12) and with "coming to hear wisdom" (11:31). The larger context of Q 11:29-32 makes clear that what is at issue is the recognition in Jesus and his activities of "something greater than Jonah or Solomon." The centurion is commended for recognizing Jesus' authority (7:9-10); John's envoys are directed to various healing and preaching activities (7:22); "this generation" is criticized for not recognizing Jesus and John for what they are: children of Sophia (7:31-35); Jesus' critics are accused of ignoring the power at work in local exorcists and Jesus (11:19-20); and Jesus' contemporaries are threatened with ultimate rejection because they fail to know, and to be known by, the "householder" (13:25-27). For Q, failure to "repent" evidently means a failure to recognize in Jesus and the Q people the presence of divine activity and authorization.

More concretely, Q's complaints about nonrecognition of Jesus and the Q people serve as an apologetic strategy to legitimize the lifestyle promoted by Q¹ and which is either under attack or not attracting the attention that the Q people feel it should. A few sayings in Q² in fact continue to promote features of Q¹'s ethos, especially its criticism of riches. Q 7:25 denigrates the wealth and finery of Antipas; 7:22 reiterates the benefits which poor and otherwise marginalized persons can expect; 10:21-24 relativizes the status of persons of great learning and social standing; and the parable of the great feast (14:16-24) depicts a failure of elite sociability, including the man's efforts to display his wealth to his peers (see Braun 1995:62–131). Q's woes against the tomb builders (11:47) and those who can command the front seats in assemblies (11:43) are, of course, attacks on persons of wealth and social standing.

This layer of Q reveals a struggle for influence and "place" in Galilean society. The opponents, by contrast, evidently already have influence or at least are perceived as likely to obtain it. The Pharisees of Q 11 claim social prominence (11:43) and the scribes (or lawyers) are in a position to impose "burdens" (11:46; cf. 11:52). They associate themselves with the memory of the prophets (11:47-51), an association to which Q vigorously objects. Q's lack of appeal to Moses can perhaps be understood as a function of this conflict. For the Pharisees and lawyers obviously claimed Moses as their authority and had the intellectual and interpretive apparatus with which to justify this claim. Q² invokes the memory of the prophets as a counterbalance.

Saldarini argues that in the early first century, Pharisees functioned principally as retainers: "literate servants of the governing class [who] had a program for Jewish society and influence with the people and their patrons" (1988a:284). Pharisees, however, were not an established presence in the Galilee and even in the second century their successors did not function as local administrators.[48] In first-century Galilee, the Pharisees were a somewhat minor and new presence; but they clearly represented the interests of Jerusalem and its priestly rulers. Saldarini suggests that Herod Antipas may even have encouraged Pharisees in his territory:

> Since the Pharisees were supporters of an ordered Jewish society and of observance of Jewish law, their goals would have been harmonious with those of Antipas, who desired to keep his predominantly Jewish kingdom in good order. The Pharisees' emphasis on tithing and practices which promoted Jewish identity could be used to promote loyalty to a Jewish king who kept the Galilee peaceful and provided a buffer between the Galilee and the Roman empire. (Saldarini 1988a:296)

The same logic would presumably apply to the reigns of Agrippa I and Agrippa II. Q's conflict with the Pharisees and their hieratic practices (purity and tithing) thus represents a struggle between indigenous Galilean piety and an incursion of Judaean and priestly influence. Q is not only silent about Moses, the hero of its opponents; David—clearly associated with both royal and southern (Judaean) interests—is also absent. To this Reed adds that Q does not mention any priests either (1996:137). This is not strictly speaking correct, since Zechariah (11:51) is probably Zechariah ben Jehoiada (2 Chron 24:20-22), a priest under Joash. Nevertheless, it is not Zechariah's priestly role but his prophetic role that is at stake for Q. Q treats his death along with

48. On the evolution of rabbis as the ruling class in third-century CE Galilee, see Goodman 1983:93–118 and L. Levine 1989.

the deaths of the prophets,[49] underscoring the irony of the fact that he was killed by the forebears of those who now claim to honor the prophets.

As Reed notes, Q's selection of figures from the epic history deliberately excludes Jerusalem. The Patriarchs, Noah, and Lot antedate the priesthood, the monarchy, and the centralization of the cult in Jerusalem. David, who embodies southern claims, is ignored, and Solomon is mentioned once as a negative example (12:27) and then for his wisdom rather than as a king (11:31). The sacrificial system is ignored as is the Decalogue. "Indeed, in terms of Q's temporal views, law has given way to the kingdom of God (16:16)" (Reed 1996:137).

Reed adduces other Galilean traditions that reflect a similar distrust of Jerusalem. The late first-century *Vitae Prophetarum* (on Jonah) has Jonah, a northern prophet, speaking an oracle against Jerusalem "that the city would be destroyed" (Schermann 1907:16). *Lamentations Rabbah* attributes to R. Simeon ben Yohai (whose traditional tomb is at Meiron in the Upper Galilee) the statement: "Ought she [Jerusalem] not have learned from the city of Jonah [Nineveh]? One prophet I sent to Nineveh and she turned in penitence; but to Israel in Jerusalem [*sic*] I sent many prophets . . . Yet she hearkened not" (*Lam. Rab.* Proem 31). "One must assume," concludes Reed, "that Galileans were attuned to such local traditions surrounding Jonah, and that the sign of Jonah [Q 11:29-30] referred not just to the preaching of Jonah but contained a barb aimed at Jerusalem and its representatives . . ." (Reed 1996:138–39).

Great and Little Tradition

A useful heuristic model for understanding the conflict in Q is that proposed by Robert Redfield for understanding religious traditions in agrarian societies. Redfield distinguishes between two levels of tradition, the "great" and the "little tradition" (1965:40–59). The two are interdependent but distinguished by the social level and social interests of their purveyors. The great tradition, systematized, rationalized, legitimized, and rendered in epic form, is the domain of the privileged: scribes, scholars, and theologians— that is, the retainers of the ruling elite. The little tradition is local, unsystematic, and mainly oral. The two traditions are not discrete and separable, however. One depends upon the other, with a bidirectional movement of intellectualization and rationalization of local tradition by scribal elite, and the parochialization, even corruption, of scribal traditions in village contexts (Marriott 1955; Scott 1977b). Despite the evident symbiosis that

---

49. While the Tanak does not call Zechariah a prophet, 2 Chron 24:20 states that the spirit of God came upon him and has him use the stock prophetic formula τάδε λέγει κύριος ("thus says the Lord"). Both Josephus (*Ant.* 9.168-69) and the *Vitae Prophetarum* treat him as a prophet, as do rabbinic sources (on which see S. Blank 1937–38). According to the *Vitae Prophetarum*, the oracular functions of the Temple ceased with Zechariah's death.

exists between the two levels of tradition, the little tradition is regularly treated as inferior: "the hypotheses of the great are considered beliefs, [but] the hypotheses of the little tradition will be considered superstitions" (Redfield 1965:49).

James Scott (1977b) has emphasized not only the interdependence and symbiosis of the great and little traditions but also the strong potential for conflict. The great tradition, since it is the formulation of privileged social strata, is naturally configured to favor their interests. It does this by legitimizing hierarchy, cultic and political centers, kingship, the extraction of surpluses, and the use of force in preserving elite privileges. Yet the great tradition cannot simply be imposed on those farther down the social ladder. It is not self-legitimating. When the rains do not come, when the crops fail, the political myths that promise prosperity are met in the peasant villages with skepticism. Skepticism and resistance increase the farther one moves down the social ladder. The fundamental peasant values of custom and subsistence "establish moral ceilings on the economic claims which the great tradition may impose on subordinate classes. A breach of these ceilings has historically threatened the relationship of subordination itself." "The law of the emperor," to quote a Vietnamese folk saying, "stops at the hedge of the village" (J. Scott 1977b:16).

According to Scott, "the material and symbolic hegemony normally exercised by ruling institutions does not preclude, but rather engenders a set of contrary values which represent in their entirety a kind of 'shadow society'" (Scott 1977b:19). For the great tradition creates a set of ideals and standards (literacy, study, etc.) which those lower on the social ladder simply cannot attain. The permanent perception of difference if not outright inferiority ultimately nurtures an opposite reaction among those at the bottom. Similarly, the hierarchy and social difference legitimated by the great tradition inevitably collides with more egalitarian expectations and norms that exist at the level of the village.[50] In the final analysis, peasants know that villages are both historically and functionally prior to cities and to the great tradition. The village, as a mostly self-supporting unit, can survive on its own. The city, the king, and the scholar cannot (Scott 1977b:18).

Even though the great and the little traditions may ostensibly share the same religious base, the actual configurations of beliefs and practices are likely to differ. This difference is most obviously visible in the routine complaints of officials about the syncretistic and superstitious character of popular piety. The village may embrace practices and beliefs associated with childbirth, puberty, marriage, death, and burial that have little place in the

---

50. J. Scott (1977a:27) stresses the norm of reciprocity that governs agrarian societies. Even patron-client relationships, based on obvious inequalities, cloak themselves in the fiction of equivalent or comparable exchange of goods or services as a means of creating legitimacy. Elsewhere, Scott and Kerkvliet (1977) have noted that patrons lose their legitimacy when the exchange of goods and services becomes too imbalanced or exploitative.

great tradition or that may even be denied and repudiated. Local, clan, and family rituals form one stratum of practice, and local saints and holy sites will assume significance that they do not and cannot have at any other level of tradition. Left to themselves, these local syncretistic compounds can function in a stable relation with the city and its learned traditions; "but when the agents of the great tradition do not tolerate petty heresy, the conflict may take the form of open resistance" (J. Scott 1977b:20).

Horsley has invoked parts of this model as a heuristic for understanding the Jesus movement and Q. Arguing that the popular resistance movements of Roman Palestine, with their prophets and popular kings, represented little tradition resistance to the Temple, tithing, hierarchy, and the various extractions that went along with these, Horsley treats the Jesus movement as a whole as a peasant movement that advocated renewed local order (1989b:90–96, 121–22, 138). This model carries over into his discussion of Q, where he draws a sharp distinction between the rulers and the ruling institutions (which encompass the scribes of all levels and the Pharisees) on the one hand, and the little tradition of peasant villages on the other (1991c:56–58). On Horsley's showing, Q advocated the "restoration of more cooperative local socio-economic relations" while at the same time offering a critique of the ruling institutions (1991c:61).

I am generally in agreement with Horsley's diagnosis of the sources of tension in Roman Galilee and his view of Q as proposing local renewal. Three important adjustments are required, however. Horsley's definition of "peasant" is too generous, including not only smallholders and tenant agriculturalists, but fishermen and craftspersons.[51] There is not much evidence in Q to sustain the supposition that the Q people were primarily peasants (i.e., agriculturalists). While Q speaks of a shepherd with a modest flock (15:4-7) and about sowing and harvesting (3:17; 10:3; 11:23; 12:18, 24; 19:20) and the milling of flour (17:35), Reed's observations (above) indicate that the framers of Q at least have little firsthand knowledge of specific agricultural practices. Second, as noted above, Horsley has a far too schematic understanding of scribalism, which in fact existed at a variety of levels of society and was far from uniformly loyal to the ruling institutions.

Finally, in the social situations described by Redfield and J. Scott and assumed by Horsley, the little tradition exists primarily as oral village tradition and is known only through the fieldwork of anthropologists. The crucial difference between these situations and that of Q is that Q is already

51. Horsley 1989b:121. Contrast Shanin 1971:240: "The peasantry consists of small agricultural producers who, with the help of simple equipment and the labour of their families, produce mainly for their own consumption and for the fulfilment of obligations to the holders of political and economic power. Such a definition implies a specific relation to land, the peasant farm and the peasant village community as the basic units of social interaction, a specific occupational structure and particular influence of past history and specific patterns of development."

the product of *scribal* activity. It is at this point that the documentary nature of Q and its organization *as a document* become important. Horsley, despite his claims to treat Q not as isolated sayings but as clusters of sayings, still operates with essentially form-critical assumptions, using Q as if it were a window on the world of oral tradition—a kind of surrogate for the modern anthropologist's field notes. It is this that allows him to skip over the literary fact of Q and to arrive immediately at peasant villages.

The main redaction of Q, no less than the construction of Q^1, is a scribal accomplishment. This level of Q is no more a random collection of sayings than was Q^1. On the contrary, it has deliberate structuring devices and repeated themes that lend it a unity (e.g., references to the Coming One, and allusions to the destruction of Sodom). The construction of its elaborated chriae creates pragmatic unities such that long segments of text are construed as belonging to the same communicative event. Although when compared to the fully narrative gospels of Matthew or Luke, Q might seem deficient, when placed in its more appropriate comparative family—chriae collections and gnomologia—Q is in fact one of the *more* sophisticated examples of the genre (Kloppenborg 1987a:322–25). This feature of Q cannot simply be dismissed as incidental.

The main redaction of Q employs more biblical allusions than Q^1 and even has one direct quotation introduced by "as it is written" (Q 7:27). Allusions to biblical stories and heroes are not, of course, solely the domain of the scribal sector. But the formula quotation brings us closer to a scribal provenance.

There are two other more telling signs of a scribal origin for Q^2, quite apart from its rather sophisticated level of organization. The first is Q 11:51, which speaks of the shedding of blood from the time of Abel to Zechariah (ben Jehoiada, of 2 Chron 24:20-22). Thus Q 11:51 assumes knowledge of the *literary* arrangement of the books of the Tanak, where 1–2 Chronicles appears toward the end of the canon.[52] Theissen aptly asks: "What lay person knows that Zechariah is the last prophet in the canon to be killed?"[53] The second indication of a scribal origin is Q's pervasive use

---

52. It should not be concluded that 1–2 Chronicles had already assumed its position as the last book of the Tanak, as is suggested by *b. B. Bat.* 14.14b-15a (which may be Tannaitic in provenance). Freedman (1992:95–96) has suggested that 1–2 Chronicles was originally the first book of the *kethûbîm* ("writings"). 4QMMT c 10-11 (II BCE) may suggest that the Psalms preceded 1–2 Chronicles at Qumran: [. . ד]כתב[נ]ו אליכה שתבין בספר מושה [ו]בספר[י הנ]ביאים ובדוי[ד [במעשׂי] דור ודור ("We have [written] to you so that you may study (carefully) the book of Moses and the books of the prophets and (the writings) of David [and the events] of ages past"). See Qimron and Strugnell 1994:58–59. In either case, however, 1–2 Chronicles still records the last prophetic death in the canon. The order of books in the LXX is much more variable: see Swete 1914:197–230.

53. Theissen 1991:228. He continues, "The exactitude of this point does not accord very well with the much less precise inclusion of Abel among the prophets" (ibid.). In fact, *T. Iss.* 5.4 suggests that Abel was the first of the "holy ones" to have his innocent blood shed, and it

of the Deuteronomistic motif of the killing of the prophets. Steck has shown that this motif was at home among scribes, wisdom teachers, and the successors of the Hasidim (1967:206–15). The motif appears at several points in early Christian literature (Mark 12:1-9; Acts 7:52; 1 Thess 2:15-16) where an examination of the context shows how ideally suited was this motif to polemical deployment, in particular against opponents who enjoyed positions of power or influence. In Q it likewise is used to combat the influence of persons who could hold themselves out as representatives of the great tradition.

Social Location

The complex of textual and rhetorical signs in Q^2 provides hints regarding the social location for its framers and addressees. This stratum of Q is composed with a measure of sophistication (when compared with other chriae collections), but does not appear to come from the highest scribal levels. It employs urban images, but normally in an negative manner. In its conflict with the Pharisees and lawyers, Q^2 does not adopt the strategy of arguing from the Torah against its opponents—a strategy that Matthew later would adopt. Instead, the strategy is one of burlesque and ridicule—probably an indication that the Q people are not in a position to confront the Pharisees directly. The Torah does not function as the self-evident starting point for argumentation; purity distinctions and tithing are a subject of ridicule (11:42ab, 39-41); and the Temple is not a symbol of sanctification and redemption. It is, on the contrary, the place where prophets are killed (Q 11:49-51; 13:34-35).

The framers of Q are scribes, to be sure, but their interests and inclinations do not coincide with the scribes and literati of Jerusalem. Nor do they appear to be very high on the social ladder, certainly not among the urban retainer class. This would account both for their negative views of the polis and for the fact that they do not directly engage the views of their opponents, but rather attack obliquely, with burlesque.[54] Of course we should not imagine that the Q people consisted only of lower-echelon scribes of Galilean towns. Although Q reflects scribal practice and values, it is not addressed to scribes. The role of scribe was a self-consciously public role: the scribe required leisure that was not available to the handworker or agriculturalist; but the scribe's responsibility was ultimately to the public and

---

is the shedding of innocent blood that is also the common denominator in 11:51. Theissen's point about the knowledge of the Hebrew canon presupposed by 11:51, however, stands.

54. In a Toronto dissertation, Han (1998:90–94) adduced the analogy of the Confucian criticism of Buddhist temples during the Koryo kingdom (918–1392 CE) in Korea. While moderate voices from within Buddhist priestly circles called for reform of the temples, the sharpest criticism originated from nonpriestly Confucian literati, either ostracized bureaucrats or village scribes who embraced neo-Confucianism.

public approbation in the form of honor and fame crowns the sage's achievement (Sir 39:1-11).[55] There is little direct reflection of the persons Q addresses beyond the likelihood that they represent no higher a social level than the scribes that framed Q. Perhaps the best that can be said is that the Q people included some of the petit bourgeois of Galilean towns and, possibly, marginalized persons from some of the cities.

I have already suggested that the role of the itinerant workers should not be exaggerated. There is little evidence that these persons founded groups, as D. Zeller and Sato would have it. Nor is there any indication that the workers were leaders in the groups addressed in Q 10:2 or that the villages which they entered were to accept them as leaders. Indeed, the social dynamics typical of towns and villages in the Levant would have made this exceedingly unlikely. Moreover, these laborers are not invested with the titles "apostle" (1 Cor 9:1; *Did.* 11.3-6), "prophet" (*Did.* 11.3-11; 13.1), or "teacher" (*Did.* 13.2), any of which would have made their role as (potential) leaders clear. Instead, the laborers were viewed as able to convey a blessing of peace upon a welcoming household (10:6)—that is, one that expressed assent to Q's program. What they did constituted work deserving of "wages" (10:7b), here understood as food and lodging (10:7a). But the very fact that Q needs to remind its addressees that such "workers" were deserving of subsistence support implies that this was not taken for granted.

Instead of imagining with Theissen that the early Jesus movement represented by Q comprised itinerants with their sometime supporters, it seems more likely that there was a network of local groups and local leaders, perhaps household heads, and that the mobile workers were dependent upon the households both materially and for the legitimation of their roles. It should also be remembered that the region of the Lower Galilee with which Q should be associated is tiny; the towns in the area along the western and northwestern shores of the Kinneret are all within a day's walk of one another. Strange calculates that a traveler starting in Sepphoris could reach any of forty villages in a short day's travel (1997:42). "Itinerancy" should not in any case be imagined on a very grand scale; it would have looked more like daylong excursions.[56]

---

55. For an exposition of scribal values, see Harrington 1980; Mack 1985.

56. Those who discuss itinerancy in Q rarely propose any concrete models for such itinerancy. The only model of which I am aware is that of the *rōchēl* (רוכל, "pedlar"), described in rabbinic literature (*m. Maʿaś.* 2.1-3; *m. Šabb.* 9.7; *m. Kelim* 2.4; *t. Qidd.* 5.14; *y. Maʿaś.* 2.49b; *b. B. Qam.* 82a; *b. ʿAbod. Zar.* 61a; *y.* . 4.44b; *y. Ber.* 2.5a; *y. Meg.* 4.75a; *ʾAbot R. Nat.* A 18 p. 34; *Lev. Rab.* 16:2). The *rōchēl* was the most important commercial link between towns and satellite villages. The circuit of the *rōchēl* appears to have been small, either allowing him to return to his own town every evening (thus *y. Maʿaś.* 2.49b, of *rochlīm* of Kefar Ḥananyah near Sepphoris), or spend a few nights in the villages (*m. Maʿaś.* 2.1-3). The standard equipment of the *rōchēl* was a box (*kuppah*), sometimes carried on a pole or staff. The description of the Q

THE FINAL FORM OF Q (Q^3)

Even though the slight extent of Q^3 materials hardly justifies its being distinguished as a discrete edition from a literary point of view, there are important features of Q^3 bearing on social location. It is only at Q^3 that the Torah and the Temple appear in a positive light. In the temptation story, both Jesus and the devil conduct their debate by quoting the Torah and the Psalms as if this is self-evidently the appropriate way to make an argument. Q 11:42c and 16:17—also secondary intrusions—likewise take the validity of Torah for granted. Q 11:42c insists on the importance of tithing, evidently inattentive to the fact that the list of items supposedly to be tithed in 11:42a does not correspond to any known tithing regime. The point of 11:42c in fact is not to insist that the items in 11:42a be tithed; rather, it is to assert the necessity of tithing as a general obligation of Torah. Similarly, Q 16:17 is obviously a qualification and limitation of any possible antinomian interpretation of 16:16 ("The law and the prophets were until John"). Whether an earlier edition of Q intended an antinomian meaning is beside the point, but probably not the case (Kosch 1989a:433–40). But the addition of 16:17 betrays the hand of a "nervous redactor" who is worried about any apparent rejection of Torah.

In Q^3 a shift in the attitude toward the Temple is also seen. While Q 11:49-51 and 13:34-35 offer a rather bleak interpretation of the Temple and its ruling elite, the second temptation (4:9-12) takes for granted that the Temple is a place where angels might naturally be present to assist holy persons. From a narrative point of view, all that the second temptation requires is altitude. Placing Jesus on any cliff or precipice or tall building would have done. The deliberate choice of the Temple location (which requires Jesus being mysteriously transported from the desert locale of the first temptation to Jerusalem) betrays a view of the Temple that is not impeded by the critique of Q^2. The Temple is now (again) a holy place.

It is also worth noting that the three temptations serve to exemplify (and hence, to legitimate) the ethics of earlier strata of Q.[57] Jesus' refusal of the devil's challenge to produce bread from stones picks up the language of 11:11 (bread/stone) and creates an image of Jesus, who, as Q 12:30-31 advises, does not seek food as his first priority. The temptation to invoke angelic support in a public display of power or self-protection exemplifies both Q's eschewing of demonstrative signs (11:29-30; 17:23-30) and its advice to fear God rather than those who might "kill the body" (12:4). The third temptation, which in the presumed original order of Q immediately

---

"workers" who travel without a staff or sandals or a bag would distinguish them immediately from *rochlîm*, even if the "workers" followed the same circuit. See further, Safrai 1994:77–81; Adan-Bayewitz 1985.

57. For paradigmatic readings of the temptation story, see Schottroff and Stegemann 1978:72–77, ET 1986:53–57; D. Zeller 1980; Kloppenborg 1987a:250–53; Tuckett 1992.

preceded the makarism regarding the poor (6:20), depicts Jesus as resisting the luster of power, privilege, and wealth, which Q elsewhere pronounces to be inimical to the service of God (16:13).

The temptation story is significant not only for the way in which the testing sequences have been made to legitimate particular aspects of Q's praxis, but for the way in which this is done. Q^1 simply pronounced the poor honorable and gave assurance via examples from family life and nature that God would bountifully provide. Q^2 stated that legitimation signs would not be forthcoming. The examples of Nineveh, the Queen of the South, and the generations of Noah and Lot illustrate that nonmiraculous activities in the present provide a sufficient reason to respond to God; signs should not be required and, in fact, will be given. Q^3, by contrast, attempts to ground practice in the Torah though a learned assemblage of texts. The technique of quotation and counterquotation, though not quite to the standards of rabbinic argument, is redolent of Matthew's argumentative practices.

Both the use of Torah quotations in argument and the evident concern for the enduring validity of the Torah strongly suggest a scribal provenance for Q^3. The level is somewhat higher and more learned than that evidenced in either Q^1 or Q^2. Nevertheless, the shift from the earlier stages of Q to Q^3 is not a matter of discontinuity but, since it is a matter of a somewhat different *scribal* practice, only a shift in level. Not enough text is available to be able to judge anything further about the audience of the final stage of Q, but it might be noted that the letter of James likewise displays important contacts with the Jesus tradition (Hartin 1991) but also evinces a view of the Torah as a legitimate starting point in argument (James 2:1-13, 14-26).

5

Reading Q in the Galilee

> Agriculture is always the kind of enterprise
> with which God has a lot to do.
> —Arthur Stinchcombe

THE PREVIOUS CHAPTER proposed a social location for Q based on the textual signs in the document itself. For such a proposal to carry conviction, however, it must also be compatible with what is known of the human geography and social culture of the Galilee. The social location deduced from the document must fit with what is otherwise known about the Galilee from historical and archaeological sources. I have suggested that Q is best situated in the Galilee. We do not possess, however, the data that would allow an exact specification of its provenance. Q's negative depiction of cities seems to exclude Tiberias or Sepphoris (Ṣippori), but this leaves several large towns such as Kefar Naḥum or Khorazin.[1] Indeed, the activities

---

1. For convenience I use the definitions of Safrai (1994:40–42, 65–67). A large town: 90–100 dunams (9–10 hectares); a medium-sized town: 30–45 dunams; a small town: more than 10 dunams; a village (כפר, *Kfar*): 8–10 dunams. On this scale, Kefar Naḥum would be a very large town (170 dunams: Tzaferis 1989:216). Determining the size of other towns in first-century Galilee is made difficult by the fact that many towns experienced dramatic growth after 135 CE. Khorazin (destroyed in the mid-fourth century) was 60 dunams at its apogee of growth (Yeivin 1973; Applebaum 1967:16), but apparently smaller before 70 CE. Meiron in the Upper Galilee was as large as 300 dunams by the latest occupational stages (Meyers, Strange, and Groh 1978:22 n. 3), but village-sized prior to 135 (Meyers, Strange, and Meyers 1981:156). Meyers, Strange, and Groh (1978:22 n. 3) estimate the size of Khirbet Shemaᶜ (Upper Galilee) to be almost 40 dunams by the Byzantine period. But prior to the early third century, when its inhabitants built a synagogue, Khirbet Shemaᶜ was treated as a satellite village of Meiron, only 500 m to the north across the Wadi Meiron (Meyers, Kraabel, and Strange 1976:15–16). Safrai (1994:65) puts the village at only 7 dunams.

Safrai estimates 10 rooms per dunam (1994:92) and hence 10 families (at 3.5–4.0 persons per nuclear family) or 35–40 persons per dunam. (This, presumably, allows for the fact that multigenerational families might live in contiguous rooms.) Thus he suggests that large towns had up to 1,000 families; medium towns had 350 families; and smaller settlements of 5–8

of Q's "workers" allow the possibility that the Q people tried to create a social network that extended over several towns or between cities and towns. If this is correct, instead of focusing on single town or village, it will be more useful to offer a reconstruction of some of the salient features of first-century Galilee in general.

This is not a simple matter. Josephus, the principal literary source in the first century, provides a very incomplete glimpse of the political and economic character of the Galilee and his account is both tendentious and self-serving. From a much later period, rabbinic literature gives a rich view of political and economic life in the Galilee (Goodman 1983; Safrai 1994). But between the first century and the time of the rabbis, the face of Galilean society changed dramatically. The failure of the Second Revolt (132–135 CE) was responsible for a large-scale displacement of Judaeans, many of whom resettled in the Galilee. Rabbinic sources, even when they describe the Galilee before the First Revolt, do so through the lens of a Galilee that had been reconfigured by waves of Judaean immigration.

The archaeological evidence that might serve as a control on our literary sources is, at present, still quite fragmentary and still open to debate. Sepphoris, Kefar Naḥum, and Gamla have been excavated in part, but other sites such as Yodefat, Tiberias, Magdala-Tarichaeae, Cana, and Bethsaida have received far less attention.[2] Cities and large towns such as Sepphoris and Kefar Naḥum understandably have received more attention than villages, but it may be that large centers are less pertinent to Q's world than towns and villages. Despite these difficulties, it is possible to assemble at least a partial view of Galilean society.

Some Key Features of the Galilee in the First Century

Obviously this is not the place for a full review of the Galilee in the early Roman period.[3] Several features of the history and archaeology of the period are, however, germane to the social location of Q. These include: (1) the ethnic complexion and ethnographic borders of the Galilee; (2) evidence of the attitudes of Galileans toward the principal Judaean political

---

dunams had 100–250 families (*sic!*). This calculus implies that Kefar Naḥum had a population of 6,000–8,000 (1,500–1,700 families). Reed (1992) has shown, however, that this figure is far too high: comparison with Roman Pompeii (125–156 per hectare) suggests that the population of Kefar Naḥum was 1,700–2,500 or 425–625 families.

2. Although some of ancient Tiberias has been exposed, the excavation is impeded by the modern city that lies on top. A synagogue was excavated at Magdala (Loffreda 1976; Corbo 1974), and Yodefat and Bethsaida are currently being excavated. On Bethsaida, see Arav and Freund 1995; on Yodefat: Adan-Bayewitz, Aviᶜam, Edwards 1997. Excavations at Cana (Ḥorvat Qana) have just begun.

3. For surveys, see Meyers 1979; 1985; 1995; Freyne 1980; 1988b; Goodman 1983; Bösen 1985; L. Levine 1992; Aviᶜam 1993; Overman 1993; Oakman 1994; Reed 1994a; Safrai 1994; Strange 1994; Horsley 1995a; 1995c; 1996.

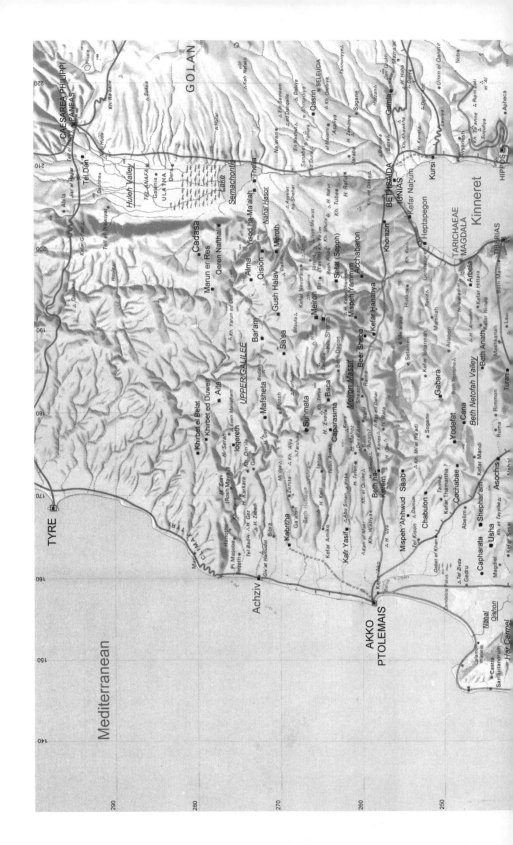

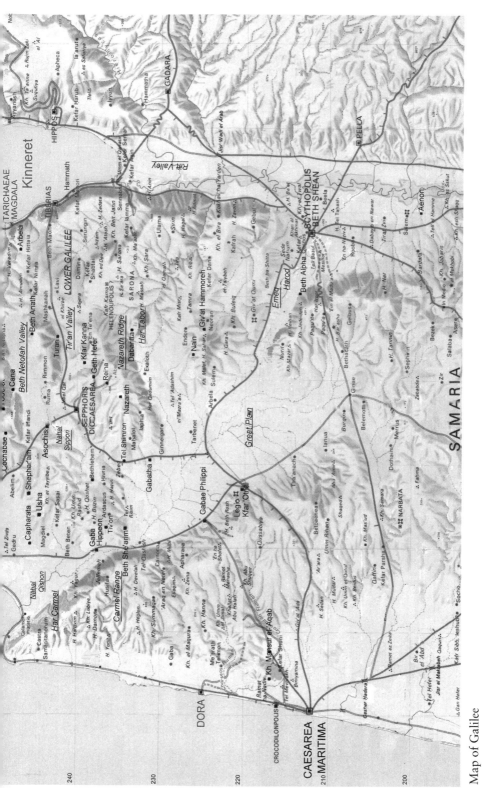

Map of Galilee

and political-religious institutions (e.g., the Temple and the Judaean Torah); (3) the pressures of urbanization; (4) the presence of priests and the priestly courses; and (5) the general economic and political climate (including levels of indebtedness, banditry, and social unrest).

THE ETHNOGRAPHIC BORDERS OF THE GALILEE

Two quite distinct geographical regions comprise the Galilee.[4] Extending north from a line defined by Miṣpeh ʾAḥihwud, Kefar Ḥananya, and Beer Sheba (of the Galilee) at the foot of the Meiron massif, the upper Galilee has a rugged terrain filled with high hills, mountains, and deep valleys.[5] The city regions (*chorai*) of Ptolemais and Tyre formed its western and northern boundaries. On the west, the village of Caparasima (Kafr Sumeiʿ) Ptolemais and Suḥmata belonged to Tyre, while Cadasa (Kedesh) in the northeast belonged to Tyre (Avi-Yonah 1977:130). This means that the effective border of the Upper Galilee probably ran northwest from Baca (Peqiʿin) to Mafsheta and then turned east, passing through ʿAlma, down the Naḥal Ḥaṣor past Qiṣion (Kh. Qasyûn) and Meroth (Kh. Marrus),[6] and terminated at Thella (Yisod ha-Maʿalah) on Lake Semachontis in the Huleh Valley (Avi-Yonah 1977:130–35). The Upper Galilee thus included the towns and villages of Baca, Saʿsa, Gush Ḥalav (Gishala), Meiron, Khirbet Shemaʿ, and Barʿam (all of which contain remains of later synagogues).[7] Later called the *tetracomia* ("union of four villages"),[8] this region did not fall within the *chora* of any city (even if Tyre sometimes encroached on the Upper Galilee). Each village probably developed its own independent administrative structure.[9] Some of these settlements experienced dramatic growth after 135 CE, when Judaeans displaced in the wake of the failed Second Revolt relocated

---

4. *M. Šeb.* 9.9 adds a third division, that of the Kinneret: "Three countries are to be distinguished in what concerns the law of removal: Judaea, beyond Jordan and the Galilee; and each of them is divided into three lands. [The Galilee is divided into] Upper Galilee, Lower Galilee and the (rift) valley: from Kefar Ḥananya upwards, wherever sycamores do not grow, is the Upper Galilee; from Kefar Ḥananya downwards, wherever sycamores grow, is the Lower Galilee; the region of Tiberias is the valley."

5. Rainfall is high, with Mount Meiron registering a mean annual rainfall of 1,000–1,100 mm.; Ṣefat only slightly less (800–900 mm). See Rosenan 1970.

6. Josephus (*War* 3.39) describes the northern border with Tyre as extending μέχρι Μηρωθ ἀπὸ Θελλᾶ (from Thella as far as Meroth). Avi-Yonah (1977:133) suggested that Meroth should be identified with Marûn er Ras, north of Barʿam, but the more likely identification is with Khirbet Marrus (map ref. 199270), located on the wadi that leads up to Qiṣion (Tsafrir, Di Segni, and Green 1994:184).

7. For bibliography, see Chiat 1982:21–65; Ilan 1987; Groh 1995; and Tsafrir, Di Segni, and Green 1994:ad loc.

8. Georgius Cyprius (ca. 600 CE), *Descriptio orbis Romani* (ed. Gelzer 1890) no. 1040.

9. Thus Goodman 1983:119–28, arguing on the analogy of a similar deployment of villages in Bashan, Hauran and Trachonitis (Harper 1928).

there. Prior to this time, however, the Upper Galilee seems to have been rather sparsely populated (Meyers, Strange, and Meyers 1981:156–58).

The Lower Galilee is a fertile region bounded in the west by the city regions of Gaba (in the Great Plain) and Ptolemais.[10] The *chora* of the cavalry settlement of Gaba Hippeon[11] and that of Ptolemais described a diagonal NNE line from the promontory of the Carmel, running inland almost as far as Shephar^cam, Chabulon, and Saab in the western Lower Galilee.[12] The area between the Meiron massif and the Nazareth ridge consists of a series of valleys on an east-west axis, finally descending over 400 meters to the Kinneret (210 m below sea level), which forms the eastern edge of the Galilee. The southern boundary of the Galilee touched the Great Plain, running along the northern length of the ^cEmeq Ḥarod to Giv^cat Hammoreh, and then to Har Tabor and along the foothills of the Nazareth ridge to Tel Shimron and the Naḥal Qishon, which separates the Carmel range from the hills of Beth She^carim. While the Lower Galilee abutted the city territories of Scythopolis and Samaria,[13] for most of the Roman period the choice land of the Great Plain was carved up into royal estates. Ceramic evidence suggests that the Nazareth ridge formed a de facto cultural and economic boundary: the pottery of Kefar Ḥananya, the major producing site in the Galilee, is found in the Upper Galilee (Meiron), the western Lower Galilee (Beth She^carim), the eastern Lower Galilee (Sepphoris), the Kinneret basin (Kefar Naḥum, Tiberias), and even in the Decapolis and the edge of the Golan (Susita-Hippos, Gamla), but not south of the Nazareth ridge.[14]

In spite of the name "Galilee of the Gentiles" (גליל הגוים, Isa 8:23),[15] the Galilee appears to have been largely Israelite by the early Roman period. The key question, however, is, what does this imply about the Galilee's political and cultural allegiances? The Galilee had been separated from

10. Mean annual rainfall is significantly less than in the Upper Galilee (Sepphoris [Ṣippori]: 500–600 mm; Nazareth Ridge 600–700 mm; Tiberias: 400–500 mm) but still more than adequate for wheat and barley production.

11. Gaba Hippeon (el Ḥarithiyeh; map ref. 160236), founded by Herod to settle cavalry veterans (Josephus, *War* 2.459), might be identical with Gabae Philippi (Tel Shosh, Mishmar ha-^cEmeq; map ref. 163224), founded by Marcus Philippus, governor of Syria in 61/60 BCE. See Tsafrir, Di Segni, and Green 1994:125, 126.

12. Josephus (*War* 2.573; *Life* 188) also mentions the fortification of Καφαρεκχώ (or Καφαράθ), which may be Kefar Ata near Shephar^cam (map ref. 160245).

13. Josephus (*War* 3.35-40) states that the Galilee extended from the *chora* of Ptolemais and Carmel in the west, to Samaria and Scythopolis in the south, to the territory of Hippos, Gadara, and Gaulanitis in the east, to the *chora* of Tyre in the north.

14. Adan-Bayewitz and Perlman 1990; Adan-Bayewitz 1992; Freyne 1995b:602. A similar distribution of stone vessels manufactured in Kefar Shikhin (Asochis) can be observed.

15. Cf. 1 Macc 5:15: Γαλιλαία ἀλλοφυλῶν, "Galilee of the foreigners." The term appears originally to have referred to the fact that this region was ringed or circled (גלל) by Canaanite cities. Even though "Galilee" had become a proper name, in the first century CE it was still ringed by Gentiles cities—Tyre and Sidon in the North, Ptolemais and Caesarea in the west, Samaria and Scythopolis in the south, and Gadara and Hippos in the east.

Judaea by the Assyrian campaign of 733/732 BCE (2 Kings 15:29) when its nobility was deported.[16] A survey of ceramic evidence from the Iron Age suggests that after 732 BCE the Lower Galilee was depopulated for more than a century.[17] In the next centuries, the region was controlled successively by the Persians, the Ptolemies, the Seleucids, and, as the Seleucids declined, by the Itureans. The Galilee did not come again under the political control of Judaea until late in the second century BCE when the Hasmonean king John Hyrcanus (134–104 BCE) began to extend the control of Judaea northward, as far as Samaria and Scythopolis (Kasher 1990:125–31).

Hyrcanus's son Aristobulus (104–103 BCE) reportedly completed his northern expansion by wresting control of all of the Galilee from the Itureans (104 BCE). Josephus reports in this connection that Aristobulus acquired Iturean territory for Judaea and "compelled the inhabitants, if they wished to remain in the country, to be circumcised and to live in accordance with the laws of the Judaeans" (*Ant.* 13.318-19; see Adam 1996). This statement is sometimes taken to mean that the inhabitants of the Galilee were Gentiles whom Aristobulus forcibly Judaized.[18] Other statements, both in 1 Maccabees and in Josephus, suggest that prior to 104 BCE substantial portions of the Galilee were deemed to be Israelite or, at least, that in a conflict they were more likely to support Judaea than Iturea or Syria.[19]

---

16. Compare the fragmentary annals of Tiglath-Pileser III (*ANET* 283), which mention the towns of [Ga]bara (?), Ḥinatuma (=Tel Ḥannathon), Kannaʾ (?), Yoṭba (? Yodefat/Jotapata), and Merom (=Tel Qarney Ḥiṭṭim, in the ʾArbela pass). See Gal 1992:108, who identifies Yoṭba with Karem el-Ras near modern Kefar Kannaʾ, a site occupied during Iron I.

17. Gal (1992:79–83) found no Assyrian pottery or its local imitations in a single site from the Lower Galilee, even though such pottery is found in Iron III sites in Samaria. These sites evidence pottery from the Persian period and later periods. See also Aviʿam forthcoming: 32:33.

18. Thus Schürer 1973–87, 1:217. Schürer (1:142) understands the report in 1 Macc 5:23 to mean that Simon evacuated the entire Jewish population of the Galilee in 164/163 BCE.

19. The evidence for a predominantly Israelite population is not unambiguously clear, but is nonetheless suggestive:

(1) The report of Simon's rescue of Jews in the Galilee (1 Macc 5:23; 164/163 BCE) should not be taken to imply that the entire Israelite population of the Galilee was under threat from the encroachments of Ptolemais, Tyre, and Sidon, but only limited areas of the western Galilee and the western part of the Great Plain. Kasher (1990:69) has plausibly argued that the reason for the conflict was an attempt by the coastal cities to expand their urban *chorai* further into the western Lower Galilee (and, presumably, the Upper Galilee).

(2) 1 Macc 9:1-2 reports that Bacchides, a Seleucid general, en route to engage Judas in 160 BCE, took the road τὴν εἰς Γαλγαλα and encamped against Μαισαλωθ τὴν ἐν Ἀρβηλοῖς, killing many of its population. Josephus (*Ant.* 12.421) understands this to mean Arbela in the Galilee (ἐν Ἀρβηλοῖς πόλει τῆς Γαλιλαίας) and refers to the caves there (anticipating his description of Herod's campaign against brigands at the caves of Arbela; cf. *War* 1.304-13; *Ant.* 14.415-30). Horsley (1995c:40) conjectures that this should be read as *har-beth-el* (the hill country of Beth-el), just north of Jerusalem, where Bacchides engaged Judas. But this leaves unexplained Γαλγαλα and ignores the fact that 1 Macc 9:50 mentions Beth-el, there using the ordinary spelling (Βαιθηλ). Goldstein (1976:372) plausibly suggests that Μαισαλωθ stands for *mesillôth* ("roads, ascents, steps"), which in that case refers to a village associated with the stepped path that leads

It is not clear how this state of affairs came about, since we have little direct evidence bearing on the repopulation of the Galilee following its devastation by the Assyrians. Ceramic evidence indicates Phoenician infiltration into the Upper Galilee during the Persian period. Avi'am suggests gradual Judaean resettlement in the western Lower Galilee.[20] Unfortunately, it is impossible to determine whether the Israelite presence in the Galilee represented the survival of tiny populations from the aftermath of the Assyrian conquest or immigrants from Judaea or some combination of the two. A dramatic rupture is signaled, however, in the late second century BCE with the abandonment of several pagan sites in the Upper Galilee and the virtual disappearance of pottery typical of the pre-Hasmonean period in a series of Galilean sites.[21] This rupture appears to correspond to the Hasmonean recovery of the Galilee.

The reestablishment of political relations between Judaea and the Galilee is suggested archaeologically by the appearance at several sites of the coins of Alexander Jannaeus (103-76 BCE) and later Hasmoneans alongside the currency of Tyre.[22] Tyre remained an important economic and political force because of its proximity; but after 104 BCE the Galilee came clearly into the orbit of Judaean control and remained so throughout the Hasmonean and early Herodian periods. If there was a pagan population, it left

---

up the Arbela pass. In any event, Bacchides' action makes sense only if the inhabitants of Arbela were presumed to be supporters of Judas against Bacchides (thus Freyne 1980:39).

(3) Describing Jonathan's operations against Demetrius II in 144 BCE, Josephus reports (*Ant.* 13.154) that Demetrius, in order to relieve pressure on Damascus, brought an army to Cadasa (Kedesh) on the nothern border of the Upper Galilee, supposing that Jonathan would move to support the Galilcans "who were of his own people."

(4) Even prior to Aristobulus's annexation of the Galilee, his brother Alexander Jannaeus is said to have been raised in the Galilee "from his birth" (Josephus, *Ant.* 13.332), which suggests that at least some parts of the Galilee were favorable to the Hasmoneans.

(5) Immediately after Aristobulus's annexation and "Judaizing" of the Galilee, Ptolemy IX Lathyrus attacked the city of Asochis (Shikhin) on the Beth Netopha plain, deliberately choosing the Sabbath for strategic reasons (Josephus, *Ant.* 13.337). As Kasher (1988:80) observes, this implies that the inhabitants of the village were not just recently converted, and makes it very unlikely that their "conversion" was under duress.

20. Avi'am (forthcoming: 33) cites Judith 1:8, where the Upper Galilee and the Great Plain seem to be treated as Gentile areas, while nothing is said of the Lower Galilee, presumably because it was Israelite.

21. Avi'am (forthcoming: 39) discusses archaeological evidence of pagan cultic sites and activities in the Hellenistic period in the Upper Galilee at Miṣpeh Yammim (see Frankel 1993) and Beeı Sheba, both abandoned at the end of the second century BCE. In these sites, and at Yodefat, Galilean Coarse Ware (GCW) is attested up to the second century BCE but not thereafter. Avi'am suggests that GCW was typical of the pagan residents of the Upper Galilee, and its disappearance coincides with the Hasmonean conquest of the Galilee.

22. On the Upper Galilee, see R. Hanson 1980:51–70; Meyers, Strange, and Meyers 1981:260–72. The earliest Hasmonean coin found in conjunction with the Galilean fishing boat is from the time of Alexander Jannaeus or Salome Alexander (Gitler 1990:104). On Tyrian influence in the Galilee, see above, chap. 4, n. 173 n. 9.

few tracks. Avi'am observes that the boundaries of Jewish Galilee are confirmed archaeologically, at least from the second century CE on: no synagogue or Jewish remains are found west of a line that runs from Tiv'on to
Shephar'am to Peqi'im[23] or north of the arc described by Sa'sa—Bar'am—
Qişion—Meroth—Yisod ha-Ma'alah.[24] Conversely, pagan temples are
found in the Carmel Range and at Cadasa (Kedesh), Khirbet Harrawi
(Qeren Naftali), Khirbet el Belat, and Khirbet ed Duweir,[25] but not south of
the Sa'sa—Yisod ha-Ma'alah line or east of the Peqi'im. Later archaeology
seems to preserve a "memory" of the earlier ethnographic boundaries of the
Galilee and confirms the essentially Israelite character of both the Galilees.

It should not be assumed too quickly that the dominant presence of an
Israelite population in the Galilee automatically meant that Galilean
Judaism[26] assumed the same contours as that of Judaea. Horsley has
insisted that the fact that the Galilee had not been under the political control of Jerusalem for eight centuries prior to 104 BCE cannot have been without consequences (1995a:8). To assume as Meyers does (1979:693–701)
that the Galilee was "Torah true" in the early Roman period because it was
predominantly Israelite is a large leap. Meyer's characterization depends in
large measure on statements of Josephus on the topic.[27] Recent analysis of

---

23. A exception to this is perhaps presented by Kfar Yāsif (9.5 km NE of Akko), well inside
the territory of Ptolemais. A dedication to Hadad and Atargatis from ca. 150 BCE is attested
(*SEG* 17.622; Avi-Yonah 1959) but the site also contains the remains of what was first
reported to be a synagogue (Chiat 1982:17–18). More recent examination of the site by
Mordechai Avi'am suggests that the mosaic floor belonged to a church rather than a synagogue
(personal correspondence).

24. Avi'am 1993:453, 455; forthcoming:10–11; cf. Meyers 1995:23.

25. Cadasa [200279] (a temple to Baalshamin/Apollo: Magness 1990; Avi'am 1985); Khirbet Harrawi [202277] (an inscription from the lintel with a dedication to Athena: Abel
1908:574–76); Khirbet el Balat (Jebel Balat [175280], 20 km SW of Tyre, containing the ruins
of a temple, perhaps to a local embodiment of Aphrodite or Venus: Guérin 1880, 2:131–33;
Conder and Kitchener 1881–83: 1:171–73); Khirbet ed Duweir [176275] (a dedication to
Diana and Apollo in southern Lebanon; Conder and Kitchener 1881–83: 1:236; Avi'am
1993:455). The cult of "Zeus Carmelos" is attested in the Carmel range—i.e., in the city territories of Ptolemais (Avi-Yonah 1952).

26. The term "Galilean Judaism" is potentially problematic insofar as it implies a unity of
belief and practice between Judaea and the Galilee that is precisely under examination in this
chapter. That "Judaism" could be used of Galilean practice and belief after the second century
CE is defensible, but only because of the large migration of Judaeans to the north as a result of
the failure of the Second Revolt. There is, however, no felicitous generic term to substitute,
and so I use "Judaism" as the generic, and (seemingly redundant) "Judaean Judaism" and
"Galilean Judaism" to denote subtypes. An analogous problem is presented by the term
Ἰουδαῖοι, normally translated "Jews," but sometimes better rendered "Judaeans," insofar as
Josephus and some of the Gospels appear to distinguish Ἰουδαῖοι (Judaeans) from Γαλιλαῖοι
(Galileans). I have used the terms "Israel/Israelite" to denote the larger groupings of those asso-
ciated in various ways with Jerusalem (in Judaea, Galilee, Peraea, and the Diaspora).

27. Meyers (1979) cites as his evidence a 1973 Duke University dissertation on Josephus by
Malinowski.

Josephus, however, has provided ample reason to conclude that Josephus exaggerated commonalities between Judaea and the Galilee for his own apologetic reasons (see below, p. 228).

Horsley thinks that the Israelite presence in pre-Hasmonean Galilee was due mainly to the remnant not deported by Assyrians in the seventh century BCE. The literary and material evidence is far too slender to know for certain. He is correct nonetheless to argue that the extension of Hasmonean control over this region and the imposition of the "laws of the Judaeans" are unlikely to have immediately assimilated Galilean practices to the Judaean forms of Judaism. Indeed, there is little evidence that the Hasmoneans promoted such an assimilation. As Israelites, the Galileans would have shared with Judaeans many traditions and practices (including, presumably, circumcision and some form of Sabbath observance). But they are also likely to have had many indigenous traditions and practices at variance with Judaean ones. These differences were probably at the root of some of the friction reported between Galileans and representatives of the Judaean hierocracy and later, with the sages who relocated in the Galilee (Horsley 1995c:46–52). The distinction between the Judaisms of the Galilee and Judaea was slowly effaced after 135 CE;[28] prior to that time, however, we should reckon on some differences.

THE GALILEE, THE TEMPLE, AND THE TORAH

The Second Temple

A key issue in gauging the complexion of Galilean Judaism has to do with attitudes toward the Temple. The case for Galilean allegiance to the Temple has been put most trenchantly by Seán Freyne, who makes three main points. First, there is no evidence that Galileans availed themselves of alternate cultic centers, as Jews in Leontopolis in Egypt did. Even had Galileans been tempted to worship at Gerizim, they would not have been welcome there.[29] A cultic site existed at Dan in the north, but Freyne rightly doubts that Galileans would have had much attachment to that site.[30] Nor is there

28. Schiffman (1992) argues that Galilean halakhah was not more "lax" than Judaean halakhah but the evidence he cites concerning the purity of wine and oil presses (*m. Hag.* 3.5), the temple tax (*m. Ned.* 2.4), and the law of removal (*t. Sanh.* 2.6) all indicates significant noncompliance with Judaean halakhah. Moreover, if Galilean observance was only nominally different from Judaean halakhah in the first century, as Schiffman maintains, it becomes difficult to account for the fact that during the second century CE, the rabbis, now relocated in the Galilee, had practically nothing to do with the Galilean masses and, conversely, the Galileans only rarely went to the rabbis for advice in affairs of religion and commerce. On the latter point, see Cohen 1992.

29. Hostilities between Samaritans and Galileans is reflected in Luke 9:53; John 4:3-42; and Josephus, *Ant.* 20.123; *War* 2.237.

30. Freyne 1988b:183–84. Biran (1981) published a dedication from a certain Zoilos (who

any positive evidence of connections with the cult of Dionysus, attested at Scythopolis and Sidon.

Second, drawing on a statement of Josephus (*Life* 63, 80), Freyne argues that Galileans supported the Temple through the half-shekel temple tax and tithes. The Pharisaic complaints regarding Galilean payment are explained as complaints about their manner of payment, not that they refused to pay the tax (1981:105, 281, 283). The issue of the half-shekel tax is complicated by several factors, however. Despite the fact that the Pharisees seem to have understood Exod 30:11-16 as instituting an *annual* temple tax (*terumah*), the levy for the temple was probably of quite recent origin. It is not mentioned in Second Temple literature before Philo.[31] At Qumran the identification of the half-shekel tax with Exodus 30 was accepted, but the covenanters insisted, in direct opposition to the Pharisaic view, that it was to be paid only once in a lifetime (4Q159).[32] The fact that susceptibility to the tax was a matter of controversy in the first century CE is also suggested by *m. Šeqal.* 1.4, which records Yoḥanan ben Zakkai's insistence against other opinions that priests were not immune from the tax.

The attitude of Galileans toward the tax is difficult to assess. *M. Ned.* 2.4 reports the view of R. Judah (b. Ilai; mid-second century CE) that certain ambiguous oaths made by Galileans are invalid "since the men of the Galilee know nothing of the *terumah* of the Temple chamber" (i.e., the half-shekel tax).[33] This report is typical of Ushan (mid-second-century) rabbinic

---

Biran thinks was a Jew) to "the God who is in Dan" (ΘΕΩΙ ΤΩ ΕΝ ΔΑΝΟΙΣ). The inscription appears to date from the Hellenistic period.

31. Philo, *Spec. Leg.* 1.77-78; Josephus, *Ant.* 18.312. See Liver 1963. An annual one-third shekel tax is mentioned in Neh 10:32 and 2 Chron 24:5, but Tobit, Ps-Aristeas, and Jubilees—all dealing with Temple offerings—fail to mention the half-shekel tax (Liver 1963:185–87; Horbury 1984:278).

32. 4Q159 (4QOrdinances[a]) 1 ii 6-7: "Concerning [ransom]: the money of the census which one gives as a ransom for his own person will be half a shekel [corresponding to the shekel of the temple, as an offering to God]. Only once will he give it in all his days." 11QTemple 60.1-15 lists tithes to be paid to priests and Levites, but makes no mention of a temple tax.

33. *M. Ned.* 2.4: "R. Judah says: If the vow was of undefined *terumah*, in Judaea it is forbidden [the oath is binding], but in the Galilee it is permitted, since the men of the Galilee know nothing of the *terumah* of the Temple chamber (שאין אנשי גליל מכירין את־תרומת הלשכן). [And if the vow of] undefined devoted things, in Judaea it is permitted, but in the Galilee it is forbidden, since the people of the Galilee know nothing of things devoted [to the use of] the priests (חרמי הכהנים)." The logic of the ruling rests on the facts that (a) *terumôt* can mean both the "heave offering" (the priestly portion), which is not intended directly for God and therefore cannot be the object of a vow, and temple tax, and that (b) "devoted things" (*ḥerem*) can be given either to the Temple directly (Lev 27:28) or to priests (Num 18:14). Galileans' ignorance creates a presumption in favor of the (nonbinding) "heave offering" and the (binding) "things devoted to the Lord." A parallel account in *t. Ned.* 1.6 ascribes the *terumah* portion to R. Judah, but the *ḥerem* portion to Eleazar b. Zaddok (Yavnean period). Citing this pericope, Schiffman 1992:149–50 argues that there was not a distinctive Galilean halakhah, but in effect concedes the point that while Galileans may have given priestly tithes, the *terumah* of the Temple chamber was not observed.

literature, which reflects "deep feelings of animosity towards those Jews known as ʿammei ha-ʾaretz," who are treated as untrustworthy in legal matters.[34] Freyne concludes that if *m. Ned.* 2.4 reflects anything about first-century attitudes—which he doubts[35]—it only means that Galileans adopted a conservative (Sadducean) interpretation regarding the responsibility for the tax,[36] not that they rejected the tax altogether (1980:280–81). Yet Freyne also cites Yoḥanan ben Zakkai's complaint, probably uttered in the wake of his remarkably unsuccessful tenure in the Galilee, that his contemporaries "were unwilling to pay the head-tax to God, 'a beka a head' [Exod 38:26]; now you are paying a head-tax of fifteen shekels under a government of your enemies" (*Mek. Exod.* 19.1).

We have in fact *no* positive evidence that Galileans accepted any form of the tax. Given the relatively recent vintage of the annual tax, the fact that its principal advocates were the Pharisees, the lack of sustained Pharisaic presence in the Galilee before 135 CE, and the complaints of second century sages, there is no good reason to think that Galileans were especially compliant with the tax. Perhaps some Galileans paid the tax. We cannot tell. The framing of the question to Peter (at Capernaum), "Does your master pay the didrachma tax?" (Matt 17:24), presumes that it could not be taken for granted that Galileans would pay. Jesus' answer (17:25-27) makes clear that Jesus did not accept liability to the tax (Horbury 1984).

Evidence of tithing is even less clear. On the one hand, Josephus reports that he was offered tithes by the Galileans but refused them, while his two companions, also priests, amassed a large sum and returned to Jerusalem (*Life* 63, 80). Josephus's account is both self-serving and designed to exaggerate Galilean loyalty to Josephus and Jerusalem in the face of a severe challenge by Justus of Tiberias (Freyne 1988b:190). But even if it were to be accepted, it must be kept in mind that the report comes from 66 CE, i.e., at

---

34. L. Levine 1989:30. Similarly, Goodman 1983:102–4, cataloguing a litany of complaints concerning disregard of purity laws, *kashrut*, the laws of mixed kinds (*kilaim*), tithes, and (more occasionally) Sabbath observance.

35. Freyne 1988b:213–18, here 214–15 (citing Neusner 1981:chap. 6): "almost all of the references to Galilee and Galileans in the earliest document, the Mishnah, would appear to be illustrative of what in Neusner's view are the basic concerns of the framers of the completed document. These were the removal of gray areas of law, the exclusion of middle ground and the resolution of doubtful cases—an agenda that was the direct result of the application of a legal imagination to the crisis besetting Jewish religious faith in the wake of the Bar Kochba war." Accordingly, most or all of the pericopae mentioning the Galilee and Galileans reflect either the experiences of *second*-century sages or are simply hypothetical scenarios designed to solve legal conundrums. They tell us little or nothing about Galilean Judaism before the two revolts.

36. See Liver 1963:189. A scholion on *Megillat Taanit* (Lichtenstein 1931:323) reports a dispute between the Boethusians (Sadducees) and the sages in which the former held that sacrifices ought to be provided privately, while the sages advocated public support via the temple tax. A similar report is found in *b. Men.* 65a.

the outbreak of the Revolt when Jerusalem felt in a strong position to exer-cise direct control over the Galilee. Prior to that time and especially after the death of Agrippa I (44 CE), there was hardly any mechanism for the collec-tion of tithes.

On the other hand, letters from Gamaliel I and, later, from R. Simeon ben Gamaliel I to upper and Lower Galilee complain of noncompliance with the law of removal of olives (Deut 26:13) and state that this has been a long-standing situation.[37] As with the temple tax, Freyne suggests that Pharisaic complaints about Galilean tithing practice are (in part) based on the Galilean adoption of Sadducean customs: payment of tithes directly to the priestly aristocracy rather than bringing them to the temple (1980:286). He pleads that the complaints of negligence in tithing after 70 CE do not trans-late into evidence of disregard of the Temple prior to 70 CE (1980:287).

Horsley thinks that the Hasmoneans, as priest-kings, consolidated the taxation system to include tithes payable to the Temple along with other tax revenues and that this system extended to all Hasmonean-controlled areas (1995c:141–43). If true, this would have made tithing much less informal than the earlier system implied by biblical texts. Unfortunately, little is known of the mechanics of the Hasmonean taxation system or its Herodian successor.

The report of Josephus (*Life* 63, 80) in fact suggests that the collection of tithes lay outside the royal revenue system. *T. Pe'a* 4.3 depicts priests and Levites coming to the threshing floors to collect the first tithe and attributes to Simeon b. Gamaliel (I) the nostalgic view that rich priests used to defer to poorer priests by taking only a token offering. The latter comment may have been formulated in direct antithesis to the accounts related by Jose-phus (*Ant.* 20.181, 205-6) of the high priests Ishmael b. Phabi (during the time of Felix) and Ananias (time of Albinus) sending their agents to appro-priate tithes forcibly at threshing floors in Judaea, thereby depriving poorer priests of their due.[38] Moreover, the entire presupposition of the second-century rabbinic discussion of *demai* produce—produce on which tithes may not have been paid—and the pervasive assumption that the 'ammei ha-'aretz are not reliable in matters of tithing indicate that tithe collection was not part of the royal (or later, Roman) revenue system and that nonpayment was common. Further, Sanders points out that rabbinic discussions take for granted that the priestly portion of the tithe (one-tenth of the first tithe) was paid but that the portion due the Levites (nine-tenths of the tithe) was

37. *T. Sanh.* 2.6; *y. Sanh.* 1.18d; *b. Sanh.* 11b; *y. Ma'aś.* 5.56b.

38. Cf. the complaint in *b. Pesaḥ.* 57a of chief priests forcibly appropriating priestly offer-ings. Ishmael b. Phabi is expressly mentioned in the accompanying woe: "Woe is me because of the house of Ishmael, the son of Phabi, woe is me because of their fists. For they are High Priests and their sons are [Temple] treasurers and their sons-in-law are trustees and their ser-vants beat the people with staves."

widely evaded (1990:152, 429–31). In prewar Galilee, where none of the priestly courses (*mishmarôt*) was resident, Freyne's conjecture that Galileans had adopted the Sadducean tithing custom runs aground. There was neither a priestly aristocracy nor significant priestly population in the Galilee to collect the tithe in the first place. That some Galileans paid tithes by bringing them to Jerusalem should not be doubted; but the difficulties entailed in collecting priestly tithes from areas outside Judaea, coupled with the later complaints of the sages, make it unlikely that observance of tithing was either widespread or regular.

Freyne is correct that Galilean "negligence" or "laxity" (from a Pharisaic perspective) does not necessarily signal opposition to the Temple. The sheer distance between the Galilee and Jerusalem meant, however, that there was likely a very low level of "exchange" between Galileans and the Temple—both material goods flowing to the Temple and nonmaterial benefits flowing from it. Temples in antiquity normally received material support from populations dwelling in the vicinity who could easily visit the cultic site, participate in festivals, and feel that the temple and its operations were conferring benefits.[39] Distance naturally decreases the level of exchange. Pressure from southern interests to increase material support for the Temple cannot have been regarded with much sympathy by Galileans, who not only were spatially separated from the Temple but belonged to a sector of Israelite society whose historical connections with the second Temple were tenuous to say the least.

Freyne's third argument for Galilean support of the Temple is based on pilgrimage. It is reasonable to suppose, he thinks, that Galileans participated in pilgrimages to Jerusalem, even though he concedes that "not all devout Jews of the province attended every festival."[40] The allegiance of Galilean peasants to the Temple is also signaled by their threat to withhold the planting of crops when Gaius Caligula announced plans to place an idolatrous statue in the Temple, a threat that would have deprived the nobility of Tiberias of its ability to pay the tribute (*Ant.* 18.273-78).

Simple mathematics ought to militate against the assumption that Galileans made pilgrimages on a grand scale. As Sanders points out, the journey from the Galilee to Jerusalem would require a week's travel each way. If one stayed in Jerusalem for even one week, attendance at Passover, Shevuôt, and Sukkôt would require a minimum of nine weeks away from one's farmstead (1992:130). This is simply not credible, quite apart from the expenses that would be involved. Tobit 1:6-8 suggests that most Galileans did *not* participate in the pilgrimage, despite Freyne's attempt to

---

39. On whether cities were "parasitic," see below p. 234.

40. Freyne 1981:104. As evidence of Galilean participation in pilgrimages, Freyne (1988b:170, 181, 187) cites Tobit 1:6-8; Luke 9:51-53; 13:1; Josephus, *War* 2.232-37; *Ant.* 20.118-23.

use it to support the opposite conclusion. Josephus's lone account of the killing of one Galilean pilgrim under Cumanus (*War* 2.232-37) cannot be ballooned into evidence of general Galilean Temple piety.[41] Horsley's estimate seems much more realistic: if even 1,000 Galileans made a pilgrimage each year, fewer than one-half of the entire population (of 100,000) would have gone to Jerusalem at any point in their lifetime (1995c:145–47, 316).

As Seth Schwartz observes, the evidence for Galilean recognition of the exclusive sanctity of the Temple is fragile (1989:389). While both Judith and Tobit assume that it is sufficient that northerners recognize the Temple in order to be considered Jews, Tob 1:4-8 concedes that most Galileans did not. Statements by Josephus form a key part in the "evidence" of Galilean support of the Temple. Schwartz, however, has exposed the strong apologetic thrust of these statements. Josephus took over the account in 1 Macc 10:22-45, which records Demetrius I's letter to John Hyrcanus proposing a definition of the Jewish kingdom as including Judaea, Samaria, and the Galilee under the authority of the high priest (10:38). Josephus's paraphrase of this letter adds mention of observation of "ancestral laws" and the exclusive recognition of the Jerusalem Temple in the northern areas (*Ant.* 13.54). Additionally, Josephus implies that Demetrius's offer was accepted by John Hyrcanus (*Ant.* 13.58), in direct contradiction of 1 Macc 10:46. Schwartz here makes two key observations: First, Josephus's account indicates that he supposed that Samaria and the Galilee did *not* observe Judaean laws or recognize the Temple prior to the time of John Hyrcanus. Second, it is remarkable that Josephus, writing in the 90s, should have to argue for the "Judaism" of the Galilee, supposedly long since Judaized. The key, for Schwartz, is that in the aftermath of the First Revolt, Galileans were freed from the influence of Judaea and its Temple and that Galilean varieties of Judaism and elements of local pre-Jewish religions reasserted themselves more fully:

> It is perhaps unlikely that 200 years after the introduction of Judaism Galilee and Peraea will have shrugged it off—whatever this non-Judaean Judaism may have consisted of—completely and reverted to some form of Greco-Semitic paganism. But it is at least worth suggesting that local varieties of Judaism will have acquired more open support from a local elite newly freed from the centripetal pull of the temple and its administrators. . . . If these suppositions are correct, many Galileans and Peraeans would have had a conception of law at variance with that of conservative Judaeans, and a conception of piety which presumably included little devotion to the memory of the temple, or to the priesthood. (Schwartz 1989:390)

Significant differences between Judaean and Galilean Judaisms may account for the fact that prior to 135 so few sages came from the Galilee.[42]

---

41. The account in *Antiquities* (20.118-123) turns this into the murder of several pilgrims.
42. Yoḥanan ben Zakkai (born in Judaea) spent 18 years in Arav, north of Sepphoris, dur-

Moreover, as Levine notes, "the animosity of first and second century sages and the *ʿammei ha-ʾaretz* (most of whom appear to have lived in the Galilee) is likewise indicative of the chasm which existed between the rabbis and segments of this population" (1989:40).

The Galilee and the Judaean Torah

Despite the supposed application of "laws of the Judaeans" to the Galilee by the Hasmoneans (*Ant.* 13.318-19), centuries of separation of the Galilee from Judaea and the development of local practices would inevitably have been responsible for differing understandings of the Torah. The fall of the Galilee in 732 BCE was more than a century before the "discovery" of Deuteronomy in the time of Josiah (2 Kings 22:3-13) and final editing of the Pentateuch during the exilic and postexilic periods. If our assumption is correct that the Galilee had a significant Israelite population even prior to the Hasmonean conquest, it is likely that such Galileans observed basic practices such as circumcision of males, Sabbath, some form of *kashruth*, and made some purity distinctions, particularly in respect to women during menstruation and after childbirth and in respect to the disposition of the dead.[43] Indeed, we have good evidence that circumcision and the Sabbath were observed in at least some parts of the Galilee from an early date.[44] This conclusion, however, is a far cry from the assertion that the Galilee was faithful to the Judaean Torah.

Freyne is doubtful that Galileans in general would be attracted to Pharisaism, but adduces three episodes perhaps indicative of their faithfulness to Torah. The first is an incident (66 CE) recorded in Josephus's *Life* (65) of the burning of Herod's palace in Tiberias, which reportedly contained representations of animals. Josephus states that the initiative for the destruction came from Jerusalem and that this proposal had been resisted by the lead-

---

ing which time he was consulted on only two halakhic matters. Yoḥanan is reported to have complained, "Galilee, Galilee, you hate the Torah. In the end you will be victimized by (Roman) oppressors" (*y. Šabb.* 16.15d). Ḥanania ben Dosa (*b. Ber.* 34b) and Yose the Galilean were both Galileans. Ḥanania was less a sage than a local holy man, secondarily made into a sage in rabbinic literature and, as Lightstone (1980) argues, Yose's traditions stand outside the mainstream of Yavnean opinions.

43. Distinction of states of purity in respect to menstruation, childbirth, and death do not set Judaism apart from other cultures of the Mediterranean and the Levant, however. See Parker 1983, and Sokolowski 1955; 1962; 1969, for purity regulations affecting entry into sanctuaries by persons who have contracted *miasma* (pollution).

44. Whatever one makes of Josephus's statement about the Judaizing of the northern region by Aristobulus (*Ant.* 13.318-19), it can hardly mean that the entire population was forcibly circumcised. The attack on Asochis (Shikhin) by Ptolemy Lathyrus in 103 BCE on the Sabbath (Josephus, *Ant.* 13.337) makes sense only if the inhabitants of that town (in the Lower Galilee) already observed the Sabbath in some form. Josephus states that he refrained from military activity on the Sabbath in order not to offend the inhabitants of Magdala-Tarichaeae (*War* 2.634; *Life* 128, 161).

ing men of Tiberias. The palace was only destroyed when locals Jesus ben
Sapphias "and a party of sailors and destitute" burned and looted the
palace (*Life* 66). Freyne suggests that opposition to the palace and its orna-
mentation was a function of newly arrived Zealot ideology (1980:311). The
opposition to iconic art cannot be traced to any special sensitivities of
Galileans in general: the palace had been in existence for nearly fifty years
without any known local criticism. Freyne's suggestion, that the episode is
an instance of political and social tensions cloaked in religious guise, is
closer to the mark, but undermines the supposition that Galileans by nature
adhered to the Judaean Torah (Freyne 1988b:207; cf. Horsley 1995c:153).
    The second incident is similar. Josephus (*Life* 112-13) reports that dur-
ing the Revolt two Gentile nobles from Trachonitis, both subjects of
Agrippa II, requested asylum in Magdala-Tarichaeae, bringing with them
arms and money, evidently to assist the Jewish resistance. Josephus states
that "the Judaeans" ('Ιουδαῖοι) wanted to have the nobles circumcised as a
condition of residence, but Josephus persuaded them to desist from this
request. Later, however, setbacks with the Roman forces were blamed on
the sorcery of the nobles and Josephus had to remove the nobles to Hippos
(*Life* 149-55).
    The incident of course takes for granted that most or all of the male
inhabitants of Tarichaeae were circumcised. It tells us little else beyond what
is obvious: that in conditions of war xenophobia prevails and that signs of
loyalty are at a premium. It tells us little useful about Galilean attitudes
toward Gentiles, if indeed Josephus is not to be taken literally when he says
that it was the *Ioudaioi* (not the Galileans) who demanded circumcision.
    The final episode concerns the situation of Jews at Caesarea Philippi, again
at the beginning of the Revolt. Josephus complained that his rival, John of
Gush Ḥalav (Gishala), profiteered by selling kosher olive oil to the Jews of
Caesarea, who evidently were unable to obtain oil from their usual sources
in the area.[45] The avoidance of Gentile oil by Jews was widespread and evidently ancient (Josephus, *Ant.* 12.120), even if it was not based on biblical
injunctions or halakhic pronouncements.[46] The incident, since it arose at the
initiative of Caesarean Jews rather than Galileans and because it was an

45. Josephus, *War* 2.591-93; *Life* 74-75. In *War* Josephus alleges that John tried to supply
"all the Jews of Syria"; but in *Life* (more realistically) limits this to the Jews of Caesarea, "who
had been shut up [in Caesarea] at the king's order" and so were deprived of their usual sources.
In *Life* Josephus admits that he authorized John's sale at inflated prices.
46. See Baumgarten 1967 and Goodman 1990:240: "The widespread custom among Jews
of avoiding gentile oil may have been based neither on biblical exegesis nor on a decision by
an accepted authority but on a pervasive religious instinct which was all the more powerful for
its lack of rationale. . . . It had no explicit connection with a concern for levitical purity . . .
[and] is best explained by social and cultural changes in the lives of Jews of this period." Judith
10:5; 12:1-4 indicate avoidance of Gentile foodstuffs, including oil. *M. ʿAbod. Zar.* 2.6 later
lists Gentile oil as prohibited, but notes that Judah ha-Nasi permitted its use.

extraordinary occurrence rather than a matter of regular supply,[47] tells us nothing about specifically Galilean observances beyond the fact that oil at Gush Ḥalav was manufactured in a manner acceptable to Caesarean Jews.

If the literary evidence from Josephus does not provide much evidence of a "Torah true" Galilee prior to the First Revolt, archaeology is only slightly more helpful. The presence of *miqwaôt* (stepped immersion pools) is often taken as an indication of Torah observance. From the existence of such pools some scholars infer widespread observance of purity laws in Roman Palestine.[48] There are several notorious problems related to these pools. Since there is little uniformity in size and design and since many of the pools lack the features that the later Mishnaic tractate *Miqwaʾôt* prescribes, it is unclear whether all such stepped pools are in fact *miqwaʾôt*.[49] Nevertheless, some pools are probably *miqwaʾôt*, since other possibilities—bathing pools, for example—seem to have been excluded (Reich 1993). While the final dating of many *miqwaʾôt* awaits the analysis of the plaster, at least some Galilean pools belong to the first century. This is true of the two *miqwaʾôt* at Gamla, one public *miqweh* and several in private homes at Sepphoris,[50] and two at Yodefat, both in private houses and one near an olive press.[51]

47. Horsley 1995c:153 suggests that the incident implies "a ruling based on some concept of an approved *eretz Israel* deleated already in the mid-first century C.E. by some recognized authorities, perhaps in Jerusalem." But the fact that the incident was ad hoc relief of a lack normally supplied by producers closer to Caesarea provides no basis for such a conclusion.

48. Sanders 1992:229: "The very wide distribution of immersion pools, so strikingly demonstrated by archaeology, shows that the purity laws were generally observed." Contrast Sawicki 1994:342, commenting on a similar assertion of Eric Meyers: "To me they [*miqwaʾôt*] assert: 'Not everyone here is Jewish *enough*, like us.' Besides certifying the propriety of the conditions of conception, the pools can also 'restore' the purity of residents after polluting contact with gentiles and 'upgrade' the ritual purity of workers, *ʿammei ha-ʾaretz*, who serve in the home by day but return to the villages at night. Thus they bespeak an ethnically diverse city, not a homogeneous one. The pools are defensive borders against threats to 'Jewishness' from without and from within."

49. See B. Wright 1997. According to *m. Miqw.* 1.4, 7; 6.7-11, a *miqweh* must contain at least 40 *seʾah* = approx. 500 litres. The more than 300 pools surveyed by Reich (1990) range in capacity from 8–10 m^3 to 1–2 m^3 (all holding well over 500 liters). Some have a divider on the steps and alternating broad and narrow steps; some have and some lack entrance and exit channels; and some have and some lack an *otzar* (a small reservoir joined to the *miqweh*).

50. Meyers 1992:325; Strange 1992:345. A recent analysis of the pools at Sepphoris has concluded, however, that none is fact is a *miqweh*. Eshel (1997) notes that (a) all of the baths at Sepphoris are smaller than the *miqwaʾôt* in Judah; (b) none has a separation line or double door; (c) none has an *otzar*; (d) and the houses in which they are found do not contain any other bathing facilities (1997:132). He observes, moreover, that since most of the pools were found at a higher level than the city aqueduct and since none has a reservoir, it would be "virtually impossible for the owners of these *miqvaot* to assure the necessary amount of water in their pools" (ibid). He concludes that they were baths for washing. The latter point seems unnecessarily to presume that water for *miqwaʾôt* should have been provided by the aqueduct, which is neither necessary nor likely: water from the aqueduct would not satisfy (later) regulations for valid water (*m. Miqw.* 5.1).

51. One of the *miqwaʾôt* at Yodefat is reported in Adan-Bayewitz, Aviʿam, and D. Edwards

Key to the assessment of *miqwaʾôt* is not merely their numbers,[52] but their location. A large number of stepped baths were discovered in private houses in the Herodian quarter in Jerusalem where members of the priestly aristocracy lived (Avigad 1989:19). A series of public *miqwaʾôt* are located at the southern steps of the Temple in front of the two Ḥuldah gates which led to the Temple platform, providing facilities for those entering the Temple to purify themselves. A large number of stepped baths are also attested at Qumran, a community that espoused ideals of priestly purity and which regarded itself as a temple. The correlation between priestly presence and *miqwaʾôt* is hardly coincidental and suggests a nuanced view in regard to the observation of purity law. Benjamin Wright argues:

> Rather than a general concern for purity among the populace, perhaps the presence of *miqvaôt* outside Jerusalem indicates that the idea of maintaining priestly purity for temple service was considered vital to the daily lives of even those priests who were not in the course of their Jerusalem service. (B. Wright 1997:213)

This might account for the *miqwaʾôt* in private houses in Yodefat and Sepphoris—if indeed the pools in Sepphoris are *miqwaʾôt* and not simply bathing facilities (see above n. 50). At Sepphoris at least there was a small priestly presence prior to the First Revolt (see below). Accepting that the pools at Sepphoris are *miqwaʾôt,* Sawicki suggests that they functioned in the rather specific context of ensuring the purity of women who would marry into priestly lineages. Sepphoris may have served "as a producer of high-caste brides" (Sawicki 1997:16). In any event the presence of stepped pools in the upper city of Sepphoris does not amount to evidence of generalized use of *miqwaʾôt* in the Galilean population.

In addition to a correlation between priestly presence and *miqwaʾôt,* immersion pools appear with some regularity at commercial installations, in particular at oil presses.[53] One of the two *miqwaʾôt* at Gamla is found in an industrial complex with a large commercial oil press and one of the

---

1997:44: "Three rock-cut water-storage installations were uncovered south of the olive press. . . . The third installation—a stepped pool, evidently a Jewish ritual bath—was hewn alongside the shallow pool and the cistern. The six extant rock-cut steps of the pool descended in a counterclockwise directions. . . . The latest material found in the stepped pool dated from the mid-1st century CE."

52. The most comprehensive study is Reich 1990, who surveys more than 300 pools (150 in Jerusalem alone), of which 163 almost certainly functioned as *miqwaʾôt* (1990:81).

53. Stepped pools have been excavated at Khirbet Manṣur el-ʿAqab (Ramat ha-Nadiv, map ref. 144216) near Caesarea Maritima (Hirschfeld and Birger-Calderon 1991), Qalandiya (169141), Jericho (192140), and Khirbet Susiya (159090, Reich 1984), all in industrial complexes. An installation similar to that at Khirbet Manṣur el-ʿAqab with four *miqwaʾôt* has recently been excavated at Naḥal Ḥaggit (map ref. 153224) in the Carmel Range (Seligman 1997). The 90x90 m installation dates from I BCE–I CE and contains a large crushing basin and two oil presses.

miqwaʾôt at Yodefat was discovered near an oil press. The same long-standing concerns that led Caesarean Jews to request kosher oil from Gush Ḥalav probably account for *miqwaʾôt* at oil production facilities. As a liquid, oil was particularly susceptible to impurity (Baumgarten 1967). Production involved several stages, each of which carried the potential for contamination. The harvested olives, wet with oil, had to be transported to the presses and the refined oil had to be transported to markets or the Temple, a major consumer of oil. The numerous points at which contamination of the oil might occur between the orchards and the markets help to account for heightened concerns about the conditions of production and the vessels in which oil was stored and transported. The use of *miqwaʾôt* undoubtedly helped to insure buyers regarding the purity of the oil.[54]

The distribution of *miqwaʾôt* at pressing complexes is quite uneven. They are absent from the villages of the Lower Galilee and from oil installations of the western Upper Galilee. Oil presses from the western Upper Galilee are of Phoenician (rather than "Galilean") type and the proximity of these installations to Akko suggests that the product was marketed in the (Gentile) coastal regions.[55] *Miqwaʾôt* would be pointless.

Oakman draws an important consequence from the uneven distribution of *miqwaʾôt* in the Lower Galilee:

> I suggest [Oakman writes] that for Jewish villagers in the Lower Galilee *miqwaʾôt* were associated with political economy, and thus with *political religion*. Therefore, Galilean peasants had ample reason to detest purity concerns, along with the product extraction linked to them. Peasant anger compromised village loyalty to the temple, since it was the temple and levitical law that mandated such arrangements. (Oakman 1994:232, emphasis original)

Oakman's point, if I understand him, is that purity concerns cannot be detached from agricultural production and the taxation associated with it. Resistance of the countryside to the cities—which were the points of product extraction—manifested itself not only in the overt hostility of the "Galileans" toward Sepphoris and Tiberias that Josephus describes in *Life* 375-79, but also in noncooperation with the purity practices associated with product extraction. It is of course difficult to prove a correlation between hostility and purity practices in connection with agricultural production. Nevertheless, it does seem clear that *miqwaʾôt* belong to highly specific aspects of Galilean culture having to do with priestly practices and the production of olive oil intended for Jewish markets (and perhaps for the

54. Later Mishnaic discussions vividly detail precautions that were taken to ensure the purity of olive oil, including the locking of workers within the press buildings during their shift (*m. Ṭohar.* 9.1—10.3).

55. Phoenician-type presses have slotted piers (rather than a niche in the wall) and lateral (rather than central) collecting basins (Frankel 1992:63).

Temple itself). These functions help to account for the places where *miqwaʾôt* occur and for their general absence elsewhere.

None of these considerations translates into a picture of a "Torah-true" Galilee, if by that rather vague term one means a population that demonstrated loyalty to the Judaean Torah by strict observation of tithing, purity regulations, and regular pilgrimages. That some Galileans observed these should not be doubted. Nor should it be doubted that Galileans practiced circumcision, kept Sabbath in some form, and observed some form of *kashruth*. To assume more than this not only would be in the absence of supporting evidence, but would render nonsensical the numerous complaints of the sages who resettled in the Galilee after the failure of the Second Revolt.

THE PRESSURES OF URBANIZATION

Several scholars draw attention to conflict between cities and the hinterland as a significant factor in Roman Galilee. Tensions between cities and their outlying regions of course were not peculiar to the Galilee. The ancient city was largely parasitic on its surrounding villages. Cities extracted agricultural surpluses through taxes and rents.[56] The benefits they supplied were of a less tangible sort: cultic services and the provision of legal and administrative apparatuses.[57] In the case of the Galilee, Jerusalem was too far

---

56. For the notion of the "consumer city," see Finley 1982. Jones (1971:293–94) illustrates the relation between city and countryside in his comments on the urbanization of Syria: "[Urbanization] was achieved partly by assigning vast territories to the old cities of the coast [of Syria] and of the desert fringe, partly by the foundation of a small number of new cities, to each of which was assigned a vast territory. The political life of the inhabitants of the agricultural belt was unaffected, their unit remained the village, and they took no part in the life of the city to which they were attached. Economically they lost by the change. The new cities performed no useful economic function, for the larger villages supplied such manufactured goods as the villagers required, and the trade of the countryside was conducted at village markets. The only effect of the foundation of cities was the creation of a wealthy landlord class which gradually stamped out peasant proprietorship. Culturally, the countryside remained utterly unaffected by the Hellenism of the cities; the peasants continued to speak Syriac down to the Arab conquest. The only function which the cities performed was administrative; they policed and collected the taxes of their territories." The notion of a "consumer city" has been modified slightly by noting that some production did occur in cities, and that taxation had the effect of stimulating the economy of the countryside, but the basic model of Finley remains in place. See Rich and Wallace-Hadrill 1991.

57. On the exchange relationship between cities and the hinterland, see Rohrbaugh 1991:132–33; Oakman 1991; Hopkins 1978:72–75; Wrigley 1978. Wrigley writes: "It is not difficult to describe a type of town . . . whose nature seems aptly described as parasitic since it is largely a centre for consumption, levying a tribute upon production in the countryside. If there is a return flow of services in the other direction they may well connote a type of benefit, like religious services, which appear intangible to a pragmatic and secular age, or take the form of the sustaining of an administrative machine whose prime object appears to be the perpetuation of the exploitation of the countryside in favour of the town" (1978:307).

removed to provide ready access to cultic benefits and the nearby cities of
Tiberias and Sepphoris provided none.

Special tensions were created in the Galilee by the recent foundation (or
refoundation) of Sepphoris and Tiberias. The foundation of a city in the
ancient world normally entailed the assigning of a city territory (*chōra*)
from which revenues could be derived (de Ste Croix 1981:9–19). From the
perspective of the countryside, the city was often socially alien and economically parasitic. It was typically the place of residence for the elite, who
were not only socially differentiated from those of the countryside but often
culturally different too. In the case of Sepphoris and Tiberias, many of the
elite were from Judaean rather than Galilean society and evidently some
were Greek. The city, moreover, consumed resources out of proportion to
its ability to create wealth. It was the locus for the collection of taxes from
the countryside and for administration of justice, which in the ancient
world, typically favored the elite over the nonelite. The liquid capital of the
civic elite allowed for investment in land (the traditional basis for wealth
and status), which encroached on peasant holdings.[58]

Although we are not well informed in regard to the taxation structure of
antiquity, it is generally assumed that the principal bases of Roman taxation
were a land tax (*tributum soli*), levied on the basis of the value of the land,
and capitation (*tributum capitis*).[59] Since the majority of the population was
rural and since the elite often enjoyed partial or total tax immunity, the burden of taxation fell disproportionately on the countryside and smallholders.
Besides direct taxation, villagers were subject to a variety of other imposi-
tions, including forced labor and the requisitioning (*angareia*) of carts and
animals for transport (Q/Matt 5:41). This further impinged on the viability
of economically marginal farming operations (Mitchell 1976). In addition
to imperial levies, cities derived revenues from capitation, rents, tolls, salt
taxes, and sales taxes.[60] In this system, large landowners enjoyed certain

58. Garnsey (1988:46) estimates the size of peasant holdings in Attica to be 2–4 hectares,
1.25–2.5 hectares in republican Italy, and many would have worked plots smaller than these.
"The essential point is that the 'basic' farm of Attica and Italy is universally considered too
small to have supported by itself a peasant family, and the shortfall was significantly greater if
animal labor was employed. It follows that access to other, typically uncultivated, land (and to
other employment) was crucial, and that the fortunes of the peasantry fluctuated significantly
with the availability of such land. Wherever there was pressure on the land, as a result of population growth or increased investment in rural property by the wealthy, the result would have
been an expansion of the area under cultivation and under private ownership, and thus a contraction of the *incolto* and reduced access to such as remained." See also J. Patterson (1991)
for a case study of the effects of urbanization on the hinterland in Samnium and Lycia.

59. See the discussion of taxation in Roman Palestine in Fiensy 1991:99–105; Sanders
1992:146–69; Udoh 1996; Hanson and Oakman 1998:113–16.

60. See the list of Seleucid taxes in 1 Macc 10:29-31; 11:34-36; Josephus, *Ant.* 13.49-51,
including the tribute, salt tax, crown tax, grain tax (one-third of the harvest), fruit tax (one-
half of the harvest), tithes, and tolls.

advantages. Because the cadastral valuation of land took into account whether it was cultivated or not, large landowners had greater opportunity to leave land fallow or use it for pasturage in the year of the valuation (Corbier 1991). Smallholders were additionally disadvantaged by the fact that taxes were extracted in kind at the time of harvest and transported to the city, leaving the farmer, in times of poor harvests, to suffer or even starve.[61]

While the Upper Galilee remained a region of villages without controlling cities, the early first century saw significant structural changes in the Lower Galilee. Sepphoris, destroyed by Varus in 4 BCE in response to an insurrection and its population enslaved (*War* 2.68; *Ant.* 17.289), was refounded by Antipas a few years later as the "ornament of all the Galilee" (*Ant.* 18.27). Josephus's comment on Sepphoris, that it had enough villages to be able to withstand a Roman attack had it so wished (*Life* 346), indicates that Sepphoris had a substantial *chōra* from which to draw revenue and produce. Reed estimates that Sepphoris's population of approximately 24,000 would have required the entire agricultural output of the Beth Netofah and Tir'an valleys as well as that of the more immediate Naḥal Ṣippori (1994b:214–15). Almost twenty years later Antipas founded Tiberias, moving his capital there.[62] This naturally entailed the allotting of lands in exchange for residence (*Ant.* 18.38).[63] The designation of Tiberias as the capital brought with it the debt archives (τὰ ἀρχαῖα) and the royal bank (βασιλικὴ τράπεζα, *Life* 38-39), eventually shifting back to Sepphoris when in 54 CE Nero transferred Tiberias and Magdala-Tarichaeae to the jurisdiction of Agrippa II (*Ant.* 20.159).

61. Garnsey and Saller 1987:97, citing Galen, *De rebus boni malique suci libellus* 6.749-50: "The famines occurring in unbroken succession over a number of years among many of the peoples subject to the Romans have demonstrated clearly, to anyone not completely devoid of intelligence, the important part played in the genesis of diseases by the consumption of unhealthy foods. For among many of the people who are subject to the Romans, the city-dwellers, *as it was their practice to collect and store enough grain for all the next year immediately after the harvest*, left what remained to the country people, that is, pulses of various kinds, and they took a good deal of these too to the city. The country people finished the pulses during the winter and so had to fall back on unhealthy foods during the spring; they ate twigs and shoots of trees and bushes, and bulbs and roots of indigestible plants; they filled themselves with wild herbs, and cooked fresh grass." This account of peasant cuisine, as Garnsey and Saller point out, is not the description of normal conditions; but the parenthesis on tax and rent collection (italicized) does indicate a normal practice.

62. The foundation of Tiberias was sometime between 17 and 23 CE. On the dating problems, see Avi-Yonah 1960; Hoehner 1972:93–95.

63. It is not clear whether Tiberias possessed a *chōra* in the technical sense of an assigned city region. *Life* 155 refers to the *chōra* of Tiberias, but earlier (*War* 2.252) Josephus mentions only the *toparchiai* (toparchic districts) associated with Tiberias (and Magdala-Tarichaeae). Jones (1971:276) and Sherwin-White (1963:127) take the view that Tiberias was given city status but its surrounding district was administered by royal officials, not the city itself, and thus did not possess a *chōra*.

Both Sepphoris and Tiberias were administrative cities. The countryside was hostile to both (*Life* 30, 39, 66, 375, 381-89), and the "Galileans," as Josephus calls the villagers, attempted to sack both cities and were involved in the destruction of Herod's palace in Tiberias. The reasons for the hostility were probably a combination of cultural and economic factors. Tiberias was the home to Herodians, other elite, and some Greeks.[64] Thus it had a population that was different from that of the countryside, no doubt with different cultural allegiances. In spite of initial gestures in the direction of revolt, Tiberias ultimately maintained its allegiance to Agrippa and Rome, opening its gates to Vespasian (*Life* 352, 391). For its part, Sepphoris resisted all invitations to revolt and admitted a Roman garrison under Cestius Gallus (*Life* 347-48).

Sepphoris and Tiberias also served as collection and storage points for tax revenues and they housed the debt archives. An index of the centrality of this function is the bitterness that the Tiberians felt toward Sepphoris when Tiberias's administrative functions—the archives and bank—were transferred to Sepphoris in 54 CE (Jones 1971:276). In this light, the attitude of the "Galileans" is perfectly comprehensible. Both cities functioned in an exploitative fashion, extracting and storing the produce of the countryside, providing few tangible (or intangible) benefits in return, and serving as a home to classes of persons whose cultural and political allegiances differed significantly from those of the countryside.[65]

Freyne stresses the significant pressures that Herodian economics in general and the foundations of Sepphoris and Tiberias in particular created (1995a:29–46). First, he suggests a shift in landowning patterns, from smallholders to larger estates, some owned by absentee landlords and run by managers. The land grants that were inevitably part of the (re)founding of Antipas's two cities may have created such estates. These estates naturally represented the better lands, acquired either by direct expropriation or resulting from smallholders defaulting on taxes or loans. The creation of such large estates allowed for more intensive cultivation of the land, greater crop specialization, and the maximization of production. This, of course, benefited the estate owners as well as royal revenues and, at least in the case

---

64. See *Life* 32-35. Several of those mentioned by Josephus have Latin names (Julius Capellus; Crispus); two evidently belonged to Herod's family (Herod son of Miarus; Herod son of Gamalus); and Agrippa I had served as the superintendent of the markets (*agoranomos*) under Antipas (*Ant.* 18.149). Josephus (*Life* 67) reports that the Greek population was massacred at the beginning of the First Revolt.

65. Peter Brunt's observations apropos of Judaea are equally applicable to the Galilee: "[E]ven in Judaea upper class Jews seem mostly to have opposed the revolt, or to have sought to sabotage it, not only because (as Josephus makes king Agrippa urge) in their judgment it was certain to fail, and it was folly to 'kick against the pricks', but because Rome guaranteed the social order; the revolt of 66 was almost as much directed against native landlords and usurers as against the heathen rulers" (1976:165–66; repr. Brunt 1990:272). Brunt further elaborates this thesis in Brunt 1977; 1990:282–87.

of olive oil production, probably contributed to the evolution of an export industry.[66]

Specialization and exploitation applied to nonagricultural endeavors as well. The Kinneret was fished intensively as is evidenced by the large number of moles, breakwaters, and anchorages that have been discovered (see Nun 1989). As K.C. Hanson has shown, the fishing industry, probably centered at Tarichaeae (from ταριχεία, "pickling" or "salting [fish]"), was controlled through layers of direct taxes, licensing fees, sales and road taxes, and its surpluses extracted for elite benefit (K.C. Hanson 1997; Hanson and Oakman 1998:106–10).

Second, the Roman period witnessed a gradual monetization of the economy, which allowed for easier storage and movement of wealth. As will be argued below, monetization also encouraged lending and, when borrowers defaulted, the seizure of their lands.

Finally, Freyne argues that the adoption by the Herodians of the lifestyle of other Hellenistic rulers and their alliance with the priestly aristocracy had the effect of eroding the older theocratic ideology that once had legitimized taxation and social inequalities. The affluence of the Herodians, noted by Q 7:24-26, could not be rationalized within the theological framework of purity and cultic necessity that had explained the social differentiation of the priesthood from other Israelites. To the extent that the priestly aristocrats aligned themselves with the Herodian household, their own sustaining ideology was subverted. In Jerusalem, Freyne argues, where one could see at first hand the magnificence of the Herodian Temple and its complex operation, the priestly ideology might still have been effective in bridging the gap between the symbolic universe and social realities (1995b:609). In the Galilee, however, the priesthood was largely absent and the Temple was distant. The foundations of Sepphoris and Tiberias only concretized and institutionalized for the Galilean peasant the erosion of traditional values in favor of a Roman agrarian economy and its naked exploitation of the hinterland (Freyne 1992; 1994; 1995b).

This picture of social change can be confirmed in part by archaeological findings. David Fiensy (1991:119–49), drawing on the survey of Samaria by Shimʿon Dar (1986), noted several significant changes in settlement patterns from the monarchic period (Iron II) to the Herodian period. First, the isolated farmstead supporting an extended family disappeared, and its peasant inhabitants moved either to villages or became tenants on large estates. Even more recent archaeological surveys of the Lower Galilee have identified a number of large farmhouses, presumably belonging to wealthy families. Existing alongside these estates are many small plots too small to support those who farmed them (Strange 1994:89). This means that poorer farmers

---

66. On oil as an export crop, see Safrai 1994:122–27; Ben-David 1974:111–12.

had to have other means of support and, no doubt, ran the danger of gradually slipping into irreversible debt, leading to the loss of their land.

Second, literary evidence suggests that the courtyard-house complexes,
with 5–6 dwelling houses opening onto a common courtyard such as those
found at Kefar Naḥum and Khorazin, probably did not belong to extended
families but housed several nonrelated families.[67] Finally, by the Herodian
period the clan (משפחה) had already largely disappeared. This was perhaps
due to the administrative patterns introduced by the Ptolemies that emphasized regional rather than kinship links, and in part to urbanization, which
privileged the urban aristocracy (some of whom were absentee landlords)
over clan elders. At the level of the village (כפר), the largest unit of peasant
settlement, the breakdown of the clans meant that villages now consisted of
both kinsmen and nonrelated neighbors (Fiensy 1991:135). Thus Fiensy
suggests significant shifts in the Herodian period in patterns of land tenure,
in the nature of the family unit, and in the structure of the villages and
towns. In sum, we get a picture of increasing pressures placed on the hinterland by the cities, subverting traditional social structures.

William Arnal (1997c) had elaborated two important corollaries of the
urbanization of the Galilee. First is a shift from a "closed" to an "open"
economy—that is, from an economy based on self-sufficiency, with luxury
items imported only occasionally, to one dependent on trade and where
export crops were produced. Strong evidence exists that the Upper Galilee
exported goods to Tyre, in particular oil. This is reflected in the statement
attributed by Acts to the people of Tyre and Sidon, who sued Agrippa I for
peace because "their country depended on the king's country for food"
(12:20).[68] While Arnal argues that first-century Galilee was still largely a
closed economy (especially at the level of small producers), pressures to
develop and maintain exports were already present in the first century, especially in the Upper Galilee. By the end of the Second Temple period, rabbinic
evidence attests a developed trade system (Arnal 1997c:288; Safrai
1994:423).

Pottery provides a partial glimpse at the developing networks of distribution. Adan-Bayewitz (1992) employed neutron activation analysis of the
chemical content of clays to determine whether the pottery found in dispersed sites in the Galilee originated at Kefar Ḥananya, a major pottery-
producing site on the border of upper and Lower Galilee. Since most pottery

67. For details of this debate, see Applebaum 1986:262 (on the size of family plots); Goodman 1987:68 (on the decreasing number of endogamous marriages); and Hachlili and Killebrew 1983:126 (on the size of Second Temple tombs).

68. *T. Dem.* 1.10 (cf. *y. Dem.* 1.22a) suggests that all of the produce that arrived in Achziv
(Ecdippa [map ref. 159272], 7 km north of Ptolemais-Akko) is to be tithed, since it is presumed
to have been grown in Galilee. See further, Safrai 1994:417–18; Meyers 1995:19, 21–22
(responding to Horsley's [1995a] minimizing of links with Tyre).

appears to have been marketed within a 50 km radius of its production site, little would have found its way outside Galilee.[69] Analysis of the village itself suggests that Kefar Ḥananya experienced significant growth in the late first century BCE and early first century CE. Adan-Bayewitz coordinates this upturn with the expansion of several Galilean settlements—he mentions Meiron, Kefar Naḥum, and Magdala-Tarichaeae. The more obvious sources of such stimulation, however, are the new foundations of Sepphoris and Tiberias, where Kefar Ḥananya pottery is particularly common.[70]

It would be premature, says Arnal, to conclude that increased production and trade was to the advantage of the primary producers.[71] On the contrary, it was more likely that the profits accrued to the cities where the goods— especially olive oil—were marketed and to the middlemen who could ship produce to the coastal regions (Arnal 1997c:285–86). Horsley puts the matter thus:

> The principal "surplus product" of Galilean or Judean peasantry, however, was under the control of the Herodian or high-priestly rulers and/or the Roman government in the form of taxes, tithes and offerings, and tribute. Trade between Judea or Galilee and Tyre was thus under the control of the very rulers who desired luxury goods Tyre had to offer—as mediated perhaps by traders working for the Judean or Roman rulers.[72]

Arnal observes that the small agricultural producer would have little use for the luxury items of Tyre or for hard currency, since most economic exchange at the village level was in kind, and for basic necessities. Trade served the interests of, and was controlled by, the elite and their agents, as indeed Acts 12:20 implies.

A second factor noted by Arnal is the monetization of the economy. Coin served several interests: those of the government for the payment of the army and urban populations for many or most transactions. It did not serve the interests of the primary (peasant) producers, who were more likely to

69. Adan-Bayewitz and Perlman (1990:157 and figure 1) report small quantities of Kefar Ḥananya pottery at Gamla and Susita-Hippos across the Kinneret.

70. Adan-Bayewitz 1992:236–37. Horsley (1996:85) suggests a direct relation between Kefar Ḥananya pottery and the needs of Tiberias and Sepphoris where, according to Adan-Bayewitz 1992:221–22, the percentage of Kefar Ḥananya pottery runs between 74 percent (Sepphoris) and 97 percent (Tiberias, though the sample size here is small).

71. Adan-Bayewitz and Perlman 1990:171–72 conclude from the distribution of Kefar Ḥananya pottery that there were nonexploitative relations between Kefar Ḥananya and Kefar Shikhin (which produced storage vessels) and nearby Sepphoris. Oakman (1994:232), however, argues that it is more likely that "powerful interests controlled the two pottery villages— especially when Shikhin was very close to Sepphoris and manufactured the basic vessels of liquid commerce—and that the distribution of these products reflects rather the outcome of monopoly rather than of a free market." The same perhaps applies to the manufacture of stone vessels at Reina, a site 5 km southeast of Sepphoris (see Gal 1991).

72. Horsley 1996:86. See now the discussion of the political economy of Roman Palestine in Hanson and Oakman 1998:99–129.

pay in kind and use coin only for extraordinary purchases or for "storage" of wealth (e.g., Q 15:8-10).[73] Arnal notes the paucity of first-century bronze and copper coins in the Galilee, indicating that at the level of most daily transactions, the economy was still unmonetized (1997c:292–94). The foundation of Tiberias and the establishing of a mint there, however, provided impetus for monetization: aniconic bronze coins of Antipas are found at Tiberias, Meiron, Gush Ḥalav, Nabratein, Arbela, Kefar Naḥum, intended evidently for local Israelite transactions (Meshorer 1982:205 n. 28). Thus, Arnal concludes,

> an effort to 'urbanize' corresponded to an effort to monetize. Monetization was unquestionably in the interests of the wealthy and ruling classes, as well as the Romans: it allowed *value* to be removed from Galilee without the burdensome requirement of transporting bulky items overland; as a result, the wealth of this very productive region could be tapped effectively and relatively cheaply.[74]

The monetization of the economy not only did not serve the interests of smallholders; it worked against them. Goodman (1982) argues that the availability of hard currency that flowed to Jerusalem through taxes and tithes found its most natural outlet in agricultural loans. This surplus, however, had the effect of intensifying the debt spiral and led to the gradual concentration of land in the hands of the elite and the dispossession of smallholders. It was during this period that the so-called *prozbul* was introduced. This legal procedure, eventually ascribed to Hillel, allowed for debts to be secured by immovable property (usually land), in spite of the provisions for sabbatical release.[75] Although the Mishnah (*Šeb.* 10.3) suggests that the *prozbul* was instituted to ensure that loans would be made even in the last year of a sabbatical cycle, the provision made foreclosure inevitable in the case of default.[76] Oakman draws attention to a gradual increase in free laborers between the Hasmonean period and the second century CE and suggests that this was the result of the loss of patrimonal lands, on the one hand, and the creation of large estates, on the other (Oakman 1997a:27).

Thus the impact of urbanization was deep and lasting. Not only were land-ownership patterns altered to the disadvantage of the smallholders, but significant shifts in the economic structures occurred. Arnal summarizes these well:

73. On high (gold, silver) versus low (bronze, copper) currency types and their social significance, see Crawford 1970.

74. Arnal 1997c:295–96; similarly, Freyne 1995a:38.

75. Although *m. Šeb.* 10.2-6, which calls for loans to be "delivered to the court" to avoid cancellation, ascribes the institution to Hillel, a text from Wadi Murabbaʿat (Mur 18; 55 CE) guards against a sabbatical release by a simple contractual stipulation.

76. Thus Oakman 1999:167, citing Neusner 1973:16: "Debtors . . . were here given a good motive to dislike Pharisees, who now rendered their debts into perpetual burdens."

a (forcible) reorientation of agriculture toward urban consumption, progressive monetization of the economy, more frequent use of hired labour, greater efficiency in the extraction of taxes and other dues, incremental concentration of land with resultant tenancy and loss of smallholdings, cash-cropping and specialization, greater trade, and a noticeable polarizing of the divide between the relatively wealthy and the very poor; in short, an incremental reduction, at a variety of levels, in the rural peasantry's standard of living. (Arnal 1997c:317)

PRIESTS AND PRIESTLY COURSES IN THE GALILEE?

Gauging the political culture of the cities and the countryside of the Galilee is a difficult, yet important matter. One key orienting factor for the cities was the presence of Herodians, who would naturally incline toward political stability and the status quo. The political kin of the Herodian family are mentioned among the prominent citizens of Tiberias.[77] Given Antipas's foundation of Sepphoris, Herodians were undoubtedly among the elite there too. Their presence helps to account for the refusal of both cities to participate in the anti-Roman activities of the First Revolt. Whether there was a significant priestly population in the Galilee is an equally important question, for large settlements of priests would undoubtedly constitute a factor in Galilean society that would have oriented it toward Jerusalem and the Temple.

Some have thought that first-century Sepphoris was a priestly town "inhabited by many well-to-do, aristocratic Jews of a priestly background."[78] Later rabbinic texts and fragmentary inscriptional evidence suggest that the twenty-four priestly courses (משמרות הכהונה) relocated in a series of Galilean towns,[79] including Sepphoris, the eventual home of the *mishmar* ("course") of Yedaʿyah (ידעיה).[80] There is no doubt that after the second century CE priests were resident in Sepphoris (S. Miller 1984:103–15), just as Sepphoris also was the home to various sages in the late second century (e.g., R. Yose b. Ḥalafta) and one of the centers of rabbinic learning in the third century.[81] There is also no doubt that 135 CE and the failure of the Second Revolt was a watershed for Galilean society, when Judaeans

77. See above, n. 64.

78. Meyers 1992:322. Similarly, Meyers, Netzer, and Meyers 1992:10; Freyne 1980:126; L. Levine 1989:172.

79. On the rabbinic evidence, see Klein 1909; Sperber 1971; on the fragmentary inscriptions containing partial lists of the *mishmarôt*, see Avi-Yonah 1962; 1964; L. Levine 1989:171–74.

80. Meyers 1992:326 thinks that the course of Yedaʿyah was located in Sepphoris "in the second half of the first century."

81. L. Levine (1989:25–33) outlines three factors key to the success of the rabbinic class in Galilee in the third century CE: urbanization, the establishing of academies (eventually located in the large urban centers), and easing of the "deep feelings of animosity towards those Jews known as the *ʿammei ha-ʾaretz*" (1989:30).

(including priests) relocated in large numbers.[82] The issue for us, however, concerns the period before the First Revolt.

Despite generalizations about the priestly population of Sepphoris, there is very little supporting evidence. Josephus reports that in 5/4 BCE the high priest Matthias was temporarily disqualified from officiating at Yom Kippur and that Herod chose a relative, Joseph son of Ellenus, to serve in his place for a single day (*Ant.* 17.165-66). Although Josephus describes Matthias as a native of Jerusalem (*Ant.* 17.78) and does not indicate the hometown of Joseph, rabbinic sources (*t. Yoma* 1.4) connect Joseph ben Elim—probably the same person—with Sepphoris. This has formed the basis for the conclusion of Freyne, Meyers, and others, not only that priests were resident in Sepphoris, but that it was the settlement of families of aristocratic priests.[83]

While there is no good reason to doubt that Joseph ben Elim was associated with Sepphoris, S. Miller rightly observes that his brief stint as high priest tells us nothing about the status that priests from Sepphoris enjoyed in Jerusalem (1984:88). Joseph's connection with Sepphoris is quite incidental; Herod chose him because he was a relative of Matthias. There is no evidence at all to connect Joseph with the *mishmar* of Yeda'yah that would eventually settle in Sepphoris, or even to suggest that prior to the First Revolt Sepphoris had a significant priestly population.

The other rabbinic tradition identifying a priest from Sepphoris comes from *t. Soṭa* 13.8, which describes a priest who took more than his portion of the sacrifices and for that reason was nicknamed "ben ha-Ḥamsan" ("the

---

82. Archaeological evidence suggests a substantial expansion of Meiron in the second and third centuries (Stratum III) (Meyers, Strange, and Meyers 1981:xix, 3), but the excavators suggest that the presence of some imported pottery in Stratum II (50 CE–135 CE) may mean that Meiron welcomed newcomers from the south even after the first revolt (1981:xix). Meyers (1981:3, 156) thinks that the priestly *mishmar* of Yehoiarib located in Meiron soon after 70 CE even though he concedes that "their impact is readily discernible in the growth and building activity of the community attested in Stratum III, or after 135 CE when village life at Meiron is truly expanding" (1981:3). The *miqweh* at Meiron belongs to Stratum III (1981:41–44).

Prior to the early third century, the village of Khirbet Shema' was treated as a satellite of Meiron, only 500 m to the north across the Wadi Meiron (Meyers, Kraabel, and Strange 1976:15–16, 258). The major expansion in population did not occur until the third century (Stratum III; 284–306 CE) when a Synagogue I was built. The synagogue, however, partially covers an earlier *miqweh* belonging to Stratum II (180–284 CE) (1976:39–41).

83. Earlier Stern (1976:272) argued (in spite of Josephus's statements to the contrary) that since Joseph was from Sepphoris and a kinsman of Matthias, the high priest Matthias must originally have come from Sepphoris. The opposite argument, however, could be made: Goodman (1987:41) suggests that since the tradition in *t. Yoma* is ascribed to a Sepphorean, Yose b. Ḥalafta, and since nothing is said about Sepphoris by Josephus, the connection with Sepphoris may be an instance of talmudic storytellers linking tales of the past to the politics and geography of their own society.

snatcher").[84] Nothing associates the anonymous priest of *t. Soṭa* with the *mishmar* of Yedaʿyah, and there is no reason to think that he was an aristocrat. The only element common to the two stories is, as Miller notes, that these two Sepphorean priests were remembered poorly, as aggressive and self-interested (Miller 1984:102). But even this cannot form the basis for a generalization, for the reports in *t. Yoma* 1.4 and *t. Soṭa* 13.8 both belong to the second century, a time when Galilean sages were in conflict with priests who had settled in the Galilee and had little good to say about them.[85]

It is now generally conceded that priestly courses were not located in the Galilee until at least after the First Revolt and probably after 135 CE. Prior to 70 most of the priestly residences were either in or in the environs of Jerusalem, for obvious reasons (Büchler 1895). Klein argued that the relocation of the twenty-four priestly courses occurred mainly in the wake of the Second Revolt (1909:94–95) and that the *mishmar* of Yedaʿyah was established in Sepphoris by the end of the tannaitic period (ca. 200 CE; Klein 1924:9). As Miller has shown, however, Yedaʿyah is not clearly associated with Sepphoris until the fourth century.[86] That the relocation of the priestly courses occurred well after 135 is also suggested by the fact that the list of courses (Klein 1909:95) gives Yodefat as the residence of the *mishmar* of Miyamin (מימין); yet the town destroyed in 67 CE was never reoccupied. Only 150 years later did a settlement develop to the north of "Old Yodefat." This means that the course of Miyamin could not have been present until sometime after 200 CE.

This does not mean that there were no priests in Sepphoris prior to the First Revolt, but it does cast rather grave doubts on the assertions that Sepphoris was a priestly city or a home to significant numbers of aristocratic priests. The presence of *miqwaʾôt* in some private houses—if that is what they are—and even a Herodian public *miqweh* might provide an archaeological indication of the presence of some priestly families (such as that of

---

84. The story is also found in *y. Yoma* 6.43c, where the nickname is "ben ʾAfun" ("son of the chickpea"), referring to the size of the priestly portion. *B. Yoma* 39ab provides another version, this time assigning the nickname "ben Ḥamṣan" ("lawless one").

85. L. Levine (1989:171–72) notes that rabbinic literature tends either to ignore the priests or to refer to them disparagingly and suggests that priestly tithes be given to deserving sages rather than priests (1989:71). Büchler (1909:69–70) collected a series of sayings that complain of the ignorance of priests and counsel against giving tithes to those who are not scholars.

86. S. Miller 1984:120–27. Klein's conclusion was based on *Qoh. Rab.* on Qoh. 7:12, which refers to the people of Sepphoris as the "sons of Yedaʿyah" (on the lips of Bar Kappara, an early third-century Tanna). However, the parallel account in *y. Kil.* 9.32b lacks this address and hence Miller treats it as an editorial embellishment, supplied by the eighth-century editor of *Qoh. Rab.* The earlier tradition attesting the connection of Yedaʿyah with Sepphoris is *y. Taʿan.* 4.68d, in the mouth of R. Berakhiah (fourth century), who offers an etymological speculation to explain the relocation of the *mishmar* to Sepphoris.

Joseph ben Elim) prior to 70 CE. Beyond that, there is no evidence of a large priestly presence in Sepphoris, still less anywhere else in the Galilee.

We are left, then, with evidence of Herodian families in Tiberias (and probably in Sepphoris) that would orient one sector of the civic culture of the Galilee to elite, perhaps southern interests. Equally in evidence is the hostility of the countryside to these cities. As to evidence of a significant priestly population that would provide an orientation toward the Temple, there is only sparse evidence for Sepphoris and none for the rest of the Galilee.

SOCIAL UNREST IN THE GALILEE

The Lower Galilee of the early first century CE was a society in flux. Urbanization and the gradual monetization of its economy were destabilizing factors that worked to the disadvantage of the nonelite. Although the tensions between the cities and the countryside increased gradually throughout the early Roman period, they became palpable in the mid-60s and by 66 CE a revolt had erupted.

Earlier generations of scholars, conflating Josephus's mention of "bandits" with the Zealots, characterized the Galilee as a hotbed of Zealotism. This characterization, as Horsley rightly pointed out, was based on a misreading of Josephus and served largely as a foil for the depiction of Jesus as an apolitical pacifist (Horsley 1987:x). His reexamination of Josephus indicated that the Zealots as a movement of rebellion did not come into existence until 67/68 CE and that there is no evidence of an organized violent resistance to Roman occupation prior to that time (Horsley and Hanson 1985).

Popular Kings and Social Bandits

As an alternative to the now-discredited zealot hypothesis, Horsley identifies three expressions of unrest: social banditry, popular kingship, and actions of the urban poor (Horsley 1979; 1995c:256–75). The sole Galilean evidence for "popular kingship" is the attack on Sepphoris by Judas, son of the bandit-chief Hezekiah following the death of Herod the Great in 4 BCE (*War* 2.56). This attack provoked action by the Syrian legate Varus, who marched on Sepphoris, burned (?) the city, and reduced its inhabitants to slavery (*War* 2.26). Horsley is right to emphasize that Judas was not simply a bandit but had royal pretensions; Josephus's account of Judas occurs in the context of a trio of stories about pretenders to the throne.[87]

---

87. See Josephus, *War* 2.56, 57-59, 60-65; *Ant.* 17.271-72, 273-77, 278-84. Josephus concludes the *Antiquities* account with the statement, "And so Judaea was filled with brigandage. Anyone might make himself king as the head of a band of rebels whom he fell in with, and then

Whether it is correct to see Judas as a "popularly acclaimed king" at the head of a "mass movement among Galilean peasants from villages around Sepphoris" (Horsley 1995c:271) is another matter entirely. Both of Josephus's accounts indicate that the principal target of Judas's attack was the royal arsenal[88] rather than, say, the debt archives, the royal stores, or some other institution that would more directly benefit the peasantry. The attack on the arsenal indicates that Judas's men were professional men of violence who knew how to use weapons—that is, either bandits or mercenaries—rather than peasant farmers. In any event, the brutal Roman retaliation,[89] coupled with the refoundation of Sepphoris as a pro-Herodian, pro-Roman city, appears to have put an end to such aspirations to kingship. We hear of no similar incidents for the remainder of the early Roman period.

The key part of Horsley's evidence for popular unrest is Josephus's accounts of banditry.[90] Here Horsley invokes Eric Hobsbawm's (1959; 1985) model of "social banditry," a prepolitical and nonorganized form of protest against injustice and resistance to occupation and its deleterious effects.[91] Horsley treats the bandits mentioned by Josephus as social bandits, suggesting that many of the brigands were dispossessed peasants. These brigands, lacking a coherent ideology or sense of an alternate political order, nevertheless took it upon themselves, like ancient Robin Hoods, to "right wrongs." The peasantry gave their support to these bandits and, Horsley suggests, occasionally even looked to them for leadership (1987:38).

While social banditry does not in general lead to popular rebellion, it could do so when two related developments occurred: if it became epidemic

---

would press on to the destruction of the community, cause trouble to few Romans, and then only to a small degree, but bringing the greatest slaughter upon their own people" (*Ant.* 17.285).

88. *War* 2.56: ἀναρρήγνυσιν τὰς βασιλικὰς ὁπλοθήκας καὶ τοὺς περὶ αὐτὸν ὁπλίσας. In *Ant.* 17.271 Josephus adds to this the vague statement that after arming his companions, he "made off with all the property (χρήματα) that was stored there."

89. The excavations at Sepphoris have failed to turn up evidence of the burning of the city mentioned by Josephus, which may mean that Josephus's account is (typically) exaggerated.

90. Horsley's third expression of unrest is the conflict, especially at Tiberias, between the aristocratic citizens, a faction of "sailors and destitute men" (apparently led by Jesus ben Sapphias), and another faction (of urban poor?) led by Justus of Tiberias (*Life* 33-42, 65-66, 271) (Horsley 1995c:272–75).

91. Hobsbawm 1985:17: "[social bandits] are peasant outlaws whom the lord and state regard as criminals, but who remain within peasant society, and are considered by their people as heroes, as champions, avengers, fighters for justice, perhaps even leaders of liberation, and in any case as men to be admired, helped and supported." It is the relation between the peasant and the social bandit that distinguishes social banditry from two other types of rural crime: the professional underworld or common robbers and groups for whom raiding is a ordinary way of life, both of whom prey on the peasants. "It would be unthinkable for a social bandit to snatch the peasants' (though not the lord's) harvest in his own territory, or perhaps even elsewhere" (ibid., 18).

and the bandits' groups were joined by more "more massive popular resistance," and if a millenarian or apocalyptic orientation prevailed in popular imagination (1987:39). This, says Horsley, is precisely what occurred in the 60s.

Horsley's invocation of social banditry is of a piece with his more general thesis that the main fault line in Roman Palestine (and the Galilee) was between the rulers and the ruled, the taxers and the taxed. For Horsley the bandits fall on the side of the peasants and their very existence is symptomatic of rural resistance to imperial domination (Horsley 1979).

There is ample attestation of banditry in the Herodian and early Roman periods, particularly in Judaea and to a lesser extent in the Galilee (Isaac 1984). It is a priori likely that an increase in banditry is symptomatic of worsening social and economic conditions,[92] although not necessarily in the way Horsley thinks. Two critical issues arise in respect to Horsley's theory, however: the extent to which banditry was a particular problem in the Galilee; and whether such banditry reflects rural opposition to the ruling structures.

Freyne (1988a) subjected Horsley's examples of Galilean banditry to a telling critique, arguing that in no instance does the model of social banditry fit. The earliest instance of Galilean banditry is from the time when Herod was still governor of the Galilee under Hyrcanus II (47 BCE). He captured and executed the "archbrigand" Hezekiah (Ezekias), who had been active along the Syrian frontier (*War* 1.204-11; *Ant.* 14.160-70). Herod's action was applauded by the Syrian villages that had been the objects of Hezekiah's attacks. It also attracted favorable notice from the Syrian legate, Sextus Julius Caesar (*War* 1.205-6). The account in *War* adds that some within the Hasmonean court, fearing Herod's growing personal power, pressed to charge Herod with a violation of the law, a charge that Hyrcanus eventually dismissed on the orders of Sextus. According to the later account in *Antiquities*, the complaint was lodged by the mothers of the men killed (*Ant.* 14.167-68).

In all this, as Freyne rightly notes, there is no support for Horsley's contention that Hezekiah was on "good terms" with the people of the Galilee and "certainly was not the enemy of the people" (1979:53). As will be argued below, the criticism of Herod's actions, as *War* 1.209 indeed makes clear, was initiated from within the Hasmonean court, jealous of Herod's personal power and afraid—with good reason, as it turned out—that it might lead to the deposition of Hyrcanus II.

The second instance of Galilean bandits comes from only a decade later (39–38 BCE), when Herod destroyed brigands who had taken refuge in the caves of Arbela (*War* 1.304-5, 309-13; *Ant.* 14.415-17, 420-30). Horsley treats these as social bandits, but the context of Josephus's discussion

---

92. See Goodman 1987:60–66; Schwartz 1994:297–300.

suggests rather that they were partisans of Herod's rival, Antigonus the high priest and king from 40 BCE until his execution by the Romans in 37 BCE.[93] This is not to say that Josephus's derogatory characterization, "bandits," was not somehow appropriate; but it indicates that these bandits were not examples of grassroots opposition to Herodian rule.[94]

Josephus depicts the period of direct Roman rule of Judaea as a time of increased banditry. Although he states that the arrest of a Judaean bandit Tholomaeus by Fadus (44–45 CE) purged Judaea of bandits (*Ant.* 20.5), he nonetheless describes protracted exploits of another bandit, Eleazar, who had been active for twenty years prior to his capture and execution by Felix in 54 CE (*War* 2.228-35, 253; *Ant.* 20.113-24, 161). Josephus also mentions a bandit attack on an imperial servant under Cumanus (48–52 CE), and later says that "the whole of Judaea was infested with bands of bandits" (*Ant.* 20.124).

By contrast, we do not hear of Galilean bandits again until the beginning of the First Revolt[95] when Josephus admits that, unable to disarm brigands in the Upper Galilee, he "pacified" them by arranging to have the people of Gush Ḥalav pay protection money (*Life* 77-78). None of this fits the picture of the social bandit. Nor does Josephus's description of a bandit gang led by a certain Jesus, whom the Sepphorites paid to defend them against Josephus (*Life* 104-11). The staunchly pro-Roman stance of Sepphoris and its function as a control city, collecting taxes from the outlying region, scarcely permits us to understand Jesus as a bandit siding with the peasantry against the elite. If anything, Josephus's description indicates precisely the opposite.

Josephus refers to his rival, John of Gush Ḥalav, as a "bandit" (*War* 2.585-94; contrast *Life* 71-76) who commanded four hundred men and who "plundered the whole of the Galilee." The allegation that John preyed

---

93. Horsley (1979:56 n. 56) tries to separate the "garrisons of Antigonus" (*War* 1.303, 314-46) from the account of the rebels at Arbela, which appears in the midst of this account (*War* 1.304-13), even though Josephus immediately connects Herod's intent to reduce the "strongholds of Galilee" with an attack on Sepphoris which drove out Antigonus's partisans (1.303) and the assault on Arbela (1.304). Despite Herod's dramatic destruction of the bandits at Arbela, he was unable to reduce Antigonus's forces, which counterattacked and killed Herod's general Ptolemy (1.314-15) and, later in 38 BCE following a victory of Antigonus, attacked Herod's partisans and drowned them in the Kinneret (1.326). It seems likely that the stronghold at Arbela, only a kilometer from the Kinneret, was still in the hands of the forces of Antigonus.

94. A third instance of banditry during Herod's reign occurred in 23 BCE, when brigands from Trachonitis were operating in the area of Damascus. The account in *Wars* (1.398-400) states that Marcus Terentius Varro, legate of Syria, was dispatched to destroy the brigands but *Antiquities* (15.343, 345, 348) credits Herod with this action after the area of Trachonitis was assigned to him.

95. Freyne 1988a:59 suggests that Eleazar son of Deineus was operating on the border between Samaria and Galilee, on the edge of the Great Plain. Josephus, however, locates Eleazar's activities in the toparchy of Achrabetene, southeast of Shechem (*War* 2.235), on the border between Judaea and Samaria.

on the Galileans—something that on Hobsbawm's definition would disqualify him as a social bandit—must be seen in the context of Josephus's
attacks on his rival and the self-serving descriptions of his own practices.
Nevertheless, nothing in Josephus's account suggests that John was a Robin
Hood figure for the peasantry. On the contrary, Josephus's descriptions of
John in *Life* 74 and *War* 2.585-89 presuppose that John was wealthy—and
hence a landowner—who controlled a significant portion of the agricultural
output (especially the oil) of the area. He controlled a force of "bandits"
active in the region between Gush Ḥalav and Tyre, with whom Josephus
also claims to have negotiated—probably a misrepresentation, since these
bandits eventually followed John to Jerusalem.

Horsley treats John as one of the rare examples of a social bandit who
became a revolutionary (1995c:267–68). As evidence, Horsley adduces
John's seizure of an imperial granary (*Life* 71-73) and his eventual flight to
Jerusalem after Titus's attack on Gush Ḥalav (*War* 4.98-120). But the claim
that peasants in Gush Ḥalav joined the bandits "in common rebellion
against both Roman domination and the representative of Jerusalem rule"
(i.e., Josephus) is contradicted by the fact that once John and his bandits
had left Gush Ḥalav, the residents opened the gates to Titus, hailing him as
a benefactor and liberator (*War* 4.112-13). That Titus in turn did not
enslave the inhabitants or burn the town and its surrounding villages, contenting himself to pull down a token portion of its wall, indicates that he did
not regard the inhabitants as rebels. John, the main force of opposition to
Rome, had fled and those who remained were agriculturalists more interested in their crops than revolution (*War* 4.84-85).

Despite Horsley's efforts to use banditry as an index of general social
unrest among the peasantry and of its eventual "politicization," there is
little evidence of two key features of social banditry: that Galilean bandits
enjoyed the support of the peasantry, and that they refrained from preying
on their own villagers.[96] Josephus's depiction of banditry in fact fits much
better the more nuanced description of banditry in the Roman Empire
offered by Brent Shaw (1984).

Shaw begins by noting that banditry was ubiquitous, representing a danger to persons of every rank, and that it enjoyed a special status as a criminal activity. Death from bandit attack was in fact common enough to give
rise to a stock funerary formula, *interfectus a latronibus* (killed by bandits).
Bandits were never treated as common criminals and the penalties imposed
were not those employed for "ordinary" criminal activity. Rather, bandits
were subject to the *summa supplicia*—the most severe punishments of condemnation to the beasts (*damnatio ad bestias*), crucifixion (*crux*), and condemnation to the mines (*metallum*; *Digest* 48.19.16.10).

Yet structural features of the empire created and tolerated banditry. On

---

96. Hobsbawm 1985:47–49; O'Malley 1979:489.

the one hand, banditry and raiding had for centuries been one of the "normal" means of livelihood.[97] Bandit numbers were enhanced by decommissioned soldiers, often given inadequate grants of land upon their release from the army. There was, moreover, a constant movement of men of violence in and out of the *auxilia* employed by the Roman army (Dyson 1975). An even greater problem, Shaw notes, was the "enforced desertion" of soldiers that resulted from the struggles between local potentates, each with his own army. The victory of one meant that the armies of the other were cut off from pay and provision. Unless they wished to become civilians, soldiers were compelled to a life of brigandage. Thus bandits were "created" by "the shifting frontiers of the definition of authority within the state itself" (1984:30).

On the other hand, the limited and ineffective nature of policing, especially in mountainous and frontier regions, left bandits to operate with few restrictions.[98] Police were mainly urban and their effectiveness declined precipitiously outside city walls. Bandits suffered from none of the limitations of the police. If they were pursued at all, they could simply disappear across a frontier and thus escape the purely regional jurisdiction of urban-based police. Only if banditry became too serious a problem might a local ruler such as Herod or the Roman army intervene. Short of this, bandits were safe in the rugged hinterland.

More importantly, there is widespread evidence that landlords, estate managers, municipalities, and even the state *employed* bandits to police their own fields and estates. This was necessary in fact, since the city was normally incapable of providing such services beyond its own walls. It is for this reason that later law codes refer to bandits operating with the support of landlords and contain provisions directed not only at the bandits themselves, but at those who harbor, employ, and extend their protection (*patrocinium*) to violent men.[99] The fact that laws carry punitive *fines* as well as corporal penalties shows, as Shaw notes, that "*honestiores* or persons of high social rank (of town decurion or higher status) were supporting bandits" (1984:38).

Keith Hopwood's study of banditry in Cilicia confirms this picture. Bandits enjoyed the support of local communities, but it was more often than not the landlords and local officials rather than the peasantry who employed the bandits (1989:182). Blok's study of the Mafia and Driessen's analysis of nineteenth-century banditry in Andalusia made similar findings: banditry exists within a pattern of rural patronage and client networks and is successful only because of the support of local potentates (Blok 1972;

97. Aristotle (*Politics* 1.3.4-5 [1256a-b]) lists banditry as one of the pure types of livelihood, along with nomadism, hunting, fishing, and agriculture. See also Thucydides 1.5-8.
98. On the structural problems of policing, see Hopwood 1989:177–80.
99. *Codex Justiniana* 9.39.2; *Codex Theod.* 2.29.2; 1.55.6; *Digest* 48.19.27.2.

Driessen 1983). There are, of course, occasional references to Robin Hood–like bandits who steal from the rich to give to the poor and who administer local justice. But this *literary* image, as Shaw has shown (1984:44–50), belongs to ideological theater: the "noble bandit" who forces economic redistribution and administers justice in the interests of the peasantry is an anti-type to the emperor and appears in literature precisely at times when the legitimacy of the emperor was under question. That there may have been the occasional altruistic bandit is not in doubt. The point of Hopwood and Shaw, rather, is that ancient banditry in general was of a very different character. "Social bandits" existed, but they existed mainly on parchment rather than in the mountains.

The descriptions of banditry by Shaw and Hopkins fit the picture of Galilean (and Judaean) banditry. The most obvious point of similarity is the case of the bandit Jesus, who operated in the border region between Ptolemais and the eastern Lower Galilee and whose services were retained by the people of Sepphoris. Josephus claims to have outwitted Jesus and to have forced him to become his own client and signify allegiance to his new patron by a demonstration of loyalty (πιστός, *Life* 110). Only because Josephus treats the incident within the context of patron-client relationships can one make sense of Josephus's otherwise odd admission that he permitted Jesus to reassemble his bandit gang (*Life* 111). Josephus had merely shifted Jesus and his gang into his own client network, either by outbidding Sepphoris or by threat of arms (or both).[100] Hopwood summarizes this type of phenomenon:

> [P]rotection in rural society is competitive. A 'protector' [which is the image Josephus promoted for himself vis-à-vis Sepphoris] has to ensure that his protection is better than that of his rivals to obtain the greater following in the community, access to more resources and so increase his standing. Such a process turns protection into a protection racket. (Hopwood 1989:181)

Josephus's earlier statements that he persuaded the people of Gush Ḥalav to employ the bandits as mercenaries rather than to submit to raids and his claim to have bound the bandits with an oath not to violate this agreement illustrate two key features of ancient banditry. First, they make clear the fluid boundary between banditry and military service; indeed, John of Gush Ḥalav had selected men of military experience for his band of bandits (*War*

100. Earlier Josephus claims to have offered protection to Sepphoris by "persuading" (πείσας ὑπὲρ αὐτῶν τὰ πλήθη) the hostile "Galileans" in the countryside to desist from their pillaging and attacks on Sepphoris (*Life* 31). Sepphoris had already declared its loyalty to Rome and was apparently relying on Cestius Gallus (the legate of Syria) for protection (though hardly for local policing of the city's interests). Despite Josephus's claims, the later account in *Life* 104-11 makes clear that Josephus failed to secure Sepphoris as a client. The deal with Jesus also seems to have collapsed, if he is the same Galilean brigand chief (also named Jesus: *Life* 200) retained by the aristocracy in Jerusalem (for "three months' pay") to accompany the delegation to Galilee and depose Josephus.

2.588). Second, Josephus's account indicates the way bandits functioned in a network of patron and client relationships. Josephus obtained the cooperation of these bandits (by payments and forced demonstrations of personal loyalty) to control the population of the town and to maintain general peace in the surrounding district. Whether Josephus's self-serving account is to be trusted is not the point here. Rather, the point is that Josephus's description of the relationship between John and himself and the bandits conforms precisely to the picture that is painted elsewhere, of local strongmen employing bandit gangs for social control.

The shifting lines between soldiers and bandits are also illustrated by the account of the "bandits"—apparently partisans of Antigonus—in the Arbela caves. To Herod they were of course outlaws, regardless of what they thought of themselves. With Antigonus's defeat, those that survived probably did become bandits, since they were now cut off from pay, provisions, and legal justification.

To Freyne's (1988a) suggestion that the bandits that Herod attacked were in fact pro-Hasmonean partisans Horsley replies, "power struggles had been happening among rival Hasmonean factions for some time, prior to and utterly unrelated to Herod's elimination of Hezekiah and his brigands in Galilee in 47 B.C.E." (Horsley 1995c:260). This reply, however, misses the function of Herod's actions. As Shaw has shown, Herod's elimination of the bandits—as also his actions three years later at Arbela, and again twenty years later in Trachonitis—was calibrated quite precisely to demonstrate his *personal power* and thereby to assert his kingly qualifications (1993:184–89). Each of his attacks on bandits occurred at a crucial juncture in his rise to power: at his initial appointment by Caesar as the governor of the Galilee in 47 BCE; during his efforts to recoup his power after the assassination of Caesar and his confirmation by the Roman Senate as king (40 BCE); and in the wake of the debacle caused by Herod's erstwhile support of Anthony against Octavian (Augustus) and his desire to retain power and to demonstrate his loyalty to Rome and Augustus after Anthony's death. The "elimination" of bandits was an excellent way to demonstrate loyalty to Herod's masters.

In all this I do not mean to suggest that the ebb and flow of banditry did not somehow reflect social and economic conditions or that bandit ranks did not sometimes include peasants. The point, rather, is to see that banditry was part of power politics. Herod's suppression of banditry is as typical of such demonstrations of personal power by the elite as is Josephus's utilization of bandits to control local populations or to outmaneuver rival strongmen.[101]

Freyne is probably correct that banditry does not appear to have been

101. Cohen's suggestion (1979:211–13) that Josephus's own forces included bandits is a priori likely.

especially characteristic of the Galilee, at least until the mid-60s. Moreover, the romantic image of the noble bandit fighting in support of the peasantry belongs not to empirical history but to ideological conflict. Nevertheless, Josephus's accounts of banditry in the Galilee at the outset of the First Revolt do suggest instability in patterns of local control. Schwartz argues that this instability was the product of the Herodian policy of urbanization. The foundation of Tiberias and Sepphoris entailed land grants to Herodian aristocracy. This created a new elite comprised of absentee landlords more interested in extraction of revenue than in local conditions. Thus Schwartz suggests a structural conflict between this new elite and the older country landlords:

> The main consequences of the foundations of Tiberias and Sepphoris in the early first century were the creation of a class of absentee landlords based in the cities, a decline in the position of the country landlords (and so a breakdown in relations between them and *their* Herodian and Roman patrons), and the impoverishment of small farmers. These processes in turn produced a partial breakdown in the patronal system, the most conspicuous manifestations of which were the development of large bands of brigands; the violent hostility between the urban upper classes and the country people which is such an important theme of Josephus's account; and finally the adherence of expanded groups of clients to the wealthier and more ambitious country landlords. (Schwartz 1994:305, emphasis original)[102]

Whether there was an absolute increase in brigandage in the Galilee cannot be known with certainty. Virtually all that we know of the Galilee in the Roman period comes from Josephus, whose account of his own brief and unhappy stay in the Galilee begins in 66 CE and ends the next year. Banditry was endemic in the empire and might reasonably be expected to be a permanent feature of mountainous regions such as the Upper Galilee. Schwartz's main point, however, that Herodian foundations destabilized social control, is probably essentially correct. Banditry as such was not a symptom of social breakdown; in fact, bandits might operate with a perfectly stable system of patron-client relationships, functioning as the means by which urban elites protect their interests in the hinterland. When the power relationships of the urban elite begin to shift, bandit activity reflects this instability. The establishment of a new aristocratic elite in Galilean society created new set of potential employers for bandits and new targets of bandit activity. These shifting power arrangements are evidenced in the conflicts between local landowners and the representatives of the Herodian and Judaean aristocracy (including Josephus) in which bandits were employed as enforcers and mercenaries. Doubtless these arrangements worked to the disadvantage of the smallholders and peasants.

---

102. On the differences between patronage of the rural poor by absentee (urban) elite and resident landlords, see Garnsey and Woolf 1989.

Unrest and the Problem of Debt

It would be unwise to exaggerate the extent of social breakdown, still less the level of anti-Roman sentiment.[103] Freyne argued that the Galilee was in less straitened circumstances than Judaea owing to the style of Herodian government (1994:94–95). We do not hear of the kinds of protests against Herodian rule at the deposition of Antipas or death of Agrippa I that were voiced in response to Archelaus's reign in Judaea. Goodman noted that in the wake of the First Revolt, Vespasian did not reinstate the Judaean rulers, as might have been expected. The reason for this, Goodman surmises, is that "the ruling class had, after all, never been seen by the rest of the population as a natural elite" (1987:234). The continuation of the direct Roman rule of Judaea amounted to Rome's realization that the Judaean ruling class was incapable of effective control. The situation in the Galilee was different. The fact that Agrippa II retained jurisdiction over Tiberias and Tarichaeae (while the rest of the Galilee remained under direct Roman control) implies that Vespasian supposed Agrippa to have exercised effective rule and considered the two Galilean cities and their respective city territories to be sufficiently peaceful to permit the continuation of a client kingship.

Whether the level of indebtedness in the Galilee was comparable to that in Judaea is difficult to know. Goodman (1982) conjectured that a major contributing cause of the First Revolt was the increasing debt spiral in Judaea. Jerusalem experienced significant growth in the first century (Josephus, *War* 5.148-55). Lavish Herodian spending and major building projects enhanced the attraction of the city to pilgrims and others. Naturally this benefited most directly the priestly aristocracy, who derived their income both from tithes and from Temple monopolies. The natural outlet for the currency that was acquired, Goodman argues, was agricultural loans (and, we might add, the outright purchase of land). The institution of the *prozbul* (see above, p. 241) about this time secured loans with immovable property (i.e., land) and effectively eliminated the recourse to a sabbatical

103. See Rappaport 1992. There is not much evidence of concerted resistance to the Roman invasion of the Galilee, despite Josephus's claims to have fortified the Galilee against the Romans (*Life* 187; *War* 2.573). Josephus's claims are at least in part fabrications: some of the cities he names were never under his control (Gamla; Gush Ḥalav), and in cases such as Meiron, there is no archaeological evidence of these alleged fortifications. The Roman assault was far from inconsequential, but neither was it completely devastating. Gabara was razed in retaliation for the defeat of Cestius Gallus at Beth Horon, even though Gabara appears not to have even closed its gates to Vespasian (*War* 3.132-34). Yodefat and Gamla (in Gaulanitis), both fortified towns, put up stout resistance; but Sepphoris and Tiberias opened their gates. Gush Ḥalav surrendered once John and his bandits had left (*War* 4.112-20). Tarichaeae was taken after a short siege (*War* 3.492-502). In both Gush Ḥalav and Tarichaeae the resident population, which had opposed the revolt, was dealt with leniently, a sign that Titus did not perceive them to be a threat.

release. Under these circumstances, default led to the loss of patrimonial lands.

Goodman does not think that the baneful influence of the Temple economy extended to the Galilee. Judaean aristocrats were more likely to buy land in Judaea and perhaps in Idumaea and Peraea (1982:421 n. 29). Nonetheless, as Schwartz notes, Queen Bernice owned an estate near Beth She'arim (*Life* 119), and the other Herodians at Tiberias (and presumably at Sepphoris) likely owned estates in the Great Plain or the more fertile areas of the Lower Galilee.[104] Whether these were acquired by confiscation or by purchase or through default on loans cannot be known; but the result would be the same: increased encroachment on smallholders. Freyne thinks that Galileans were on balance better off than those in Judaea; but the hostility that Josephus reports between the "Galileans" and the cities of Sepphoris and Tiberias—where the elite lived and where the debt archives were located—raises the suspicion that debt and other forms of exploitation were among the sources of this hostility.[105] In the final analysis, whether debt conditions were better or worse in the Galilee may be moot; Josephus's account of conditions in the Galilee assumes that smallholders, like their Judaean counterparts, lived close enough to the threshold of destitution that one failed harvest could drive large numbers from the land, producing a "harvest of banditry" (*Ant.* 18.274).

Reading Q in the Galilee

From the standpoint of method, what remains is to determine whether the actual shape of Q's rhetoric (as described in chapter 4) can plausibly be seen within the horizon of first-century Galilee, as reconstructed on the basis of documents and sources other than Q (in order to avoid circularity). Both what Q takes for granted—and therefore does not need to argue—and what it argues in detail ought to be plausible, given what is known of Galilean social, political, and religious dynamics. Such an exercise does not of course prove that Q derives from the Galilee; at best, one can make a case that the

---

104. Schwartz 1994:295–96. Crispus, one of the aristocrats at Tiberias, owned estates across the Jordan (*Life* 33).

105. Freyne (1988a:62) adds that there is no record of an attempt to destroy debt archives in the Galilee parallel to what occurred in Jerusalem when the Judaean bandits entered the city (*War* 2.427-48). This does not take into account the fact that the debt archives for the Lower Galilee were from 54 CE on in Sepphoris, which was fortified and solidly pro-Roman throughout the Revolt. Josephus reports only one attack on Sepphoris by the "Galileans" (with whom he appears to have collaborated), an attack that did not succeed in taking the citadel and which seems to have lasted only briefly (*Life* 373-80). It is not known where the debt archives in Sepphoris were housed, but the archives in Jerusalem were located in an area near or in the citadel (ἡ Ἄκρα), and near the council chamber (τὸ βουλευτήριον) and the Ophel (ὁ Ὀφλᾶς), all of which are within the first wall. One must presume that the debt archives of Sepphoris were also in a secure area.

Galilee provides a plausible locale for Q's rhetoric and theology. If, on the other hand, the rhetoric of Q or its assumed world were not to fit with what is otherwise known of the Galilee, one would have to seek another geographical and social locale for the document, or reassess one's understanding of its rhetoric.

In fact Q coheres reasonably well with what we know of the Galilee. At all three redactional levels, the document presumes a largely or exclusively Israelite audience. Although Q[1] lacks most specific references to Israelite figures and institutions, it takes for granted that the addressees know of Solomon's proverbial wealth (12:27). Q employs the Aramaic words Gehenna (γεεννα, 12:5) and mammon (μαμωνα, 16:13) without any need to translate or explain them. Q 6:33 and 12:30 invoke presumed Gentile behavior as stereotypically "other." At the level of Q[2] there are frequent appeals to Israelite epic traditions and the spatial world of Q is constructed concentrically, with three Galilean towns at the center: Kefar Naḥum, Khorazin, and Bethsaida (Reed 1995). Both Jerusalem and Tyre, whose economic and political pull on the Galilee is otherwise well documented, are viewed as negative, though evidently significant points on Q's horizon. It is perhaps surprising that neither Tiberias nor Sepphoris is mentioned given the immediate and baneful influences that these two cities exerted on the rest of the Lower Galilee. On the other hand, Q refers (again negatively) to institutions that would have been present in these cities—the ἀγορά (marketplace: 7:31; 11:43), the law courts (12:58-59), and possibly to a πλατεῖα (broad street, plaza: 10:10?; 13:26; 14:21). Actual and imaginary Gentiles make their appearance at this stage of Q. There were, of course, Greeks in the Galilee (as Josephus's account makes clear), but they function in Q's rhetoric primarily to shame the principally Israelite audience (cf. Q 7:1-10; 10:12-15; 11:31-32; 13:28-29). The final stage of Q likewise appears to assume a largely Israelite audience, appealing to Torah as a basis for argument (4:1-13), and affirming the enduring validity of the Torah (11:42c; 16:17).

The ambivalent attitude of Galileans toward the Temple and the Judaean Torah helps to make sense of Q's distinctive rhetoric. Q nowhere challenges circumcision (unlike Paul) or Sabbath observance (unlike Mark) and appears to assume as self-evident the distinction between Jews and Gentiles (6:33; 12:30). Given these features, it is likely that the Q people, as other Galileans, took for granted the principal distinguishing marks of Israelite identity—circumcision, some form of Sabbath observance, and probably certain dietary observances. The critical points in Q's rhetoric are precisely those that we have suggested were controverted in the Galilean population as a whole: purity distinctions (11:39-41), tithing (11:42), and the role of Jerusalem and the Temple in social and religious economy of the north (11:49-51; 13:34-35).

If the woes in Q 11:39-52 are correctly understood as burlesque, they represent a form of resistance to the pressures (probably via the periodic presence of Pharisees) to extend Judaean forms of Temple-oriented practices to the Galilee. The topics of the woes in 11:39-44, purity and tithing, are rooted in the economy of the Second Temple. Q's response is not to reject purity distinctions out of hand or even to reject tithing in principle. Such a wholesale rejection of purity distinctions would have been most unlikely in any Mediterranean society and certainly in Israelite society. Q 11:44, which accuses the Pharisees of being like unmarked graves, takes for granted that death brings defilement and that graves ought to be avoided (except by those who have familial obligations toward their own dead).[106] Rather, Q's woes lampoon the highly specific purity practices of the Pharisees who adopted the articulated purity regime of the priestly caste of Judaea.

What is especially noteworthy about Q 11:39-41 is its specific focus. The woe has to do with *vessels*, and thus belongs to the broader concern about the production, storage, transport, sale, and consumption of agricultural products, in particular, wine and oil. Q's woe should not be taken to imply that the Q people disregarded the purity of agricultural produce. Perhaps, like at least some other Galileans, they observed some form of purity distinctions regarding the production of olive oil or wine. Such speculations cannot be controlled given the lack of data. What the woe does suggest is that the Q people resisted any further articulation of purity distinctions, which would have represented heightened symbolic (or actual) control of agricultural production with few or no compensatory benefits. The fact that *miqwaʾôt* in first-century Galilee are restricted to places of priestly settlement, a few private homes, and locations associated with oil production indicates that the Q people were not alone in resisting (or ignoring) a greater extension of purity practices.

The woe on tithing may be interpreted analogously, as popular resistance to any extension of practices designed specifically in support of the Temple in the south. It is not that Q (or most Galileans, for that matter) opposed the Temple as such. The threatened strike mentioned by Josephus (*Ant.* 18.273-78) indicates that threats to the Temple might spur Galileans to actions in its support. But whether such attitudes translated into unconditional or widespread monetary support for the priestly caste is another matter entirely. There is little evidence to indicate widespread Galilean payment of the half-shekel tax, and it is not likely that there was regular payment of priestly tithes either. Q 11:42ab registers the complaint that the Pharisees (and those whom they represent), who are known to be concerned with

---

106. Tiberias was founded on an ancient cemetery and this created an obstacle to its settlement (Josephus, *Ant.* 18.38). It is sometimes implied that only Pharisees would have found this location problematic; but it must be recognized that the dead were almost universally regarded to be a source of pollution throughout the Mediterranean world and normally buried outside city walls (see Parker 1983). On the foundation and eventual purification of Tiberias, see Avi-Yonah 1960; L. Levine 1974.

produce that is susceptible to the tithe down to rather small seeds, are negligent when it comes to values key to the villagers from whom the tithes are supposed to be extracted.

The woes regarding tithing and the purity of vessels—both related to agricultural production—occur alongside the woe concerning Pharisaic presence in the marketplaces (ἀγοραί) and assemblies (συναγωγαί, 11:43), both urban phenomena. This seems significant, since the cities and their markets were key points for the extraction of agricultural surpluses. The point of both 11:39-41 and 11:42ab is that the Pharisees promote an articulated system of purity and tithing and in doing so mirror the "rapacious" appetites of elite interests—Q 11:39 accuses the Pharisees of ἁρπαγή (rapacity)—but do little to promote justice (κρίσις) and the love of God, which would confer more general benefits.[107] The various complaints of second-century rabbis about the unreliability of the ʿammei ha-ʾaretz in respect to tithing suggests that the Q people were not alone in resisting the system of tithing.

That the Pharisees are aligned with Jerusalem and the Temple is indicated by the ease with which Q shifts from woes directed specifically against the Pharisees and scribes (or lawyers) to Jerusalem and the Temple (11:49-51). While Q employs the synthetic term "this generation," in the context of 11:49-51 the Temple personnel are probably in view. Q 13:34-35 likewise represents "Jerusalem"—again, the priestly hierarchy—as inimical to the prophets and, by extension, the Q people.

The absence of direct mention in Q of the cities of Sepphoris and Tiberias might initially seem puzzling, but as already noted, Q treats the urban institutions and landmarks—the ἀγορά (7:31; 11:43), the law courts and prisons (12:58-59), and the πλατεῖα (10:10?; 13:26)—negatively, as places where Q's opponents may be found, or where there is equivocal support for Jesus and his message, or where there are other dangers. Oakman has recently suggested that the locales in which the early Jesus movement was found—mainly villages—and its absence from, or lack of mention of, towns such as Yodefat, Cana, Kefar Naḥum, and Magdala-Tarichaeae or the cities of Sepphoris and Tiberias have political and economic correlates. These cities and towns were the domiciles of the political kin of Herod and of the Judaean elite and the points of extraction of taxes and tolls (Oakman 1994:229). This is to suggest that the avoidance of Tiberias and Sepphoris and the critical views that Q 10:13-15 expresses toward Kefar Naḥum (which was a point of tax extraction: Mark 1:29) and, one could add, Bethsaida, are to be seen at least in part as a function of tensions between the hinterland and points of revenue and resource collection that were exacerbated by the urbanization of the Galilee in the first century.

---

107. Whether such accusations were true or fair is beside the point; the rhetoric of Q indicates that the Q people aligned the Pharisees with the hierocratic interests in Judaea.

Oakman (1997b) also makes important observations that bear on money and monetization. Beginning with the proposition that it is important to distinguish higher (silver, gold) from lower (copper, bronze) denominations, elite from nonelite usage, and various functions of money,[108] Oakman notes that Q is aware of the storage function of silver (Q 10:4; 19:20) and provides the only direct reference in the Jesus tradition to using money to make money (Q 19:23). Q, however, in fact counsels *against* the carrying of silver (10:4) and treats the investors of the Parable of the Entrusted Money negatively (Rohrbaugh 1993; Kloppenborg 1995b:295–300). It might be added that persons who are in a position to make large-scale purchases, doubtless involving silver, are likewise treated negatively, as can be seen in Q's Parable of the Great Feast (14:18-19).

Oakman urges that Q's references to bronze coinage reflect the nonelite realities of Galilee (1997b:7). Q 12:6 invokes money barter in local markets (five sparrows for two *assaria*) while 12:59 points to the grim reality of debt extraction, extending to the smallest bronze (Roman) denomination, the *quadrans*. Q 16:13 represents a key point of resistance to the monetizing of the economy. The contrast between *mammon* (ממון from אמן "to trust"), literally meaning "deposit money," and God signals a "piercing critique of a political order where loans, indebtedness, and safety deposits defy God's purposes" (Oakman 1997b:9). It could be added that the very construction of Q 16:13 and its use of δουλεύειν, "to be a slave to," underscores the stark contrast that Q sees between a money- and deposit-based economy (which naturally benefited the elite) and reliance on God's providential care. A similar contrast is witnessed in the construction of Q 12:16-20, 22-31, which juxtaposes the wealthy fool's reliance on stored surpluses with the subsistence provisions offered by God.

Running throughout Q is a tension between "natural," agricultural, and familial processes, which are characterized as sources of insight and models for emulation,[109] and the "higher" elements of culture, mostly associated with urban centers, are treated negatively.[110] This coheres with the account of the urbanization and monetization of the Galilean economy given by

108. Oakman (1997b:4) distinguishes five functions: F1: storage of value; F2: measurement of value; F3: standard of payment; F4: exchange value (which assumes the universal utility of money); and F5: use value (the use of money in barter). See also Hanson and Oakman 1998:120–25.

109. Q 6:43-44 (arboriculture), 47-49 (flash floods); 9:58 (the dens and nests of animals and birds); 9:59-60 (funerary obligations in families); 10:2 (harvest); 11:11-13 (parental behavior); 12:6 (sale of sparrows), 24 (ravens), 27-28 (field flowers), 33-34, 39 (housebreaking), 54-56 (weather signs); 13:18-21 (mustard and leaven); 15:4-7 (sheep herding), 8-10 (nonélite money storage); and 17:3b-4 (conflict resolution).

110. Q 7:25 (royalty and other elite), 31 (the agora); 11:43 (assemblies and the agora), 51 (Jerusalem); 12:11-12 (assemblies and rulers), 42-46 (large estates and managers), 58-59 (courts); 13:34-35 (Jerusalem); 14:16-24 (dining practices of the elite); 16:13 ("mammon"); and 19:12-27 (large-scale investors and their retainers).

Freyne and Arnal and suggests that Q's various discourses on "low" versus
"high" aspects of culture reflect a resistance to those developments. Arthur
Stinchcombe puts the matter well: for agriculturalists subject to exploitation from rentiers, "agriculture is always the kind of enterprise with which
God has a lot to do."[111] The dangerous variability in income levels experienced by smallholders and tenants that are the combined result of the vicis-
situdes of nature and the extractions of the elite is counterbalanced by an
appeal to God's reign and providential care as the appropriate sources of
confidence and renewal. Understood in this context, Q's discourse on the
kingdom of God represents resistance to the imposition of a political and
economic culture that would benefit urban elites at the expense of the small
producers.[112]

Q betrays few signs of a "revolutionary" environment. At the level of Q[1],
mention is made of local conflict (Q 6:27-29), of forced labor or corvée
(ἀγγαρεύω Q/Matt 5:41), of loans and debt (Q 6:30; 11:3), and of robbery
and housebreaking (Q 6:29;[113] 12:33-34 [and Q[2]: 12:39]). These phenomena are treated as "normal" and almost predictable happenings rather than
as signs of rapidly escalating social conflict. Sayings at the main redactional
level (Q[2]) convey a greater impression of impending disaster (Q 3:3, 7-9;
11:50-51; 12:49, 51, 54-56; 13:34-35) but there is no obvious reflection of
the events of 66–70 CE. If the Q people are aware of the machinations of the
elite or of "revolutionary" sentiments, they betray few signs. The cryptic
warning of Q 17:23 not to "go out" (ἐξέλθητε) into the wilderness or follow (διώξητε) persons into secret chambers (ἐν τοῖς ταμείοις) may signal
some awareness of clandestine activities. But in the elaboration of this
warning, it becomes clear that Q assumes that the day of the Son of Man
will occur suddenly and quite unexpectedly, in the midst of the everyday and
perfectly ordinary domestic activities (17:26-30, 34-35), not in the context
of a general collapse of the political and social order (contrast Mark 13:12-
13, 14-26).

111. Stinchcombe 1961–62:186. He continues: "With the commercialization of agriculture,
the enterprise is further subject to fluctuation in the gross income from its produce. Rentiers,
especially if they are capitalists investing in land rather than aristocrats receiving incomes from
a feudal patrimony, shift as much of the risk of failure as possible to the tenants. Whether the
rent is share or cash, the variability of the income of the peasantry is almost never less, and is
often more than the variability of the rentier's income. This makes the income of the peasantry
highly variable, contributing to their political sensitization."

112. Similarly, Oakman 1994:235: "Jesus as an advocate of non-elite interests in the Galilee
envisions the emergence of an alternative social order under God's reign; this reign implies a
community of fictive kinship. Its emergence, however, is hindered as long as the prevailing
political order remains. There are indications in very ancient Jesus material of a critique of the
political order."

113. On whether Q 6:29 envisages a scenario of robbery or a lawsuit, see Piper 1995b and
Steinhauser 1992.

In this regard, too, Q seems to cohere with the situation of the Galilee before the First Revolt: subject to steady pressures from urbanization and the monetization of the economy and in a situation where older forms of rural patronage were threatened by the presence of a new urban elite, small-holders were in an increasingly fragile state. One bad harvest or one serious misfortune might mean the loss of everything, since the new patronal class, already viewed with distrust (Q 7:24-26; 14:16-24; 16:13; 19:12-26), could not be depended upon for help.

In reaction to this, the Sayings Gospel and the scribes who framed it proposed a model of local cooperation based on strategies of tension reduction, debt release, and forgiveness, and appealing to an image of God as a generous patron and parent who could be depended upon for sustenance. These scribes also resisted any efforts to impose a southern, hierocratically-defined vision of Israel in which human affairs are centered on a central sanctuary and its priestly officers. This is not opposition to the Temple; but it is also not an endorsement of the hierocratic worldview of either the priestly aristocracy or the Pharisees, both of whom come in for serious criticism. Q is thus engaged in a struggle on two fronts: in support of town and village culture against the encroachments of the cities, and in support of local forms of Israelite religion in the face of pressures from the hierocratic worldview of Judaea.

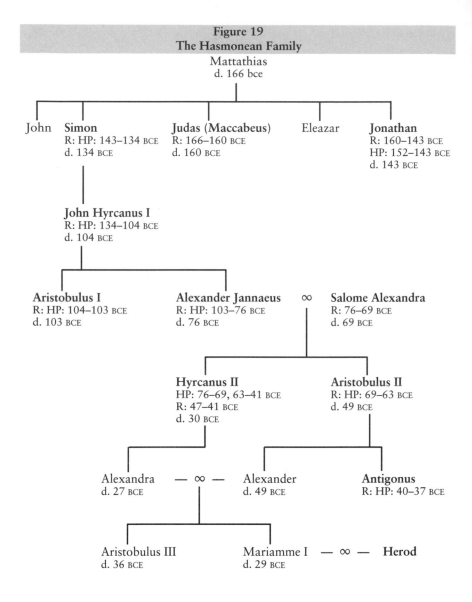

Figure 19
The Hasmonean Family

Mattathias
d. 166 bce

John

Simon
R: HP: 143–134 BCE
d. 134 BCE

Judas (Maccabeus)
R: 166–160 BCE
d. 160 BCE

Eleazar

Jonathan
R: 160–143 BCE
HP: 152–143 BCE
d. 143 BCE

John Hyrcanus I
R: HP: 134–104 BCE
d. 104 BCE

Aristobulus I
R: HP: 104–103 BCE
d. 103 BCE

Alexander Jannaeus   ∞   Salome Alexandra
R: HP: 103–76 BCE   R: 76–69 BCE
d. 76 BCE   d. 69 BCE

Hyrcanus II
HP: 76–69, 63–41 BCE
R: 47–41 BCE
d. 30 BCE

Aristobulus II
R: HP: 69–63 BCE
d. 49 BCE

Alexandra — ∞ — Alexander
d. 27 BCE   d. 49 BCE

Antigonus
R: HP: 40–37 BCE

Aristobulus III
d. 36 BCE

Mariamme I — ∞ — Herod
d. 29 BCE

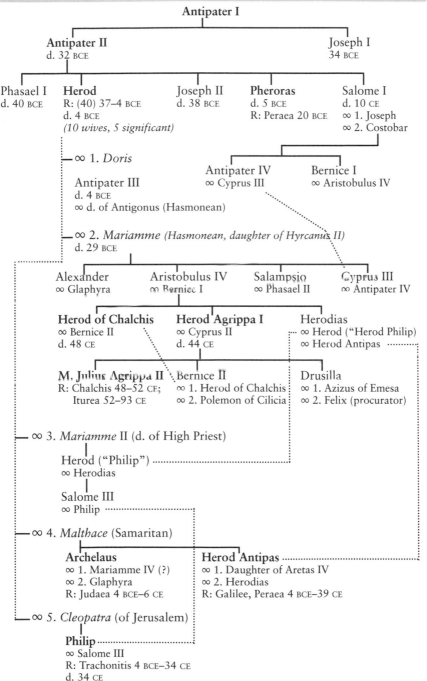

Figure 20
The Herodian Family

Antipater I

Antipater II
d. 32 BCE

Joseph I
34 BCE

Phasael I
d. 40 BCE

Herod
R: (40) 37–4 BCE
d. 4 BCE
(10 wives, 5 significant)

Joseph II
d. 38 BCE

Pheroras
d. 5 BCE
R: Peraea 20 BCE

Salome I
d. 10 CE
∞ 1. Joseph
∞ 2. Costobar

∞ 1. *Doris*

Antipater III
d. 4 BCE
∞ d. of Antigonus (Hasmonean)

Antipater IV
∞ Cyprus III

Bernice I
∞ Aristobulus IV

∞ 2. *Mariamme (Hasmonean, daughter of Hyrcanus II)*
d. 29 BCE

Alexander
∞ Glaphyra

Aristobulus IV
∞ Bernice I

Salampsio
∞ Phasael II

Cyprus III
∞ Antipater IV

Herod of Chalchis
∞ Bernice II
d. 48 CE

Herod Agrippa I
∞ Cyprus II
d. 44 CE

Herodias
∞ Herod ("Herod Philip)
∞ Herod Antipas

M. Julius Agrippa II
R: Chalchis 48–52 CE;
Iturea 52–93 CE

Bernice II
∞ 1. Herod of Chalchis
∞ 2. Polemon of Cilicia

Drusilla
∞ 1. Azizus of Emesa
∞ 2. Felix (procurator)

∞ 3. *Mariamme* II (d. of High Priest)

Herod ("Philip")
∞ Herodias

Salome III
∞ Philip

∞ 4. *Malthace* (Samaritan)

Archelaus
∞ 1. Mariamme IV (?)
∞ 2. Glaphyra
R: Judaea 4 BCE–6 CE

Herod Antipas
∞ 1. Daughter of Aretas IV
∞ 2. Herodias
R: Galilee, Peraea 4 BCE–39 CE

∞ 5. *Cleopatra* (of Jerusalem)

Philip
∞ Salome III
R: Trachonitis 4 BCE–34 CE
d. 34 CE

Part II

THEOLOGY AND IDEOLOGY

Kefar Naḥum. Rolling olive press, made of black basalt.

Theology and Ideology

T HE FIRST FIVE CHAPTERS considered issues in the Synoptic Problem and Q from the standpoint of the available textual and historical data, and constructed arguments for the existence of Q and its documentary character, composition, genre, and social location based on those data. In chapter 1, for example, it was argued that solutions to the Synoptic Problem should be based on two sets of arguments. The first set derives from the patterns of agreements and disagreements among the Synoptics and the logical inferences that these patterns permit. Since these data point to the medial nature of Mark but not necessarily to its priority, progress toward a solution must be conducted by means of a second set of arguments having to do with the literary and editorial plausibility of the various possible solutions. Thus the respective plausibilities of Mark's use of Matthew or of Matthew's use of Mark, Luke's use of Matthew, or their independence, must be measured on a register of editorial considerations. A solution that can provide a generally plausible accounting of most of the textual data most of the time is preferable to one that provides a less plausible accounting.

The 2DH measures well on this scale. The multiple transformations of Mark and Q by Matthew and Luke that are entailed by the 2DH can be accounted for by means of a coherent set of assumptions about Matthew's and Luke's respective (and differing) penchants for stylistic improvement, expansion, and reconfiguration. The assumption of the 2DH yields a generally coherent picture of Matthew and Luke as stylists and as editors with identifiable theological profiles. Thus it is an effective literary hypothesis. I have also suggested that the 2DH scores significantly better than the 2GH or the Farrer-Goulder hypothesis, notwithstanding a residue of Synoptic data—a handful of "minor agreements"—that remain problematic and which perhaps call for a somewhat more complex version of the hypothesis.

267

Discussions of the Synoptic Problem and Q do not occur in a vacuum, however. They have taken place and still occur for the most part in the context of general theological scholarship where issues of doctrine, faith, church polity, pastoral practice, and Christian self-understanding are keenly debated. Scholarship on Christian origins, including the literary-critical issue of the relationship among the Gospels, may have implications for some of these debated issues. For example, the attempt to write a history of christological doctrine would differ depending on whether one began with the 2GH or the 2DH. This is not only because Matthew's Christology is richer and more diversified than Mark's but because Mark lacks key Matthaean notions such as Jesus as an eschatological judge.[1] The 2DH seems to imply a line of christological elaboration that accords with (some) modern theological convictions that christological doctrine tended toward increasingly high expressions. Or again, one solution to the Synoptic Problem might imply a point of origin for the Gospels with characteristics that are particularly appealing to other contemporary theological and social concerns. For example, Matthaean priorists sometimes point out that Matthew is far more "Jewish" than Mark and thus better expresses the Jewish origins of the Jesus movement.[2] Alternatively, advocates of the 2DH might reply that Mark and especially Q are much more acutely concerned with actual poverty and the declaration of God's advocacy for the poor than either Matthew or Luke and thus the 2DH is a better positioned for use by liberation theology.

It is a fundamental error, however, to allow considerations of nonliterary utility or advantage to influence the solutions to a literary problem.[3] As an

---

1. See the discussion of these problems in Head 1997.

2. This sort of argument is not especially telling, since Q is equally "Jewish." Moreover, the fact that the earliest Jesus movement was Judaean and Galilean has no bearing on whether the first gospel came from the Jewish Jesus movement or from Gentile Christian circles.

3. Although Farmer's support of the 2GH is based on the literary evidence (Farmer 1964), the closing peroration of his recent book comes perilously close to just such an appeal (1994:199). Countering the 2DH's argument of *literary utility*, he asserts that the 2DH "can be useful" to those who (1) deny that Jesus taught his disciples the Lord's Prayer, (2) treat the Last Supper as a cult legend, (3) deny contact between Paul's doctrine of justification and the teachings of Jesus, (4) downplay the role of women in the Gospel tradition, (5) discount the emphasis on God's preferential option for the poor, (6) discount the role of Peter, (7) discount the importance of the Torah and the prophets for Christians, (8) think of Jesus as un-Jewish, (9) wish to dismantle the church's canon, (10) wish to value Q, the *Gospel of Thomas,* and other apocrypha equally with the New Testament in understanding Christian origins, (11) reject the idea of Jesus' redemptive death as "normative," (12) think that Q had no idea of Jesus' redemptive death, (13) downplay the importance of Isaiah 53 in the teachings of the historical Jesus, (14) view Paul as "corrupting" the earliest form of Christianity, and (15) those "liberal Catholic theologians and Bible scholars who feel alienated from a hierarchically dominated church."

It would tedious and perhaps pointless to refute these allegations individually, but it ought to be obvious some of these supposed implications of the 2DH are simply wrong and the rest

essentially literary issue, the Synoptic Problem must be addressed on the level of literary evidence and argument—the sorts of data and arguments presented in chapter one. That the 2DH turns out to be convenient for other purposes is not additional "evidence" in its favor. Nor conversely is the fact that the 2DH is perceived to cause theological difficulties a strike against it. The confusion of literary arguments with arguments from theological utility, and the confusion of criteria with consequences are serious failures of argumentative logic.

As the history of the discussion of the Synoptic Problem and Q makes clear, the distinction between literary-critical and historical arguments and the theological utility of hypotheses has not always been observed strictly. Even if solutions to the Synoptic Problem were originally constructed on the basis of literary data, their appeal sometimes derived from nonliterary considerations. The birth of the Synoptic Problem was in fact attended by a theological midwife. At various points along the way, the perceived utility of various solutions to the Synoptic Problem has played a role in concealing their weaknesses or in eliminating competing solutions without real warrant.

In the final four chapters, I will revisit the topics discussed in the first five and in each case inquire into the larger theological or ideological framework within which the more technical literary and historical questions have had their place. The point is twofold: first, to understand why the Synoptic Problem and various issues concerning Q became problems in the first place and how they fit with or challenge broader theological scholarship; and second, to notice the ways in which this broader theological or ideological climate has sometimes encouraged an uncritical acceptance of dubious or at least debatable conclusions from literary criticism, and at other times has disinclined scholars from embracing possible or even plausible literary and historical scenarios, presumably because they had (or are perceived to have) entailments that collided with prevailing theological convictions. From a methodological point of view, the lionizing of literary-critical hypotheses is every bit as dubious a procedure as resisting solid historical and literary-critical hypotheses merely because they interfere with long-held views of the historical Jesus or the character and development of early Christian theology. Nevertheless, attention both to phases of uncritical acceptance of

---

are quite irrelevant. The Lord's Prayer (1), women (4), the poor (5), the Torah (7), and Jesus' "Jewishness" (8) are features of Q! Peter (6) and the Lord's Supper (2) are from Mark. Whether the Lord's Supper is a cult legend (2) and whether Pauline doctrine is related to Jesus' teachings (3) must be decided quite independently of particular solutions to the Synoptic Problem. The endorsing of the 2DH is not logically related to the valuation or devaluation of apocryphal gospels (10). As to scholars' judgments on the issues of canon (9), the theological normativity of redemptive views of Jesus' death (11), whether Paul "corrupted" Jesus' teachings (who now holds such a view?), or hierarchy (14, 15), these simply have no bearing on solutions to the Synoptic Problem.

hypotheses, and to those junctures where sound literary hypotheses were either ignored or resisted, are extremely telling of the larger intellectual context within which Synoptic scholarship is pursued.

Throughout these chapters, I will insist that the congeniality of the 2DH with larger theological projects and sensibilities is irrelevant to a critical assessment of its plausibility as a literary and historical account. If, however, we wish to develop a self-critical understanding of the 2DH and appreciate its full impact, it is necessary to understand how the discourse on literary criticism of the Gospels intersects with other discourses on Christian origins and Christian theology.

6

The Jesus of History
and the History of Dogma
Theological Currents
in the Synoptic Problem

STANDARD NEW TESTAMENT introductions normally discuss the Synoptic Problem by beginning with a brief typology of solutions to the Synoptic Problem and then proceed rather rapidly to a survey of the key historical developments that led to the birth and eventual triumph of the Two Document Hypothesis. Given the wide acceptance of the 2DH today, this approach is perhaps understandable. Yet such treatments tend inevitably to become, as William Farmer (1980a) has lamented, "school histories" in which earlier contributors to the Synoptic Problem are selected and interpreted from the point of view of what would later emerge as the dominant solution. Competing hypotheses are discussed only in light of the eventual ascendancy of the 2DH, while deficiencies in the arguments of the early advocates of the 2DH are glossed over. Little attention is given to the theological or ideological factors that helped to commend one solution over all others.

It should not be surprising that such school histories provoked sharp criticism by advocates of competing solutions. They rightly point out that some of the arguments employed by earlier advocates of the 2DH were inconclusive or even fallacious and that arguments in favor of other solutions were ignored.[1] Unfortunately, no critical history of the Synoptic Problem yet exists which provides a comprehensive survey and evaluation of the varied

1. Most helpful in this regard are the surveys by Farmer 1964; Meijboom 1866 (ET 1991); and Dungan 1999. Stoldt's (1980) history should be used in consultation with the works he cites, since he often quotes them partially or *contra sensum auctoris*. Linnemann's book (1992) is virtually worthless: she ignores most of the technical literature on the Synoptic Problem of the last two centuries and misrepresents much of what she does report.

source-critical theories advanced from the eighteenth century until now, although several local studies have illumined various aspects of that history.[2]

Obviously it is impossible to undertake a full history of the Synoptic Problem here. Instead, I wish to sketch the horizon within which the Synoptic Problem first became an issue worthy of attention and the theological preoccupations which energized this inquiry and which eventually promoted the acceptance of the Two Document hypothesis and with it, the hypothesis of a Q source. The question is not so much *how* the 2DH came to dominate but *why* it did.

It was not an antiquarian interest in the sources of the Gospels nor a literary conundrum of how the Gospels were composed that gave birth to the Synoptic Problem. Instead, the issue was theological: how the Gospels could be used theologically once it was recognized that they painted four significantly different and potentially incompatible portraits of Jesus. On the heels of this recognition followed the imperative to formulate criteria that would allow the Gospels to be differentiated, either in terms of their historical priority or within a larger framework of theological development.

From Lessing to Holtzmann

REIMARUS AND THE CREDIBILITY OF THE GOSPELS

The idea of a source for the sayings of Jesus is not new. Over one hundred and sixty years ago Friedrich Schleiermacher (1768-1834) hypothesized the existence of a sayings collection used by Matthew (1832). What attracted his attention was the statement of Papias (*floruit* ca. 110 CE) that "Matthew compiled the λόγια ("oracles") in the Hebrew language and everyone interpreted them as they were able" (cited in Eusebius, *Hist. eccl.* 3.39.16). Unable to reconcile this description of Matthew's Gospel as Hebrew *logia* with the canonical Gospel of Matthew—which clearly was composed in Greek and is hardly a collection of "oracles"—Schleiermacher surmised that Papias was speaking of a collection of sayings of Jesus that canonical Matthew translated and used in Matthew 5–7; 10; 13:1-52; 18; 23–25. For its narrative materials, canonical Matthew used another source that Papias described as Peter's memoirs as collected by Mark, containing the things "said and done by the Lord" (cited in Eusebius, *Hist. eccl.* 3.39.15). Thus, for Schleiermacher, Gospel origins were to be located in *two* pre-canonical collections, one consisting largely of sayings and one of narratives (later to be called *Ur-Markus*).

Neither the concern to identify sources behind the Synoptic Gospels nor the problem of their pedigree was adventitious. It was the collapse of confi-

2. In addition to the works of Farmer and Meijboom (n. 1), see Devisch 1975; M. Lang 1993a 1993b; 1993c; 1993d; Peabody 1987; 1995; Reicke 1976; 1986:1–25; 1987; 1990.

dence in Protestant orthodoxy and its naive assumption that dogmatic statements could be derived from the biblical text that created an urgent need for a new approach. The architect of this collapse was Hermann Samuel Reimarus (1694–1768), whose essay, "The Purpose of Jesus and his Disciples," Gotthold Lessing published as the last in a series of anonymous "fragments." But the story begins even earlier.

From an early date, discrepancies among the Gospels were recognized (Merkel 1971). About 270 CE the pagan philosopher Porphyry composed *Adversus christianos*, in which he assembled lists of contradictions and implausibilities within the Gospels (Dungan 1999:89–97). Slightly after 400 CE the Porphyrian lists came to Augustine's attention and he composed in response *De consensu evangelistarum*, "On the Harmony of the Evangelists." In this work Augustine argued that the Gospels were written in canonical order and that each evangelist knew the work of his predecessor.[3] Disagreements among the Gospels only illustrated the fact that the evangelists (and the Holy Spirit) wished to provide different yet ultimately compatible depictions of Christ, Matthew focusing on royalty, Mark on humanity, Luke on priesthood, and John on divinity. Each evangelist knew the original sequence of historical events but sometimes chose other arrangements for pragmatic reasons. Some of the variations in detail were due to textual corruption and those that were not could be harmonized or explained simply as differences in idiom or as attempts to communicate the "mystical meaning" of the incident.[4]

By the sixteenth and seventeenth centuries, what was supposed to be the "Augustinian" solution—that the Gospels were composed in canonical sequence and that Luke used *both* Mark and Matthew and that John used all three[5]—was normative, finding such distinguished champions as Martin

---

3. Augustine, *De consensu evangelistarum libri quattuor* 1.2.3 (CSEL 43:3): isti igitur quattuor evangelistae universo terrarum orbe notissimi . . . hoc ordine scripsisse perhibentur: primus Mattheus, deinde Marcus, tertio Lucas, ultimo Iohannes, unde alius eis fuit ordo cognoscendi adque praedicandi, alius autem scribendi. "Therefore those four evangelists who are most notable throughout the entire world . . . are believed to have been written in the following order: first Matthew, then Mark, thirdly Luke, and finally John." 1.2.4 (CSEL 43.4): horum sane quattuor solus Mattheus Hebraeo scripsisse perhibetur eloquio, ceteri Graeco. et quamvis singuli suum quendam narrandi ordinem tenuisse videantur, non tamen unusquisque eorum velut alterius praecedentis ignarus voluisse scribere repperitur vel ignorata praetermisisse, quae scripsisse alius invenitur, sed sicut unicuique inspiratum est non superfluam cooperationem sui laboris adiunxit. "Of these four, only Matthew is said to have been composed in Hebrew; the others were in Greek. And although each may appear to have retained a certain order of events proper to himself, yet in fact each writer chose to write not in ignorance of what his predecessor had done, or left out as unknown what the other writer is found to have included; on the contary, in accordance with the inspiration proper to each, each refrained from adding anything superfluous to his labour."

4. See the discussion of Augustine's interpretive strategies in Dungan 1999:116–36.

5. H. de Jonge (1992a; 1992b) points out that Augustine (above, n. 3) uses the singular (alterius praecedentis, "the other one, namely, his predecessor") rather than the plural, and

Chemnitz (1593) and Hugo Grotius (1641). Most of their contemporaries, Protestant and Catholic, agreed and more than a century later Reimarus simply took over the "Augustinian" view from the prolegomenon to John Mill's *Novum Testamentum* (1707).[6]

Yet a key shift in the understanding of the Gospels had occurred. For Augustine, neither the differences in the sequence of pericopae nor differences in the wording in parallel accounts constituted real contradictions, for these only illustrated the variations that are naturally to be expected in four equally inspired accounts. Sequential and verbal variation could not compromise the truth of the narratives.[7] Given this view, it was a relatively simple matter to construct a harmony of the Gospels and thus to produce a life of Jesus.[8] By the sixteenth century, however, Augustine's approach to sequential and verbal disagreements came under pressure from a new verbally based doctrine of inspiration. Andreas Osiander's *Harmonia evangelica* (1537) insisted that even small variations in seemingly parallel accounts were significant and indicated different historical events. Thus he desynchronized pericopae that earlier harmonists had treated as parallel, a policy that produced in his synopsis and those that followed him a string of absurd repetitions. Thus Osiander, for example, had three healings of blind men near Jericho, three centurions' sons healed, three anointings of Jesus, and the Temple cleansed three times.[9]

---

hence probably favored a straight line solution (Matthew → Mark → Luke), if indeed he intended to draw literary critical conclusions—which de Jonge rightly doubts (see chap. 1 n. 38). Peabody (1983) contends that Augustine's assertion that in *De consensu evangelistarum* 4.10.11 that Mark is the "companion of Matthew" and "walks with both" (cum ambobus incedit) Matthew and Luke implies that Augustine believed that Mark used both Matthew and Luke. De Jonge (1992b:420 n. 38) and Tuckett (1990:51 n. 15), however, are right in concluding that Augustine was not discussing literary relationships in that text, but only the contrast between the Synoptics, epitomized by Mark, which focus on the humanity of Jesus, and John, whose interest lies on the divinity of Christ.

6. Reimarus (1780–68) 1972, 2:530–31, 533, 539. See the discussion of this point in H. de Jonge 1992b:411–12, 417.

7. *De consensu evangelistarum* 2.12.28 (CSEL 43:129): quod ad doctrinam fidelem maxime pertinet, intellegeremus non tam verborum quam rerum quaerendam vel amplectendam esse veritatem, quando eos qui non eadem locutione utuntur, cum rebus sententiisque non discrepant, in eadem veritate constitisse adprobamus. "As far as faithful doctrine is concerned, we understand that it is the truth of the things themselves rather than mere words that is to be sought and embraced; for when [the evangelists] do not employ the same locution, if they are not discrepant as far as the facts or the sentiments themselves are concerned, we accept them as abiding by the same truth."

8. Augustine did not produce a harmony of the Gospels; by 1800, however, Fabricius (1790–1809, 4:882–89) could count almost 150 harmonies.

9. See the discussion of pre-Griesbach synopses in McArthur 1966:85–101 and M. Lang 1993b. The first to compile a synopsis with the Gospels arranged in three parallel columns was Jean Calvin (1555, ET 1972). Calvin was not concerned to produce a life of Jesus, a fact that gave him considerable freedom in the arrangement of parallels and allowed him to abandon the procedure of the harmonies, which used the Fourth Gospel as the overall frame. All of the

This view of the Gospels made an easy target. In his final fragment, Reimarus mounted a full-scale attack on the historicity of the Gospels and, by extension, the dogma that was supposed to flow from the Gospel accounts. The Gospels could not be taken as expressions of Jesus' intentions, for the disciples had systematically and fraudulently transformed Jesus' simple (and not especially unique) piety into a fantastic account of miracles, prophecies, angels, the resurrection and the Parousia.[10]

Reimarus's method was naive but devastatingly effective. He turned the approach of the conservative harmonists against itself, pitting the plain sense of one gospel against the plain sense of another, thereby assembling a long list of contradictions and incongruities. Harmonization was impossible and Osiander's expedient led to gross absurdities. Since Reimarus accepted the "Augustinian" model, which did not attempt to establish a literary and historical hierarchy among the Gospels, Reimarus did not try to determine which of the various versions of a story or saying was the earliest. Instead he took the contradictions he had identified as indications that all the Gospels were falsifications of the portrait of Jesus. Jesus' real intention (*Zweck*) could be fathomed only by understanding contemporary Jewish eschatological expectations. Reimarus thus employed literary criticism to deconstruct and discredit the Gospels and historical comparison to reconstruct a Jesus whose aims were at variance with those claimed for him by his followers.

The wedges that Reimarus had driven among the Gospels and between the Gospels and Jesus would prove impossible to extract. Shock waves were felt not only by the orthodox at whom Reimarus had aimed his attack but by scholars who had no investment in orthodox dogmatism. The response elicited by Reimarus has been programmatic for Synoptic studies in the succeeding two centuries. On the one hand, a concerted effort was made to define the literary relationship among the Gospels, not in the Augustinian sense of literary complementarity but in a genealogical manner. Such a genealogy would allow the disagreements among the Gospels to be refereed by an appeal to the "more original" version. Key contributions in this regard were made by Lessing himself and by Eichhorn and Herder, whose solutions invoked lost sources behind the Gospels, and by Griesbach, who sought to determine a literary (and hence historical) hierarchy among the extant Gospels. On the other hand, Lessing also recognized that Reimarus's narrow and literalist reading of the Gospels did not do them justice: the Gospels were not the *sources* of early Christian theology but *expressions* of that theology. Their "truth" or adequacy did not depend upon—and hence

synopses that followed Calvin and preceded Griesbach, however, reverted to the use of John and were in fact "harmonies in the form of a synopsis" (M. Lang 1993b:603).

10. Reimarus 1778 (ET 1970:67–68 [=I 7]) describes Jesus' *sole* intention as "man's repentance, conversion and betterment, insofar as these consist of a true inner and upright love of God, of one's neighbor, and of all that is good."

viewed in the context of the larger sweep of ecclesiastical and dogmatic history in which they were embedded.

The same year he published Reimarus's final fragment, Lessing himself
composed a response (published posthumously in 1784). As its title, "New
Hypothesis concerning the Evangelists Regarded as Merely Human Historians," suggests, Lessing was one with Reimarus in rejecting the naïveté of
orthodoxy's use of the Bible. Nevertheless, it was Reimarus who was naive
in assuming that contradictions among the Gospel accounts justified his vil-
ification of the disciples and his conclusion that the Gospel accounts were
sheer fabrications.

Lessing suggested that the *Gospel of the Hebrews* or the *Gospel of the
Nazarenes* mentioned by Epiphanius and Jerome was an extensive Aramaic
proto-gospel—existing in several different versions—from which the canonical Gospels were translated (see figure 21a).[11] He accounted for Papias's
statements about Matthew quite differently than Schleiermacher would,
arguing that Matthew had been associated with this Gospel because he had
been the first to *translate* the Aramaic Gospel into Greek and because his
version was the most complete. The original Aramaic Gospel, however, was
not the work of Matthew but of a wider group and originally bore Jerome's
other designation *evangelium iuxta apostolos* ("the Gospel according to the
Apostles"). By positing an *Urgospel* which each of the evangelists used, but
used differently, Lessing both allowed for the differing Gospel accounts and
implied a more reliable antecedent:

> For we need only remind ourselves of the actual origins of the Gospel of the
> Nazarenes—from honest people who had had personal converse with Christ,
> and who thus must have been completely convinced of Christ as man, and
> apart from Christ's own words, which they had more faithfully impressed upon
> their memory than clearly grasped in their understanding, could not relate any-
> thing about him which could not have been true of a mere man, though doing
> miracles by an endowment of power from on high. (Lessing 1784, ET
> 1956b:79)

As Barth observed, Lessing had posited a Gospel to serve as "the historical truth with the power of proof *before* the Bible" (1972:256). But Lessing

---

11. Lessing was also first to recognize that the Fourth Gospel belonged to a completely different class. Like the Synoptics, John had used the *Gospel of the Nazarenes*, but he had transformed it into "the Gospel of the Spirit" which "gave the Christian religion its true
consistency" (1784, ET 1956b:81). His characterization of John implied that it was less valuable for historical data about Jesus. This distinction, however, introduced a new phase of Jesus
scholarship which would debate whether John or the Synoptics was the better starting point
for a life of Jesus, a debate which lasted until Strauss's attack on Schleiermacher (Strauss 1865,
ET 1977), who thought that the Fourth Gospel was a better source than the Synoptics for his
life of Jesus (1864, ET 1975:37–44), notwithstanding his analysis of Papias's statements (see
above).

Figure 21
Lessing, Eichhorn, and Herder

Figure 21a: Lessing

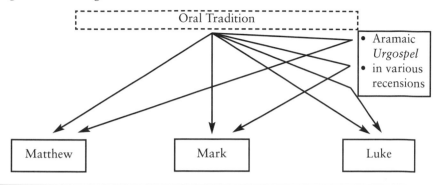

Figure 21b: Eichhorn

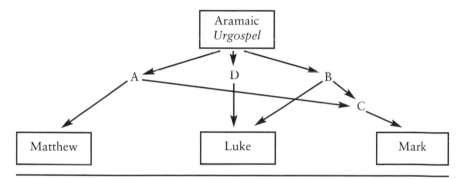

Figure 21c: Herder

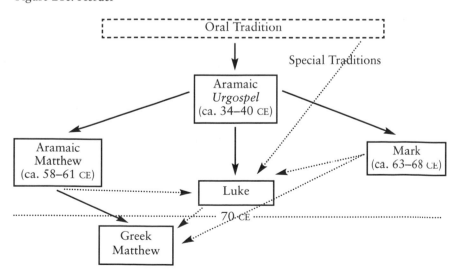

also distinguished the question of the historicity of the Gospels from that of the truth of the Christian religion: "the accidental truths of history can never become the proof of necessary truths of reason."[12] The rule of faith (*regula fidei*) existed both before and independently of all New Testament documents and after them, serving as the criterion for their inclusion in the canon (1778, ET 1956a:62–63). This *regula fidei* was not susceptible to historical proof or disproof. Rather, its truth and power are verified intuitively as they were grasped by the subject. In this sense history itself—that is, eighteen hundred years of reception and recognition of Christianity—becomes the only proof possible (1777, ET 1956c:55). Lessing viewed history as the process of education of the human race, so that, anticipating Hegel and nineteenth-century idealism, history itself was revelation.

Lessing's notion found an elaborate embodiment in the work of Johann Gottfried Eichhorn (1752–1827), who also traced the Synoptic gospels back to an Aramaic *Urgospel*. In order, however, to account for the complex combination of agreements and disagreements among the Gospels, Eichhorn posited four intermediate documents (figure 21b).[13] His theory was so complex that it found few adherents. But Eichhorn articulated a critical principle that would command more approval when he argued that certain portions of the Gospels, notably the infancy accounts, represented later embellishments of the *Urgospel*. The goal of Synoptic criticism was to reconstruct the *Urgospel* and "to reduce the Gospels solely to their apostolic content and to free them again from the additions and embellishments that were made at a later time in the course of their reworking."[14] This critical task was not just historically possible; it was theologically responsible and apologetically urgent:

> What articles of faith would be endangered? What doctrine would the Christian religion have to give up? If a few theological speculations should get into trouble and lose the apparent support on which they have heretofore rested, what harm can come of that? Should the inner credibility and truth of the gospel story be abandoned, or exposed to the mockery of witty or witless opponents of religion, in order to maintain a few theological speculations?[15]

While Lessing and Eichhorn met the challenge of Reimarus with a reliable Aramaic document underlying the Gospels, Johann Gottfried Herder (1744–1803), influenced by recent hypotheses regarding the oral character of the Homeric epics, argued that the *Urgospel* was oral (figure 21c). The

---

12. Lessing 1956c:53; cf. H. Allison 1966:96.

13. Eichhorn (1794) posited several revisions of the *Urgospel*: A (the main source of Matthew); B (the main source of Luke); C (a combination of A and B that served as the basis for Mark); and D (another revision of the *Urgospel*, to explain the Matthew–Luke agreements against Mark).

14. Eichhorn 1804–27, 1:458; quoted by Kümmel 1972:79.

15. Eichhorn 1804–27, 1:458–49; quoted by Kümmel 1972:79.

differences among the Gospels resulted from individual performances of a "fixed sacred Saga" in which sayings and deeds of Jesus variously arranged in a schema defined by the three "heavenly signs," baptism, transfiguration, and resurrection (1796).[16] For this reason Herder rejected harmonization, insisting on the individual complexion of each Gospel. Of the three Synoptics, Mark most closely approximated oral style:

> No gospel had so few scribal characteristics and so much of the *living voice of a narrator* as [Mark]. Hence the pervasive use of "and" or "and immediately" or "and he said to them" that begins every clause, as well as the Syrianisms which are found in Codex Beza and the old Latin versions. It is the popular tone of a Palestinian narrator—hence at various points, the lists of wonders that Jesus performed, of illnesses that he healed, serving as transitions and summaries; and again, in the narration of *individual* wonders, the numerous small details which are natural to a narrator. Matthew and Luke group such accounts together, for they are not *speaking*, but writing. (1796 [1994]:688–89, emphasis original)

The genealogies, infancy stories, and temptation account likewise bore the impress of the "living rhapsodist." Instead of stressing the unhistorical character of these items, however, Herder, anticipating form criticism, emphasized how the evangelists' artful use of these materials—and indeed all the Gospel stories—advanced key theological expressions. The varying arrangement and complexions of the Synoptics in no way detracted from their theological value. For, like Lessing, Herder rejected the view that the norms of faith were derived from the writings of the New Testament; on the contrary, the *regula fidei* was chronologically and logically prior to the Gospels, even the *Urgospel* (1796 [1994]:674–75).

The final key development came from Johann Jacob Griesbach (1789–90), himself already a distinguished textual critic. Two years before the appearance of Reimarus's final fragment, Griesbach had published what would be the first modern synopsis of the Synoptic Gospels (1776).[17] It allowed careful comparison of the Gospels, both in the wording and in the sequence of pericopae. Griesbach saw that the Fourth Gospel was significantly different from the Synoptics and so omitted it from his synopsis. This omission portended a significant shift in agenda: the issue to be solved was not deciding how to force four Gospels into a single historical narrative, as the harmonists had attempted to do. Instead, the issue was the *literary*

---

16. Herder (1797) thought that Mark produced an Aramaic version of the oral gospel (ca. 34–40 CE), later translating it into Greek in Rome (ca. 63–68) (1797:394–95). Matthew composed his own gospel, using Aramaic Mark, about 58–61, and translated it into Greek after 70. Luke also translated the Aramaic *Urgospel* prior to 70. In order to account for verbal agreements among the Gospels in Greek, Herder argued that Luke was aware of Mark's Greek, and that Matthew knew both Luke and Mark (Greek). See Schmithals 1985:81.

17. Actually, the *Synopsis* appeared in 1774 as part of Griesbach's *Libri historici Novi Testamenti graece* (Halle 1774) but was printed as a separate volume two years later.

relation of the three gospels that were most similar. The preface served notice of his complete rejection of the harmonizing expedient:

> I doubt very much that it is possible to compose a harmonious narrative from the books of the evangelists that accords with reality with regard to chronology and is constructed on sure footings. How could it be, when none of the evangelists anywhere has followed precisely the temporal sequence? and when there are insufficient indications by which one might decide which evangelist has departed from the chronological order, and in what points. Well, I confess to this heresy! (1776:viii)

In 1783, a year after the appearance of an essay by J. B. Koppe (1782) that refuted the "Augustinian" hypothesis, Griesbach published his own analysis of the resurrection accounts in which he proposed that Mark, not Luke, was the final Synoptic and that Mark had conflated Matthew and Luke. A more comprehensive outline of his hypothesis followed in 1789–90 in which he argued that the contents of Mark could be explained on the supposition that Mark alternately followed Matthew, then Luke, and at various points conflated what he saw in his two sources (figure 22a).

Griesbach was not the first to make this proposal. He seems to have known a similar hypothesis of Henry Owen (1764). But in the wake of Reimarus's challenge Griesbach's hypothesis acquired a crucial apologetic function. By rejecting harmonization Griesbach refereed the disagreements among the Gospels by proposing a literary pedigree and implicitly, at least, a historical ranking.[18] Griesbach also rejected the use of patristic testimonies regarding the Gospels, considering them to be sheer fabrications and conjectures—this in spite of the fact that he accepted without argument the eyewitness character of Matthew.

The models of Eichhorn, Herder, and Griesbach collided on a variety of points: whether patristic statements were valid starting points or not; whether one needed pre-Synoptic or only inner-Synoptic relationships to account for the final form of the Synoptics; and whether a documentary solution or an appeal to oral tradition was preferable. They agreed, however, in four key respects. First, harmonization was both impossible and illegitimate. In this Reimarus was correct. This recognition, however, was only the point of departure for more sophisticated solutions that avoided Reimarus's skepticism. Second, the differences between John and the Synoptics implied that two separate problems had to be distinguished within the problem of Gospel origins, the Synoptic Problem, and the Johannine Problem. Third, it was illegitimate to use the plain sense of one Gospel against another. On the contrary, the Synoptics could be comprehended adequately only by grasping the process of their composition. And finally,

18. M. Lang (1993b:606) observes that Griesbach's 1783 essay, by praising those who affirm the reliability of the resurrection stories, appears to be offering a critique of Reimarus, whose starting point was precisely the inconsistencies in the resurrection stories.

Figure 22
Griesbach, de Wette, and F. C. Baur

Figure 22a: Griesbach

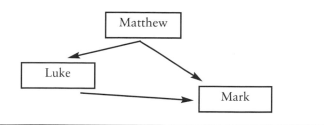

Figure 22b: de Wette

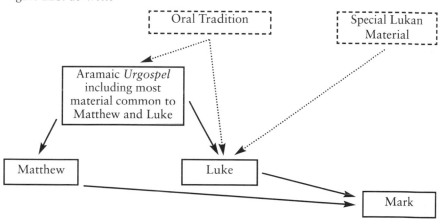

Figure 22c: F. C. Baur

The Gospel of the Hebrews
(=Papias's Aramaic
Matthew)

↓

ca. 130 CE   Matthew
a Jewish-Christian gospel,
with a few universalizing
tendencies (Matt 28:18-20)

ca. 140–50 CE   Luke
anti-Marcionite; a
revision of Matthew
uner the influence of
Pauline universalism

mid-second century CE   Mark
harmonistic; indifferent and
neutral; a reconciliation of the
Jewish-Pauline Controversy

3 Their dodge!

the relation between the text of the Gospels and dogmatics was reconfigured. The Gospels now belonged to the history of dogmatics, whose individual moments they variously and sporadically illustrated. History—compositional history and the history of Christian thought—had become the matrix in which the Synoptics should be viewed. The task of Synoptic criticism was to assist in describing a literary and theological "archaeology."

Reimarus had created an urgent need for a Gospel archaeology, either one that peered underneath the Gospels to now-lost sources or one that arranged the Gospels in discrete strata and thus created a model for understanding their commonalities and differences. By more recent standards, many of the arguments adduced in support of either type of solution were flawed: vague or dubious patristic references were used to manufacture primitive sources; and impressionistic and question-begging arguments were used to "establish" literary genealogies. None of this seemed to matter, for the pressing matter was to offer a response to Reimarus and his skepticism, which threatened the dogmatic edifice of Christian theology.

THE GOSPELS AND THE HISTORY OF DOGMA

By the beginning of the nineteenth century the basic choice in literary theories was threefold:[19] (a) "utilization hypotheses" (*Benutzungshypothesen*) such as Griesbach's, assuming the direct dependence of one Gospel upon another; (b) those that posited the independent use of an *Urgospel*, usually thought to be written in Aramaic (*Urevangeliumshypothese*, the "proto-gospel hypothesis"); and (c) variations of Herder's "oral tradition hypothesis."

Griesbach's version of the utilization hypothesis received little notice until it was adopted in 1825 by a student of Schleiermacher, Heinrich Saunier. Saunier offered an exposition of Mark's procedure on the Griesbach Hypothesis (GH), arguing that Mark was unintelligible apart from a knowledge of Matthew and Luke. The following year Griesbach's view of Mark was endorsed by another Berliner, Wilhelm Martin Leberecht de Wette (1780–1849), who undertook a painstaking demonstration of Mark's alternating use of Matthew and Luke (1826:128–71). De Wette, who had studied with Herder at Weimar as well as Griesbach at Jena, rejected Griesbach's view of the relation of Luke to Matthew. Instead he proposed that while Matthew was prior to Luke, both drew on oral tradition and an Aramaic *Urgospel* (figure 22b). Anticipating F. C. Baur, de Wette also mapped the theological terrain of primitive Christianity, distinguishing three types of belief: Jewish Christianity, to which Matthew (as well as the Petrine epistles, James, Jude, and the Apocalypse) belonged; Alexandrian or Hellenistic

19. This taxonomy is already standard in the introductions of Credner 1836:170–71; de Wette 1826:136, and Holtzmann 1863:15–67; cf. earlier, Gieseler 1818:32.

Christianity (John, Hebrews); and Pauline Christianity, whose universalism had influenced Luke (1813:19–20). The center of gravity of his Synoptic analysis, however, was on the secondary nature of Mark.[20]

Until 1860 the GH enjoyed wide acceptance—de Wette counted fifteen major advocates from 1805 to 1853,[21] and the more extensive bibliography of Neirynck and Van Segbroeck (1978) lists almost forty titles before 1880. Noteworthy also is the qualified endorsement of the GH by Roman Catholics—notably Johann E. Kuhn (1838) and Franz Josef Schwarz (1844) at Tübingen, Adalbert Maier (1852) at Freiburg, and Josef Langen (1868) at Bonn—even if they modified Griesbach's view of Mark by positing direct Petrine influence. But the fate of the hypothesis was significantly affected by what Reicke (1976; 1978) has termed its "dogmatic abuse" by the Protestant Tübingen school, most importantly D. F. Strauss (1808–74) and F. C. Baur (1792–1860). It has been suggested, in fact, that the eventual demise of the GH had more to do with this "abuse" than it did with the merits or demerits of the hypothesis itself.[22]

Tübingen's Appropriation of the Griesbach Hypothesis

Despite its title, Strauss's *The Life of Jesus, critically examined* (1835–36, ET 1972), was less interested in recovering a life of Jesus than it was in documenting and interpreting the use of myth in Gospel narratives. Unlike most of his predecessors, for whom the recognition of the mythic character of biblical narratives robbed them of dogmatic import, Strauss treated myth positively. Myth was not a pejorative term; on the contrary, mythic narrative, though unhistorical, was the product of an *idea*, and the key idea at work in the Gospels was that of "God-manhood." Strauss's debt here is usually thought to be to Hegel, who understood history as the progressive and dialectical realization of Absolute Spirit and the Incarnation as a key moment in this realization.[23] Strauss indeed counted himself among the "left-Hegelians," denying that the Absolute could be realized in any historical individual. The extent to which the historical Jesus realized "God-man-

---

20. See further, Reicke 1978:58–62. De Wette's *Introduction to the New Testament* was very influential, being reprinted five times during de Wette's lifetime, translated into English (1858) and reissued in an expanded edition in 1860.

21. De Wette [6]1860:150–52.

22. Farmer 1964:58: "The real enemy [of liberal theology] was the Tübingen school and only incidentally the Griesbach hypothesis, which Baur had accepted"; more cautiously, 1980b:5–6; Stoldt 1980:227–35; Kiwiet 1991. Reicke (1987:21) is more tentative on this point.

23. Hegel 1827 [1984], 312: "the substantiality of the unity of divine and human nature comes to consciousness for humanity in such a way that a human being appears to consciousness as God, and God appears to it as a human being." 314: "There are two conditions for this appearance. The first is that consciousness can achieve this content, this substantial unity, the consciousness of which is given and which is its reconciliation. The second condition is the consciousness of the determinate form of this exclusive singularity [i.e., Christ as the God-man]."

hood" was irrelevant. What was important was that the *idea* of God-man-hood had entered human history:

> Faith, in her [*sic*] early stages, is governed by the senses, and therefore contemplates a temporal history; what she [*sic*] holds to be true is the external, ordinary event, the evidence for which is of the historical, forensic kind. . . . But mind having once taken occasion by this external fact, to bring under its consciousness the idea of humanity as one with God, sees in this history only the presentation of that idea; the object of faith is completely changed; instead of a sensible, empirical fact, it has become a spiritual and divine idea, which has its confirmation no longer in history but in philosophy. (1835–36, ET 1972:780–81)

In fact Hegel's influence appears only at the end of the volume, not in the analytical portions where other influences were more decisive.[24] Eichhorn and de Wette had already recognized the pervasive presence of myth in the Hebrew Bible and Eichhorn had even identified mythical aspects of the Gospels, if only to set them aside as nonapostolic. Strauss was critical both of the failure to extend mythic analysis to the Gospels as a whole and of what he regarded as a misunderstanding of myth itself. At the same time he was encouraged by several obscure articles which appeared between 1796 and 1832 arguing that key Gospel narratives, especially from the infancy, temptation, and transfiguration accounts,[25] represented the clothing of religious ideas drawn from the Hebrew Bible in historical forms. Strauss's achievement was to apply this principle consistently and systematically to the whole of the Gospels.

The enfant terrible of Tübingen was no source critic, however. He simply declared his allegiance to the GH, citing Griesbach as having demonstrated the hypothesis adequately but dismissing Schleiermacher's analysis of Papias as strained (1835–36, ET 1972:71). Indeed source-critical considerations played almost no role in Strauss's volume apart from the fact that the use of the GH enabled him to begin with the Matthaean (and Lukan) birth narratives and thus to see in the two earliest Gospels mythological content right from the beginning. Schweitzer later explained that Strauss's animus toward Mark—whom he dismissed as having invented graphic details and exaggerated the miraculous (1835–36, ET 1972:448)—had to do with Strauss's rejection of interpreters such as Paulus who had relied heavily on Mark's descriptions for their historicizing and rationalist accounts of the miracles (Schweitzer 1910:88).

Like his notorious student, F. C. Baur was less concerned to reconstruct a portrait of the historical Jesus than he was to discern the theological tendencies immanent in early Christian literature and to situate those ten-

---

24. See H. Harris 1973:259–73. That Strauss's mythical principle was essentially independent of Hegel is also the conclusion of Hartlich and Sachs 1952:121–47.

25. Especially Anonymous 1816; Usteri 1832, discussed in H. Harris 1973:266–70.

dencies with the greater sweep of the history of dogma.[26] Baur's lasting contribution and that of the Tübingen school was a comprehensive theory of the history of dogma based on the fundamental opposition between Jewish Christianity and Paulinism and the eventual resolution of this conflict in Catholicism. This opposition not only could be seen in Paul's letters themselves, as one of his earliest essays on 1 Corinthians (1831) tried to demonstrate, but extended throughout the first two centuries.[27]

When in 1847 Baur turned to the Synoptics, he adopted the GH, although not primarily for the literary-critical reasons that Griesbach or de Wette had proposed. Instead, "tendency criticism" confirmed its adequacy: the "indifferent and neutral" character of Mark and its harmonistic nature were consistent with a date after the midpoint of the second century.[28] Matthew was clearly of a Jewish-Christian pedigree and was therefore the earliest Gospel.[29] Matthew preserved much of the character of his Jewish-Christian source, but had introduced a few elements of universalism (Matt 28:18-20). Luke represented an irenic blend of Pauline and Jewish elements, written in response to Marcion's use of an earlier draft of Luke, but incorporating a decidedly Pauline and universalist outlook[30] (see figure 22c). Baur saw in Matthew 24 an allusion to the Bar Kochba Revolt of 132–35 CE and so dated Matthew to that era. Luke, consequently, came later and Mark's harmony, sometime after 150 CE.[31]

Strauss and Baur had moved the debate far beyond the initial reaction to Reimarus—Strauss, by offering a positive interpretation of the mythic elements of the Gospels, and Baur, by proposing a framework within which to resolve the varying perspectives taken in New Testament documents and a model for grasping their mutual relations. Baur's concentration on the "tendency" of each of the Gospels anticipated by more than a century the development of redaction criticism[32] and his oppositional model for understanding the landscape of primitive Christianity finds many echoes today.

26. Baur 1847:73: "Since all history is transmitted to us by way of the author who recounts it, the primary question is not to what degree some story informs us about reality, but in what relation this story stands to the consciousness of the author. Through the mediation of the author the historical data becomes for us objects of research, which is true also for the criticism of Gospel history."

27. This view was worked out in Schwegler 1846. For a discussion, see H. Harris 1975:198–207.

28. Baur 1847:567; cf. H. Harris 1975:209–13; Baird 1992:258–69.

29. Baur (1847:571) saw Papias's statements on Matthew as confirmation of his view and was even prepared to admit that there may have been an earlier Aramaic collection ("the Gospel of the Hebrews") that formed the basis of Greek Matthew.

30. Baur's view of Luke was influenced by the earlier analysis of Luke by E. Zeller 1843b.

31. See also Baur 1851:110. A convenient summary of Baur's dating of all NT books is given in H. Harris 1975:237.

32. In 1846 Baur credited Strauss with first having rejected harmonization in favor of attending to the peculiarities of the Gospels individually: it is necessary "to investigate the particular tendency . . . of each of the four gospels" (596).

Reactions to the Griesbach Hypothesis

The adoption of the GH by Strauss and Baur had a profound effect on the fate of the hypothesis. In 1850 Adolf Hilgenfeld—not a proponent of the GH—could observe that it was the majority opinion of scholars (1850:8); yet scarcely ten years later support for the hypothesis had all but collapsed. Stoldt claimed that the opponents of Strauss and Baur "preferred to strike at [Strauss] indirectly, by endeavoring to disprove his source theory" and that Griesbach, consequently, "got his ears boxed posthumously" (1980:227). This is a highly dubious claim, since the key views of the Tübingen school did not depend on the GH. Nevertheless, the endorsement of the GH by Tübingen scholars, both Protestant and Catholic, initially had a buoyant effect on the fortunes of the GH and the collapse of Baur's school affected it adversely.

The period leading up to the 1848 liberal revolution and its failure the following year was one of profound intellectual ferment and bitter conflict. Strauss's *Life of Jesus* unleashed a storm of protest that cost him an academic career. Baur spent his career enmeshed in theological and personal struggles with the orthodox Ernst W. Hengstenberg (Berlin) and the pietist August Tholuck (Halle).[33] While Hengstenberg paid no attention to the Synoptic Problem, Tholuck attacked both Strauss and the GH, describing it as "laughable" (without, however, ever engaging Griesbach's arguments).[34] Even C. H. Weisse's careful response, whose title *Die evangelische Geschichte: Kritisch und philosophisch bearbeitet* expressly evoked Strauss's volume, did not devote significant space to a refutation of the GH. Weisse was more exercised about Herder's tradition hypothesis, which allowed for a long period of oral development of Gospel traditions, and saw this as the real basis of Strauss's views.[35] Weisse apparently simply accepted Lachmann's observations that on Griesbach's view, Mark was a "bungling dilettante, unsure of his way, borne hither and thither between Matthew's and Luke's Gospel by boredom, desire, carelessness, folly or design."[36] Nothing more was needed by way of refutation.

Weisse had no interest in maintaining the absolute historicity of the Gospels and was by no means opposed in principle to Strauss's mythological interpretation. He declared that Mark "is not like the work of an eyewitness nor is it like the work of someone who had the immediate opportunity to fill in the gaps through a careful, searching examination of eyewitnesses . . ." (1838, 1:69). Like others of his day, he suggested that various narratives such as the temptation story or the transfiguration were transformations of metaphorical expressions and hence should not be read

33. See Bigler 1972; H. Harris 1975; Massey 1983.
34. Tholuck 1838:248, 257. See Baird 1992:285.
35. Weisse 1838, 1:4, 10; cf. Reicke 1977:358.
36. Lachmann 1835, ET Palmer 1966–67:372; Weisse 1838, 1:39.

naively as history. What he disliked was Strauss's late dating of the Gospels and the thoroughgoing nature of his mythological interpretation. Equally, he rejected what he saw as the consensus of contemporary theology following Schleiermacher to base an "aesthetic-historical" conception of the person of Christ on the Gospel of John. As a philosopher he insisted that "the picture of the divine personality of the savior . . . [to which] the individual can give living expression in his own soul" must be discovered not only in the elaborated and reformulated image of Christ in the church, but also in "the individual, historical figure of the personal Christ" (1838, 2:501). As a historian, he concluded that Mark provided the best access to this figure. Mark was not the latest of the Gospels, as Strauss and Baur supposed, but the earliest. In support of this conclusion, Weisse cited the vivid imagery of the Gospel, its Semitic style, and its "Petrine" character (1838, 1:67–68). It was more likely, Weisse argued, that Semitisms and vivid language would be eliminated in the course of editing than that they would be added.

The same year that Weisse published his answer to Strauss, Johann Kuhn, then professor of Catholic exegesis at Tübingen and strongly influenced by Hegel, published *Das Leben Jesu, wissenschaftlich bearbeitet*, in which he tried to show, against Strauss's historical skepticism, that the messianic consciousness of Christ could be formed in a Jewish milieu. Nevertheless, Kuhn accepted the GH and the posteriority of Mark even if he also criticized Griesbach's "mechanical" accounting for the production of Mark's Gospel (1838:33–34).

Thus the first reaction to Strauss, contrary to Stoldt's suggestion, did not take the form of an attack on Griesbach. Strauss invoked the GH only in passing and his program of mythological interpretation was hardly dependent upon that or any other source theory.[37] For that reason it was hardly relevant whether one only qualified Griesbach's theory (Kuhn) or rejected it in favor of Markan priority (Weisse); for it was Strauss's thoroughgoing historical skepticism that was under attack.

The GH was more important to Baur than it ever was to Strauss since it seemed to confirm Baur's view of the principal oppositions in the history of dogma. Horton Harris in fact surmised that Baur, who otherwise might have been expected to endorse Markan priority, could not do so because "he would have been forced to revise completely his whole tendency approach; for if he had misjudged the tendency of Mark, how could his judgment about the other New Testament books have been trusted?" (1975:213).

Baur seems to have known Griesbach only via the work of Saunier and adopted from him the view that Mark's omissions could be explained by his alternating use of Matthew and Luke (Baur 1847:544; Fuller 1978a:357).

---

37. Later, as support for the GH collapsed, Strauss (1864, ET 1879) felt obliged to offer a defense of the GH.

He offered additional criteria for determining the direction of dependence in the case of parallel narratives: a shorter account is secondary to a more detailed one when the former, despite its brevity, presupposes knowledge of the longer; abbreviation may lead to various difficulties (*Unklarheiten*), for example, the disciples' unmotivated fear in Mark 9:5; and a secondary gospel may fill out the narrative by adding details that his sources merely take for granted (Baur 1847:548–54; Fuller 1978a:358). On all counts Baur found Mark to be secondary, and characterized Mark as

> a writer who in an artful manner was clever enough to conceal the emptiness of his historical material, the poverty of his own information, on the one hand by abridging and summarizing a detailed portrayal, on the other hand by filling out and amplifying certain facts. . . . (1847:560; cf. Harris 1975:211)

Mark's omission of both Matthew's Sermon on the Mount with its Jewish-Christian tendencies and the allegedly Pauline features of Luke were indications of his "neutral" tendency (1847:562).

Baur's directional criteria, however, were easily reversible and hence, inconclusive. From within the Tübingen school, Adolf Hilgenfeld[38] published a book on Mark arguing on the basis of "tendency criticism" and literary-critical observations that Mark was prior, not posterior to, Luke (1850:8–30). Mark lacked distinctively Lukan tendencies and it was not Mark but Luke who had disturbed the balance (*Angemessenheit*). For example, Luke moved the Nazareth sermon (Luke 4:16-30), which recalls earlier miracles, to a point at which miracles had not yet been performed. For Hilgenfeld it was not that tendency criticism was wrong; rather, it was that Mark's medial position better accommodated the basic insights of the Tübingen school.[39]

Baur suffered another reverse when another Tübingener, Albrecht Ritschl, deserted in favor of Markan priority, albeit on rather insubstantial grounds.[40] Soon after, other members of the school, Karl Köstlin (1853) and Gustav Volkmar (1857), abandoned the GH in favor of various forms of Markan priority. These defections, coupled with the increasingly strained relations among Baur, Ritschl, and Hilgenfeld, the departure of several of the younger members of the school to pursue philosophical interests (E. Zeller, Planck) or from theology altogether (Schwegler), and the death of the

38. On the career of Hilgenfeld, see H. Harris 1975:113–26.
39. See Fuller 1978a:366: "Hilgenfeld thought that Mark stood halfway between Matthew and Luke and that Luke was reconciling Matthew and Mark by soft-pedalling the disciples' fear. The real issue therefore between Baur and Hilgenfeld is, which order of the gospels best does justice to the early history of Christianity as the Tübingen School understood it."
40. Ritschl 1851. Ritschl argued that Mark emphasized Jesus' secrecy commands and the incomprehension of the disciples, both of which are downplayed by Matthew and Luke, and that Matthew's quotations of the Old Testament are mixed, those shared with Mark being Septuagintal but those added by Matthew showing more influence of the Masoretic text. The first two arguments are reversible and hence, inconclusive. On the third, see below.

Tübingen journal, *Theologische Jahrbücher*, meant that by the time Baur died in 1860 his school had collapsed. There were few left to carry Gries-bach's torch.[41] Baur's successor at Tübingen, Carl Weizsäcker, was a Markan priorist.

In answering Stoldt and Farmer, C. M. Tuckett observed that for later members of the Tübingen school, "the Griesbach Hypothesis was by no means integral to the Tübingen school's theories, with regard to either their use of *Tendenzkritik* or to a skeptical attitude to the historicity of the Gospels" (1979:34). While this may strictly speaking be correct, Markan posteriority was associated sufficiently closely with Baur personally, the centre of the Tübingen school, for Hilgenfeld to be able to refer to it as a "school dogma" in a letter that he wrote to Baur in 1860 (H. Harris 1975:245).

It was in the work of Baur's erstwhile colleague at Tübingen, Heinrich Ewald, that opposition to Baur's theological views and Markan posterior-ity coalesced. Ewald, one of the "Göttingen Seven" expelled from Hannover in 1837 for their refusal to rescind allegiance to an earlier liberalizing con-stitution, had accepted an appointment at Tübingen (1838–48). In the con-text of the rising German nationalism of 1850s, he saw his own efforts as restoring the credibility of "German scholarship" after it had been com-promised by the Tübingen school. He even expressed the hope that his analysis of the Gospels would persuade the German public of the truth of Christianity and bring about German unity![42] Ewald's own solution, which involved a proto-Mark, the *logia* source, two editions of Mark, a "Book of Higher History," canonical Matthew, three intermediate Gospels, and finally Luke—ten documents in all!—was far too complicated to commend itself. His case for the primitive character of Mark—based on its vivid descriptions, lack of a consistent chronological framework, lack of infancy materials, and use of Aramaic words (1849:203–6)—was, nonetheless, con-vincing enough to "convert" Heinrich A. W. Meyer to the theory of Markan priority in the third edition of his commentary on Matthew (1853).[43]

<hr>

41. Neirynck's bibliography of the Griesbach Hypothesis (Neirynck and VanSegbroeck 1978) lists only ten items that appeared between 1863 and the publication of William Farmer's book in 1964.

42. H. Ewald 1848; 1849; 1850b; 1850a, esp. 1850a:vi, xviii–xix; cf. Reicke 1990:296.

43. Meijboom (1866:68; ET 1991:67) credits H. Ewald as the definitive influence on Ritschl and Tobler, stating that the latter had declared in 1858 that "after Ewald's conclusive exposi-tion" the Markan hypothesis should not longer be considered a "hypothesis." Neither state-ment is correct. As Farmer notes (1964:28), Ritschl was very critical of Ewald. And what Tobler actually said of Ewald is much more modest: "Following what Ewald has already basi-cally accomplished, I hope to show that the understanding of the origin, composition, and interrelationships of our canonical gospels should no longer be considered to be as uncertain and controverted as it still appears to be in the subjective pronouncements of the Tübingen school" (1858:10).

The GH suffered even more from the critiques of Bernhard Weiss (1827–1918) and H. J. Holtzmann (1832–1910). The main point of attack was not Luke's use of Matthew but the status of Mark as a late, conflated Gospel. Tuckett rightly notes against Stoldt that both B. Weiss and Holtzmann were perfectly aware that the Tübingen school and the GH were not coterminus. Hence they separated their arguments against advocates of the GH such as de Wette and Bleek from those against Baur and Strauss.[44]

Weiss first concentrated on the view of Mark's editorial procedure that the GH assumed. In particular he attacked Griesbach's suggestion that Mark, wishing to avoid the discourse material of Matthew and Luke, shifted from one source to the other when he encountered speech material.[45] After rehearsing Griesbach's argument, Weiss noted a variety of points (a) where Griesbach's solution simply did not supply satisfactory explanations of Mark's text, or (b) where Mark was inconsistent with the editorial procedure that Griesbach suggested (e.g., by including parabolic material from Luke), or (c) where Mark's compositional procedure would be unimaginably complex (1861:680–87). Weiss notes that on the GH Mark does not merely shift between Gospels at the end of long blocks but would have had to make numerous small insertions from Matthew even when he was following Luke as his main source, and vice versa.[46] Moreover, the reasons for Mark's preference of one Gospel over the other are anything but clear. Weiss concluded that "the hypothesis remains an abstract possibility that shrinks from every concrete test case" (686).

One of the attractions of the GH concerned instances where Mark's double expressions seem to have originated from a conflation of Matthew and Luke. A typical example is Mark 1:32, ὀψίας δὲ γενομένης, ὅτε ἔδυ ὁ ἥλιος, "when it was evening, when the sun had set," where Matthew (8:16) has ὀψίας δὲ γενομένης ("when it was evening") and Luke (4:40) has δύνοντος δὲ τοῦ ἡλίου ("when the sun had set"). Weiss, however, argued that Mark's double expression was neither tautological nor secondary but necessary and original: since for Mark, the incident occurred on the Sabbath (1:21), it was important to stipulate that the sun had set so that the fact that the sick now came to Jesus was explicable. Luke, who also dates the incident to a sabbath, preserved the mention of the setting of the sun, but in a form that betrays knowledge of Mark's genitive absolute (ὀψίας δὲ γενομένης). In Matthew, however, the healings do not occur on a sabbath, and thus it was not necessary for him to preserve the precise temporal reference (Weiss 1861:683).

In Weiss's view the GH made Mark's treatment of Luke puzzling:

---

44. Tuckett 1979:40; see B. Weiss 1861:680–89, 689–92; Holtzmann 1863:113.
45. Griesbach 1789–90, ET 1978:109–10.
46. So Holtzmann 1863:117. See below, n. 48.

Of the rich historical material that this gospel has beyond Matthew, [Mark] has taken over nothing except one exorcism that is hardly peculiar in comparison with the others (1:23-28), the brief notice about the first journey of Christ (1:35-38) and the selection of apostles (3:13-15), and the commissioning and return of the disciples (6:12, 13, 30, 31) as well as the story of the widow's mite (12:41-44); of the much richer discourse material, only the sayings of Christ in 9:38-40 and the group of sayings (4:21-25), which in Matthew are found differently located. . . . (1861:696)

Holtzmann echoed several of Weiss's points but added his own: if Mark used Matthew and Luke, one would expect that the favorite vocabulary of his two sources would appear in Mark. Mark, however, lacks Matthew's βασιλεία τῶν οὐρανῶν ("kingdom of the heavens"), ἐρρέθην ("it has been said"), ὥσπερ ("just as"), ἀδελφός (used of neighbors), καλεῖν (used of calling), ἡγεμών ("leader"), ἕως οὗ ("until"), κελεύειν ("order"), ὕστερον ("finally"), φρόνιμος ("wise"), and ἐν ἐκείνῳ τῷ καιρῷ ("at that time"), and numerous Lukanisms.[47] Such results, Holtzmann thought, posed insuperable obstacles to the view that Mark conflated Matthew and Luke for it is almost unimaginable that he could systematically eliminate the favorite vocabulary of his sources. He noted too that de Wette's explanation of how Mark worked through Matthew and Luke would have led to "unimaginable procedures."[48]

The criticisms of Weiss and Holtzmann went largely unanswered. In 1866 Hajo Uden Meijboom wrote a critical assessment of the Markan hypothesis

---

47. Holtzmann 1863:345. Holtzmann also drew upon the statistics of E. Zeller (1843a) compiled in support of the GH. Zeller (1843a:527–28) took the case of words or phrases that appeared in two gospels: in gospel "A" only where gospel "B" also evidenced them, but at several other points in gospel "B." He reasoned that the phrases were "characteristic" of gospel B and that A depended upon B. Zeller's results were mixed, with 78 words and phrases allegedly supporting Matthaean priority and 31 Markan priority. Despite the seemingly inconclusive nature of his statistics, Zeller declared that there was an "overburdening proportion" favoring Matthew. Tuckett (1979:69 n. 57) noted that Zeller's list includes many instances where a word that occurs once in Mark and twice in Matthew or twice in Mark and three times in Matthew is declared to be "characteristically Matthaean." Holtzmann, moreover, noted that Zeller's own admission that Luke's constant use of Matthew might have prompted him to take over and develop Matthew's vocabulary as his own could be used in support of Holtzmann's view that Matthew had been influenced by the vocabulary of A (Mark) (1863:353). The same point has been made by Goulder (1984:100) against Farmer's reiteration of Zeller's argument (see Farmer's reply [1984]). Yet as Tuckett points out (1995:35–36), Goulder himself uses the argument that he declared to be fallacious in his 1989 book on Luke.

Since Zeller's principle is reversible—the vocabulary in "A" appealed to the author of "B" who expanded its usage—it is invalid for determining the direction of dependence. For a critical but more positive evaluation of Zeller's contribution, see Peabody 1987:62–65.

48. Holtzmann 1863:117–18. E.g., Mark, who *ex hypothesi* was closely following Matthew from Mark 6:45—10:14, suddenly made additions from the parallel accounts in Luke 9:26, 39, 42, 45, and 48–50; and in Mark 1:22—3:6 where Mark was following Luke, he nonetheless omitted Luke 5:39 following Matthew.

which included a defense of the GH, but passed over the criticisms of Weiss and Holtzmann in silence.[49] Moreover, it was never published in anything but its dissertation form and evidently did not attain significant circulation until more than a century later when it was translated into English (1991). Meanwhile, support for the GH within the Tübingen school had collapsed and only a handful of supporters remained outside the school.[50]

The story of the Griesbach hypothesis is not a simple one. First articulated in the context of responses to Reimarus's attack on the theological utility of the Gospels, it achieved no great distinction. The GH was simply one among several ways of answering Reimarus. Saunier and de Wette placed the hypothesis on a firmer basis by means of careful literary argument and additional support was supplied by E. Zeller and Meijboom. But a key factor in its appeal was theological. In the hands of Strauss and especially Baur, the GH seemed to cohere with and to illustrate a particular understanding of the evolution of dogma.

The decline of the GH after 1860 is also a complex matter. While it is correct that the fate of the GH was intertwined with that of the Tübingen school, it is an error to assert that opponents of the Tübingen school preferred to attack the school indirectly through the GH. The GH was not just an inadvertent casualty of the anti-Tübingen reaction.[51] It was attacked by

49. The third part of Meijboom's dissertation (1866, ET 1991:151–206) is the least coherent, for he alternates between defending the GH and attacking the Markan hypothesis but without achieving comparative parity. His discussion of Griesbach's observation of Mark's alternating agreement with Matthew and Luke is perhaps the clearest available to date; but instead of continuing with a defense of Mark's procedure on the GH, he shifts to the problem that omissions of Markan material by Matthew and Luke create for the Markan hypothesis instead of the far more serious problems that Mark's omission of Matthaean and Lukan material pose for the GH. Then he tries to respond to Lachmann's criticism of the GH with a long apologia for the care the gospel writers took with their sources (165–71). He rightly criticizes proponents of the Markan hypothesis for drawing too many conclusions about the intentions of the later evangelists in their treatment of Mark. But he seems not to recognize that in order to render the GH plausible, the GH requires recourse to authorial intention even more than the 2DH (see chap. 1). Then, curiously, he attacks the implication of the Markan hypothesis that Matthew, for example, would have had to alternate between Mark and the *logia* (172), not noticing that the same criticism, mutatis mutandis, had been leveled at Griesbach by Weiss and Holtzmann (see the previous note). When he described Matthew as "tumbling through his sources," he merely echoed the very language that he had just rejected in Lachmann!

50. E. Zeller continued to support Markan posteriority (1864; 1865), but his transfer to the philosophical faculty at Marburg in 1849 diminished his role within the Tübingen school. Outside the school only a few wrote in support of the GH: Keim 1867–72, 1:86; Davidson 1868 (²1882:352–500, 533–84); Langen 1868 (²1873), 55–56, 60–61; Nippel 1876; Nösgen 1880:116–18; Pasquier 1911. Peabody (1995) provides an extremely useful account of Holtzmann's colleagues at Strasbourg and elsewhere, detailing the personal, institutional, and political events (especially the Franco-Prussian War) that contributed to the diminution of criticism of Holtzmann's hypothesis.

51. Compare the slightly different assessment of Tuckett (1979:43): "There seems thus to be little justification for the view that the demise of the Griesbach hypothesis was closely tied

Weiss and Holtzmann on grounds that had nothing to do with Tübingen. That not all of their criticisms were of equal force does not diminish the fact that they were also not answered.[52]

Could they have been answered? Perhaps. With Baur's death and Zeller's shift to philosophy, however, the GH lost the brilliant minds that might have offered adequate responses to Weiss and Holtzmann. Moreover, the influence of Sieffert's 1832 argument that placed Matthew beyond the eyewitness period coupled with the relative chronology implied by the GH (Matthew—Luke—Mark) almost inevitably put Matthew late in the first century and Luke and Mark much later.[53] This dating did not trouble Strauss or Baur, interested in elaborating the mythic nature of early Christian discourse or in describing a history of dogmatic evolution. With the birth of liberal theology, however, attention rapidly shifted from attempts to define a comprehensive theory of the history of dogma to the quest of the Jesus of history. Tübingen's historical skepticism and the dating of the Gospels implied by the GH posed obstacles to such a quest.

Holtzmann's *Die synoptischen Evangelien* signaled a resurgence of interest in the historical Jesus—the other target of Reimarus's attack and a casualty of Strauss's skepticism. In the opening paragraphs Holtzmann referred to Strauss and Baur, disapproving of both Strauss's reduction of the life of Jesus to the "mythmaking fantasies of the early church" and Baur's tracing of the Gospels to "the intentional literary activity of specific early Christian parties" (1863:3). In place of these Holtzmann proposed a conservative defense of the historical reliability of the Synoptics. His purpose was to "recover the historical figure of the one to whom Christianity owes not only its name and existence but whose person it has also made central

---

up with the demise of the Tübingen school, or with a desire to find a reliable tradition in the gospels. This may have been the case in the minds of those who sought to establish the theory of Markan priority, but if so it never reached the stage of being a significant factor in the arguments which were adduced to oppose the Griesbach hypothesis. There was a clear awareness that the Griesbach hypothesis and the Tübingen school were not to be identified without remainder on either side, and that many people adhered to Griesbach's hypothesis without sharing the presuppositions of the Tübingen school. What is true, and can be examined scientifically, is that specific arguments were brought against the Griesbach hypothesis considered in its own right."

52. Davidson (1868; [2]1882) offered his own defense of the GH, but without the sophistication of de Wette or Meijboom. Instead, after concluding that a literary relationship must exist among the Gospels, he gratuitously averred that Matthew most closely approximated the "exact chronological sequence" (1882:358) even though he placed the Sermon on the Mount "too early" (1882:386). Davidson's assumption of Matthaean priority, like Griesbach's, and his assumption that Luke "probably" would have used Matthew, implied that Mark must be in third place as a conflation of Matthew and Luke. Davidson replied to none of the objections voiced against the GH, and his own case was so assumption-laden that it is hardly surprising that it was not taken seriously.

53. On the influence of Sieffert's essay, see Farmer 1964:18–19, 22, 26.

to its unique religious outlook, in a way that satisfies all the impartial demands of the advanced historical-critical sciences" (1863:1).

Whether the GH could have been reconfigured and its component parts redated so as to respond to the altered theological sensibilities of the 1860s and 1870s is perhaps moot. The GH had been compromised by the theological company it kept, by the unanswered literary-critical objections leveled by B. Weiss and Holtzmann, and by its loss of advocates capable of mounting a convincing defense. For whatever reasons, some perhaps ideological and some literary, the GH simply lost support. Its demise after 1870 should not be laid at the feet of the Tübingen school, in spite of the fact that opposition to Tübingen was *one* factor in its demise. Though it was a literary hypothesis, constructed on literary-critical grounds, the GH was not immune from ideological use (or abuse). As its recent revival has amply demonstrated, the GH is also sufficiently independent of nineteenth-century theological concerns to be promoted on new literary grounds and for theological reasons which are virtually the antithesis of those of Strauss and Baur.[54]

THE SYNOPTICS AND THE LIFE OF JESUS: THE MARKAN HYPOTHESIS

The history of the Markan hypothesis and its corollary of a sayings source parallels in significant ways the history of the Griesbach hypothesis. Emerging from the ferment caused by Reimarus, Markan priority was advanced initially on literary grounds—in an effort to account for textual phenomena. Like the GH, it was generally ignored until, much later, its congeniality with certain theological interests was recognized. Although the 2DH survived much longer than the GH, its appeal, like that of the GH, sometimes had more to do with ideological considerations than with its logical architecture or the way it solved literary problems.

Part of Lessing's response to Reimarus was to challenge Reimarus's attempt to disconnect the Gospels from the history of dogma. For Lessing, inconsistencies in the Gospels could never gainsay the truth of the Christian faith. On the contrary, its truth was verified intuitively by the believing subject and reconfirmed repeatedly in eighteen hundred years of reception. Baur's brilliant theory of dogmatic development went a step further by coordinating the literary development of the Gospels with the rational unfolding of dogma. Thus he reconnected literary history with doctrine. The other part of Lessing's response to Reimarus involved the positing of

---

54. The revived Griesbach hypothesis has shed the earlier associations with a late dating of Matthew and with Baur's dogmatic project. Dungan (1983:427–34) argued that both Matthew and Luke were composed prior to 70 CE and Mark shortly after 70 CE. Farmer's 1994 monograph argued that the 2GH carries with it various historical and theological benefits, in the main by rooting eucharistic practice and the Petrine ministry in the early Jesus tradition and by minimizing the distance between Jesus and Paul (see above, p. 268 n. 3).

sources behind the Gospels and the wholly undefended claim that such sources were the product of "honest people who had had personal converse with Christ" (1784, ET 1956b:79). The appeal of this kind of approach rested on the desire to trace gospel origins to documents rooted in the immediate circle of Jesus' followers. It mattered less whether the final forms of the Gospels were dated early or late. Primitive gospel sources provided a means by which to account *historically* for the transmission of the Synoptic tradition and the origin of the Gospels.

Lessing's own proposal of a single *Urgospel* did not attract much of a following, perhaps because it was so speculative. Instead, two publications in 1832 initiated another development. That year Schleiermacher's essay on Papias's fragments appeared, positing a *logia* collection and a narrative source behind Matthew.[55] Then Friedrich Sieffert published an influential essay which argued that Matthew's Gospel did not belong to the eyewitness period (1832). This finding was no more a problem for Schleiermacher than it would later be for Strauss or Baur, since Schleiermacher's *Life of Jesus* (1864, ET 1975) was based more upon John than on the Synoptics.

The attraction of Schleiermacher's thesis lay not only in the idea of proto-gospels but in his connecting the two primitive sources with Papias's statements about Peter, Mark, and Matthew. His *logia* and his proto-Mark offered an anchor for the contents of the later Gospels in the eyewitness period. This mooring, moreover, seemed to be guaranteed by the external testimony of a patristic writer. According to Schleiermacher it was only Matthew, not Luke, who had access to these two sources. Unlike exponents of the 2DH, Schleiermacher did not think that Mark was early. For he too had been convinced by Griesbach (figure 23a).

Like Lessing's argument, Schleiermacher's was constructed almost exclusively on a credulous reading of patristic testimony. Three years later Karl Lachmann (1793–1851) turned to internal evidence and concluded from his examination of the order of the Synoptic tradition that canonical Mark better resembled the order of the primitive narrative gospel than either Matthew or Luke (1835; ET Palmer 1966–67). Lachmann accepted Schleiermacher's conclusions about the *logia* as "obviously true,"[56] as well as his supposition of a narrative source (figure 23b). But his examination of the content of the Synoptic tradition convinced him that Schleiermacher and Griesbach had underestimated the importance of Mark. When one compared the order of the pericopae in the Synoptics, the greatest degree of

---

55. Schleiermacher had not been the first to think that there was a sayings collection lying behind the Gospels. Thirty years earlier, the Lady Margaret Professor of Divinity at Cambridge, Herbert Marsh (1801, 3:161–409), proposed that the Synoptics derived from two sources, א (aleph), a Semitic proto-gospel, available both in Aramaic and in slightly differing Greek recensions, and a sayings collection, ב (beth), containing both the material common to Matthew and Luke and many of the parables and sayings used by only Matthew or Luke.

56. Lachmann 1835:577: ita veritas rei primo aspectu patet.

Figure 23
Schleiermacher, Lachmann, and Credner

Figure 23a: Schleiermacher

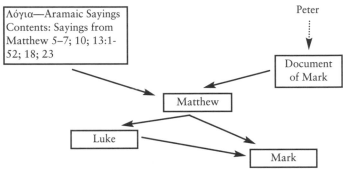

Figure 23b: Lachmann

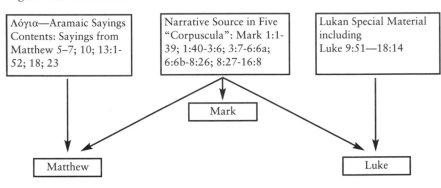

Figure 23c: Credner

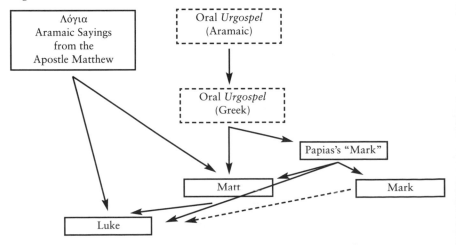

disagreement was registered between Matthew and Luke; Mark tended to agree with either one or the other. Lachmann concluded that Mark better represented the primitive order than Matthew or Luke. He did not commit the "Lachmann fallacy," as B. C. Butler (1951a) misleadingly christened the fallacious inference of Markan priority from the fact that Matthew and Luke do not tend to agree against Mark in the positioning of triple tradition material. Instead, Lachmann argued that in the cases of disagreements between Matthew and Mark, no good reason could be found for Mark's altering the order, but good reasons why the Markan (=Lukan) order would not suit Matthew's purposes. The same argument could be made mutatis mutandis for the Mark–Luke disagreements. Hence, as far as sequence was concerned, it was Mark, not Matthew or Luke, that stood closer to the primitive arrangement of materials.

Lachmann stood Griesbach's solution on its head, giving Mark pride of place. Now the road lay open for the emergence of the 2DH. In the next year, Karl Credner in Giessen suggested that the *Urgospel* used by Matthew, Mark, and Luke was none other than Papias's Mark. Credner also reckoned with the influence on Matthew and Luke of the oral proto-gospel used by Mark, with Luke's use of Matthew, and with the possible influence of Mark on Luke (1836:201–5) (figure 23c). Credner's solution accounted for the agreements of Matthew and Luke with Mark (via use of Papias' "Mark"), for the double tradition material (from the Λόγια source and Luke's use of Matthew), and even for the minor agreements of Matthew and Luke against Mark, since Papias's Mark may have differed from canonical Mark, and since Luke had direct access to Matthew. Thus Credner's model not only responded to an analysis of the patterns of agreements and disagreements in the Synoptics, but also seemed to derive support, however unearned, from Papias's testimony.

In 1838 two works appeared, consolidating the solutions of Lachmann and Credner. First, Christian Gottlob Wilke (1786–1854) attacked Herder's tradition hypothesis as it had been developed by Gieseler (1818) as well as Eichhorn's *Urgospel* hypothesis (figure 24a). The pattern and extent of the agreements and disagreements among the Synoptics excluded both possibilities. Curiously, it was not the verbatim and sequential agreements among the Synoptics that told against the tradition hypothesis, but the disagreements. Wilke assumed that an oral apostolic tradition would have attained too high a degree of fixity to allow for the degree of variation that is observed in the Synoptics. This variation is explicable, according to Wilke, with written sources, since these would allow greater intervention by the evangelists (1838:26–161). Wilke also noticed that in matters both of order and wording, Mark tended to be medial: Mark agreed with either Matthew or Luke (or both), and when Matthew or Luke departed from Mark, they did not agree with each other. But he rejected the possibility that this pattern of agreement resulted from Mark's conflation of Matthew and

Luke (Griesbach), for in that case Mark would not have been "an abbreviator or an epitomiser or an excerptor, but a castrator of the other texts—what else should one call the mutilator of borrowed sentences, the mixer of the mutilated?" (433).

In the same year Christian Hermann Weisse (1801–66), impressed by Sieffert, Schleiermacher, and Lachmann, made the case for Markan priority in great detail: canonical Mark and Papias's Mark were identical, for not only did Mark seem to be the common denominator between Matthew and Luke, but Mark also seemed more primitive. Whereas Wilke had explained the non-Markan material in Matthew and Luke by the supposition that Matthew used Luke,[57] Weisse argued that Luke had, like canonical Matthew, used both Mark and the *logia* source. With this the Two Document Hypothesis was born (figure 24b).[58]

Had Weisse's solution been embraced and developed, the discussion of the Synoptic Problem and Q might have more rapidly reached the consensus that was achieved only a century later with the publication of B. H. Streeter's *The Four Gospels* (1924). Despite the fact that Weisse wrote in response to Strauss, however, his solution did not immediately present a clear alternative, at least as far as the historical evaluation of the Gospels was concerned. Hilgenfeld later commented that Weisse dismissed too much of the Gospels as unhistorical for his opposition to Strauss to achieve a significant following (1854:11). Whether for this reason or because of the dominance of the Tübingen school, Weisse's 1838 precursor to the 2DH was ignored for a generation, as he himself was later to complain (1856:85).

When Weisse revisited the Synoptic Problem in 1856, he felt obliged to modify his hypothesis, reintroducing *Ur-Markus*. In his 1838 work, Weisse had expressed some embarrassment over the fact that the two initial pericopae in the *logia* source, Luke 3:7-9, 16-17; 4:1-13, were either not sayings *of Jesus* or not sayings at all (1838, 2:5). Moreover, the source also contained a narrative about the centurion's serving boy and the Beelzebul accusation. Weisse had relieved this embarrassment by suggesting that the sayings now attributed to the Baptist were originally dominical sayings about John and that the temptation story originated as a "parable" of Jesus that had been turned into a narrative (1838, 2:8, 17–26)—a suggestion that was at least as old as Schleiermacher's 1832 lectures on Jesus.[59] He solved

---

57. Wilke (1838:685) argued for Matthew's dependence upon Luke on the basis of the Sermon on the Mount/Plain. Since Luke's shorter version indisputably represented an older form, Matthew's longer version must be an expansion of Luke.

58. Weisse 1838, 1:34, 48, 54. Weisse (1838, 2:83) was undecided whether Matthew and Luke consulted the Sayings Source in Aramaic or in a Greek translation.

59. Schleiermacher 1864 [1832], ET 1975:153–55. Stoldt (1980:52–53) mistakenly treats Weisse's explanation of the origins of the temptation story as if it were Weisse's own coinage, designed to rescue his hypothesis from a serious "obstacle."

Figure 24
Wilke (1838), Weisse (1838), and Weisse (1856)

Figure 24a: Wilke (1838)

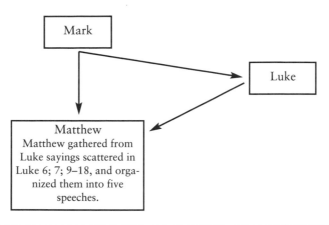

Figure 24b: Weisse (1838)

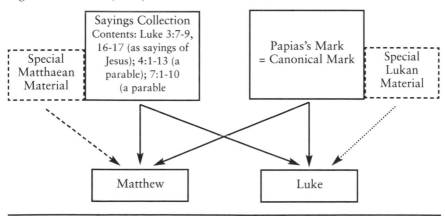

Figure 24c: Weisse (1856)

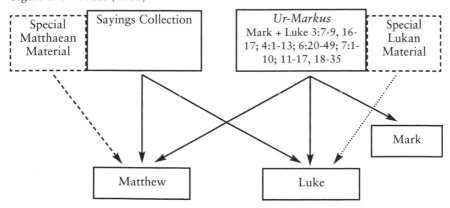

the problem of the healing of the centurion's serving boy similarly: it had been a parable that was converted into a narrative (1838, 2:53–55).

By the time he wrote *Die Evangelienfrage in ihrem gegenwärtigen Stadium* (1856) Weisse decided, evidently out of loyalty to Schleiermacher's understanding of *logia*, that it was better to attribute at least John's sayings (Luke 3:7-9, 16-17), the temptation story, and the story of the centurion, and probably also John's inquiry and related sayings (Luke 7:18-35), the Beelzebul accusation and an abridged version of the Sermon on the Mount, to an *Ur-Markus* (1856:156-57). Hence, canonical Mark abbreviated *Ur-Markus*, while Matthew and Luke fused *Ur-Markus* with the *logia* source (figure 24c).

Up to this time the Markan hypothesis was still overshadowed by the GH. Weisse's 1838 book had not attracted followers, and his 1856 book was not much more successful. The turning point in the discussion of the Synoptic Problem came seven years later with the publication of Holtzmann's *Die synoptischen Evangelien* (1863). Holtzmann is often credited with having established definitively the Two Document Hypothesis.[60] Yet Holtzmann's achievement itself requires careful assessment, for what he accomplished and what he was seen to have accomplished are quite different matters.

H. J. Holtzmann

Holtzmann's solution differs in significant respects from what later emerged with Wernle and Streeter. Rather than building on the simplicity of Weisse's 1838 solution, Holtzmann was influenced by Weisse's 1856 proposals, in particular, the notion of an *Ur-Markus*. Although canonical Mark was closer to *Ur-Markus* than the other Synoptics, it differed from *Ur-Markus* ("A") in five important respects: (1) At several points Mark contained obscurities that were produced by abbreviation;[61] (2) Mark betrays legendary—and hence secondary—elements not found in the parallel accounts (e.g., Mark 7:24-31); (3) Mark may have shortened the originally longer speeches of John the Baptist and Jesus; (4) the minor agreements of Matthew and Luke against Mark (Holtzmann lists 36) suggest that canonical Mark is secondary; and (5) at some points Matthaean and Lukan scenes

---

60. E.g., Sanday 1872:9; 1893a; Kümmel 1972:151. Albert Schweitzer, Holtzmann's erstwhile student at Strasbourg, would say of it: "[t]he [Markan] hypothesis has a literary existence, indeed it is carried out by Holtzmann to such a degree of demonstration that it can no longer be called a mere hypothesis" (1906, ET 1910, 1968:202). V. Stanton (1899:237) locates the turning point earlier: "The chief critical work of the last 40 years or so has been the lineal continuation and development of that of Weisse and Wilke."

61. Holtzmann (1863:60) mentions (a) Mark 3:22, which he takes to be an abbreviated version of Matt 12:22-24; (b) Mark 1:13, which presupposes the longer temptation narrative of Matthew and Luke; and (c) Mark 14:65 ("prophesy"), which presupposes Luke 22:64, "who struck you?"

Figure 25
Holtzmann (1863) and Hilgenfeld

Figure 25a: Holtzmann (1863)

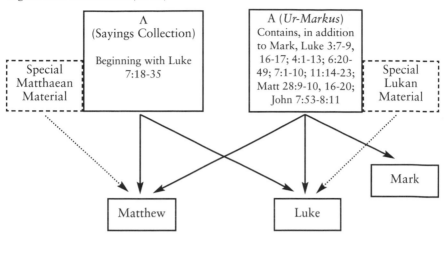

Figure 25b: Hilgenfeld

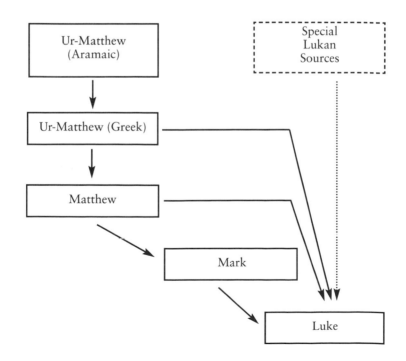

display better internal coherence than the Markan parallel (e.g., Mark 10:23; 10:49).

This meant that *Ur-Markus* ("A") contained a longer form of the words of the Baptist (Matt 3:7-12; Luke 3:7-9, 16-17) than was present in Mark, the long form of the temptation story, a version of the Sermon on the Mount (Luke 6:20-49), the story of the centurion's serving boy (Matt 8:5-13; Luke 7:1-10), and an expanded version of the Beelzebul accusation. Holtzmann also assigned to "A" the story of the adulterous woman from John (7:53—8:11) and the great commissioning from Matthew (28:9-10, 16-20). Correspondingly, this implied that the other source, Λ, lacked the double tradition material in Luke 3, 4, 6 and 7:1-10 (figure 25a).

This conclusion may appear puzzling, since the Sermon in Luke 6:20-49 in particular would seem to fit better with Holtzmann's Λ. What had influenced both Weisse and Holtzmann was a "textual gap" detected by Ewald at Mark 3:19/20, at the words "and he went home" after the call of the Twelve.[62] Ewald surmised that the Sermon on the Mount and the story of the centurion's serving boy originally filled this "gap."[63] Neither Weisse nor Holtzmann believed that the lengthy Matthaean Sermon occurred here, but agreed in assigning to *Ur-Markus* the substance of the shorter Lukan sermon (6:20-49). Weisse included with this the stories that followed in Luke 7—the healing of the centurion's serving boy (7:1-10), the raising of the son of the widow from Nain (7:11-17), and the question of John the Baptist and Jesus' reply (7:18-35) (1856:161–62). The fact that the Sermon was followed immediately by the healing in Luke 7:1-10 and almost immediately in Matt 8:5-13 inclined Holtzmann to agree with Weisse on Luke 7:1-10; but Holtzmann ascribed Luke 7:11-17 to a Lukan source and 7:18-35 to Λ.

Holtzmann agreed with Weisse on another crucial point: to have included in Λ narratives such as the temptation story and the healing in Luke 7, as well as the sayings of John the Baptist in Luke 3, would have made of it an "evangelical narrative" with the very characteristics of the canonical Gospels. This in turn would mean that the second Synoptic source, "which ought to contain only authentic sayings of Jesus," was not unitary.[64] Hence, Holtzmann withheld from Λ any narrative elements. He detected, nevertheless, a certain appropriateness in having the second source begin with Luke 7:18-35:

> Just as A began with the appearance of the Baptist, so Λ began appropriately with a statement of Jesus concerning the significance and import of John (Luke

62. The versification of this section of Mark varies. Luther, Westcott-Hort, Vogels, Merk, NA[25], NA[26] begins v. 20 with καὶ ἔρχεται εἰς οἶκον, "and he went home," while in earlier editions of the Greek New Testament and translations (some editions of the Textus Receptus; Tischendorf; KJV; RSV; NRSV) that is the conclusion of v. 19.

63. H. Ewald 1850a:208–9; cf. Weisse 1856:159–60; Holtzmann 1863:75.

64. Holtzmann 1863:142, referring to Weisse 1856:156, 164.

7:18-35 = Matt 11:2-11, 16-19) relating to this ἀρχὴ τοῦ εὐαγγελίου ("beginning of the gospel"). (1863:143)

In both Weisse (of 1856) and Holtzmann the lasting influence of Schleiermacher's *logia* can be seen, dictating a reconstruction of the second Synoptic source in accordance with an implicit and wholly undefended notion of generic purity: the *logia* source can only have included sayings. This is ironic in the case of Holtzmann, for notwithstanding his use of the terms Λ (for λόγια) and *Urmatthäus*, the testimony of Papias played very little role in Holtzmann's argument. Instead, the positing of Λ followed from his argument that A was prior to Matthew and Luke, and that Matthew was independent of Luke. That is, he posited Λ on purely internal and literary grounds. Only once he had provided the logical grounds for positing a sayings source did he consider Papias's testimony, treating it as ancilliary confimation of his proposal.[65] While previous speculations on the *logia* source had begun with Matthew's five well-organized speeches, Holtzmann made the critical observation that Matthew appears to have rearranged the speech material, conflating it with pericopae from "A." Luke better represented the order and character of Λ.

> From the outset it seems that brief sentences, pithy sayings and gnomai were probably written down earlier than long discourses, whose composition would require much deliberation. . . . Which is the more likely: that Luke willfully destroyed the grand constructions [of Matthew] and scattered the wreckage to the four winds, or that Matthew constructed his wall from Luke's [i.e., Λ's] pile of stones? (1863:130)

Holtzmann's "second Synoptic source" bore little real resemblance to Papias's putative Aramaic "oracles" or to Schleiermacher's collection of Matthaean speeches, except insofar as they too were exclusively sayings. The first exorcism on Papias's ghost had been performed, but the ghost would occasionally haunt the study of Q for another generation.

Holtzmann's role in mounting arguments against the GH has already been described. Assessment of Holtzmann's positive contribution to the establishment of the 2DH is a more complex matter. From a methodologi-

---

65. Holtzmann 1863:252: "Whether and how the document [mentioned by Papias] was related to our [canonical] Matthew must be investigated on separate grounds. Since, however, we have proceeded from a completely different basis and have in §10 ["the second principal source"] discovered a collection of speeches among the sources of the Synoptics, nothing should stop us now from identifying these two convergent results and to place our [canonical] Matthew in the same relation to the apostolic work mentioned by Papias as the Λ source." Holtzmann (ibid.) saw some additional confirmation of the apostolic (Matthaean) origin of Λ and his reconstruction of Λ beginning with Luke 7:18-35 (par. Matt 11:2-19) in the fact "that Λ is not connected to any one of [Matthew's] discourses which in A [*Ur-Markus*] appeared prior to the call of Matthew [Mark 2:14-17; Matt 9:9-13] and the apostles [Mark 3:13-16; Matt 10:1-4]. In general the source [Λ] represents mostly memoirs from the later period, since Jesus already publicly appeared as the Messiah."

cal perspective, he shifted the debate from the external to the internal evidence and insisted on literary criticism over "tendency criticism." Unlike most of his predecessors, Holtzmann did not begin with patristic testimony. Instead, he adopted literary criticism as his method, and in this respect was both an heir to the Tübingen school and its opponent. Holtzmann's most immediate dialogue partner was Hilgenfeld, who had used literary and tendency criticism to overturn Baur's view of the relation of Mark to Luke (figure 25b).[66] But as Holtzmann saw matters, Hilgenfeld had not gone far enough:

> As much as [Hilgenfeld] is concerned to depict his procedure as different from that of the Tübingen method and as clearly as one might see that Hilgenfeld took a step beyond Baur, insofar as he does not try to account for Mark on the basis of Luke and does not put a Marcionite version of Luke prior to canonical Luke,[67] his method, nevertheless, is in complete accord with Baur's regarding Matthew. He does not try to determine the origin of Matthew by means of a thorough comparison with the text of Mark and Luke but abruptly, by means of various dogmatic perspectives that he shares with Baur. (1863:39)

The "dogmatic perspective" that Holtzmann had in mind was one of the main pillars of "tendency criticism": the a priori assumption that as a "Jewish Christian" gospel, Matthew preceded the other Gospels. Against this Holtzmann insisted: "We begin instead with the purely critical investigation of the linguistic and logical relationships of sections of text, in order that our opinions concerning the tendentious character of our Gospels may at the conclusion of our study appear as a result that has been legitimately achieved" (1863:57).

By recent standards the architecture of Holtzmann's argument for "the Markan hypothesis" leaves much to be desired. Farmer complained that Holtzmann's argument and those that followed him were "not based upon a firm grasp of the primary phenomena of the Gospels themselves, but upon an artificial and deceptive consensus among scholars of differing traditions of Gospel criticism" (1964:38).

It is certainly true that Holtzmann did not begin with a detailed analysis of the patterns of agreements and disagreements among the Gospels in sequence and in wording and the logical inferences that these permit. In this, however, he was not alone: in the Synoptic Problem literature of the nineteenth century it is difficult to find clear statements of the "Synoptic facts" and an easy matter to find assumption-laden, impressionistic, easily reversible, and simply irrelevant arguments made on *all* sides of the debate.

---

66. Hilgenfeld 1854; 1861; Baur 1851. On this, see Fuller 1978a.

67. The allusion is to Ritschl's 1846 book, which argued that Luke's conciliatory tendency vis-à-vis Jewish Christianity and Paulinism and his anti-Marcionite tendency implied that Luke had written in reaction to Marcion's anti-Jewish gospel. Ritschl later (1851) retracted his view, but Baur had in the meantime adopted it (Baur 1846).

Holtzmann proceeded at first by cataloguing and evaluating the solutions proposed to date. Neither the *Urgospel* hypothesis nor the tradition hypothesis was plausible, since the various minute agreements among the Synoptics in the use of rare words (such as ἐπιούσιος in Matt 6:11 / Luke 11:3) or in phrases with complex word order (e.g., Matt 12:27-28 / Luke 11:19-20) were simply inexplicable on hypotheses that posited independent translations of an Aramaic document or independent renditions of oral tradition. Turning to the "utilization hypotheses," he listed all logically possible versions with their adherents, but reduced the basic choice to two: either Matthew was primary and Mark secondary, or vice versa, since Lukan priority was no longer seriously defended.

Holtzmann focused on Hilgenfeld as the chief advocate of the Matthew → Mark order. (Griesbach, it will be remembered, simply *assumed* that Matthew was first, which meant that Mark must have been derivative.) Hilgenfeld had argued that Mark's dependence on Matthew was demonstrated by the fact that Mark 12:1-12 reflected the editorial *Tendenz* of Matthew to emphasize the "hardening" of Israel and the conversion of the Gentiles.[68] This argument was invalid of course because it was so easily reversed: Mark (or *Ur-Markus*) might be the source of the hardening theory. Holtzmann took this as a prime example of the ineffectiveness of tendency criticism. In its place he insisted that conclusions about the direction of dependence be based on literary-critical and vocabularic considerations. In fact, neither Matthew nor Mark could be primary, for research had shown that Matthew was a *mixtum compositum*[69] and his own analysis of Mark (above p. 291) indicated that canonical Mark was secondary.

At this point, Holtzmann invoked what he saw as a consensus of Synoptic scholarship: apart from the GH, which in his view was "without foundation" (*haltungslos*), all agreed that the Synoptics depended upon a common *Grundschrift*. Here the consensus collapsed. Some favored an *Ur-Matthäus*, others favored an *Ur-Markus*; some explained Luke with reference to *Ur-Markus*, others with reference to Matthew (1863:66).

What is problematic about Holtzmann's procedure at this point is not, as Farmer claims, that he invoked an artificial consensus regarding a common *Grundschrift*—Holtzmann was clearly aware that there were fundamental disagreements about the nature of the alleged *Grundschrift*. What is problematic, rather, is that he moved immediately to an exposition of his own solution without resolving those outstanding disagreements. His procedure was to offer a "proof of the pudding" argument: to show that a satisfactory explanation of all Synoptic data could be provided on the assumption of

---

68. Hilgenfeld 1857:417. The Matthaean texts Hilgenfeld cites are Matt 8:11-12; 20:1-16; 21:33-44; 22:1-14; 24:14; and 28:19. On this, see Holtzmann 1863:57.

69. Holtzmann (1863:58) cites Lachmann (1835) as having shown the secondary nature of Matthew's sequence of pericopae.

Mark's redaction of *Ur-Markus* (A), and Matthew and Luke's independent combination of A with Λ.

Accordingly, he devoted a chapter to Matthew's redaction of A and Λ, offering various motives for Matthew's treatment, and occasionally arguing why other directions of dependence (Matthew → Mark/A; Matthew → Luke) were implausible.[70] Similarly with Luke, he tried to show how Luke variously supplemented, modified, and improved A. For example, at 9:28-36 Luke dropped A's (=Mark's) statement that the disciples did not understand "the unambiguous saying about Jesus' resurrection from the dead" (1863:224-25). His treatment of the editorial activities of Matthew and Luke, however, fell far short of a comprehensive demonstration of the priority of A and Λ to these two Gospels. Instead, Holtzmann was content to give a plausible accounting of the later evangelists' procedures, given the *assumption* of their dependence on A and Λ, and only occasionally offered arguments concerning the direction of dependence.

In a similar vein, Holtzmann considered the phenomenon of doublets, indicating how his solution could provide an explanation of the presence in Matthew and Luke of *some* of the doublets. Logically, however, this functioned more as an illustration of the hypothesis rather than as a proof; as Meijboom observed, Holtzmann's categorization of the doublets into four groups[71] "immediately creates the impression that these categories of doublets have been constructed on the basis of the supposedly proven Marcan hypothesis" (1866, ET 1991:76).

Holtzmann's treatment of citations from the Hebrew Bible offered more clearly directional arguments, for he observed that whereas all of the citations taken from A (Mark) were essentially Septuagintal,[72] those added by Matthew showed more affinities with the Masoretic text (MT).[73] For Holtz-

---

70. E.g., on Matt 8:14-15 Holtzmann (1863:178) argues that it is more likely that Matthew compressed the scene so that Jesus immediately sees Peter's mother-in-law than that Mark (=Luke) added the additional step of the disciples informing Jesus about the patient. On Matt 5:3-12 (1863:176) he notes that Luke lacks the characteristically Matthaean words τῷ πνεύματι (v. 3), τὴν δικαιοσύνην (v. 6), and ἕνεκεν δικσιοσύνης (v. 10). The unstated argument seems to be that Luke would have had no reason to omit such vocabulary.

71. Holtzmann (1863:254–58) divides the doublets into four groups: (1) doublets that already existed in A (=Mark); (2) doublets in Matthew and Luke that result from the conflation of A and Λ; (3) doublets in *either* Matthew *or* Luke that result from the conflation of A and Λ; and (4) repetition of a saying taken from one of the sources in various contexts in a gospel (e.g., Matt 3:7; 12:34, both from A). To the second category, Holtzmann assigns (a) Mark 4:25 / Matt 13:12 / Luke 8:18; Matt 25:29 / Luke 19:26; (b) Mark 8:34-35 / Matt 16:24-25 / Luke 9:23-24; Matt 10:38-39 / Luke 14:27, 33; (c) Mark 8:38 / Matt 16:27 / Luke 9:26; Matt 10:32-33 / Luke 12:8-9; and (d) Mark 13:9-13 / Matt 24:8-14 / Luke 21:12-19; Matt 10:17-22 / Luke 12:11-12.

72. Holtzmann notes that Mark 1:2 (Mal 3:1) deviates from the LXX, while in Matt 1:23 (Isa 7:14) Matthew preferred the LXX reading for obvious theological reasons.

73. The mixed nature of Matthew's citations was one of the key reasons Ritschl abandoned the GH in favor of Markan priority: Ritschl 1851:522.

mann, it was rather unlikely that Mark could have used Matthew but avoided the bulk of Matthew's MT-leaning citations.[74]

More persuasive also were Holtzmann's remarks on Matthew's and Luke's alterations of A. He noted that Matthew tended to be more concise than Mark but had also made sentences more complete in the interest of clarity. Matthew also introduced various improvements, for example, replacing the awkward parenthesis in Mark 11:32 with a participial phrase and replacing Mark's dangling ἀλλ᾽ ἵνα πληρωθῶσιν αἱ γραφαί ("but in order that the scriptures be fulfilled," 14:49) with τοῦτο δὲ ὅλον γέγονεν ἵνα πληρωθῶσιν αἱ γραφαὶ τῶν προφητῶν ("all this happened so that the writings of the prophets would be fulfilled," Matt 26:56). Holtzmann found Luke to make analogous improvements, using the optative mood in questions and replacing Mark's direct discourse with the more classical accusative-infinitive construction (Mark 1:44). Moreover, he noted various points where Luke inadvertently betrayed knowledge of what was in Mark, even though he omitted the relevant portions of Mark. For example, although Luke omitted Mark's explanation of the reason for Judas's kiss (Mark 14:44; cf. Luke 22:47-48) because he does not have Judas actually kiss Jesus, he presupposed that explanation.[75]

Assessing Holtzmann's Contribution

If one looks to Holtzmann for a systematic proof of the 2DH one will be disappointed. What he offered was a detailed exposition of the Markan hypothesis, showing how it might plausibly account for the data. In this it must be said that he was generally successful. But it must also be made clear that his "defense" of the Markan hypothesis did not logically imply the invalidity of other hypotheses, even if his successors assumed that it did. When his positive accomplishments were coupled with his and Weiss's unanswered criticism of the GH, it is not difficult to understand how his hypothesis could achieve hegemony, however unearned that hegemony was. Supporters of the GH were few and evidently ineffective, as was Hilgenfeld in promoting his version of the "Augustinian" hypothesis.[76]

---

74. Meijboom's response (1866, ET 1991:87) ignored Holtzmann's case and focused on the earlier proposal of Ritschl (1851), dismissing it with reference to a "multiplicity of exceptions" (*sic!*). David New's (1993) investigation concludes (1) that the evidence is consistent with the 2DH; (2) that none of the evidence clearly favors the GH; and (3) that eleven citations could be argued either way (1993:121).

75. Holtzmann 1863:331–32. He also notes that while Luke has altered Mark 4:7 εἰς τὰς ἀκάνθας to ἐν μέσῳ τῶν ἀκανθῶν (8:7), he preserves the Markan locution later in 8:14. (The same argument could be made of Matthew at this point.)

76. Hilgenfeld was also rather marginal in the German university system, having been passed over for prestigious chairs several times apparently because of his poor teaching and acerbic style. See H. Harris 1975:117–26.

Of course there were criticisms of the Markan hypothesis, most notably in a Dutch dissertation by Meijboom (1866). From the works of Weisse and Ewald in particular, Meijboom distilled three principal arguments used to "establish" Markan priority, each of them inconclusive: the brevity of Mark; Mark's use of graphic or vivid description; and the relative unity and consistency of Mark when compared with Matthew. He rightly pointed out that brevity was equally explicable on the basis of Markan *intention* to abbreviate; that the use of vivid language does not necessarily imply an eye-witness account, but might simply point to the author's purpose and creative imagination; and that the distinction between Mark and *Ur-Markus* was dubious.[77] Since neither the first nor the second point had been parts of Holtzmann's argument, as Meijboom himself conceded (1991:79), and since the observations regarding the natural unity of "A" was a conclusion rather than a criterion for Holtzmann, none of Meijboom's quite valid points affected Holtzmann's argument in the least.

Eventually, Holtzmann modified the most awkward part of his hypothesis, namely, the A (*Ur-Markus*) source. In 1863 he had attempted to explain Mark's omission of the Sermon in A (=Luke 6:20-49) because the Sermon was "too long for him" (1863:116). As Stoldt has pointed out, however, Mark's apocalypse (13:5-35) and his parables discourse (4:1-34) are both longer than Luke 6:20-49 (1980:76). Later on in his book Holtzmann added that perhaps the Sermon had been too Ebionite for Mark (1863:386). In his *Lehrbuch der historisch-kritischen Einleitung in das Neue Testament*, however, Holtzmann dropped the idea of an *Ur-Markus* entirely (1886:363–65; [3]1892:350). Although he did not offer a new catalogue of the contents of Λ, it would presumably now have contained some of the double tradition prior to Luke 7:18-35. Abandoning a pre-Markan source, however, also meant that Holtzmann lost a convenient way in which to explain the minor agreements of Matthew and Luke against Mark, and so he speculated on the possibility of sporadic influence of Matthew on Luke (figure 26).

Holtzmann's argument was so effective that subsequent generations of Synoptic scholars would simply take his solution for granted. In the decades between the publication of his book and William Sanday's *Oxford Studies in the Synoptic Problem* (1911), only Meijboom's dissertation (1866) and Wernle's monograph (1899) qualify as substantial reviews of the problem.[78] Holtzmann had been effective, however, less in proving Markan priority

---

77. Against the Markan hypothesis, Meijboom tried to mount a case for the advanced rather than primitive character of Mark, but fell prey to his own objection against the Markan hypothesis that stylistic and theological characteristics are not univocal in indicating relative age.

78. One might add Pasquier (1911), who attempted a defense of a modified version of the GH, with Mark being the conflation of Matthew and Luke, but Luke knowing Matt[Aram] only indirectly, via small "packets." Pasquier's "solution" was mired in self-contradictions, as Lagrange's (1912) systematic refutation pointed out.

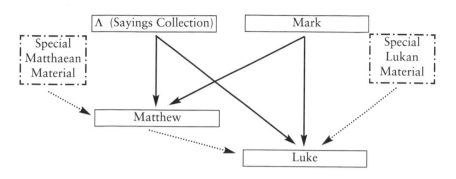

Figure 26
Holtzmann (1886)

than in illustrating the economy of the Markan hypothesis in accounting for the Synoptic data. Indeed, the appeal of his solution probably rested more upon its literary and theological "usefulness" than upon its logical rigor.

The Reception of the Markan Hypothesis

Why was the Markan hypothesis embraced with such enthusiasm, when Holtzmann's demonstration of it left so much to be desired? In part it was due to the vacuum created by demise of the Tübingen school, the failure of the few remaining proponents of the GH to offer a defense, and the lack of any other credible alternative, including Hilgenfeld's "Augustinian" solution. Such an explanation is incomplete, for it is hardly the case that Holtzmann's solution won the day simply by default. In searching for positive reasons for Holtzmann's success, one might consider the possible appeal of nonextant sources, especially when it is remembered that these played so important a role in the solutions of Lessing, Schleiermacher, Eichhorn, and Lachmann. Yet in spite of Holtzmann's positing of a sayings source lying behind Matthew and Luke, there is no evidence that the appeal of Holtzmann's solution lay in the notion of pre-Gospel sources. Indeed it is surprising how little Λ figured in Holtzmann's book. Although he isolated the source and even described its linguistic character, his real interest was A and the way it might serve as the basis for a life of Jesus.

I suggest that two theological factors contributed to the success of the Markan hypothesis, one for liberal Protestant theology and another for Catholics prior to 1911.

Jesus as Religious Genius

In fewer than thirty pages Holtzmann sketched a "Life of Jesus according to the A Source" in which he used Markan material to circumscribe the development of Jesus' consciousness in seven identifiable stages (1863:468–96). In fact Holtzmann described this accomplishment as the most valuable result of his investigations.[79] His statement turned out to be prophetic. This portrait, as Schweitzer described it, became "the creed and catechism of all who handled the subject during the following decades" (1906, ET 1910:204). Holtzmann's treament of Papias's testimony on Mark is a telling index of his confidence in the reliability of Mark's framework. According to Papias, Mark recorded what Jesus had said and done "carefully, but not in order" (ἀκριβῶς ἔγραψεν, οὐ μέντοι τάξει, Eusebius, *Hist. eccl.* 3.39.15).[80] For Holtzmann, Mark's narrative outline was a reliable guide for a construction of the life of Jesus.

On Holtzmann's showing, Mark (or A) lacked the "dogmatic" features that were so evident in both Matthew and Luke. Mark depicted Jesus as "the image of a purity and harmony of that which constitutes vigorous humanity, a constant interplay of intellect, feeling, contemplation, intuition" (1863:496)—a depiction that eminently served the theological goals of liberal theology, with its strong antidogmatic agenda. Indeed, Schweitzer is probably correct in stating that "[t]he victory . . . belonged, not to the Marcan hypothesis pure and simple, but to the Marcan hypothesis as psychologically interpreted by a liberal theology" (1906, ET 1910:204).[81]

During the next four decades a string of "lives of Jesus" were published, all capitalizing on Holtzmann's view of Mark: Schenkel (1864, ET 1869), Weizsäcker (1864), Keim (1867–72, ET 1873–83), Hase (1876), Beyschlag (1885), and B. Weiss ([2]1884, ET 1883–84). Typical of these "lives" was the interpretation of the kingdom of God as a spiritual kingdom of repentance and the conviction, based on Holtzmann's reading of Mark, that Jesus' messianic consciousness developed, precipitated principally by a "Galilean crisis" in which Jesus came to face the failure of his mission. The spell of Mark would not be broken until Wrede demonstrated that the "messianic con-

---

79. Meijboom (1866, ET 1991:74) suggested that Holtzmann's motivation was the desire for a historically reliable source. Be this as it may, the fact remains that Holtzmann did base his *argument* for Markan priority upon its alleged historical reliability; hence Meijboom's comment, even if correct, is irrelevant as a criticism of Holtzmann's argument.

80. Holtzmann (1863:253–54) argued that Papias's statement was prompted by his comparing A to either John or (more likely) (canonical) Matthew and hence A *appeared* deficient in this company.

81. Peabody (1995) points out that Schweitzer's statement that the Markan hypothesis should no longer be considered merely a hypothesis (above, n. 60) should be qualified by his later opinion that "the literary question [of the dependence of the Gospels] is scarcely possible to answer" and that Matthew should be given equal weight with Mark, in the 1950 preface to *Von Reimarus zu Wrede*. Peabody makes much of this, but fails to note that the authenticity of portions of Matthew 10–11, especially Matt 10:23, was crucial to the whole edifice of Schweitzer's view of Jesus. Moreover, Schweitzer's statement cannot be taken as an endorsement of Matthaean priority in literary-critical terms, only an acknowledgment that Matthew contains reliable materials lacking in Mark.

sciousness" that the liberal lives had attempted to detail was a creation of Mark (Wrede 1901, ET 1971).

Some of the appeal of Holtzmann's Jesus—and of the source-critical theory that sustained it—can be traced to its congruence with a growing attraction of the figure of the individual genius, the hero of bourgeois Christianity. The works of Goethe (1749–1832) and Thomas Carlyle (1795–1881) promoted the idea of the heroic personality (Kahlert 1984). Ernest Renan's enormously popular *Life of Jesus* (1863), published the same year as Holtzmann's book on the Synoptics, illustrates the tendency in nineteenth-century thought to depict Jesus as rural romantic hero "full of unspoiled naïveté but at the same time full of dignity and wisdom, the ideal image of bourgeois nostalgia" (Georgi 1992:78).

Prior to the 1860s the heroic Jesus was eclipsed as a dominant emphasis by Baur's focus on post-Easter dogmatic developments as the locus of theological significance, even though, as Holtzmann observed, Baur himself was paying more attention to the historical Jesus in his later works.[82] In 1838 Weisse had espoused the theological importance of the historical Jesus based on Mark but his efforts languished in the shadow of Strauss's mythic approach and Baur's history of dogma. After the 1860s, however, the tide changed. Holtzmann's critically constructed Jesus became the model of vigorous yet undogmatic humanity. In A, Holtzmann found

> the hardiness of a real genius and of a special—indeed a miraculous—endowment from the depths of the divine which itself marks more ordinary persons for enigmatic mysteries. There is a special strength of will, resolve, and direction that in its fullness and passion transcends what is seen elsewhere and that is absorbed in the depths of his own spirit and in the revelation of God in humanity. (1863:489)

Such a portrait of Jesus, as Georgi puts it, was "sufficiently human to allow identification with him, but also sufficiently lifted above the masses that he could be seen as a beacon" (1992:78).

As long as the nineteenth-century fascination with the notions of religious genius and embodied ideal humanity held sway, Holtzmann's reconstruction of the historical Jesus appeared self-evidently correct. His Jesus was vigorous, introspective, and nondogmatic, and espoused the superior morality of A's Sermon (Luke 6:20-49). It is startling to note that Holtzmann's treatment passed over Mark 13 in silence—a text that hardly gives the impression of an undogmatic speaker. It was Johannes Weiss's "rediscovery" of the apocalyptic strands in the Jesus tradition and the popularization of apocalypticism by Albert Schweitzer—ironically, a pupil of Holtzmann—that led eventually to the deconstruction of the liberal Jesus. There was, however, no corresponding denouement for Markan priority, as

---

82. Holtzmann 1863:469–70, referring to Baur 1853.

there had been for the Griesbach hypothesis after 1860. The 2DH outlived liberal theology and, insofar as J. Weiss and Wilhelm Wrede both accepted the 2DH, it played a role in that deconstruction.

CATHOLIC–PROTESTANT POLEMICS AND MARKAN PRIORITY

Farmer has offered a different account of the triumph of Markan priority after 1870. Whereas prior to 1870, Matthaean priority had been associated with the radical Tübingen school, after 1870 it came to be identified with Catholic ultramontanism and extreme papal claims. Accordingly, it was rejected by most Protestants during the course of Bismarck's struggle with Pius IX. Farmer argues:

> In 1870, the Marcan hypothesis was no more than an increasingly popular *wissenschaftliche Hypothese*. But certainly by 1914, probably by 1890, and possibly as early as 1880 this popular hypothesis implicitly converted into a German Protestant dogma. Why? I wish to suggest that in the cultural struggle between church and state the ideas of Marcan primacy and the existence of "Q" took on ideational and ideological roles. (1992:2492 = 1995:32; cf. 1994:148–60)

The period of *Kulturkampf* began soon after Vatican I's declaration on Petrine primacy (1869–70) and ended with Pius IX's death in 1878 and the concord between Bismarck and Leo XIII. This period was marked by bitter Catholic–Protestant polemics, especially in Prussia, exacerbated by the arrest, imprisonment, and expulsion of Catholic clerics in Germany and by inflammatory statements from Rome.[83]

It is hardly imaginable that such polemics did not affect theological dispositions. Theologians, in particular those who taught at state-funded universities and whose appointments were a matter of state interest, did not live in a vacuum. It is very difficult, however, to gauge the influence of *Kulturkampf* on Synoptic scholarship since Farmer does not refer to any exegetes, either Catholic or Protestant, who showed signs of being influenced by such polemics. At the height of the conflict between Bismarck and Pius IX, Bismarck contrasted the infallible Pius IX with Peter, who sinned, wept bitterly, and repented (Farmer 1995:31). Farmer conjectures that it was in Berlin's interest to appoint professors sensitive to this conflict and prepared to contribute to the struggle by affirming Markan primacy and to deny Matthaean priority:

> To have well placed professors in the universities, whose publications supported Markan primacy would clearly serve the interests of the state. Conversely, any professor whose published work proceeded from the traditional position that the Gospel of Matthew is our earliest Gospel [Farmer names

---

83. Farmer 1992:2496 (= 1995:37) suggests that the reception of the 2DH in Britain was also a function of anti-Roman Catholic sentiments.

Hilgenfeld], would be out of step with the interest of the state, and could expect, under the new Reich, to wither on the vine. (1995:32).

There is little to support Farmer's inference that Holtzmann's appointment at Strasbourg in 1874 or Bernard Weiss's appointment to Berlin in 1876 had anything to do with anti-Vatican politics. Reventlow's examination of the archive at Strasbourg led him to conclude, on the contrary, that

> the documents do not confirm the theses of W. Farmer . . . according to which the appointment of Holtzmann to a chair in the Theological Faculty of the university of Strasbourg was an act of imperial politics belonging to Bismarck's anti-Roman measures during the *Kulturkampf*. On the contrary, they show that the Emperor and his Chancellor in Berlin only very reluctantly, and after having imposed important restrictions on Holtzmann, accepted his nomination, the initiative for which did not come from Berlin but from the faculty in Strasbourg itself. (1995:284)

Or again:

> In any case: the Markan Hypothesis played no role whatever in Holtzmann's appointment so far as the government was concerned. In the scientific world, Holtzmann was a scholar of fame. Whatever one might think about liberal theology in general, about the Markan hypothesis in particular, the testimonies we have about the personality of Holtzmann and the breadth of his universal knowledge are impressive. (1995:290)[84]

Another test of Farmer's thesis that Markan priority figured as a weapon in the ideological warfare between Catholics and Protestants is to look at exegetes themselves. It is of course correct that by 1900 Markan priority had been fully secured in Protestant circles. Yet it is significant that Adolf von Harnack's *What Is Christianity?* (1900, ET 1901), with its undisguised polemic against Roman Catholicism and papal primacy, never used the 2DH as a weapon. On the other hand, there are no signs at all that the 2DH had been seen as potentially anti-Catholic, at least during the pontificate of Leo XIII (1878–1903). A good test case is the exegesis of Matt 16:17-19, attested only in Matthew and historically used in connection with the doctrine of the primacy of the Roman pontiff.

Biblical scholars, both Protestant and Catholic, challenged both the interpretation and the authenticity of the words to Peter (Matt 16:17-19). Since

---

84. Professor Farmer informs me by letter (September 7, 1998) that the chronology of his and Reventlow's papers is complex. Reventlow's (1995) paper was not a response to Farmer's 1995 paper but to an earlier form prepared for a conference in Dartmouth (1990) and later published in a revised form in the Neirynck Festschrift (1992). Nevertheless, Farmer's 1995 position (quoted above) still implies state "interest" in the Markan hypothesis and Reventlow's 1995 rejoinder finds no evidence of such interest. In the introduction to the 1995 volume Reventlow and Farmer agree that the Strasbourg archive "does not contain express statements which could contribute to a solution to the problem" (1995:11) but disagree on "how far it is possible for the historian to speak of state *Interesse* in the appointment of Holtzmann" (ibid.).

at least the 1790s German Catholic scholars had argued against the rising tide of ultramontanism, that Petrine primacy could not be sustained on the basis of this text alone.[85] During the nineteenth century various Protestants suggested that Matt 16:17-19 must be a legendary accretion to Matthew, since it so obviously conflicted with the stinging rebute given to Peter only a few verses later (Matt 16:23).[86] Holtzmann himself recognized the conflict between Matt 16:17-19 and Matt 16:23; but in 1863 he merely drew the conclusion that the two sayings could not have been spoken by Jesus on the same occasion (1863:193).[87] What is important to note is that with the possible exception of Bruno Bauer (1841–42, 3:8–9), no Protestant exegete employed Markan priority and Matthaean posteriority as a blunt instrument by which to dispatch Matt 16:17-19. Scholars on all sides of the Synoptic Problem debate raised doubts about the text because of the tension with Matt 16:23 or its putative "legendary" character. They questioned its historicity because of its singular use of the term *ekklēsia* and because of the partial overlap with Matt 18:18—Meijboom's teacher Johann Heinrich Scholten as well as Adolf von Harnack. Critics on all sides—Griesbach supporter Josef Langen and Matthaean priorist Theodor Zahn, as well as Heinrich Meyer, Albert Schweitzer, and M. J. Lagrange—saw a genuine saying in Matt 16:17-19 and responded to the objections voiced against it either by relocating it elsewhere in the life of Jesus, or by arguing that its interpretation had developed, or by invoking special Matthaean sources. In other words, the fault line in this important dogmatic debate did not run alongside the rift in Synoptic source theories, but repeatedly crisscrossed it.

Leo XIII's encyclical *Providentissimus Deus* (1893) expressed concern about a variety of topics in biblical interpretation, but Markan priority was not among them. The encyclical in fact provided the impetus for an energetic phase of Catholic biblical scholarship inaugurated by the Dominican founder of the École biblique et archéologique française de Jérusalem, M. J. Lagrange. Lagrange was widely read in German Protestant Synoptic criticism and favored Markan priority (1895; 1896; 1911). He disagreed with the limitation of Q (or the *logia*) to sayings of Jesus, arguing that it probably contained narratives including those of the passion and resurrection. But Lagrange's reasons for expanding Q in this way had nothing to do with answering Protestant polemics.

---

85. See the survey of views in Burgess 1976. Doubts as to the authenticity of Matt 16:17-19 were raised as early as 1781 (F. A. Stroth). German Catholics such as T. A. Dereser, P. A. Gratz, and J. A. Möhler apparently accepted the authenticity of the saying but rejected the ultramontane interpretation.

86. H. Meyer 1832:118 (contrast all later editions); Wilke 1838:358; Weisse 1838, 1:398; 2:94 (contrast 1856:238–39).

87. Later Holtzmann (1892:381; 1911, 1:269) described the passage as an "insertion" and as "unhistorical."

By 1903 Lagrange referred to the 2DH as "généralement admise."[88] In 1911 he was able to offer a long list of Catholic exegetes, all of whom had endorsed Markan priority and many who accepted the 2DH in its classical form:[89] in England, Msgr. A. S. Barnes (1905) and the Benedictine John Chapman[90] (1905); in Germany, Joseph Sickenberger (1911) and Friedrich Maier (1912); and in France, Eugène Jacquier (1903–07),[91] Joseph Huby (1910),[92] and especially Abbé Pierre Batiffol, who described Q as a "source évangélique . . . sorte de recueil des *Dits du Seigneur*" that served as the source of Matthew and Luke and that was probably also known to Mark (1897:69, emphasis original). Camerlynck and Coppieters, whose synopsis of the Gospels was published in 1908, indicated Mark as the source of Matthew and Luke and accepted Harnack's description of the extent and nature of the second Synoptic source, Q.[93] Even more tellingly, the article on the Synoptic Gospels by the Abbé Eugène Mangenot (probably written before 1897) that appeared in the influential *Dictionnaire de la Bible*, while ultimately remaining undecided on the Synoptic Problem, clearly leaned in the direction of the 2DH and Markan priority. In regard to theories of Markan priority, Mangenot concluded that "they offer nothing that is

88. Lagrange (1903, [2]1904:249): "I cannot criticize Loisy for taking this hypothesis [the 2DH] as his basis: you yourself, my friend [Pierre Batiffol], have accepted it in your lectures on the Gospels because it is generally accepted." Batiffol (1897:69) had already indicated that the 2DH was accepted by the "majority of critics." Batiffol's history of ancient Christian literature (1901:26–30) likewise espoused the 2DH (including Mark's use of Q). Batiffol quotes Resch's work (1897; cf. 1906) but does not appear to have adopted Resch's much-expanded *Urgospel* thesis. Batiffol did, however, borrow Resch's term דברי ישוע as a designation for the Semitic *logia*.

89. Lagrange 1911:xxxv–xxxvii; also Soiron 1916:15–17. In 1903, Lagrange himself almost seemed to endorse the 2DH: "Criticism seems to be agreed on this point that Saint Mark can be considered, along with another document named *logia*, as a source for Saint Matthew and Saint Luke" (1903, [2]1904:248).

90. See below, n. 98.

91. See Jacquier 1903–07, 2:328–55. Jacquier's summation (355) is much more ambiguous than his analysis, where he describes Mark as the "middle term" between Matthew and Luke (323); Matthew and Luke have corrected Mark (324–26); Matthew and Luke used a "collection of *logia*" but in different recensions (337).

92. Huby, a Jesuit, was living in England in 1910, probably owing to the persecution of religious orders in France. All of his writings were in French and so he is included among the French.

93. Camerlynck and Coppieters 1908:xxvi–xxvii. In the second (1910) and third (1921) editions of their synopsis Camerlynck and Coppieters show increasing hesitation regarding Q. The list of the contents of Q is dropped in the 1910 edition and in the 1921 edition the 2DH is described with the words: "Other authors, rationalists and Protestants [quoting Harnack, Wellhausen, and B. Weiss] . . . almost unanimously ascribe those passages common to Matthew and Luke but missing in second Gospel to a source, usually called 'the logia.'" (1921:lxviii). Compare the [2]1910 edition: "Other authors justly (*aeque*) favouring the priority of Mark nevertheless are strongly inclined to derive those passages found in the first and third Gospels from a common source usually called the 'logia.'"

formally opposed to the Catholic faith, because the dating of the Gospels and the order of their publication are not specified by ecclesiastical tradition with a precision that would inevitably require our assent" (1895–1912a, 2:2098).

The significance of this statement lies in the fact that the *Dictionnaire* was edited by the Abbé Fulcran Vigouroux, a principal representative of conservative Catholic exegesis during the 1890s and the secretary of the Pontifical Biblical Commission (PBC) from 1903 to 1914.[94] Mangenot, himself named a consultant to the PBC, wrote further articles on Mark and Matthew (probably in 1903 [=1895–1912b,c]) during the period of increasing tensions over biblical scholarship. This was followed by a monograph (1911) in which he endorsed the 2DH.[95] Evidently neither Vigouroux nor Mangenot felt that Markan priority or the existence of Q presented a serious challenge to the primacy of the Roman pontiff or was incompatible with ecclesiastical tradition. Only in 1911–12, when the PBC expressed its views on the Synoptic Problem (*EB* §404–5), did the dogmatic importance of Matt 16:17-19 become the object of express attention (*EB* §394). The commission, which under Pius X (1903–14) was filled with neo-scholastics and now included the ultraconservative secretary of state, Rafael Cardinal Merry del Val,[96] rejected the 2DH and the notion of a sayings collection underlying Matthew and Luke ("collectio sic dicta sermonum Domini," *EB*

94. See Levie 1958, ET 1961:45, 75. On the history of the commission, see Fitzmyer 1991:119–25.

95. Mangenot 1911:45–65 (based on lectures in the summer of 1910 in Paris). To the question, "Is the 2DH compatible with ecclesiastical tradition and Catholic thought?" Mangenot responded: "It fits well, provided that one does not regard it as a conclusion that is certain and proven—which it is not—but as a simple critical hypothesis, reasonable in itself and functioning to explain the similarities and differences [among the gospels] by the free use which they have made of [Mark]" (1911:59). That Mangenot wrote this scarcely more than a year before the PBC's outright rejection of the 2DH (June 26, 1912) is an index of the extent to which even moderate and otherwise influential Catholic scholars were totally unaware of and unprepared for the Vatican's wholesale repudiation of historical criticism of the Bible.

96. Kurtz 1986:44: "At first, it seemed as though the commission might allow (if not facilitate) the development of biblical criticism, but within a year [i.e., 1903], its original twelve members were overshadowed by the addition of twenty-eight more. According to von Hügel, the new members were either scholastic-trained, noncritical scholars or men without scholarly reputations at all. The Biblical Commission's real task [under Pius X], it seemed, was to guide biblical studies away from critical historiography and towards methods more compatible with neo-Thomist presuppositions." Of the PBC's constitution after 1906, Rollmann (1995:213) writes: "The Pontifical Biblical Commission, envisioned as an ecclesiastical forum for biblical questions by competent theologians, was emptied of its scholars who were replaced with neo-scholastic theologians and church officials, who reduced the differentiating probability judgments of history to the final propositional statements 'negative' or 'positive.'" While both Mangenot and Lagrange were named as consultors to the PBC, Lagrange (in Jerusalem) was never consulted on any matter and, given Mangenot's (in Toulouse) ignorance in 1910/1911 of the coming condemnation of the 2DH, it would appear that he was not an active member either.

§405) and declared instead that canonical Matthew was "substantially identical" (*quoad substantiam*) with a Semitic original (*EB* §392). This was not, however, a reaction to Protestant exegesis but to Catholic modernists such as Loisy whose intent and sophistication the Commission failed to understand, much less appreciate.[97]

Even after 1911–12 when Catholic scholars abandoned under duress the simplest expression of the 2DH, there was no return to the "Augustinian" solution or the GH.[98] Instead, what triumphed was Lagrange's supposition of an expanded Q or rather, an Aramaic predecessor of Matthew whose contents it approximated.[99] Lagrange had argued in 1895–96 that Mark was the source for both Luke and the Greek of Matthew, that Matthew derived from an Aramaic predecessor, and that Luke shows no signs of influence from canonical Matthew (1896). Nevertheless, since Luke shared with Matthew non-Markan materials, sometimes displaying near-verbatim agreement, it was most probable that Luke used "partial translations" (in Greek) of Matt[Aram] (figure 27a).

Variations of this "modified" or "Catholic two source hypothesis" quickly gained popularity,[100] so that Dausch, an opponent of the 2DH, complained that in spite of the PBC's decrees, "a growing number of Catholic theologians are sympathetic to this hypothesis [the 2DH] and even agree with it" (1932:30). While Wikenhauser, for example, argued that Matt[Aram] was more than a *Spruchsammlung*, neither he nor the others were very precise on what else it might have contained. The main critical problem that "Aramaic Matthew" solved was precisely the same problem that Q solved in the classical forms of the 2DH: the presence of the double

---

97. See, e.g., Loisy 1907–08, 1:529; 2:5–15. Ironically, Loisy himself, who regarded Matt 16:17-19 as post-Easter prophetic saying attributed to Jesus, argued that this in no way compromised its truth or threatened the primacy of the Roman pontiff.

98. The most important exception is Chapman who recanted his 1905 endorsement of Markan priority in favor of the "Augustinian hypothesis" (1937). Chapman was an Anglican who converted to the Roman church. His colleague at Downside Abbey, B. C. Butler, also advocated the "Augustinian hypothesis." Pasquier (1911) was the only Catholic of note favoring the GH, though in a modified form.

99. Lagrange's objection to a sayings source had to do with the silence of the tradition on a sayings collection and the a priori implausibility of such a collection: 1896:27: "If the *logia* are an evangelical work that contained only the sayings of the Savior, a work composed in Aramaic, transmitted in Greek to the church and used by the author of the first Gospel who would have added the narrative components, I refuse to recognize this primitive Matthew, of which I can find no trace in early Christian tradition, and which cannot be posited on the basis of an internal examination (of the gospels)." Lagrange 1911:civ: "No book, if it were a collection of proverbs, could have been written in this way, and it is impossible to suppose that virtually all the sayings of Jesus were arranged without any setting that explained their occasion."

100. See Sickenberger 1911; 1916; 1933; Camerlynck and Coppieters 1921; Huby 1924; 1929, ET 1931; Vogels 1925; Vosté 1928; Pölzl and Innitzer 1932:xx (the latter elevated to Cardinal Archbishop of Vienna); Meinertz 1932; Wikenhauser 1937:953; cf. 1931. The work of Josef Schmid (1930) laid the groundwork of the eventual Catholic acceptance of the 2DH.

Figure 27
M. J. Lagrange and the "Catholic Two Document Hypothesis"

Figure 27a: Lagrange

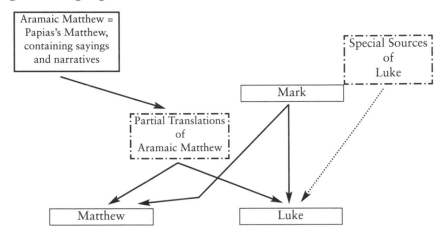

Figure 27b: The "Catholic Two Document Hypothesis"

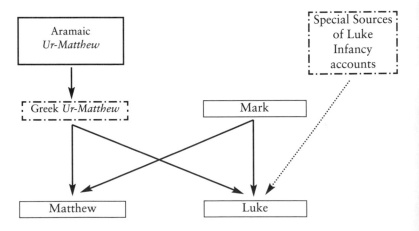

Figure 28
Catholic Source Criticism before 1955

Figure 28a: Lucien Cerfaux (1935, 1938, 1951, 1952, 1954)

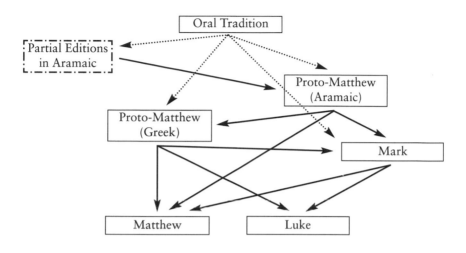

Figure 28b: Pierre Benoit (1950)

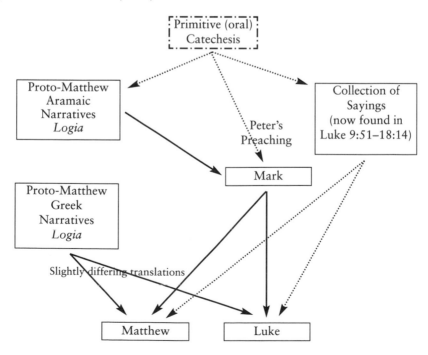

tradition (mostly sayings) in canonical Matthew and Luke. Moreover, Wikenhauser allowed for considerable difference between the Matt^Aram and canonical Matthew by declaring that the latter was not a "slavish" translation of Matt^Aram but a "reworking" (*Bearbeitung*) in which an "unknown author had utilized the Gospel of Mark in some expressions and in the ordering of the material, as well as various Markan materials" to produce the Gospel. Luke used Mark and a Greek translation of Matt^Aram (1937). The differences between this "Catholic two source hypothesis" and the simpler forms lay mostly in the name.

Lagrange's model was also elaborated along different and more complicated lines by Cerfaux (1935; 1938; 1954), Benoit (1950) and Vaganay (1954), each of whom posited an additional connection between Matt^Aram and Mark (see figure 28). This development had several effects, including the implication that Matt^Aram was far more like canonical Matthew than earlier proponents of the "Catholic two source hypothesis" allowed. It also required a highly complex model for understanding the editorial procedures of the later evangelists, since, for example, Luke would have access both to Mark (whose general outline he followed) and Greek proto-Matthew (Mg), whose contents he took over but whose structure he evidently ignored. Moreover, if Mark knew Mg, one would have to explain both his abbreviation of the source and his complete reordering of it. Such solutions, while ostensibly starting with Lagrange's solution, undermined Lagrange's basic insight that Luke betrayed no knowledge of Matthew's structure (and hence, no knowledge of the putative structure of Matt^Aram; Lagrange 1896).

These solutions, although far less parsimonious than the 2DH, had the advantage of preserving the critical insights of Holtzmann and Wernle on the priority of Mark to Matthew and Luke, and Benoit even included a source to account for the sayings now found in Luke 9:51—18:14, mostly Q sayings. By assigning great value to patristic reports, they also in effect created solutions that, in an era marked by suspicion and hostility to critical scholarship, could be regarded as faithful to ecclesiastical tradition while still preserving some of the insights of Lagrange and others.

With the retraction of the PBC restrictions of 1907–15[101] and the

---

101. The PBC decrees of 1907–15 were effectively annulled in statements of the secretary (A. Miller 1955) and subsecretary (Kleinhans 1955). They introduced a distinction between decisions touching on faith and morals and those dealing with literary criticism, authorship, integrity, date, historicity. While the former remained valid, the latter were to be considered as contingent upon the particular circumstances in which they were issued [the Modernist crisis]. Exegetes could now work with full liberty (*plena libertate*, "in aller Freiheit") in regard to these questions. The inertia behind the retraction of the PBC earlier decrees might more generally be traced to Pius XII's liberalizing *Divino Afflante Spiritu* (1943; *EB* 538–69 = *AAS* 35 [1943] 297–326). Rollmann (1995:215) has noted the contacts between Baron Friedrich von Hügel, a friend of Holtzmann and an advocate of his source theory, and the young Eugenio Pacelli, the future Pius XII.

resumption of critical Catholic Synoptic scholarship, the theory of an Aramaic Matthew, already under attack by Catholics,[102] was abandoned in Germany and North America and the 2DH embraced.[103] As will be suggested in the next chapter, an Aramaic proto-Matthew had been a necessary postulate not for literary reasons, but as a symbol of deference to ecclesiastical authority. With the reactionary PBC decrees abolished, such symbols were unnecessary.

Farmer's claims notwithstanding, there is no persuasive evidence that the German Protestant endorsement of Markan priority had much to do with anti-Catholic or antipapal sentiments or, conversely, that Catholic scholars wishing to defend the Petrine primacy rejected Markan priority. Nor is it true that only Catholic modernists endorsed Markan priority and the 2DH. Lagrange, Batiffol, and Mangenot certainly did not belong in that company.[104] Neither before nor after 1912 did Catholics see any conflict between the 2DH (or the "Catholic 2DH," figure 27b) and the authenticity of Matt 16:17-19. For neither Catholics nor Protestants strictly coordinated source criticism with judgments concerning authenticity; to explain elements in secondary Gospels such as Matthew or Luke it was always quite possible to invoke oral tradition or other sources in order to explain the presence of special materials in Matthew (or Luke).

Catholic Interest in Markan Priority

It is worthwhile asking why Catholics were attracted to Markan priority and the 2DH prior to 1912 and in its modified form after 1912 and not, for example, to the Griesbach or the "Augustinian" hypotheses. Lagrange insisted on the strict separation of historical critical decisions from dogmatic interests, confident that the findings of historical criticism would not be incompatible with dogma. Dogma could not be invoked in the midst of a historical examination without vitiating its scientific character. Thus, his

102. See Schmid 1953; 1964; Schnackenburg 1953; Neirynck 1967.

103. This change was anticipated in 1948 in the influential *Initiation biblique* of A. Robert and A. Tricot (under the imprimatur of the Cardinal Archbishop of Paris and with a preface by Achille Cardinal Liénart of Lille). Tricot added an "appendix" on the Synoptic Problem (not present in the first [1939] edition) in which he endorsed the 2DH as "une excellente *work-hypothesis*" (1948:332) and offered an ingenious argument that the 2DH "agrees in substance with the directives given by the Pontifical Biblical Commission" of 1911–12 (1948:332–33). In the third edition Tricot added a section criticizing Lagrange and (especially) Benoit and a summary where he described Q as "un recueil composé en araméen" whose tenor and style Matthew preserved, but whose order Luke preserved (1954:371–72). Virtually simultaneous with the 1953 PBC statements, Wikenhauser (1953:178–82, ET 1958:249–53) openly endorsed the 2DH. He was followed quickly by Solages (1959, with a preface by Eugène Cardinal Tisserant and the imprimatur of the archbishop of Toulouse), who espoused both Markan priority and the dependence of Matthew and Luke on "X" (which was equivalent to Q).

104. Theobald (1992) classifies Lagrange and Batiffol as part of the "progressive right."

own solution to the Synoptic Problem was professedly not based on its dogmatic utility but only on literary critical considerations. Nevertheless, he
perceived an apologetic value in scientific criticism. In his review of Holtzmann's *Lehrbuch der neutestamentlichen Theologie* he stated:

> I do not demand that [the Catholic exegete] be a theologian, although I wish
> that he would be one; but I expect that he place himself on the terrain of our
> adversaries, leaving aside the contemporary expression of dogma when it
> comes to his study, in order to demonstrate in the end that it is only the *logical
> development* of the teaching of the New Testament. (1897:474, emphasis
> added)

The presence of secondary elements within the Gospels could be acknowledged forthrightly. According to Mangenot,

> it is appropriate, in the [Gospel] narratives and even in the discourses that they
> attribute to Jesus, to begin with what is historical and what is interpretive, with
> what was actually said by the divine Master, and what was a later *development
> of the tradition* and the work of an evangelist in the redaction of the stories and
> the sayings which they received from the tradition. (1911:69, emphasis added;
> cf. 1908:395)

As Lagrange indicated and Mangenot reiterated, historical criticism
could be used for apologetic purposes—to show that differences in teaching
represented *legitimate developments* rather than corruptions: "Secondary
traditions express precisely what the second generation of Christians
thought about Jesus, his life and his teachings, through the legitimate interpretation of the primitive tradition. This was not a deformation of that tradition" (Mangenot 1911:86). In Lagrange's view, to embrace the notion of
the evolution or development of doctrine relieved the exegete of the burden
of "finding" later dogmas, even in germinal form, within the Scriptures
themselves (1903:29).

When seen in the light of the theological interest in dogmatic development, it is perhaps clearer why Markan priority and the 2DH proved
broadly attractive. For the respective expansions and redactions of Mark by
Matthew and Luke themselves illustrated a kind of theological development
within the canon and afforded a historical paradigm for defending dogmatic
development in the subsequent eras of church history. The "Augustinian
hypothesis" and (still less) the GH were incapable of serving this function,
since on either view Mark could hardly be seen as a development of
Matthew (or Luke), and Luke's treatment of Matthew's discourses could
only have been regarded as a deconstruction.

Vatican Suppression of Critical Scholarship

Developments along these lines had been abruptly curtailed with the
decrees of the Pontifical Biblical Commission (1906–15), the declarations

against Modernism (*Lamentabili sane* [1907]; *Pascendi domini gregis* [1907]), and the excommunication of Alfred Loisy (1908). The Vatican officials rejected the 2DH along with the idea of a sayings source, and canonical Matthew was declared to be "substantially identical" (*quoad substantiam*) with its supposed Semitic original. This was not, however, an official endorsement of the Augustinian or Griesbach hypothesis over the 2DH. It was, on the contrary, a wholesale and undifferentiated rejection of *all* historical and literary-critical theories. This rejection included not only theories of Synoptic composition but also those regarding the composition and authorship of the Pentateuch, the textual criticism of 1 John, the historicity of Johannine narratives, literary criticism of Isaiah, the mythological nature in Genesis 1–11, and the authorship of the Psalms.

Even these lamentable occurrences must be seen in context. The period from the pontificates of Pius IX (1846–78) to Pius X (1903–14) was one of wild shifts as far as scholarship was concerned (Dansette 1961). The Vatican under Pius IX had been embattled by waves of anticlericalism in France and Italy; the church had lost control of its schools in France; and the pope had himself been driven from Rome in 1848. The security of religious truths seemed to have been undermined, on the one side by the publication of Darwin's *Origin of Species* (1859) and on the other by growing liberal democratic movements, which criticized the monarchic alignments of the church. Pius IX's reaction came in the issuing of the *Syllabus of Errors* (1864) and the promulgation of the doctrine of papal infallibility (*Dei filius* [1870]).

Leo XIII's reaction was different.[105] Moderately progressive, he promoted an intellectual revival in the church by encouraging the study of Aquinas, convinced that a speculative reason which took its starting point from revelation was best equipped to provide convincing answers to modern challenges (Daly 1980). Leo's encyclical *Providentissimus Deus* (1893) gingerly encouraged the study of oriental languages—the impulse that had encouraged scholars like Lagrange. The overall tone of the encyclical was cautious, affirming the inerrancy of the Bible; but it was permeated by the confidence that careful study of the Bible could only produce results that were consistent with the theological deductions of neo-scholasticism.

This confidence was misplaced. Neo-Thomism lacked any real sense of history and had an essentially static notion of truth. On both points, a collision with the major course of nineteenth-century thought was inevitable. But such historically minded scholars as Lagrange, Batiffol, and Loisy responded to Leo's encyclical with enthusiasm, undertaking a variety of historical and archaeological studies, sharing Leo's confidence that they would

---

105. Unlike Pius IX, Leo recognized the legitimacy of democratic governments in France. An important sign of his intellectual interests was his opening of the long-closed Vatican archives to researchers, including Protestant scholars. See Chadwick 1978.

only shed light upon and confirm the faith of the church. Even when Leo created the Pontifical Biblical Commission in 1902, its function was to encourage and guide serious scholarship; it was, in Leo's words, to provide the "divine text" with "the most thorough interpretation which is demanded by our times."[106]

By the following year and the accession of Pius X, the situation changed drastically. A Spanish aristocrat, Merry del Val, himself neither a scholar nor a theologian, became Pius X's secretary of state, and under his influence the PBC quickly became a mechanism of ecclesiastical control, handing down simple "affirmative" and "negative" verdicts on a variety of complicated topics.[107] By 1906 the views of Loisy, Tyrrell, and other Modernists were condemned; but no attempt was made to distinguish between the theological and philosophical underpinnings of Modernism and the results of their historical studies, which they shared with many others. The wholesale dismissal of the 2DH had the effect of rejecting the moderate views of Batiffol, Lagrange, and Mangenot, all of whom insisted that critical scholarship and ecclesiastical dogma were not in conflict. As Lester Kurtz aptly remarks: "The real enemy of the Vatican at the time of the Modernist crisis was not Alfred Loisy or Baron von Hügel or George Tyrrell, or any other individual within the church, but the widespread attack on the Vatican's authority" (Kurtz 1986:34). The "official solution" was to impose blind traditionalism and to reject both historiographic methods and the notion of historical development—hence, to affirm without argument the Mosaic authorship of the Pentateuch, the unity of Isaiah, the authenticity of the "Johannine comma" (1 John 5:7-8), and the apostolic character of Matthew. It was a crude effort to maintain a hold on truth and moral authority in an age of increasing rationalism.

Ultimately, the strategy of Merry del Val and Pius X failed. Catholic investment in historical criticism continued in the works of Lagrange, Sickenberger, Maier, Schmid, and Wikenhauser, albeit in a form that often wrapped itself in the watchwords of the PBC (Levie 1954). During the 1920s and 1930s Aquinas's thought—the ostensible basis of neo-scholasticism—was itself subjected to historical-critical analysis in the works of Chenu and others. In 1943 a more moderate Pius XII, who as a young man was befriended by "Modernist" Baron von Hügel, published *Divino afflante spiritu* to encourage Catholic study of the Bible.[108] It was during his

---

106. Leo XIII, *Vigilantiae* [October 1902; *EB* 137–48, here 137]. Lagrange took *Vigilantiae* as encouragement "to cultivate actively the study of philology and its attendant sciences, and to foster their continuous progress" (1985:89).

107. On the change of membership, see above, n. 96.

108. In 1936 a number of Catholic scholars offered a defense of historical criticism, sent to Pius XI via Eugène Cardinal Tisserant (see Guitton 1992:231–45). It was not until Pius XII that such overtures were successful, when Tisserant, Bruno de Solages, and Jacques Marie Vosté—

pontificate that the PBC degrees of 1906–15 were retracted. By the time of Vatican II, the notion of the development of dogma, actively promoted by the works of Yves Congar and Karl Rahner, was firmly entrenched in Roman Catholic theology. By that time too, the 2DH had become commonplace, especially in Germany, the center of postwar Catholic exegesis.

The Region of History: Theological Interest and the Synoptic Problem

This chapter has argued two main theses. First, it should not come as a surprise that factors other than the configuration of literary data and arguments based on them have played a role in commending the 2DH. The Synoptic Problem originated not as a literary problem but as a theological one—not as an innocent, antiquarian excursion into the literature of primitive Christianity, but as a response to the *theological* problem created by Reimarus. The quest to specify the literary relationships among the Gospels and to discover pre-Gospel sources was from the beginning tied to an endeavor to preserve the link between Gospel history and theological discourse that Reimarus had threatened to sever.

Once, however, scholars began in earnest to think about the literary relationships among the Gospels, genuinely literary arguments were mounted. Attention increasingly shifted from external (patristic) accounts to internal data. Important advances were made by Lachmann, de Wette, Baur, Weisse, Weiss, Holtzmann, and Hilgenfeld. Though it originated as a theological problem, the Synoptic Problem, with its array of literary-critical observations, soon came to deconstruct the theological solutions it was initially thought to sustain. The Griesbach hypothesis came under attack both from inside and outside the Tübingen school, not just on theological grounds but because it seemed to offer an inadequate *literary* account of the data. Likewise, the theory of Markan priority slowly rid itself of dependence on patristic statements and gradually came to terms with internal Synoptic data. In doing so, it had to change form, from the versions initially proposed by Weisse to those of Holtzmann in 1863—influenced by an uncritical reading of Papias—to those of the later Holtzmann and finally to Wernle's solution. The Synoptic Problem may have begun as a theological problem, but it did not remain so. In fact, the maturing of Synoptic literary criticism had the effect of undermining various theological systems it was once seen to support.

The second thesis is that despite the increasingly autonomous and distinct

---

the latter two both students of Lagrange—encouraged Pius XII to publish *Divino afflante spiritu* (ghostwritten by Augustin [later cardinal] Bea and Vosté). The 1936 letter played an important role in the draft of the encyclical. On Tisserant's role elsewhere, see above, n. 103.

grounds on which solutions to the Synoptic Problem were formulated, their appeal was often not simply a matter of how effectively they solved literary conundrums. Literary-critical solutions were "discovered" and utilized within larger ideological or apologetic frameworks, frameworks that helped to promote their acceptance, disguise their weaknesses, and eliminate competitors without real warrant. This is as true of the Griesbach hypothesis as it is of Markan priority.

Although Griesbach did not develop his hypothesis with dogmatic history in view, the GH was adopted by Baur because it seemed transparent to the general conviction that dogma developed from a Jewish Christian to a Gentile Christian and then to a Catholic synthesis. The evident appeal of this scenario seems to have made it difficult for Baur, at least, to see the weaknesses in the literary hypothesis. Conversely, Weisse's early version of the 2DH met with so poor a reception probably because the appeal of Baur's solution before 1848 made it difficult to imagine substituting a differently based literary solution and a differently configured theological argument.

As I have suggested, the Markan hypothesis also served larger theological interests, and its wide appeal seems to have hidden from view the fact that Holtzmann's "demonstration" of his hypothesis was notably defective. The 2DH was seen to cohere with key aspects both of liberal theology and of Roman Catholic convictions about dogmatic development. Those appeals may have had something to do with the lack of real consideration that the GH received after 1860, but I have suggested that many personal factors are involved as well.

The decline of idealist philosophy and the rise of historicism especially after 1848 constituted another important background to the reception of Markan priority. After Sieffert's 1832 book and especially in the wake of the Tübingen school's exposé of the mythological and seemingly late character of Matthew, few Protestant exegetes in the nineteenth century could base a life of Jesus solely or principally upon the first Gospel. The attempts of Strauss and Baur (and later Meijboom) to demonstrate that Mark was even later (on the basis of its allegedly "neutral" character) amounted to special pleading, and Weiss's and Holtzmann's attacks on the GH and its view of Mark seemed to rule out the GH on literary-critical grounds. When the edifice of Baur's theoretical system collapsed, the road lay open to the reception of Mark, or something very near Mark, as the historical source closest to Jesus.

The triumph of the Markan hypothesis should not, however, be seen as the inevitable result of Holtzmann's literary analysis nor, as Stoldt and others would have it, as the perverse disregard for the counterarguments of its detractors. Holtzmann's case was far from comprehensive and begged many questions, but Meijboom's objections and Davidson's defense of the GH equally lacked rigor. What commended the Markan hypothesis was, as

Schweitzer suggested, the fact that the "life of Jesus" that it allowed proved congenial with the interests of liberal theology.

The strong investment of late nineteenth- and early twentieth-century Protestant scholarship in finding a historical Jesus near the surface of at least one Gospel is key to an assessment of the history of the Synoptic Problem. The scores of liberal lives of Jesus that appeared in the four decades following Holtzmann's little "life of Jesus" (above, p. 310) took for granted Holtzmann's demonstration of Markan priority and assumed the essential reliability of either Mark or *Ur-Markus*. Even in the wake of Wrede's demonstration of pervasive theological structuring in Mark and its implied rejection of the psychological lives of Jesus, F. C. Burkitt could in 1901 still plead on Mark's behalf: "But we are still in the region of history" (1901:51). The endorsement of Markan priority seems to have been as much based on the *assumption* of Mark's reliability as it was on literary-critical arguments.

In a sense, one might view Lagrange and his successors as taking over, but completely inverting, Baur's ambitious and brilliant program. Catholics, like Baur and unlike Holtzmann, were less interested in reconstructing the historical Jesus than they were in describing the unfolding of dogma and its relation to the Bible. Unlike Baur, however, Catholic exegetes from the 1890s on began not "at the top" with the theory of the dialectical development of dogma, but "at the bottom," with the literary and historical data. The "Catholic 2DH" rejected and inverted Baur's own conclusions about the Synoptics, placing Mark before canonical Matthew and Luke. It was this hypothesis, not the GH, that allowed intracanonical doctrinal development to be seen most clearly. In spite of the pressures of 1911–12 to suppress historical criticism, Catholic exegetes maintained its essentials. By Vatican II both the 2DH and an articulated theory of dogmatic development were in full swing and emerged with the blessing of the council.

The fact that Holtzmann's life of Jesus based on Mark (or A) found a sympathetic ear in the liberal theology of the nineteenth century should not obscure the fact that this was not the *basis* of his view of Synoptic relationships, but its *result*. The congeniality of the 2DH with Catholic theories of dogmatic development does not diminish the *literary* arguments of Lagrange and others. Likewise, the fact that Strauss and Baur saw the GH as usefully illustrating their theological and historical views should not permit us to ignore the solid literary work done by Saunier and de Wette in articulating the hypothesis. It is important to stress that the uses to which a particular hypothesis is put are extrinsic to the logical and evidentiary basis of the hypothesis itself. It is fallacious to suppose that the attraction of liberal theology to the 2DH after 1870, or the eclipse of liberal theology after World War I, or the Catholic use of the 2DH, or Strauss's use of the GH, necessarily compromise the hypotheses involved. Indeed, Walter Schmithals is correct in observing that the fact that the 2DH outlived and, indeed, played a part in bringing about, the demise of many of the intellectual constructions that once lent it support, demonstrates how just little it depended for its key elements upon an "ideological foundation" (1985:197).

To recognize that theological interests were present at the conception and birth of solutions to the Synoptic Problem is not to suggest that the 2DH *depends* on liberal theological assumptions or that these solutions to the Synoptic Problem are simply disguised theological apologetics. That would be naive and would trivialize the serious and substantial literary-critical observations that were adduced by B. Weiss and Holtzmann and later Lagrange (whose work had nothing to do with theological liberalism). Although the 2DH has indeed served various theological interests, its essential foundations are the observations, outlined in chapter 1, of the special pattern of agreements and disagreements among the Synoptics and the logical inferences that these permit.

On the other hand, it is clear from the history of scholarship that the *Rezeptionsgeschichte* of various solutions had as much to do with their perceived utility as it had with their logical and literary appeals. Baur's use of the GH and the liberal use of the 2DH are equally clear instances. This is a particularly important point, since we shall see that it recurs throughout the twentieth century as well, affecting the fortunes of essentially literary and historical arguments regarding the documentary character, genre, composition, and theological affinities of Q.

7

Putting Q on the Map

D ESPITE THEIR FLIRTATION with the *logia*, scholars in the nineteenth century were mostly uninterested in the questions surrounding the reconstruction of Q, being captivated both historically and theologically by Mark
(or *Ur-Markus*). Wendt, to be sure, was a conspicuous exception when,
alongside Mark, he considered the "Logia of Matthew" and "the groundwork of the sayings of Jesus in the fourth Gospel" as reliable bases for a life
of Jesus (1886, ET 1892, 1:22). Holtzmann had gone so far as to catalogue
the linguistic profile of "Λ" (1863:335–44). In the main, however, few
looked to the *logia* as a key historical or theological source and fewer still
expended any effort trying to give the document a definite shape.

The sayings source was overshadowed by Mark/*Ur-Markus* because the
latter was thought to provide the most reliable access to the historical Jesus,
at least after Holtzmann's *Die synoptischen Evangelien*. Q was of interest
only insofar as it helped to account for Mark. It was the *idea* of a document
beside Mark rather than the document itself that was exploited. The sayings
source served as a kind of algebraic unknown, capable of expansion and
contraction. The extent of Q depended on whether Matthew and Luke were
derived from canonical Mark or from an *Ur-Markus* containing some of the
double tradition, and on whether the reconstruction of the life of Jesus
could be satisfied with canonical Mark or whether it needed some of the
double tradition (e.g., the Sermon on the Mount) as well. For the Weisse of
1838, the double tradition and the sayings source were more or less coextensive. But for the Weisse of 1856, who included the temptation story
and well as much of Luke 7 in *Ur-Markus*, or the Holtzmann of 1863,
whose *Ur-Markus* included the words of the Baptist, the temptation story,
a short version of the Sermon on the Mount and the healing of the centurion's serving boy, the sayings source was considerably shorter than the
double tradition. Only when confidence in Mark as a historical source was

destroyed in the wake of Wrede's *Das Messiasgeheimnis in den Evangelien*[1]
and after the rejection of the *Ur-Markus* hypothesis that ensued from
Wernle's *Die synoptische Frage* (1899) could attention shift to the Sayings
Source, by this time christened "Q" (for *Quelle*, "source") by Johannes
Weiss (1890:557).[2]

At the beginning of the twentieth century there was a rather short-lived
turn to Q as a source for the Jesus tradition in its pristine purity. According
to Adolf von Harnack, Q provided access to the historical Jesus in a way
that Mark could not. It was both homogeneous and ancient, unpreoccupied
with the miraculous (even in Q 7:1-10), apologetics, or the "exaggerated"
apocalypticism of Mark; instead its focus was on pure morality (1908:233,
237, 250–51).

> Q is a compilation of discourses and sayings of our Lord, the arrangement of
> which has no reference to the Passion, with an horizon which is as good as
> absolutely bounded by Galilee, without any clearly discernible bias, whether
> apologetic, didactic, ecclesiastical, national or anti-national. (1908:171)

Harnack had declared the so-called Johannine *logion* (Q 10:21-22) to be a
key to Jesus' self-understanding and as "the basis of faith and of theology"
(1894–97, 3:902, ET 1896–99, 7:273). Wernle shared this optimistic view
of Q's reliability, declaring that it expressed the "free, almost revolutionary
Gospel of Jesus himself" even though he recognized the presence of some
late "Jewish Christian" elements.[3]

Such a rosy assessment of the historical veracity of Q soon came under
attack by both Catholic and Protestant exegetes. In his penetrating analysis
of the Synoptics, Loisy argued that many Q sayings, including Q 10:21-22,
were not authentic sayings of Jesus at all but the utterances of Christian
prophets speaking in Jesus' name. For Loisy, this did not constitute a problematic discontinuity; on the contrary, the sentiments of such sayings as Q
10:21-22 conform to those of Jesus. Much of the secondary development of
Q was perfectly intelligible as the logical unfolding of the message of Jesus
(1907–8, 1:907). It was, nonetheless, secondary and nonauthentic.

For his part, Wellhausen compared Q and Mark where the two overlapped and argued that Q consistently displayed theological developments
beyond what was present in Mark.[4] From this he concluded that Q was *lit-*

---

1. Wrede 1901, ET *The Messianic Secret* (1971); cf. later K. Schmidt 1919.
2. Neirynck (1991e:474) points out, however, that J. Weiss may have been influenced by
Simons (1880:4, 22, 29, 30, 68), whose principal designation for the sayings source was Λ (or
"die apostolischen Quelle" or "die zweite Hauptquelle") but who occasionally referred to "die
Weiss'sche Quelle" or "die W.'sche Q" and "Λ (Q)."
3. Wernle 1899:229–30; similarly 1904:64–65: "It is ultimately the entire stock of these discourses that conveys to us the kernel of the gospel in unmixed purity and freedom." Similarly,
Jülicher 1904:359.
4. Wellhausen 1905: §8; 1911: §6. Cf. 1911:159–60: "On the surface the difference is that
while Mark combines narrative and didactic material, the other documentary source restricts

erarily dependent upon Mark. In retrospect, most of his arguments are unconvincing and even among his contemporaries there was little support for placing Q after Mark. At the time, however, Wellhausen's analysis, coupled with those of Loisy and others, was sufficient to inscribe *caveat lector* (reader beware) over any attempt to read a life of Jesus directly from Q. Scholars such as Burkitt (1906), interested in recovering historical tradition from the Synoptics, now used Q along with Mark but knew that a judicious and critical sifting of both sources was required.

The two main issues of Synoptic research that emerged in the nineteenth century—the historical Jesus and the developments of early Christian theologies—continued to be discussed actively but with a difference in focus. It was no longer a question of determining a sequence of *documents*, either in order to plot them against the various identifiable *Tendenzen* in the history of dogma or in order to arrive at a single document that could deliver a reliable portrait of the historical Jesus. In the meantime the idea of "the Synoptic tradition" had been born—the totality of the Jesus tradition contained in Matthew, Mark, and Luke (some would also include some of the early noncanonical gospels).[5]

Scholars were now prepared to imagine a much more complicated process of tradition whereby the Jesus tradition was carried via several means, initially in multiple oral strands and eventually several written documents. They were prepared to cope with a much more diverse field of combinations and configurations of the available traditions, not playing one against the other but treating them as varied expressions of "*the* tradition."[6] The task of reconstructing the life or teachings of the historical Jesus would necessarily entail the analysis of the tradition as a whole, with its various oral and written components. Indeed, this was implicit in the very title of F. C. Burkitt's book, *The Gospel History and Its Transmission* (1906). Likewise, the description of the history and development of primitive Christianity would draw on "the tradition" and from it distill multiple discrete and contrasting expressions, some successive, some simultaneous.

---

itself mainly to the didactic. It omits the narrative *intentionally*. That it knew the passion, which it passes over in silence, goes without saying. . . . Thus it is not out of the question that it presupposes and attempts to elaborate on Mark" (emphasis added).

5. An analogous shift occurred in NT textual criticism, with the replacing of the "genealogical method," which thought in terms of successions of discrete documents and recensions and aimed at the construction of relatively simple stemma diagrams, with a much more complex model that envisaged the transmission of the NT as a "process" entailing multiple influences and cross-fertilization. See Metzger 1963; Epp 1989.

6. Farmer (1964:21–22) contrasts this with the documentary approach of de Wette and Bleek: "The Synoptic Problem has now become a great jigsaw puzzle, and the critic is busy trying to fit all the pieces together. Eventually the critic will actually begin to refer to the 'Synoptic-tradition,' meaning the total mass of the Gospel materials making up Matthew, Mark, and Luke. Thus, the integrity of the Gospels as literary wholes is dissolved, and the distinctive intentions of the Evangelists tend to become obscured."

Q, the Synoptic Tradition, and the Historical Jesus

Although Harnack failed to replace Mark with Q as a source for the historical Jesus, his efforts contributed to a much larger paradigm shift in Synoptic studies. The nineteenth century had begun in a spirit of enthusiastic and, at times, unbridled intellectual experimentation regarding the origins of the Gospels, and throughout most of the century several source hypotheses vied for supremacy. By the beginning of the twentieth century the 2DH had outlived all its rivals; source-critical experimentation ended. Harnack in Berlin, Julius Wellhausen in Göttingen (1905), F. C. Burkitt at Cambridge (1906), Heinrich Julius Holtzmann at Strasbourg (1907), B. W. Bacon at Yale (1908b), and Kirsopp Lake in Leiden (1909) lent their considerable prestige to the 2DH and declared the battle over; only a tiny handful of dissidents remained.[7]

Problematic aspects of the 2DH lingered, to be sure, as some of its proponents admitted. Rival source hypotheses had not been dispatched quite as successfully as proponents of the 2DH thought; nevertheless, no other hypothesis was seen to solve the Synoptic Problem with the efficiency and plausibility of the 2DH and none gained any following of note. This new consensus significantly reshaped the agenda for Synoptic studies and for the study of Q. The question was no longer, which Gospel is the earliest? Almost everyone thought that it was Mark. Nor was the agenda defined by the dogmatic problem created by Reimarus: diversity within the New Testament and what dogmatic sense could be made of such diversity. For in Protestantism, the intense historical analysis and critique of dogma in the latter part of the nineteenth century relativized the importance of dogma itself.[8] The task now was to understand the transmission of the Jesus tradition in its variety and complexity and from it to reconstruct a critical portrait of the historical Jesus.

PUTTING Q ON THE MAP

The new sense of security in the 2DH had immediate consequences for the study of Q. The casual, almost whimsical, use of the *idea* of a second Synoptic source came to an abrupt end and Q became now a *documentary*

---

7. Holtzmann 1907:19–20: "On this point virtually all agree, Germans as well as others, Europeans and Americans, and for the vast majority the Markan hypothesis is no longer just a hypothesis." Holtzmann mentioned as dissenters only Klostermann, Zahn, Hilgenfeld, and Merx, as well as Holsten and Keim, who continued to advocate the views of Baur and Strauss.

8. See Lührmann's wry comment: "In our own time this relationship [of exegesis to dogmatics] can perhaps be most clearly seen in the conflict which Catholic colleagues have with papal teaching authorities, where there is historical criticism of the dogma that has been handed down. They still have a dogma which can be criticized. In the Protestant domain, historical criticism has long won the victory over dogma and there is no binding church teaching or at least, hardly any" (1993:57).

source, susceptible to analysis and precise description. With the 2DH "secured," reconstruction now became a priority. In rapid succession important studies appeared that articulated the principles for reconstructing Q[9] and three scholarly reconstructions of the Greek text.[10] The first to appear, and certainly the most influential, was Harnack's full Greek reconstruction, which he furnished with a vocabularic and syntactic analysis and discussions of its date, character, and importance (1907, ET 1908). In the next few years there followed outlines and commentaries on the contents of Q (Stanton 1903–20, 2:102–4) and finally a series of technical studies discussing the order, extent, and integrity of Q.[11]

To be sure, disputes continued about the precise extent and wording of the document. But gone were the times when Q could be used algebraically and expanded or contracted on demand. So secure would the profile of Q become that in the decades that followed, Q, along with other sources, could be integrated into "documentary maps" depicting the evolution of Gospel tradition. Thus, for example, B. H. Streeter's influential *The Four Gospels* (1924:150) proposed a stemma diagram of Synoptic relationships that localized each Gospel and each Gospel source in space and time (figure 29a). Published a few years later in the United States, F. C. Grant's *The Growth of the Gospels* (1933:66) and its successor, *The Gospels: Their Origin and Their Growth* (1957:51), incorporated the Fourth Gospel into the stemma, adding further sources and nuance to Streeter's diagram (figure 29b).[12]

My interest in drawing attention to these maps is not whether they are adequate or not. Few scholars today would endorse them. What is striking about such diagrams is the degree to which they resemble classical text-

---

9. Hawkins 1899:88–92; [2]1909:107–13; 1911; J. A. Robinson 1902:86–102; V. Stanton 1903–20, 2:76–79; Fridrichsen 1913. Burton (1904:esp. 41–49) offered a valuable discussion of the logical principles for reconstructing the common Matthew–Luke material even though he espoused a somewhat more complicated solution to the Synoptic Problem (see above, chap. 2 n. 69).

10. Harnack 1907, ET 1908; B. Weiss 1907:1–96; Haupt 1913:7–87. In 1886 Wendt proposed a reconstruction (without actually providing a Greek text) of the "Matthäuslogia," in which he included not only the double tradition but much special Matthaean and Lukan material ([2]1901:23–33). Resch (1898) actually attempted a reconstruction of "the Logia" (דברי ישׁוע) in both Greek and Hebrew (!). His "reconstruction," however, was indiscriminate and idiosyncratic, and included the double tradition (sometimes broken up and rearranged), supplemented by selected Markan narratives, special Matthaean and Lukan materials, and scattered sayings and stories from the *agrapha*. Neither Wendt's nor Resch's "reconstruction" found any real following.

11. Streeter 1911a; 1911b; 1911c; Castor 1912; Patton 1915.

12. Figure 29b reproduces Grant's 1957 diagram. There are only minor differences between the 1933 and the 1957 stemmata: the sources of Matthew's infancy accounts (Syria [1933]; Syria-Palestine [1957]); L (Palestine-Syria [1933], Caesarea [1957]); and various Asiatic (1933) or Antiochene, Alexandrian, and Judaean (1957) sources for the Fourth Gospel.

Figure 29
B. H. Streeter and F. C. Grant on Gospel Relations

Figure 29a: B. H. Streeter
From: B. H. Streeter, *The Four Gospels* (London: Macmillan, 1924) 150

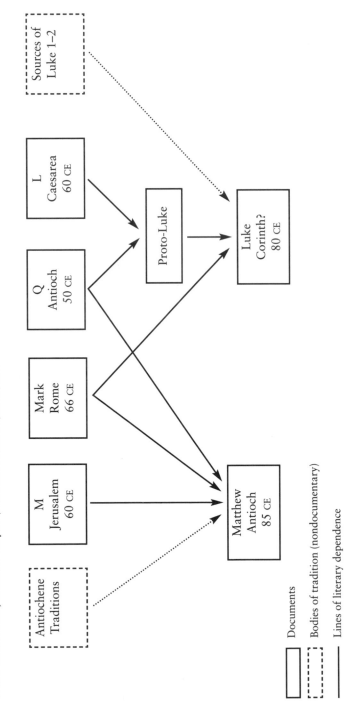

Documents

Bodies of tradition (nondocumentary)

Lines of literary dependence

Oral influences

Figure 29b: F. C. Grant

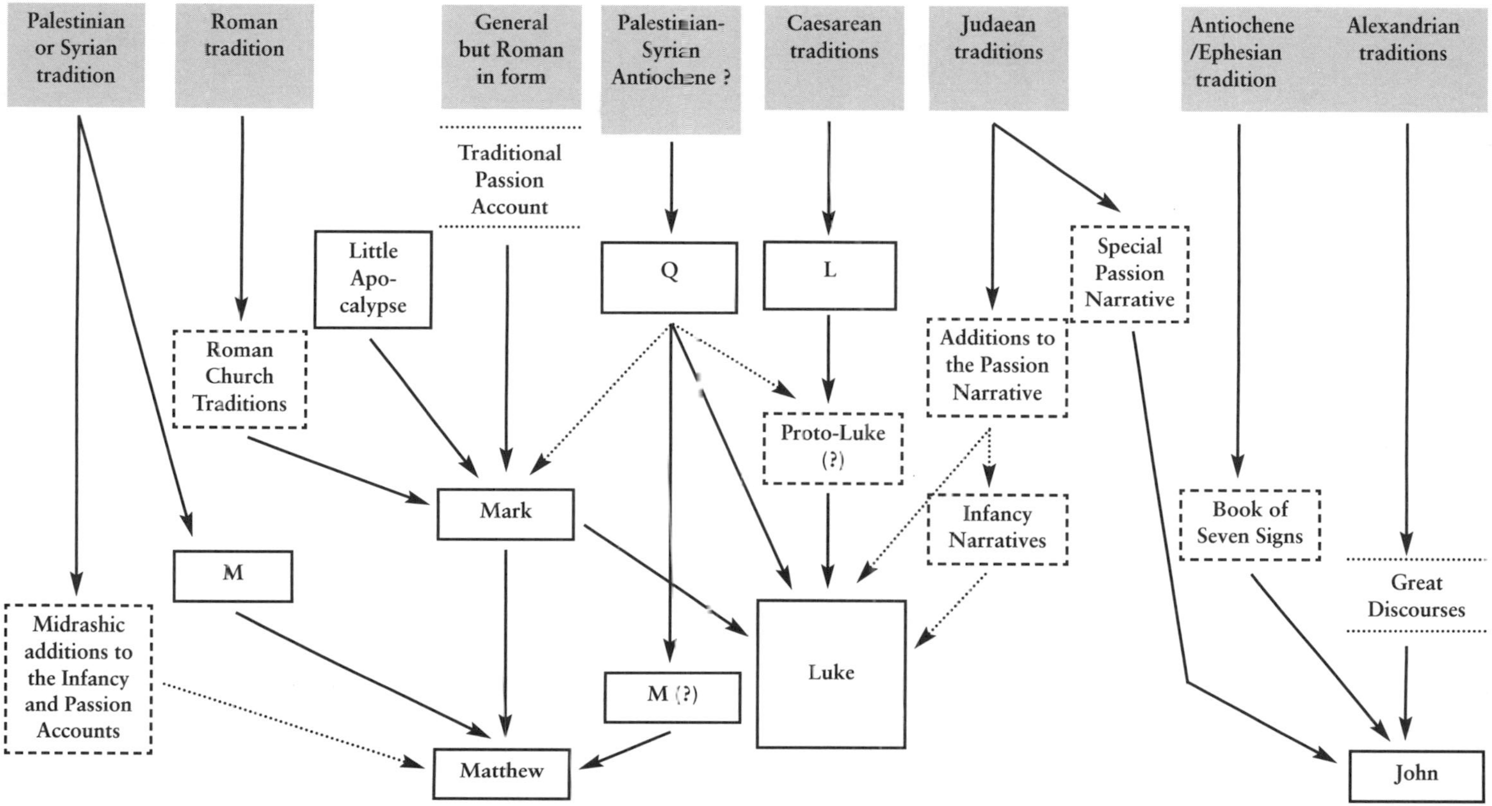

From: F. C. Grant, *The Gospels: Their Origin and Growth* (New York: Harper & Row, 1957) 51

critical stemmata which map the textual history of a particular document or documents by means of a series of exemplars and parent documents, each situated both geographically and temporally. That Streeter would view the Gospel tradition through the optic of text criticism is not really surprising when one recalls that Streeter was himself a distinguished text critic and that the first quarter of *The Four Gospels* dealt with text criticism (1924:25–148). Streeter discussed the pre-Byzantine manuscript tradition of the Gospels based on a theory of "local texts"—Alexandrian, Western (i.e., North African, and Italo-Gallic), Ephesian, Antiochene, and Caesarean—each associated with a particular center. The theory of local texts provided a model for compassing the diversity and complexity of three centuries of transmission of the New Testament. Streeter saw an explicit analogy with the study of the Gospels. Just as one could determine the local characteristics of manuscripts by an intensive examination of each, so also the Gospels (and their sources) should, he argued, be studied individually, so that their local characteristics could be set in relief. Streeter's diagram of the pedigree of the Gospels thus paralleled his earlier chapter "The Texts of the Great Sees" (1924:53–76). The model of text criticism had simply been transposed backwards from the period of scribal transmission of the New Testament that extended from the origins of the five local recensions to their displacement by Lucianic recension (and later, the *Textus Receptus*), to the period that began with the formation of the major source documents and ended with the inscribing of the Gospels. Q was another "manuscript" to be fit into space and time in the great flow of the Gospel tradition.

The influence of text criticism may also be seen in the methods used in the reconstruction of Q. Indeed, the very notion of "reconstruction" or restoration was congenial with the discipline of text criticism, and many of the principles used in restoring Q are principles adapted from text criticism: giving priority to the more difficult reading, the less editorialized version, the reading showing less harmonization with Mark, and the reading that explains the others.

That text-critical principles would be applied to the study of Q was, of course, quite natural in the early twentieth century. It was a time of consolidation of the great advances that had been made in the textual criticism of the New Testament: Codex Sinaiticus (א) had been "discovered" in 1844, and Codex Vaticanus (B) was published in 1857. The appearance of Tischendorf's *Novum Testamentum graece* (1869–72) and of Westcott and Hort's *The New Testament in the Original Greek* (1881) marked high-water points in the critical study of the New Testament. It was now thought possible to describe the transmission of the text of the New Testament with precision and to understand with the same precision how changes were introduced. Above all it was possible to "reconstruct" the *original* text of the New Testament. With the refinement of text-critical methods, the same principles—and the same mentality—could be transferred to the Synoptic tradition. Most of those, in fact, who contributed to this stage of scholarship on the Synoptic Problem debates were themselves distinguished text critics: F. C. Burkitt, A. Harnack, G. D. Kilpatrick, Kirsopp Lake, M. J. Lagrange, J. A. Robinson, William Sanday, Josef Schmid, B. H. Streeter, Vincent Taylor, H. J. Vogels, to name only the more prominent.

To view Q through the lens of text criticism conferred on it a tangibility that the earlier, more abstract notion of a "lost source" or *Urgospel* did not. Q was no longer just an idea that assisted in the solution of a source-critical problem; it was a definable point in a documentary history that could be reconstructed with reference to other points and by means of the scientific methods of textual criticism established by Griesbach, Lachmann, Tischendorf, and Westcott and Hort.

A quite unexpected discovery further enhanced the tangibility of Q. In 1898 B. P. Grenfell and A. S. Hunt published their first volume of the *Oxyrhynchus Papyri*, a spectacular find of papyri from Upper Egypt. The first document in volume one was an unknown collection of sayings of Jesus that would later be identified conclusively as part of the *Gospel of Thomas*, now known in full from a Coptic version (Attridge 1989). At the time of their discovery Grenfell and Hunt simply christened *P.Oxy.* 1 Λόγια Ἰησοῦ (the "Logia of Jesus"), adapting the common designation of Q.[13] The significance of *P.Oxy.* 1 was not lost on them: "In any case we may have got for the first time a concrete example of what was meant by the Logia which Papias tells us were compiled by St. Matthew, and the λόγια κυριακά upon which Papias himself wrote a commentary" (Grenfell and Hunt 1897:18).

Of course Grenfell and Hunt did not imagine that they had discovered a copy of Papias's *logia* or that they had in their hands parts of Q. *P.Oxy.* 1 and *P.Oxy.* 654, however, confirmed that archaic sayings collections lacking a narrative framework did exist.[14] As Lührmann noted, the Oxy-

---

13. Grenfell and Hunt 1898:no. 1 (pp. 1–3); 1897; 1904a. Lock (in Lock and Sanday 1897:16) pointed out that since λόγια in early Christian usage referred either to the whole of the Tanak or the whole gospel, λόγοι Ἰησοῦ was a better title for the collection (so Lake 1904:333). Lock's astute conjecture was confirmed with the discovery of *P.Oxy.* 654 (Grenfell and Hunt 1904b), whose first fragment begins: οὗτοι οἱ λόγοι οἱ [ἀπόκρυφοι οὓς ἐλά]λησεν Ἰη(σοῦ)ς ὁ ζῶν κ[αὶ ἔγραψεν Ἰούδα ὁ] καὶ Θῶμα ("These are the secret sayings which the living Jesus spoke and which Judas, who is called Thomas, wrote down"). Despite Lock's suggestion and its subsequent confirmation, it was Grenfell and Hunt's title that continued in use (e.g., White 1920:xxvi). Lock anticipated by more than sixty years a similar suggestion by J. M. Robinson (1964), that λόγοι rather than λόγια was the appropriate generic designation for Q.

14. Grenfell and Hunt's dating of *P.Oxy.* 1 and *P.Oxy.* 654 to the early third century (1904a:1; 1904b:14–15) suggested that the *terminus ad quem* for composition was 140 CE, and perhaps as early as the first century (1898:2). Given the fact that in 1900 the early NT papyri (𝔓⁴⁵, 𝔓⁴⁶, 𝔓⁵², 𝔓⁷⁴, 𝔓⁷⁵) had not yet been discovered, Grenfell and Hunt's discoveries made the Oxyrhynchus sayings among the earliest gospel-related manuscripts extant. Lake (1904) took the fragments as confirmation of the existence of a sayings collection, contemporary with Mark and used by Matthew and Luke.

rhynchus fragments seemed "to give Q a foundation from archaeological evidence."[15]

FROM ARAMAIC *LOGIA* TO GREEK Q

There is a notable irony here. Just as the Oxyrhynchus fragments were identified as "the *logia*," and just as their discovery seemed to demonstrate that the idea of a collection of Jesus' sayings was not merely a fancy of Synoptic scholarship, the connection between Q and Papias's *logia* was being severed. This development was rather gradual and took a different course in Protestant scholarship than it did among Catholic writers. The result was nevertheless the same. Reconstruction of Q suggested two conclusions: Q was not an Aramaic document, at least in its immediate pre-Matthaean and pre-Lukan forms; and it was less Matthaean than Lukan. The two key links with Papias were broken.

An important methodological shift had already occurred in German Protestant scholarship during the nineteenth century, from source hypotheses based exclusively upon patristic testimony (e.g., Lessing and Schleiermacher) to those based on a consideration of the internal Synoptic data, beginning with Lachmann, but in full bloom with B. Weiss and Holtzmann. By the end of the century both Protestants and Catholics alike would begin with the internal evidence, even though Catholics tended to value patristic testimony, not as a starting point, but as relevant nonetheless. It was obvious that Matthew and Luke had consulted Q in *Greek*, and hence the burden of proof would shift to those who wished to posit something else behind this Greek source. Moreover, by the end of the nineteenth century many German Protestants held that Papias, however erroneously, was describing canonical Matthew, not some other source. Hence his testimony was worthless in regard to Q.[16]

Other signs of the ferment are already visible with Holtzmann. His solution to the Synoptic Problem, while adducing Papias's testimony as sec-

---

15. Lührmann 1995:114. See earlier, Bacon 1908a:45: "The discovery of Grenfell and Hunt of papyri of the 2nd and 3rd century, in which sayings attributed to Jesus are agglutinated with no more of narrative framework than the bare words 'Jesus saith' (λέγει Ἰησοῦς), proves that such compilations actually circulated, fulfilling a function similar to the *Pirke Aboth*, or the 'Sayings of the Fathers' in the contemporary and earlier Synagogue."

16. Wernle 1899:117–20; Jülicher 1900:280; Wellhausen 1911:158. Farmer (1964:20–21) claims that Papias's testimony was a "powerful factor" in winning and sustaining support for the 2DH during the nineteenth century. Given Holtzmann's indifference to patristic testimony and the rejection of Papias's statements by later German scholars, this claim needs to be reevaluated. It is truer of British scholarship at the turn of the century when, for example, Sanday (1899–1900) argued that "nothing fits Papias's logia better than what remains of Matthew and Luke over above Mark" (responding to Allen 1899–1900). Nonetheless, most British scholars were aware of the problem with Papias's testimony; Allen, Burkitt, and J. A. Robinson rejected its value completely.

ondary, corroborative evidence, did not use it to delineate the character of
"the second main source." Nonetheless he designated his source with the
siglum Λ (λόγια) *"subject to a more precise demonstration of its nature"*
(1863:128, emphasis added). By 1900 even Holtzmann's provisional designation was rejected by W. C. Allen and by J. A. Robinson, who refused to
use the "question-begging" term *logia* to describe the non-Markan Greek
document.[17] *Logia* meant "oracles" and there was no evidence prior to
Papias that sayings of Jesus were thought of as oracles. Allen's and Robinson's reservations were soon echoed by Burkitt, Bacon, and Hawkins.[18]

Still, some maintained that Papias's testimony applied to Q. Harnack
cited Papias's statements in support of the view that Q was an apostolic
composition in Aramaic, quoting Wellhausen as having demonstrated the
Aramaic substratum of Q. Harnack, it should be noted, also held that
Matthew best represented the order of Q's sayings, in spite of the fact that
he was unable to adduce reasons for Luke's editorial procedures on that
supposition.[19] Well aware of the problematic character of Papias's testimony, Hawkins was also reluctant to sever the connection with Papias; nevertheless, he based his case for an Aramaic Q on Wellhausen's translation
variants rather than on Papias's statements (1911:104); the same is true of
Castor (1912:17–18), who explicitly cited Wellhausen.[20]

The link between Q and Matthew was cut decisively with the works of
Streeter (1911b), Castor (1912), and Patton (1915), all of whom concluded
that Luke best preserved the original order of Q. Holtzmann, in fact, had
argued for Lukan order in the face of an earlier consensus,[21] as did Wellhausen against Harnack (1905:67; 1911:59). By the second decade of the
twentieth century these arguments had won the day. Given the fact that
Luke did not substantially interfere with Mark's order and given that
Matthew's presentation of the double tradition was far more organized than
Luke's, it was clearly preferable to suppose that Luke had preserved the
order of Q and that Matthew had rearranged it, as he had rearranged Mark.
Thus a key connection with Papias's testimony was undermined: the Q say-
ings were now neither *logia* nor especially Matthaean.

In his introduction to Castor's volume B. W. Bacon rejected the entire

17. J. A. Robinson 1902:70. Allen 1899–1900:425: ". . . it is greatly to be hoped that the
term Logia as a title for the supposed Greek source of Mt and Lk may cease to haunt the writings of serious students." Papias's Aramaic source should not be confused with Matthew and
Luke's *Greek* source.

18. Burkitt 1906:127, 130; Bacon 1908a:49; 1908b:55; Hawkins 1909:107 [but not in the
1899 edition]; 1911:107.

19. Harnack 1908:247–49; also Godet 1893–99, 2/1:199–200, 217–20.

20. See also Manson 1949:18; Koester 1980:108 n. 12; 1982, 2:172.

21. Holtzmann (1863:128) notes that up to the time of Tobler, Matthew had been assumed
to represent Q. Tobler (1858:15–18) assumed (with Schleiermacher) that the conclusions to the
Matthaean sermons (7:28-29; 11:1; 13:53; 19:1; 26:1) derived from the sayings source
(*Spruchsammlung*), noting the coincidence of its fivefold structure with that of the Pentateuch.

connection between Q and Papias, including the thesis that it was composed in Aramaic (1918:18). Despite Wellhausen's "translation variants," the language of Q was Greek, not Aramaic.[22] Nothing in Q indicated apostolic authorship. Most important, internal examination of the double tradition provided strong evidence that *Luke*, not Matthew, best preserved the basic structure of Q. With this, Q was cut completely free of Papias.

Catholic scholarship followed a rather different path. For Lagrange, whose discussion of the Synoptic Problem began from his astute observations of the internal data (1895; 1896), it was nonetheless important that the final solution be consistent with ecclesiastical tradition. It was this concern that seemed to incline him to reject the idea of a source composed entirely of sayings.[23] But for Batiffol and Mangenot the 2DH offered nothing incompatible with ecclesiastical tradition. Indeed, an Aramaic sayings collection authored by Matthew seemed perfectly compatible with Papias's testimony.[24]

Even after the Pontifical Biblical Commission's statements of 1911 and 1912 seemed to close the door to the 2DH, a significant number of Catholics used an Aramaic Q, now called "Aramaic Matthew," to protect the 2DH from criticism. In the *responsum* of June 19, 1911, the PBC rejected the view that Matthew's source was merely a "collection of sayings or sermons of Christ" (*collectio dictorum seu sermonum Christi*), insisting that it was "properly and strictly" (*proprie et stricte*) a gospel (*EB* §391). Joseph Sickenberger answered that most (Catholic) proponents of the 2DH agreed: "For them, the siglum Q also represents 'proprie et stricte' a gospel, just as Papias apparently regarded the λόγια that he attributed to Matthew as τὰ ὑπὸ τοῦ κυρίου ἢ λεχθέντα ἢ πραχθέντα (the things said and done by the Lord)—in other words, a proper gospel" (1911:393).

As to whether canonical Matthew preserved his source substantially (*quoad substantiam,* *EB* 392), Sickenberger conceded that whoever interpreted this to imply absolute identity could not hold the 2DH. However,

> whoever conceives of the activity of the translator as that of free redaction and thinks it possible that this redaction took into account the Markan material that already existed in Greek and both made insertions into the Matthaean original and systematized the material, can with justification adhere both to the authorship of Matthew that is conveyed by tradition as well as to the Two Source hypothesis, based on numerous textual comparisons.[25]

---

22. Ironically, Wellhausen himself agreed. Although he noted that the degree of agreement between Matthew and Luke varies and suggests that "a few variants can be explained most satisfactorily only as divergent readings or translations of an Aramaic original," Wellhausen insisted that Matthew and Luke "knew [Q] only in a Greek translation," although he allowed that there may have been two slightly different Greek recensions (1911:59–60).

23. Lagrange 1896:27. See chap. 6, n. 99.

24. Batiffol 1897:69–70; 1901:26–30; Mangenot 1911:54, 59, 60.

25. Sickenberger 1911:393–94. Sickenberger's introduction to the New Testament, written

Another Catholic, Friedrich Maier, tried to answer Lagrange's objection about the lack of traditional attestation of Q:

> The so-called sayings source (which must have also contained narratives as well) is unattested as such in early church tradition. It must have been translated into Greek very early on and thus been deprived of its own existence, leaving no detectable remains outside of the two longer synoptic gospels in which it survived in two new translations and adaptations.[26]

After 1955 a few Catholic critics continued to maintain the probability of an Aramaic Q (rather than Matt^{Aram}),[27] even though its evidentiary basis had been severely compromised and its apologetic usefulness had virtually disappeared. Ironically, Wikenhauser and Schmid, who held this view, also insisted that the variations between Matthew and Luke are not due to translation variants and rejected even the likelihood of two Greek versions (Q^{Matt}, Q^{Luke}); such assumptions were unnecessary as long as one could trace the differences to the evangelists themselves (Wikenhauser 1973:287). One wonders why similar reasoning was not applied to the theory of an Aramaic Q, since on their own logic an Aramaic Q is equally unnecessary. Once the PBC had nullified its predecessor's decisions, there was no apologetic need for heroic attempts to harmonize patristic statements with the internal Synoptic data. Significantly, the first book-length treatment of Q by

---

after the PBC decree of June 26, 1912, which cast doubt on the 2DH as "nullo fulti traditionis testimonia nec historico argumento" (*EB* §405), nonetheless maintained a source-critical solution that was equivalent to the 2DH, but without stipulating the contents of Matt^{Aram}: Mark was prior to, and the source of, Greek Matthew and Luke; both Matthew and Luke used Matt^{Aram} (=Matthew *quoad substantiam*) via a Greek translation (Matt^{Greek}); and Luke had special sources. Since he refused to indicate the precise extent to which Matthew also used special sources, but argued that Luke did *not* know Matthew's infancy or resurrection stories or his genealogy and that Luke's order of sayings is closer to that of Matt^{Greek} than canonical Matthew, Sickenberger in effect preserved most of the essential features of the 2DH without using the name (1916; [2]1920:77–78). In a later article that challenged the priority of (Greek) Matthew to Mark, he states that he personally avoided the term "Two Source Hypothesis" since Luke 1:1-4 suggests that there were several sources available to him (1933:2). Despite the terminological quibble, Sickenberger's acceptance of the 2DH seems not to have changed.

26. F. Maier 1912:49; cf. Wikenhauser 1953:182. Maier (1883–1957) was a *Privatdozent* (lecturer) at Strasbourg 1910–13. Because of the 1911–12 PBC decrees, he broke off his Synoptic commentary after only the second fascicle (1910–12), which probably would have been accepted as his *Habilitationsschrift* had he completed it. After serving in chaplaincy positions (1913–1921), he was habilitated in Breslau (1920), becoming "Ordentlicher Professor" in 1924 and remaining there until 1945. In 1938 he received a *Ruf* ("call") from Munich to succeed Sickenberger (professor, 1924–38); but the Nazis did not confirm the appointment, so Maier had to remain in Breslau. The following year (1939) the Nazis closed the Catholic Theological Department at Munich. It was reopened in 1946 in Früstenried (a southern suburb of Munich) and later relocated to Munich, but already in November 1945 Maier was named "Ordentlicher Professor für Neues Testament." He remained in Munich until his retirement in 1951. (I owe the clarification of the sequence of events to Dr. Christoph Heil, Universität Bamberg.)

27. Wikenhauser and Schmid 1973:286; Zimmermann 1974:87; R. Collins 1983:132.

a Catholic, Athanasius Polag, rejected the notion of the composition of Q in Aramaic even though Polag reckoned on the Greek collector's use of tradition that had been formulated first in Aramaic (1977:31–32).[28]

The apologetic function of an Aramaic source is as clear in the case of nineteenth-century Protestant scholarship as it is for Catholics before 1955. For Catholics, an Aramaic source was a symbol of fidelity to ecclesiastical tradition. Protestant scholarship of the latter part of the nineteenth century had a deep investment in answering the late dating of the Gospels by D. F. Strauss and F. C. Baur and the unreliability of the tradition that this dating implied—even if nineteenth-century scholars had generally conceded that canonical Matthew was not apostolic in origin and was late. If doubts persisted about the Petrine character of Mark, a source in Aramaic and, presumably, proximate to Jesus (if not apostolic) was an excellent guarantor of the tradition.

After the 1920s in Protestant scholarship and after the 1950s in Catholic scholarship the need to posit an Aramaic Q was not so acutely felt, perhaps because the challenge of Strauss and Baur was also not so pressing. In the meantime the discoveries of $\mathfrak{P}^{52}$ (P. Rylands 457), the Chester Beatty Papyri, and the Bodmer Papyri moved the earliest manuscript evidence of the Gospels more than a century earlier than the manuscripts used by Tischendorf and Westcott and Hort.[29] $\mathfrak{P}^{52}$ provided a manuscript fragment of John from the early second century, a few decades *before* Baur had placed the composition of the Gospel!

Another reason that the theory of an Aramaic Q could be de-emphasized is that the "text-critical model" described above came to function as a kind of guarantor of the general reliability of the Jesus tradition. As a text critic, Streeter was perfectly aware of the numerous variations that had been introduced into the manuscripts of the NT; but his theory of local texts and the principles he invoked for determining the better reading afforded him the confidence to judge among those variations. The analogy he suggested between textual criticism and source criticism allowed him to conceive the task of bridging the gap between Jesus and the Gospels similarly. Streeter's "map" of early Christian documents offered an orderly accounting of the transmission and evolution of the Gospel tradition from 50 CE to the compilation of Matthew and Luke in the 80s (1924:22). Its very orderliness and fixity evinced the confidence that, in spite of some elements of variation, the Jesus tradition could be known, plotted, and reconstructed. Scholars from Harnack to Streeter addressed the technical problems of the order and extent of Q, but it was Streeter's *model* that lent to Q a tangibility as a doc-

---

28. Polag's licenciate thesis at Trier (supervised by Wilhelm Thüsing) was completed in 1966; his doctoral dissertation, also at Trier, was accepted in 1969 but published only in 1977.

29. See Metzger 1964; Aland 1989. The Chester Beatty papyri ($\mathfrak{P}^{45-47}$) were acquired in 1930–31, $\mathfrak{P}^{52}$ was published in 1934, and the Bodmer Papyri ($\mathfrak{P}^{66, 74-75}$) were acquired and published 1956–61.

ument that it had hitherto lacked. Streeter had put Q, both figuratively and actually, on the map of primitive Christianity.

The use of just such a map to achieve a critical reconstruction of the teachings of Jesus may be seen most clearly in the work of T. W. Manson, to whom we also owe the first commentary on Q (1937). Manson knew that it was no longer possible to write a biography of Jesus; but he could trace in a fairly precise manner the "history of the tradition," as he called it, from its oral stages, to its inscription in small collections, through the compilation of the documents Q and "M" and the collection of Luke's "L" materials, to their "amalgamation" in the Synoptic Gospels. No less than Streeter, Manson pictured the tradition through the lens of a documentary map on which he plotted its most significant stations: Q in Antioch somewhat before 50 CE, a Judaean M-source just before the First Revolt, and L in Caesarea ca. 60 (1949:11–28). Although Manson thought that Papias's testimony applied to Q, appeal to a putative Aramaic substratum of Q played only a minor role in his argument. It was, rather, the assured existence of Q, its clear contours, its early date, and the reliability of its contents that conferred on Q its importance.[30]

With the advent of form criticism in Germany, however, no written source was safe. Form critics showed the extent to which all written sources, no matter how early, showed the impress of the post-Easter Christian community and, consequently, none could serve purely and simply as the basis for a life of Jesus.

The Synoptic Tradition and the Life of the Early Church

FORM CRITICISM AND THE DISAPPEARANCE OF Q

Harnack might justly be accused of harboring the same naïveté toward Q that his predecessors did toward Mark. His positive assessment of the historicity of Q was not to last long, however. The year following the publication of his volume on Q, Bacon (1908b) argued that neither Mark nor Q was a primitive composition and used Q to describe, not the life of Jesus, but the course of the development of Gospel tradition. Wellhausen also answered Harnack's optimistic evaluation of Q by showing the extent to which Q was more theologically developed than Mark and hence, just as unreliable as a source for the historical Jesus (1911:63–79).

Two years later, Rudolf Bultmann published his first and only essay devoted solely to Q, an essay that represents a significant turning point in

30. Manson's book contains no discussion of the Synoptic Problem but begins with the general consensus of Harnack, Bussmann, and Streeter in the extent of Q, modifying this only slightly. "The existence of a common source being taken for granted, the next thing is to see what can be learnt about it, to attempt to restore it from the remains preserved in Mt. and Lk., to speculate about its probable date, authorship, place of origin, and the like" (1949:15).

Gospel research. While Bultmann acknowledged that Q was the source closest to the primitive church, it was not for him a quarry of materials relating
to the historical Jesus. For despite its age, Q was not unalloyed: the scribes
who had framed it had collected sayings of Jesus but had also introduced
pieces of secular wisdom and various "foreign influences" (1913, ET
1994:23). Accordingly, Q was to be used as a source for the *Urgemeinde*
("the primitive community"), attesting its diverging theological currents
and eddies. Q reflected the "eschatological mood" of the early church, its
freedom of spirit, and the gradual emergence of church regulation. It evidenced both imminent expectation of the end and the relaxation of that
expectation, both enthusiastic admonitions and bits of ordinary "secular
wisdom," both spirit-filled freedom from the law and the "spirit of order."
Significantly, Bultmann quoted Wellhausen extensively, but never Harnack.

Two important shifts were in progress. While British and American
scholars pursued the reconstruction of Q, culminating in Manson's "commentary" (1937), Bultmann began his essay by problematizing the reconstruction of the order, wording, and extent of Q. This did not deter
Bultmann's investigation, however, since he was not concerned, as his
British and American counterparts were, with Q as a document. Instead, Q
evidenced the varying moods, habits, and theological tendencies of the
primitive community. Bultmann's model was not text-critical at all. For him,
what was of interest were the traditions behind the written Gospels. The act
of Q's literary inscription was quite incidental and so too, therefore, was the
task of documentary reconstruction.[31] Almost as soon as Q had appeared
as a document, it began to disappear.

The second shift was theological. With the rise of neoorthodoxy after
World War I, theological attention was focused on the kerygma of the crucified and risen Lord rather than on the historical Jesus. This choice placed
Bultmann in the train of D. F. Strauss, for whom Christianity was not based
on the pre-Easter Jesus but upon the Easter faith (Georgi 1985:78). Since
the kerygma of the crucified and risen Jesus was conspicuously missing in
Q, the tendency was to regard Q as paraenesis or catechetics rather than as
the theological heart of Christianity. This theological evaluation of Q was
also shared by British scholars, Streeter (1924:292) and Manson (1949:9),
both of whom argued that Q knew and presupposed the passion kerygma
while functioning itself as a catechetical supplement.

Q "disappeared," not because Bultmann doubted the 2DH, but because
his method had scant place for documents. The primary fault lines in early
Christianity were not between Mark and Q or between John and the Synoptics or between written documents and oral tradition, but rather between

---

31. Bultmann (1968:6): "it is . . . a matter of indifference whether the traditions were oral
or written, because on account of the unliterary character of the material one of the chief differences between oral and written traditions is lacking."

Palestinian Jewish-Christian and Hellenistic Christian layers of tradition. According to Bultmann, all of our written sources already contained a mixture of both; for that reason, none of the early gospel documents, including Q, could receive a distinctive literary or theological profile.

Bultmann has been criticized for his undue skepticism concerning the historical value of the tradition, for his assumption that much of what was attributed to Jesus was the creation of early Christians, and for his schematic division of the Jesus tradition into two more or less sequential phases, Palestinian and Hellenistic. All are fair criticisms. At the same time, Bultmann's achievement was to demonstrate through close analysis of the text the great diversity in the forms, theologies, and literary affinities of the materials that make up the Jesus tradition, and in viewing the tradition in the context of the life of the various communities which preserved and employed it. In this sense, he prepared both for redaction criticism and for social analyses of the Gospels that would emerge after the Second World War.

THE DISCOVERY OF KERYGMATIC DIVERSITY

Q continued to be invoked in the many studies of the Synoptic Gospels in the period between the world wars, but hardly with the enthusiasm that had motivated Harnack. It was with Heinz Eduard Tödt's 1956 Heidelberg dissertation that Q began to recover its distinctive theological profile (1959, ET 1965). Tödt demonstrated, on the one hand, that form-critical analysis did not support the supposition that Q was paraenetic: pericopae such as the Beelzebul accusation (Q 11:14-26), the request for a sign (Q 11:29-32), and the thanksgiving for revelation (Q 10:21-22) betrayed no paraenetic interests. Elsewhere Q resumed Jesus' own preaching of the kingdom (Q 6:20b-23; 9:60; 10:9) (1965:249–50). On the other hand, Tödt showed that in Q christological cognition was in full swing and that this was not merely a function of the tradition embedded in Q, but rather a result of the deliberate literary activity of compiling the document (1965:253). This cognition—that Jesus was the coming Son of Man and that as such he also possessed authority (ἐξουσία) on earth—functioned as the hermeneutical equivalent of the "Easter faith," impelling the Q people to collect and represent Jesus' sayings afresh:

> The community which preserved the Q-material for us, concentrating its attention almost exclusively on Jesus' preaching, was convinced that Jesus' pointing to the coming of God's reign had not lost its meaning in the post-Easter situation, but must be proclaimed anew. The group of the disciples was regarded as authorized to resume this teaching (Luke 10:16). The meaning of the hortatory sections, too, was not understood separately but in connexion with "the most essential subject of our Lord's preaching, namely, that the kingdom of God is at hand." The nature of these sections is thus not determined by the passion but by the imminence of God's reign. (Tödt 1965:249; quoting Dibelius 1953:98)

Q, thus, did not represent a supplement to the passion kerygma but a "second sphere" of Christianity whose theological center lay in eschatology and Christology rather than the passion (1965:268).

Tödt's treatment of Q was symptomatic of a much larger shift that occurred in Synoptic studies, with the transition from form criticism, which focused on individual, discrete units of tradition as they circulated in pre-literary forms, to redaction criticism, which drew attention to the theological and literary accomplishments of the individual Synoptic evangelists as authors. Correspondingly there was also a shift from the anonymity of oral tradition vaguely associated with *the* "Palestinian" or *the* "Hellenistic church" to the particularity of individual writers, each engaged with the concerns of a specific Christian community. The method of redaction criticism produced a consciousness of the diversity and variety of primitive Christianity: Mark's gospel was quite distinct from Matthew's and from Luke's, and each represented a distinct "church." Redaction criticism, with its distinction between inherited tradition and theologically self-conscious redaction, provided the categories which could account for a significant theological pluralism within the early church while still drawing lines of continuity and commonality.

The attention devoted to theological diversity in primitive Christianity in technical NT studies after 1950 did not arise in a vacuum. During precisely the same period theological and practical diversity among Christian churches became the focus of attention in a way that it had not been before. The efforts on the part of Christian churches to respond to the devastation of World War II and at the same time to create a basis for mutual understanding sparked almost endless investigations of "unity and diversity,"[32] including many studies of the NT.[33] The recognition of striking diversity within the New Testament served the important role of providing historical precedents for the equally striking diversity of the present.

Unity was as important as diversity, however. Starting with the World Council of Churches' Faith and Order Conference in Lund (1952) and the WCC assembly in Evanston (1954), great stress was laid on eschatology as both fundamental to Christian identity and the basis for the churches' tran-

32. The evidences of the recognition of diversity are legion: the birth of the ecumenical movement; the establishing of the World Council of Churches (WCC) (1948) and of the Vatican Secretariat for Promoting Christian Unity (1960); Vatican II's documents on the church (*Lumen Gentium*) and the church in the world (*Gaudium et Spes*); the founding of the *Journal of Ecumenical Studies* (1964); and hundreds of articles and monographs on "unity and diversity" in various aspects of Christian tradition, mainly from the late 1950s and 1960s (see World Council of Churches 1972, 2:191–99).

The period after World War II also began a process (still to be completed) of decolonialization and with it, the beginning of the recognition of the legitimacy of other cultures. See Kloppenborg 1996a.

33. An early manifestation of this can be found in the debate between Ernst Käsemann and Raymond E. Brown at the 1963 Faith and Order Conference in Montreal.

sition from diversity to unity (see Clapsis 1991).[34] The importance of eschatology was highlighted among scholars of Christian origins by the discovery of the Dead Sea Scrolls in the late 1940s and their subsequent
publication, since the scrolls seemed to provide adventitious confirmation
that primitive Christian documents shared with Qumran similar eschatological hopes. Unity, diversity, and the importance of eschatology, far from
being isolated preoccupations of biblical exegetes, were symptomatic of a
much deeper concern in systematic and practical theology to establish a
framework with which to compass diversity. Eschatology in fact became a
determining aspect in two great Protestant theologians, Jürgen Moltmann
and Wolfhart Pannenberg.

It was at this point also that the Oxyrhynchus fragments (*P.Oxy.* 1; 654;
655) reentered the scene, by this time conclusively identified as parts of the
Gospel of Thomas. A complete Coptic version had been discovered in 1945
in the Egyptian hamlet of Nag Hammadi (Guillaumont 1959). Lines were
quickly drawn on the issue of whether Thomas depended on the final form
of the Synoptics or whether it provided independent access to the early
stages of the tradition. Although this debate raged without a consensus
emerging, one matter became quite clear: Thomas demonstrated that it was
possible to organize a gospel without reference to the Passion and Resurrection and without a narrative framework. James M. Robinson was one of
the first to grasp this fact, a fact that Grenfell, Hunt, and Bacon had recognized but which had in the meantime been forgotten.[35] Already in his 1962
review of German scholarship, Robinson treated Q as a discrete and
autonomous sphere of theologizing, independent of the passion kerygma.
The density of language relating to heavenly Wisdom (Sophia) and the Spirit
suggested a reading of Q that placed it on a theological trajectory stretching from the personification of Sophia in *1 Enoch* 42.2, through the wisdom
Christology of the Corinthian pneumatics, and ending in the Sophia speculations of the *Hypostasis of the Archons* from Nag Hammadi Codex II
(1962:82–83).

34. E.g., Käsemann 1963:295: "The unity of the Church has been, is and remains primarily an eschatological datum, which is only achieved insofar as it is received as a gift."

35. Perhaps because the Oxyrhynchus fragments and the *Gospel of Thomas* were treated as
"apocryphal" was it was illegitimately assumed that they had nothing to contribute to the
study of the Synoptics. Austin Farrer put the matter baldly: "We have no reason to suppose
documents of the Q type to have been plentiful. . . . No, in postulating Q we are postulating
the unique, and that is to commit a *prima facie* offense against the principle of economy in
explanation" (1955; repr. 1985:325). Farrer's argument is specious of course since it is quite
irrelevant whether sayings collections were common or not; *gospels* are not very plentiful
either. In any case, by 1955 a sayings gospel such as the *Gospel of Thomas* was already
published, and the Oxyrhynchus fragments had been available for more than half a century.
In addition, there were dozens of "documents of the Q type" in the form of Greek and Latin
gnomologia and chriae collections and in the form of Egyptian and other Near Eastern
instructions.

Two years later Robinson worked out this insight in much greater detail in his highly influential essay for the Bultmann Festschrift, "ΛΟΓΟΙ ΣΟΦΩΝ: Zur Gattung der Spruchquelle Q" (1964; ET 1971b). In this essay he traced the process by which Jesus' sayings were collected and tried to specify the hermeneutical principles at work in such collections. Robinson located Q on a trajectory of wisdom collections that extended from the Sayings of Amenemope, Ahikar, and Prov 22:17—24:22, through Sirach and the *Testaments of the Twelve Patriarchs*, and ending with the *Gospel of Thomas, Thomas the Contender*, and the *Pistis Sophia* in gnostic circles, the *Sentences of Sextus* in orthodoxy, and the *m. ʾAbot* in rabbinic circles. Moreover, he argued that other early Christian collections of λόγοι could be detected underlying, for example, Mark 4 and *1 Clem.* 13.2; 46.7-8.

According to Robinson, the presentation of sayings of Jesus in the genre of "sayings of sages" (λόγοι σοφῶν) activated one of the important theological dynamics of the genre: to associate and eventually to identify the speaker with the Heavenly Sophia, the source of wisdom. It was within this genre that a Sophia-Christology could emerge, as it does in Q 10:21-22 and especially in the *Gospel of Thomas* (esp. saying 28).[36] Once the generic tendencies of "sayings of the sages" are coordinated with the late-antique development of the Jewish Sophia into the gnostic redeemer, the continuities between Q, the *Gospel of Thomas*, and the *Pistis Sophia* become evident. Robinson conjectured that it was the gnosticizing associations that disinclined the orthodox church from continuing the use of the genre.

In a single stroke, Robinson had offered an explanation both for the generic peculiarities of Q—its lack of narrative framework and its concentration upon sayings—and for its theological distinctiveness—its association of Jesus with the Heavenly Sophia (Q 7:35; 11:49-51 and probably 13:34-35 and 10:21-22) and the absence of any interest in developing a salvific understanding of Jesus' death. Streeter had been convinced on literary grounds of the existence of Q but was unable to imagine any function for such a collection that did not presuppose the passion kerygma. Tödt demonstrated just how implausible Streeter's imagined catechetical *Sitz im Leben* for Q was, but it was Robinson who provided a literary and theological accounting for the existence of Q that had hitherto been lacking.

The recognition of the theological pluralism that redaction criticism had encouraged was manifest in another way in a resurgence of interest in heresy. Walter Bauer's *Rechtgläubigkeit und Ketzerei im ältesten Christentum* had been published in 1934, but now appeared in English in 1971 as *Orthodoxy and Heresy in Earliest Christianity*. Helmut Koester, one of Bultmann's last students, developed Bauer's thesis of the diverse nature of

---

36. This association is discussed briefly in J. M. Robinson's essay but worked out in much greater detail by Kloppenborg (1987a:274–76, 284–87, 319–22), not as an imminent or necessary tendency of wisdom collections, but as one of the usual hermeneutical options.

primitive Christianity. Instead of assuming the theological normativity of a ubiquitous passion kerygma, Koester described the variety of early Christian *kerygmata*, first by geographical region, analyzing the various forms and theological tendencies in evidence in Syria and western Palestine, Edessa, and the countries around the Aegean (1965; repr. 1971a), and then in a later essay, by literary form (1968; repr. 1971b).

In the 1968 essay, "One Jesus and Four Primitive Gospels," Koester advanced the hypotheses that (a) underlying the canonical Gospels are several primitive gospel forms, none of which is organized on the pattern of the passion kerygma, and that (b) the primary theological tendencies of these gospel forms are often most clearly visible not in the canonical Gospels but in the apocryphal Gospels. Alongside the genres of aretalogy (collections of miracles) and revelation discourse, Koester sketched the contents and theological tendencies of the "sayings gospel," which he had already described as "the most original *gattung* of the Jesus tradition" (1971a:135). In accord with the second part of his hypothesis, Koester's treatment of the "sayings gospel" took the *Gospel of Thomas* as its starting point and focus. It is in *Thomas* that he discerned the primary internal principle of the genre:

> [It is] the authority of the word of wisdom as such, which rests in the assumption that the teacher is present in the word which he has spoken. If there is any "Easter experience" to provide a Christology congenial to this concept of the *logoi*, it is here the belief in "Jesus, the Living One" (incipit of the *Gospel of Thomas*). (1971a:138–39)

Robinson and Koester thus clarified and legitimated Tödt's modest conclusions concerning the nature of Q within the framework of a comprehensive theory of Gospel origins. Q was not only a plausible postulate of source criticism; it was now a new landmark on the map of primitive Christian theologizing.

The Fourth Synoptic

Following the preliminary explorations of Tödt and the more comprehensive theses of Robinson and Koester, Q entered the landscape of New Testament studies in a new way. Prior to 1970 introductions to the New Testament and to the Synoptic Gospels typically treated Q briefly, normally as a subdivision of a section on the Synoptic Problem. This is true even of one of the more detailed and influential treatments of Q by W. G. Kümmel.[37] Starting with Howard Clark Kee's chapter on Q in *Jesus in History*

---

37. Kümmel [14]1965, ET 1966; [17]1973, ET 1975. Several more recent introductions reflect the same pattern: Conzelmann and Lindemann 1975; [6]1982:63–69, ET 1988:53–59; and R. F. Collins 1983:130–33. L. T. Johnson's introduction (1986) acknowledges the 2DH as the most probable solution to the Synoptic Problem but sidesteps any discussion of Q, explaining that he prefers literary and narrative approaches to diachronic analyses (145). Since one could offer a synchronic analysis of Q, it seems probable that it is rather Johnson's biblicism that allows

(1970),[38] however, chapters devoted to the composition and theology of Q could be found *alongside* and parallel to those treating each of the Synoptic Gospels.[39] Full-scale and popular commentaries on Q appeared[40] and since 1983, the major bibliographical index, *Elenchus bibliographicus* in the periodical *Ephemerides theologicae lovanienses* includes a separate section entitled "Quelle" in its larger unit on "Jesus et evangelia."[41] Q had become the fourth Synoptic Gospel. One cannot make Robinson and Koester responsible for the whole of this development, especially since some of the contributors to this phase of Q scholarship held positions quite distinct from them. Nevertheless, the liberation of Q from servitude to the passion kerygma and the recognition of theological pluralism in earliest Christianity that was typical of Robinson and Koester epitomized a larger transition in scholarly habits in regard to Q.

It is perhaps a natural outcome of these theological shifts that renewed attention should be devoted to the reconstruction of Q. Several developments are worthy of note: the full reconstructions of Q by Polag (1979, ET 1986) and Schenk (1981); the production of two synopses designed to aid in the reconstruction of Q (Kloppenborg 1988a; Neirynck 1988);

him to exclude Q from consideration. Johnson's revised edition pays slightly more attention to Q (1999:155–57), but source-critical concerns still play very little role in the analysis. Conservative evangelical introductions tend to ignore the Synoptic Problem entirely.

38. In personal correspondence (October 10, 1994), Kee indicated that what impressed him to include a chapter on Q was, first, that his examination of the Q material in the Huck–Lietzmann synopsis indicated, rather to his surprise, that Q had a coherent perspective on Jesus and was "by no means a random selection of supplemental material." He also had come to the conviction that "Judaism and Christianity must be understood as a spectrum of communities from which, and in service of which the Jewish and early Christian literature emerged. The history of post-exilic Judaism makes clear how and why this range of options arose, and sheds essential light on why the Jesus movement was also diverse from the outset."

39. Kee 1970; 1977:76–120; 1996b:74–115 (Q is given its own chapter, before those devoted to Mark, Matthew, Luke, and John); Perrin 1974:74–77; Perrin and Duling 1982: 100–106 (Q is discussed along with other expressions of apocalyptic Christianity); completely reorganized in Duling and Perrin 1994:115–17 ("A Brief Social History of Early Christianity"), 147–54 ("The Earliest Non-Pauline Christians"); Vielhauer 1975:260–80 ("die Zwei-Quellen-Theorie"), 311–29 ("Die Spruchquelle"); Schmithals 1985:215–33 ("die Logiensammlung," under "Die synoptische Quellenkritik"), 384–404 ("Die Logiensammlung"); Koester 1982a:583–86, ET 1982b:147–50; 1990:128–71 ("The Synoptic Sayings Source"); Ehrman 1997:75–78. Neirynck's second volume of collected essays now has a section (comprising six essays) devoted to Q: Neirynck 1991c:409–568 ("the Sayings of Jesus"); as does the Festschrift for Neirynck (Van Segbroeck, Tuckett, Van Belle and Verheyden 1992, 1:359–688).

40. Schulz 1972; Schenk 1981; D. Zeller 1984. Commentaries on Q are also in preparation by Paul Hoffmann (Evangelisch-Katholischer Kommentar zum Neuen Testament [Benziger and Neukirchener Verlag]) and James M. Robinson (Hermeneia [Fortress Press]).

41. See also Neirynck and Van Segbroeck 1982 (supplement 1986); Neirynck, Verheyden, and Corstjens 1998 and David M. Scholer's continuing bibliography of works on Q beginning in 1986 and yearly updates in the *Society of Biblical Literature Seminar Papers* should also be mentioned. The technical problems involved in library cataloguing materials on Q are now discussed by Haverly 1997.

Neirynck's lists of the vocabulary of the double tradition in *New Testament Vocabulary* (1984); numerous partial reconstructions of Q; and especially, the work of the International Q Project (IQP).[42]

In one sense, the method of reconstruction has not changed much since the time of Harnack, Stanton, or Manson, although the IQP aims at a degree of completeness in reporting and a methodological rigor that are hitherto unmatched. One may still be convinced at a given point by Harnack's or Manson's reconstruction and for precisely the reasons that they gave. The key difference between the older phase of reconstruction and the more recent one has to do with their respective purposes. While Harnack and V. Stanton were interested in Q because they thought it provided access to the historical Jesus, both form and redaction criticism have taught us in the meantime that Q, once reconstructed, provides only a perspectival glimpse on the Jesus tradition treasured and transmitted by a particular group of Galilean followers.

Indeed, one might employ Q in a reconstruction of the teachings of Jesus, as John Dominic Crossan has done with great care and sophistication (1991). But neither Crossan nor most of the recent specialists in Q suppose that the contents of Q exhaust what can responsibly be said of Jesus, nor, more important, that Q's particular construal of Jesus represents *the* historical Jesus. This point needs to be underscored, since it is so widely misunderstood.[43] The majority of recent analyses of Q, whether they take a stratigraphic or a synchronic approach, are about Q, its composition, and the particular group it represented and *not* about the historical Jesus. It should be obvious that there is much about Jesus that Q neglects, most especially, the events surrounding his death and the mighty deeds to which Mark devotes so much attention. Redaction criticism, in particular the groundbreaking work of Werner Kelber (1983), should also have taught us that the choice of genre and the organizational patterns employed by the written Gospels are the choices of the *authors* involved; they cannot be used as indices by which to characterize the historical Jesus. The *literary choice* to feature sapiential and prophetic sayings and to ignore the miracle and passion traditions tells us in the first place about Q, not about the historical Jesus. It renders evidence of the persons who collected and framed its sayings. *Their* interests must be probed and *their* techniques analyzed. Only

---

42. See chap. 2, p. 101, and Neirynck 1993.

43. See, e.g., Fuller 1994, who expresses concern at the Q studies by Kloppenborg (1987a) and Mack (1988b) because "Jesus is *reduced* to a teacher of wisdom" or a "popular sage" (emphasis added). Apart from this highly misleading characterization, Fuller misses the point that these studies are of *Q*, not Jesus, and that I have expressly stated that my analysis has to do with the *literary* arrangement and composition of Q and *not* with the ultimate provenance or authenticity of its sayings. That a particular saying is used in a secondary compositional form by Q does *not* thereby imply that it is inauthentic, nor, conversely, should it be assumed that the sayings used in the formative stratum are necessarily authentic. "Tradition-history is not convertible with *literary* history . . ." (Kloppenborg 1987a:245; emphasis original).

when these are clear might it become possible to inquire behind Q, with the help of other traditions found in Mark, the *Gospel of Thomas*, John, and Paul, and piece together a portrait of Jesus.

In this sense, the modern study of Q belongs to the legacy of F. C. Baur and Rudolf Bultmann—this despite the facts that Baur's source theory did not involve Q at all and that Bultmann did not understand Q as a discrete expression of primitive Christian theologizing. Q tells in the first place about one particular sector of the Jesus movement, its literary and theological expressions, and its eventual transformation in the Gospels of Matthew and Luke. To be sure, Q is an important source for the historical Jesus, but it is only one of several. It is neither complete nor is it unalloyed. Q is again on the map—as a documentary point in the literary history of the Jesus tradition; as a theological point in the history of early Christian reflections; and, as chapter 4 has shown, as a site where the social practices of one sector of the Jesus movement may be seen.

8

Making Difference

> The real problem of the sayings source
> is its theology.
> —Athanasius Polag (1991:101)

THE LAST TWENTY YEARS of scholarship on Q have raised problems that have spilled over into other areas of scholarship on Christian origins. Studies of Q have now been employed in revisiting the problem of the historical Jesus and in redrawing intellectual and social maps of primitive Christianity.[1] Q scholarship has also attracted strong criticism because it is seen, rightly or wrongly, to endanger long-held views about the historical Jesus and the development of early Christian theology. This is an irony perhaps, given the fact that the Synoptic Problem was born from a concern to resecure the links between the Jesus of history, the Gospels, and dogmatic theology that Reimarus's critique had threatened to sever.

This current state of affairs is the cumulative result of a long phase of Synoptic scholarship outlined in the preceding two chapters. Q was hardly even noticed as raising theological issues during the nineteenth century. The main fault lines of the theological debate ran between Tübingen's theological construal of the GH and liberal theology's privileging of (proto-)Mark. While this debate was running its course, technical and literary studies of the Synoptic Problem increasingly favored the 2DH with its postulate of a sayings source. In the second main phase of Q scholarship outlined in chapter 7, Q emerged as a definable point on the map of early Christian literary history. Efforts to reconstruct Q and to determine its original order and shape—to transform the "double tradition" from an algebraic variable into a document—inevitably raised *theological* questions: where did it fit and how was its theological differentness to be cashed out? Now, with redaction critical and social historical analyses in full swing, and in a context that is

---

1. Mack 1988b:53–77; 1993; B. Scott 1990; Crossan 1991; 1998; Kosch 1992; Kloppenborg 1996b.

prepared to acknowledge much greater ranges of intellectual and practical diversification in early Christianity, Q has again become a site of theological as well as literary and historical debate.

From Diversity to Difference

When, following World War II, redaction criticism was developed and applied to the Synoptic Gospels in order to describe their compositional features and distinctive theologies, it was only a matter of time before it would be tried on other documents of primitive Christianity, including Q. It is perhaps not surprising that the first important studies of the composition and theology of Q were written by students of those who pioneered redaction criticism: Dieter Lührmann (a student of Günther Bornkamm), Paul Hoffmann (a student of Josef Schmid), and Richard Edwards (who studied with Norman Perrin).[2]

The period following the war also saw the flourishing of the Biblical Theology Movement, which sought to define the larger theological unities in the New Testament—indeed, in the entire Bible. Redaction criticism was not directly invested in the quest for a common biblical theology but nonetheless presumed some levels of common discourse and theological commitments. As was suggested in chapter 7, the development of redaction criticism should be seen in the broader context defined by an interest in comprehending legitimate theological diversity within a presumed unity. The discursive idiom adopted by redaction criticism—"tradition" and "redaction," continuity and innovation—epitomized this larger theological as well as historical investment in unity and diversity. The discovery of diversity-in-unity at the very heart of the New Testament canon seemed to provide unimpeachable support for analogous ecumenical quests in ecclesiological and doctrinal arenas. In the long run, however, redaction criticism's penchant for working contrastively, distinguishing redaction from tradition and contrasting the compositional effect of the arrangement of pericopae in one gospel with that in another gospel, meant that redaction criticism was far better equipped to describe difference than it was to articulate continuities. Eventually the results of redaction criticism almost completely undermined the approach of biblical theology and, along with it, the notion of a theological center.

---

2. Lührmann (1969) dedicated his *Habilitationsschrift* to Bornkamm; Hoffmann dedicated his 1972 *Habilitationsschrift* to Schmid (whose 1930 study of Matthew and Luke was a forerunner of redaction criticism), and to Ernst Haenchen and Willi Marxsen, both of whom were responsible for seminal studies on Mark (Marxsen 1956; Haenchen 1966) and Luke-Acts (Haenchen 1956). Edwards's more limited study of Q 11:29-32 (1971) was based on a 1968 Chicago dissertation, supervised by Norman Perrin, an American pioneer of redaction criticism (Perrin 1969).

Beginning in the late 1960s works appeared that posited fundamental discontinuities and dissonances within primitive Christianity. Much of the attention focused on Mark's interaction with prior tradition and rejected the form-critical assumption of a basic continuity between oral units of tradition and their written expression in Mark. On the contrary, Theodore Weeden saw Mark's gospel as a reaction to and rejection of a construal of Jesus' miracles by "heretics," who claimed the authority of the original disciples.[3] These "heretics," represented narratively by the Markan disciples, espoused a "divine man" Christology that took no account of Jesus' death. Mark's negative depiction of the disciples and his contrasting affirmation of the necessity of Jesus' suffering were meant to counteract this heretical Christology.[4] Of course not all redactional studies of Mark conceived the oppositions so sharply, but almost all were prepared to allow Mark a considerable measure of creative interaction with and modification of the inherited tradition.

By the 1970s another important development occurred. Against the older form-critical view that Mark took over and adapted a narrative of Jesus' death, some argued that Mark was the creator of his Passion narrative.[5] If correct, this meant that the inscription of the Gospel of Mark represented a significant reinterpretation of the Jesus tradition. While acknowledging Mark's debt to oral tradition, Werner Kelber nonetheless argued:

> If Mark has a deep investment in Jesus' death, in the demise of the disciples and the fall of the temple, whereas oral tradition by and large does not, and if he writes not to continue but to overcome oral mentality, and if indeed he is the creator of the textualization of Jesus' life and death, what prevents us from crediting him with the composition of the bulk of the passion narrative? (Kelber 1983:196)

Thus Mark's relationship to prior oral tradition is highly ambivalent. He is extraordinarily sparing in placing sayings on Jesus' lips and what he ascribes to Jesus is qualified as riddling or parabolic speech rather than as direct and open address. In these habits Kelber saw Mark as a critic of older representations of the risen Jesus continually present to his followers in the prophetic activities of the Spirit and in the re-presentation of Jesus through the performance of his sayings. Mark's Jesus, by contrast, is not only absent; he is silent too (Kelber 1983:207–11).

3. Weeden 1968. The notion of discontinuity is explicit, both in the title of Weeden's 1964 Claremont dissertation, "The Heresy That Necessitated Mark's Gospel," and in its 1971 published form, *Mark—Traditions in Conflict*. A similar thesis, that Mark was combating a royal Christology espoused by the Jerusalem church, was proposed by Tyson (1961).

4. More recently, Boring (1982) and Kelber (1983) argued that Mark reacted to Christian prophecy that focused on the exalted Jesus present in the community in ecstatic utterance rather than the crucified and "absent" Jesus. Both suggest that Q evinces a prophetic understanding of Jesus.

5. Donahue 1973; Kelber 1976; Matera 1982; Mack 1988b.

Whether Weeden or Kelber or others who argued for fissures and discontinuities within "the gospel tradition" are correct is not the point. Many
qualifications and nuances might be added. The point, rather, is to observe
that the inherent logic of redaction criticism could and did produce representations of primitive Christianity that were no longer a matter of "diversity in unity" but rather of *difference* in varying degrees of starkness.

Other developments during the 1970s weakened the "unity" side of the
earlier redaction critical equation. With the discovery of the Coptic gnostic
library at Nag Hammadi it became clear that the intellectual landscape of
primitive Christianity was far more varied than hitherto thought. For the
first time it was possible to trace not only developments from the earliest
kerygmatic statements to the great orthodox syntheses of the second and
third centuries; the pedigrees of several parallel and divergent developments, ending in heterodox syntheses, also became visible. For James M.
Robinson these divergences were "not simply a case of random variety, of
pluralism. A more penetrating analysis reveals individual items to be exponents of intelligible movements" (1971a:10).

Robinson argued that these diverging strands were not deviations from
an originary creedal statement or kerygma nor could they be measured
against what eventually came to be recognized as orthodox. On the contrary, both orthodox and heretical expressions could be traced back to common starting points. Their various and divergent elaborations described
"trajectories" that could be traced through documents of the first two or
three centuries of Christian literature. Not even the canon could be treated
as a unifying construct:

> The monolithic concept of one church history gives way to a series of trajecto-
> ries, each determined in part by the course of history in the differing regions
> and in part by interactions of an inner-Christian nature. The various ways in
> which "Jesus" as the ultimate force behind such diversified theological devel-
> opments reappeared in different cultural contexts draws attention to the dialec-
> tic structure of the Christian's appropriation of both his tradition and his
> environment. The writings now bound together in the New Testament "canon"
> emerge as conflicting witnesses to this process, in which they often contradict
> each other, or appear as theological compromises of only passing historical sig-
> nificance. (Robinson 1971a:18)

For Robinson the theologically unifying feature is the "Jesus" who stands
behind these diversified developments. Robinson later described the development of understandings of Easter using a similar model: the originally
"luminous" Easter experiences were visualized by means of two ultimately
divergent models: one stressing the visionary and incorporeal nature of the
resurrection; the other insisting (against the first) on a bodily, fully tangible
resurrection (Robinson 1982). Q itself expressed the ambivalence of the
originary, for Q does not yet imagine Easter as a narratable event. Q 10:21-
22 ("All things have been delivered to me by my Father"), which contains

the impress of Easter and expresses the divine authorization of Jesus' words, falls *in the middle* of the collection, not at the end as a kind of substitution for a resurrection narrative. This does not mean, however, that the first half of Q is pre-Easter and the latter postresurrectional. On the contrary, "Easter does not fall here, or at the beginning, or at the end, or anywhere in Q. Q has the timelessness of eternal truth, or at least of wisdom literature" (Robinson 1982:23). Later editing of the sayings traditions resolved this ambivalence, either by framing Jesus' sayings as gnostic postresurrectional dialogues or by embedding them in an orthodox pre-Easter "life of Jesus."

A similar model for comprehending diversity is at work in Koester's "One Jesus and Four Primitive Gospels" (1971b) and "The Structure and Criteria of Early Christian Beliefs" (1971c). Koester isolated four creedal patterns, each having a foundation in the historical Jesus and each selecting, construing, and elaborating historical tradition in a congenial manner: Jesus as Lord of the future, Jesus as the Divine Man, Jesus as Sophia's Envoy, and Jesus raised from the dead. Though perspectival and diverse, these creeds are normed theologically not by some other creed or by arbitrarily giving preeminence to one of the four, but by the Jesus who stands behind and gives rise to these diverse kerygmatic formulations.[6]

Others, acknowledging the profound kerygmatic diversity in early Christianity, seek nevertheless to discern underlying structural unities between Jesus' proclamation of the reign of God and the (canonical) post-Easter kerygma in which Jesus functions centrally. James Dunn (1977), for example, resists the temptation to construct a single kerygma lying behind the variety of kerygmata in the New Testament. There is no single NT writing that attests such a reduction and any attempt to reconstruct a common kerygma would inevitably abstract individual kerygmata from the concrete historical settings in which they had meaning. Nevertheless, Dunn suggests that there are elements common to the diverse NT kerygmata: the proclamation of a risen, exalted Jesus; a call for faith and acceptance of what Jesus proclaimed; and the promises held out to faith—variously expressed as the gift of the Spirit, forgiveness, salvation, life, or abiding fellowship with the exalted Christ (1977:29–32).

---

6. Koester 1971c:230–31; Schillebeeckx 1979:403–38: "[W]e can discover even now that there were in circulation all kinds of pre-canonical independent Christological interpretations of Jesus, each having evident points of contact with particular facets of Jesus' life on earth, albeit on a selective basis for each local community. The historical continuity between each distinctive *kerygma* and particular aspects of the earthly Jesus is a striking fact about all such primitive Christian 'creeds'. Equally striking, however, is their perspectival view of Jesus, in other words the one-sidedness of these pre-canonical interpretations of Jesus. Despite that, however, it turns out that in each and every case, allowing for the particular *kerygma* and the religious milieu supplying them with the specific language in which to speak of him, Jesus of Nazareth himself was the criterion and norm" (403).

Dunn also argues that meaningful continuities can be found between the historical Jesus and post-Easter proclamations, not at the level of explicit statement but in what is implicit in Jesus' message. It is probable, Dunn contends, that Jesus "looked beyond his death to some sort of vindication" and perhaps even conceived his death as vicarious suffering (1977:210–11); he understood his disciples' relationship with God as in some way dependent on their relationship with him—their *abba* depended upon his *Abba*— (1977:212–13); and Jesus thought himself to be endowed by the Spirit to a unique degree (1977:213–15). The points of contact between these three dimensions of the historical Jesus and the elements common to early Christian kerygmata are obvious and mean, for Dunn, that "there are sufficiently clear foreshadowings of the centrality of the kerygmatic Christ in the self-understanding of Jesus during his ministry for us to recognize the kerygmata of the early churches as a development from Jesus' own proclamation in the light of his resurrection" (Dunn 1977:216).

According to John Galvin, it not just that continuities and congruities between the historical Jesus and Christian proclamations can be demonstrated; they *must* be present if the kerygma is to remain credible. If later Christology is to have justification, there must have been some "intrinsic connection between Jesus' person and his message"; Jesus cannot merely have been the "theologically insignificant bearer" of some message (1994:264).[7] There must be an indication, however implicit, of Jesus' self-understanding as God's definitive salvific representative.[8] Tension between the presence and absence of salvation in Jesus' preaching—between the realized and future dimensions of the reign of God—is necessary if the same tensions in Christian theology are to be sustained.[9] Galvin, along with some

---

7. Apropos of Schillebeeckx's appeal to Jesus' "abba experience," for example, Galvin notes: "To find a basis for one's own life in the trustworthiness of Jesus, and ultimately of his *Abba* experience (through which Jesus discovers the ground of his own life in God) is of course an act of faith in Jesus, which is thus—and *ipso facto*—an act attesting faith in God. On purely historical grounds this cannot be verified, since such an *Abba* experience may be disqualified as an illusion. On the other hand for someone who acknowledges and in faith confesses this trustworthiness of Jesus as grounded in truth and reality, the trustworthiness acquires visible contours in the actual life of Jesus of Nazareth . . ." (1979:270).

8. Galvin carefully distinguishes this from the issue of whether or not the historical Jesus used epithets such as "Messiah" of himself, which in the context would have been construed in a political or priestly way. "While valid ascription of a particular title to Jesus does not depend upon his personal use or acceptance of that terminology with reference to himself, and would even be compatible with explicit rejection of that title in a different historical context, Jesus' personal self-assessment as God's definitive salvific representative (whether articulated in particular terminology or simply reflected indirectly in his words and deeds) is a necessary though not sufficient condition for the Christian conviction that he is *the* Christ, a salvific figure of unequalled and insurpassable religious and theological importance" (1994:265–66, emphasis original).

9. Galvin (1994:266–67) has in mind both nineteenth-century liberal theology, which rejected the apocalyptic element of Jesus' preaching and with it "all the external hope for the future," and Schweitzer's completely apocalyptic and mistaken Jesus.

other Roman Catholic theologians, is not as insistent as Dunn that the historical Jesus attributed saving significance to his death,[10] although "historical knowledge of Jesus' free acceptance of death is essential for soteriology" (1994:268).[11]

In sharp contrast to the concerns of Robinson, Koester, Dunn, Galvin, and others to articulate continuities between Jesus and later theological syntheses is the work of Burton Mack. By 1988 the fruits of redaction criticism, rhetorical analysis, and social theory came together in Mack's study of Mark entitled *A Myth of Innocence: Mark and Christian Origins* (1988b). He began his book with a survey of the variety of embodiments of the Jesus movement: Galilean itinerants [Q]; the "pillars" in Jerusalem; those claiming family ties to Jesus; bearers of the pre-Markan miracle traditions ("the Congregation of Israel"); a reform movement in Galilean and Syrian synagogues who formulated pre-Markan pronouncement stories; and the "Congregations of the Christ" (Pauline churches). Mark knew and was indebted to each of these. But unlike earlier treatments of Mark, Mack was prepared to argue that something new happened with the framing of the gospel: a Christian myth of origins had been created. Mark wrote a mythic narrative that presented Jesus

> as the king of the kingdom of God, predicted by the prophets and acknowledged by his Father as the legitimate heir of all the promises ever made for Israel among the nations. Packed into this sovereign figure, suddenly appearing on the scene just before Jerusalem's sorry end, was absolute authority (pronouncement stories), power (miracle stories), and knowledge (Sayings Source). (1988b:320)

In order to account for the failure and demise of this Jesus, Mark composed the passion narrative as the climax of his gospel, combining the notion taken from Q of Jesus' rejection by "this generation" with the martyrological schema and its logic of a vicarious death borrowed from the Hellenistic Christ cult (1988b:320–21).

10. Galvin 1994:268–69, citing Schillebeeckx (1979:310–19), who regards Jesus' death as a prophetic sign which was left to be interpreted by his followers both in light of Jesus' life and against the background of various cultural and religious concepts (1979:319). Karl Rahner (1978:248–49) leaves "open" several issues, including "whether and to what extent and in what sense the pre-resurrectional Jesus explicitly ascribed a soteriological function to his death," but offers as certain that "he faced his death resolutely and accepted it at least as the inevitable consequence of fidelity to his mission and as imposed on him by God." Others such as Schürmann (1979; 1983) suggest on the basis of the words of institution that Jesus not only anticipated his own vindication (Mark 14:25b) but came to see his death as a death "for" others (Luke 22:19b–20).

11. Galvin (1994:270) adds as a desideratum of systematic theology that there should be some continuity between the historical Jesus and the church, not insofar as Jesus envisaged a church, but that he called disciples or constituted the Twelve as a distinct group or performed words and actions at the Last Supper that served as the basis for the Eucharist. It is not clear from his discussion, however, that he considers this to be a sine qua non.

"Mythmaking" served the immediate social needs of the Markan community. Mark offered to a group which had failed as a reform movement among diaspora synagogues[12] and which had subsequently withdrawn into a sectarian mentality a comprehensive picture of Jesus, whose death was associated with rejection in the synagogue and, ultimately, with the destruction of the Temple.

> [N]either the Jesus movements [Q] nor the congregations of the Christ [Pauline groups] had imagined Second Temple institutions as their nemesis. When Mark did make that connection the Christian myth of succession or substitution was born. Jesus had been the rightful heir to a kingdom in conflict with Second Temple Judaism. Its leaders had sought to destroy him, but had succeeded only in destroying themselves. Jesus, the once and future king, now was to reign in the place of the vanquished high priests. It was a myth written during a brief period of threat to a particular Jesus movement in danger of losing its bearings, its confidence, its cool. (1988b:355–56)

Mack thus posed an alternative not only to the conventional model of Christian origins that posited a structural coherence between Jesus' preaching and the theological configurations of the post-Easter churches; he also rejected the model advanced by Robinson (and Koester) of (an) originary moment(s) to which all diversity can be traced, whether it be Jesus or Easter. Here Q became important, for Mack saw recent scholarship on Q as having reinforced the fundamental fissures and discontinuities in the early Christian landscape. This landscape had already begun to change with the dissolution of the older consensus that the historical Jesus was an apocalyptic prophetic, for it had been this equation that supplied the essential links between Jesus and the subsequent proclamation of Jesus' resurrection as an apocalyptic event.[13] The absence of reference to the kerygma of the cross and resurrection in Q and the *Gospel of Thomas* demonstrated, according to Mack, that "the kerygmatic formulation of Christian origins was only one way of understanding Jesus as a founder figure among the many movements of the first century" (Mack 1990a:6). Moreover, the stratigraphical analysis of Q suggested a formative "sapiential" layer and this implied that it was quite possible to organize Jesus traditions without regard to either the passion kerygma or an apocalyptic understanding of history.[14]

---

12. Mack later retracted the notion of a "reform movement" (1991a:148–52, esp. 151–52).

13. Mack 1990a:5: "The kerygmatic proclamation, it was understood, was both 'eschatological' (in reference to the dramatic significance of the resurrection) and apocalyptic (in reference to the future appearance of Jesus and his kingdom). Thus the apocalyptic hypothesis served as a bridge from the historical Jesus to the kerygmatic Christ. This produced a tidy reconstruction of Christian origins, supported by the assumption of widespread apocalyptic fervor in Galilean Judaism and sealed by pointing to the apocalyptic frame of the earliest gospel (Mark)."

14. Robinson in the meantime has modified his earlier unqualified association of Jesus with apocalypticism (1982:6) by accepting the hypothesis of a "sapiential" formative stratum of Q.

Mack treated apocalyptic elements not as formative and primary but having rather specific rhetorical functions in respect to what was primary. Q's apocalyptic language served as a mythic rationalization of the rejection of the Q people's preaching:

> This means that apocalyptic language in the Q tradition is a later, secondary development at a particular stage of social formation and experience. It does not represent the discourse that attracted Q people to the movement in the first place. Neither does it represent the "preaching" of the Q tradents to others. The speeches of judgment composed for Jesus are highly crafted fictions written after other conversations had broken down and decisions had been made either to agree or not to agree about Jesus and the Jesus movement. (Mack 1990a:9)

Even though Q eventually dressed itself in apocalyptic language, its formative impulse did not derive from apocalyptic any more than it did from an interpretation of the death and resurrection of Jesus. Thus, for at least Q (and the *Gospel of Thomas*) one could not, according to Mack, plot a hermeneutical trajectory such as Robinson had described, originating in the ambivalent "Easter event." Instead, for Q and the *Gospel of Thomas* Jesus "was rather a sage whose sayings and the wisdom to be derived from them made all the difference that mattered" (Mack 1990a:18).

For Mack the models of continuity with the Jesus of history and congruence with other kerygmata that are so important for others have been replaced by a view of early Christianity as a series of social experiments, each engaged in more or less autonomous forms of mythmaking. What is common for Mack is the novel notion of the kingdom of God—but without any necessary connection to Jesus as a savior and without any necessary apocalyptic attachments. This notion "called for reimagining society and . . . contained both a critical (countercultural) and a constructive (utopian) edge" (Mack 1995:11). Once unleashed, the kingdom of God triggered multiple social experiments. Christian origins for Mack are not traced to a particular individual (Jesus), whose complex genius can account for subsequent developments, or to a single event (the so-called "Easter event"), providing the social and theological counterpart to the Big Bang. Rather, Christian origins are understood through social anthropology, as more or less discrete acts of mythmaking and social formation; they were pluriform and divergent.

Diversities or even anomalies in the intellectual landscape of the Jesus movement do not automatically translate into theological problems. The

---

He suggests, further, that while John the Baptist and Paul were apocalypticists, Jesus (and Q[1]) did not continue John's apocalypticism in a "straight line way." "The earlier layer of Q would seem to be oriented heavily to sapiential traditions (though not without apocalyptic flickers or interpolations)"; it was only in the later layer that "re-apocalypticizing" is evidenced (1991b:192).

fact that Q and the *Gospel of Thomas* focus on the kingdom of God rather than Jesus' death and resurrection makes for a much more variegated picture of early Christian *thought*, but it does not automatically subvert the theological efforts to articulate theological continuities within the early Jesus movement.

It might be argued, for example, that since neither Q nor the *Gospel of Thomas* is canonical, New Testament theology need not concern itself with them any more than with the Signs Source lying behind the Fourth Gospel, the Logos hymn embedded in John 1:1-18, pre-Pauline confessional formulas, or the hypothetical pre-Markan passion account. Q is naturally a part of any consideration of the history of early Christian thought and practice but not a part of New Testament theology. To judge from the anxiety that studies of Q continue to raise, however, such an expedient apparently is not viewed as entirely satisfying. This is perhaps because of the way in which the canon has itself been problematized, such that any attempt to restrict "theological" discourse to intracanonical documents appears parochial, apologetic, and ultimately ahistorical. Moreover, while it has always been possible to bracket noncanonical texts out of consideration, it is perhaps more difficult when it comes to a precanonical text that is at least as substantial as many NT writings and arguably a "gospel."

Even if one defines Q (and the *Gospel of Thomas*) out the problem of constructing a theology of the Jesus movement, one is still left with the potential challenges that Q and the *Gospel of Thomas* pose to a reconstruction of the historical Jesus. If these two documents provoke a major recalibration of understandings of the historical Jesus, some of the notions of continuity and coherence between Jesus and later Christian kerygmata might also have to be rethought. For example, if Q's silence concerning a salvific interpretation of Jesus' fate makes it difficult or impossible to conclude that the historical Jesus considered his own death vicarious (as Dunn would have it), one might still wish to claim the notion of Jesus' death "for us" (1 Cor 15:3) as a key Christian theologoumenon, but it would be difficult to affirm any rootedness of this doctrine in the historical Jesus.

Another way to avoid the potential theological difficulties posed by Q is to treat it, in John Meier's words, as a "grab bag," without a clear genre, a coherent theology, or a supporting "community" (1994:181, 271). Meier's refusal to inquire into Q's editorial and theological profile appears to be a part of the concern to leave Q as an untrammeled source of sayings of the historical Jesus. He prescinds from the literary and historical questions of Q's origin, tradents, and editorial tendencies and uses it simply as a "distinct and valuable source for sayings . . . of Jesus and John" (1994:181), much as Harnack did, as a document without editorial bias. This anemic, unreal view of Q also renders it innocuous theologically; a document compiled for no particular group, with no particular intent or guiding principle, would not constitute a theological problem at all. It is doubtful, however, that such an approach will convince many for very long. Such a view obviously conflicts with the general assumptions of redaction criticism. Even miscellanies—and Q is far from a miscellany—have specifiable genres, functions, and principles of selection. Minimally, Q's portrait of Jesus is affected by the principles of selection employed by its framers and by the rhetorical situation and purpose of the document. Given what has been said about the production of ancient literature in chapter 4, it makes little sense to posit the existence of an editorially "neutral" and "audience-less" composition.

We are thrown back to the initial problem. It seems unsatisfactory to dispense with Q either by a canonical stipulation or by asserting that is it a document to which the ordinary rules of literary analysis somehow should not apply. But what of the various models of theological continuity and unity that have been proposed which attempt to integrate Q—whether "trajectories" emanating from a common originary point, or diverse kerygmata all sharing a basic structure or repertoire of concerns, or foreshadowings of later doctrines in earlier expressions? The choice of one model over another is not a historical or an exegetical decision, but a theological one, prompted (at least in part) by other considerations. A model, for example, that treats Q either as a "foreshadowing" or as an incomplete expression of later doctrinal developments assumes an implicit theological teleology ultimately affirming "orthodox" outcomes, whereas the "trajectories" model might be employed to display counterexamples and counterdevelopments precisely in an effort to deconstruct or problematize orthodoxies. Mack's model of disparate acts of mythmaking, all employing a notion of the kingdom of God, leaves virtually no room for talk of unity and continuity at all.

In what follows, I will not defend a particular model for imagining theological unity and continuity within the early Jesus movement; but I will insist that any model that offers a construal of Q does so in a manner that is responsive to what can be said *exegetically* about Q, and not merely asserted. I shall argue that Q exhibits greater commonalities with other "theologies" of the early Jesus movement than detractors sometime suppose; but at the same time, Q's "differentness" is substantial and that difference has the potential of undermining some of the tidy models for imagining theological continuity. Three issues in particular are worth consideration: the relationship between Q and kerygmata in which Jesus' death and exaltation figure prominently; the interrelation of sapiential and prophetic or apocalyptic strands in Q; and whether or not Q ought to be called a "gospel."

Q and "Easter Faith"

Throughout the twentieth century it was generally accepted that Q contained no passion account, allusions to Jesus' resurrection, or appearance narratives. Prior to World War II these lacunae were rendered theologically inconsequential by the assumption that Q was employed for catechetical purposes in communities that also knew and used a primitive version of the passion narrative and the Easter kerygma.[15]

Tödt's monograph on the Son of Man offered another way to account for Q's silence: for Q the resurrection was not an item to be preached but was instead a confirmation of the abiding authority of the earthly Jesus and his identity with the coming Son of Man. The resurrection thus constituted the enablement to continue preaching Jesus' sayings and the validation of that preaching (Tödt 1965:249–50, 252–53). With regard to the passion kerygma, Tödt argued, "only after the redemptive significance of the death [of Jesus] had been recognized and expounded could the passion kerygma have been presented and transmitted as the central concept." This is clearly not the case for Q, which locates saving significance in the re-presentation of Jesus' words (1965:251).

Tödt's treatment of Q as an independent kerygma rather than a supplement to the Easter kerygma created a potential theological problem, since it seemed to challenge a hitherto prevailing notion of the ubiquity of the passion kerygma. The application of redaction criticism to Q after Tödt further exacerbated the problem. The idiom of redaction criticism made it easy to speak of discrete "communities," each with its own distinctive theology. Within such a framework it became increasingly usual to describe Q as belonging to a "second sphere" of Christian preaching whose soteriology was not based on the passion of Jesus.[16] Siegfried Schulz, for example, argued that Q located the saving event not with Mark in the history of Jesus or with Paul in the death and resurrection, but in Jesus' "messianic Torah, his prophetic-apocalyptic proclamation, and his priestly instruction" (1964:139). Schulz assumed further that the Q people did not commemorate the Lord's Supper with its salvific interpretation of Jesus' death but as Jews would have continued to observe the Passover.[17]

15. Thus, e.g., Wellhausen 1911:159–60 ("That [Q] knew the passion, which it passes over in silence, goes without saying"); Streeter 1911a:215, 219; 1924:292; Dibelius 1935:28, 238; Manson 1949:9. I have argued (1987:19–22) that while Bultmann's *History of the Synoptic Tradition* (1931, ET 1968) treated Q as paraenesis, functioning alongside the Easter kerygma (1931:338, ET 1968:393), in the later *Theology of the New Testament* (1948–53, ET 1951–55) he began to view Q as an imperfect or inadequate attempt in its own right to grasp the kerygmatic significance of Jesus' preaching.

16. E.g., Lührmann 1969:94–95 (ET 1994:67–68); Kloppenborg 1990b; Jacobson 1992b:27–30; Seeley 1992; Tuckett 1996:221. Schmithals (1994:47) argues that the core of Q (containing nonchristological, nonkerygmatic sayings) derived from a community isolated from those influenced by the passion kerygma, but suggests that the final form of Q comes from the Markan community (1994:51).

17. Schulz 1972:169–70: "[The Q people] celebrated with their ancestors the Passover meal and knew no sacraments. Instead, the eschatological baptismal purification was probably practiced as a purification from sins in view of the approaching Parousia of the Son of Man, which amounted to a 'rite of initiation of the eschatological community'. . . [In Q] no kerygmatic interpretation of the passion of Jesus was known, nor an explicit theology of Easter, and the

There was, of course, and continues to be resistance to such a conclusion. Kümmel's widely used *Introduction to the New Testament* asserts:

> [W]e must consider that in the Palestinian community in which Q must have originated . . . the passion kerygma repeated by Paul was formulated at a very early date and that it attests the redemptive significance of the death of Jesus. In that case the collecting of the words of Jesus could not have taken place in conscious disregard of this basic confession. (Kümmel 1975:73)

Neither of Kümmel's assumptions—that there was a single "Palestinian community" and that the confessional formula in 1 Cor 15:3b-5 derived from that "community"—is very plausible. Still, Q's silence on passion theology might be explicable on the assumption that it had a limited *Sitz im Leben* or ecclesial function: not proclamation as such, but instructions for missionaries, for example.[18] Even if this were so, however, the fact remains that Q does not betray the slightest hint of knowledge of the passion kerygma, which would be at least curious had passion theology been so central. Thus Kümmel's supposition that Q derives from the same "community" as the passion kerygma is just that: pure supposition.

At issue here is not whether Q and its framers knew of the death of Jesus; it would be difficult to imagine that they did not. Nor is there much room for doubt that the Q people held Jesus to have been vindicated and his ignominious death thereby overcome. The question is, *how* did they conceive this vindication? Polag wonders rhetorically whether there ever was a Christian community "for which the resurrection of Jesus was not the *central confession* and the *pivotal point of the teaching*" (1991:101, emphasis added).[19] The answer is yes. Neither Q nor the *Gospel of Thomas* is preoccupied with the resurrection of Jesus. It is more appropriate to ask two questions: First, in a document whose focus is the kingdom of God, is there *any* special salvific meaning assigned to the death of Jesus? And second, how was Jesus' vindication represented in a document in circulation long before the appearance stories of Matthew, Luke, and John are attested, and at roughly the same time that the bare formula of 1 Cor 15:3b-5 was circulating in Antioch and in the Pauline churches?

---

only thing that had the significance of being given 'for the sake of' (ὑπέρ) was the Torah that had been given to Israel" (quoting Bultmann 1948–53, 1:42).

18. Thus Käsemann 1969:119–20; Steck 1967:288 n. 1; Gnilka 1994:134. Wilckens 1967:13–14 suggests that Q was part of the didactic activity of the "Christian synagogue."

19. Polag says of Q: "By the resurrection of Christ his importance for the history of the kingdom in its manifestation in Israel has not only been confirmed by God; rather, a renewed possibility of deciding for or against Jesus and his mission has been opened up; Jesus now lives with God and *is nevertheless present in his Church* in such a way that in this Church of disciples there is a possibility of meeting him *in another form*. From now on, *until Jesus returns and is visible to every eye in the events of judgement, the offer of access to salvation stands*" (1991:102, emphasis added). This summary seems unduly influenced by Matthaean theology of the presence of the Risen Lord within the community and Luke's salvation history.

Q AS THEOLOGICALLY "DEFICIENT"

Dunn agrees that Q lacked both a passion narrative and passion predictions and refuses Kümmel's gratuitous expedient of assuming Q's knowledge of the passion kerygma. He wishes nonetheless to avoid any hint of heterodoxy in Q. Even though he agrees that the *Gospel of Thomas* and Q derive from the same stream of tradition, he rejects the implication that Q evinces to the "gnosticizing wisdom trajectory" represented by the *Gospel of Thomas*—a case that had been argued in Robinson's influential essay, "ΛΟΓΟΙ ΣΟΦΩΝ" (1964, ET 1971b). Q, Dunn countered, did not identify Jesus with Sophia and it is "thoroughly eschatological" (1977:285–86). The *Gospel of Thomas*, by contrast, represents a secondary development, both in terms of its Sophialogy and its de-eschatologized version of Jesus' sayings. Dunn thus rejects both Robinson's assessment of the theological tendency immanent in Q and Helmut Koester's conclusion that the *Gospel of Thomas* reflects a very primitive theological stratum, lacking both the appeal of a passion kerygma and apocalyptic sayings.[20] For in that case one would have a rather "unorthodox" theological configuration as a primitive level of the Synoptic tradition.

To dissociate Q from the *Gospel of Thomas* does not alleviate Dunn's dilemma, however. Q still lacks one of the three key marks of continuity that Dunn posits to establish the congruences between the historical Jesus and later kerygmata: an expectation of Jesus' vindication and a perhaps a salvific view of his death. Hence he suggests that "it looks rather as though Q presents Jesus' teaching as guidance for living in the last days rather than as kerygma, with Jesus understood as one whose words have eschatological significance quite apart from any question of his dying or rising" (1977:287)

It is not clear from Dunn's comments whether he thinks that the framers of Q had something in addition to Q for their "kerygma" or whether Q should be regarded as an immature or incomplete theology, though the latter seems more likely. He speculates that the reason for Q's ultimate disappearance was that it was "not treated as gospel by most of the early Christians" and perhaps even that it came to be perceived as too amenable to gnosticizing distortions (1977:287).

This leads Dunn to a general theological assessment: early Christians thought crucial the unity and continuity of the human Jesus with the exalted Christ. Although Q presented Jesus as both a sage and the coming Son of

---

20. Koester 1971b:186: "Faith is understood as belief in Jesus' words, a belief which makes what Jesus proclaimed present and real for the believer. The catalyst which has caused the crystallization of these sayings into a 'gospel' is the view that the kingdom is uniquely present in Jesus' eschatological preaching and that eternal wisdom about man's true self is disclosed in his words. The gnostic proclivity of this concept needs no further elaboration." On the non-apocalyptic character of the formative components of Q, see also Koester 1980:113; 1990:150.

Man, this balance was "found inadequate to serve as an expression of the Christian gospel, since it lacked precisely the emphasis that Jesus is the crucified and risen one as well as the teacher of wisdom and Son of Man coming in glory" (1977:287).

Dunn treats together two issues that are better kept quite distinct: the *disappearance of Q*, on the one hand, and the implications of Q's *existence* for a history of theology, on the other. In fact we do not know why Q disappeared. It is completely illegitimate to assume that the reason for its disappearance was theological. Long ago Kilpatrick (1941) offered a *literary* explanation: if Q had been almost completely absorbed by Matthew and Luke, it may have been quite simple for Q to disappear. The obvious objection, of course, is that the same ought then to have happened with Mark. More recently Dieter Lührmann has observed that before the fourth century, "the circumstances of the transmission of the Jesus tradition are so haphazard that Q would have had to be known in Egypt for us to possess a fragment of it. Even for the Gospel of Mark . . . there is only a single manuscript [from Egypt, i.e., $\mathfrak{P}^{45}$], and that derives from circles which already accepted the canon of Irenaeus" (1995.113).

Q's disappearance may simply have been a function of failing to be "adopted" by one of the consolidating forces of the second and third centuries; or, it may have been an accident of geography: Q was never copied in Egypt. Few would argue on Dunn's analogy that the lost Pauline or deutero-Pauline letters to the Corinthians (1 Cor 5.9) and to the Laodiceans (Col 4:16) were not copied because they were heterodox or inadequate. Their disappearances are accidents of transmission. To suppose that Q's disappearance was a judgment on its theology assumes anachronistically that the earliest Christians developed an acute sense of theological adequacy and inadequacy. If such a sense had existed, it would be difficult to account for the transmission and reception of James or the *Didache*.

Dunn's argument, once stripped of its speculation about the disappearance of Q, amounts to arguing that Q is theologically inadequate because it is not Pauline. This judgment is stipulative and retrospective, defining the essential continuities between Jesus and early kerygmata on the basis of one particular theological stream.

Q AND THE CANONICAL "DIRECTION"

Brevard Childs (1993) takes a different approach. Like Dunn, he disputes the theses of Robinson and Koester that Q is located on a trajectory leading to Gnosticism and, in particular, Koester's suggestion that the incorporation of Q into Matthew and Luke represented a radical alteration of Q's immanent tendency.[21] Childs is also concerned with my suggestion that Q

---

21. Koester 1971a:135: "[T]he *Gospel of Thomas* continues . . . the most original gattung of the Jesus tradition—the *logoi sophon*—which, in the canonical gospels, became acceptable

originated as a set of instructions that were later expanded, ultimately taking on a proto-biographical cast.[22] His objection is that "these literary construals ultimately do not succeed in illuminating theologically the final form of the canonical Gospels, but are left mired in a murky pre-literary projection" (Childs 1993:257).

The objection is curious. Since Childs is otherwise acutely interested in the "canonical shape" of individual biblical books—the way that the canon creates a particular construal of the writings it compasses—one might wonder why judgments about the shape of *pre*-Gospel sources—murky or not— should be relevant to the illumination of the "final form of the canonical Gospels." Even if Q should turn out to be proto-gnostic—which I do not think it was—the incorporation of Q into two *non-gnostic* Gospels and the juxtaposition of Matthew and Luke with the *anti-gnostic* polemic of the Pastoral epistles would, presumably, effectively mitigate its supposed "Gnosticism." Clearly, Childs is concerned with diachronic aspects of the tradition, which he calls the "depth dimension within the kerygma" (e.g., 1993:216–17, 263). A critical recovery of this dimension is important, he suggests, for it indicates the "direction in which the tradition grew." It aids in correlating "the witness to the concrete life of the early church with its changing historical and cultural situation," and it indicates the "range of kerygmatic diversity as well as establishing the nature of its unity" (1993:216–17).

When he comes to summarize the core of the earliest Christian kerygma, Childs describes as a "fixed content" the affirmation of the death and resurrection of Jesus as the promised Messiah, even though he allows for considerable latitude in the growth and elaboration of this message (1993:224). He also insists that, despite significant discontinuities with Israel's traditions, "the Jewish scriptures provided the only authoritative context by which the marvelous, yet confusing events of Easter, could be understood, and from which perspective the earthly life of Jesus could also be comprehended" (1993:227). He continues:

> [T]he central role of the Old Testament [*sic*] in the early church's understanding and interpreting the death and resurrection of Christ is incontestable. Psalm 110 provided the imagery for seeing Jesus exalted at God's right hand and reigning sovereign over the powers of death. . . . Psalm 89 formed the link to Christ's humiliation . . . and Psalm 22 spoke of his righteous suffering. . . .

---

to the orthodox church only by a radical critical alteration, not only of the form, but also of the theological intention of this primitive gattung. Such critical evaluation of the gattung, *logoi*, was achieved by Matthew and Luke through imposing the Marcan narrative-kerygma frame upon the sayings tradition represented by Q." See further below, p. 383.

22. Childs's summary (1993:256–57) focuses on the allegedly "subordinate" role of prophetic speech patterns in Q; this is not an accurate reflection of my argument, which acknowledges the importance of prophetic speech patterns in the main redaction of Q (see above, chapter 3).

Psalm 2 and II Samuel 7 provided the language for the royal messianic office as Son of God . . . and Daniel 7 spoke of the eschatological hope of his kingdom. . . . (1993:229)

Significantly, Q lacks *all* of these elements.

At this point it becomes clear why Q poses a problem. As Childs admits, "the crucial theological issues" in respect to Q are its uncertain "christological *Tendenz*," its lack of a passion narrative, and its infrequent citation of the Tanak (1993:255). Simply put, if one accepts Childs's "fixed content" of the earliest Christian kerygma as normative, Q is an anomaly at the heart of this early kerygma. Alternatively, Q offers an instances of early theologizing that threatens to undermine both Childs's view of the kerygmatic unity of early Christian proclamation and the relative uniformity of the "depth dimension" of the canonical witness to faith. It is significant that Childs treats Q only *after* he produced his summary of the earliest kerygma; had he included Q in his calculations from the beginning, a different picture of both primitive kerygmata and the significance of the creation of the canon might have emerged.

Q AND JESUS' DEATH

Despite the fact that Q lacks a narrative of Jesus' death or sayings that refer specifically to his death, Q is not as silent, as either its detractors or some of its advocates have supposed

Arland Hultgren provides perhaps the most useful discussion of the problem to date, distinguishing carefully between the issues of whether Q knows of the passion kerygma—there is no evidence of this—and whether there are any reflections on Jesus' death (1994:31–41). In part, he wants to demonstrate that Q is aware of elements that also appeared in the passion narratives. He makes three suggestions.

First, Hultgren argues that Q 14:27 ("whoever does not take up his cross and follow me cannot be my disciple") presupposes knowledge of Jesus' cross and recalls the story of either Jesus or Simon of Cyrene carrying the cross. If this is so, Q betrays knowledge of some form of a passion narrative. Hultgren's conclusion, however, seems unlikely. Not even Mark, who has a version of Q 14:27 (Mark 8:34), makes any effort to assimilate the description of Simon to Mark 8:34 and thus to depict him in the role of a disciple. Nothing in Q 14:27 itself makes the connection: Q speaks of the disciple *"receiving* his [own] cross" (λαμβάνει τὸν σταυρὸν αὐτοῦ) and "following after" (ἀκολουθεῖ ὀπίσω), while Mark's description of Simon uses "*lift up* his [Jesus'] cross" (ἄρη τὸν σταυρὸν αὐτοῦ) and makes no mention of Simon *following* Jesus.[23] Nevertheless, Hultgren is right that Q 14:27

23. Only in Luke 23:26 is the description of Simon of Cyrene assimilated to Luke 14:27 with the addition of "after Jesus" (ὄπισθεν τοῦ Ἰησοῦ).

would inevitably be interpreted with Jesus' death in view. More than this, the saying suggests that discipleship be seen as inextricably connected with the willingness to undergo the same shameful death as Jesus. This does not make Jesus' death salvific, but it does imply that Jesus' fate was an integral part of his identity and activity.

Second, Hultgren argues that Q's quotation of Psalm 118:26, "You will not see me until you say, 'Blessed is the one who comes in the name of the Lord'," in Q 13:35b recalls the acclamation of the crowds at the triumphal entry (Mark 11:9 and parr.) (1994:33–34). This is also doubtful in my view, for Q uses the participial phrase ὁ ἐρχόμενος ("the one who comes") in a quasi-titular fashion to refer to a figure coming in judgment (Q 3:16). This is hardly the Jesus of Mark 11. Moreover, the difficulty with Hultgren's suggestion is that it requires some narrative framework within which "you will not see me *until* you say" makes sense and implies that 13:34-35 is spoken before some unnarrated entrance story. Q contains neither a narrative sequence surrounding 13:34-35 nor an entry scene. The more likely referent is the hiatus preceding the coming of the Son of Man.[24] Nonetheless, since 13:35b is framed in the first person ("me") and concludes the Jerusalem saying with its reference to the killing of the prophets, it is a reasonable conjecture that Jesus is included among those "prophets and messengers" killed and is the one who is specifically vindicated with the coming of the Son of Man.[25]

Finally, Hultgren suggests that Q 9:58 (the homeless Son of Man) and Q 19:12-27 (the Parable of the Entrusted Money) represent reflections on the death of Jesus (1994:34). It is not at all obvious to me that 9:58 would be so understood by the readers/auditors of Q. And while the departing and returning master (κύριος) of 19:12-27 would undoubtedly be understood as Jesus—in particular since the parable is sandwiched between Q 17:23-37 (on the coming of the Son of Man) and Q 22:28-30 (where his followers are rewarded), the parable itself offers no particular construal of Jesus' death.

A better candidate for a saying that implies a construal of Jesus' death is Q 6:22-23. While not expressly speaking of Jesus, this beatitude describes the ill-treatment that Jesus' followers endure "for the sake of the Son of Man" and compares this with the treatment of the prophets. Since the Deuteronomistic view of the prophets invoked here regularly also speaks of the killing of the prophets, it does not require too much imagination to suppose that Q 6:22-23 has in view Jesus' fate and, like 14:27, associates the disciples' fates with that of their teacher. This does not make Jesus' death

---

24. Q 13:35b, like 10:12 and 11:51b, probably derives from Q redaction (see above, chapter 3, n. 66). All three refer to the coming judgment.

25. See below, p. 377, on D. Zeller's suggestion that Q 13:35b conceives Jesus' role on the analogy of Elijah and Enoch, who were removed to heaven. If this is so, it is Mark who has *historicized* Ps 118:26, referring it to Jesus' entry into Jerusalem rather than his return as Son of Man.

salvific any more than the prophets' deaths are salvific; but it does mean that Q viewed Jesus' fate as inextricably related to his other activities and asserts that discipleship involves a complete mimesis of Jesus' behavior and character.

Again it is necessary to insist that at issue is not whether Q knows of Jesus' death and includes sayings that comment on it at least indirectly. The various references to persecution and opposition (6:22-23; 11:49-51; 13:34-35) and the explicit use of "cross" (14:27) were most likely read with Jesus' death in mind. The issue is whether a *soteriological function* was assigned to that death. Hultgren rightly observes that in the tendency to suppose that Q must have known other passion traditions "lurks the habit of measuring all forms of proclamation in light of the Pauline kerygma" (1994:38).

Hultgren raises the important issue of the extent to which one may rely on arguments from silence in reconstructing Q's system of beliefs. He agrees that Q does not offer a complete catalogue of the Q group's beliefs (1994:38, citing Kloppenborg 1991:79). We know nothing of the ritual structure of the Q group. We do not know whether the Q group(s) had adopted a eucharistic practice and, if so, whether it was more like the Pauline or Markan form than that preserved in the *Didache* 9–10. Nor can we verify Schulz's assertion that the Q people had celebrated the Passover rather than sacraments. Arguments from silence are precarious, but assumptions that Q "must have observed" certain practices are even more problematic. All that we have to go on is what the text of Q itself offers.

A key problem is how to know whether Q's relative silence on Jesus' death means that it is indifferent to that death, or that it presupposes (and so does not repeat) the conventional pre-Pauline solution or a pre-Markan passion narrative, or that it has understood Jesus' death within a different framework. As should already be clear, I do not think the first option is viable. Yet it is also not the case, as some scholars have intimated, that all conclusions regarding Q's (lack of) understanding of Jesus' death are based on elaborate arguments from silence.

George Nickelsburg's (1980) study of the narrative structure of the Markan passion narrative supplies important clues for Q. Nickelsburg showed that the Markan passion narrative was framed on the pattern of the genre of the "wisdom tale" which depicts the persecution, sometimes death, and vindication of the righteous one. Examples of the genre are found in the Joseph story (Genesis 37–42), Ahiqar, Esther, Daniel 3 and 6, Susanna, Wisdom of Solomon 2–5, and 3 Maccabees. The essential narrative elements (which are italicized) can be illustrated from Wisdom 2–5:

> The actions and professed knowledge of God of the righteous man (2:12-13, 16) prove to be a *provocation* to his opponents, who form a *conspiracy* against him (2:12a). That leads to a *trial* and *condemnation* (2:20), resulting in an *ordeal* (2:17, 19) and, eventually, a "shameful death" (2:20). This portion of

the story may also depict the *decision* of the hero when faced with the choice of obedience or disobedience to God and his *trust* in God, often framed as a *prayer*. It may also contain a *protest* and the mention of *assistance* rendered to the protagonist by helpers. The second main part of the tale relates the *rescue* of the wise man who, in Wisdom, only "*appears*" to die (3:2-4) but in fact possesses immortality (3:4b). He is *vindicated* in the presence of his persecutors, *exalted and acclaimed* (5:1-5) while his enemies react in dismay (5:2) and experience *punishment* (5:9-14). (Kloppenborg 1990b:78, summarizing Nickelsburg 1972:170)

Nickelsburg's interest was to show that although Mark 14–15 conforms to this genre, the passion narrative is not Mark's creation, since not all of the features of the wisdom tale are homogeneous with Markan editorial intent (1980:182–84). For our purposes, however, what is important is that although Q does not *narrativize* or emplot these elements, most of the narrative functions of the wisdom tale are present.

> While there are no elements in Q which express the elements of provocation and conspiracy, the sequences of *trial* and *condemnation* are presupposed. Q 12:11 expressly mentions judicial proceedings, and hostilities and persecution of a more general sort are alluded to in Q 6:22-23; 11:47-51 and 13:34-35. In connection with the judicial proceedings (12:11), the *assistance* of the Spirit plays a role (12:12). *Ordeal* in connection with such proceedings is probably implied by 12:4-5 (cf. also 6:22-23) and, as in the Wisdom of Solomon, the ignominy of an unjust death is compensated and overcome through the parental care that God exhibits for his own (12:6-7). [One should add that both *decision* and *trust* are implicit here.] *Vindication* is expressed variously: the persecuted are, paradoxically, blessed (6:22-23b) and are included in the company of God's prophets (6:23c; 11:49-51; 13:34-35). In spite of opposition, they speak with the voice of Jesus and ultimately, God (10:16), and are the ones who may claim knowledge of God (10:21-22). Both the promise of a "reward in heaven" (6:22b; cf. 6:35b) and the promise that Jesus' followers will sit on thrones, judging Israel imply vindication and *exaltation* (22:28-30; cf. 13:28-29). Various *acclamations* are present: Jesus and John are identified as Sophia's children (7:35); Jesus' followers are set above the sages because of their superior grasp of revelation (10:21-22); and they are pronounced more blessed than prophets and kings because of what they have witnessed (10:23-24). The predicted *punishment* of the persecutors is evidenced at Q 11:50-51: "The blood shed by all the prophets . . . will be required of this generation." (Kloppenborg 1990b:79)

Not only does Q include most of the narrative functions that constitute the wisdom tale; it also assumes a "narrative world" in which the death of Jesus *could* have appeared as an emplotted element.[26] Far from being

---

26. Here I invoke Petersen's (1978:49–80) distinction between "plotted time"—the elements of a text that are arranged into a plot—and "story time" or "narrative world"—the lexicon of temporal references which define a larger "world" within which the plot occurs.

atemporal exhortations, Q has a rather developed "narrative world" which extends from Abel and the foundations of the world (11:49-51) to the coming of the Son of Man (17:23-30) and includes the time of the Patriarchs (13:28-29), Lot (10:12; 17:28-29), Solomon (11:31; 12:27), Jonah (11:30, 32), the death of Zechariah (11:51a), John the Baptist (7:18-35), and the projected activities of Jesus' disciples (10:2-3, 16; 12:2-12, 22-31) and the hostilities they will encounter.

Instead of choosing to emplot the death of Jesus as a specific station in this narrative world, however, Q chose rather to treat the narrative elements of the wisdom tale *collectively*. The elements of the wisdom tale refer not exclusively to Jesus' fate but *generally* to the Q people and to the sages and prophets who preceded them. This accords with some other instances of the wisdom tale. In Second Temple Judaism the wisdom tale and the psalms of complaint are often applied not to the suffering and vindication of an individual but to collectivities. Such is clearly the case with Wisdom 2–5, where the "wise man" is not a specific individual but stands for Alexandrian Jews who are under pressure. The same is the case with 1QS 8.3-10, 1QSa 1.1-3, and, in part, 1QH 2.8-9, 20-30 (Marcus 1995:223–24).

A well-known feature of the passion narratives is the dense texture of quotations of and allusions to the "Psalms of the Righteous Sufferer" or "Psalms of Complaint": Pss 22, 27, 31, 34, 35, 38, 41, 43, 43, 69, and 109.[27] Elements from these Psalms provide much of the detail of the passion narratives, not only in Mark but in John and the *Gospel of Peter*, supplying such details as the offer of wine mixed with gall (Ps 69:22) and the division of Jesus' clothing (Ps 22:19). Those who framed the passion narratives appear to have used the genre of the wisdom tale and consciously assimilated the account of Jesus' ordeal and death to the language of the Psalms of the Righteous Sufferer. What is important to note in this regard is that Q *does not reflect the language of the Psalms* to any measurable extent.[28]

What are the implications of these findings? On the one hand, it seems clear not only that Q is well aware of the death of Jesus but that it has also invoked a framework by which to understand its significance. The Deuteronomistic understanding of the prophets is common in Q and thus it seems plausible that Q understands Jesus' death as an instance of the "typical"—perhaps climactic—prophetic death. Jesus' death is also seen within the context of a collective interpretation of the "wisdom tale." Persecution, rejection, suffering, and death are the fate of *all* God's envoys and the righteous. Jesus' fate is an instance of this fate. When one asks, is there any

27. Kee (1975) has noted over two hundred biblical quotations and allusions in Mark 11–14, including twenty-six from the Psalms in Mark 14–15. Marcus (1995:207–9) provides a convenient tabulation of the use of the Psalms in the passion narratives.

28. The only allusions to these psalms are found in textually uncertain aspects of Q 6:22. On this, see Kloppenborg 1990b:80–81.

reason to suppose that Q knows a pre-Markan passion account or a salvific interpretation of Jesus' death, the answer must be, no. This is because at the numerous points where Q might have borrowed from either the individualistic reading of the wisdom tale or its rich texture of the Psalms of the Righteous Sufferer or from the passion kerygma's salvific construal of Jesus' death, *it consistently fails to do so*. It would be hard to imagine that this silence is a matter of Q consciously rejecting such construals of Jesus' death. Rather, the only plausible solution is that Q simply does not know them.

This finding has significant consequences in the writing of a history of the beliefs of the early Jesus movement. But does it have theological consequences? It would be mistaken, I think, to imagine that Q represents a theological backwater, much less gives an aberrant reading of Jesus' fate. Hultgren, for example, is concerned lest the Q community be treated as if it were "walled off from the rest of early Christianity" (1994:38). Such a conclusion is hardly necessary. Rather, Q appears to represent an *early* treatment of Jesus' death, one that is probably earlier than Mark's privatizing narrative and perhaps at least as early as Paul's view of Jesus' death. Q's depiction is still barely visible, preserved in Matthew and Luke, but its distinctiveness has been effaced by Matthew's and Luke's incorporation of Mark's passion narrative. The non-emplotted and collective interpretation of ordeal and death has been lost from view.

Q's treatment of Jesus' death might be treated theologically as a trajectory that went nowhere or as a preliminary stage in the development of a wisdom tale that eventually focused on Jesus exclusively. But Q's view of ordeal and death is arguably as early as Paul's and, unless one wishes to invoke a canonical stipulation, deserves careful consideration alongside Pauline views. Moreover, Q's absolute silence on Jesus' death in particular casts into doubt the assertions that Jesus must have viewed his own death as vicarious (see above, p. 358). Even Galvin's requirement that Jesus accepted his own death freely (see above, p. 359) ought to be adjusted, for Q does not appear to treat Jesus as special in this regard: the prophets and Jesus' followers also accepted the likelihood of persecution and death.

A Resurrection in Q?

The apparent absence of a mention of Jesus' resurrection in Q presents a problem similar to, but not identical with, that of its relative silence on the death of Jesus. On the one hand, there are scarcely any texts that can be called to our aid. On the other, Marinus de Jonge is certainly right to conclude that

> [i]t is extremely unlikely . . . that communities in which the sayings of the Q collection were handed down knew no other traditions about Jesus' life, death, and resurrection/exaltation. . . . For one thing, one could not speak of Jesus' rejection by Israel's leaders without telling what happened afterward. One had

to explain why the kingdom of God was a present dynamic reality and not an illusion of people who did not want to admit that their master had deluded both them and himself. Those who handed down the Q material believed in a God who had vindicated Jesus, his work and his message, and they believed that he would come again to share with them the full bliss of the kingdom of God. (1988:83–84)

In an earlier essay (1990b) I suggested that the lack of a resurrection account was in part due to the genre of Q. Mapping the generic typicalities of the instructional genre as well as other sayings genres, it was observed that while virtually all wisdom collections trace themselves to dead sages, the death of the sage is rarely if ever an issue. Nor do such collections imagine the exaltation or vindication of the sage. The sayings receive their authority not from a postmortem rescue of the speaker but by means of other strategies, either a testing sequence at the beginning of the collection, or, most commonly, by asserting or implying that the sage speaks for Sophia/God or that Sophia is speaking in the sage's words.

Q in fact employs both strategies. The temptation story demonstrates the reliable moral character of its principal character and shows behavior consistent with the teachings that will follow (Kloppenborg 1987a:248–56; Tuckett 1992). Q affirms that John and Jesus are "children of Sophia" (7:35) and that Jesus is the exclusive conduit of the knowledge of God among humans (Q 10:21-22), a claim that applies to Jesus' language commonly associated with Sophia (Kloppenborg 1978). The intimate association between Jesus and God is also expressed in Q 10:16, also in language that resembles, but goes rather beyond, the idiom of sententious wisdom collections. Hence, I suggested:

> Rather than invoking the apocalyptic metaphor of resurrection, Q understands the authorization of Jesus' soteriologically intensified words by implying a functional identification of Jesus and Sophia. Thus the speaker of the wise words is *never* without legitimation for his sayings, although it is always legitimation *coram Deo* and not necessarily *coram hominibus*—in the human forum. No special moment of vindication is required. If one wishes to speak of Easter at all, one must say that what the Markan and post-Markan Easter traditions localize and particularize by narration, Q assumes to have always been a characteristic of Jesus' words as the words of Sophia. Sophia's envoy is always justified, and conversely, Sophia is justified in the activities of her children, though this vindication is not manifest empirically in history. (Kloppenborg 1990b:90–91)

Hultgren is right to question whether this formulation does not ascribe too determinative a role to genre (1994:37). He points out, for example, that in the papers of Martin Luther King Jr., references to the cross and resurrection are wanting, no doubt owing to the genre of the papers. The point is well taken and suggests a reformulation of the thesis: the genre employed by those who transmitted the Q materials had a ready place for pericopae such as the temptation story or Q 10:21-22, for such fitted eminently well with the legitimation strategies customarily used by sayings genres. This, however, should not exclude the possibility that the Q people may have used other legitimating strategies on other occasions, but it does perhaps help to account for the fact that their document does not include direct appeals to Jesus' resurrection.

Hultgren's corrective comment, it should be noted, is not intended as a resort to Kümmel's facile assumption that Q "must" have known and used the passion kerygma. On the contrary, he insists that "to claim that the Q community had other sources, traditions, and theological emphases is to argue from silence no less than it is to say that Q contains all that the community thought significant about Jesus" (1994:38).

De Jonge's point, however, deserves careful consideration. Notwithstanding the genre of Q and the force it may have exerted on the type of materials present in Q, it remains that Q, unlike most other wisdom collections, has as its speaker a figure who not only was executed in a particularly ignominious manner but whom the document itself treats as vindicated and identified with an eschatological figure with a role at the judgment. Whether or not the genre of Q provided adequate "room" to voice this dimension, it is worthwhile wondering how the Q people might have imagined the vindication to have occurred.

The textual evidence is slender. Perhaps the most widely held view is that the identification of Jesus with the Son of Man presupposes a specific exegesis of Dan 7:13-14 by means of Ps 110:1 and in view of "resurrection experiences."[29] Perrin argued that as a result of the resurrection experiences, Jesus' earliest followers concluded that he had been exalted by God to his right hand (Ps 110:1) as "Lord" (*mar*, (מר) and that he was the heavenly Son of Man (Dan 7:13). Such a linkage may be seen both in Stephen's vision (Acts 7:56) and in Mark 14:62 (1974a:12–13). Boring adds that the reason that all of the Son of Man sayings appear on Jesus' lips is that it was Christian prophets, speaking as mouthpieces of Jesus, who first articulated this equation: "They did this in association with the first Easter experiences, as the risen Jesus addressed the community through them. Their sayings from the risen Jesus formed the transition point from the proclaimer to the proclaimed" (Boring 1982:244–45). If this line of argument were correct, one could argue that the resurrection (or at least a "resurrection experience") is implicit in Q's very application of the Son of Man title to Jesus.

There are significant difficulties with this scenario when applied to Q, however. For Q shows no traces at all of Ps 110:1 and it is not even clear

29. Perrin 1968 (repr. 1974a:57–83); R. Edwards 1971:85; Boring 1982:244–45. This, presumably, is also the logic for those who, like Yarbro Collins (1987), think that some of the coming Son of Man sayings such as Q 17:24 and 17:26-27 (which do not specifically identify Jesus with the Son of Man) are authentic: on the basis of Jesus' resurrection, his followers identified the (now exalted) Jesus as the Danielic Son of Man.

that Q's use of the Son of Man term presupposes Dan 7:13-14.[30] In order to maintain the thesis of Perrin and Boring, it is also necessary to assume that the allusions to Daniel 7 and Psalm 110, by which the original exegetical equation that identified Jesus with the exalted Son of Man was effected, were completely effaced. All that remained was the title itself. Such a disappearance is theoretically possible, of course; but given the early date of Q, one would also have to suppose that the two texts were effaced almost immediately—a supposition that is inconvenient, to say the least.[31]

Dieter Zeller (1985) has made a plausible alternate case that Q conceived Jesus' role on the analogy of Elijah or Enoch, both of whom were removed to heaven and held in reserve for a further role. He finds the clue in 13:35b, which on other grounds should be ascribed to Q redaction (above p. 148). The claim that the Jerusalemites "will no longer see me" recalls the description of Elijah: as 2 Kings 2:12 states, Elisha "no longer saw him" (καὶ οὐκ εἶδεν αὐτὸν ἔτι).[32] This premature disappearance encouraged in biblical and post-biblical tradition the expectation that Elijah would return in a forensic role (Haufe 1961). Elijah is not the only such figure to disappear. The removal of a figure and his installation as Son of Man is found in *1 Enoch* 70–71,[33] and both Baruch and Ezra were said to have been assumed to await some eschatological function.[34]

30. Opinion is sharply divided: on the one hand, Casey 1980:194; Jacobson 1992a:416: "the evidence of influence of Dan 7,13-14 on the Son of Man in Q is very scant; by contrast, it is quite clear in Mk 13,26 and 14,62." Contrast Caragounis 1986:203: "The connections [of Q 12:8-9] with Dan 7:13f. are so obvious that it is unnecessary to belabor the point"; Tuckett 1996:266–76.

31. Tödt himself noticed that the "apocalyptic elaborations" in Q's coming Son of Man sayings were "radically cut down" (1965:66) and that they were completely absent from the present Son of Man sayings (1965:124–25). Robinson (1994b:327) observes: "But once Tödt conceded that the future Son of Man sayings do not betray the coloring of the Jewish apocalyptic tradition, and that the present Son of Man sayings do not derive their elevated status for Jesus from the apocalyptic Son of Man (but rather from the activity of the kingdom of God in Jesus' public ministry), then his whole thesis becomes so improbable that the converse theory is indeed suggested: Jesus used of himself the idiom Son of Man. The idiom was then put on his tongue by his disciples as characteristic of his language. Once an apocalyptic role was ascribed to him, the idiom would be used here as well."

32. As Lohfink 1971:41–42 points out, the terminology most commonly associated with the assumption of a figure has to do with being removed from sight: ἀφανίζω, ἀφανίζομαι, ἀφανὴς γίνομαι, ἄφαντος γίγνομαι, *non (nusquam) compareo*, and *nusquam appareo*. A second frequent word group is derives from ἁρπάζω, and a third from μεθίστημι. The motif of non-appearance is already seen in Gen 5:24: καὶ εὐηρέστησεν Ἐνὼχ τῷ θεῷ καὶ οὐχ ηὑρίσκετο, ὅτι μετέθηκεν αὐτὸν ὁ θεός; *1 Enoch* 12.1: καὶ οὐδεὶς τῶν ἀνθρώπων ἔγνω ποῦ ἐλίμφθη καὶ ποῦ ἐστιν καὶ τί ἐγένετο αὐτῷ; Wisdom 4:10-11: εὐάρεστος θεῷ γενόμενος ἠγαπήθη καὶ ζῶν μεταξὺ ἁμαρτωλῶν μετετέθη· ἡρπάγη, μὴ κακία ἀλλάξῃ σύνεσιν αὐτοῦ ἢ δόλος ἀπατήσῃ ψυχὴν αὐτοῦ.

33. D. Zeller 1985:516–17. J. Collins 1995:179–80 points out that *1 Enoch* 70.1 distinguishes Enoch and the Son of Man, but 71.14 has the angel asserting that Enoch is the Son of Man. Collins suggests that the latter is a rejoinder to the Christian identification of Jesus as the Son of Man.

34. See *2 Apoc. Bar.* 13.3; 25.1; 76.2; *4 Ezra* 14.9; 50 [Syriac]. Of the righteous in general:

While such figures as Elijah and Enoch were assumed prior to death, the Wisdom of Solomon describes the "just man," a victim of a violent death, being "transported" (μετετέθη) and "snatched away" (ἡρπάγη) by God, only to confront and shame his erstwhile oppressors at the judgment (Wis 4:10—5:23). Zeller notes how congenial the notion of the rescue of God's envoy through assumption was with the Deuteronomistic view of the prophets seen in Q 13:34-35a. By means of assumption, God both preserves the just from contamination (Wis 4:11; 2 *Apoc. Bar.* 48.29-30) and spares them from the coming eschatological catastrophe (4 *Ezra* 14.15). Assumption and the Deuteronomistic view of the prophets are found combined in the Animal Apocalypse (1 *Enoch* 85-90): Elijah's assumption (2 Kings 2:1-18) is made the *direct* result of the persecution of the prophets, which 1 Kings 19:14 locates much earlier in the Elijah cycle (see 1 *Enoch* 89.51; D. Zeller 1985:518).

To understand Q 13:35b on the analogy of these assumption texts suggests that the Q people may have regarded Jesus' death as the death of a just man or a prophet whom God had assumed, pending some future eschatological function. This accounts for the fact that Q accords Jesus' death no special salvific significance, but jumps immediately to Jesus' return as the Son of Man (11:49-51; 13:34-35). In the parallel texts from Second Temple Judaism, it is not the death of the sage or prophet that is soteriologically significant (despite its typicality), but rather the figure's assumption and expected postmortem vindication.

It must be admitted that there is practically nothing to go on when discussing Q's view of the "resurrection" of Jesus. Q 13:35b is virtually the only clue we have, beyond the general conviction that Q must have imagined some sort of vindication of its hero. Nevertheless, three facts must be kept in view. First, Q never comments directly on Jesus' death but seems instead to treat opposition and persecution as a collective matter. Second, a fortiori, Q does not speak of Jesus' death (or the deaths of God's envoys) as salvific and, as important, does not betray the slightest knowledge of the exegetical strategies based on the Psalms that are employed in the early passion narratives. Finally, Q displays no signs of applying *resurrection* language to Jesus—this in spite of the fact that Q 11:31-32 speaks of the Queen of the South and the Ninevites being raised (ἐγερθήσεται, ἀναστήσονται) at the judgment to serve as the accusers of "this generation." There are several points in Q that speak of persecution or opposition where one might have included allusions to the resurrection of Jesus as a model for endurance. But Q is silent in this regard. Instead, the only text that directly concerns vindication invokes a death–assumption–judgment scenario, not the death–

---

4 *Ezra* 6.26; 7.38; 13.52. Although it does not specifically mention assumption, the *Test. Abr.* [A] 13.2-3 depicts Abel, the first murder victim, sitting on the throne of judgment, waiting to judge the righteous and sinners.

resurrection pattern that was to become common in Christian thinking after Paul.

The conclusion to be drawn is not that Q was oblivious to the issues of the death and vindication of Jesus but that Q's approach to these issues is *significantly different* from those of Paul (and his immediate predecessors) and the Markan and post-Markan gospels. Whether this alleviates the theological problem presented by Q is a different question.

Can Q be regarded as "fitting" with other kerygmatic expressions? Minimally, the fact that the diverse Christian kerygmata all select *Jesus* as their focal point means that, at one level of discourse at least, we can speak meaningfully of a unity. Whether particular kerygmata are too incomplete to be "full members" of the kerygmatic club or too divergent[35] is another question and depends on some normative definition of what is kerygmatic. Dunn in one way, and Childs in another, work retrospectively. Dunn selects some features in some early Christian kerygmata and then uses them as the criteria for assessing whether Q is fully kerygmatic. Childs, curiously, seems to require that the "depth dimension" of the Gospels conform materially and formally to the kerygmatic structure of the canonical gospels.

Such criteria, in my view, are far too restrictive and are predesigned to filter out as ultimately insignificant different voices. They inevitably lose sight of the experimental and tentative nature of the efforts of Jesus' earliest followers to create a framework by which to grasp the significance of his teachings and his fate. Such criteria, by defining unity and continuity in conceptual terms, also subordinate the ethical aspects of Jesus' teachings to the more obviously "theological" aspects and miss the continuities in social posture and social practice that existed between Jesus and the Q people. Since Q, as one of our earliest embodiments of the Jesus tradition, is acutely and obviously concerned with encouraging a social practice based on Jesus' teachings, this subordination seems needlessly tendentious.

Apocalyptic and Wisdom in Q

A second key problem in the assessment of Q has to do with its theological taxonomy and immanent tendencies. This debate, for better or worse, has centered on the terms "wisdom," "apocalyptic," and "prophecy," but is beset with numerous conceptual, ideological, and definitional problems. There are two distinguishable sets of issues here and much of the confusion that has attended the debate arises from a failure to make appropriate

---

35. Meadors (1992; 1995) misrepresents Q scholarship since Lührmann by suggesting that it posits an "unorthodox" and "heretical" kerygma. Meadors's own efforts to posit an essential theological unity between Mark and Q are at the cost of all that is distinctive of both documents and in his reduction of Mark and Q to banalities he misses their deeper common theological commitments.

distinctions. One set of issues is properly literary-critical, the other is a matter of theological taxonomy.

As to the issue of literary genre, it was noted in chapter 3 that there are, broadly speaking, two main proposals. The first is that Q should be viewed on the analogy of a prophetic book. According to this view, most clearly articulated by Migaku Sato (1988), both the major framing features of the collection and many of its individual components recall the features of prophetic books of the Tanak. To be sure, nonprophetic elements are present, but these have been subjugated systematically to the overall prophetic features of the book (Sato 1995). Moreover, it is generally conceded by proponents of this view that Q does not *simply* represent Jesus as a prophet among other prophets—whose messages were not intrinsically tied to their persons—but treats Jesus' prophetic preaching and his person as intimately related.

The other main proposal acknowledges the presence of prophetic speech forms but argues that other generic strategies are at work at the formative level of Q, best situated in the field of ancient Mediterranean instructional literature. The subsequent expansions of Q can be seen in the context of the literary transformations typical of that literature (Kloppenborg 1987a), which includes a development in the direction of a *bios* (Downing 1994). It is likewise clear that Jesus is not represented "merely" as a sage, but bears a definitive, "soteriologically intensified" message (Kloppenborg 1990b).

While the determination of the genre of Q has important implications for understanding how its framers conceived of their work, it is important to be clear about the basis for genre determination and about the limited nature of its consequences. As I have argued in chapter 3, the discussion of the genre of Q should proceed *not* on the basis of subjective judgments regarding its contents, still less on a priori assumptions about the theological or social history of the earliest Jesus movements. Instead, genre determination must proceed on the basis of more conceptually neutral features: framing devices; the dominant grammatical forms; the nature of argumentation (its warrants and methods); the nature of the authorial "voice"; and finally, the typical idioms and tropes. The determination of genre is not a matter of form-critical "nose counting"—whether proverbs, for example, are outnumbered by woe oracles or vice versa—but rather by attention to the *hierarchy of forms* that is created by literary composition.

There are several reasons for insisting on formal and compositional features and for avoiding the theological terms "sapiential," "apocalyptic," and "prophetic" in genre definition and in compositional analysis. First, it is well known that prophetic books employ sapiential forms and that wisdom books such as Proverbs and Sirach have taken over prophetic motifs.[36]

---

36. On the prophetic use of sapiential forms, see Wolff 1964; ET 1973; Whedbee 1971. Some (e.g., Fichtner 1949, ET 1976) have tried to argue that some prophets were sages; for a convincing critique of this, see Van Leeuwen 1990. The most obvious instance of the

That does not turn Isaiah into wisdom or Proverbs into prophecy, for what determines genre are the framing devices, both at the level of individual discourse and at the level of the book as a whole, and the construction of the (implied) author's voice. That a variety of forms should occur in Q is hardly surprising. Its genre, however, is not a matter for form criticism, which treats individual units, but rather the result of a compositional analysis, which attends to the construction of larger units of discourse, their argumentative strategies, and their "voice."[37]

Second and correlatively, the terms "sapiential" and "apocalyptic," insofar as they are used to characterize the theological orientation of Q's component sayings, have been avoided entirely or given a much reduced role in compositional and generic analysis precisely so that tradition-historical and theological assumptions not determine the outcome of what are properly literary decisions. Simply put, the assessment of the genre of Q is not dependent upon whether its hero, Jesus, was (historically speaking) a prophet or a sage or an apocalypticist, or some combination of the three, or none of the three; it is a function of the literary decisions taken by the framers of Q. In the same way the Solomonic collections of proverbs represent Solomon as a sage, to the exclusion of the many other possible depictions of Solomon.[38]

Finally, theological characterization of the content of Q has been avoided in the discussion of literary-critical matters because it is so often ambiguous. Q 16:13 ("No one can serve two masters") is clearly a wisdom sentence, and Sophia's prophecy against "this generation" in Q 11:49b–51a conforms closely to the prophecies of judgment in the Tanak. But what of "blessed are you poor, for yours is the kingdom of God"? Is this an instance of a conventional sapiential saying that has been given innovative content designed to challenge the common assumption that God blesses with prosperity those who are pious?[39] Or has it become something else? Tuckett, for example,

---

"prophetizing" of Wisdom is Prov 1:20-33. On prophetic forms in Sirach, see Gammie 1990b:370–72; Ceresko 1997.

37. No one to my knowledge has proposed that Q is an apocalypse, although many have argued that it contains apocalyptic features. The reason is simple: Q lacks the macrostructural framing devices of apocalypses—including a narrative framework in which revelation is mediated by a dream, vision, otherworldy journey, discovery of a lost document, or other means (see J. Collins 1979). Conzelmann referred to Q 17:23-37 as the "logia apocalypse" (1969:135), a designation that I earlier adopted (1987a:154), but subsequently rejected as inappropriate (1987b:301).

38. The *Testament of Solomon*, for example, exercises other options, presenting a first person testamentary report that describes his building of the Temple, his struggle with demons, and his eventual succumbing to idols.

39. Betz 1985a:33–34 calls the Matthaean parallel (Matt 5:3) an "anti-macarism" which unmasks "a naive, but religiously sanctioned, materialism." I have found particularly helpful the suggestion of B. Scott (1990:412), who argues that the Q sayings should be seen in the context of a contest between anonymous common wisdom and the "distinctive voice" of Jesus which "innovates in the common wisdom tradition by playing in minor keys and using wisdom images against themselves."

wonders whether such a beatitude has stretched wisdom to the "breaking point" and should no longer be considered wisdom (1996:337). Tuckett's questions highlight the problem with theological approaches: they depend upon a priori definitions of what is sapiential or prophetic.[40] This is unproblematic when the form and content of the material under review fall neatly within the conventional definitions. But when there is innovation and when there is a critical manipulation of the content within a conventional form, theologically laden criteria—especially when narrowly defined—collapse and are unable to be productive as heuristic constructs.[41]

Genre definition and content are not unrelated. Nevertheless, I have given preference to formal rather than material criteria when discussing composition and genre and have tried to avoid slippery theological characterizations. I have also adopted a descriptive and heuristic approach to genre rather than a normative-prescriptive approach. This means treating genre definitions as "family resemblances" rather than as strict conformity to some abstract normative definition;[42] and it allows one to see transformations and adaptation of basic forms to meet changing situations without having to imagine complete disjunctions in genre. This means that one may treat the formative portions of Q as instructional despite the fact that Q does not exhibit every characteristic of the older representatives of the

40. Tuckett 1996:334 emphasizes the collective nature of wisdom: "wisdom is an attempt to 'explain' things on the basis of collective experience; prophecy is the claim to 'announce' on the basis of direct revelation." This definition, in my view, fits only what Perdue has called the "paradigm of order" but not the "paradigm of conflict" which is equally characteristic of wisdom books (esp. Job, Qoheleth), or the view of wisdom articulated by B. Scott (above, n. 39). Perdue describes the world of the "critical sages" thus: "The experience of the catastrophic dissolution of social and political order, occasioned by historical disasters, led to the destabilization and ultimately fragmentation of the cultural and religious traditions that [the] paradigm [of order] had produced. To attack the old order and to forge new traditions of meaning required a major paradigm shift for the critical sages. Without new formulations, the fragmentation of old traditions would ultimately result in either the submergence of wisdom's critical stance within an unquestioning naïveté or in the dissolution of the sapiential communities themselves" (Perdue 1990:469). Perdue's sketch of Qoheleth's situation might apply equally to the situation of Roman Palestine.

41. More problematically, theologically laden criteria allow for quite illegitimate inferences. For example, Tuckett (1989) devotes an article to refuting the "Cynic" nature of Q and, having done so, simply virtually concludes ex nihilo that Q must therefore be "prophetic" (1989:376), as if whatever is not Cynic is prophetic! He later corrected this approach in his more comprehensive work (1996), but still devotes a full chapter to wisdom, designed to question the characterization of the *genre* of Q as sapiential (1996:325–54), without including a comparable chapter on the assessment of *genre* of Q as prophetic. Having argued that Q is not sapiential, he then concludes that it "shows greater affinity with prophetic collections" (while still acknowledging the "powerful critique" of Sato's views by Robinson and Downing) (1996:354 n. 87).

42. On family resemblance, see Wittgenstein 1958:§67. Wittgenstein's example is of the similarities between members of a family (hair color, gait, height, etc.). No members might share any one characteristic, and yet one still speaks meaningfully of family resemblance.

instruction genre. It does not, for example, purvey "conventional" wisdom and does not have the sage speak in the role of parent; yet it preserves other key features of the instructional genre.

This brings me to the issue that is central to this chapter, that of the theological taxonomy of Q. Although the genre of Q ought not be established on the basis of its supposed theological orientation, the place of Q within the theological landscape of primitive Christianity is in part a function of, though not fully reducible to, its genre.

It is safe to say that the theological characterizations that have generated the most discussion and opposition have been those of James M. Robinson and Helmut Koester. Robinson argued that Q belonged to the genre of "sayings of the sages" (λόγοι σοφῶν) whose immanent theological tendency was to treat the speaker as a sage, then to associate the sage with Heavenly Sophia, and ultimately to identify the speaker as Sophia herself or depict the speaker as a gnostic revealer (Robinson 1964, ET 1971b). Robinson described a "trajectory" that extended from Proverbs through Q and the *Gospel of Thomas*, ending in the *Pistis Sophia*. The *Tendenz* of the genre was not inevitably gnosticizing, for he suggested that *m. ʾAbot* and *1 Clem* 13.2; 46.7-8 were also expressions of the genre. Nevertheless, historically speaking, one of the main developmental lines of this genre ran parallel to a development of the Jewish Sophia into a gnostic redeemer and it was this parallel that accounts both for the popularity of sayings (and eventually dialogue) genres in Gnosticism, and for the eventual disappearance of the genre in orthodox circles.

Koester accepted Robinson's generic designation for Q but argued additionally the theses that underlying the canonical Gospels are several primitive Gospel forms, none of which is organized on the pattern of the passion kerygma, and that the primary theological tendencies of these Gospel forms are often most clearly visible not in the canonical Gospels, but in the apocryphal Gospels (1971b:166). The *Gospel of Thomas* provided the best illustration of a "sayings gospel," which Koester had already described as "the most original *Gattung* of the Jesus tradition" (1971a:135). The overriding theological tendency of this genre derives from

> the authority of the word of wisdom as such, which rests in the assumption that the teacher is present in the word which he has spoken. If there is any "Easter experience" to provide a Christology congenial to this concept of the *logoi*, it is here the belief in "Jesus, the Living One" (incipit of the *Gospel of Thomas*). (1971a:138–39)

In spite of the lack of a passion kerygma, the "wisdom gospel" had a genuinely theological basis:

> Faith is understood as belief in Jesus' words, a belief which makes what Jesus proclaimed present and real for the believer. The catalyst which caused the crystallization of these sayings into a "Gospel" is the view that the kingdom is

uniquely present in Jesus' eschatological preaching and that eternal wisdom about man's true self is disclosed in his words. The gnostic proclivity of this concept needs no further elaboration. (Koester 1971b:186)

This theological characterization of Q's genre was coupled by Koester with a conclusion about its compositional history derived from the fact that the *Gospel of Thomas* lacked entirely apocalyptic Son of Man sayings:[43]

> If the genre of the wisdom book was the catalyst for the composition of sayings of Jesus into a "Gospel," and if the christological concept of Jesus as the teacher of wisdom and as the presence of heavenly Wisdom dominated its creation, the apocalyptic orientation of the *Synoptic Sayings Source* with its christology of the coming Son of man is due to a secondary redaction of an older wisdom book. (1980:113)

Koester thus suggested two stages by which the sayings of Jesus were rendered acceptable, first, through the introduction of apocalyptic Son of Man sayings into Q, and then by fusion of Q with Mark:

> [S]uch sayings collections [as the *Gospel of Thomas*] with explicit theological tendencies were in use quite early, and not only in Aramaic-speaking circles in Syria; [this would prove] that the source "Q," used by Matthew and Luke, was a secondary version of such a "gospel," into which the apocalyptic expectation of the Son of man had been introduced to check the gnosticizing tendencies of this sayings gospel; and that the *Gos. Thom.*, stemming from a more primitive stage of such a "gospel," attests its further growth into a gnostic theology. (1971b:186–87)

It is this assessment of the *Tendenz* of Q that clearly has worried several scholars. Dunn, for example, devotes an excursus to the "Gnosticizing proclivity in Q" (1977:285–87) in which he argues that while the *Gospel of Thomas* is clearly gnostic, there is nothing gnostic about Q. He insists on the thoroughly "eschatological" character of Q and rejects Koester's treatment of the apocalyptic sayings in Q. Thus he argues that the sapiential character of Q should not be "overemphasized" and concludes that Q "was certainly not content to portray Jesus simply as the teacher of wisdom who lives on in and through his words" (1977:287). Instead, the depiction of Jesus as the coming Son of Man is integral to Q's message.[44] This does not

---

43. Koester notes that *GThom* 86 (=Q 9:58) uses "Son of Man" in a nontitular way, and with Bultmann (1968:98; also Tödt 1965:122) argued that this saying is a proverb in which *Son of Man* is no honorific title, but simply means "man," as contrasted with the animals. He wonders: "The decisive question is whether *Thomas* presupposes a stage of the Synoptic tradition in which a titular usage of the term *Son of Man* had not yet developed" (1971:170–71 n. 34).

44. Dunn misrepresents Koester's argument in the sense that Koester does not deny the presence of "eschatological" sayings in both Q and the *Gospel of Thomas*. Koester's argument concerns the presence of apocalyptic Son of Man sayings in the *Gospel of Thomas* and in the earliest level of Q. Hence, Dunn's defense of the eschatological character of Jesus' preaching

end Dunn's worries, since he also ventures that Q was ultimately abandoned because early Christians "recognized the danger of presenting Jesus simply as a revealer and teacher of wisdom" (287). Thus, in spite of a stout defense, Dunn cannot avoid the suspicion that Q was somehow "inadequate."

WISDOM LITERATURE, SOCIAL ORDER, AND ESCHATOLOGY

Some of the discomfiture regarding the genre of Q derives from inadequate understandings of the nature of "wisdom" and, even more, from caricatures of scholarship on Q.[45] Although some of the *literary forms*—the instruction, for example—adopted by sages demonstrate remarkable stability over a millennium or more, the *content* of the wisdom tradition is itself remarkably diverse and adaptable. Some scholars, however, seem to consider the allegedly sapiential character of Q to be antithetical to its having a futuristic eschatology. It is true that the older wisdom instructions tend to be prudential and oriented toward action in the present life. But several wisdom texts from Qumran display elements of future eschatology.[46] The

---

(1977:318–22)—which merely collects futuristic sayings without supplying any *argument* for authenticity—does not meet Koester's point.

45. This is especially evident in the careless treatment of Q ventured by N. T. Wright (1992:435–43), who represents as the "majority" view of recent Q scholarship that the formative stratum of Q presented Jesus as "a teacher of aphoristic, quasi-Gnostic, quasi-Cynic teaching" (437)—he later adds "Platonic" (442)—devoid of "apocalyptic future expectation" (437) and characterized by "realized eschatology." It is difficult to imagine whom Wright has in mind in offering this silly caricature: while Q is by nature largely aphoristic, neither Koester, nor Robinson, nor I, depicts its formative stratum as devoid of eschatological hopes, and none of us argues that Q^1 is "Cynic"; Downing, Mack, and Vaage, who *have* adduced comparisons with Cynicism, do not think that Q at any level is "gnostic." I likewise reject the thesis of an inherently gnosticizing *Tendenz*. An even sloppier reporting of recent Q scholarship is given by Kee, who (like Wright) misrepresents the basis for positing an early stratum of Q (1995:230) and curiously asserts that I have argued for a *Cynic* Q (!) that is "free of eschatological features" (233; contrast Kloppenborg 1987a:324; 1987b:passim). He adds: "As Horsley notes, most of the Q sayings that Kloppenborg classifies as sapiential are in fact strongly eschatological or even apocalyptic in their essence" (233). Contrast what Horsley actually says: "Kloppenborg and Burton Mack have both pointed out that Q is much less apocalyptic than previously imagined. But we can press that critical realization far more sharply: *there are virtually no apocalyptic motifs in the supposedly apocalyptic stratum of Q*" (1991a:197, emphasis added). Kee's most recent expedition into Q scholarship (1996a) should be read only in conjunction with the authors he purports to represent.

46. 4Q185 displays many similarities to Proverbs and Sirach, but speaks of Wisdom as a gift to Israel (ii 10-11), by which "he has saved all his people but has destroyed . . . [. . .]." 4Q525 (4QBéat) begins with a string of makarisms similar to those found in Proverbs, extolling piety and the pursuit of the Law and of Wisdom (2 ii 1-10) but seems to invoke the specter of apocalyptic punishments and rewards toward the end of the document (15-16, 21-23). Tobin (1990) argues that 4Q185 is not a composition of the Qumran community, since it lacks many of Qumran's distinctive sectarian features, but was a text taken over and used by the community. In any event, the covenanters apparently did not see any conflict between 4Q185 and their own much more pronounced eschatology. See now Harrington 1996.

Wisdom of Solomon similarly entertains the hopes of an intervention of God in history that will exalt the righteous and punish the impious (3:7-9; 4:20–5:23).

This accords quite well with trajectories in Jewish wisdom literature plotted by John Gammie (1990a). Using the coordinates of "the family," "the king," and "nation and other nations," Gammie traces three transformations within wisdom literature.

The valorization of the family is evident in older wisdom literature—one should add, in most Near Eastern instructions and Hellenistic gnomologia. This changed, however, in the Hellenistic period, with the rise of more individualistic notions of the self and more defined beliefs in the afterlife. Gammie observes that the family is virtually ignored in books such as Daniel and the Wisdom of Solomon, and suggests:

> The reason is apparent: once belief emerged in a realm beyond death in which the inequities of the present world would be resolved, the family as an intellectual construct with which to defend theodicy was no longer so urgently needed. The function of the concept of the solidarity of the family to explain the anomaly of the prosperous sinner or the suffering righteous had been supplanted. The way was thus opened up for the sages to celebrate the blessedness of married or unmarried persons who would produce no physical offspring. (Gammie 1990a:485)

This observation fits well what is seen in Q, where the repertoire of social transactions, attitudes, and rituals employed to express and maintain family solidarity is rendered questionable (6:32-33; 9:59-60; 12:51-53; 14:26). For Q, the primary allegiance expected is not toward a sage speaking in the role of parent and representing a divine order that permeates and sustains the current order of things, from king down to individual clans and families. Instead, Q promotes allegiance to a God who overcomes the deprivations of the present and relativizes its inequities. It locates the solution to the problems of poverty and suffering (6:20b-21), persecution (6:22-23; 12:4-9), conflict (6:35), and vindication of the righteous and punishment of the impious (7:35; 10:12-15; 11:47-51; 13:34-35) in the "reign of God," which stands over against this-worldly order, and in the assurance of God's loving surveillance and the eventuality of reward and punishment.

Gammie's second point concerns kingship in wisdom literature. The social location of sages in the older scribal schools—most often in royal courts—accounts for the fact that they were rarely very critical of kingship as such. Instead, one finds extravagant estimates of royal accomplishments and human kingship being given a place within divine rule. This did not, of course, prevent the older wisdom literature from contrasting enlightened rule with its opposite, or from contrasting the ephemeral nature of human kingship with divine rule. By the Hellenistic period, however, not only was the ephemerality of kings increasingly stressed (Sir 10:10; 46:20), but human rule was set over against an everlasting kingdom that would supplant all competitors (Dan 7:13, 27).

This shift in Israelite wisdom literature is part of a larger cultural change. Downing (1995a) has drawn attention to expectations of the golden age or "life under Cronos" current, in a wide of variety of guises, among such diverse groups as Stoics, Cynics, Roman poets, and hellenized Jews. In this context, discourse about the "reign of God" not only had a positive function, associating the ethos of a particular group with the everlasting reign of God, but also assumed an implicitly critical function, offering an alternative to current politics and the utopian visions occasionally promoted by such as Augustus or Herod. To proclaim the appearance of the *basileia tou theou* (reign of God) implies the end of other *basileiai*.

Q belongs squarely within this development. It assumes the coming of God's reign, which will transform and invert the current order of things (Q 6:20b-23) and in which Jesus' followers will assume positions of privilege (Q 22:28-30). Since the framers of Q, like the later sages, were not retainers of the court, their posture toward established power also takes on a critical tone: Solomon, despite his accomplishments, can be outdone (12:27); and earlier kings and prophets were not privileged with knowledge of the kingdom (10:23-24). In a remarkable show of self-transcendence, the framers of Q concede that the sages themselves could lack insight (Q 10:21-22). Sophia herself speaks against the permanence of the current order: the reckoning for the persecution of the prophets will occur imminently (11:49-51), and the Temple and its priestly caste will be made desolate (13:34-35). While lacking most of the apocalyptic elements of Mark or 2 Thessalonians or the Apocalypse—detailed previews, timetables, and elaborated scenarios of judgment and reward—Q clearly undergirds its ethical appeals by invoking the impermanence of the present and the hope of a divinely established future.

Under the third heading, nation and the nations, Gammie traces the development of wisdom from the internationalism of early collections, to an emphasis on the Torah and a particularism that is held in tension with internationalism. This trajectory ends in an insistence on the privileged position of Israel in the possession of Wisdom (Sirach 24 and—one could add—4Q185 ii 10-11). This emphasis was not narrowly particularist, for one finds concessions that other states and peoples possessed wisdom too. Ultimately, however, the righteous of Israel would rule the nations (Wis 3:8). This transformation of wisdom also provided a platform from which to criticize the idolatrous practices of other peoples and hence to absorb elements of the prophetic prophecies against foreign states (Gammie 1990a:489–96).

Q represents a particular transformation of this tendency. For while the Q people clearly assume that they, through Jesus and John, are in unique contact with Wisdom (Q 7:35), it is not the Torah that especially enshrines that wisdom. Indeed, the appeals to the Torah are rare, all either relics of earlier configurations or later glosses.[47] Additionally, Q's main target is not foreign states but "this generation"—which evidently includes the ruling elite of Jerusalem. In the service of its polemic Q invokes internationalism—both the Ninevites and the Queen of the South are called to serve as witnesses against "this generation" (11:31-32); and the oracles against foreign states that play so important a role in prophetic literature (Isa 23; Jer 29 [47]; Ezek 28:11-12, 22-23; Zech 9:2-4; Amos 1:9-10; Joel 4:4-8) are both invoked and inverted: even the enemy cities of Tyre and Sidon will fare better than unrepentant Israelite towns (Q 10:13-15).

Gammie thus describes three parallel movements in the development of wisdom: the eschatologizing, "torahizing," and "prophetizing" of wisdom, especially through the introduction of temporal perspectives and through the incorporation of the prophetic doctrines of election and sacred history (Gammie 1990a:497). Of these, Q most clearly exhibits the first and the third. In its lack of "torahizing" Q is closer to the Wisdom of Solomon than to Sirach.[48]

To characterize Q as "sapiential" is not, therefore, to imply a depiction of Jesus as a teacher of this-worldly, prudential wisdom, or still less to imply an intellectual world that was hermetically sealed against eschatology, prophetic traditions, and the epic traditions of Israel. Q indeed contains elements that *might have developed* toward a completely contemporizing, noneschatological presentation of Jesus and his message. That, after all, is the way the Jesus tradition was deployed in the *Gospel of Thomas*. Most of those elements, however, were equally capable of transformations in a modestly eschatological direction, and that is the form in which they are encountered in Q. The formative stratum (Q[1]) does not present Jesus' sayings as secret words requiring special interpretation but instead conforms to the tone of other Near Eastern instructions. Nor are there obvious signs of gnosticizing tendencies in the main redaction of Q (Q[2]), which absorbed prophetic tropes and forms. The introduction of chriae exploits the biographical potential of saying genre, a development that is further advanced with the addition of the temptation story.

THE THEOLOGICAL "CENTER" OF Q

A second concern arising from the depiction of Q as "sapiential" has to do with the type of soteriology and authority claims present in Q. In general, German treatments of Q have avoided this issue by focusing almost exclusively on the christological claims of Q and, in particular, on the identification of Jesus as the coming Son of Man.[49] Alfons Weiser's view is typical:

47. For the former view, see Kosch 1989a:443, 451–67; for the latter, Kloppenborg 1990c.
48. On the "torahizing" of wisdom and the "sapientializing" of Torah, see Sheppard 1980.
49. This is the legacy of Tödt 1959, ET 1965. See also Hoffmann 1972:142–47; D. Zeller 1975:76; Hengel 1979:177; Sand 1992:128: "'The community which used the Q material was

The focal point of the Son of Man sayings in Q is the interpretation of the Son of Man as an exalted-authoritative figure in the eschatological events of consummation and judgment. At the judgment he will stand as an advocate before God for those have acknowledged Jesus publicly and will disavow those who have disavowed Jesus (Q 12:8-9; Q 11:30). . . . A personalization of the eschatological events is effected by the sayings concerning the Son of Man who is expected at the consummation. It is Jesus who lived homeless on earth (Q 9), who called people to discipleship (Q 9), who used the goods of the earth and was a friend of sinners (Q 7), and whom is awaited as the Coming One (Q 12:40), who will appear with power (Q 17), and who will intercede for the salvation of his own (Q 6; 12) but will condemn his opponents among "this generation" (Q 11:30-32; 12:8-9). (Weiser 1993:36–37)

Weiser concludes that the very act of collecting Jesus' sayings implies a Christology and a soteriology: the stance one assumes toward Jesus and his sayings determines the basis of salvation (1993:31).

It is obvious that if Koester is right and the coming Son of Man sayings in Q are secondary additions, Weiser's soteriological center of Q would evaporate in all but its final redaction. Even if we leave aside the issue of stratigraphy, however, it seems quite unwarranted to conclude that Son of Man Christology (and its attendant soteriology) represents the theological core of Q. As D. R. A. Hare has observed, the first four Son of Man sayings in Q (6:22; 7:34; 9:58; 11:30) do not feature a coming Son of Man at all. He asks:

Is it reasonable to suppose that the redactor or redactors of the collection would have been content to defer allusions to the central article of faith of the Q community ("Jesus is the coming Son of Man") to so late a point [i.e., 12:8-9, 40] when in fact the presence of the judgment motif encouraged such allusions at a number of earlier locations (i.e., not only at Luke 6:46-49 but also 7:31-35; 10:10-14; 11:29-32, 37-52)?[50]

Tödt in fact tried to argue that the Son of Man designation, even when it appears in such contexts as 6:22, 7:34, and 9:58, nonetheless implies Jesus' sovereignty.[51] He stopped short of claiming that the so-called present Son of Man sayings imputed to Jesus the full authority of the coming Son of Man sayings but insisted that "Son of Man" ascribed to Jesus "a unique sover-

---

definitely anticipating the arrival of Jesus as Son of Man in the near future.' In this rigorously eschatological orientation lies *the* decisive element of Q theology" (quoting R. Edwards 1976:43). Gnilka (1994:134–37) characterizes Q as "messianic-eschatological instruction" and stresses the combination of expectation of the coming of Jesus as the Son of Man and the motif of judgment. He observes: "If this is correct, Q may have de-emphasized the preaching of Jesus as it was assimilated to the preaching of the Baptist. For what was most urgent for Jesus was the saving offer of the Kingdom, from which the judgment followed secondarily; but for the Baptist, the reverse was the case" (136–37).

50. Hare 1990:220. One should add Q 3:7-9, 16-17 to Hare's list of judgment texts.
51. Tödt 1965:116 [Q 7:34], 119 [Q 12:10], 122-23 [Q 9:58], 123 [Q 6:22].

eignty " and "Christological dignity."[52] This conclusion, however, is doubtful. Tuckett has subjected Tödt's conclusions to a searching analysis and concludes in each case that far too much is read into the texts in question. Q 7:34 concerns not the authority of the Son of Man/Jesus, but his rejection; and Q 6:22 and 9:58 are more statements about the cost of discipleship than they are about the one who calls to discipleship.[53]

Reviewing Tödt's argument, Robinson points out several additional difficulties. First, in the coming Son of Man sayings that Tödt ascribed to the historical Jesus, Tödt noted the dearth of traditional apocalyptic elements actually present and that only "as the distance from Jesus' preaching increases, an increasing number of traditional features are channeled secondarily into the Son of Man sayings of Jesus or of the community" (1965:66). Robinson observes:

> Nothing would seem to be clearer documentation for the *Tendenz* of the synoptic gospels to merge secondarily the Jewish apocalyptic traditions to which Daniel, the Similitudes of Enoch and 4 Ezra attest, with the Q tradition of apocalyptic son of man sayings where the tradition was originally lacking. The normal inference would be that the apocalyptic son of man sayings of Q were not originally derived from that Jewish apocalyptic tradition. (1994b:326)

When Tödt says of the present Son of Man sayings that they lack entirely the "attributes of the transcendent [i.e., apocalyptic] Son of Man" (1965:116) and employs this as a refutation of the thesis that Jesus spoke of himself as the Son of Man (1965:125), Robinson retorts: "Yet no answer is given to the obvious initial question as to why the son of man sayings referring to the public ministry, if nonauthentic and derived from the authentic

---

52. Tödt 1965:124. See also Hoffmann (1972:145–46), who states, apropos of the (alleged) origin of the earthly Son of Man sayings in the coming Son of Man sayings: "On the basis of this origin, [the Son of Man title] in the sayings concerning the earthly Son of Man cannot be understood any longer as an expression of earthly authority; instead, it is an expression of the identity of the early Jesus with the coming Son of Man. It is not the Son of Man title that is reinterpreted, but the authority of Jesus. . . . Undoubtedly the earthly Jesus made certain claims to authority, but now the authority of the earthly one, who proclaimed the Son of Man and made claims about his authority, is perceived as the authority of the Son of Man himself."

53. Tuckett 1996:254–56. Curiously, Tuckett then concludes that the Son of Man title in Q is an "intentional allusion" to Daniel 7 and that "in Q, the whole stratum of the tradition presupposes that, as SM [Son of Man], Jesus will act as agent in the final judgement in a way not dissimilar to the figure described in *1 Enoch* or *4 Ezra*, and given the fact that the latter texts clearly develop Dan 7, it seems reasonable to conclude that Q's use of the 'SM' does the same" (1996:274). The basis for this conclusion is the observation that the present Son of Man sayings all have to do with rejection or persecution. By arguing for the convergence of Daniel 7 with the exegetical tradition developed from Isaiah 53 in *1 Enoch* 62 and Wisdom 2–5 that describes the persecution and vindication of the righteous, Tuckett then reads all of Q's Son of Man references in light of this exegetical tradition. Tuckett's objections to Tödt's overinterpretation of the present Son of Man sayings, however, apply equally to his own attempt to read Daniel 7 into those texts.

apocalyptic son of man sayings, do not somewhere betray this origin" (1994b:327).

At issue here is not whether Q ultimately identifies Jesus as the Son of Man or whether the Son of Man, especially after Q 12:8-9, is given eschatological functions. The issue is whether this identification constitutes the theological *center* and warrant for Q's soteriology. Simply put, is the "christological cognition" of Jesus as the exalted Son of Man who is to come in judgment the *theologoumenon* that energizes Q's message? The observations of Hare, Robinson, and Tuckett—in spite of Tuckett's attempt to read Daniel 7 into Q—cast this into grave doubt. In contrast to Mark, whose entire structure is dominated by a christological question and its resolution, a christological agenda is far less prominent in Q.[54]

Q is concerned that Jesus be identified as John's "Coming One," and this requires something of a redefinition of the role that is first sketched in Q 3:16-17 (cf. Q 7:18-23). This, however, can hardly be considered as the theological center of Q. The implicit christological question raised in the challenge of Q 11:15, "it is by Beelzebul, prince of the demons, that he casts out demons," is not answered directly by a christological claim but indirectly, by a reductio ad absurdum (11:17-19) and a saying about the coming of the *kingdom* (11:20). Likewise, Q 11:30, which compares Jonah and the Son of Man insofar as both were preachers, could have gone on to make a christological claim. Instead Q asserts that some*thing* (not some*one*) greater than Jonah (and Solomon) is here (11:31-32). That something is undoubtedly the kingdom.

The center of Q's theology is not Christology but the reign of God.[55] In the first stratum of Q the focal point is the characterization of that reign, seen as an expansive power (13:18-21) that is able to subvert or invert con-

---

54. Similarly, Jacobson 1992a:418: "What is really at issue in the discussion as to whether Q is apocalyptic is the question as to whether the apocalyptic paradigm will be admitted as the primary or organizing paradigm for interpreting Q as a whole. . . . Often, Q is alleged to be dominated by a Son of Man christology, as we have seen. Yet there is surprisingly little specifically apocalyptic language to be found in the Q Son of Man sayings. Most are so ambiguous or brief that they can be read as apocalyptic only by reading into them a great deal that is not there."

55. Jacobson (1992a:416) has noted "the absence of any link between Kingdom and a radical ethic" (cf. D. Zeller 1977:181). It is indeed the case that βασιλεία τοῦ θεοῦ does not appear in any of Q's imperatives except Q 12:31, but the term does appear in the programmatic sayings in 6:20 (introducing a string of imperatives), 11:2, and 12:31 (summarizing the preceding instruction on anxiety). Piper (whom Jacobson cites in this connection) observes that Q's imperatives are not sanctioned by means of an appeal to "eschatological motifs," except in Q 12:2-9. Even there "[t]he common ground between experiential wisdom and the eschatological outlook is found primarily in an emphasis on the extent of God's effective care for those who trust in him, a care which encompasses both this world and the world to come, and a recognition of the correspondence between present action (one's confession) and future consequence (judgement)." In Q 12:31, the kingdom "is something to be sought in the present, and implicit in its presence is not judgement but God's care" (Piper 1989:76).

ventional relationships, benefiting especially the disadvantaged (6:20; 11:2; 12:31) and the sick (10:9). The kingdom sayings of Q¹ are connected with exhortations to a countercultural lifestyle that includes love of enemies, nonretaliation, debt forgiveness, and a willingness to expose oneself to danger, all undergirded by appeals to the superabundant care of a provident God. Both of the Son of Man sayings found in this stratum (6:22b; 9:58) function in appeals to emulate the exposed and endangered lifestyle of Jesus.

Even at the main redactional phase (Q²), where christological statements are more in evidence, these remain embedded in a broader strategy of defending the ethos of the Q group and threatening those who are seen as opponents. Thus Q 7:34 illustrates the petulant and nonresponsive reaction of "this generation" to John and Jesus that is elsewhere documented in Sophia's woe against this generation (11:49-51a), the lament over Jerusalem (13:34-35), the Beelzebul accusation (11:14-23), and the request for a sign (11:16, 29-32), where the "Son of Man" is also featured (11:30) along with Jonah and Solomon. The Son of Man appears in four warnings (12:40; 17:24, 26, 30) where what is elaborated is not the person or function of the Son of Man, but rather the unanticipated nature of the judgment. This is also the theme of John's oracle (3:7-9) and Q 12:54-56, 57-59. Indeed, it is rather surprising just how little is actually said of the Son of Man by way of concrete characterization, especially when one compares Mark's descriptions in Mark 13:26 and 14:62 and the later Matthaean and Lukan elaborations. Although it is clear that the Son of Man is a part of the scenario of judgment, he functions as an advocate rather than a judge (Q 12:8-9).[56] In Q 12:40; 17:24, 26, and 30 the warnings of the sudden coming of the Son of Man seem semantically equivalent to warnings of the Day of the Lord, and Q 17:26 even uses the phrase "in the day of the Son of Man."[57] In other words, the Son of Man sayings are part of a larger fabric of Q's announce-

---

56. Schweizer 1959:198; Higgins 1964:59; Lindars 1983:50; Jacobson 1992a:418 and others. The simple contrast in Q between confession/denial in the human and divine forums is fused in Mark 8:38 with Parousia language ("when he comes in the glory of his father with the holy angels"), which Matthew expands with a reference to judgment ("and he will then repay each according to their deeds," 16:27; cf. 25:31). As Lindars observes, through this embellishment of the saying with details from Daniel, the original "contrast between the tribunal of men and the tribunal of God disappears" (1983:51).

57. The IQP reconstruction of 17:26 is (conjecturally): [[Καθὼς [( )] ἐγένετο ἐν ταῖς ἡμέραις]] Νῶε, οὕτως ἔσται καὶ [[ἐν τῇ ἡμέρᾳ]] τοῦ υἱοῦ τοῦ ἀνθρώπου. The phrase "the day of the Son of Man" also appears in 17:24: ὥσπερ γὰρ ἡ ἀστραπὴ ἐξέρχεται [[ἀπὸ ἀνατολῶν]] καὶ [[φαίνεται ἕως δυσμῶν]], οὕτως ἔσται ἡ [[<ἡμέρα>]] τοῦ υἱοῦ τοῦ ἀνθρώπου; and 17:30: οὕτως ἔσται καὶ [[ᾗ ἡμέρα ὁ]] υἱὸ[[ς]] τοῦ ἀνθρώπου ἀποκαλύπτεται. Cf. Jacobson 1992a:415: "Indeed, it might be argued that the Son of Man has been introduced secondarily (at an earlier stage of the tradition, not by the redactor) into the Q 'apocalypse', or that 'the day of the Son of Man' was simply a circumlocution for the day of Judgment."

ment of judgment against this generation, but not its defining characteristic or theological core.[58]

This does not mean, however, that Q treats Jesus simply as a messenger. What Dunn and Galvin have called for—a necessary connection between the person of Jesus and the message—and what is generally thought to be absent from "wisdom" documents (and prophetic documents, for that matter), is in fact present in Q, if only incipiently. At the level of Q^1 this connection is asserted through the compositional devices. For example, the mission speech begins with a chria (9:57-58) that takes the unattached and peripatetic lifestyle of Jesus as a model for discipleship. The main part of the speech begins by depicting God (the Lord of the harvest) as able to "send" workers (10:2), a commissioning that is immediately reiterated by Jesus himself ("Behold I send you," 10:3). In 10:4, an itinerant and exposed lifestyle is enjoined on the "workers" and in 10:9 it is learned that the "workers" are to heal and proclaim the kingdom, which Jesus has already announced in Q 6:20b. These diverse materials yield, by the algebra of association, a Christocentric conclusion: it is the specific lifestyle, therapeutic practice, and kingdom message of *Jesus* that defines the activities of the "workers" and these are traced back ultimately to the "sending" of God. Q 10:16 assembles the scattered parts of this equation into a whole: "Whoever welcomes you welcomes me, and whoever welcomes me welcomes the One who sent me."

The structure of the inaugural sermon (Q 6:20b-49) yields a similar equation. It begins with a pronouncement about the kingdom of God (6:20b) and buttresses its first set of admonitions with the statement that by observing them, Jesus' followers will become "children of the Most High" (6:35). The discourse ends with its mild rebuke to those followers who call Jesus master (κύριε) but do not emulate his teachings and the admonition to hear and obey "*my*" words (6:47-49). From this it is clear that Jesus himself is represented as a necessary link in the communication of the ethos of the kingdom that is elaborated in 6:20b-45. While many wisdom collections

---

58. Vaage (1991:124) puts the point even more starkly: "In every case, the figure's [Son of Man's] contribution to the saying itself is quite abstract; we would even say mathematical, providing an unseen but implied point of reference. . . . Logically, in every case we could replace 'Son of Man' with an x and still grasp whatever is at stake. The only thing added by the actual words 'Son of Man' in the text of Q's redaction is semantic contact with a certain intertextual (apocalyptic) field of play." Similarly, Hare 1990:224: "[N]one of the so-called authentic logia [those thought authentic by Tödt] is formulated in such a way that would suggest that Jesus announced the imminent coming of the Son of man to *nondisciples*; in each, 'your Lord' could be substituted without changing the force of the saying." Vaage's formulation is too strong, for the use of the Son of Man phrase not only makes possible associations that later evangelists would exploit, but also *personalizes* the judgment, even if rather vaguely, and connects it directly with the hero of the Q community.

conclude with an exhortation to attention, Q has personalized this by drawing specific attention to *Jesus'* words.[59]

The particular connection between Jesus and his message that is found in Q^1 is not so much a matter of christological claim—Jesus' self-consciousness as a bringer of salvation and his followers' thematizing of that in christological epithets—as it is a matter of the emulation of a specific ethos and practice associated with the kingdom of God. Crossan has put it succinctly: "The continuity is not in mnemonics but in mimetics, not in remembrance but in imitation, not in word but in deed" (1996:117). This, it should be noted, is not quite the same as the "gnosticizing" view, suggested by Koester, "that the kingdom is uniquely present in Jesus' eschatological preaching and that eternal wisdom about man's true self is disclosed in his words" (1971b:186). Little in Q falls under the rubric of anthropological revelations, and the few texts that might be so classified (Q 6:43-45; 11:34-36) are used in the service of other argumentative goals. Instead, Q represents an elongation of the standard sapiential view that the sage learns to assimilate and emulate the divine ethos—in her knowledge but, more importantly, in her *conduct*—and exemplifies it to others (see Sir 39:1-11). What makes Q^1 distinctive is the degree to which the speaker's own person comes into focus as a privileged exponent of that divine ethos, which Q calls "the kingdom of God."

The polemical and defensive cast of the main redaction inevitably extended what was already in play in Q^1. Not only does Q engage the epic history of Israel, aligning Jesus and the Q people with Abraham, Lot, and the Patriarchs (3:2-3, 7-9; 13:28-29; 17:28-30, 34-35), Jonah (11:30, 32), Solomon (11:31), Abel and Zechariah (11:51), and John (7:34-35). It is also here that the central role of Jesus in the soteriological equation emerges more clearly, for example, in Q 12:8-9, where one's stance toward Jesus is a criterion in the judgment, and in 10:22, where an exclusive mediation of saving knowledge is assigned to Jesus.[60]

---

59. Q 6:46-49 is often read as depicting Jesus as an "eschatological judge" and thus a role not otherwise assigned to Jesus by Q is smuggled in. However, a comparative analysis of instructions shows that warnings, threats, and promises often conclude the admonitions, and the figure of a ruined house is especially common in biblical wisdom literature (Kloppenborg 1987a:186–87; Jacobson 1978:110 n. 84). Crossan (1996:115) draws attention to the fact that Q makes a somewhat unusual distinction between hearing and doing, or hearing and not doing.

60. See Kloppenborg 1978. Jacobson 1987:289 = 1992b:51; Horsley 1994:735; and Tuckett 1996:351–52 have treated the presence of "sapiential" traditions in Q^2 as a flaw in my (1987a) analysis. (Horsley also wrongly reports that I ascribed Q 10:21-22 to the "sapiential stratum"; contrast Kloppenborg 1987a:203.) This would only be an apt criticism if I had argued that the two strata were entirely discontinuous and if the basis for strata delineation had been tradition-historical (which is it not). Of course, no such a discontinuity has been asserted and would, in fact, be ludicrous. More importantly, Horsley misses the obvious: that there are different forms of sapiential discourse (see, e.g., J. Collins 1993:168), some directly or indirectly admonitory, such as the imperatives in Q^1 or Prov 2:1-22; 3:1-12, etc., and others

To conclude this section: in both strata of Q Jesus is represented as intimately associated with the reign of God and not merely as its messenger. The focus of Q, which is less on christological characterization than on the message of the kingdom and its defense, did not require explicit christological developments; these would come later. Q's "intensified soteriology," which includes the person of Jesus, might be seen to take Q out of the orbit of wisdom. Tuckett seems to think so, but the basis for his doubts is a very narrow theological definition of "wisdom" that would exclude most of the developments that Gammie traced. For Tuckett, the presence of a "powerful eschatological/prophetic element" makes Q more prophetic than sapiential (1996:353). As I have suggested, however, this reflects a caricature of wisdom, which by the Hellenistic period had accommodated itself to temporal dualisms and had made prophetizing adaptations. In any case, the fact that Q "personalizes" the kingdom by linking Jesus with his message does not make Q "prophetic" simply because such a linkage is not typically sapiential; for such a development is just as foreign to prophecy as it is to older wisdom.

Q AND ITS WARRANTS

The debate about the *theological* taxonomy of Q—whether Q belongs to wisdom discourse, to prophecy, or to apocalyptic—is in one sense moot, since most contributors to the discussion, or recent contributors at least, are prepared to admit that Q does not fit neatly into any of the stereotyped synthetic categories used by modern theology. Yet one cannot simply dismiss the debate as irrelevant or insoluble, since it is patent that deep theological nerves have been touched, even though there is very little frank discussion of what theological issues are seen to be at stake.

Hermann von Lips is right to suggest that the key theological problem is that of the authority that informs Q's sayings (1990:225). This is, on the one hand, an issue of Christology (what kind of "Jesus" is behind Q) and, on the other, a matter of the ultimacy of its claims. The worry with a sapiential denomination of Q appears to be that wisdom does not supply a sufficiently robust set of warrants, either christologically or soteriologically, and that wisdom is always in danger of drifting off into Gnosticism.

---

reflective, offering theological or anthropological reflections on the relation of creation and humanity to the divine, such as encountered in Proverbs 8, Sirach 24, Wis 7:27; Q 7:34; 10:21-22, and John 1:1-18. These represent fundamentally different *levels* of discourse and accomplish different argumentative goals. Obviously, the two forms can subsist in the same document, as they do in Proverbs, Sirach, Wisdom, and Q. Whether they in fact subsist at the *same compositional level* is a matter for compositional analysis. Robinson (1993:388) rightly stresses the continuity between Q[1] and Q[2]: "Even if the later stratum of Q cannot any longer be designated exclusively as λόγοι σοφῶν, at least the fact that it is Sophia who sends out her envoys and who is justified by her children, John and Jesus, should warn against ignoring the older λόγοι σοφῶν stratum of Q."

These worries are partly founded on caricatures. In the first place, there is nothing inevitable about the development of wisdom theology into Gnosticism. Although one of the *possible* transformations of sayings genres was in the direction of Gnosticism, that was not the only possibility, and Q shows no signs at all of moving in that direction. Second, to argue that Q belongs to the orbit of sapiential theology is not to assert that Jesus is "merely" a teacher of wisdom. Q leaves little doubt that the message of the kingdom, itself definitive, is connected to the person of Jesus. Hence, there is at least implicitly a Christology, even if it is not elaborated. Finally, there is no fundamental incompatibilty between wisdom genres and the presentation of definitive teaching. Careful study of wisdom literature shows that the attempts to distinguish it from prophecy on the basis that the former is anthropocentric, eudaemonistic, and fundamentally debatable are quite mistaken. On the contrary, such texts as Proverbs 8, Sirach 24, and Wisdom 6–9 illustrate the thoroughly theocentric and categorical claims made on wisdom's behalf. On the issue of the authority of wisdom pronouncements, James Crenshaw concludes: "In short, between 'Thus saith the Lord' and 'Listen, my son, to your father's advice' there is no fundamental difference" (1971:123).

Seen in this context, there should be little problem in locating Q *generally* within a sapiential current, acknowledging both the authority claims proper to the wisdom tradition and the special claims that Q made.[61] If Q 13:35b

61. Lips (1990) makes several important observations on Q: First, Q reflects all of the major thematic domains of wisdom literature: the individual; relations with others; social/societal relations; humanity as a creation of God; other nations; and the cosmos (215–16). Second, wisdom discourse arises from reflection on the ambivalent character of several types of human experience: (a) the necessity of planning *versus* the operation of fate; (b) the necessity of labor *versus* the anxiety it brings; (c) wealth and possessions as helpful and as dangerous; (d) the appropriateness of doing good *versus* the experience that not all do good; and (e) the conviction that the cosmos is a creation of God *versus* the experience of evil in the cosmos (217–23). Lips notes that Q's sayings are in tension with the wisdom tradition in two ways: (a) some of the "extreme positions in Q are expressed within the bounds of sapiential ambivalence. That is, many statements in Q which stand in opposition to the statements of the sapiential tradition can be derived from the ambivalence of sapiential sayings. But for Q it is typical that it is not the ambivalence that is affirmed, but either one or the other of the possible alternate positions" (223–24). At the same time, he notes (b) sayings such as Q 9:60 and 14:26 that cannot easily be derived from sapiential ambivalences. "The tensions with the wisdom tradition listed under both (a) and (b) must be clearly distinguished from one another. For with (a) it is clear that the statements belong completely within the wisdom tradition and, above all, that the argument here is expressly sapiential (starting from experience). On the other hand, the statements listed under (b) are characterized by an eschatological aspect and can be recognized as such by their terminology, for example, when in Q 9:58-60 there is a connection made with the kingdom of God or in other instances where christological references (Son of Man) can be seen" (224). He wonders whether the latter more radical sayings can be explained by reference to an eschatological situation that elicited such unusual behavior, or whether this is a matter of "wisdom of the lower classes" (see Mayer 1983).

is an allusion to the assumption of Jesus, this fits eminently well in the wisdom tradition, which knows of the assumptions of other such sages (Baruch, Ezra, the sage of the Wisdom of Solomon).

It is easy to appreciate the appeal of the principal alternate: viewing Jesus as an "eschatological prophet" and treating Q's sayings serving as "instructions" of this prophet (Gnilka 1994:134–35). For such a characterization implies a clear christological and soteriological direction—the more so if it is coupled with the supposition that Son of Man Christology presupposes a specific interpretation of the resurrection of Jesus. Additionally, the invocation of "eschatology" has the key apologetic effect of rendering Q (and Jesus) definitive and incomparable. In reflecting on Bultmann's use of eschatology as a descriptive category, Dieter Georgi has shrewdly observed that Bultmann

> opposes what he calls the relativism of the history-of-religions school. Again I need to mention the term "eschatological." It works for Bultmann and for many New Testament scholars and systematic theologians ever since as a magic wand. Whereas for the history-of-religions school the term "eschatological" described the foreignness of Jesus and of the early church—together with Jewish apocalypticism and other comparable ancient eschatologies—for Bultmann . . . the term "eschatological" stands for the novelty of Christianity, its incomparable superiority, the uniqueness of the victorious religion, deservedly victorious. Wherever a comparison is ventured, wherever analogies lift their head, wherever challenges are heard from other religious options but the canonical ones, the invocation of the "eschatological" is made, and the demons, the shadows have to disappear. (Georgi 1985:82)

The difficulty with the denomination of Q as "eschatological prophecy," quite apart from the literary problems described in chapter 3, is that far too many christological equations need to be read into Q's use of the term "Son of Man," and too much needs to be imported into the term "kingdom of God."[62] There is no doubt that once Q was absorbed into Matthew and Luke, a large repertoire of eschatological and apocalyptic motifs from Daniel 7 and elsewhere became available, so that the Matthaean Son of Man could be represented as "coming in his kingdom" (16:28), "sitting on his throne" (25:31), and rewarding the faithful with "a kingdom that had been prepared since the foundation of the cosmos" (25:34). But it would be a mistake to read these developments back into Q, whose "Christology" is far more modest and tentative and whose depiction of the kingdom of God is not furnished with Danielic imagery.

The evidentiary basis for describing Q as "eschatological prophecy" is

---

62. Jacobson (1992a:416), building on Vielhauer's observation that the "kingdom of God" and the "Son of Man" do not appear in the same context, notes: "This becomes especially curious if one supposes some influence from Dan 7,13-14 on the early Christian notion of the Son of Man, for in Daniel Son of Man and kingdom are linked." One might observe, conversely, that the kingdom of God in Q has also not acquired the apocalyptic coloration.

simply lacking. From a generic point of view, Q is not prophecy and Q's Christology—such as it exists at all—scarcely depicts Jesus as *the* definitive eschatological prophet. As convenient as such a characterization might be from the standpoint of theological apologetics, it is simply not authorized by the evidence. On the other hand, to argue that Q belongs essentially to the orbit of Second Temple Jewish wisdom is not a de facto endorsement of an anemic view of Q's Jesus as a "mere" sage, still less a "teacher of timeless wisdom." For such a characterization ignores both features that are key in Q's architecture and the characteristics of wisdom in the Second Temple period, if not wisdom as a whole.

The debates over Q's relation to the passion and resurrection traditions and over its theological taxonomy illustrate, as Georgi rightly notes, the ease with which historical and literary description succumbs to apologetic impulses. It is quite clear that the appearance of Q as a definable literary, social, and theological point on the map has engendered two distinct but related theological anxieties. On the one hand, Q's theological "differentness" on the key *theologoumena* of the cross and resurrection are regularly seen to endanger some presumed unity of primitive Christian thinking, a danger that is made acute by the fact of Q's antiquity and its fundamental contribution to the contents of the canonical gospels. On the other hand, Q represents a chink in the armor of the view that has been promoted in various guises, that apocalyptic eschatology was a theological foundation, either for Jesus' own preachment (J. Weiss 1892; Schweitzer 1906) or for that of the post-Easter church (Käsemann 1960, ET 1969). Modern scholarship on Q thus endangers the notion of a stable and consistent theological core. It also raises serious questions about the way in which eschatology, not simply as a descriptive historical category but as a *theological* category, has been allowed to control discourse on early Christianity. To this topic I shall return in the last chapter.

Q as a "Gospel": What's in a Name?

The debate over whether Q is a legitimate expression of early Christian theology is epitomized in the seemingly trivial question of nomenclature. Should we call Q a "gospel" or not? Scholars such as Dunn assure us that Q "was not treated as gospel by most of the early Christians" (1977:287). On the other hand, since 1990 it has become increasingly more common to refer to the sayings collection used by Matthew and Luke as the *Sayings Gospel Q*.[63]

---

63. The English term originated in the SBL Q Seminar (1987), the suggestion of John Dominic Crossan. Ron Cameron first used "the Synoptic Sayings Gospel" (1986:3 n.1), and the shorter "Sayings Gospel Q" first appeared in a paper by Kloppenborg (1988b) and in print two years later (Kloppenborg 1990b). See also the recent publications by Jacobson (1992b),

This is a debate that would have been unthinkable two generations ago. From the 1920s until well after the Second World War, "gospel" functioned as both a theological and a literary category whose essential contours were defined by the intracanonical Gospels. Karl Ludwig Schmidt (1923) had in fact argued that the Gospels were sui generis, the unliterary outcome of a process of sedimentation of oral traditions under the auspices of the kerygma. They were not "high literature" (*Hochliteratur*) but popular books, not "biographies, but cult legends" (1923:76). Of course, non-canonical gospels were known which did not conform to the narrative format of the canonical Gospels, but these could easily be dismissed as late degenerations.[64]

The congeniality of sui generis gospels with the theological program of neoorthodoxy did not escape Schmidt's notice:

> Thus the form-critical approach is a theological matter. The general philosophical question about content and form carries over into the theological question of God and the world, Christianity and culture. Radical and positive consideration of the Gospels is a function of the basic theological question. (1923:134)[65]

To claim that the gospels were sui generis served as an important corollary to the neoorthodox notion that the Christian kerygma was entirely discontinuous with human culture, including all forms of human piety. Christianity was not a religion among religions but the authentic communication

Mack (1993), Kloppenborg (1994b, 1995a), Piper (1995a), and Uro (1996), all of which use "gospel." Earlier, Crossan (1983:ix) referred to Q as a "discourse gospel" and now refers to it as "the Sayings Gospel Q" (1991:passim) or the "Q Gospel" (1994:passim; 1996). Koester (1984:1512–24) described a set of nonnarrative gospels as "Spruchevangelien," designating Q as "das älteste christliche Spruchevangelium" (1515). Koester's usage was an influence on the English term, even though Koester himself shows some ambivalence to "the Sayings Gospel," referring to Q as "die Spruchquelle" (1984:1515) and "the Synoptic Sayings Source Q" (1990:128), notwithstanding his inclusion of Q in a volume entitled *Ancient Christian Gospels*. The use of "gospel" is still resisted in Germany, but with a notable exceptions: Dormeyer 1993: 219 (see below, p. 406); Kristen 1995:39: "Thus Q may rightly be called a sayings Gospel (*Spruchevangelium*). This designation is much better justified for Q than the term 'logia source' (*Logienquelle*), which is indeed widespread; but neither of its component parts is adequate." See now the discussion of the history of usage by Neirynck (1995c).

64. Meagher 1983:208 summarizes Schmidt's views aptly: "The gospel genre therefore derives its uniqueness from the cultic tradition, mediated by the sheer absence of any self-conscious literary character, and derives its intelligibility from its rootedness in the early Christian communal cult. It is the signet impress of primitive Christian religious life. And as its source of uniqueness determined its emergence, so it determined its deterioration. Hellenistic culture nibbled at successive gospels, from Mark to Matthew, and then Luke, and finally the apocryphal gospels and John: 'This movement signals a constantly strengthening *secularization* of the gospels'" (citing K. Schmidt 1923:131, emphasis original).

65. Similarly, Bultmann 1928:419, ET 1969b:89: "Thus [the gospels] are a unique phenomenon in the history of literature and at the same time are symbolic of the distinctive nature of the Christian religion as such."

of God. It was a *novum* and its earliest literary expressions were likewise discontinuous with contemporary literature. For Schmidt, what distinguished the Gospels from contemporary biographies—their lack of interest in providing an account of the "inner and outer development" Jesus' personality (1923:79–80)—was their theological advantage. The Gospels did not present Jesus as a founder-figure, because "[b]y the standard of primitive Christianity, to seek to present Jesus in this sense as the originator of Christianity and the founder of the Christian Church is a misleading and Pelagian idea" (Schmidt 1929:105, ET 1969:102). Given the necessary link Schmidt forged between the kerygma and the Gospel "form," it is unthinkable that Q could have been regarded as a gospel, for it lacked all elements of the passion kerygma and any hint of "cult legends."

It would take almost a half century for this view of the Gospels to change. The erosion of neoorthodox theology, the discovery of more documents that called themselves gospels but which did not conform to the narrative format of the intracanonical Gospels, the recognition of the diversity of early Christian kerygmata, and the effect of redaction criticism's insistence on the authorial role of the evangelists all conspired to reopen the issue of the place of the Gospels within the field of ancient literature. By the 1970s a change of climate was signaled by James M. Robinson: "in view of the plurality of kerygmatic trends in primitive Christianity, and their history-of-religions parallels, the view that one distinctive *Gattung* Gospel emerged sui generis from the uniqueness of Christianity seems hardly tenable" (1970–71:104)

When studies began to appear that argued that the canonical Gospels belonged to the larger genre of *bios*, Schmidt's link between the theological and the literary identity of "gospel" dissolved. Instead of treating the gospel genre as the result of the autonomous expansion of the kerygma, Charles Talbert, David Aune, and others contended that careful comparative analysis justified seeing the Gospels as types of biographies.[66] Two important methodological shifts had occurred: on the one hand, as Meagher has observed, the normal canons of procedure in literary history were very much against Schmidt's literary claim of uniqueness:

> [T]he literary historian assumes generic nonuniqueness on both small scale and large, and recognizes that controlled conventionality is really the only way to set up an intelligible uniqueness at all—for an unintelligible uniqueness is of no use. . . . To shift from an emphasis on the uniqueness of the gospels is therefore to shift towards the normal procedures of literary research and accordingly to invite the possibility of enhanced interpretive control. (Meagher 1983:212)

On the other, the neoorthodox attempt to link literary and theological conclusions was rejected: the issue of genre was not a theological problem at all

---

66. See, for varying perspectives on this problem, Talbert 1977; Aune 1981; 1987:17–76; Shuler 1982; Burridge 1992; Dormeyer 1993:212.

but one of literary taxonomy. Theological uniqueness cannot ride in on the coat tails of dubious literary conclusions.

There has been, to be sure, resistance to such conclusions: Childs laments the "theological tone-deafness" of Talbert and Aune, rejecting their efforts to classify the Gospels as biographies and preferring instead to delineate a structural correlation (and apparently, a genetic link) between the kerygma of the resurrected one and the Gospels, seen as *anemnesis* of the earthly Jesus in view of the resurrection.[67] But Childs's dismissing of available literary parallels looks like special pleading and his alternative is merely asserted rather than defended. Meagher's comment on Schmidt's efforts applies equally to Childs:

> Interpretations that try to see the gospels as prosecuting any one consistent pre-possession, be it Schimdt's own notion of the incarnation of the logos or the more common modern supposition that they attest consistently to "the" kerygma, seem to me not only unpersuasive but negligent, foundering not only on their failure to account for some of the less cooperative of the individual pericopae but also on the puzzling features in the overall shape of the gospel's behavior. . . . The assumption of a unique, unified, and consistent early confession has yielded under scrutiny to the more temperate recognition of a variety of early Christian ways to understand and formulate what had taken place. (Meagher 1983:228–29)

The collapse of Schmidt's view of the Gospels as incommensurable had important, if unanticipated, effects on the theological taxonomy of Q. If the intracanonical Gospels could be situated on the field of ancient literature, then so could other documents, including Q. Such an inquiry was strictly one of comparative literary analysis; it was an investigation of how ancient readers would have regarded the texts in question and not a clandestine apologetic effort to distinguish emergent Christianity from its environment. Moreover, once the term "gospel" was stripped of its pseudogeneric character and seen as a theological category, it could be used to characterize the theological *content* of the intracanonical Gospels as well as other documents. Robert Fortna (1970) applied the term "Gospel of Signs" to a

---

67. Childs 1993:253–55, citing Dahl 1976. Similarly, Stuhlmacher's response (1990) to Shuler (1990) and Shuler's "Nachtrag." Stuhlmacher rejects Shuler's comparative literary analysis, substituting a purely theological one: "The biographical accentuation of the presentation of the evangelists is entirely undeniable, but it is better taken into consideration when we call the Gospels' presentation of the history of Jesus as 'salvation event' (*Heilsgeschehen*). The Gospels cannot be incorporated into the genre of the *vita* or βίος. Their subject matter, purpose and use all indicate that they are to be considered independent books. They summarize the Jesus-tradition according to the pattern established in the narrative preaching about Jesus (cf. Acts 10:36ff.) and are intended to be read in the gatherings of the community for the purpose of instruction and edification." The Shuler-Stuhlmacher debate makes clear how theological categories are invoked to derail literary comparison. This is not history, but apologetics.

miracle collection and passion narrative that he posited as the principal source for the Fourth Gospel. In striking contrast to Schmidt, some argued that the term could be used *legitimately* of noncanonical Gospels to designate documents that offer an accounting of the words and/or deeds of Jesus (Patterson 1992b).

Again it is essential to be clear. There is no textual evidence recoverable from the incipit of Q that might solve the debate at the literary level. The issue is not one of the *title* or *incipit* of Q. Since *euaggelion* was not a generic designation in the first century, it is scarcely likely it occurred as the title of Q (which would have normally appeared in the colophon, at the end), and there is no reason to suppose that it appeared in a nongeneric sense in the incipit (as it does in Mark 1:1). The issue, rather, is a matter of scholarly conventions that signal the importance of Q relative to other documents for both the historical reconstruction and the theological history of primitive Christianity.

The usage of the term "gospel" has been defended in at least three distinct registers: the first, at the level of sheer convention, the second, of theological trajectory, and the third, of literary trajectory.

1. Neither of the two earlier designations, *logia* and *Quelle*, has been entirely satisfactory. The earliest designation, *logia*,[68] which derived from Papias's term, must now be regarded as inappropriate: the logical basis for positing Q has nothing to do with Papias, and Q is not aptly designated as *logia* ("oracles"). *Logia* is in fact "question-begging," as J. A. Robinson rightly observed (1902:70), and was abandoned by English scholarship early in the twentieth century. The terms *la source des Logia* and *Logienquelle* persisted in French and German, but this persistence probably had less to do with Papias than with the fact that Bultmann's chapter on the sayings tradition was entitled "Logia (Jesus as the Teacher of Wisdom)" (1968:69–108).

After Johannes Weiss, the terms of choice became the "sayings source" or the "Q source" in English and *la source des Logia* or *la source Q* in French, all deriving from the German *Quelle, Logienquelle, Spruchquelle,* or *Rede(n)quelle.* What is common to these designations and indeed implicit in the very siglum Q (=*Quelle*, source) is the notion that Q is first and foremost a "source" for something else. Of course, Q was a literary source for two of the Synoptic evangelists, as was Mark's Gospel. It was also, presumably, a literary and theological work in its own right and in this respect deserves a designation that acknowledges its integrity and independent value as a document of early Christianity. No one, after all, calls the second gospel "the Markan source" merely because it was used by Matthew and Luke.

68. Holtzmann referred to Q as Λ or "die zweite Hauptquelle" (the second main source), while others used the *Logia* (Sanday 1899–1900) or "the Logian source" (V. Stanton 1903–20, 2:102).

Why the Sayings *Gospel* Q? In view of the preceding survey of the theological currents that carried Q research forward, the term should be far from unexpected. Once Tödt's discovery had sunk in and once Q came to be placed *alongside* the Synoptics in the standard introductions to the Gospels, it was a very small and altogether natural step to call Q a gospel, even if Kee, Perrin, Vielhauer, and Schmithals did not take this step. Yet the designation deserves a better defense than merely the adducing of a "tendency" of scholarship.

To call Q "the Sayings Gospel Q" rather than a source is to argue that the *analogy* with the canonical Gospels is both reasonable and apt. First, it allows one to take Q seriously in a way that calling it a "source" does not. Q belongs, as much as the canonical Gospels do, to the literary endeavors that sought to define the salient features of the Jesus movement with reference to the sayings and deeds of Jesus. Second, it is to argue that Q, as much as any of the other gospels, functioned as a touchstone or point of reference for those who treasured and transmitted it. Finally, it is to argue that Q deserves serious attention as a *document* of primitive Christianity.

This usage of the term "gospel" is unabashedly "provocative" (Jacobson 1992b:3) or, as I would prefer, "argumentative." This provocative or argumentative use can be defended by noting, on the one hand, that the intracanonical Gospels can no longer claim proprietary privilege in respect to the term. In the first place, "gospel" is not a proper literary category. Second, we now know of other documents from antiquity that were called "gospels" but which do not have a narrative or biographical cast at all. The *Gospel of Thomas* (NHC II,2), the *Gospel of Philip* (NHC II,3), and probably the *Gospel of the Egyptians* (mentioned by patristic writers) are gnomologia or chriae collections; the *Gospel of Truth* (NHC I,3) is a tractate. This means that to call Q a gospel is not to imply a particular literary organization.

Q may be treated as a legitimate gospel analogous to at least the canonical Gospels under two conditions: first, if the term "gospel" is recognized as making a theological claim—that the materials so designated represent "a coherent theological perspective and thus capable of standing alone";[69] and second, if the argument in the two preceding sections is cogent, that Q does have a view of Jesus' death and vindication, and that it assumes, if only implicitly, a necessary connection between Jesus and his message of the kingdom.

Of course, objections can be raised. Some insist that a gospel must have a narrative format (Frankemölle 1988:149). This objection is purely stipulative, and has the disadvantage of disqualifying as "gospels" several non-narrative documents that we know to have been so designated. It also runs

---

69. Jacobson 1992b:30. Similarly, Kristen 1995:39. Less happily, Jacobson declares that "there is nothing specifically *Christian* about this [Q's Deuteronomistic] view of Jesus' death" (1992b:30, emphasis added). Jacobson does not explain what a "Christian" view might be.

the risk of appearing arbitrary and disingenuous.[70] It could be maintained that Q's theology is not sufficiently "mainstream" to be treated on the analogy to the canonical Gospels or the Pauline gospel; or it could be doubted that Q indeed represents a coherent theological perspective. This is a question that evidence will probably not settle; some critics will be satisfied that Q embodies a coherent perspective and others will not. It is a matter of making a theological wager, and allowing this to guide one's reconstruction of the Jesus movement. But, I hasten to add, there is no neutral position here. Treating Q as a gospel is one form of wager; denying it that status is equally a wager and one that yields a different (and narrower) theological history of primitive Christianity.

2. Robinson has attempted to secure the use of the term "gospel" by arguing for the existence of a theological trajectory from Q to the use of *euaggelion* in Matthew.

> Although Q does not use the noun εὐαγγέλιον, the synonym κήρυγμα occurs both as verb (Q 12:3) and as noun (Q 11:32). Here πλεῖον Ἰωνᾶ, where the *tertium comparationis* is τὸ κήρυγμα Ἰωνᾶ, would seem to refer to the message of Q as itself κήρυγμα. Thus, in distinction from modern theological usage, "kerygma" in primitive Christianity referred not only to the Pauline kerygma of the cross and resurrection . . . but also to the message of the Q community. The same must be true of εὐαγγέλιον, even if the noun does not occur in Q. It is this terminological usage embedded in the sayings tradition . . . that ultimately led to the Gospels being designated as Gospels. (Robinson 1992b: 370–71)

Robinson's argument regarding kerygma is not especially convincing. While the term assumed great importance in twentieth-century theology, there is no evidence that it connoted anything more than "preaching" in Q. Thus, Q 11:32 only implies that Jesus' preaching (and by extension, that of the Q people) is greater than Jonah's.

The more important argument concerns the influence of the verb *euaggelizesthai* in Q 7:22, where it appears in the phrase "the poor are given the good news."[71] Robinson argues against the prevailing view that *euaggelion* in Mark 1:1 determined the use of that term in Matthew and Luke. He pointed out that *euaggelizesthai* and the other allusions to Isa 61:1-2 in Q

---

70. The counterobjection that "gospel" in the *Gospel of Thomas* is probably a secondary designation, added in the colophon, applies equally to the canonical Gospels, where the phrase "the gospel according to NN" is obviously a secondary title, presupposing a collection of gospels. Robinson (1992b:372) makes the important observation that "gospel" in the *Gospel of Truth* is *not* a secondary addition, but part of the incipit. "This modern usage [i.e., referring to NHC I,2 as "the Gospel of Truth"] hence does seem to represent the intention of the text to be presenting a (or, more precisely, *the* only true) Gospel. Irenaeus, *Haer.* 3,11.9 seems to have interpreted it correctly as such an invidious title."

71. The verb also appears in the Lukan version of Q 16:16 ("the kingdom of God is proclaimed"), but that is normally ascribed to Lukan redaction.

7:22 form an *inclusio* with Q 6:20b-21. Thus they construe the whole inaugural sermon as an act of "evangelizing" (1992b:371). This usage, Robinson contends, is reflected in the Matthaean summaries that surround his Sermon on the Mount (Matt 4:23; 9:35), which refer to Jesus "preaching the gospel of the kingdom" and performing various healings—healings that are also mentioned in Q 7:22. Thus, Matthew's use of *to euaggelion tēs basileias* is merely the logical continuation of a trajectory begun in Q (Robinson 1995:32–33).

It might be argued that Matthew's usage in 4:23 is simply a compensation for his omission of Mark 1:14 (κηρύσσων τὸ εὐαγγέλιον τοῦ θεοῦ) (thus Neirynck 1995c:426). Nevertheless, Matt 4:23 does not summarize what goes before, as the corresponding Markan phrase (1:39) does, for Matthew either omitted or relocated most of Mark 1:16-38. Instead, Matt 4:23 is an introduction to the large block of material beginning with the Sermon on the Mount and reaching at least to 9:35 and perhaps to 19:1 (Luz 1989:204). This being the case, the phrase "the gospel of the kingdom" takes on a programmatic function with respect to Matthew's Sermon, a function that the verb *euaggelizesthai* clearly has in Matthew's retrospective comments in Matt 11:5 (citing Q 7:22). To derive Matthew's use of *to euaggelion* in 4:23 exclusively from Mark 1:14, as Neirynck wants to do, seems unnecessarily restrictive and mechanical, especially when Matthew clearly treats the substantive (4:23) and the verb (11:5 = Q) as equivalent, and when a text such as 4Q521 also uses the verb (יבשר) to describe in a programmatic fashion the activities of the Messiah.[72] Robinson's argument depends on positing a trajectory of the programmatic use of *euaggelizesthai* that Matthew recognized and elaborated.

Robinson may be right. But it is impossible to peer into Matthew's mind and know whether it was Mark 1:14 or Q 7:22 that inclined him to describe the material following Matt 4:23 as "the gospel of the kingdom." Nor is it obvious that Q used *euaggelizesthai* programmatically, despite the important role that 7:18-23 plays in the structure of Q in establishing Jesus' identity. What may be said is that irrespective of whether Q saw special significance in the word *euaggelizesthai*, Q 7:22 characterizes Jesus' *discourse* and the *events* attending his ministry as salvific in a manner analogous to what the use of the term *euaggelion* accomplishes in Mark.

3. A third possible line of defense for the term "gospel" is based on a literary trajectory. Dormeyer argues that the addition to Q of a temptation

---

72. Where Robinson has stressed the specific associations between Q 7:22 and Isa 61:1-2 (1992b:364) and now even prefers (against the IQP) to reconstruct Q 6:20b-21 with vocabulary from Isa 61:1-2 (1996:93!), Neirynck (1995c:427) stresses that Q 7:22 makes use of other Isaian texts (e.g., Isa 29:18-19). This point, however, is partially mooted by the occurrence of most of the items listed in Q 7:22 (except deafness and leprosy) in 4Q521. It would appear that a synthesis of Isaian texts was *already* in circulation by the time of the composition of Q (and certainly, Matthew) and that Q 7:22 reflects this exegetical development.

story and other narrative elements at the beginning of Q, and the inclusion
of a few narrative features throughout, justifies the designation gospel:

> The redactor of Q therefore could not have referred to a schematized, Old
> Testament genre of "Prophetic book" (*pace* Sato 1988), but continued the syn-
> thesizing practices of the post-exilic period. In analogy to second Temple Jew-
> ish and hellenistic sayings collections, and under the influence of the Old
> Testament ideal biography, he created a particular genre of ideal biography: the
> "Sayings-Gospel" (*Spruch-Evangelium*). . . .[73]

Dormeyer's conclusion is tied to an argument that the intracanonical
Gospels represent a subtype of the *bios* genre (1993:212) and to the obser-
vation that Q 7:22, no less than the intracanonical Gospels, characterizes
Jesus as the final bringer of salvation:

> The citation [of Isaiah] refers directly back to the miracle story of the Centu-
> rion of Capernaum and the programmtic inaugural sermon. With the citation
> occurring at this point, what is expressed is the fulfillment of the expectations
> of salvation which are connected with the eschatological messengers of joy
> mentioned in Trito-Isaiah. Jesus shows himself by word and deed to be the final
> messenger who decisively brings salvation. Jesus' sayings and deeds are there-
> fore "gospel," just as the later gospels. (1993:217)

Hence, if the intracanonical Gospels as "kerygmatic ideal biographies" are
Gospels, then Q with its narrativizing tendency and its kerygmatic content
is no less a gospel (1993:212). Dormeyer even suggests that it was the proximity of the genre of Q to that of Mark that facilitated the editorial work of
Matthew and Luke in fusing the two.

Although Dormeyer may associate the term "gospel" too closely with a
narrative format and hence exclude other gospels from this nomenclature,
he is surely correct that the distance between Q and the later intracanonical
Gospels is not as far as has been supposed. This is true both in terms of Q's
narrativizing tendency,[74] and in terms of its message. I prefer not to identify

---

73. Dormeyer 1993:219. The term "ideal biography" is Baltzer's (1975), who treats the
"biographies" of David (2 Sam 23:1-7), Gideon (Judges 6–8), and Moses (Exodus 2—
Deuteronomy 34) as examples of this subtype of biography, which focuses on office and function rather than on the personality of the figure. Baltzer argues that the intracanonical Gospels
are also examples of this type.

74. The argument made in Kloppenborg 1987a:325–28, that the final redaction of Q moved
the collection more strongly in the direction of a *bios*, is accepted by Strecker 1992:169 and
Dormeyer 1993:219. In an earlier work, Dormeyer was less clear on including Q as a gospel,
even though he recognized its narrativizing tendency: "Under the circumstances, Q can be
regarded as a intermediate stage between a collection of materials of similar form arranged topically, and a distinctively formed 'gospel' biography" (1989:189). Aune (1987:52) treats Q as
a sayings collection rather than as a gospel/biography, but fails to note the way in which the
opening pericopae create a narrativizing frame. According to his own statement, that "since
the ancients regarded a person's actions and words as revelations of character, collections of
chreiai had a fundamentally biographical function" (1987:34), Q would have strong biographical tendencies.

too closely the theological category of Gospel with the literary category of biography; nonetheless, *in both respects*, Q is already very close to the later intracanonical Gospels.

Un évangile presque tout en maximes

To think of Q as a gospel is not, after all, very new. A century ago Abbé Pierre Batiffol was able to describe this important collection of Jesus traditions quite simply:

> If one compares the three editions [of the Gospels], one can easily confirm that Matthew and Luke are independent of one another and that of the three, Mark is the most original. . . . But Matthew and Luke have in common a series of isolated maxims, parables and prophecies: our two evangelists reproduced them with the same degree of variation and verbal agreement that one observes when they copy Mark. We can thus conclude that they depended on a gospel different from Mark, more ancient than Mark, known to Mark, and which will have been a gospel composed almost completely of maxims, parables and discourses of Jesus (*un évangile presque tout en maximes, en paraboles, en discours de Jésus*), a gospel that began with the preaching of John the Baptist. (1897: 66–67)

The debate about whether Q is a "gospel" or not is not a question of reconstruction. It will not be settled by recovering this or that word or phrase behind Matthew's or Luke's redaction. Rather, it is about deeper descriptive habits and theological choices—habits and choices that are not unrelated to the literary sources and reconstruction, but are not reducible to them. One may adduce the precedents of such scholars as Batiffol, who evidently did not blush at calling Q a gospel. One may adduce features of Q that might well render reasonable the application of the term "gospel." One may offer arguments justifying the nomenclature on theological or literary grounds. In the final analysis the designation is provocative or, as I would prefer, argumentative.

By this I do not mean merely disputatious. To call Q a gospel is argumentative in the same way that the earlier designation *logia* was not merely a name but represented an argument. It advanced the claimed that Q was somehow rooted in the memory of the early church represented by Papias. Even though this usage eventually foundered, it should not go unnoticed that in the age of Lessing and Schleiermacher, when it was widely assumed that patristic literature preserved the memory of documents of the first Christian generation now lost, but of key importance to unraveling the web of tradition, it was perfectly ordinary and, indeed, reasonable to invoke Papias as part of the defense of Q. Logically speaking, this invocation was completely irrelevant to the intrinsic credibility of the hypothesis of a sayings source; but it was intimately related to the explanatory habits of the time. To call Q a gospel is argumentative in the same way that, in another age with different sensibilities, Streeter rendered his understanding of Q, Mark, M, L, Matthew, and Luke plausible by being able to place them on a documentary map of the primitive Gospel tradition. Streeter's map was pure construct. He did not derive it from some additional evidence about the Synoptics which happily harmonized with his documentary hypothesis. His map of Synoptic relationships was derived entirely from his own hypothesis. Yet his ability to create such a map served a much larger concern to have a model by which to grasp both constancy and change in "*the* Gospel tradition" that reached from Jesus to the great recensions of the fourth century.

To call Q "the Sayings Gospel Q" is analogously to argue for the essential plausibility of a reconstruction of primitive Christianity that compasses difference and diversity, that entertains the possibility of other gospels which cannot any longer simple be dismissed in an instinctual antiheretical reflex, and that is willing to imagine the possibility of theological and social experimentation—experiments that perhaps failed, but whose failure is nonetheless worth a closer look. It should be clear by now that to deny the designation "gospel" to Q is no less argumentative. There is no default position any longer, no assured or neutral point of departure that can be claimed. The *difference* of Q—its different way of thinking of death and vindication, and its differentness in framing a message of salvation—makes a difference, whether it is acknowledged and factored into one's reconstruction of primitive Christianity, or whether it is factored out as inadequate, incomplete, or simply irrelevant.

9

Social Characterizations
in Theological Perspective

OR THE FIRST THREE-QUARTERS of the twentieth century, New Testament
scholars treated documents chiefly as the repositories of ideas. The
scholar's tasks were to extract these ideas, articulate the "theology" of texts,
locate their constituent themes with respect to antecedent stages of thought,
note developments, and observe potential or actual conflicts with other
ideas. Little consideration was given to the persons who produced or embraced those ideas, their social location, their economic and political status,
and the ways their ideas and behavior fit within Mediterranean societies.

The Context of Social-Historical Criticism

At the beginning of the 1970s a new direction in scholarship developed that
raised questions of the social location of the Jesus movement and the relationship between social location and theology. No longer were bare ideas
enough. Texts were now treated as the productions of particular persons or
groups with specific social locations and therefore with particular ways of
viewing themselves in relation to their world. These socially located persons
had interests which required defense and aspirations and behavioral patterns that required justification. Ideas were still important, but the focus
had shifted to ideas as they are expressive of and embedded in the social
world of the persons who held them.

Inquiry into the social matrix of early Christianity was partially anticipated in form criticism's quest for various *Sitze im Leben* (social or ecclesial
settings) of the units that made up the Synoptic tradition. But form criticism
rarely moved beyond correlating units of tradition with narrowly conceived
ecclesial functions such as paraenesis, controversy, apologetics, liturgy, and
so forth. There was almost no effort to address the broader questions of the
social status and economic level of early Jesus movement or to adopt theoretical models that could help to clarify the relationship between the social

location of early Christians and the particular characteristics of their discourse.

The dominant idealist predeliction of scholarship prior to the 1970s proved a stubborn obstacle to genuine social analysis. To be sure, a few scholars prior to the 1970s offered social descriptions and explanations, but their insights gained little footing at the time.[1] The major development of social-scientific approaches had to await larger political and social developments—something that occurred in the late 1960s and early 1970s.

It is no coincidence that the seminal articles and monographs which began to take social location seriously and which argued that early Christians adopted noticeably countercultural social and political profiles were written in the wake of the 1968 student riots in France and Germany and a series of events in North America: the height of American involvement in Vietnam, Laos, and Cambodia; the 1968 Democratic convention in Chicago; and the killing of students at Kent State University by the National Guard. These events problematized the relationship between intellectuals and their universities on the one hand, and the political and cultural institutions that universities had once been seen to support, on the other. The widening gap that appeared between political-military cultures and those of universities made it easier to see how ideology and commitment could be correlated with social location. It was also clear how ideology often served specific social interests.

The tensions of the 1960s and 1970s created a "space" in which many new issues were promoted to prominence, including feminism, civil rights, ecology, the moral responsibility of science, social justice, just war theory, and the appropriate role of major cultural institutions (including churches) in political advocacy. Universities adopted a more prominent stance as countercultural institutions, spawning vocal critics of prevailing political and social arrangements.

Embedded in university culture, scholars of the earliest Jesus movements began to ask whether these groups might have been similarly "countercultural." This was not simply a case of reading one's own experience and attitudes into history. Rather, the situation of the late 1960s and early 1970s created room for scholars to ask questions that hitherto would hardly have been raised. Once we saw the correlation of social location and ideology in our own culture, it seemed a natural step to ask about the social location of the early Christians and to correlate this with its ideology and social practice.

Robin Scroggs's 1975 essay entitled "The Earliest Christian Communities as Sectarian Movement" typifies the shift I am describing, from an approach mainly interested in ideas to one that tried to set ideas within social contexts. His hypothesis was that the earliest Christians can be

---

1. Schmidt 1885; Mathews 1897; Bigelmair 1902; Deissmann 1908; Kautsky 1908, ET 1925; Case 1914; 1923; Grant 1926; Riddle 1936; Alfaric 1959; Judge 1960.

described meaningfully as a sect whose members were mainly disadvantaged persons reacting to economic and social repression and whose ideology promoted an inclusive and egalitarian ethos and rejection of key values of the macrosociety. Scroggs paid express attention to social location, using models borrowed from the social sciences, and characterized early Christian groups as countercultural in their social practice. In the context of the 1970s Scroggs's essay exemplified the growing conviction that the early Jesus movement was not just about ideas, even "radical" ideas, but represented in its practices a criticism of, or resistance to, the dominant Roman culture. The tools of the exegete now had to include methods by which those social practices could be described and evaluated.[2]

In the decades that followed, many studies appeared asking broadly sociological questions. Some inquired into social *realia* (occupations, food, housing, travel, etc.) of the early Christians; some constructed social histories by attending to economic, social, and political data alongside the "theological" ideas; some examined social institutions; still others made express use of sociological and anthropological theory in describing the social world of the Jesus movement and attempted to provide explanatory accounts of various aspects of the Jesus movement (see Smith 1975a). Where earlier approaches had avoided intellectual anachronism by contextualizing the ideas of the New Testament, relating them to antecedent ideas, now, in order to avoid ethnocentricism, exegesis required a clarification of social and cultural details. Texts had to be viewed as the products of specific social groupings, with social needs, values, interests, and perspectives. These texts belonged not to post-Enlightenment, North American, or North European cultures, which values the individual, mobility, progress and the future, and political and social equality, but to an ancient Mediterranean culture, which emphasized much more the family and collective values, honor and shame, purity, the past, and social hierarchy.

It had always seemed important, for example, to interpret Q 6:27-28 (on loving one's enemies) in relation to the ethical ideas of the Tanak (e.g., Lev 19:18) and of surrounding cultures. Now, it became also important to understand how Q 6:27-28 would be heard in the context of agonistic Mediterranean social relationships (especially among males), characterized by challenge and riposte, retaliation, and blood feud. In this context Q 6:27-28 does not articulate an abstract altruistic principle, as earlier exegetes were inclined to think, but represents a strategy for dealing with quite concrete local conflict. One also had to inquire into the social location of those who transmitted Q 6:27-28. In the mouth of someone of senatorial rank, "love

2. In the preface to the 1993 reprint of the essay Scroggs now explains that it was precisely the tumult of the 1970s and his interest in countercultural interpreters such as Herbert Marcuse and Norman O. Brown that had brought him to sociological analysis and given him the scientific tools by which to describe the religious sectarianism and countercultural nature of the early Christians.

your enemies" might signal a strategy of political accommodation among the
elite; in the mouth of a small-town scribe in Jewish Palestine it would have a
rather different set of connotations. This new attention to the social values
and social location of the Jesus movement—its attitude(s) toward the values
of honor and shame, distinctions between pure and impure, and numerous
assumptions about the human body, the family, marriage, gender relations,
children, wealth, slavery, coming from a "good family," and so forth—
allowed for a more comprehensive contextualization of more abstract theological ideas. By suggesting how ideas were related to and embodied in
specific social practices and specific social locations, this approach also provided a more adequate basis for accounting for the appeal of the Jesus movement and the points of resistance the movement encountered.

From one point of view, social-historical approaches merely enlarged and
refined the historical-critical method. Attention to the social fabric of Jewish Palestine allowed for a "thicker" historical description of the Jesus
movement and, hence, one that was better equipped to account for its
impact. The turn toward social history also coincided with a redefinition of
theology itself, which included reflection not only on doctrine but on the
praxis of Christian communities. In the last two decades numerous voices
have called for a rethinking of the structure of theological discourse so that
it begins not with speculative philosophical principles but with the concrete
experience of persons in the world, whether it be the disenfranchisement of
women, or the systemic oppression of the poor in the Third World, or the
fact of the Holocaust. To orient theological discourse in this way naturally
requires analysis of current social realities; but if it is to be responsible in its
appropriation of the foundational documents of Christianity, it must also
pay close attention to the social realities that those texts reflect.[3]

Social History and Its Theological Consequences

Recent scholarship on the Sayings Gospel Q belongs squarely within the
more general developments I have just outlined. Whether Hoffmann's political reading of the temptation story; or Horsley's suggestion that the Q
people were engaged in a program of local revitalization and prophetic
resistance to imperialist domination; or the use by Vaage and Mack of the
analogy of Cynic critique and social experimentalism; or the theses of
Freyne and Arnal concerning the urbanization and monetization of the

3. Much of the criticism of the early forms of liberation theology was that its use of biblical
texts was naive. Since that time, exegetes such as Horsley (1987) and Myers (1988) have given
social-historical accounts of the Jesus movement that are obviously pertinent to liberation theology. Similarly, much of the focus of feminist theology had been on a rereading of biblical
texts and a critical recovery of the role of women in early Judaism and the Jesus movement
(Corley 1993; 1996; Schüssler Fiorenza 1983; 1995; A. J. Levine 1990; 1991; 1994; Plaskow
1990).

Galilean economy; or the conjectures by myself and Piper regarding lower-echelon scribal disenfranchisement, resistance to encroachments by the south and from Herodian cities, and Q's advocacy of a model of local cooperation—all are attempts to situate the Q people within a particular social and political context and read Q's discourse as seriously engaged with that context. None is satisfied with narrowly ideational answers.

ARE THERE THEOLOGICAL CONSEQUENCES?

Social-historical approaches to Q cohere with the general thrust of *historical criticism* to situate documents and social phenomena in their environment in as detailed and nuanced a fashion possible. But does the social history of Q have *theological* consequences? None, automatically. One could argue that pre- or noncanonical documents are theologically irrelevant. Or, it could be asserted that theological ideas, but not their social contextualizations, are the stuff of Christian theology. Two comments are in order here.

First, it is a defensible position that New Testament theology should be constructed on the basis of canonical documents or some subset of canonical documents, but need not take into account pre- and noncanonical developments. Bultmann, for example, argued that the preaching of Jesus (with which he associated Q) "belongs to the presuppositions of the theology of the New Testament and is not part of New Testament theology itself" (1948 53:1). The key notions of New Testament theology, that the proclaimer had become the proclaimed and the paradoxical nature of the eschatological proclamation, are seen most clearly in the Pauline gospel of the crucified Messiah and John's announcement of the Logos-become-flesh. Pre-Gospel sources such as Q, the Signs Source lying behind the Fourth Gospel and pre-Markan miracle catenae might have a legitimate place in a literary and social *history* of the early Jesus movement, but they are germane to the enterprise of establishing what is *theologically normative* in that history. This approach to New Testament theology would also render innocuous the facts discussed in the previous chapters that Q lacks certain features that became integral to Christian theology and that its notion of the vindication of Jesus is strikingly different from the one that eventually prevailed. A fortiori, Bultmann's view would also make irrelevant any consideration of Q's social practice or social location.

Bultmann's position has often been criticized, however, for distinguishing theology too sharply from its ostensible subject, Jesus. An approach to New Testament theology that privileges the canon (or some subset of canonical documents), and accordingly minimizes or disregards both precanonical document such as Q and noncanonical documents such as the *Gospel of Thomas*, is in some tension with the fact that Christian theology has to do with the proclamation of God's action *in history*. Although Bultmann held that all that New Testament theology need presuppose about the historical Jesus were the bare facts of his life and execution, subsequent theologians show a stronger tendency to root theology in the words and activities of the historical Jesus.[4] As soon as the historical Jesus is treated as theologically germane to the project of New Testament theology, it becomes methodologically problematic to ignore documentary sources like Q and the *Gospel of Thomas,* which represent significant sources of knowledge about the historical Jesus.

It is not only because Q is an important source for historical Jesus tradition that it is arguably theologically relevant, however. The Sayings Gospel represents a substantial inscription of the Jesus tradition, expressing a generally coherent view of Jesus' significance, and inscribed by persons who were geographically, culturally, and chronologically proximate to the historical Jesus. It cannot reasonably be treated as a backwater or footnote, since Q served as a foundational document for two of the canonical Gospels. Q can thus claim antiquity, proximity to the subject of New Testament theology, and influence. A strict Bultmannian approach to New Testament theology might still choose to disregard Q; but to the extent continuities between the historical Jesus and theological affirmations are thought to be a necessary part of New Testament theology, Q assumes greater theological importance.

A second reason that social-scientific approaches to Q might not be deemed to be theologically relevant has to do with the fact that theology has sometimes been interested not in what is culture- and situation-bound but in those aspects of the Jesus movement that supposedly transcend the particulars of specific expressions of the Christian faith. These normally have to do with ideas—views of God, of Jesus, salvation, discipleship, etc. It is not that the ideas of the Jesus movement are treated uncritically, as timeless truths. On the contrary, it is usual to acknowledge development, extension, and qualification of theological ideas from the first century to the modern period. Such an approach to theology maintained a critical perspective by situating theological ideas in relation to the history of ideas, but felt no pressing need to contextualize them further in regard to their social location and social interest.

With the decentering of theological discourse from its European and North American axes and the emergence of feminist, womanist, African, Asian, Latin American, and liberationist theologies, the dominant ideational paradigm for theology has come under increasing pressure.

---

4. As noted in chapter 8, even Childs, who privileges canonical interpretation, does not ignore the diachronic aspects of biblical theology, referring to them as the "depth dimension" of the kerygma (Childs 1993:216–17). This, for Childs, has to do with understanding "the direction in which the tradition grew" (1993:216) and aids the interpreter in grasping "the range of kerygmatic diversity" and "the nature of its unity" (1993:217).

African theologian Itumeleng Mosala, for example, insists on theology's awareness of the fact that the Bible itself is the product of ruling-class ideology and can be employed for liberative ends only when this is taken into account:

> The insistence on the Bible as the Word of God must be seen for what it is: an ideological maneuver whereby ruling-class interests evident in the Bible are converted into a faith that transcends social, political, racial, sexual, and economic divisions. In this way the Bible becomes an ahistorical, interclassist document. (Mosala 1989:18)

Instead of endorsing the notion that the Word of God is a transhistorical reality that finds various contextualizations in history, Mosala insists that the texts of the Bible are indelibly and radically marked by their origin in history. The Word of God cannot be disengaged from its historical and social context; on the contrary, the locus of truth is found in the crucible of historical struggle. This means, for Mosala, that "the social, cultural, political, and economic world of the black working class and peasantry constitutes the only valid hermeneutical starting point for a black theology of liberation" (Mosala 1989:21).[5]

That the text of the Bible bears the marks of the patriarchal and hegemonic practices of those who composed and transmitted it is also a basic insight in some recent feminist scholarship. Elisabeth Schüssler Fiorenza insists that the *text* of the New Testament cannot be the starting point of theological discourse since its very inscription has come under the influence of "kyriarchy" and potentially or actually nonliberative practices (Schüssler Fiorenza 1995).[6] To use the Bible naively leads to the reinscription and validation of the practices that liberative theologies oppose. Instead, the documents of the New Testament must be subjected to a critique that arises from a critical recovery of the liberative praxis of the early Jesus movement. In such approaches to the theology of New Testament, the social practices and social location of the Jesus movement matter very much, for they

5. Mosala (1989:43–66) is also critical of the early attempts at a sociological analysis of biblical texts (W. Meeks, J. Gager, R. Wilson, and G. Theissen) for failing to attend sufficiently to the material conditions presupposed by the texts and concentrating instead on the ideological conflicts occasioned by the material conditions.

6. Schüssler Fiorenza (1983:52) earlier noted that the process of selecting a canon "manufactured the historical marginality of women" and thus distorted the reality of the early Jesus movement, which presented itself as "an *alternative* option to the dominant patriarchal structures" (107) and emphasized inclusiveness and the presence of the reign of God. The liberative praxis of the Jesus movement became the criterion for evaluating other aspects of piety: "Temple and Torah praxis must be *measured* and *evaluated* by whether or not they are inclusive of every person in Israel and whether they engender the wholeness of every human person" (120).

provide one of the bases for a critical analysis and (re)appropriation of the
Jesus tradition.

The Sayings Gospel Q has now been featured in theological syntheses
which do not exclude a priori non- and precanonical documents and which
take seriously not only the intellectual context of statements of faith, but the
social values and interests which they embody. More than two decades ago,
Q's theology found a place in Edward Schillebeeckx's work on the development of Christology (1975, ET 1979), where it served to illustrate one of
the three or four early patterns for articulating the saving significance of
Jesus. Now Indian theologian Rasiah S. Sugirtharajah has argued that wisdom theology and particular characteristics of Q—its use of common wisdom and tropes, its endorsement of universal human values such as
forgiveness, its claim that God is available to all, and in particular, its rejection of class distinctions and its attention to issues of poverty and margin-
alization—should be given special place in the articulation of an Indian
theology, faced with the dual problems of confrontation with other faiths
and systemic issues of poverty (Sugirtharajah 1990b). He suggests that the
image of the subversive sage is more compatible with Third World theologies than that of the apocalyptic prophet or the triumphalist and vanquish-
ing Christ, which, more often than not, has been employed to validate the
vested class and ideological interests of the privileged (Sugirtharajah 1990a;
1990b; 1991). The place that Schillebeeckx gave to Q had mainly to do with
its ideas; Sugirtharajah's conclusions have very much to do with the social
location and social interests of Q's subversive sage Christology.

Social historical studies of Q are still too recent to have made a wide
impact on theological syntheses, but there is at least some reason to believe
that they might influence theologies that are attentive to the issues of
renewal of local communities and the critique of ruling structures. In any
event, the Sayings Gospel, insofar as it represents a formulation of a rather
declassé social stratum and insofar as it differs notably in its shape from
formulations that derived from urban, wealthier, social locations (e.g., the
Pauline letters), provides an excellent site at which to examine the relation
between social location and ideological commitment.

The Rejection of Social Historical Studies of Q

As chapter 4 makes clear, there is disagreement as to how the social location
of the Q group is best characterized. There are some, however, who dissent
from the entire enterprise of inquiring into Q's social location. In some cases
the objection is framed quite generally—even dismissively—suggesting that
it is pure folly to speculate on the nature of a "Q community" (Hengel
1994:336). Such doubts are usually registered without any serious engagement with the existing methodological discussions of how one might

reasonably move from text to social location.[7] In a few cases, however, real arguments are given.

Meier, for example, questions the existence of a Q "community" by arguing (a) that there is no "historical proof that one and only one community either created, gathered, or carried the Q tradition," (b) that Q's use by Matthew and Luke "tells against [the] idea of one Q community," and (c) that a coherent theology cannot be reconstructed for Q (1994:179).[8] The argument fails on all three counts, however. First, most of the recent discussion of Q is *not* predicated on the assumption of a *single* "Q community." As I have noted above (p. 170), the very term "community" (*Gemeinde*) is problematic insofar as it inappropriately applies conceptual models from urban settings to that of largely rural Galilee. What is argued is that Q represents *one* textual response of Galilean Jesus people to the particular social and cultural circumstances in Galilee (mainly) prior to the First Revolt. One does not have to assume any particular *geographical* location of the Galilean Jesus people in one particular town or village in order to discuss their *social* location.

Meier's second argument is simply a non sequitur. The fact that Q was used by other persons or groups indicates little about its original composers or tradents. The fact that Mark was used by Matthew and Luke does not tell against the notions of a Markan community or of a social location for the second Gospel.

The third point—that Q lacks a coherent theological outlook—is both overstated and probably simply wrong. The discussion in chapter 3 has indicated that there is a broad consensus on several theological themes which give Q coherence. It has also been shown that Q exhibits fairly consistent rhetorical patterns. Social inferences may be drawn from both. If Meier's point is that not every saying in Q can be compassed by Q's overarching theological constructs or rhetorical patterns, the point is correct but overstated. It would be absurd to insist on a level of internal coherence for Q that no other New Testament writing exhibits either. The odd and seemingly contrary sayings found in the intracanonical Gospels and the divergent

7. See the discussions of method in J. H. Elliott 1993:60–83; Robbins 1996a; 1996b; Kloppenborg 1991.

8. Meier misadapts Wittgenstein's Tractarian proposition 7 ("Wovon man nicht sprechen kann, darüber muss man schweigen," "Whereof one cannot speak, thereof one must be silent": Wittgenstein 1922) to a situation of lacunae in historical *knowledge*. His use of Wittgenstein is inappropriate: *Tractatus* #7 concerns the situation of *speaking* of the sublime (logic, ethics, God), which is for Wittgenstein "nonsense" insofar as the one who speaks of the sublime has "given no meaning to certain signs in his propositions" because they do not belong to the propositions of natural science (# 6.52). Meier's hesitations about knowledge do not prevent him from "speaking" about Matthew's "community" or many other topics where historical knowledge is far from complete. (I am grateful to my wife Hami Verbin for explaining this passage in Wittgenstein.)

elements in the letters of Paul do not (and should not) prevent one from discussing the social location of such documents.

Meier's argument is also based on a false supposition. He wishes to characterize Q as a "grab bag" and seems to assume that social conclusions cannot be drawn from such miscellanies. But even miscellanies betray the
values of their composers and intended audiences. It is difficult to imagine
any ancient composer creating a document, and others transcribing and
transmitting that document, without the social location and values of its
author(s), tradents, and intended audience(s) being inscribed in the document. Q, however, is very far from being a miscellany or a random collection of sayings and, as chapter 4 has suggested, betrays a roughly coherent
set of data about its compilers and users.

The reticence to discuss the social location of Q is curious, since those
who doubt the existence of a social formation that supported the Sayings
Gospel normally do not register the same doubts about other documents
such as the Synoptic Gospels or John. This reticence seems to be a part of
the concern to leave Q as an untrammeled source of sayings of the historical Jesus. Meier's characterization of Q as a "grab bag" without a coherent
theology or a supporting "community" allows him to prescind from the literary and historical questions of its origin, tradents, and editorial tendencies, and to use Q simply as a "distinct and valuable source for sayings . . .
of Jesus and John" (1994:179–81). Meier uses Q much as Harnack did, as
a document without editorial bias. To skirt the issue of the social embed-
dedness of Q likewise allows him to avoid asking whether a particular saying ascribed by Q to Jesus has been colored by Q's social practice or perhaps
even created by those who framed the document.

Few today would treat any of the other Gospels analogously. Redaction
criticism insists that an analysis of the way in which a saying is deployed in
a literary setting is a fundamental first step, before asking anything about
prior or originary stages of the tradition. Social-historical criticism analogously insists that the Jesus tradition (say) in Luke is deployed in the first
place in such a way as to reflect and respond to the social situation of urban
Gentile Christians in the late first century. Sayings that are too congenial
with the overall editorial concerns of a particular evangelist or which
appear to be thoroughly colored by the social location of the evangelist are
normally suspect when it comes to judgments about authenticity. The same
consideration ought to apply to Q.[9] Of course, the social distance between

---

9. A case in point is Q 22:28-30, which is often treated as authentic (including by Meier
1997:653–59). Meier notes that both the Matthaean and Lukan locations are secondary and
that both locations provoke some redactional alterations. But then, without examining the
function and context of the saying in Q, Meier jumps to a judgment about authenticity, failing
to note that its concluding position in Q, the use of *krinō* (to judge) and the motif of judgment
of Israel all cohere rather well with Q's theology (Kloppenborg 1996b:326–28). It is at this
point that the consequences of Meier's treatment of Q as a "grab bag" become clear, for it

Jesus and the Jesus movement in Galilee in the 50s or 60s is not as great as the distance between Jesus and urban Lukan Christians in the 90s. But to circumvent issues of the redaction and transmissional context of Q is to treat Q by rules other than those applied to the Synoptic Gospels.

In other cases, resistance to the discussion of Q's social location and social posture seems to be a function of much deeper theological worries. Some of the worry is methodological. Traditional theological scholarship on the Gospels has privileged the categories of Christology, soteriology, and ecclesiology. Thus, for example, we have numerous treatments of Matthaean Christology, the function of the Torah in Matthaean soteriology, and Matthew's "church." Similar theological topics are discussed in respect to the other three Gospels, Pauline and pseudo-Pauline letters, James, Hebrews, and other books of the New Testament. It is a relatively simple matter to assemble the results of such studies and discuss "unity and diversity in New Testament theology," either as an end in itself or as a prolegomenon to a discussion of modern theological issues. Social-historical studies, by contrast, are by their nature tied to highly specific situations and cannot easily be pried loose or generalized. The analytic categories are demographics, social catchment, literacy levels, familial and political relations, marital patterns, mobility, economic relations, conflict and conflict management, patronage and clientalia, and so forth. The focus is not ideas but social practice, not in establishing antecedents for later ecclesial practices in other parts of the world but in understanding the practice and discourse of the Q people in their own environment.

It is not that Christology is unimportant or unworthy of investigation. Debates about the historical Jesus—whether he is best understood as a "charismatic" or an "eschatological prophet" or a "messianic sage" or a "visionary"—employ frames of reference that focus on *personal* characteristics of Jesus and thus permit an easy opening for christological discourse. By contrast, social-historical approaches are more likely to select categories that focus on social relationships and ask about the conditions under which a particular figure might have appeal to a particular social sector.

Crossan (1997), for example, is critical of Theissen's use of "charisma" as a quality of individuals. Crossan argues, following Bryan Wilson, that "charisma" is less a matter of personal characteristics than of relationships between a leader and a following:

> *Charisma* is a sociological, and not a psychological concept. . . . [I]t expresses the balance of claim and acceptance—it is not a dynamic, causally explanatory, concept; it relates to an established state of affairs, when the leader is already accepted, not to the power of one man to cause events to move in a particular direction. (Wilson 1973:499)

---

allows him to sidestep an otherwise serious difficulty in defending the authenticity of the saying.

A social-historical account of Jesus as a "charismatic" will inquire not into Jesus' self-consciousness or intentions but into the social state of affairs that accounts for the particular appeal that Jesus (or an image of Jesus) had for his following and the social endowment of power expressed through their endorsement of the leader. That is, social-historical approaches are much more likely to treat "Christology" not as description of the unique characteristics of Jesus but as the collective act of a group, employing a memory of Jesus in its articulation of a symbolic universe.

It is the invoking of a different explanatory framework—one based on social relationships and the ways in which beliefs and ideas are socially situated—that occasions deeps concerns about social-historical analyses. It should be obvious that the results of social-historical criticism are not as immediately amenable to theological conversion as those of ideational approaches to the early Jesus movement. In some instances, social-scientific approaches have been rejected as reductionist, that is, as treating the whole of the early Christian phenomenon as strictly a function of unconscious social, sociopsychological, and economic factors. This charge is unfair: social-historical approaches are not necessarily any more reductionist than other historical approaches. As Scroggs notes, however, by underscoring the highly specific social circumstances that accompanied particular beliefs, a social-historical approach "increases the awareness of the *contextualism* of the New Testament statements. . . . Sociological analysis thus makes it more obviously problematic to claim those statements as directly revelatory for other social contexts" (1986:140, emphasis original). Thus at least some of the resistance to the social-historical treatment of Q and other documents of the Jesus movement seems to derive from the fear that it will evacuate or render questionable theological applications.

A Dog among the Pigeons: A Cynic Q?

A particularly telling instance of the collision of traditional scholarship with social-historical approaches is provided by the recent debate about the "cynic-like Q."[10] The course of the debate exposes the often-unstated ideological concerns that lurk beneath the surface of supposedly critical historiography and exemplify how Q scholarship has become a lightning rod for such ideological concerns.

The thesis propounded by Leif Vaage, Gerald Downing, and Burton Mack and outlined in chapter 4 is that the closest analogy to Q's social

---

10. I use "cynic-like" and "cynic hypothesis" (both without capitalization) rather than "Cynic" to underscore the point that Vaage and Mack (and Crossan, on the historical Jesus) do not argue that Q (or Jesus) was "influenced" or "dependent" on Greco-Roman Cynics, but rather that Cynicism provides a particularly apt *analogy* for understanding Q (or Jesus). The term "cynic hypothesis" will refer to the hypothesis advanced by Vaage and Mack without the genealogical assumptions that are often falsely ascribed to it.

posture is found in Greco-Roman Cynicism.[11] It has provoked muscular opposition.[12] Many of the objections that have been voiced take the *form* of historical arguments—that the data do not fit the argument, or that the data admit of too many other interpretations, or that the data are just too sparce to permit certain conclusions. It is only when one compares the objections raised against the cynic hypothesis with the way in which other conclusions about Q are established that one begins to wonder whether more is at stake.

Although there has not yet been a thoroughgoing analysis that responds to the hypothesis at the same level of detail with which it has been propounded, preliminary criticism has raised several types of objections: (1) diversity within Cynicism, both synchronic and diachronic, makes the comparison of Q and Cynicism difficult; (2) the dearth of Cynic sources from the time of Cercidas (III BCE) to Demetrius (mid-I CE) raises the possibility that Cynicism lacked real influence during the intervening centuries; (3) the supposition that Cynics were present in Galilee may be no more than, in Betz's words, "a fanciful conjecture";[13] (4) the genre and structure of Q are not sufficiently close to Cynic lives to make for a cogent comparison; (5) stratigraphical and compositional analyses of Q do not support its characterization as cynic-like; and (6) some of the alleged Cynic parallels are either not exclusively Cynic or not Cynic at all; or there is an imperfect overlap of the standard topoi of Cynicism and those of Q; or that despite some similarities between Cynics and the Q people, their respective presuppositions and motivations were quite different.[14]

11. Downing 1988a; 1988b; 1992; 1994; Vaage 1987; 1994; 1995; Mack 1988b; 1993. See also Cameron 1990b; Seeley 1992.

12. For critiques, see Tuckett 1989; 1996:368–91; Horsley 1991c; Betz 1994; Robinson 1994a; 1996; 1997; Ebner 1996; Eddy 1996; Arnal 1997d; Aune 1997. Witherington (1994:117–45; 1995:58–92, esp. 59–64) offers a popularizing critique of characterizations of Jesus as a Cynic but gives scant attention either to the primary evidence or to recent studies of Cynicism.

13. Betz 1994:471; repeated by Eddy 1996:467; Witherington 1995:61 ("for the most part conjecture").

14. Betz (1994:462–70) offers an erudite account of the rebirth of interest in ancient Cynicism in Schopenhauer, Schlegel, and Nietzsche and shows that Nietzsche came very close to regarding Jesus as a Cynic. But Betz's criticism that the current interest in a Cynic Jesus (or Cynic Q) is "severely compromised by its proponents' failure to examine the history of reception and interpretation, in particular its version in the nineteenth and twentieth centuries" (p. 474) is vacuous. Betz himself makes no effort to indicate *how* the history of the nineteenth- and twentieth-century reception of Cynicism may affect our evaluation of the comparison of Q or Jesus with Cynicism. Does the association of Cynicism with Nietzsche help to account for the panic that is seen when scholars of Christian origins dare to associate Q and Cynicism? Has the revival of interest in Cynicism in the nineteenth century allowed for valid historical comparisons to be made? Or does it obscure much better analogies? What interests are served by such a comparison? What interests are threatened by the comparison? Until Betz clarifies some of these questions, it remains wholly unclear just how the thesis is "severely compromised."

While all of these points have some merit, many have been rebutted effectively by Vaage, Seeley, and Downing.[15] Here is not the place to review the evidence that has been mustered for and against the hypothesis. Instead, I wish to draw attention to the *conduct* of the debate and, in particular, the lack of comparative parity in assessing evidence and argument. The reaction to the cynic hypothesis seems out of proportion to the nature of the evidence and argument adduced by its proponents. By this I mean that the comparison with Cynicism is defended by Vaage, Downing, and Mack in much the same way that other comparisons are ventured: by assembling a series of parallel texts which approximate the language of Q, accompanied by an attempt to read Q in a coherent manner with such texts in view. It is a rather easy matter to find analogous attempts to read Q as a sapiential text, as a prophetic text, or as a set of apocalyptic traditions, employing precisely the same forms of argument. The effort to read Q alongside Cynic texts, however, has met vigorous opposition and the ad hoc imposition of standards of comparison which, if applied to these more usual comparisons, would equally rule them out of court. The fact that these other comparisons have not been criticized with a similar energy and that critical parity has not been achieved (or even attempted) in the assessment of the cynic hypothesis suggests that it has touched a very deep nerve. I will suggest that this nerve is not historiographic, but theological.

None of the objections to the cynic hypothesis, so far as I am aware, is explicitly theological in form. That is, no one objects, "Q cannot be cynic-like, because such a view would render a particular theological commitment or conclusion problematic." Nevertheless, I wish to suggest that the best way to account for the curious conduct of the argument against the cynic hypothesis is to suppose that theological, rather than merely historiographic, interests play a role in assessment. This is itself a dangerous venture, for I am trying to peer beneath the ostensible arguments to the deeper ideological issues that lurk beneath the surface. In doing so, I do not wish to suggest that the scholars such as Tuckett[16] who have raised objection to Vaage, Mack, and Downing are simply cloaking their theological objections in historical dress. That would be unfairly demeaning and would grossly underestimate the care and erudition with which Tuckett mounts his arguments. I do wish to suggest, however, that the cynic hypothesis and its criticism have exposed important theoretical issues bearing on the relationship between historical data, social-historical modeling, and theological scholar-

15. Vaage 1995 (responding to Tuckett); Seeley 1996; 1997 (a response to Eddy); Downing 1998 (also responding to Eddy).

16. Tuckett 1989; 1996:369–73. I focus on Tuckett's arguments precisely because they are so carefully presented. Others (e.g., Witherington 1995:58–64) have dismissed the Cynic analogy, merely echoing Tuckett. My interest in all this is not to single out Tuckett's otherwise outstanding volume for special criticism, but rather to draw attention to a rather pervasive failure to achieve argumentative parity in the assessment of comparative data.

ship. An analysis of portions of the debate will allow us to see how the cynic hypothesis has problematized various dearly held theological positions.

Before inquiring into the theological issues that are engaged by the cynic hypothesis, it will be useful to illustrate my point about comparative parity, with special reference to three of the objections listed above. The first has to do with the dating of Cynic parallel texts; the second concerns the question of whether there were Cynics in Galilee; and the third, diversity in Cynicism.

THE DATING OF CYNIC PARALLELS

One of the criticisms that has been offered has to do with the dating of the Cynic materials. Tuckett, for example, argues that Cynicism "seems to have faded away quite considerably in the second and first centuries BCE, but to have revived in importance in the second half of the first century CE with figures such as Demetrius and Epictetus writing about the Cynic ideal."[17]

Tuckett here relies on the classic position articulated by D. R. Dudley a generation ago that between the time of Cercidas (ca. 290–220 BCE) and Demetrius (I CE), Cynicism was largely eclipsed (even though the figure of the Cynic sometimes appeared in literature).[18] Tuckett concedes to Downing that Cicero knew some of the Cynic epistles in first-century BCE Rome (*Tusculan Disputations* 5.90) but passes over rather too quickly Downing's long list of evidence of Cynicism in the first centuries BCE and CE. Other evidence includes the *Epistles* of Pseudo-Crates 1–29, which Malherbe places in the first century BCE, the *Epistles* of Heraclitus (first century CE), and the

---

17. Tuckett 1996:373. Eddy (1996:451) first refers to the "debate" concerning whether Cynicism truly "died out" during the second and first centuries BCE, or "merely suffered a low profile" (citing Billerbeck 1991 for the first view, and Moles 1983 for the second). But by the end of the article (p. 467) he seems to have decided in favor of Billerbeck, but without any argument: "The dating problem is exacerbated by the fact that the Imperial revival of Cynicism, which replaced its dearth from the second century BCE on, is not attested until the *middle* of the first century—and thus *after* the death of Jesus and the birth of the Christian movement" (emphasis original).

18. Dudley 1937:esp. 117–124. A similar view is taken by Billerbeck 1979; 1991:esp. 148. A careful reading of Dudley shows that his position is not as blunt as is often implied by those who cite him against advocates of the cynic hypothesis. Dudley point out that there is evidence of Cynicism in this period, though it suggests that Cynicism was "obscure and unimportant" (1937:117). Yet he also notes that "street preachers were familiar enough in Rome towards the end of the first century B.C., as we gather from Horace's references to such persons as Fabius, Crispinus and Stertinius," and that there is "nothing to distinguish them from the Cynics of Hellenistic times as far as their creed goes," even though they called themselves Stoics. Moreover, Dudley points out that in the Greek East the evidence of survival is scant though less ambiguous, referring to Meleager, Diocles of Magnesia (Diogenes Laertius 6.104), and Antipater of Thessalonica; *P. Berol.* inv. 13044 (ca. 100 BCE); the Vienna Diogenes Papyrus (i.e., *P. Vindob.* G. 29946; I BCE); and some of the Cynic epistles, which date from the Augustan period (1937:123).

Epistles of Pseudo-Socrates 1–7 (first century CE or earlier).[19] To this should be added Moles's observation that Cicero treated Cynicism as a live option in his day.[20] More recently Griffen (1996) has shown that in the late Republic it was necessary for Stoics to disown certain sorts of behavior as Cynic, which would be hardly necessary if Cynics were simply a literary memory.

To the list of contemporary Cynics we should add Avidienus (Horace, *Satires* 2.2.55-62) from the first century BCE, and Carneades (Eunapius, *Vita Philosophorum* 2.1.5), Didymus (Plutarch, *De defectu oraculorum* 7.412F-413D), Hermodotus (in an epigram by Lucilius in the *Anthologia Graeca* 11.154), Menestratus (*Anthologia Graeca* 11.153) from the first century CE. In the 60s of the common era, Seneca had a Cynic friend, Demetrius of Corinth; other Cynics are mentioned during the time of Nero (Isidorus: Suetonius, *Nero* 39.5-6; Menippus of Lycia: Eunapius, *Vita Philosophorum* 2.1.5; Philostratus, *Vita Apollonii* 4.25) and Vespasian (Diogenes the Sophist and Heras: Cassius Dio 65.15).[21]

While much of this evidence pertains to Rome, there are data from the East: Meleager of Gadara (135–50 BCE), who moved to Tyre and Cos, and his contemporary Diocles of Magnesia (in Asia Minor). Allusions to Cynicism are found in Antipater of Thessalonica (time of Augustus, *Anthologia Graeca* 11.158), and the awareness of Cynicism is displayed by Dio Chrysostom (40–after 112 CE).[22] Just as important are papyri with Cynic chriae or allusions to Cynic teachings: *P. Berol.* inv. 13044, dated by Wilcken to 100 BCE and echoing Onesicritus's account of Alexander's meeting with the gynosophists, wearing Cynic mantles;[23] and *P. Vindob. G.* 29946, a fragmentary collection of Diogenes chriae dating from the first

---

19. On Pseudo-Crates: Malherbe 1977:10; the *Epistle* of Heraclitus: Malherbe 1977:22; Attridge 1976; Ps-Socrates 1-7: Malherbe 1977:27. For the problem of Cynicism in the first century, see in general Hock 1992.

20. See Moles 1983:esp. 120–23, who revisits Dudley's argument concerning the eclipse of Cynicism in the second and first centuries BCE. Moles points to several evidences of the continuous survival of Cynicism, especially Cicero, *De Officiis* 1.128; 1.148; *De Finibus* 3.68, where Cicero treats Cynicism as "an option at the time of writing" (1983:122). He suggests against Dudley that the apparent demise of Cynicism in this period is a matter of scant sources rather than of actual demise.

21. See Goulet-Cazé, 1990; 1996; Billerbeck 1979. Varro (116–27 BCE) was known by some as a Cynic because he imitated Cynic satire (Cicero, *Academica* 1.8; Aulus Gellius, *Attic Nights* 2.18; Tertullian, *Apologeticus* 14.9) and Horace (65–8 BCE) has one of his characters enunciate Cynic teachings (*Satire* 2.7.83-88). But, as Dudley points out, "there is no reason to suppose that in the Republic Diogenes would have commanded a much better rate of exchange" and that Varro's imitation of Cynic style does not make him a Cynic (1937:119).

22. On Philo of Alexandria (ca. 30 BCE–45 CE) as a witness to Cynicism, see Dudley (1937:186–87), who argues that the influence is purely literary.

23. Diels 1904 (cf. Pack 1965:no. 2068). On the dating, see Wilcken 1923. The pairing of gynosophists with the Cynics seems to have begun with Onesicritus, a companion of Alexander (Strabo 15.1.63–65; Plutarch, *Alexander*, 65).

century BCE.[24] Finally, as Downing has more recently noted, the pervasive influence of the Diogenes tradition on the *Progymnasmata*, textbooks for elementary rhetorical instruction, suggests that those studying rhetoric would encounter Cynics, on the page at least, if not in person: "anyone learning Greek in Palestine would be likely to be introduced to Cynicism, in this way if in no other, and be provided with good stories and witty comments—and a radical ethos—to pass on, in the original or in translation" (Downing 1998:102).

Technically, Tuckett is correct. We have Cynic data from the late republican Rome and the time of Augustus, and again, from the time of Nero. But when Tuckett refers to the "awkward gap in our extant evidence" about the actual activity of Cynics in the first half of the first century CE" (1989:373), he imposes a standard on the evidence that, if extended to other sets of data, would disqualify all comparisons and analogies. The Dead Sea Scrolls, which have been exploited widely to establish the context for all sorts of beliefs of the early Jesus movement, date mainly from the second and first century BCE, not the first century CE. The same is true of *1 Enoch* and Sirach. Rabbinic evidence is derived from a document compiled in the early third century CE. *2 Baruch* and *4 Ezra* are at least half a century after Q. Yet no one speaks of an "awkward gap" in our knowledge of Judaism at the time of Q. Of course many gaps exist in our documentation of practically every social, political, economic, and religious aspect of antiquity. Such gaps, however, do not paralyze scholarship. Rather, they invite cautious and disciplined extrapolations of the existing data, just as is routinely and unblinkingly done in the case of the standard reconstructions of "Judaism in the time of Jesus."

It is often forgotten that the conclusions drawn by Dudley on the eclipse of Cynicism between Cercidas and Demetrius pertain mainly to Rome. For the Greek East Dudley himself concluded that Cynicism survived "in obscurity, attracting far less attention than had been the case in the third century" (when it had been highly visible) (1937:124). But he also concludes that Cynic literature continued to have a "considerable influence." Copies of Diogenes chriae on papyri and the use of Diogenes chriae in *Progymnasmata* indeed suggest that sufficient Cynic materials were in principle available to persons in the first half of the first century.

The cynic hypothesis does not require that Cynics be attested in large numbers in the early first century CE. It does not require that there were any contemporary high-profile Cynics such as Diogenes or Demetrius. It only requires one of two assumptions: either that there were still *some* Cynics or persons who would be identified as cynic-like on the basis of their dress, behavior, or teaching; or that the *literary* figure of the Cynic and the basic

---

24. Wessely 1902 [I BCE] (=Pack 1965:no. 1987; cited in Kloppenborg 1987a:340). See also Crönert 1906:49–53.

profile of Cynic behavior and teaching were sufficiently well known to be recognized when they were encountered in a *literary* presentation of Jesus—which is, after all, precisely what Q is. It is clear from the data cited above that both of these assumptions are reasonable. The dismissal of Cynic parallels on grounds of date would appear to misuse Dudley and to overlook several of important evidences.

CYNICS IN GALILEE?

A second type of objection rests on the assumption that, irrespective of the dating of Cynic materials, Cynics were not likely to have been found near the persons responsible for Q. The general point it made (and tediously repeated) was that Cynicism was an urban phenomenon, while the cultural setting of the Galilee was mainly rural.[25] This appears to ignore Downing's observation that "there is actually much more evidence for Cynics out of town in the sources, even if not in the standard generalizations. And many moved around—that is, through the countryside, on foot, at walking pace, where else and how else?"[26]

Of course no one ignores the fact that the Galilee contained two large cosmopolitan centers, Sepphoris and Tiberias, both with mixed populations (Galileans, Judaeans, some Greeks, ruling elite, retainers, and others). The population of the Galilee in general appears to be rather high,[27] and both Tiberias and Sepphoris had populations of perhaps 24,000.[28] While such populations do not rival the great metropolises of Alexandria, Antioch, or Rome, the Galilean cities were far from insignificant. A decade ago, in commenting on Downing's thesis, Hengel seemed to have no difficulty in imagining the presence of Cynics in Sepphoris:

---

25. Tuckett 1989:358; Eddy 1996:462; Aune 197:191.

26. Downing 1998:99–100 and n. 16, citing Downing 1992:26–56, esp. 26–30, 45–52, 82–84, 148–149; Lucian, *Demonax* 1 (referring to an otherwise unknown Sostratus who lived in the open on Mount Parnassus) and *Philosophies for Sale*, 10 (which advises the would-be Cynic to "frequent the *most crowded place* and in those very places desire to be solitary and uncommunicative, greeting neither friend nor stranger"). The latter text seems not to support Downing's point.

27. Broshi (1979) sets the population of Western Palestine at about one million, making it one of the more densely populated regions of the empire. Safrai (1994:436) suggests that Broshi's figures, which are based on maximum estimates of grain-growing capacity, may be too low for the Byzantine period, when the available land may have been farmed more intensively than Broshi assumed. Goodman (1983:32) estimates the population of the Galilee about 135 CE at 300,000—the bulk of which would be in the Lower Galilee.

28. Reed (1994:213–14) estimates Tiberias at 24,000, based on a probable size of 80 hectares and a population coefficient of 300 persons per hectare. See also Avi-Yonah 1960. Overman (1988:164) estimated Sepphoris at 30,000, but Reed has reduced this to 24,000, based on an area of 50–60 hectares within the walls and another 50 hectares outside. Josephus (*War* 2.608) puts the population of Magdala-Taricheae at 40,000, but this appears too high.

Why should not the craftsman Jesus, who grew up in the neighbourhood of Sepphoris, have made contact with Cynic itinerant preachers, especially as he himself spoke some Greek? . . . These affinities between Gospel traditions and Cynic religious and social criticism [discussed by Downing] go right back to Jesus himself. (Hengel 1989:44)

In the meantime, however, opponents of the cynic hypothesis have attempted to obviate this possibility. Tuckett observes rightly that the Gospels (and Q) refer to small towns and villages in the Galilee (but not to Sepphoris and Tiberias). This, he claims, "would appear to make the theory of Cynic influence rather less probable" (1989:358). To this Eddy adds two points: (a) that while the Galilee might have been hellenized, hellenization would probably not have affected very deeply the local populations, being restricted mainly to the rulers and administrative hopefuls; and (b) that the political and economic rift between urbanized, hellenized centers and the surrounding villages implies that, if anything, Jesus (and, presumably Q) would not have been influenced positively by Sepphoris (Eddy 1996: 464–65).

As a general comment, one might observe that there is again a glaring lack of comparative parity between the evaluation of the cynic hypothesis and other claims of ideological "influence." There is a large body of scholarship, for example, that claims influence on the Jesus movement, including Q, from Qumran. The Qumran covenanters, however, were not rural, Galilean, peasant farmers, or artisans. They enjoyed a much higher literacy standard than the largely illiterate population of the Galilee. They were relatively inaccessible to Galileans—even those traveling to Jerusalem. And they espoused a priestly ideology and communal practice that are not likely to have had much currency in the Galilee. Yet it would be rare to find in the studies that wish to relate the Qumran texts to the world of the Galilean Jesus movement any reflections on the geopolitical, social, and ideological gulfs between Qumran and Galilee that would make direct influence rather unlikely. When detractors of the cynic hypothesis insist on careful attention to the highly differentiated social and ideological map of Jewish Palestine and do not do the same when assessing other hypotheses, the insistence looks oddly disingenuous.

Tuckett's inference that Cynics, were they in Sepphoris, would still not likely have influenced the Q folk, ignores much of the available literature on the interactions between city and countryside in antiquity.[29] The well-known phenomenon of periodic market days, regional markets, and fairs, all well attested in Roman Palestine, would naturally have brought inhabitants of the villages of the Lower Galilee into periodic contact with urban areas. Eddy's supposition that hellenization (and hence, presumably, Cynic

29. See, e.g., Rich and Wallace-Hadrill 1991; Rich 1992. On Galilee specifically: Adan-Bayewitz and Perlman 1990; Overman 1993.

influence) would have pertained mainly to the ruling gentry is curious, since if anything is clear it is that Cynics, though present mainly in cities, were consistently critical of the polis and used the gentry as their typical targets (Moles 1996). His conclusion that Jesus (and the Q people) would not likely have been inclined in that direction assumes a monolithic view of culture and a single and uniform model of adhesion and repulsion. This is plainly not the way in which cultural interaction works. It would be tedious to point out the numerous examples of cultural critique that takes the form of adopting aspects of the dominant or opponent culture in order to criticize it more effectively. The imitation of colonialist religions in so-called cargo cults (Worsley 1969) or the adoption of Western computer and communication technology by Islamic fundamentalists as instruments for their ideological opposition to "Western values" are cases in point.[30]

Without appealing to Cynics at all, Freyne and Arnal have made a plausible case for assuming that much of Q's rhetoric is born from anxieties over the urbanization and monetization of the Galilee and the baneful effects on land-ownership patterns, taxation, and local economies that resulted from this.[31] City–countryside friction, amply attested in Josephus, provides a social context in which cynic-*like* critique of the polis and its functionaries might plausibly take root and flourish.

Still, the historical question remains: were there Cynics in Sepphoris or Tiberias? Tuckett observes that Josephus, who is otherwise well informed about the Galilee, says nothing of Cynics (1996:375). Eddy adds that the cynic hypothesis presupposes a thoroughly hellenized situation in the Lower Galilee, which is not supported by archaeological evidence.[32] He concedes that Cynics were indeed present across the Kinneret in Gadara,[33] but seems to agree with Betz's assessment:

> The presumed presence of Cynics in the Galilean society in which Jesus lived is mostly a fanciful conjecture. The evidence for Cynicism is limited to Gadara and Tyre, Hellenistic cities outside the Galilee, though smaller cities existed in Galilee itself, especially Sepphoris. It is, therefore, wrong to make up for our lack of evidence by projecting a sophisticated urban culture replete with Cynics into every part of Galilee and then to place a Cynic-inspired sayings source Q together with the Jesus movement in this Galilee.[34]

---

30. Seeley (1997:710) make a similar point, adducing 4 Maccabees' use of Greek, Hellenistic rhetoric, and Hellenistic philosophy in its critique of Greek culture.

31. Freyne 1995a; 1995b; 1997; Arnal 1997d. See also Piper 1995.

32. Eddy 1996:466–67. Similarly, Aune 1997:188: "There is, furthermore, no literary or archaeological evidence for a Cynic presence in first-century Galilee." One wonders just what sort of archaeological evidence Aune has in mind that would indicate Cynic presence.

33. See Downing 1992:147; Tuckett 1996:374. Cynics at Gadara include Menippus of Gadara (early III BCE), Meleager of Gadara (135–50 BCE), and Oenomaus of Gadara (II CE).

34. Betz 1994:471–72; similarly, Tuckett 1996:374.

Of course none of the proponents of a cynic-like Q imagines a "sophisticated urban culture replete with Cynics into every part of Galilee." Apart of its obvious overstatement, however, Betz's point is unfortunate, for he seems not to be aware of the strong economic ties between Tyre and both the upper and Lower Galilee.[35] Moreover, the trade route that lead from Gadara to Akko-Ptolemais passed through Tiberias before turning west at Arbela, crossing the Tir'an Valley, and along to Sepphoris. One branch of the main road from Damascus to the coastal plain passed Bethaida, Kefar Naḥum, and Tarichaeae (Magdala) before joining the road to Akko-Ptolemais. Another branch passed Khorazin before going west along the base of Meiron massif. Hence, while it is perfectly correct that we have no reports of Cynics in the Galilee, circumstantial evidence ought to lead us to expect that those who lived along these major routes were likely to have come into contact with all sorts of persons—soldiers, traveling merchants, refugees, magicians, hucksters, scribes, philosophers—even Cynics.

To be sure, we do not have positive evidence of Cynics at Sepphoris or Tiberias. We do not have much evidence about the demography of these two cities at all. Josephus is virtually our only source for the period. His interests in detailing the course of war with Rome—or, to be more precise, the short period between 66 and 67 CE when he was captured at Yodefat—and the principal groups he variously exploited and opposed would hardly have extended to the description of unorganized, individual dissenters whose political impact was mostly likely negligible. If there were Cynics in the Galilee, Josephus is unlikely to have been bothered to mention them. His silence tells us very little.

Again, my point is here is not to defend the contention that there were Cynics in the Galilee. I simply do not know. Rather, the point is to observe that the *dismissal* of the possibility of a Cynic presence in the Galilee is utterly premature, based either on an ignorance of physical geography or on a priori notions of what Galileans "could" and "could not" have been or have known, or both.

DIVERSITY IN CYNICISM AND THE COGENCY OF PARALLELS

A third area which illustrates lapses in argumentative logic has to do with the definition of ancient Cynicism and the analysis of alleged parallels.[36]

---

35. Most of the Upper Galilee is within a 25 km radius of Tyre. There is ample numismatic evidence of the economic dominance of Tyre in the region.

36. Betz 1994:474 lists two "problems" with the cynic hypothesis in regard to the use of parallels. First, he points out that "we have different versions of Q, among which a given saying may be close to Cynic parallels in one version, and quite different in another." Parallels with Cynicism are not restricted to Q "but can be found in other parts of the New Testament as well." This hardly constitutes a serious objection: whether or not other NT documents have Cynic parallels is irrelevant to the case with regard to Q. Even if Betz is correct that there are multiple versions of Q and that some are closer to Cynicism than others, it is hard to see how

Tuckett makes the sensible points that Cynic sources are diverse, that some of Downing's parallels (in Musonius Rufus, Seneca, and Epictetus outside Book Three) are Stoic rather than Cynic, that some of characteristics cited as Cynic are not exclusively Cynic, and that there were real differences among Cynics, some adopting austere forms, and others milder or "hedonistic" forms.[37] Betz also notes the diversity within Cynicism, suggests treating Cynic figures individually, and calls for careful distinctions between idealizations, satirical depictions, school traditions, and so forth.[38]

One might have expected the point about diversity to issue in an effort to lay out a spectrum of Cynic types and to inquire whether Q might be compassed by this diversity. Oddly, however, it is presented as an objection to the hypothesis. Needless to say, diversity within Judaism has not prevented scholars from discussing Q's place within Judaism.

A seemingly contradictory objection is make with respect to specific parallels. Apropos of Downing's citation of Epictetus's description of the Cynic's duty to love those who beat him (*Diss.* 3.22.53-54) as a parallel to Q 6:27-28, Tuckett objects that "Diogenes is often portrayed as very far from exhibiting such a generous attitude to his 'enemies.'"[39] This makes Diogenes of Sinope into the benchmark for all Cynic behavior and ignores both the fact that a Cynic such as Crates was far more philanthropic than Diogenes, and that Q 11:39-52 portrays Jesus as using rather strong and insulting words against his opponents. Thus, it both ignores the prior objection about Cynic diversity and just as conveniently ignores the non-philanthropic aspects of Q's Jesus.

---

this is a "problem" for Downing or Vaage. Second, Betz states: "Although Downing's collection may be useful at this point, a more precise interpretation of the material is still a desideratum." But Betz does not offer one, and so, even if we agree with his general and innocuous point that precise interpretation of the parallel materials will be important, Betz provides no concrete reason for thinking that a particular parallel is a good or poor one, let alone that the entire assemblage of parallels is telling or not. The criticism is vacuous.

37. Tuckett 1989:351–52; similarly, Eddy 1996:459. For the distinction of austere and hedonistic Cynicism, see Dudley 1937:42–53, comparing the more austere Diogenes with the "philanthropic" Crates, and Malherbe 1978; 1982.

38. Betz 1994:473: "Consequently, every Cynic philosopher at this time has to be treated in his own special way. Also, one needs to make literary distinctions between school traditions, idealized and satirical portraits, and attempts, such as that by Diogenes Laertius, to create a Cynic school on the analogy of other philosophical schools." None of this, of course, constitutes a "major problem" for the cynic hypothesis, only a list of desiderata in careful historical comparison.

39. Tuckett 1989:366. Witherington (1995:124) makes the dubious distinction that Jesus, unlike the Cynics, did not engage in acts of public indecency (he has in mind accounts of Diogenes defecating and masturbating in public). Like Tuckett, Witherington arbitrarily selects *one* Cynic figure (Diogenes of Sinope) and treats him as the measure of all Cynic behavior. (Witherington shows very little acquaintance with primary sources, but seems largely dependent upon the treatment of Cynicism in Ferguson 1993.) Apparently for Witherington, Jesus' eating with disreputables, speaking with women in public, breaching Sabbath customs, and disrupting the Temple are somehow not cases of public indecency.

A yet more striking instance of an odd argument is the tedious point that Q's prohibition of the *pera* and staff (10:4) was a conscious rejection of Cynic behavior,[40] especially when this is coupled with the two preceding arguments—as it is in Tuckett and Eddy—that Cynics could not have influenced Q by reason of the date of Cynic sources and geography. It is patently illogical to wish to have it both ways. Either Cynics were present to influence Q's depiction of Jesus, whether positively or negatively, or they were not, in which case Q 10:4 cannot be "anti-Cynic." One cannot gnaw one's Cynic bone and bury it.

The objection to the parallel, however, is itself problematic, since it reifies one *typical* portrait of Cynic attire and falsely makes it the *criterion* for all Cynics. It is simply not the case that all Cynics carried a staff and a *pera*, though both were often part of Cynic attire. Teles, for example, advised against taking a *pera* (O'Neil 1977:47) and Diogenes is said to have gone without a staff (Dio 6.60).[41] The point made by Downing and Vaage is that the mention in Q of the trio "sandals —staff—*pera*" would likely recall typical Cynic attire and thereby invite comparison with Cynics.

James M. Robinson, not a supporter of the hypothesis, nonetheless acknowledges the striking character of some of the parallels adduced and calls on critics to "desist from their shocked, indeed reproachful tone about the Cynic comparison until they have shown that Q 12:22-31 has a closer matrix elsewhere."[42] In fact, the Cynic comparison gains at least part of its plausibility from the inability of interpreters to supply similarly close analogies for various of Q's sayings, in particular Q 9:59-60; 10:4; and 12:22-31.

I do not wish to suggest that the cynic hypothesis is without more substantial objections as a historical thesis.[43] In my view, the case for a cynic-like Q has yet to be made effectively. There are, nevertheless, interesting and puzzling parallels with Cynicism that cry out for exploration, not simple dismissal. Beyond the many literary and argumentative parallels is the fact, adduced by Goulet-Cazé (1990), that in Roman times Cynicism flourished

40. Tuckett 1989:367–68, citing Kee 1980:58: "The fact that the restrictions on the Christian itinerants were more severe than those placed on Cynic preachers . . . suggests that *there was a conscious differentiation* between the Christian charismatics and the cynics, even though the basic methods of itinerancy and public preaching were so similar." (The italics are not Kee's but Tuckett's.) A similar argument was made by Theissen 1973:259, and the point is repeated by Horsley 1989b:117 ("almost as *anti*-Cynic"); Eddy 1996:462 (citing Horsley approvingly).
41. See Vaage 1995:208–10, citing Diogenes Laertius 6.22-23 (on the staff) and 6.102 (on the rough cloak); Seeley 1997:706; Downing 1998:98; Aune 1997:183. See now the essay by Clay (1996), which details significant variations in the portraiture of Diogenes.
42. Robinson 1997:225. Witherington (1995:133–34) offers Prov 6:6 as a better parallel but does not appear to notice that the point is *opposite* to the Cynic point of Dio 10.15-16.
43. Aune (1997) makes the important point that while there are interesting parallels with individual Cynics' sayings, there is less evidence of the structurally central Cynic virtue of *autarcheia* (self-sufficiency) and *askesis* (training). See the further discussion in Robinson 1997; Kloppenborg Verbin 1999.

among disenfranchised persons. This is especially significant in light of current inclinations to see Q as representing Galileans who experienced a significant degree of disenfranchisement. It is also worth pondering the fact that Cynicism, at least in Rome, assumed a critical posture vis-à-vis the elite (including the emperor)—so much so that Stoics felt obliged to purge their Cynic heritage—and that Q's rhetoric is deeply committed to a proclamation of the coming reign of God which will invert (and does invert) social privilege (Q 14:11, 16-24) and economic patterns (Q 6:20, 30; 11:4). This does not make Q Cynic, though it is perhaps cynic-like. It does call for serious inquiry.

Theological Subtexts in Historical Criticism

The usual alternative to a cynic-like Q is to assert that Q reflects a prophetic movement, either endorsing the renewal of village life in Galilee or anticipating the imminent inauguration of the reign of God. Horsley is perhaps the most vocal advocate of the former option and opponent of the cynic hypothesis. Koester, who espouses a stratigraphy of Q not unlike mine, has recently argued that the Jesus of Q is "an eschatological prophet who announces the presence of the kingdom."[44] Tuckett concludes his article on Q and Cynicism with the simple statement:

> By contrast, Q does appeal frequently to the Jewish prophetic traditions as providing such precedents [viz. of the persecution of Christians 6:22, etc.]. In his recent book, M. Sato has impressively portrayed the strength of the parallels between Q and Jewish prophetic traditions. "Q und Prophetie" seems perhaps a more promising avenue of approach for the analysis of Q than an allegedly Cynic Q. (Tuckett 1989:376)

What is noteworthy here is that having dispensed with the Cynic analogy on the grounds of the dating and provenance of the comparative materials or the nonexact "fit" of parallel traditions, no one seems to feel obliged to defend the "prophetic analogy" similarly. Were there prophets in the Galilee? If there were, they are not mentioned by Josephus, who describes prophetic figures active in Judaea, one in Samaria, but *none* in the Galilee during the first century CE.[45] Freyne observes that "none of the [prophetic]

---

44. Koester 1997:153. Similarly, Tuckett 1996:391–92: "rather than being a demonstration of Cynic virtues of freedom from possessions, the [wandering] life-style demonstrates, in a kind of prophetic symbolic 'sign' analogous to prophetic actions in the OT, the total trust and confidence in God who is about the inaugurate the kingdom. . . ."

45. Horsley (1995c:268–71) mentions Judas son of Hezekiah (Josephus, *Ant.* 17.271; *War* 2.56), who led an abortive uprising in Sepphoris in 4 BCE, and whose brigand-father had been killed by Herod at the caves of Arbela (*War* 1.204, 311; *Ant.* 14.429-30). Horsley wishes to view Hezekiah as a "social bandit" and thereby see him as broadly part of "prophetic movements" in the Galilee. Freyne (1988a), however, casts Horsley's model into grave doubt. Judas

movements in question occurred in or near Galilee, nor, insofar as we are informed, did any Galilean participate."[46] If a scholar wishes to argue that Galileans Jews were involved in an imaginative recovery of the prophetic heritage of the Hebrew Bible, she will have to point to some evidence to that effect, if indeed we are to achieve comparative parity with the case *against* Cynicism. That no one advances such evidence or, evidently, thinks it necessary flows from a pervasive explanatory habit that takes for granted the a priori plausibility of any "biblical" explanation but demands disproportionate argument in support of a nonbiblical explanation.

Why should the cynic hypothesis call forth such a muscular reaction and why should "biblical" analogies slip by under so weak a degree of scrutiny? Why should rigorous standards of comparison be applied for the cynic hypothesis and relaxed standards employed when it comes to the more comfortable analogies of biblical prophecy or, for that matter, the comparison of Jesus (or the Q people) with sages? When critical assessment of the cynic hypothesis comes close to exorcism, we must ask why.

I have no full answer to my own question, only four tentative suggestions to offer. Each has to do, not with the plausibility of the cynic hypothesis *as a historical account* of Q, but with the fact that the hypothesis is either mistakenly supposed to endanger important theological notions, or that it exposes the fact that theological conclusions are not as securely history-based as previously supposed. That is, I will suggest that some of the opposition to the cynic hypothesis has less to do with its explanatory plausibility than with its ideological utility.

THE "JEWISHNESS" OF Q AND ANTI-SEMITISM

The debate about a cynic-like Q is peppered with perplexing disagreements. Detractors speak as if "Cynic" and "prophetic" are polar opposites; yet Mack states: "[a] more balanced view [of ancient Cynics] would see the Cynics as the Greek analogue to the Hebrew prophets" (1993:114). For some critics, a "cynic Q" is taken to mean a "non-Jewish Q." N. T. Wright, for example, ventures the claim that according to the majority view, Q is seen as purveying a "quasi-Gnostic, quasi-Cynic wisdom" (1992:437 n. 64).[47] This he contrasts with Tuckett's and Sato's view of Q as "prophetic and Jewish-Christian." The distinction that Wright wishes to make is of

---

the Galilean, who founded the "Fourth Philosophy" in 6 CE, was active not in the Galilee but in Judaea (*War* 2.118).

46. Freyne 1988a:195. Freyne notes that the long rule of Antipas insulated the Galilee from the hardships of direct Roman rule. He observes: "One must surmise that a census was held in the Galilee similar to that in Judaea when eventually the former territory came under direct Roman rule in 44 CE. Yet there is no trace of any extreme nationalism similar to that displayed by Judas the Galilean in Judaea when his call for freedom and acceptance of the sole rule of God occasioned the emergence of the Fourth Philosophy" (Freyne 1981:101).

47. See the analysis and refutation of Wright's views in Kloppenborg Verbin 1999.

course a false one, for none of the advocates of a cynic-like Q imagines that the Q people were anything but Galilean Jews.[48] In criticizing the cynic hypothesis, one critic has even raised the specter of the de-Judaized Jesus produced by scholars of the Third Reich.[49] When one sees instances of such odd argument and rhetorical excess and when one sees the Jewishness of Q affirmed by all sides, but described as if it were a matter of sharp controversy, it is time to ask what deeper issues lurk beneath the surface.

The pertinent question to ask, as Arnal reminds us, is not whether Q was "Jewish" but *what kind* of Israelite traditions and piety it presupposes (1997c:309). Current scholarship on Q reflects a range of views, from the bare assertion that Q was "Jewish" (as if this were somehow self-explanatory), to arguments that the Galilee (and therefore Q) was "Torah-true" (based mainly on the discovery of some first-century *miqwaʾôt* in Sepphoris), to the efforts by Freyne and others to define more precisely the ideological ties between the Galilee and Judah, to the arguments of Horsley, Oakman, and myself that differentiate Galilean and Judaean Judaisms somewhat more sharply.

Vaage and Mack create a further level of differentiation, not by arguing that the Galilee was not "Jewish" (which would be absurd), but by situating the Q people more broadly within the social and intellectual dynamics of the Greco-Roman world. Implicit in this procedure is the assumption that Jewish Palestine was not a separate (and unified) cultural realm, isolated within a sea of Hellenism. On the contrary, Galilee was at the intersection of a variety of cultural streams, some Israelite, some Judaean, some local, some Hellenistic, some Roman. The economies of Tyre and Jerusalem impinged on the Galilee; some of its architecture is Hellenistic; some was indigenous; a minority of its (elite) population was Greek; some were Judaean; others Herodian; some dwelled in the royal foundations of Tiberias and Sepphoris; and the majority lived in villages. Tensions existed between the Jewish regions and the Gentile periphery, between city and village, between Galilee and Judah, and, no doubt, between Galileans and the Roman forces in Judah and the coastal plain. The statement that Q is Jewish poses the question of identity within one cultural frame of reference but ignores the fact that multiple overlapping frames of reference existed, all contributing to cultural identity.

48. Wright (1996:41) even accuses my own work as promoting a non-Jewish Q, a characterization that I find utterly perplexing.

49. Pearson (1995:334) accuses the Jesus Seminar (with which the cynic hypothesis is sometimes associated) of having "performed a forcible epispasm on the historical Jesus, a surgical procedure removing the marks of his circumcision." He then recalls the Aryan Jesus produced by German scholars in the 1930s and 1940 (e.g., Grundmann 1940) but concludes by volunteering that the Jesus of the Jesus Seminar "is much too banal to cause us to think that the ideology producing him is like that which produced the 'Aryan Jesus' of the 1930." Pearson's combination of innuendo and disingenuousness is an isolated though regrettable piece of polemic.

The emphasizing of one frame of reference over another is neither innocent nor objective. Freyne is forthright on the matter when he states that his insistence on a "Jewish" Jesus is important as an antidote to the anti-Semitism latent in much Christian thought. It is not just historically necessary but an important *theological* desideratum to acknowledge that the Christian understanding of God is grounded in the Jewish understanding of God, "active within history, hidden and mysterious, yet present and living, a God who suffers because it is God's nature to care, to care ultimately about the whole of God's creation, especially its most fragile and broken elements. . ." (Freyne 1997:91). Such an insistence is also medicine against the lurking supersessionism that infects much Christian thinking. Even if one wishes to claim ultimacy or finality on Jesus' behalf (as Freyne does), it remains true that Jesus' God was the God of Israel, not some other deity.

Eliminating the toxic waste of anti-Semitism and supersessionism ranks high on my own list of theoretical interests and in this context one may applaud Freyne's insistence on the Jewishness of Q. Such concerns now belong to a broad spectrum of scholarship on Christian origins after the Shoah, which dramatically underscored the roles that persistent misreading of texts of the Jesus movement and the conceptual apparatus of Christian theology have played in both encouraging anti-Semitism and blinding Christians to the utter horror of the Shoah.[50] Yet Vaage is also correct in his response to Freyne, that there is no necessary reason to believe that identifying *other* family resemblances between Jesus (or Q) and the wider Mediterranean world should displace a Jewish Jesus and lead to anti-Semitism (Vaage 1997:186).

Vaage suggests that behind the spirited insistence of a "Jewish" Jesus (as a false alternative to a cynic-like Jesus) is an excessively narrow view of Jewish identity, both in antiquity and today. Philo and Josephus are a good instance of persons who were members of several distinguishable but not separate cultural frameworks. Vaage argues that the possibility of Jesus (or Q's Jesus) being such a person

> can only be denied in principle if we were somehow obliged to imagine (as, in fact, modern capitalist Eurocentric civilizations and their colonizing sciences, including biblical scholarship, have endeavored to maintain) that persons in antiquity (and, by extension, today) must somehow really and necessarily choose to live in one and only one cultural frame of reference. Such an assumption, I am convinced, simply cannot be sustained as a sufficient description of human social life (however much it may still be apparent as political will). (Vaage 1997:186)

It ought to be clear that Vaage rejects a dichotomous relation of "Judaism" to "Cynicism." The either/or mentality, the desire to precipitate

50. Especially prominent in the efforts to undo anti-Semitism in scholarship on Christian origins are the works of Sanders (1977; 1985).

clear choices in favor of one cultural framework over another, are symptomatic of a view that affirms the permanence of traditional identities (a com-
forting fantasy when culture is under severe pressure) and is unable to
countenance significant deviance from that identity, especially when it concerns a "religious" hero. Vaage's constrasting affirmation of such a mestizo
possibility allows him the theoretical framework within which to imagine a
Q that is simultaneously Jewish and cynic-like, participating in Jewish culture and at the same time bitingly critical of certain aspects of that culture.

Part of the anxiety expressed toward a cynic-like Q thus seems to rest on
a fundamental misunderstanding of what is claimed. Nothing in the cynic
hypothesis entails a non- or anti-Jewish posture. It only *sounds* anti-Semitic
if one makes the false collateral assumption that Judaism and Cynicism are
polar opposites, and the equally false assumption that the culture of Jewish
Palestine was monolithic. Conjecturing a Jesus movement that simultaneously reflected multiple cultural discourses—some critical, some constructive, some conventional—in fact is part of the rigorous contextualization
characteristic of social-historical approaches. It is not social and historical
contextualization that is to blame for anti-Semitism; on the contrary, it is
the lurking supersessionist tendencies of Christian theology, which try to
absolutize the fine differentiations that intellectual and social history detects
between the (Jewish Galilean) Jesus people and their (Jewish Galilean)
environment and turn them into points of ultimate disagreement and transcendence.

A Cynic Q and Biblical Theology

I have already noted N. T. Wright's efforts to create a false dichotomy
between the cynic hypothesis and the characterization of Q as Jewish.
Behind his treatment of Q scholarship seems to be the worry that a
"cynic"—by which he seems to mean pagan and Hellenistic—Q would represent a rupture in the supposed unitary fabric of "Jewish stories" and
"Jewish worldview" that he posits as the necessary matrix for the theological history of early Christianity.[51] The fear is groundless, since the denomination of Q as cynic scarcely excludes its being "Jewish." After all, more
than three decades ago Fischel argued that *m. ʾAbot* was influenced by

---

51. Wright is prepared to admit a considerable degree of diversity within the Jesus movement in attitudes toward Rome, toward the Temple, toward the application of circumcision,
purity practices, and dietary laws, and even concedes that "some may well have placed little
emphasis on the salvific effect of the cross" while "others, by no means only in the Pauline tradition, emphasized it as central to the divine plan of salvation" (1992:454–55, here 455). What
held this diversity together (from a theological point of view) was that early Christians "told,
and lived, a form of Israel's story which reached its climax in Jesus and which then issued in
their spirit-given new life and task" (1992:456). The worldview of the early Christians was
"first, emphatically Jewish rather than pagan, and then second, emphatically Christian rather
than Jewish in the sense of an ethnic and Torah-based identity" (ibid.).

Cynic chriae without thereby implying that this rabbinic document had somehow become un-Jewish (Fischel 1968).

The categorical separation of Judaism from Hellenism, as J. Z. Smith (1990) observed, has served in contemporary scholarship not a historiographic goal, but an apologetic one—as a way to insulate Jesus and the early Jesus movement from its broader Hellenistic environment and to help secure claims to uniqueness. For Wright the separation functions to preserve the essentially "biblical" pedigree of the Jesus movement. Wright also insists on a double structure to early Christian practice that expresses both its Jewishness and its emphatic christocentricity. Baptism, for example, *both* linked early Christians with "the imagery of a Jewish sect (including exodus-typology)" and represented "the mode of entry into the eschatological people of Israel's god" *and* involved a "specific historical reference to Jesus himself, and to his death and resurrection" (1992:447). Similarly, the Eucharist was associated with the Exodus, Passover, and the (Davidic) kingdom and (insofar as it occurred on the first day of the week) with the events of Jesus' death and resurrection. Wright's theological schema thus both anchors the thought of the Jesus movement firmly within a biblical world, sharply distinguished from its wider (pagan) environment, and ultimately distinguishes the Jesus movement from its biblical world itself by virtue of its Christocentricity. Because Wright mistakes "cynic-like" for "non-Jewish," a cynic-like Q violates the putative unity of the "Jewish world" he posits.

Again Arnal's reminder is pertinent: the issue is not whether Jesus (or Q) was either "Jewish" or "Cynic/Hellenistic" but instead *what kind of Judaism* Jesus (or Q) represents. The insistence that "Q is Jewish" of course rightly locates Q with respect to the history, culture, and institutions of Israel. But all too often it also embodies a tacit assumption that "Jewish" means "religious" and that "religion" is a discrete and bounded realm of cultural discourse, separate from social (family, village) and political structures. Thus the assertion serves to isolate Q, not only from the context of the other cultural discourses of the Mediterranean but from the social and political culture of Jewish Galilee itself. The cynic hypothesis, whatever its other failings, assumes that religion is embedded in other cultural and social forms. Hence, the tensions between Q's Jesus and his culture should not be interpreted as narrowly defined "religious" opposition, isolated from other cultural possibilities. On the cynic hypothesis, without ceasing to be Galilean and Jewish, Q was *also* simultaneously part of intersecting discourses critical of certain institutions and patterns of Galilean and Judaean culture and *analogous to* Cynic criticism of Greek urban culture (Vaage 1997:186). The cynic comparison implicitly resists compartmentalization: the compartmentalization of "religion" within ancient society; of "Judaism" within the ancient world; and "biblical religion" as an apologetic construct. Instead, it tries to locate Jesus at the conjunction of multiple intersecting discourses.

CYNICISM, ESCHATOLOGY, AND CHRISTOLOGY

The third theological issue has to do with the dominance of eschatology and apocalypticism in discourse on Christian origins and its singular importance in systematic theology since the end of World War II.

Almost a century ago Schweitzer proposed an apocalyptic Jesus, basing this understanding on the apocalyptic documents of Second Temple Judaism (Schweitzer 1901; 1906). His Jesus was thus consistent with the supposedly thoroughgoing apocalyptic climate of the first century. Schweitzer's Jesus, however, was a stranger to the world of the early 1900s, for at the time Schweitzer wrote apocalypticism was regarded in European culture with distaste and disdain. For Schweitzer himself it was not the mistaken apocalypticist of the remote past who was theologically important but the "spiritual Christ" who continues to animate the Christian church. Schweitzer's use of apocalyptic eschatology as a *descriptive* category, on the one hand, underscored the *commonalities* between Jesus and his environment, and the profound *distance* between Jesus and early twentieth-century Christian theology, on the other. Schweitzer's historical Jesus was part of the first century but not part of the twentieth.

Ironically, since Schweitzer's time a complete reversal has occurred. The terms "eschatological" and "apocalyptic"—usually stripped of their most blatantly predictive aspects—are regularly used in order to *distinguish* Jesus from his environment.[52] Thus, for example, Hengel's study of discipleship uses the category of "eschatological charismatic" in order to render Jesus incommensurable and unique within Judaism and the Hellenistic world (1981:69). At the same time, however, eschatology was elevated to a central theological category by such systematic theologians as Pannenberg and Moltmann, so that Jesus' announcement of an imminent and decisive transformation of human reality happily coincided with what was now seen to be at the heart of the Christian theological project. Analogously, emphasis on the eschatological orientation of Q serves to cement Q and its Jesus to contemporary Christian theological interests rather than to distance him from modern sensibilities.

The importance of the connection between eschatology and Christology is underscored by John Galvin. Commenting on the historical Jesus as reconstructed by J. Meier (1994) and Gnilka (1990, ET 1997), he observes that both balance the futuristic and present aspects of Jesus' expectations

---

52. Apropos of Bultmann, Georgi (1985:82) observed: "Whereas for the history-of-religions school the term 'eschatological' described the foreignness of Jesus and of the early church—together with Jewish apocalypticism and other comparable ancient eschatologies—for Bultmann . . . the term 'eschatological' stands for the novelty of Christianity, its incomparable superiority, the uniqueness of the victorious religion, deservedly victorious. Wherever a comparison is ventured, wherever analogies lift their head, wherever challenges are heard from other religious options but the canonical ones, the invocation of the 'eschatological' is made, and the demons, the shadows have to disappear. Historical criticism thus turns into exorcism."

and both provide sufficient purchase for the idea that Jesus saw his own activities as part of the eschatological events he proclaimed. Thereby these portraits allow traditional christological affirmations to be seen "as a plausible, though not rationally compelling, interpretation of Jesus and of the events of his public ministry" (1996:375; also 1994:264–65).[53]

Freyne is forthright on the point. The insistence on the eschatological nature of Jesus' career, he says,

> arises from my concern regarding the claims of ultimacy that Christian faith makes in terms of Jesus. . . . In the absence of an eschatological dimension to Jesus' utterances it would be impossible to see how any christological claims could be grounded in his earthly life, which is precisely the issue that gave rise to the quest for the historical Jesus in the first place as both an ecclesial and academic exercise.[54]

The declarations by Galvin and Freyne are important for they make clear the theoretical and theological interests—Christology and ultimacy—that are served by highlighting Jesus' (and Q's) eschatology. "Eschatology" stands as a cipher for finality and ultimacy. Only if Jesus made ultimate and final claims about the reign of God, and only if there is some connection, however implicit, between those claims and the person of Jesus himself, can christological claims be sustained. Freyne expresses hesitations about this admission, fearing that it will destroy the credibility of his historical reconstruction. It should have no such effect. For Freyne can hardly be accused of engaging in covert apologetics or of smuggling theology into his historical analysis.[55] But his admission clarifies why eschatology—however it is construed—has achieved so central a place in some treatments of the historical Jesus.

It should now be clear why the cynic hypothesis is seen to undermine christological interests. Cynicism is viewed by some as lacking an eschatol-

---

53. The use of eschatology in relation to "uniqueness" and Christology is explicit in Pannenberg (1990:100–101): "In fact, Jesus' emphasis on the anticipatory presence of God's kingdom in his own activity (Lk 11,20) involved his own person in a way that essentially implies what later on was explicated by incarnational language and by titles like Son of God. But then, the uniqueness attributed to Jesus by the incarnational theology of the church was already characteristic of his own eschatological message and activity. . . . The Christian claim to uniqueness is not based on any Christian experience. If this were so, it would be fair to argue that there are other experiences of uniqueness within world religions. But the claim to uniqueness concerning the person of Jesus is bound up with his own eschatological message, especially the eschatological finality of God's kingdom as becoming present in his activity."

54. Freyne 1997:90. A similar view is expressed, apropos of Crossan's Jesus, by Galvin 1996.

55. The same cannot be said of Witherington's *Christology of Jesus* (1990), which tries to make a historical case for Jesus thinking of himself as Wisdom incarnate as well as proclaiming (with some equivocation) the impending end. Witherington's defense of the authenticity of the sayings upon which he bases this view, however, is feeble or nonexistent. For a critique of Witherington's Jesus, see R. Miller 1997.

ogy—probably incorrectly (Downing 1995b; Koester 1992). While some Cynics may have thought of themselves as messengers of heaven, there is no reason to suppose that any Cynic thought himself to be the final or definitive messenger. A cynic Q with a cynic-like Jesus without a strong eschatological outlook and message is not so amenable to christological discourse as the "eschatological prophet" with a message of a partially imminent, partly realized, but wholly definitive intervention by God.

It is at this point that the distinction between "Cynic" and "cynic-like" Q is important. Neither Vaage nor Mack claims that Q was *influenced* by Greco-Roman Cynics. Hence, the whole discussion about whether there were Cynics in Galilee and about the dating of Cynic sources is moot. Moreover, even though neither Vaage nor Mack makes much of Q's eschatology, the assertion that Q is cynic-like need not necessarily entail the claim that is is noneschatological. The term itself, however, would have to be used cautiously, given the fact that it carries with it not only historical-descriptive connotations, but theological nuances as well.

Again, I wish to be clear. I am not defending the cynic hypothesis, only pointing out that the reaction to the cynic hypothesis seems as much moved by theological worries as by concerns for a defensible social-historical reconstruction. These are worries that a cynic-like Q cannot bear the weight of claims to ultimacy and incommensurability that are regularly attributed to the ideology of the Jesus movement, and worries that a cynic-like Jesus cannot be seen to be in plausible continuity with the exalted Lord of later christological confessions. Such concerns are not historical but theological. Each may have its place; but it is a dangerous venture to confuse the two and to turn historical explanation into apologetics.

DEGREES OF DEVIANCE

A final reason for reticence toward the cynic hypothesis has to do with the way it implicitly labels the Q people deviant. In some contexts, this label might well be taken as a mark in its favor, in particular in discursive contexts that wish to highlight the ethical and political oppositions between the Jesus movement and imperial culture. Such a portrayal is only an extrapolation of earlier, more conventional, representations of Jesus as a countercultural figure. In the last generation of studies of the historical Jesus, such adjectives as "novel," "striking," "countercultural," "radical," "marginal," or "world-subverting" have been employed with such tedious regularity that they seem no longer to require any justification.

Curiously, when it comes to the characterization of the Q folk as cynic-like, justification is required. Why? It seems that while it is quite comfortable to call them "radical," a line is crossed when they are labeled as cynic. Vaage observes how in the resistance to the cynic hypothesis numerous assumptions are made regarding what was "personally possible" for a Galilean Jews. These assumptions, he notes, are rarely brought to the level of direct examination.

> [I]f we conclude in our historiographic repertoire the question of what was "personally possible" in antiquity, we can begin to consider how a given person might have resisted the standard options for social identification in his or her historical context, or have blended them into a singular combination." (Vaage 1997:184)

Vaage wonders about how much the social location of modern biblical scholarship in universities and seminaries (all embedded in institutions of power) has fueled the disinclination to regard Jesus (or Q's Jesus) as specifically countercultural and opposed to key institutions of power. Lest Vaage's arguments be construed *contra sensum auctoris*, it needs to be added that he is not advocating some bizarre reconstruction of Jesus; rather, he merely draws attention to the fact that the location of scholarship—for the most part within affluent universities and in some association with ecclesial communities—must be an object of critical reflection when one asks what was and was not possible for relatively underprivileged Galilean Jews living in the shadow of Rome and her client kings.

In fact it is not viewing the Q people as radical that distinguishes the cynic hypothesis from other views. Rather, it is the emphasis on the critical, almost rootless, posture of the Q people and the rejection of the notion that they were interested in corporate, national, or local renewal. Rather than adopting the customary strategy of rooting the metaphor of the reign of God in Israelite royal ideology and its later transformations, Vaage treats it largely as empty of positive content, functioning primarily as "a discursive instrument of ongoing socio-political destabilization" (Vaage 1996:56). In both the use of this metaphor and in the woes (11:39b-48, 52), Q does not offer a utopian alternative or a program of renewal, restoration, or reform. It is satisfied instead with an attack on the self-evident character of the current order of things.

This depiction of Q is likely to appear unsatisfying to those who are more inclined to see Q either as advocating local renewal in the face of regional economic and political changes or expecting imminent transformation of the cosmos as a whole. Might it be the case that the stratum represented by Q^1 was sharply critical of hierarchy and privilege and offered limited strategies for local survival, but did not embrace any fantastic scenarios of local or national transformation? The possibility can scarcely be denied in principle, except by importing sayings from Q^2 into Q^1 or by insisting on reading Q's sometimes ambiguous terminology in a determinate way which obviates such a possibility. The possibility cannot be denied that the Q people were far more deviant than pious Christians or cautious scholars would prefer. Herein lies one of the threats of the cynic hypothesis, that it places the possibility of serious social deviance too near to the historical Jesus and too near to the canonical Gospels.

As has been made clear in chapters 4 and 5, I believe that there are sufficient elements in Q¹ to sustain the thesis that the Q people articulated a model of local cooperation based on strategies of tension reduction, debt release, and forgiveness. They appealed to an image of God as a generous patron and parent who could be depended upon for sustenance. This suggests that the reign of God is not "merely a discursive instrument of ongoing socio-political destabilization" but offered a real, though spare, alternative in the present. By Q² this alternative was more clearly spelled out in scenarios of renewal and judgment (Q 13:28-29; 22:28-30). At the same time, the scribes responsible for Q resisted the efforts to impose a southern, hierocratically defined vision of Israel in which human affairs are centered on a central sanctuary, its priestly officers, and their retainers.

Nevertheless, the cynic hypothesis underscores the possibility that at Q's earliest layer the early Jesus movement adopted postures that were significantly deviant and socially experimental. This clearly conflicts with the ways in which other early Christian authors, notably Luke, 1 Peter, and later apologists, wished to portray the Jesus movement as nondeviant, at least as far as the political culture of the empire was concerned. The main redaction of Q (Q²) seems to have already felt obliged to defend the novelty of Q¹ by consciously aligning Jesus, John, and the Q people with eminent figures of Israel's past—the prophets. Even in this alignment, a memory of deviance is preserved, for the prophets themselves were remembered as similarly uncooperative persons, opposing kings, objecting to political strategies, and decrying the exploitation of the poor and dispossessed. It is only when the prophets are reread through a pious and biblicizing lens that their deviance is effaced and the possible deviance of Q¹ implied by the cynic hypothesis begins to look atypical and disruptive of a more general "Christian" ethos. But this too is more apologetics than it is a defensible social history.

Conclusion

In the assessment of a historical hypothesis, judgments as to its antecedent probability play a significant role in the standards of proof that are required. A lower burden of proof is required of hypotheses that are deemed to have high antecedent probability. Higher standards are imposed on views that are judged to be improbable or, for some other reason, undesirable.

In this chapter I have suggested that judgments of antecedent probability have influenced the way in which the cynic hypothesis has been evaluated, and that these judgments have to do, largely though not exclusively, with theological concerns rather than with historiographic considerations. If I may borrow and adapt a term from feminist historiography, they have to do with a reconstruction of a "theologically usable history"—a construal of the past that is cooperative with theological interests. These concerns include a synthesis of historical data that implies maximal coherence and continuity within "biblical" history and the mitigation of "influences" that appear to represent disruptions, ruptures, or breaks in that supposed history.

Characteristically, the Biblical Theology Movement takes narrative (rather than social history) as the paradigm for theological historiography, and consequently resists any historical data or social-historical constructions that do not appear to fit the narrative syntax of the particular "story" it wishes to tell. Other instances of resistance to the cynic hypothesis seem to be a function of a confusion regarding what "cynic-like" means, coupled with an excessively narrow notion of cultural participation. Whether or not one ultimately embraces the hypothesis as plausible or not, the debate has exposed the abiding conceptual muddles that plague the study of Christian origins.

Christological concerns and concerns about the social and political posture of the Q folk also seem to hover on the edges of the debate and play a key role in determining the antecedent probability of historical hypotheses. It seems clear that historical constructions which appear to be amenable to christological transformation and adaptation, and which can be aligned easily with the social and political postures of other sectors of the Jesus movement, are deemed to be "more likely" that those which are not. But to recognize this is also to recognize the way in which *our* preferences bend interpretation and, at times, serve to manufacture evidence.

I should not wish to imply that a "neutral" historiography is possible or desirable. On the contrary. A similar analysis of many of the historiographic endeavors in the field of Christian origins will show, I think, that ideological (theological as well as antitheological) subtexts lurk beneath the often pretended objectivity of criticism. That is not a defect of criticism. It is what makes historical criticism of interest in the first place. On the other hand, however, it is important not to confuse theological or ideological subtexts with historical method or to allow spurious historical arguments their place merely because they seem to cooperate with those subtexts. Theological (and antitheological) commitments cannot be allowed either to manufacture or to obscure data. If theological cases are to be made, they must stand on their own feet.

The cynic hypothesis, whether or not it is ultimately judged to be an adequate *historical* hypothesis, is of intellectual interest precisely because it has helped to expose the interface between historiography and theology and to clarify what might be at stake in comparison. To suggest, for example, that the Q people might meaningfully be compared (*not* equated) with Cynics is *not* to deny their Israelite identity. The fact that later Christian writers, in particular Matthew but arguably Q^2 as well, would look back on earlier stages of the tradition and propose a synthetic model in which Jesus and the Jesus movement were viewed though the biblicizing lens of Israel's story, the continuing legacy of Israelite prophets, and, eventually, a representation of Jesus as a Torah scholar, and the fact that second-century theologians would endorse against Marcion the fundamental unities of the testaments, should not obscure the real, though disturbing, possibility that the early Jesus movement represented by Q—maybe Jesus himself—was not in all regards "man's best friend" and at least occasionally barked and bit.

The cynic hypothesis, of course, is not the only location where it is possible to analyze and clarify the complex relationship between historiography and theological interest. Historical Jesus studies provide another location where historical reconstruction is seen to have important theological consequences. Some recent scholarship on the historical Jesus at least has begun to avoid a reification of "religion" and instead provides a description of the Jesus movement that draws on multiple dimensions of ancient Galilean society and places the Jesus movement at the intersection of the "little tradition" of peasant culture, the "great tradition" of the retainers of the aristocracy, exploitation by ruling powers, and various strategies of local resistance (e.g., Horsley and Freyne). Commitment to humane values has led to a recasting and enlarging of the typical analytic categories in order to describe in a way that corresponds better to *our* interests what the ancient Jesus movements were all about. Such a recasting of categories, with a view to contemporary concerns, is not a matter of trying to read the ancient world through modern lenses. On the contrary, it is the effort to give a responsible account of ancient texts that at the same time will *matter* to us.

Epilogue

W HY SHOULD SO MUCH INK be spilled on a document that has, after all, gone missing, whose existence is inferred from a hypothesis that accounts for much of the Synoptic data but which also admits of counterevidence, whose original contours cannot be reconstructed with complete or satisfying clarity, whose theology was effaced by the redaction of Matthew and Luke, and whose supporting social networks apparently disappeared in the wake of the First Revolt?

What makes the Sayings Gospel Q a particularly strong site of investigation is precisely what is *not* known securely about it and therefore what can be discussed as our plausible intellectual constructs. This book began by insisting both on the hypothetical character of the Two Document hypothesis (from which the existence of Q is inferred) and on the fact that the 2DH is an *effective* hypothesis that renders intelligible most of the Synoptic data most of the time. The larger argument of the book flows from both sides of the previous statement: on the one hand, good hypotheses are constructed from an intensive and extensive examination of the relevant data and are constructed in such a way as to render a coherent account of those data. This is true whether one is discussing issues of the Synoptic Problem, or the original language or order or wording of Q, or its compositional features, or its theological structure, or genre, or the social setting it presupposed.

On the other hand, it is important to be able to distinguish between the data, on the one hand, and the way our hypotheses configure that data, and the ideological interests that inform such intellectual constructions in the first place, on the other. It is here that retrospective analysis of the previous two centuries proves helpful, for this allows us to see that interest in Q did not arise in a vacuum, out of the pure intellectual drive to solve a problem that disagreements and agreements among the Synoptic accounts raised. Rather, it arose out of deep theological and ideological concerns generated by Reimarus and his successors. It arose in a broader stream of opposition to absolutism and orthodoxy. Later stages of Q scholarship variously reflected concerns to draw a theological and documentary "map" of the earliest Jesus movements, to comprehend and manage theological diversity, and to coordinate early Christian discourse with social practice. In each

445

case, Q scholarship has played an exemplary role in these broader discussions. Perhaps because the very existence of Q is itself the product of hypothesis building, Q scholarship has become an important "site" at which to understand the role of hypotheses and ideologically invested intellectual constructs within NT scholarship in general.

What difference does Q make? Solutions to the Synoptic Problem in general and the Two Document hypothesis in particular were originally generated as a response to the theological problems raised by Reimarus and his attack on eighteenth-century dogmatic theology. Although the threat of Reimarus is past, the implications of the 2DH and its postulate, Q, turn out to be of significant moment for understanding the history of the Jesus movement, its theology, and its social practice. The initial positing of Q has had consequences that extend far beyond responding to Reimarus's problematizing of the relationship between Jesus, the Gospels, and dogmatic assertions, but ironically has created a new set of intellectual conundrums and challenges.

If we take the 2DH seriously—and we must do so or be prepared to advance an alternative hypothesis that accounts for the Synoptic data at the same or a better level of detail—then we must also be prepared to take seriously the consequences of Q as a document, probably from the Galilee, written in Greek about the time of the First Revolt, and offering a perspectival account of the Jesus tradition. If we take Q seriously as a document— and we must do so or be prepared to offer some other account of the manifold agreements in wording and order in the double tradition—then we must also take seriously that it is a product of editors, who did not begin tabula rasa but worked within the framework of available ancient genres, selecting and deploying materials in accordance with their argumentative and rhetorical concerns. Taking Q's composition and theology seriously means in turn taking Q's *different* theology seriously and adjusting our views of the theological history of primitive Christianity accordingly. If we take Q seriously as an expression of part of the Jesus movement in Galilee— and we must do so or be prepared to justify the anomaly of documentary production without a social context—then we must also endeavor to understand how Q's "theology" was embedded in a particular social location and consonant with a particular set of social practices.

Each of these consequences has consequences, no less important than earlier realizations that the Gospels differ from one another in significant ways, or that the Pastorals and Hebrews are not from the pen of Paul, or that Acts and Paul have measurably different portraits of Paul. Such differences matter. Q, for all its fragility, is different enough on several registers to be able to prompt rethinking and renovation of some of the conceptual apparatus of the discipline and the achieving of a new level of self-awareness and deliberation in the way we imagine the Jesus movement, and the reasons for which we might think that important.

Glossary

2DH → Two Document hypothesis

2GH → Griesbach hypothesis

4SH → Four Source hypothesis

"Augustinian hypothesis"—Associated with Augustine of Hippo's comments in *De consensu evangelistarum* 1.2.4 and held by a few scholars today. The hypothesis suggests that the Gospels were written in canonical order (Matthew → Mark → Luke → John), and that each evangelist knew the works of his predecessor(s). Quotation marks are used because it is not clear that Augustine's comments were intended to advance a theory of literary courses.

chria—According to Aelius Theon of Alexandria, a *chria* is a "brief statement or action fittingly attributed to a definite person or something analogous to person." This is the ancient rhetorical designation for what have later been termed "apophthegms" or "pronouncement stories" and include declaratory (NN said: "..."), responsive (Being asked about *x*, NN replied: "..."), and circumstantial forms (Seeing *x*, NN said: "...").

double tradition—Synoptic pericopae found in Matthew and Luke, but not in Mark (e.g., Matt 3:7-10 / Luke 3:7-9), or where Mark's form is significantly different from those of Matthew and Luke (e.g., Matt 4:1-11 / Luke 4:1-13; cf. Mark 1:12-13).

dunam—1,000 m² or about 0.25 acre. Originally a Turkish unit of measure, it is now used principally in Israel.

Farrer-Goulder hypothesis—Associated with Austin Farrer and Michael Goulder. The hypothesis holds Mark to be the first Gospel, Matthew expanded Mark, and Luke used both Mark and Matthew.

Four Source hypothesis (4SH)—Associated with B. H. Streeter, this hypothesis is a form of the Two Document hypothesis (see below). In addition to asserting the priority of Mark and Q, the 4SH accounts for special Matthaean material by means of a discrete document (M) and special Lukan material by a fourth source, L.

GH → Griesbach hypothesis

gnomologium—A form of wisdom literature consisting solely or mainly of gnomic verses, ethical or philosophical sayings.

Griesbach hypothesis (GH; Owen-Griesbach hypothesis; Two-Gospel hypothesis, 2GH)—Associated with Henry Owen and J. J. Griesbach. The hypothesis holds that Matthew is the first Gospel to be written, Luke used Matthew, and Mark

447

conflated and abbreviated Matthew and Luke. The modern revival of the GH prefers the name "the Two Gospel hypothesis" (2GH).

hectare—2.471 acres = 100 ares (1 are = 10x10 m). The town of Kefar Naḥum is about 17 hectares 2 acres 168 dunams.

IQP—The International Q Project, with a membership of thirty Q specialists from the United States, Canada, Germany, the United Kingdom, Finland, and South Africa, was established by the Society of Biblical Literature to edit a critical edition of Q and a comprehensive database on the reconstruction of Q.

lectio difficilior ("the more difficult reading")—A principle employed in text criticism which recognizes that scribes and editors tend to clarify obscurities and remove difficult or problematic aspects of texts. In choosing between two or more variants, the variant that is more difficult (grammatically or in its content) it usually taken to be the better or more original reading.

minimal Q—Those portions of the double tradition (q.v.) where there is verbatim agreement between Matthew and Luke and hence a very high degree of confidence as to the original wording of Q.

Modernism—A movement within Roman Catholic theology associated with Alfred F. Loisy, George Tyrrell, and others. Modernism was in part a Catholic response to the rise of historical criticism in Protestant circles and an attempt to defend the idea of the evolution or development of doctrine. Modernism was condemned by Pius X in several decrees (*Lamentabili sane* [1907]; *Pascendi domini gregis* [1907]), and Loisy was excommunicated in 1908.

Pontifical Biblical Commission (PBC)—A Vatican commission, originally established by Leo XIII in 1903 as a forum for Roman Catholic biblical scholarship, which became under Pius X (1903–14) a watchdog of "orthodoxy." Between 1907 and 1915 the PBC issued declarations on exegetical and historical opinions that could and could not be held by Catholic exegetes. Most of these were retracted in 1955 by the PBC.

Proto-Luke hypothesis—A complex form of the Two Document hypothesis (2DH) or Four Source Hypothesis (4SH) which holds that Luke's Gospel was composed on the basis of a prior combination of Q+L (=Proto-Luke), to which Mark was eventually added.

qal weḥomer—A form of exegetical argument found in rabbinic literature, taking the form: if a legal principle applies to x (the lesser situation), it also applies to y (the greater situation).

Sondergut ("special material")—Sayings or stories that are peculiar to one evangelist (e.g., the Parable of the Prodigal Son [Luke 10:30-37]).

triple tradition—Synoptic pericopae found in all three Synoptics (e.g., the baptism of Jesus, Mark 1:9-11 / Matt 3:13-17 / Luke 3:21-22).

Tübingen school—An influential group of nineteenth-century historians and theologians associated with F. C. Baur (1792–1860) that included D. F. Strauss, A. Ritschl, E. Zeller, A. Hilgenfeld, Bruno Bauer, and Karl Köstlin. Many of its members (apart from Hilgenfeld) originally endorsed a form of the Griesbach hypothesis. The school lost much of its influence after Baur's death.

Two Document hypothesis (2DH)—First associated with C. H. Weisse, later with H. J. Holtzmann, and held by most Synoptic scholars today, the hypothesis affirms the priority of Mark and the independent use of Mark by Matthew and

Luke. This requires as a corollary the positing of a second source beside Mark in order to account for the double tradition (see above). This source is now called "Q" or the "Sayings Gospel Q."

Two-Gospel hypothesis → Griesbach hypothesis

Ur-Markus—A theory generally associated with the hypothesis of Markan priority which holds that the canonical Gospel of Mark was composed from an early version of Mark, usually longer than canonical Mark (containing, e.g., Luke 3:7-9, 16-17; 4:1-13; 6:20b-49). Both C. H. Weisse (1856) and H. J. Holtzmann (1863) held forms of the *Ur-Markus* hypothesis. It was rejected by Paul Wernle (1899) but has more recently reappeared, either in connection with resolving the problem of the "minor agreements" or as part of the efforts to understand the relationship of the Secret Gospel of Mark to canonical Mark (Koester 1983).

Sites and Geographical Features

	Map Location
Acchabaron (ᶜAkbara) [S]	[197260]
Achziv (Ecdippa, ez Zib)	[159272]
Aita (ᶜAita esh Shaub)	[181277]
AKKO (PTOLEMAIS, ᶜAkka, Acre)	[155259]
ᶜAlma [S]	[196273]
Arbela (Ḥorvat Arbel, Khirbet ᶜIrbid) [S]	[195246]
Asochis (Shikhin, Kefar Shihin, Tel Ḥannaton, Tell el Bedawye)	[174243]
Baca (Peqiᶜin, El-Buqeiᶜah) [S]	[181264]
Barᶜam (Kefar Barᶜam) [S]	[189272]
Beer Sheba (Khirbet Anu esh Shiba)	[189259]
Beth Alpha (Hefsibah) [S]	[190213]
Beth Netofah Valley	
BETHSAIDA (IULIAS, et Tell) [S]	[208257]
Beth Sheᶜarim (esh Sheikh Ibreik) [S]	[162234]
Cadasa (Kedesh, Qadas, Tel Qedesh) [T]	[200279]
CAESAREA MARITIMA (Qesaria, Qaiṣāriyeh) [T, S]	[140212]
CAESAREA PHILIPPI (Panias, Banyas) [T]	[215295]
Cana (Ḥorvat Qana?)	[178247]
Caparasima (Kafr Sumeiᶜ)	[178264]
Capernaum → Kefar Naḥum	[204254]
Capharata (Caphareccho, Kefar Ata, Ḥorvat Ata)	[160245]
Carmel Range	
Chabulon (Kabul)	[170252]
Chorazin → Khorazin	[203257]
Cochabae (Kaukab)	[173248]
Dabaritta (Dabburiye)	[185233]
Ecdippa → Achziv	[159272]

Naḥal Hasor
Naḥal Qishon (Pacida Rivus)
Naḥal Ṣippori
Nain (Givʿat Naʿim)   [183226]
Nazareth   [178234]
Nazareth Ridge
Panias → Caesarea Philippi   [215295]
Peqiʿim → Baca   [181264]
PTOLEMAIS → AKKO   [155259]
Qadas → Cadasa   [200279]
Qaṣrin [S]   [216266]
Qeren Naftali [T]   [202277]
Qiṣion (Qiẓion, Khirbet Qasyûn) [S]   [199272]
Reina   [179236]
Saab (Shaʾab)   [173255]
Samaria (SEBASTE, Sebastiya) [T]   [168187]
Saʿsa [S]   [187270]
SCYTHOPOLIS (Beth Shean, Beisan) [T]   [197211]
Ṣepph (Ṣefat)   [196263]
SEPPHORIS (Ṣippori, Diocaesarea, Saffuriye) [S]   [176239]
Shepharʿam (Shefarʿam, Shafa ʿAmr) [S?]   [166245]
Shikhin → Asochis   [174243]
Suḥmata   [178267]
Susita → HIPPOS   [211242]
TARICHAEAE (Magdala, Migdal Nunia, Migdal Sebaya, Mejdel)   [198247]
Tel Shimron   [170234]
Thella (Yisod ha-Maʿalah, Tuleil) [S]   [208272]
TIBERIAS [S]   [201242]
Tirʾan Valley
Tivʿon (Tabun)   [162236]
Turan (Turan)   [185242]
TYRE (Sur)   [168298]
Usha (Khirbet Hushe)   [163244]
Yisod ha-Maʿalah [S]   [207273]
Yodefat (Jotapata, Khirbet Shifat)   [176248]

Abbreviations

Modern Works and Organizations

AAS	*Acta apostolici sedis*
AB	Anchor Bible
ABD	*Anchor Bible Dictionary*
AJS	*American Journal of Sociology*
ANET	*Ancient Near Eastern Texts Relating to the Old Testament,* 3d ed. 1969, ed. James B. Pritchard
ANRW	*Aufstieg und Niedergang der römischen Welt*
ARW	*Archiv für Religionswissenschaft*
AsiaJourTheol	*Asian Journal of Theology*
ATR	*Anglican Theological Review*
BAR	*Biblical Archaeology Review*
BASOR	*Bulletin of the American Schools of Oriental Research*
BASP	*Bulletin of the American Society of Papyrologists*
BBB	Bonner biblische Beiträge
BBET	Beiträge zur biblischen Exegese und Theologie
BETL	Bibilotheca ephemeridum theologicarum lovaniensium
BHK	*Biblia Hebraica,* ed. Rudolph Kittel
Bib	*Biblica*
BJS	Brown Judaic Studies
BR	*Biblical Research*
BTB	*Biblical Theology Bulletin*
BZ	*Biblische Zeitschrift*
BZAW	Beihefte zur ZAW
CBQ	*Catholic Biblical Quarterly*
CBQMS	CBQ Monograph Series
ConBNT	Coniectanea biblica, New Testament
CR	*Classical Review*
CRBS	*Currents in Research: Biblical Studies*
CRINT	Compendia Rerum Iudaicarum ad Novum Testamentum
CSEL	Corpus scriptorum ecclesiasticorum latinorum
DJD	Discoveries in the Judaean Desert
EB	*Enchirion biblicum*
EBib	Études bibliques
EI	*Eretz Israel*
EKKNT	Evangelisch-katholischer Kommentar zum Neuen Testament
EncJud	*Encyclopaedia Judaica*

ESCJ	Studies in Christianity and Judaism / Études sur le christianisme et le judaïsme
ET	English translation
ETL	*Ephemerides theologicaerum lovanienses*
EvT	*Evangelische Theologie*
ExpT	*Expository Times*
FilolNT	Filologia neotestamentaria
FOTL	Forms of the Old Testament Literature
FRLANT	Forschungen zur Religion und Literatur des Alten und Neuen Testaments
FzB	Forschung zur Bibel
FZPT	*Freiburger Zeitschrift für Philosophie und Theologie*
Greg	*Gregorianum*
HervTeoStud	*Hervormde teologiese studies*
HibJ	*Hibbert Journal*
HSCP	*Harvard Studies in Classical Philology*
HTKNT	Herders theologischer Kommentar zum Neuen Testament
HTR	*Harvard Theological Review*
HTS	Harvard Theological Studies
HUCA	*Hebrew Union College Annual*
ICC	International Critical Commentary
IEJ	*Israel Exploration Journal*
IQP	International Q Project
JAC	*Jahrbuch für Antike und Christentum*
JBL	*Journal of Biblical Literature*
JBW	*Jahrbuch der biblischen Wissenschaft*
JHC	*Journal of Higher Criticism*
JHS	*Journal of Hellenic Studies*
JJS	*Journal of Jewish Studies*
JPS	*Journal of Peasant Studies*
JR	*Journal of Religion*
JRS	*Journal of Roman Studies*
JSJ	*Journal for the Study of Judaism*
JSNT	*Journal for the Study of the New Testament*
JSNTSup	Journal for the Study of the New Testament Supplement Series
JSP	*Journal for the Study of the Pseudepigrapha*
JTS	*Journal of Theological Studies*
LTK	*Lexikon für Theologie und Kirche*
LTP	*Laval Théologique et Philosophique*
MeyerK	H. A. W. Meyer, Kritisch-exegetischer Kommentar über das Neue Testament
MTSR	*Method and Theory in the Study of Religion*
NA^{25}	Nestle-Aland, *Novum Testamentum Graece*, 25th ed., 1963
NA^{26}	Nestle-Aland, *Novum Testamentum Graece*, 26th ed., 1979
NA^{27}	Nestle-Aland, *Novum Testamentum Graece*, 27th ed., 1993
Neot	*Neotestamentica*
NF	Neue Folge (new series)

NHC	Nag Hammadi Codices
NHS	Nag Hammadi Studies
NorTT	*Norsk Teologisk Tidsskrift*
NovT	*Novum Testamentum*
NovTSup	Supplements to Novum Testamentum
NRT	*La nouvelle revue théologique*
NTAbh	Neutestamentliche Abhandlungen
NTOA	Novum Testamentum et Orbis Antiquus
NTTS	New Testament Tools and Studies
OBO	Orbis biblicus et orientalis
ÖTKNT	Ökumenische Taschenbucher-Kommentar zum Neuen Testament
PBC	Pontifical Biblical Commission
P&P	*Past & Present*
PEQ	*Palestine Exploration Quarterly*
QD	Quaestiones disputatae
RB	*Revue biblique*
RCF	*Revue du clergé français*
RevQ	*Revue de Qumrân*
RGG	*Religion in Geschichte und Gegenwart*
RHPR	*Revue d'histoire et de philosophie religieuses*
RSR	*Religious Studies Review*
SA	*Sociological Analysis*
SANT	Studien zum Alten und Neuen Testament
SBL	Society of Biblical Literature
SBLDS	SBL Dissertation Series
SBLSBS	SBL Sources for Biblical Study
SBLSP	SBL Seminar Papers
SBLTT	SBL Texts and Translations
SBS	Stuttgarter Bibelstudien
SBT	Studies in Biblical Theology
SCS	Septuagint and Cognate Studies
SE	*Studia Evangelica*
SecCent	*Second Century*
SEG	*Supplementum epigraphicum graecum*
SJLA	Studies in Judaism in Late Antiquity
SNTSMS	Society for New Testament Studies Monograph Series
SNTU/A	Studien zum Neuen Testament und seiner Umwelt/Abhandlungen
SPB	Studia Postbiblica
SpeechM	*Speech Monographs*
ST	*Studia Theologica*
SUC	Schriften des Urchristentums
TAPA	*Transactions of the American Philological Association*
ThJb(T)	*Theologische Jahrbücher (Tübingen)*
THKNT	Theologischer Handkommentar zum Neuen Testament
TJT	*Toronto Journal of Theology*
TLZ	*Theologische Literaturzeitung*

TQ	*Theologische Quartalschrift*
TSK	*Theologische Studien und Kritiken*
TS	*Theological Studies*
TTZ	*Trier theologische Zeitschrift*
TU	Texte und Untersuchungen
TynBul	*Tyndale Bulletin*
TZ	*Theologische Zeitschrift*
UBS	United Bible Societies
UNT	Untersuchungen zum Neuen Testament
WCC	World Council of Churches
WMANT	Wissenschaftliche Monographien zum Alten und Neuen Testament
WUNT	Wissenschaftliche Untersuchungen zum Neuen Testament
YCS	*Yale Classical Studies*
ZNW	*Zeitschrift für neutestamentliche Wissenschaft*
ZPE	*Zeitschrift für Papyrologie und Epigraphik*
ZRGG	*Zeitschrift für Religions- und Geistesgeschichte*
ZTK	*Zeitschrift für Theologie und Kirche*
ZWT	*Zeitschrift für wissenschaftliche Theologie*

Ancient Authors and Works

1QH	Hodayot (Hymn Scroll) 1QHymns[a]
1QpHab	Habakkuk Pesher (Commentary)
1QS	Rule of the Community from Cave 1
1QSa	Rule of the Congregation (1Q28a); eschatological appendix to 1QS
2 Apoc. Bar.	*2 Apocalypse of Baruch*
4Q159	4QOrdinances
4Q185	4QSapiential Work
4Q246	Aramaic Apocalypse
4Q415-418	Fragments of multiple copies of 4QSapientialWork[A] (see 4Q185 and 424)
4Q420/421	Fragments of copies of 4QWays of Righteousness
4Q424	4QSapiential Work[C]
4Q521	Messianic Apocalypse
4Q525	4QBeatitudes (4QBéat)
4QDibHam	Words of the Luminaries (4Q504, 505, 506)
4QMMT	Halakhic Letter (6 copies: 4Q394, 395, 396, 397, 398, 399)
4QS[a]	Rule of the Community from Cave 4 (4Q255)
4QSapientialWork[A]	Sapiential Work[A] (4QSap. Work A)
4QSapientialWork[C]	Sapiential Work[C] (4QSap. Work C; 4Q424)
ʿAbod. Zar.	*ʿAbodah Zara*
ʾAbot R. Nat.	*ʾAbot de Rabbi Nathan*
Ant.	Josephus, *Antiquities of the Jews*
b.	Babylonian Talmud (Bavli) tractates

B. Bat.	*Baba Batra*
Ber.	*Berakot*
Bib. Ant.	Pseudo-Philo, *Biblical Antiquities*
B. Qam.	*Baba Qama*
CDC	Cairo Damascus Document
Codex Theod.	*Codex Theodotianus*
Dem.	*Demai*
Did.	*Didache*
Diss.	Epictetus, *Dissertationes*
GThom	*Gospel of Thomas*
Haer.	Irenaeus, *Adversus haereses* (Against the Heresies)
Ḥag.	*Ḥagiga*
Hist.	Tacitus, *Historia* (History)
Hist. eccl.	Eusebius, *Historia ecclesiastica* (Church History)
Jub.	*Jubilees*
Kil.	*Kilʾayim*
Lam. Rab.	*Lamentations Rabbah*
Legatio	Philo, *Legatio ad Gaium* (Embassy to Gaius)
Lev. Rab.	*Leviticus Rabbah*
LXX	Septuagint
m.	Mishnah tractates
Maʿaś. S	*Maʿaśer Seni*
Meg.	*Megilla*
Mek.	*Mekilta*
Men.	*Menaḥot*
Miqw.	*Miqwaʾôt*
Ned.	*Nedarim*
𝔓[52]	Rylands Papyrus 457; a fragment of John 18 and 19
P. Berol.	*Papyrus Berolinensis* (Berlin Papyrus)
P. Bouriant	*Papyri Bouriant*
P. Hibeh	*Hibeh Papyri* (1906–55)
P. Insinger	*Payrus Insinger*; an Egyptian wisdom text (1st cent. CE)
P. Louvre D.	2414 *Louvre Demotic Papyrus* 2414
P. Mich.	*Michigan Papyri*
P. Oxy.	*Oxyrhynchus Papyri* (1898–)
P. Vindob. G.	29946 *Vienna Diogenes Papyrus*
Pesaḥ.	*Pesaḥim*
Ps.-Philo	Pseudo-Philo
Pss. Sol.	*Psalms of Solomon*
Qidd.	*Qiddušin*
Qoh. Rab.	*Qohelet Rabbah*
Šabb.	*Šabbat*
Sanh.	*Sanhedrin*
Šeb.	*Šebiʿit*
Šeq.	*Šeqalim*
Spec. Leg.	Philo, *Specialibus legibus* (Special Laws)
t.	Tosefta tractates
T. Abr.	*Testament of Abraham*

T. Asher	*Testament of Asher*
T. Dan	*Testament of Dan*
T. Isaac	*Testament of Isaac*
T. Iss.	*Testament of Issachar*
T. Jud.	*Testament of Judah*
T. Levi	*Testament of Levi*
T. Naph.	*Testament of Naphtali*
T. Zeb.	*Testament of Zebulon*
Taʿan.	*Taʿanit*
Tohar.	*Toharot*
War	Josephus, *War of the Jews*
y.	Jerusalem Talmud (Yerushalmi) tractates

Gospel Sigla and Terms

2DH	Two Document hypothesis
2GH	Two Gospel (Griesbach) hypothesis
4SH	Four Source Hypothesis
A	*Ur-Markus* (Holtzmann)
{A}	the highest rating of a Q passage by the IQP
{B}	the second-level rating of a Q passage by the IQP
{C}	the third-level rating of a Q passage by the IQP
{D}	the lowest rating of a Q passage by the IQP
GH	Griesbach hypothesis
GThom	*Gospel of Thomas*
Λ	*Logia*: Holtzmann's reconstruction of Q [Λ]
L	pre-Lukan source material
M	pre-Matthaean source material
Mark^{int}	intermediate Mark (Boismard); proto-Mark
Matt^{Aram}	an Aramaic form of Matthew (Lagrange and Wikenhauser)
Matt^{int}	intermediate Matthew (Boismard); proto-Matthew
Matt^{R}	Matthew's redaction of Mark
Mg	Greek translation of M, the Matthean *Urgospel* in Aramaic (Vaganay)
MT	Masoretic text
Q	the Sayings Gospel
Q^{1}	the formative stratum of Q: hortatory instructions (Kloppenborg)
Q^{2}	the main redaction of Q: editing and insertion of Deuteronomistic materials (Kloppenborg)
Q^{3}	final glosses on Q (Kloppenborg)
Q^{J}	a Judaized version of Q (Wernle)
Q^{Luke}	a version of Q used by Luke
Q^{Matt}	a version of Q used by Matthew
Q^{Red}	Q redaction, or work of Q's editor
R	*Redequelle*: Aramaic source used by Matthew and Luke (Bussmann)

Redaction A	the first constituent, originally independent, collection of Q (Sato)
Redaction B	the second constituent, originally independent, collection of Q (Sato)
Redaction C	the secondary compositional stratum of Q (Sato)
S	pre-Synoptic Source in Aramaic (Vaganay)
Sg	Greek translation of S (Vaganay)
S^L	Lukan *Sondergut*: material unique to Luke
S^M	Mattaean *Sondergut*: material unique to Matthew
T	*Täufer* (Baptist): Greek source used by Matthew and Luke (Bussmann)
Ur-Markus	a version of Mark, earlier than the final form
Ur-Matthäus	a version of Matthew, earlier than the final form

Works Cited

(Dates in pointed brackets (<1933>) refer, in the case of translations, to the date of the original German or French editions or, in the case of reprints, to the original date of publication.)

Abel, Felix Marie. 1908. "Inscriptions de Transjordanie et de Haute Galilée." *RB* 17:566–78.

Adam, A. K. M. 1996. "According to Whose Law? Aristobulus, Galilee and the Νόμοι τῶν Ἰουδαίων." *JSP* 14:15–21.

Adan-Bayewitz, David. 1985. "חרוכל בארץ־ישראל: המאה ה־2 עד המאה ה־4 לספירה" (The Itinerant Peddler in Roman Palestine from the Second to the Fourth Century CE)." In יהודים בכלכלה: קובץ מאמרים *(Jews in Economic Life: Collected Essays)*, ed. Nachum Gross, 67–85. Jerusalem: Merkaz Zalman Shazar.

———. 1992. *Common Pottery in Roman Galilee: A Study of Local Trade.* Ramat Gan: Bar Ilan Univ.

Adan-Bayewitz, David, Mordechai Aviʿam, and Douglas R. Edwards. 1977. "Yodefat—1992." *Excavations and Surveys in Israel* 16:42–44.

Adan-Bayewitz, David, and Isadore Perlman. 1990. "The Local Trade of Sepphoris in the Roman Period." *IEJ* 40(2–3):153–72.

Aland, Kurt. 1963. *Synopsis Quattuor Evangeliorum.* Stuttgart: Württembergische Bibelanstalt.

———. 1985. *Synopsis Quattuor Evangeliorum: locis parallelis evangeliorum apocryphorum et patrum adhibit.* 13th ed., revised. Stuttgart: Deutsche Bibelgesellschaft.

———. 1989. *The Text of the New Testament: An Introduction to the Critical Editions.* 2d ed., revised and enlarged. Grand Rapids, Mich.: Eerdmans.

Alfaric, Prosper. 1959. *Origines sociales du christianisme.* Ouvrage Inédit Présenté par Jacqueline Marchand. Paris: Publications de l'Union Rationaliste.

Allen, W. C. 1899–1900. "Did St Matthew and St Luke Use the Logia?" *ExpT* 11:424–26.

Allison, Dale C. 1980. "The Authorship of 1 Q S III,13 – IV,14." *RevQ* 10(38):257–68.

———. 1997. *The Jesus Tradition in Q.* Valley Forge, Pa.: Trinity Press International.

Allison, Henry E. 1966. *Lessing and the Enlightenment: His Philosophy of Religion and Its Relation to Eighteenth-Century.* Ann Arbor, Mich.: Univ. of Michigan Press.

Anonymous. 1816. "Die verschiedenen Rücksichten in welchen und für welche der Biograph Jesus arbeiten kann." *Kritisches Journal der neuesten theologischen Literatur* 5:225–45.

Applebaum, Shimon. 1967. *Israel and Her Vicinity in the Roman and Byzantine Periods.* Tel Aviv: Tel Aviv Univ.

———. 1986. "The Settlement Pattern of Western Samaria from Hellenistic to Byzantine Times: A Historical Commentary." In *Landscape and Pattern: An Archaeological Survey of Samaria 800 B.C.E.–636 C.E.,* by Shimʿon Dar, 255–69, 309–13. BAT International Series 308. 2 vols. Oxford: B.A.R.

———. 1989. "The Roman Colony of Ptolemais-ʿAke and Its Territory." In *Judaea in Hellenistic and Roman Times: Historical and Archaeological Essays,* 70–96. SJLA 40. Leiden: E. J. Brill.

Arav, Rami, and Cecilia Meier. 1995. "Bethsaida Excavations: Preliminary Report 1987–1993." In *Bethsaida: A City by the North Shore of the Sea of Galilee,* 3–63. Bethsaida Excavations Project 1. Kirksville, Mo.: Thomas Jefferson Univ. Press.

Arav, Rami, and Richard S. Freund. 1995. *Bethsaida: A City by the North Shore of the Sea of Galilee.* Bethsaida Excavations Project 1. Kirksville, Mo.: Thomas Jefferson Univ. Press.

Argyle, A. W. 1952–53. "The Accounts of the Temptation of Jesus in Relation to the Q-Hypothesis." *ExpT* 64:382.

Arnal, William E. 1995. "The Rhetoric of Marginality: Apocalypticism, Gnosticism and Sayings Gospels." *HTR* 88:471–94.

———. 1997a. "Gendered Couplets in Q and Legal Formulations: From Rhetoric to Social History." *JBL* 116:75–94.

———. 1997b. "Major Episodes in the Biography of Jesus: An Assessment of the Historicity of the Narrative Tradition." *TJT* 13:201–26.

———. 1997c. "Making and Re-Making the Jesus-Sign: Contemporary Markings on the Body of Christ." In Arnal and Desjardins 1997:308–19.

———. 1997d. "The Rhetoric of Deracination in Q: A Reappraisal." Ph.D. diss., Centre for the Study of Religion, Univ. of Toronto.

Arnal, William E., and Michel Desjardins, eds. 1997. *Whose Historical Jesus?* ESCJ 7. Waterloo, Ontario: Canadian Corporation for Studies in Religion/Corporation Canadienne des Sciences Religieuses by Wilfrid Laurier Univ. Press.

Attridge, Harold W. 1976. *First-Century Cynicism in the Epistles of Heraclitus.* HTS 29. Missoula, Mont.: Scholars Press.

———. 1979. "The Original Text of Gos. Thom., Saying 30." *BASP* 16:153–57.

———. 1989. "The Gospel of Thomas: The Greek Fragments." In *Nag Hammadi Codex II,2-7 Together with XIII,2*, Brit. Lib. Or. 4926(1), and P.Oxy. 1, 654, 655,* ed. Bentley Layton, 95–128. NHS 20. Leiden: E. J. Brill.

———. 1991. "Reflections on Research Into Q." In Kloppenborg and Vaage 1991a:223–34.

Audet, Jean Paul. 1958. *La Didachè: Instructions des apôtres.* EBib. Paris: J. Gabalda et Cie.

Aune, David E. 1981. "The Problem of the Genre of the Gospels: A Critique of C. H. Talbert's *What Is a Gospel?*" In *Gospel Perspectives II,* ed. R. T. France and David Wenham, 9–60. Sheffield: JSOT Press.

———. 1987. *The New Testament in Its Literary Environment.* Library of Early Christianity 8. Philadelphia: Westminster.

———. 1997. "Jesus and Cynics in First-Century Palestine: Some Critical Considerations." In *Hillel and Jesus: Comparative Studies of Two Major Religious Leaders*, ed. James H. Charlesworth and Loren L. Johns, 177–92. Minneapolis: Fortress Press.

Avi-Yonah, Michael. 1952. "Mount Carmel and the God of Baalbak." *IEJ* 2:118–24.

———. 1959. "Syrian Gods at Ptolemais-Accho." *IEJ* 9:1–12.

———. 1960. "The Foundation of Tiberias." *IEJ* 1:160–69.

———. 1962. "A List of Priestly Courses from Caesarea." *IEJ* 12:137–39.

———. 1964. "The Caesarea Inscription of the Twenty-four Priestly Courses." In *The Teacher's Yoke: Studies in Memory of Henry Trantham*, ed. E. Jerry Vardaman et al., 46–57. Waco, Tex.: Baylor Univ. Press.

———. 1977. *The Holy Land: From the Persian to the Arab Conquests (536 B.C. to A.D. 640).* Rev. ed. Grand Rapids, Mich.: Baker.

Avigad, Nahman. [1989]. *The Herodian Quarter in Jerusalem: Wohl Archaeological Museum.* Jerusalem: Keter Publishing House.

Aviʿam, Mordechai. 1985. "The Roman Temple at Kedesh in the Light of Certain Northern Syrian City Coins." *Tel Aviv* 12:212–14.

———. 1993. "Galilee: The Hellenistic to the Byzantine Periods." In *The New Encyclopedia of Archaeological Excavations in the Holy Land*, ed. Ephraim Stern and Ayelet Lewinson-Gilboa, 2:452–58. Jerusalem: Israel Exploration Society & Carta; New York and Toronto: Simon & Schuster.

———. Forthcoming. *Jews, Pagans and Christians in the Galilee: Archaeological Surveys and Excavations.*

Bacon, Benjamin Wiser. 1908a. "Logia." In *A Dictionary of Christ and the Gospels*, ed. James Hastings, 2:45–49. New York: Charles Scribner's Sons; Edinburgh: T. & T. Clark.

———. 1908b. "A Turning Point in Synoptic Criticism." *HTR* 1:48–69.

———. 1918. "Introduction." In *Matthew's Sayings of Jesus: The Non-Marcan Common Source of Matthew and Luke*, by George DeWitt Castor, 1–6. Chicago: Univ. of Chicago Press.

Bagnall, Roger S. 1989. "Official and Private Violence in Roman Egypt." *BASP* 26:201–16.

Bailey, Kenneth E. 1991. "Informal Controlled Oral Tradition and the Synoptic Gospels." *AsiaJourTheol* 5:34–54.

Baines, John. 1983. "Literacy in Ancient Egyptian Society." *Man* n.s. 18:572–99.

Baird, William. 1992. *History of New Testament Research.* Vol. 1: *From Deism to Tübingen.* Minneapolis: Fortress Press.

Baltzer, Klaus. 1975. *Die Biographie der Propheten.* Neukirchen-Vluyn: Neukirchener Verlag.

Bammel, Ernst. 1965. "John Did No Miracle: John 10:41." In *Miracles*, ed. C. F. D. Moule, 179–202. London: A. R. Mowbray.

Bar-Ilan, Meir. 1992. "Illiteracy in the Land of Israel in the First Centuries C.E." In *Essays in the Social Scientific Study of Judaism and Jewish Society.* Vol. 2, ed. Simcha Fishbane and Stuart Schoenfeld, 46–61. Hoboken, N.J.: Ktav.

Barnes, A. S. 1905. "Suggestions on the Origin of the Gospel according to St Matthew." *JTS* 6:187–203.

Barrett, C. K. 1943. "Q: A Re-examination." *ExpT* 54:320–23.

Barth, Karl. 1972. *Protestant Theology in the Nineteenth Century: Its Background and History.* Trans. John Bowden. London: SCM.

Batiffol, Pierre. 1897. *Six leçons sur les Évangiles.* 2d ed. Paris: Victor Lecoffre.

———. 1901. *Anciennes littératures chrétiennes. La littérature grecque.* 3d ed. Bibliothèque de l'enseignement de l'histoire ecclésiastique. Paris: Victor Lecoffre.

Batten, Alicia. 1994. "More Queries for Q: Women and Christian Origins." *BTB* 24:44–51.

Bauer, Bruno. 1841–42. *Kritik der evangelischen Geschichte der Synoptiker.* 3 vols. Leipzig: O. Wigand.

Bauer, Walter. 1934. *Rechtgläubigkeit und Ketzerei im ältesten Christentum.* Beiträge zur historischen Theologie 10. Tübingen: J. C. B. Mohr (Paul Siebeck); 2. Aufl. hrsg. von Georg Strecker, 1964.

———. 1971 <1964>. *Orthodoxy and Heresy in Earliest Christianity.* Ed. Robert A. Kraft and Gerhard Krodel. Appendices by Georg Strecker. Philadelphia: Fortress Press.

Baumgarten, Joseph M. 1967. "The Essene Avoidance of Oil and the Laws of Purity." *RevQ* 6:184–92.

Baur, Ferdinand Christian. 1831. "Die Christuspartei in der korinthinischen Gemeinde, der Gegensatz des petrinischen und paulinischen Christenthums in der ältesten Kirche, der Apostel Petrus in Rom." *Tübinger Zeitschrift für Theologie* 4:61–206.

———. 1846. "Der Ursprung und Character des Lukasevangeliums, mit Rücksicht auf die neuesten Untersuchungen." *ThJb(T)* 5:453–615.

———. 1847. *Kritische Untersuchungen über die kanonischen Evangelien, ihr Verhältnis zueinander, ihren Charakter und Ursprung.* Tübingen: Ludwig Friedrich Fues.

———. 1851. *Das Markusevangelium nach seinem Ursprung und Charakter nebst einem Anhang über das Evangelium Marcions.* Tübingen: Ludwig Friedrich Fues.

———. 1853. *Das Christentum und die christliche Kirche der drei ersten Jahrhunderte.* Tübingen: Ludwig Friedrich Fues.

Bellinzoni, Arthur J., ed. 1985. *The Two-Source Hypothesis: A Critical Appraisal.* Macon, Ga.: Mercer Univ. Press.

Ben-David, Arye. 1974. *Talmudische Ökonomie: die Wirtschaft des jüdischen Palästina zur Zeit der Mischna und des Talmud.* Hildesheim: Georg Olms.

Benoit, Pierre. 1950. *L'Évangile selon saint Matthieu.* Paris: Les Éditions du Cerf.

Benoit, Pierre, and Marie-Émile Boismard. 1965. *Synopse des quatre évangiles en français avec parallèles des apocryphes et des Pères.* Tome 1: *Textes.* Paris: Les Éditions du Cerf.

Bergemann, Thomas. 1993. *Q auf dem Prüfstand: Die Zuordnung des Mt/Lk-Stoffes zu Q am Beispiel der Bergpredigt.* FRLANT 158. Göttingen: Vandenhoeck & Ruprecht.

Bernand, Étienne. 1969. *Inscriptions métriques de l'Égypte gréco-romaine: Recherches sur la poésie épigrammatique des Grecs en Égypte.* Besançon Université, Annales littéraires 98. Paris: Société d'édition "Les Belles Lettres."

Betz, Hans Dieter. 1985a. "The Beatitudes of the Sermon on the Mount (Matt.

5:3-12): Observations on Their Literary Form and Theological Significance." In *Essays on the Sermon on the Mount*, Hans Dieter Betz, 17–39. Philadelphia: Fortress Press.

———. 1985b. *Essays on the Sermon on the Mount*. Philadelphia: Fortress Press.

———. 1991. "The Sermon on the Mount: In Defence of a Hypothesis." *BR* 36:74–80.

———. 1994. "Jesus and the Cynics: Survey and Analysis of a Hypothesis." *JR* 74:453–75.

———. 1995. *The Sermon on the Mount: A Commentary on the Sermon on the Mount*. Hermeneia. Minneapolis: Fortress Press.

Beyschlag, Willibald. 1885. *Das Leben Jesu*. 2 vols. Halle: E. Strien.

Bigelmair, Andreas. 1902. *Die Beteiligung der Christen am öffentlichen Leben in vorconstantinischer Zeit ein Beitrag zur ältesten Kirchengeschichte*. Munich: J. J. Lentner.

Bigler, Robert M. 1972. *The Politics of German Protestantism: The Rise of the Protestant Church Elite in Prussia, 1815–1848*. Berkeley: Univ. of California Press.

Bilde, Per. 1978. "The Roman Emperor Gaius (Caligula)'s Attempt to Erect His Statue in the Temple of Jerusalem." *ST* 32:67–93.

Billerbeck, Margarethe. 1979. *Der Kyniker Demetrius: Ein Beitrag zur Geschichte der frühkaiserzeitlichen Popularphilosophie*. Philosophia antiqua 36. Leiden: E. J. Brill.

———. 1991. "Greek Cynicism in Imperial Rome." In *Die Kyniker in der modernen Forschung*, ed. Margarethe Billerbeck, 147–66. Amsterdam: Grüner.

Biran, Avraham. 1981. "To the God Who Is in Dan." In *Temples and High Places in Biblical Times*, ed. Avraham Biran, 142–51. Jerusalem: Nelson Glueck School of Biblical Archaeology.

Bitzer, Lloyd F. 1968. "The Rhetorical Situation." *Philosophy and Rhetoric* 1:1–14.

Black, Matthew. 1967. *An Aramaic Approach to the Gospels and Acts; with an Appendix on the Son of Man*. 3d ed. Oxford: Clarendon.

———. 1989. "The Use of Rhetorical Terminology in Papias on Mark and Matthew." *JSNT* 37:31–41.

———. 1990. "The Aramaic Dimension in Q with Notes on Luke 17.22 Matthew 24.26 (Luke 17.23)." *JSNT* 40:33–41.

Blank, Sheldon H. 1937–38. "The Death of Zechariah in Rabbinic Literature." *HUCA* 12–13:327–46.

Blasi, Anthony J. 1986. "Role Structures in the Early Hellenistic Church." *SA* 47:226–48.

———. 1989. *Early Christianity as a Social Movement*. Toronto Studies in Religion 5. New York: Peter Lang.

Bleek, Friedrich. 1862. *Synoptische Erklärung der drei ersten Evangelien*, ed. H. J. Holtzmann. 2 vols. Leipzig: Wilhelm Engelmann.

Blok, Anton. 1972. "The Peasant and the Brigand: Social Banditry Reconsidered." *Comparative Studies in Society and History* 14:494–503.

Boismard, Marie-Émile. 1972. *Synopse des quatre évangiles en français*. Tome 2: *Commentaire*. Paris: Les Éditions du Cerf.

———. 1979–80. "The Two Source Theory at an Impasse." *NTS* 26:1–17.

———. 1990. "The Multiple Stage Hypothesis." In Dungan 1990a:231–88.

————. 1991. *Évangile de Marc: sa préhistoire.* Études biblique, nouvelle série 26. Paris: Les Éditions du Cerf.

Boismard, Marie-Émile, and A. Lamouille. 1986. *Synopsis Graeca Quattuor Evangeliorum.* Louvain and Paris: Peeters.

Booth, A. D. 1979. "The Schooling of Slaves in First-Century Rome." *TAPA* 109:11–19.

Boring, M. Eugene. 1982. *Sayings of the Risen Jesus: Christian Prophecy in the Synoptic Tradition.* SNTSMS 46. Cambridge: Cambridge Univ. Press.

Bösen, D. W. 1985. *Galiläa als Lebensraum und Wirkungsfeld Jesu: Eine zeitgeschichtliche und theologische Untersuchung.* Freiburg: Herder.

Bovon, François. 1989. *Das Evangelium nach Lukas.* 1. Teilband: *Lk 1,1-9,50.* EKKNT 3/1. Zürich: Benzinger; Neukirchen-Vluyn: Neukirchener Verlag.

Branham, R. Bracht, and Marie-Odile Goulet-Cazé. 1996. *The Cynics: The Cynic Movement in Antiquity and Its Legacy.* Hellenistic Culture and Society 23. Berkeley and Los Angeles: Univ. of California Press.

Braun, Willi. 1995. *Feasting and Social Rhetoric in Luke 14.* SNTSMS 85. Cambridge and New York: Cambridge Univ. Press.

Broer, Ingo. 1980. *Freiheit vom Gesetz und Radikalisierung des Gesetzes: Ein Beitrag zur Theologie des Evangelisten Matthäus.* SBS 98. Stuttgart: Katholisches Bibelwerk.

Broshi, Magan. 1979. "The Population of Western Palestine in the Roman-Byzantine Period." *BASOR* 236:1–10.

Brown, Raymond E. 1963. "Unity and Diversity in New Testament Ecclesiology." *NovT* 6:298–308.

Brunner, Helmut. 1970. "Die Lehren." In *Handbuch der Orientalistik. Erste Abteilung, Erster Band: Ägyptologie. Zweiter Abschnitt: Literatur.* 2 Aufl., ed. Hermann Kees, 113–39. Leiden: E. J. Brill.

Brunt, P. A. 1976. "The Romanization of the Local Ruling Classes in the Roman Empire." In *Assimilation et résistance à la culture gréco-romaine dans le monde ancien: travaux du VIe Congrès International d'Études Classiques (Madrid, Septembre 1974),* ed. D. M. Pippidi, 161–73. Bucharest: Editura Academiei; Paris: Société d'édition "Les Belles Lettres."

————. 1977. "Josephus on Social Conflicts in Roman Judaea." *Klio* 59:149–53.

————. 1990. *Roman Imperial Themes.* Oxford: Clarendon.

Büchler, Adolf. 1895. *Die Priester und der Cultus im letzten Jahrzehnt des jerusalemischen Tempels.* Vienna: Alfred Hölder.

————. 1909. *The Political and Social Leaders of the Jewish Community of Sepphoris.* Jews' College, London, Publication 1. London: Oxford Univ. Press for Jews' College.

Bultmann, Rudolf K. 1913. "Was lasst die Spruchquelle über die Urgemeinde erkennen?" *Oldenburgisches Kirchenblatt* 19:35–37, 41–44.

————. 1928. "Evangelien, gattungsgeschichtlich (formgeschichtlich)." *RGG²* 2:418–22.

————. 1931. *Die Geschichte der synoptischen Tradition.* 2. Aufl. FRLANT 29. Göttingen: Vandenhoeck & Ruprecht; 1. Aufl. 1921; 8. Aufl. 1970; 10. Aufl. 1995, mit einem Nachwort von Gerd Theißen.

————. 1948–53. *Theologie des Neuen Testaments.* 2 vols. Tübingen: J. C. B. Mohr

(Paul Siebeck); 2. Aufl. 1954; 9. Aufl, 1984, durchgesehen und ergänzt von Otto Merk.

———. 1951–55 <1948–53>. *Theology of the New Testament.* 2 vols. Trans. K. Grobel. New York: Charles Scribner's Sons.

———. 1968 <1931>. *The History of the Synoptic Tradition.* Rev. ed. Trans. John Marsh. Oxford: Basil Blackwell.

———. 1969 <1928>. "The Gospels (Form)." In *Twentieth Century Theology in the Making,* ed. Jaroslav Pelikan, trans. R. A. Wilson, 86–92. London and New York: Collins; Harper & Row.

———. 1994 <1913>. "What the Saying Source Reveals about the Early Church." In Kloppenborg 1994b:23–34.

Bundy, Walter E. 1955. *Jesus and the First Three Gospels.* Cambridge: Harvard Univ. Press.

Burgess, Joseph A. 1976. "A History of the Exegesis of Matthew 16:17-19 from 1781 to 1965." Dr. Theol. diss., Univ. of Basel, 1966. Ann Arbor, Mich.: Edwards Brothers.

Burke, Kenneth. 1968. *Counter-Statement.* 2d ed. Berkeley: Univ. of California Press.

Burkitt, F. Crawford. 1901. *Two Lectures on the Gospels.* London and New York: Macmillan.

———. 1906. *The Gospel History and Its Transmission.* Edinburgh: T. & T. Clark.

Burney, C. F. 1925. *The Poetry of Our Lord.* Cambridge: Cambridge Univ. Press.

Burridge, Richard A. 1992. *What Are the Gospels? A Comparison with Graeco-Roman Biography.* SNTSMS 70. Cambridge and New York: Cambridge Univ. Press.

Burton, Ernest de Witt. 1904. *Some Principles of Literary Criticism and Their Application to the Synoptic Problem.* The Decennial Publications. First Series 5. Chicago: Univ. of Chicago Press.

———. 1912. "Some Phases in the Synoptic Problem." *JBL* 31:95–113.

Burton, Ernest de Witt, and Edgar Johnson Goodspeed. 1920. *A Harmony of the Synoptic Gospels in Greek.* Chicago: Univ. of Chicago Press.

Bussby, Frederick. 1954. "Is Q an Aramaic Document?" *ExpT* 65:272–75.

Bussmann, Wilhelm. 1929. *Synoptische Studien: 2. Heft. Zur Redenquelle.* Halle [Saale]: Buchhandlung des Waisenhauses.

Butler, B. C. 1951a. "The Lachmann Fallacy." In *The Originality of St. Matthew: A Critique of the Two-Document Hypothesis,* 62–71. Cambridge: Cambridge Univ. Press.

———. 1951b. *The Originality of St. Matthew: A Critique of the Two-Document Hypothesis.* Cambridge: Cambridge Univ. Press.

Butts, James R. 1986. "The Chreia in the Synoptic Gospels." *BTB* 16:132–38.

Cadbury, Henry Joel. 1961. *The Making of Luke-Acts.* 2d ed. London: SPCK.

Calvin, Jean. 1555. *Harmonia ex evangelistis: tribus composita, Matthaeo, Marco, et Luca.* Geneva: Eustathii Vignon.

———. 1972. *A Harmony of the Gospels, Matthew, Mark and Luke.* Ed. A. W. Morrison and T. H. L. Parker. Calvin's New Testament Commentaries 1–3. 3 vols. Grand Rapids, Mich.: Eerdmans.

Camerlynck, Achille, and H. Coppieters. 1908. *Evangeliorum secundum Matthaeum, Marcum et Lucam synopsis juxta Vulgatam editionem.* Commentarii Brugenses in Sacram Scripturam. Bruges: Carl Beyaert; 2d ed., 1910; 3d ed. 1921.

Cameron, Ron. 1984. *Sayings Traditions in the Apocryphon of James*. HTS 34. Philadelphia: Fortress Press.

———. 1986. "Parable and Interpretation in the Gospel of Thomas." *Forum* 2,2:3–39.

———, ed. 1990a. *The Apocryphal Jesus and Christian Origins*. Semeia 49. Atlanta: Scholars Press.

———. 1990b. "'What Have You Come Out to See?' Characterizations of John and Jesus in the Gospels." In Cameron 1990a:35–69.

———. 1996. "The Sayings Gospel Q and the Quest of the Historical Jesus: A Response to John S. Kloppenborg." *HTR* 89:351–54.

Caragounis, Chrys C. 1986. *The Son of Man*. WUNT 2/38. Tübingen: J. C. B. Mohr (Paul Siebeck).

Carlston, Charles E., and Dennis Norlin. 1971. "Once More—Statistics and Q." *HTR* 64:59–78.

———. 1999. "Statistics and Q—Some Further Observations." *NovT* 41:108–123.

Carruth, Shawn. 1992. "Persuasion in Q: A Rhetorical Critical Study of Q 6:20-49." Ph.D. diss., Claremont Graduate School.

———. 1995. "Strategies of Authority: A Rhetorical Study of the Character of the Speaker in Q 6:20-49." In Kloppenborg 1995a:98–115.

Carruth, Shawn, and Albrecht Garsky. 1996. *Q 11:2b-4*, ed. Stanley D. Anderson. In *Documenta Q: Reconstructions of Q through Two Centuries of Gospel Research Excerpted, Sorted and Evaluated*. Louvain: Peeters.

Carruth, Shawn, and James M. Robinson. 1996. *Q 4:1-13,16*, ed. Christoph Heil. In *Documenta Q: Reconstructions of Q through Two Centuries of Gospel Research Excerpted, Sorted and Evaluated*. Louvain: Peeters.

Case, Shirley Jackson. 1914. *The Evolution of Early Christianity*. Chicago: Univ. of Chicago Press.

———. 1923. *The Social Origins of Christianity*. Chicago: Univ. of Chicago Press.

Casey, Maurice. 1980. *Son of Man: The Interpretation and Influence of Daniel 7*. London: SPCK.

Castelli, Elizabeth, and Hal Taussig, eds. 1996. *Reimagining Christian Origins: A Colloquium Honoring Burton L. Mack*. Valley Forge, Pa.: Trinity Press International.

Castor, George DeWitt. 1912 [1918]. *Matthew's Sayings of Jesus: The Non-Marcan Common Source of Matthew and Luke*. (Ph.D. diss., Univ. of Chicago, 1907). Chicago: Univ. of Chicago Press (completed 1912; imprint, 1918).

Catchpole, David R. 1991. "The Mission Charge in Q." In Kloppenborg and Vaage 1991a:147–74.

———. 1992a. "The Beginning of Q: A Proposal." *NTS* 38:205–21.

———. 1992b. "The Question of Q." *Sewanee Theological Review* 36:33–44.

———. 1993. *The Quest for Q*. Edinburgh: T. & T. Clark.

Ceresko, Anthony R. 1997. "The Liberative Strategy of Ben Sira: The Sage as Prophet." *TJT* 13:169–85.

Cerfaux, Lucien. 1935. "À propos des sources du troisième évangile: proto-Luc ou proto-Matthieu?" *ETL* 12:5–27.

———. 1938. "Encore la question synoptique." *ETL* 15:330–37.

———. 1954. "Le problème synoptique." *NRT* 76:494–505.

Chadwick, Owen. 1978. *Catholicism and History: The Opening of the Vatican Archives*. Cambridge and New York: Cambridge Univ. Press.

Chapman, John. 1905. "Le témoignage de Jean le Presbyte au sujet de S. Marc et de S. Luc." *Revue Bénédictine* 22:357–76.

———. 1937. *Matthew, Mark and Luke: A Study in the Order and Interrelation of the Synoptic Gospels*. Ed. John M. T. Barton. London: Longmans, Green.

Chemnitz, Martinus, and Polycarp Leyser. 1593–1626. *Harmoniae evangelicae . . . libri quinque*. Frankfurt and Hamburg: Iohannes Iacobus Porsius.

———. 1646. *Harmoniae evangelistarum Chemnitio-Lyserianae continuatio*. New ed. Ed. Johann Gerhard. Rotterdam: Arnold Leers.

Chiat, Marilyn J. 1982. *Handbook of Synagogue Architecture*. Brown Judaic Studies 29. Chico, Calif.: Scholars Press.

Childs, Brevard S. 1993. *Biblical Theology of the Old and New Testaments: Theological Reflection on the Christian Bible*. Philadelphia: Fortress Press.

Chilton, Bruce. 1984. "The Gospel according to Thomas as a Source of Jesus' Teaching." In *The Jesus Tradition outside the Gospels*, ed. David Wenham, 155–75. Gospel Perspectives 5. Sheffield: JSOT Press.

Clapsis, Emmanuel. 1991. "Eschatology." In *Dictionary of the Ecumenical Movement*, ed. Nicholas Lossky et al., 361–64. Geneva: WCC Publications; Grand Rapids, Mich.: Eerdmans.

Clay, Diskin. 1996. "Picturing Diogenes." In Branham and Goulet-Cazé 1996:366–86.

Cohen, Shaye J. D. 1979. *Josephus in Galilee and Rome: His Vita and Development as a Historian*. Columbia Studies in the Classical Tradition 8. Leiden: E. J. Brill.

———. 1992. "The Place of the Rabbi in Jewish Society of the Second Century." In L. I. Levine 1992:157–73.

Collins, John J., ed. 1979. *Apocalypse: The Morphology of a Genre*. Semeia 14. Missoula, Mont.: Scholars Press.

———. 1993. "Wisdom, Apocalypticism, and Generic Compatibility." In Perdue et al. 1993:165–85.

———. 1994. "The Works of the Messiah." *Dead Sea Discoveries* 1:98–112.

———. 1995. *The Scepter and the Star: The Messiahs of the Dead Sea Scrolls and Other Ancient Literature*. The Anchor Bible Reference Library. Garden City, N.Y.: Doubleday.

Collins, Raymond F. 1983. *Introduction to the New Testament*. Garden City, N.Y.: Doubleday.

Colson, F. H. 1921. "Quintilian I.9 and the 'Chria' in Ancient Education." *CR* 35:150–54.

Conder, C. R., and H. H. Kitchener. 1881–83. *The Survey of Western Palestine: Memoirs of the Topography, Orography, Hydrography, and Archaeology*. Palestine Exploration Fund. Publications. 3 vols. London: Palestine Exploration Fund.

Conzelmann, Hans. 1960 <1967>. *The Theology of St. Luke*. Trans. Geoffrey Buswell. New York: Harper & Row.

———. 1969 <1967>. *An Outline of the Theology of the New Testament*. Trans. John Bowden. London: SCM.

Conzelmann, Hans, and Andreas Lindemann. 1975. *Arbeitsbuch zum Neuen Testament*. Uni-Taschenbücher 52. Tübingen: J. C. B. Mohr (Paul Siebeck); 6. Aufl. 1982; 8. Aufl. 1985; 12. Aufl. 1998.

———. 1988 <1975>. *Interpreting the New Testament: An Introduction to the Principles and Methods of N.T. Exegesis.* Trans. Siegfried S. Schatzmann. Peabody, Mass.: Hendrickson.

Cope, Lamar, David L. Dungan, William R. Farmer, Allan J. McNicol, David L. Peabody, and Philip L. Shuler. 1992. "Narrative Outline of the Composition of Luke according to the Two Gospel Hypothesis." In *Society of Biblical Literature 1992 Seminar Papers,* ed. Eugene H. Lovering, 98–120. SBLSP 31. Atlanta: Scholars Press.

———. 1993. "Narrative Outline of the Composition of Luke according to the Two Gospel Hypothesis [2]." In *Society of Biblical Literature 1993 Seminar Papers,* ed. Eugene H. Lovering, 303–33. SBLSP 32. Atlanta: Scholars Press.

———. 1994. "Narrative Outline of the Composition of Luke according to the Two Gospel Hypothesis [3]." In *Society of Biblical Literature 1994 Seminar Papers,* ed. Eugene H. Lovering, 516–73. SBLSP 33. Atlanta: Scholars Press.

———. 1995. "Narrative Outline of the Composition of Luke according to the Two Gospel Hypothesis [4]." In *Society of Biblical Literature 1995 Seminar Papers,* ed. Eugene H. Lovering, 636–87. SBLSP 34. Atlanta: Scholars Press.

Corbier, Mireille. 1991. "City, Territory and Taxation." In Rich and Wallace-Hadrill 1991:211–39.

Corbo, Virgilio. 1974. "Scavi archeologici a Magdala (1971–1973)." *Liber Annuus* 24:5–37.

Corley, Kathleen E. 1993. *Private Women, Public Meals: Social Conflict in the Synoptic Tradition.* Peabody, Mass.: Hendrickson.

———. 1996. "Feminist Myths of Christian Origins." In Castelli and Taussig 1996:51–67.

Crawford, Michael. 1970. "Money and Exchange in the Roman World." *JRS* 60:40–48.

Credner, Karl August. 1836. *Einleitung in das Neue Testament.* Halle: Buchhandlung des Waisenhauses.

Crenshaw, James L. 1971. "ʿeṣā and *dabar:* The Problem of Authority/Certitude in Wisdom and Prophetic Literature." In *Prophetic Conflict: Its Effect Upon Israelite Religion,* 116–23. BZAW 124. Berlin: Walter de Gruyter.

Cribiore, Raffaella. 1996. *Writing, Teachers, and Students in Graeco-Roman Egypt.* American Studies in Papyrology 36. Atlanta: Scholars Press.

Crönert, Wilhelm. 1906. *Kolotes und Menedemos: Texte und Untersuchungen zur Philosophen- und Literaturgeschichte.* Studien zur Palaeographie und Papyruskunde 6. Leipzig: E. Avenarius.

Crossan, John Dominic. 1983. *Fragments: The Aphorisms of Jesus.* San Francisco: Harper & Row.

———. 1991. *The Historical Jesus: The Life of a Mediterranean Jewish Peasant.* San Francisco: Harper & Row.

———. 1994. *Jesus: A Revolutionary Biography.* San Francisco: HarperSanFrancisco.

———. 1996. "Itinerants and Householders in the Earliest Kingdom Movement." In Castelli and Taussig 1996:113–29.

———. 1997. "Itinerants and Householders in the Early Jesus Movement." In Arnal and Desjardins 1997:7–24.

———. 1998. *The Birth of Christianity: Discovering What Happened in the Years Immediately after the Execution of Jesus.* San Francisco: HarperSanFrancisco.

Crum, J. M. C. 1927. *The Original Jerusalem Gospel: Being Essays on the Document Q.* London: Constable & Constable.

Dahl, Nils Alstrup. 1976. "Anamnesis: Memory and Commemoration in Early Christianity." In *Jesus in the Memory of the Early Church,* 11–29. Minneapolis: Augsburg.

Dalman, Gustaf Hermann. 1930. *Die Worte Jesu mit Berücksichtigung des nachkanonischen jüdischen Schrifttums.* Band I: *Einleitung und wichtige Begriffe.* 2. Aufl. Leipzig: J. C. Hinrichs.

Daly, Gabriel. 1980. *Transcendence and Immanence: A Study in Catholic Modernism and Integralism.* Oxford: Clarendon.

Dansette, Adrien. 1961. *Religious History of Modern France.* 2 vols. New York: Herder & Herder.

Dar, Shimᶜon. *Landscape and Pattern: An Archaeological Survey of Samaria 800 B.C.E.–636 C.E.* 2 vols. BAR international series 308. Oxford: B.A.R.

Dausch, Petrus. 1932. *Die heilige Schrift des Neuen Testaments.* Ed. Fritz Tillmann. Vol. 2. *Die drei älteren Evangelien übersetzt und erklärt.* 4. Aufl. Bonn: Peter Hanstein.

Davidson, Samuel. 1868. *An Introduction to the Study of the New Testament: Critical, Exegetical, and Theological.* 2 vols. London: Longmans, Green.

Davies, W. D., and Dale C. Allison. 1988–97. *A Critical and Exegetical Commentary on Matthew.* 3 vols. ICC. Edinburgh: T. & T. Clark.

Deiss, Lucien. 1963. *Synopse de Matthieu, Marc et Luc avec les parallèles de Jean. 2: Textes.* Bruges: Desclée de Brouwer.

Deissmann, Adolf. 1908. *Das Urchristentum und die unteren Schichten.* Göttingen: Vandenhoeck & Ruprecht.

Delobel, Joël. 1982. *Logia: Les paroles de Jésus—The Sayings of Jesus: Mémorial Joseph Coppens.* BETL 59. Louvain: Peeters; Louvain Univ. Press.

Denaux, Adelbert. 1995. "Criteria for Identifying Q-Passages: A Critical Review of a Recent Work by T. Bergemann." *NovT* 37:105–29.

Dentzer, Jean-Marie. 1985. "Les villages de la Syrie romaine dans une tradition d'urbanisme oriental," in collaboration with François Villeneuve. In *De l'Indus aux Balkans: Recueil à la mémoire de Jean Deshayes,* ed. J. L. Huot, M. Yon, and Y. Calbet, 213–48. Paris: Éditions Recherches sur le Civilisations.

Derrenbacker, Robert A. 1998. "The Relationship among the Gospels Reconsidered [Review Article of A. J. McNicol, *Beyond the Q Impasse: Luke's Use of Matthew* (Valley Forge: Trinity Press International, 1996)]." *TJT* 14:83–88.

Devisch, Michel. 1972. "Le document Q, source de Matthieu: Problématique actuelle." In *L'Évangile selon Matthieu: Rédaction et théologie,* ed. M. Didier, 71–97. BETL 29. Gembloux: Duculot.

———. 1975. "De geschiednis van de Quelle-hypothese: 1. Van J. G. Eichhorn tot B. H. Streeter; 2. De recente exegese." Dr. Theol. diss., Katholieke Universiteit Te Louvain.

Dewey, Joanna. 1987–88. "Order in the Synoptic Gospels: A Critique." *SecCent* 6:68–82.

de Jonge, Henk J. 1992a. "Augustine on the Interrelations of the Gospels." In Van Segbroeck et al. 1992:2409–17.

———. 1992b. "The Loss of Faith in the Historicity of the Gospel." In *John and the Synoptics,* ed. Adelbert Denaux, 409–21. BETL 101. Louvain: Peeters; Louvain Univ. Press.

de Jonge, Marinus. 1988. *Christology in Context: The Earliest Christian Responses to Jesus*. Philadelphia: Westminster.

de Ste Croix, G. E. M. 1981. *The Class Struggle in the Ancient Greek World*. London: Duckworth; Ithaca, N.Y.: Cornell Univ. Press.

de Wette, Wilhelm M. L. 1813. *Lehrbuch der christlichen Dogmatik in ihrer historischen Entwicklung dargestellt. Erster Theil: Die biblische Dogmatik Alten und Neuen Testaments*. Berlin: Georg Reimer.

———. 1826. *Lehrbuch der historisch kritischen Einleitung in die kanonischen Bücher des Neuen Testaments*. Lehrbuch der historisch kritischen Einleitung in die Bibel Alten und Neuen Testaments 2. Berlin: Georg Reimer; 2. Aufl. 1830; 3. Aufl. 1834; 4. Aufl. 1842; 5. Aufl. 1848; 6. Aufl. 1860.

———. 1858 <1848>. *An Historico-critical Introduction to the Canonical Books of the New Testament*. Trans. Frederick Frothingham. Boston: Crosby, Nichols.

Dibelius, Martin. 1935 <1933>. *From Tradition to Gospel*. Trans. B. L. Woolf. New York: Charles Scribner's Sons.

———. 1953. *Botschaft und Geschichte*. Tübingen: J. C. B. Mohr (Paul Siebeck).

Diels, Hermann. 1904. "Laterculi Alexandrini aus einem Papyrus Ptolemäischer Zeit." In *Abhandlungen der königlichen preussischen Akademie der Wissenschaften*, 1–16. Philosophisch-Historische Klasse 2. Berlin: Verlag der Königlichen Akademie der Wissenschaften.

Donahue, John R. 1973. *Are You the Christ? The Trial Narrative in the Gospel of Mark*. SBLDS 10. Missoula, Mont.: Society of Biblical Literature.

Dormeyer, Detlev. 1989. *Evangelium als literarische und theologische Gattung*. Erträge der Forschung 263. Darmstadt: Wissenschaftliche Buchgesellschaft.

———. 1993. *Das Neue Testament im Rahmen der antiken Literaturgeschichte: Eine Einführung*. Die Altertumswissenschaft. Darmstadt: Wissenschaftliche Buchgesellschaft.

Douglas, Rees Conrad. 1995. "'Love Your Enemies': Rhetoric, Tradents, and Ethos." In Kloppenborg 1995a:116–31.

Downing, F. Gerald. 1984. "Cynics and Christians." *NTS* 30:584–93.

———. 1988a. *Christ and the Cynics: Jesus and Other Radical Preachers in First-Century Tradition*. JSOT Manuals 4. Sheffield: JSOT Press.

———. 1988b. "Quite like Q: A Genre for 'Q': The 'Lives' of Cynic Philosophers." *Bib* 69:196–225.

———. 1992. *Cynics and Christian Origins*. Edinburgh: T. & T. Clark.

———. 1994. "A Genre for Q and a Socio-Cultural Context for Q: Comparing Sets of Similarities with Sets of Differences." *JSNT* 55:3–26.

———. 1995a. "Common Strands in Pagan, Jewish and Christian Eschatologies in the First Century." *TZ* 51:196–211.

———. 1995b. "Cosmic Eschatology in the First Century—'Pagan', Jewish and Christian." *L'Antiquité Classique* 64:99–109.

———. 1996. "Word-Processing in the Ancient World: The Social Production and Performance of Q." *JSNT* 64:29–48.

———. 1998. "Deeper Reflections on the Jewish Cynic Jesus." *JBL* 117:97–104.

Driessen, Henk. 1983. "The 'Noble Bandit' and the Bandits of the Nobles: Brigandage and Local Community in Nineteenth-Century Andalusia." *Archives Européennes de Sociologie* 24:96–114.

Dudley, Donald R. 1937. *A History of Cynicism from Diogenes to the 6th Century A.D.* London: Methuen.

Duling, Dennis C., and Norman Perrin. 1994. *The New Testament: Proclamation and Parenesis, Myth and History.* 3d ed. Fort Worth: Harcourt Brace College Publishers.

Dunderberg, Ismo. 1995. "Q and the Beginning of Mark." *NTS* 41:501–11.

Dungan, David L. 1980. "Theory of Synopsis Construction." *Bib* 61:305–29.

———. 1983. "The Purpose and Provenance of the Gospel of Mark according to the Two-Gospel (Owen-Griesbach) Hypothesis." In *New Synoptic Studies: The Cambridge Gospel Conference and Beyond,* ed. William R. Farmer, 411–40. Macon: Mercer Univ. Press.

———. 1985. "Synopses of the Future." *Bib* 66:457–92.

———. 1990a. *The Interrelations of the Gospels: A Symposium Led by M.-É. Boismard — W. R. Farmer — F. Neirynck.* Jerusalem 1984. BETL 95. Louvain: Louvain Univ. Press and Peeters.

———. 1990b. "Synopses of the Future." In Dungan 1990a:317–47.

———. 1999. *A History of the Synoptic Problem: The Canon, the Text, the Composition, and the Interpretation of the Gospels.* Anchor Bible Reference Library. New York, London, and Toronto: Doubleday.

Dunn, James D. G. 1977. *Unity and Diversity in the New Testament: An Inquiry into the Character of Earliest Christianity.* Philadelphia: Westminster.

Dupont, Jacques. 1958. *Les Béatitudes I: Le problème littéraire — Les deux versions du Sermon sur la montagne et des Béatitudes.* EBib. Bruges: Abbaye de Saint André; repr. Louvain: Nauwelaerts; Paris: J. Gabalda, 1969.

———. 1964. "Le Logion de douze trônes (Mt 19,28; Lc 22,28-30)." *Bib* 45:355–92.

———. 1968. "La Parabole de la brebis perdue (Mt 18,12-14; Lc 15,4-7)." *Greg* 49:265–87.

———. 1975. "Le Couple parabolique du sénevé et du levain (Mt 13,31-33; Lc 13,18-21)." In *Jesus Christus in Historie und Theologie: Festschrift für Hans Conzelmann zum 60. Geburtstag,* ed. Georg Strecker, 331–45. Tübingen: J. C. B. Mohr (Paul Siebeck).

———. 1985. *Études sur les évangiles synoptiques.* Ed. Frans Neirynck. BETL 70A–B. Louvain: Peeters; Louvain Univ. Press.

Dyson, Stephen L. 1975. "Native Revolt Patterns in the Roman Empire." *ANRW* II.3:138–75.

Easton, Burton Scott. 1926. *The Gospel according to St. Luke: A Critical and Exegetical Commentary.* Edinburgh: T. & T. Clark.

Ebner, Martin. 1996. "Kynische Jesusinterpretation—«disciplined exaggeration»? Eine Anfrage." *BZ* 40:93–100.

Eddy, Paul Rhodes. 1996. "Jesus as Diogenes? Reflections on the Cynic Jesus." *JBL* 115:449–69.

Edwards, Douglas R., and C. Thomas McCollough, eds. 1997. *Archaeology and the Galilee: Texts and Contexts in the Graeco-Roman and Byzantine Periods.* South Florida Studies in the History of Judaism 143. Atlanta: Scholars Press.

Edwards, Richard A. 1971. *The Sign of Jonah in the Theology of the Evangelists and Q.* SBT 2/18. London: SCM.

———. 1976. *A Theology of Q.* Philadelphia: Fortress Press.

Ehrman, Bart D. 1997. *The New Testament: A Historical Introduction to the Early Christian Writings.* London and New York: Oxford Univ. Press.

Eichhorn, Johann Gottfried. 1794. "Ueber die drey ersten Evangelien: Einige Beyträge zu ihrer künftigen kritischen Behandlung." In *Allgemeine Bibliothek der biblischen Literatur* 5:759–996. Leipzig: Weidmann.

———. 1804–7. *Einleitung in das Neue Testament.* 5 vols. Leipzig: Weidmann.

Elgvin, Torleif. 1995a. "The Reconstruction of Sapiential Work A." *RevQ* 16(64): 559–80.

———. 1995b. "Wisdom, Revelation, and Eschatology in an Early Essene Writing." In *Society of Biblical Literature 1995 Seminar Papers*, ed. Eugene H. Lovering, 440–63. SBLSP 34. Atlanta: Scholars Press.

———. 1996. "Wisdom in the *yaḥad:* 4QWays of Righteousness." *RevQ* 17(65–68):205–32.

Elliott, J. K. 1990. "The Relevance of Textual Criticism to the Synoptic Problem." In Dungan 1990a:348–59.

———. 1991. "Which Is the Best Synopsis?" *ExpT* 102:200–204.

———. 1993. "Resolving the Synoptic Problem Using the Text of Printed Greek Synopses." *FilolNT* 6:51–58.

Elliott, John H. 1993. *What Is Social-Scientific Criticism?* Guides to Biblical Scholarship: New Testament Series. Minneapolis: Fortress Press.

Enchiridion Biblicum: Documenta ecclesiastica sacram scripturam spectantia 1961. Editio quarta aucta et recognita. Naples: M. D'Auria Pontificius; Rome: A. Arnodo.

Ennulat, Andreas. 1994. *Die "Minor Agreements": Untersuchung zu einer offenen Frage des synoptischen Problems.* WUNT 2/62. Tübingen: J. C. B. Mohr (Paul Siebeck).

Epp, Eldon Jay. 1989. "Textual Criticism." In *The New Testament and Its Modern Interpreters*, ed. Eldon Jay Epp and George W. MacRae, 75–126. Bible and Its Modern Interpreters 3. Philadelphia: Fortress Press; Atlanta: Scholars Press.

Eshel, Hanan. 1997. "A Note on 'Miqvaot' at Sepphoris." In Edwards and McCollough 1997:131–33.

Evelyn White, H. G. 1920. *The Sayings of Jesus from Oxyrhynchus.* Cambridge: Cambridge Univ. Press.

Ewald, Heinrich. 1848. "Ursprung und Wesen der Evangelien." *JBW* 1:113–54.

———. 1849. "Ursprung und Wesen der Evangelien." *JBW* 2:180–224.

———. 1850a. *Die drei ersten Evangelien übersetzt und erklärt.* Göttingen: Vandenhoeck & Ruprecht.

———. 1850b. "Ursprung und Wesen der Evangelien." *JBW* 3:140–77.

Ewald, Paul. 1890. *Das Hauptproblem der Evangelienfrage und der Weg zu seiner Lösung: Eine akademische Vorlesung nebst Exkursen.* Leipzig: J. C. Hinrichs.

Fabricius, Johannes A. 1790–1809. *Bibliotheca graeca.* Editio quarta. Ed. Gottlieb Christophoros Harles. 12 vols. Hamburg: Carolus Ernestus Bohn.

Fallon, Francis T., and Ron Cameron. 1988. "The Gospel of Thomas: A Forschungsbericht and Analysis." *ANRW* II.25,6:4195–251.

Farmer, William R. 1964. *The Synoptic Problem: A Critical Analysis.* New York: Macmillan.

———. 1975. "A Fresh Approach to Q." In *Christianity, Judaism and Other Greco-Roman Cults: Essays for Morton Smith at Sixty*, ed. Jacob Neusner, 1:39–50. SJLA 12. Leiden: E. J. Brill.

———. 1977. "Modern Developments of Griesbach's Hypothesis." *NTS* 23:275–95.

———. 1980a. "Critical Reflections on Werner Georg Kümmel's History of New Testament Research." In *Occasional Notes on Some Points of Interest in New Testament Studies*, ed. William R. Farmer, 21–30. [Dallas]: N.p.

———. 1980b. "A Note on the Ideological Background of the Marcan Hypothesis." In *Occasional Notes on Some Points of Interest in New Testament Studies*, ed. William R. Farmer, 1–6. [Dallas]: N.p.

———. 1984. "Reply to Michael Goulder." In *Synoptic Studies: The Ampleforth Conferences of 1982 and 1983*, ed. Christopher M. Tuckett, 105–9. JSNTSup 7. Sheffield: JSOT Press.

———. 1987. "Luke's Use of Matthew: A Christological Inquiry." *Perkins Journal* 40(3):39–50.

———. 1990. "The Two-Gospel Hypothesis: The Statement of the Hypothesis." In Dungan 1990a:125–56.

———. 1992. "State *Interesse* and Marcan Primacy, 1870–1914." In Van Segbroeck et al. 1992:2477–98.

———. 1994. *The Gospel of Jesus: The Pastoral Relevance of the Synoptic Problem*. Louisville: Westminster John Knox.

———. 1995. "State *Interesse* and Marcan Primacy: 1870–1914." In Reventlow and Farmer 1995:15–49.

Farrer, Austin M. 1955. "On Dispensing with Q." In *Studies in the Gospels in Memory of R. H. Lightfoot*, ed. Dennis E. Nineham, 57–88. Oxford: Basil Blackwell.

———. 1985 <1955>. "On Dispensing with Q." In *The Two-Source Hypothesis: A Critical Appraisal*, ed. Arthur J. Bellinzoni, 321–56. Macon, Ga.: Mercer Univ. Press.

Fee, Gordon D. 1980. "A Text-Critical Look at the Synoptic Problem." *NovT* 22:12–28.

Ferguson, Everett. 1993. *Backgrounds of Early Christianity*. 2d ed. Grand Rapids, Mich.: Eerdmans.

Fichtner, Johannes. 1949. "Jesaja unter den Weisen." *TLZ* 74:75–80.

———. 1976 <1949>. "Isaiah among the Wise." In *Studies in Ancient Israelite Wisdom*, ed. James L. Crenshaw, 429–38. The Library of Biblical Studies. New York: Ktav.

Fieger, Michael. 1991. *Das Thomasevangelium: Einleitung, Kommentar und Systematik*. Neutestamentliche Abhandlungen 22. Münster: Verlag Aschendorff.

Fields, Weston W. 1992. "Sodom and Gomorrah: Tradition, Motif, and Message: A Traditio-Literary Study of Genesis 19 and Related Biblical Narratives." Ph.D. diss., Hebrew Univ. of Jerusalem.

Fiensy, David A. 1991. *The Social History of Palestine in the Herodian Period: The Land Is Mine*. Studies in the Bible and Early Christianity 20. Lewiston: Edwin Mellen.

Finley, Moses I. 1982. "The Ancient City: From Fustel de Coulanges to Max Weber and Beyond." In *Economy and Society in Ancient Greece*, ed. Richard P. Saller and Brent D. Shaw, 3–23. New York: Viking.

Fischel, H. A. 1968. "Studies in Cynicism and the Ancient Near East: The Transformation of a Chreia." In *Religions in Antiquity: Essays in Memory of Erwin Ransdall Goodenough*, ed. Jacob Neusner, 372–411. Studies in the History of Religions 14. Leiden: E. J. Brill.

Fitzmyer, Joseph A. 1970. "The Priority of Mark and the 'Q' Source in Luke." In *Jesus and Man's Hope: Pittsburgh Festival on the Gospels, 1970*, ed. David G. Buttrick, 1:131–70. Perspective 11/1–2. Pittsburgh: Pittsburgh Theological Seminary.

———. 1981. *The Gospel according to Luke I–IX*. AB 28. Garden City, N.Y.: Doubleday.

———. 1985. *The Gospel according to Luke X–XXIV*. AB 28A. Garden City, N.Y.: Doubleday.

———. 1991. *A Christological Catechism: New Testament Answers*. Rev. ed. New York and Mahwah, N.J.: Paulist.

Fleddermann, Harry T. 1981. "The Discipleship Discourse (Mark 9:33-50)." *CBQ* 43:57–75.

———. 1995. *Mark and Q: A Study of the Overlap Texts*. BETL 122. Louvain: Louvain Univ. Press; Peeters.

Fortna, Robert Tomson. 1970. *The Gospel of Signs: A Reconstruction of the Narrative Source Underlying the Fourth Gospel*. SNTSMS 11. London: Cambridge Univ. Press.

Fowler, Henry Thatcher. 1924. "Paul, Q, and the Jerusalem Church." *JBL* 43:9–14.

Frankel, Rafael. 1992. "Some Oil Presses from Western Galilee." *BASOR* 286:39–71.

———. 1993. "Mizpe Yammim, Mount." In *The New Encyclopedia of Archaeological Excavations in the Holy Land*, ed. Ephraim Stern and Ayelet Lewinson-Gilboa, 3:1061–63. Jerusalem: Israel Exploration Society & Carta; New York and Toronto: Simon & Schuster.

Frankemölle, Hubert. 1988. *Evangelium — Begriff und Gattung: Ein Forschungsbericht*. Stuttgarter biblische Beiträge 15. Stuttgart: Katholisches Bibelwerk.

Freedman, David Noel. 1992. "The Symmetry of the Hebrew Bible." *ST* 46:81–108.

Freyne, Seán. 1980. *Galilee from Alexander the Great to Hadrian, 323 B.C.E. to 135 C.E.: A Study of Second Temple Judaism*. Wilmington, Del.: Michael Glazier.

———. 1981. "Galilean Religion of the First Century C.E. against Its Social Background." *Proceedings of the Irish Biblical Association* 5:91–114.

———. 1988a. "Bandits in Galilee: A Contribution to the Study of Social Conditions in First Century Palestine." In *The Social World of Formative Christianity and Judaism: Essays in Tribute of Howard Clark Kee*, ed. Jacob Neusner et al., 50–67. Philadelphia: Fortress Press.

———. 1988b. *Galilee, Jesus and the Gospels: Literary Approaches and Historical Investigations*. Philadelphia: Fortress Press.

———. 1992. "Urban-Rural Relations in First-Century Galilee: Some Suggestions from the Literary Sources." In L. I. Levine 1992:75–91.

———. 1994. "The Geography, Politics, and Economics of Galilee and the Quest for the Historical Jesus." In *Studying the Historical Jesus: Evaluations of the State of Current Research*, ed. Bruce Chilton and Craig A. Evans, 75–121. NTTS 19. Leiden: E. J. Brill.

———. 1995a. "Herodian Economics in Galilee." In *Modelling Early Christianity: Social-Scientific Studies of the New Testament in Its Context*, ed. Philip F. Esler, 23–46. London and New York: Routledge.

———. 1995b. "Jesus and the Urban Culture of Galilee." In *Texts and Contexts: Biblical Texts in Their Textual and Situational Contexts. Essays in Honor of Lars*

Hartman, ed. Tord Fornberg and David Hellholm, 597–622. Oslo, Copenhagen, Stockholm, and Boston: Scandinavian Univ. Press.

———. 1997a. "Galilean Questions to Crossan's Mediterranean Jesus." In Arnal and Desjardins 1997:61–91.

———. 1997b. "Town and Country Once More: The Case of Roman Galilee." In Edwards and McCollough 1997:49–56.

Fridrichsen, Anton. 1913. "De nyere rekonstruktionen av Logiakilden (Q)." *NorTT* 14:193–244.

Friedrichsen, Timothy A. 1989. "The Matthew-Luke Agreements against Mark: A Survey of Recent Studies: 1974–1989." In *L'évangile de Luc: Problèmes littéraires et théologiques. Mémorial Lucien Cerfaux*. Revised and enlarged edition, ed. Frans Neirynck, 335–92. BETL 32. Louvain: Peeters.

———. 1991. "New Dissertations on the Minor Agreements." *ETL* 67:373–94.

Fuller, Reginald H. 1975. "The Synoptic Problem: After Ten Years." *Perkins Journal* 28(2):63–74.

———. 1978a. "Baur versus Hilgenfeld: A Forgotten Chapter in the Debate on the Synoptic Problem." *NTS* 24:355–70.

———. 1978b. "The Double Commandment of Love: A Test Case for the Criteria of Authenticity." In *Essays on the Love Commandment*, ed. Luise Schottroff, 41–56. Philadelphia: Fortress Press.

———. 1994. "Biblical Studies, 1955–1990." *ATR* 76:160–70.

Fusco, Vittorio. 1982. "L'accord mineur Mt 13,11a/Lc 8,10a contre Mc 4,11a." In Delobel 1982:355–61.

Gaboury, Antonio. 1970. *La structure des évangiles synoptiques: La structure-type à l'origine des synoptiques*. NovTSup 22. Leiden: E. J. Brill.

Gal, Zvi. 1991. "אבן כלי תעשיית בגליל התחתון" (A Stone-Vessel Manufacturing Site in the Lower Galilee). *'Atiqot* 20:25–26, 179–80 (English summary).

———. 1992. *Lower Galilee during the Iron Age*. Trans. Marcia Reines Josephy. Dissertation series, American Schools of Oriental Research 8. Winona Lake, Ind.: Eisenbrauns.

Gallo, Italo, ed. 1975–80. *Frammenti biografici da papiri*. Testi e commenti 1/6. Rome: Edizioni dell'Ateneo.

Galvin, John P. 1994. "From the Humanity of Christ to the Jesus of History: A Paradigm Shift in Catholic Christology." *TS* 55:252–73.

———. 1996. "'I Believe . . . in Jesus Christ, His Only Son, Our Lord': The Earthly Jesus and the Christ of Faith." *Interpretation* 50:373–82.

Gamble, Harry Y. 1995. *Books and Readers in the Early Church: A History of Early Christian Texts*. New Haven: Yale Univ. Press.

Gammie, John G. 1990a. "From Prudentialism to Apocalypticism: The Houses of the Sages amid the Varying Forms of Wisdom." In Gammie and Perdue 1990:479–97.

———. 1990b. "The Sage in Sirach." In Gammie and Perdue 1990:355–72.

Gammie, John G., and Leo G. Perdue, eds. 1990. *The Sage in Israel and the Ancient Near East*. Winona Lake, Ind.: Eisenbrauns.

Garnsey, Peter. 1970. *Social Status and Legal Privilege in the Roman Empire*. Oxford: Clarendon.

———. 1988. *Famine and Food Supply in the Graeco-Roman World: Responses to Risk and Crisis*. Cambridge: Cambridge Univ. Press.

Garnsey, Peter, and Richard Saller. 1987. *The Roman Empire: Economy, Society and Culture.* London: Duckworth; Berkeley: Univ. of California Press.

Garnsey, Peter, and Greg Woolf. 1989. "Patronage of the Rural Poor in the Roman World." In *Patronage in Ancient Society*, ed. Andrew Wallace-Hadrill, 153–70. London and New York: Routledge.

Garsky, Albrecht, Christoph Heil, Thomas Hieke, and Josef Amon. 1997. *Q 12:49-59*, ed. Shawn Carruth. In *Documenta Q: Reconstructions of Q through Two Centuries of Gospel Research Excerpted, Sorted and Evaluated.* Louvain: Peeters.

Gelzer, Heinrich, ed. 1890. *Georgii Cyprii Descriptio orbis Romani.* Bibliotheca scriptorum Graecorum et Romanorum Teubneriana. Leipzig: B. G. Teubner.

Georgi, Dieter. 1985. "Rudolf Bultmann's *Theology of the New Testament Revisited.*" In *Bultmann, Retrospect, and Prospect: The Centenary Symposium at Wellesley*, ed. Edward C. Hobbs, 75–87. HTS 35. Philadelphia: Fortress Press.

———. 1992. "The Interest in Life of Jesus Theology as a Paradigm for the Social History of Biblical Criticism." *HTR* 85:51–83.

Gewiess, Josef. 1957. "Friedrich Wilhelm Maier." *TRev* 53:273–74.

Gieseler, Johann Carl Ludwig. 1818. *Historisch-kritischer Versuch über die Entstehung und die frühesten Schicksale der schriftlichen Evangelien.* Leipzig: Wilhelm Engelmann.

Giet, Stanislaus. 1970. *L'énigme de la Didachè.* Paris: Éditions Ophrys.

Gitler, Haim. 1990. "The Coins." *'Atiqot* 19:101–6.

Gnilka, Joachim. 1990. *Jesus von Nazaret: Botschaft und Geschichte.* HTKNT Supplementband 3. Freiburg: Herder.

———. 1994. *Theologie des Neuen Testaments.* HTKNT Supplementband 5. Freiburg: Herder.

———. 1997 <1990>. *Jesus of Nazareth: Message and History.* Trans. Siegfried S. Schatzmann. Peabody, Mass.: Hendrickson.

Godet, Frédéric L. 1893–99. *Introduction au Nouveau Testament.* 2 vols. Neuchâtel and Paris: Librairie Fischbacher.

Goldstein, Jonathan A. 1976. *I Maccabees: A New Translation, with Introduction and Commentary.* AB 41. Garden City, N.Y.: Doubleday.

Goodacre, Mark S. 1996. *Goulder and the Gospels: An Examination of a New Paradigm.* JSNTSup 133. Sheffield: JSOT Press.

Goodman, Martin. 1982. "The First Jewish Revolt: Social Conflict and the Problem of Debt." In *Essays in Honour of Yigael Yadin*, ed. Geza Vermes and Jacob Neusner, 417–27. Journal of Jewish Studies 33. Totowa, N.J.: Allanheld Osmus.

———. 1983. *State and Society in Roman Galilee, A.D. 132–212.* Oxford Centre for Postgraduate Hebrew Studies. Totowa, N.J.: Rowman & Allanheld.

———. 1987. *The Ruling Class of Judaea: The Origins of the Jewish Revolt against Rome, A.D. 66–70.* Cambridge and New York: Cambridge Univ. Press.

———. 1990. "Kosher Olive Oil in Antiquity." In *A Tribute to Geza Vermes: Essays on Jewish and Christian Literature and History*, ed. Philip R. Davies and Richard T. White, 227–45. JSOTSup 100. Sheffield: JSOT Press.

Goulder, Michael D. 1984. "Some Observations on Professor Farmer's 'Certain Results. . . .'" In *Synoptic Studies: The Ampleforth Conferences of 1982 and 1983*, ed. Christopher M. Tuckett, 99–104, with Farmer's reply (105–9). JSNTSup 7. Sheffield: JSOT Press.

———. 1989. *Luke: A New Paradigm.* 2 vols. JSNTSup 20. Sheffield: JSOT Press.

————. 1996. "Is Q a Juggernaut?" *JBL* 115:667–81.

Goulet-Cazé, Marie-Odile. 1990. "Le cynicisme à l'époque impériale." *ANRW* II.36.4:2720–823.

————. 1996. "Catalogue of Known Cynic Philosophers." In Branham and Goulet-Cazé 1996:389–413.

Grant, F. C. 1926. *The Economic Background of the Gospels.* London: Oxford Univ. Press and H. Milford.

————. 1933. *The Growth of the Gospels.* New York: Abingdon.

————. 1957. *The Gospels: Their Origin and Growth.* New York: Harper & Row.

Greeven, Heinrich. 1978. "The Gospel Synopsis from 1776 to the Present Day." In *J. J. Griesbach, Synoptic and Text Critical Studies, 1776–1976,* ed. Bernard Orchard and Thomas R. W. Longstaff, 22–49. SNTSMS 34. Cambridge and New York: Cambridge Univ. Press.

Grenfell, B. P., and A. S. Hunt. 1897. *ΛΟΓΙΑ ΙΗΣΟΥ: The Sayings of Our Lord from an Early Greek Papyrus.* London: Henry Frowde for the Egypt Exploration Fund.

————. 1898. *The Oxyrhynchus Papyri. Part I.* Egypt Exploration Society. Graeco-Roman Memoirs 1. London: Egypt Exploration Society.

————. 1904a. *New Sayings of Jesus and Fragments of a Lost Gospel from Oxyrhynchus.* Egypt Exploration Fund: Graeco-Roman Branch. London: Henry Frowde for the Egypt Exploration Fund.

————. 1904b. *The Oxyrhynchus Papyri. Part IV.* Egypt Exploration Society. Graeco-Roman Memoirs 4. London: Egypt Exploration Society.

Griesbach, Johann Jakob. 1776. *Synopsis Evangeliorum Matthaei, Marci et Lucae. Textum graecum ad fidem codicum, versionum et patrum emendavit et lectionis varietatem adiecit Io. Iac. Griesbach.* Halle: J. J. Curtius Haerdes; 2. Aufl. 1797; 3. Aufl. 1809; 4. Aufl. 1822.

————. 1783. *Inquisitio in fontes, unde evangelistae suas de resurrectione Domini narrationes hauserint.* Jena: J. C. G. Goepferdt.

————. 1789–90. *Commentatio qua Marci Evangelium totum e Matthaei et Lucae commentariis decerptum esse monstratur.* Jena: J. C. G. Goepferdt.

————. 1794. "Commentatio qua Marci Evangelium totum e Matthaei et Lucae commentariis decerptum esse monstratur." *Commentationes Theologicae* (Leipzig) 1:360–434.

————. 1978 <1789–90>. "A Demonstration That Mark Was Written after Matthew and Luke." In *J. J. Griesbach, Synoptic and Text Critical Studies, 1776–1976,* ed. Bernard Orchard and Thomas R. W. Longstaff, 103–35. SNTSMS 34. Cambridge and New York: Cambridge Univ. Press.

Griffin, Miriam. 1996. "Cynicism and the Romans: Attraction and Repulsion." In Branham and Goulet-Cazé 1996:190–204.

Groh, Dennis E. 1995. "The Stratigraphic Chronology of the Galilean Synagogue from the Early Roman Period through the Early Byzantine Period (ca. 420 C.E.)." In *Ancient Synagogues: Historical Analyses and Archaeological Discovery,* ed. Dan Urman and Paul V. M. Flesher, 1:51–69. 2 vols. SPB 47/1–2. Leiden: E. J. Brill.

Grotius, Hugo. 1641. *Annotationes in libros evangeliorum.* Amsterdam: J. Blaev.

Grundmann, Walter. 1940. *Jesus der Galiläer und das Judentum.* Veröffentlichungen des Instituts zur Erforschung des jüdischen Einflusses auf das Deutsche Kirchliche Leben. Leipzig: Georg Wigand.

———. 1961. *Das Evangelium nach Lukas.* 9. Aufl. THKNT 3. Berlin: Evangelische Verlagsanstalt.

Guérin, Victor. 1880. *Description géographique, historique et archéologique de la Palestine. III: Galilée.* 2 vols. Paris: Imprimé par autorisation de L'empereur à L'Impr. Impériale.

Guillaumont, Antoine. 1959. *The Gospel according to Thomas: Coptic Text.* Leiden: E. J. Brill; New York: Harper & Row.

Guitton, Jean. 1992. *Portrait du père Lagrange. Celui qui a réconcilié la science et la foi.* Paris: Robert Laffont.

Gundry, Robert H. 1982. *Matthew: A Commentary on His Literary and Theological Art.* Grand Rapids, Mich.: Eerdmans.

Hachlili, Rachel, and A. Killebrew. 1983. "Jewish Funerary Customs during the Second Temple Period, in the Light of the Excavations at the Jericho Necropolis." *PEQ* 115:115–26.

Haenchen, Ernst. 1956. *Die Apostelgeschichte.* 10. Aufl. MeyerK 3. Göttingen: Vandenhoeck & Ruprecht.

———. 1966. *Der Weg Jesu: Eine Erklärung des Markus-Evangeliums und der kanonischen Parallelen.* Berlin: Alfred Töpelmann.

Han, Kyu Sam. 1998. "Q and the Temple: The Q Community's Attitude toward the Temple." Th.D. diss., Knox College, Toronto School of Theology.

Hanson, K. C. 1994. "How Honorable! How Shameful! A Cultural Analysis of Matthew's Makarisms and Reproaches." *Semeia* 68:81–111.

———. 1997. "The Galilean Fishing Economy and the Jesus Tradition." *BTB* 27(1):99–111.

Hanson, K. C., and Douglas E. Oakman. 1998. *Palestine in the Time of Jesus: Social Structures and Social Conflicts.* Minneapolis: Fortress Press.

Hanson, Richard S. 1980. *Tyrian Influences in Upper Galilee.* Meiron Excavation Project 2. Cambridge, Mass.: American Schools of Oriental Research.

Hare, Douglas R. A. 1990. *The Son of Man Tradition.* Minneapolis: Fortress Press.

Harnack, Adolf von. 1894–97. *Lehrbuch der Dogmengeschichte.* 3. Aufl. 3 vols. Freiburg im Breisgau: J. C. B. Mohr (Paul Siebeck).

———. 1896–99 <1894–97>. *History of Dogma.* Trans. Neil Buchanan. 7 vols. London and Boston: Williams & Norgate; Roberts.

———. 1900. *Das Wesen des Christentums.* Leipzig: J. C. Hinrichs.

———. 1901 <1900>. *What Is Christianity?* Trans. T. B. Saunders. London: Williams & Norgate; repr. Gloucester: Peter Smith, 1957; repr. 1978.

———. 1907. *Sprüche und Reden Jesu: Die zweite Quelle des Matthäus und Lukas.* Beiträge zur Einleitung in das Neue Testament 2. Leipzig: J. C. Hinrichs.

———. 1908 <1907>. *The Sayings of Jesus: The Second Source of St. Matthew and St. Luke.* Trans. John Richard Wilkinson. New Testament Studies 2. London: Williams & Norgate; New York: G. P. Putnam's Sons.

Harper, G. Maclean. 1928. "Village Administration in the Roman Province of Syria." *YCS* 1:102–68.

Harrington, Daniel J. 1980. "The Wisdom of the Scribe according to Ben Sira." In *Ideal Figures in Ancient Judaism,* ed. George W. E. Nickelsburg and John J. Collins, 181–88. Chico, Calif.: Scholars Press.

———. 1996. *Wisdom Texts from Qumran.* London and New York: Routledge.

Harris, Horton. 1973. *David Friedrich Strauss and His Theology.* Monograph Supplements to the Scottish Journal of Theology. Cambridge: Cambridge Univ. Press.

———. 1975. *The Tübingen School.* Oxford: Clarendon.

Harris, William V. 1989. *Ancient Literacy.* Cambridge: Harvard Univ. Press.

Hartin, Patrick J. 1991. *James and the "Q" Sayings of Jesus.* JSNTSup 47. Sheffield: Sheffield Academic Press.

Hartlich, Christian, and Walter Sachs. 1952. *Der Ursprung des Mythosbegriffes in der modernen Bibelwissenschaft.* Schriften der Studiengemeinschaft der Evangelischen Akademien 2. Tübingen: J. C. B. Mohr (Paul Siebeck).

Hartman, Lars. 1979. *Asking for a Meaning: A Study of 1 Enoch 1–5.* ConBNT 12. Lund: CWK Gleerup.

Hase, Karl von. 1876. *Geschichte Jesu nach akademischen Vorlesungen.* Leipzig: Breitkopf und Härtel.

Haufe, Günter. 1961. "Entrückung und eschatologische Funktion im Spätjudentum." *ZRGG* 13:105–13.

Haupt, Walther. 1913. *Worte Jesu und Gemeindeüberlieferung: Eine Untersuchung zur Quellengeschichte des Synopse.* UNT 3. Leipzig: J. C. Hinrichs.

Havener, Ivan. 1987. *Q: The Sayings of Jesus.* Good News Studies 19. Wilmington, Del.: Michael Glazier.

Haverly, Thomas. 1997. "Cataloguing Q(s): The Quest for Q and Its Literary History." In *Summary of Proceedings: Fiftieth Annual Conference of the ATLA,* ed. M. S. Chartier, 188–203. Evanston, Ill.: ATLA.

Hawkins, J. C. 1899. *Horae Synopticae: Contributions to the Study of the Synoptic Problem.* Oxford: Clarendon.

———. 1909. *Horae Synopticae: Contributions to the Study of the Synoptic Problem.* 2d ed. Oxford: Clarendon.

———. 1911. "Probabilities as to the So-called Double Tradition of St. Matthew and St. Luke." In Sanday 1911:95–140.

Hedrick, Charles W. 1984. "The Role of 'Summary Statements' in the Composition of the Gospel of Mark: A Dialog with Karl Schmidt and Norman Perrin." *NovT* 26:289–311.

Hegel, Georg Wilhelm Friedrich. 1984. *Lectures on the Philosophy of Religion.* Ed. Peter C. Hodgson. Trans. R. F. Brown, P. C. Hodgson, and J. M. Stewart. 3 vols. Berkeley: Univ. of California Press.

Hengel, Martin. 1968. *Nachfolge und Charisma: Eine exegetisch-religionsgeschichtliche Studie zu Mt. 8, 21f. und Jesu Ruf in die Nachfolge.* BZNW 34. Berlin: Walter de Gruyter.

———. 1979. "Jesus als messianischer Lehrer der Weisheit und die Anfänge der Christologie." In *Sagesse et religion:* [Actes du] Colloque de Strasbourg, Octobre 1976, 147–88. Bibliothèque des centres d'études supérieures spécialisées. Travaux de Centre d'études supérieures spécialisées d'histoire des religions de Strasbourg. Paris: Presses Universitaires de France.

———. 1981 <1968>. *The Charismatic Leader and His Followers.* Trans. J. C. G. Greig. Edinburgh: T. & T. Clark; New York: Crossroad.

———. 1989. *The "Hellenization" of Judaea in the First Century after Christ.* Trans. John Bowden. Philadelphia: Trinity Press International; London: SCM.

———. 1994. "Aufgaben der neutestamentlichen Wissenschaft." *NTS* 40:321–57.

Herder, Johann Gottfried. [1796–97] 1994. "Vom Erlöser der Menschen." In

Johann Gottfried Herder Theologische Schriften, ed. Christoph Bultmann and Thomas Zippert, 609–724. Johann Gottfried Herder Werke 9/1. Frankfurt am Main: Deutsche Klassiker Verlag (composed, 1796–97; published 1994).

———. [1797] 1877–1913. "Von Gottes Sohn, der Welt Heiland." In *Sämmtliche Werke*, ed. Bernhard Suphan, 19:253–424. Berlin: Weidmann.

Hickling, C. J. A. 1982. "The Plurality of Q." In Delobel 1982:425–29.

Hieke, Thomas. 1998. "Methoden und Möglichkeiten griechischer Synopsen zu den ersten drei Evangelien." In *Wenn drei das gleiche sagen: Studien zu den ersten drei Evangelien. Mit einer Werkstattübersetzung des Q-Textes*, ed. Stefan Brandenburger and Thomas Hieke, 1–36. Theologie 14. Münster: LIT-Verlag.

Higgins, A. J. B. 1964. *Jesus and the Son of Man*. Philadelphia: Fortress Press.

Hilgenfeld, Adolf. 1850. *Das Markus-evangelium, nach seiner Composition, seiner Stellung in der Evangelien-literatur, seinem Ursprung und Charakter*. Leipzig: Breitkopf und Härtel.

———. 1854. *Die Evangelien, nach ihrer Entstehung und geistlichen Bedeutung*. Leipzig: S. Hirzel.

———. 1857. "Die Evangelienfrage und ihre neuesten Behandlung von Weisse, Volkmar und Meyer." *ThJb(T)* 16:381–440, 498–532.

———. 1861. "Die Evangelien-Forschung nach ihrem Verlaufe und gegenwärtigen Stande." *ZWT* 4:1–71, 137–204.

Hirschfeld, Yizhar, and R. Birger-Calderon. 1991. "Early Roman and Byzantine Estates near Caesarea." *IEJ* 41:81–111.

Hobsbawm, Eric J. 1959. "The Social Bandit." In *Primitive Rebels: Studies in Archaic Forms of Social Movement in the 19th and 20th Centuries*, 13–29. Manchester: Manchester Univ. Press.

———. 1985. *Bandits*. 2d ed. Harmondsworth: Penguin.

Hobson, Deborah W. 1993. "The Impact of Law on Village Life in Roman Egypt." In *Law, Politics and Society in the Ancient Mediterranean World*, ed. Baruch Halpern and Deborah W. Hobson, 193–219. Sheffield: Sheffield Academic Press.

Hock, Ronald F. 1992. "Cynics." *ABD* 1:1221–26.

Hock, Ronald F., and Edward N. O'Neil. 1986. *The Chreia in Ancient Rhetoric*. Vol. 1: *The Progymnasmata*. SBLTT 27; Graeco-Roman Religion Series 9. Atlanta: Scholars Press.

Hoehner, Harold W. 1972. *Herod Antipas*. SNTSMS 17. Cambridge: Cambridge Univ. Press.

Hoffmann, Paul. 1969. "Die Versuchungsgeschichte in der Logienquelle." *BZ NF* 13:207–23.

———. 1972. *Studien zur Theologie der Logienquelle*. NTAbh NF 8. Münster: Verlag Aschendorff.

———. 1984. "Tradition und Situation: Zur 'Verbindlichkeit' des Gebots der Feindesliebe in der synoptischen Überlieferung und in der gegenwärtigen Friedensdiskussion." In *Ethik im Neuen Testament*, ed. Karl Kertelge and Franz Böckle, 50–117. QD 102. Freiburg: Herder.

———. 1989. "Jesu Verbot des Sorgens und seine Nachgeschichte in der synoptischen Überlieferung." In *Jesu Rede von Gott und ihre Nachgeschichte im frühen Christentum: Beiträge zur Verkündigung Jesu und zum Kerygma der Kirche: Festschrift für Willi Marxsen zum 70. Geburtstag*, ed. Dietrich-Alex Koch, 116–41. Gütersloh: Gerd Mohn.

————. 1992. "QR und der Menschensohn: Eine vorläufige Skizze." In Van Segbroeck et al. 1992:421–56.

————. 1995. "The Redaction of Q and the Son of Man: A Preliminary Sketch." In Piper 1995a:159–98.

Hoffmann, Paul, Josef Amon, Thomas Hieke, M. E. Boring, and Jon Ma. Asgeirsson. 1997. *Q 12:8-12*, ed. Christoph Heil. In *Documenta Q: Reconstructions of Q through Two Centuries of Gospel Research Excerpted, Sorted and Evaluated.* Louvain: Peeters.

Holtzmann, Heinrich Julius. 1863. *Die synoptischen Evangelien: Ihr Ursprung und geschichtlicher Charakter.* Leipzig: Wilhelm Engelmann.

————. 1886. *Lehrbuch der historisch-kritischen Einleitung in das Neue Testament.* 2. Aufl. Rev. [and] enl. Freiburg im Breisgau: J. C. B. Mohr (Paul Siebeck).

————. 1892. *Lehrbuch der historisch-kritischen Einleitung in das Neue Testament.* 3. Verbesserte und Vermehrte Aufl. Freiburg im Breisgau: J. C. B. Mohr (Paul Siebeck).

————. 1907. "Die Marcus-Kontroverse in ihrer heutigen Gestalt." *ARW* 10:18–40, 161–200.

————. 1911. *Lehrbuch der neutestamentlichen Theologie.* 2. Aufl. Ed. Adolf Jülicher and Walter Bauer. 2 vols. Sammlung theologischer Lehrbücher. Freiburg im Breisgau: J. C. B. Mohr (Paul Siebeck).

Honoré, Anthony M. 1968. "A Statistical Study of the Synoptic Problem." *NovT* 10:95–147.

Hopkins, Keith. 1978. "Economic Growth and Towns in Classical Antiquity." In *Towns in Societies: Essays in Economic History and Historical Sociology,* ed. Philip Abrams and Edward Anthony Wrigley, 35–77. Cambridge and New York: Cambridge Univ. Press.

Hopwood, Keith. 1989. "Bandits, Elites and Rural Order." In *Patronage in Ancient Society,* ed. Andrew Wallace-Hadrill, 171–87. London and New York: Routledge.

Horbury, William. 1984. "The Temple Tax." In *Jesus and the Politics of His Day,* ed. Ernst Bammel and C. F. D. Moule, 265–86. Cambridge: Cambridge Univ. Press.

Horsley, Richard A. 1979. "Josephus and the Bandits." *JSJ* 10:37–63.

————. 1987. *Jesus and the Spiral of Violence: Popular Jewish Resistance in Roman Palestine.* San Francisco: Harper & Row.

————. 1989a. "Questions about Redactional Strata and the Social Relations Reflected in Q." In *Society of Biblical Literature 1989 Seminar Papers,* ed. David J. Lull, 186–203. SBLSP 28. Atlanta: Scholars Press.

————. 1989b. *Sociology and the Jesus Movement.* New York: Crossroad.

————. 1991a. "Logoi Prophētōn: Reflections on the Genre of Q." In *The Future of Early Christianity: Essays in Honor of Helmut Koester,* ed. Birger A. Pearson, 195–209. Minneapolis: Fortress Press.

————. 1991b. "Q and Jesus: Assumptions, Approaches, and Analyses." In Kloppenborg and Vaage 1991a:175–209.

————. 1991c. "The Q People: Renovation, not Radicalism." *Continuum* 1:49–63.

————. 1994. "Wisdom Justified by All Her Children: Examining Allegedly Disparate Traditions in Q." In *Society of Biblical Literature 1994 Seminar Papers,* ed. Eugene H. Lovering, 733–51. SBLSP 33. Atlanta: Scholars Press.

————. 1995a. "Archaeology and the Villages of Upper Galilee: A Dialogue with Archaeologists." *BASOR* 297:5–16.

———. 1995b. "Archaeology of Galilee and the Historical Context of Jesus." *Neot* 29:221–29.

———. 1995c. *Galilee: History, Politics, People.* Valley Forge, Pa.: Trinity Press International.

———. 1995d. "Social Conflict in the Synoptic Sayings Source Q." In Kloppenborg 1995a:37–52.

———. 1996a. *Archaeology, History and Society in Galilee: The Social Context of Jesus and the Rabbis.* Valley Forge, Pa.: Trinity Press International.

———. 1996b. "What Has Galilee to Do with Jerusalem? Political Aspects of the Jesus Movement." *HervTeoStud* 52:88–104.

Horsley, Richard A., and John S. Hanson. 1985. *Bandits, Prophets, and Messiahs: Popular Movements in the Time of Jesus.* Minneapolis: Winston.

Huby, Joseph. 1910. "Sur un passage du second évangile." *Recherches de Science Religieuse* 1:168–74.

———. 1924. "Bulletin d'exégèse du Nouveau Testament: Autour de la question synoptique." *Recherches de Science Religieuse* 14:78–94.

———. 1929. *L'évangile et les évangiles.* Collection "La vie chrétienne" 7. Paris: Bernard Grasset.

———. 1931 <1929>. *The Church and the Gospels.* Trans. Fenton Moran. New York: Sheed and Ward.

Huck, Albert. 1898. *Synopse der drei ersten Evangelien.* 2. Aufl. Tübingen: J. C. B. Mohr (Paul Siebeck); 4. Aufl., 1910.

Huck, Albert, and Hans Lietzmann. 1935. *Synopse der drei ersten Evangelien.* 9. Aufl. Tübingen: J. C. B. Mohr (Paul Siebeck); 10. Aufl. 1950; 11. Aufl. 1970; 12. Aufl. 1975.

Huck, Albert, and Heinrich Greeven. 1981. *Synopse der drei ersten Evangelien: mit Beigabe der johanneischen Parallelstellen. Synopsis of the Three Gospels.* 13. Aufl. Tübingen: J. C. B. Mohr (Paul Siebeck).

Hultgren, Arland J. 1994. *The Rise of Normative Christianity.* Minneapolis: Fortress Press.

Hurd, John C. 1986. "Paul ahead of His Time: 1 Thess. 2:13-16." In *Anti-Judaism in Early Christianity: Vol. 1, Paul and the Gospels,* ed. Peter Richardson, 21–36. ESCJ 2. Waterloo: Wilfrid Laurier Univ. Press.

Ilan, Zvi. 1987. "סקר בתי־כנסת קדומים בגליל" (A Survey of Ancient Synagogues in Galilee)." *EI* 19:170–98; *77–78 (English summary).

Isaac, Benjamin. 1984. "Bandits in Judaea and Arabia." *HSCP* 88:171–203.

Jacobson, Arland D. 1978. "Wisdom Christology in Q." Ph.D. diss., Claremont Graduate School.

———. 1982a. "The Literary Unity of Q." *JBL* 101:365–89.

———. 1982b. "The Literary Unity of Q: Lc 10,2-16 and Parallels as a Test Case." In Delobel 1982:419–23.

———. 1987. "The History of the Composition of the Synoptic Sayings Source." In *Society of Biblical Literature 1987 Seminar Papers,* ed. Kent H. Richards, 285–94. SBLSP 26. Atlanta: Scholars Press.

———. 1992a. "Apocalyptic and the Synoptic Sayings Source Q." In Van Segbroeck et al. 1992:403–19.

———. 1992b. *The First Gospel: An Introduction to Q.* Sonoma, Calif.: Polebridge.

———. 1994. "The Literary Unity of Q." In Kloppenborg 1994b:98–115.

Jacquier, Eugène. 1903-8. *Histoire des livres du Nouveau Testament.* 4 vols. Paris: Victor Lecoffre; J. Gabalda et Cie.

Jastrow, Marcus. 1985. *A Dictionary of the Targumim, the Talmud Babli and Yerushalmi, and the Midrashic Literature.* New York: Judaica.

Jefford, Clayton N. 1989. *The Sayings of Jesus in the Teachings of the Twelve Apostles.* Supplements to Vigiliae Christianae 11. Leiden: E. J. Brill.

————, ed. 1995. *The Didache in Context: Essays on Its Text, History and Transmission.* NovTSup 77. Leiden: E. J. Brill.

Jeremias, Joachim. 1930. "Zur Hypothese einer schriftlichen Logienquelle Q." *ZNW* 29:147–49.

————. 1958. *Heiligengräber in Jesu Umwelt (Mt. 23, 29; Lk. 11, 47): eine Untersuchung zur Volksreligion der Zeit Jesu.* Göttingen: Vandenhoeck & Ruprecht.

————. 1972 <1970>. *The Parables of Jesus.* Rev. ed. Trans. S. H. Hooke. New York: Charles Scribner's Sons; London: SCM.

Johnson, Luke Timothy. 1986. *The Writings of the New Testament: An Interpretation.* Philadelphia: Fortress Press.

————. 1995. *The Letter of James: A New Translation with Introduction and Commentary.* AB 37A. Garden City, N.Y.: Doubleday.

————. 1999. *The Writings of the New Testament: An Interpretation.* Rev. ed., with Todd C. Penner. Minneapolis: Fortress Press.

Jolliffe, Ron. 1990. "The Woes on the Pharisees: A Critical Text and Commentary on Q 11:46, 43, 52, 42, 39-40, 47-48." Ph.D. diss., Claremont Graduate School.

Jones, A. H. M. 1931. "The Urbanization of Palestine." *JRS* 21:78–85.

————. 1971. *The Cities of the Eastern Roman Provinces.* 2d ed. Revised by Michael Avi-Yonah. Oxford: Clarendon.

Jouguet, Pierre, and P. Perdizet. 1906. "Le Papyrus Bouriant n. 1. Un cahier d'écolier grec d'Égypte." In *Kolotes und Menedemos,* by Wilhelm Crönert, 148–61. Studien zur Paläographie und Papyruskunde 6. Leipzig: E. Avenarius.

Judge, E. A. 1960. *The Social Pattern of Christian Groups in the First Century: Some Prolegomena to the Study of New Testament Ideas of Social Obligation.* London: Tyndale.

Jülicher, Adolf. 1900. *Einleitung in das Neue Testament.* 2. Aufl. Tübingen: J. C. B. Mohr (Paul Siebeck).

————. 1904 <1900>. *An Introduction to the New Testament.* Trans. Janet Penrose Ward. London: Smith, Elder.

Kahlert, Heinrich. 1984. *Der Held und seine Gemeinde: Untersuchungen zum Verhältnis von Stifterpersönlichkeit und Verehrergemeinschaft in der Theologie des freien Protestantismus.* Europäische Hochschulschriften: 23. Reihe: Theologie 238. Frankfurt: Peter Lang.

Käsemann, Ernst. 1960. "Die Anfänge christlicher Theologie." *ZTK* 57:162–85.

————. 1963. "Unity and Diversity in New Testament Ecclesiology." *NovT* 6:290–97.

————. 1969a. "The Beginnings of Christian Theology." In *New Testament Questions of Today,* by Ernst Käsemann, trans. W. J. Montague, 82–107. London: SCM.

————. 1969b. "On the Subject of Primitive Christian Apocalyptic." In *New Testament Questions of Today,* by Ernst Käsemann, trans. W. J. Montague, 108–37. London: SCM.

Kasher, Aryeh. 1988. *Jews, Idumaeans, and Ancient Arabs: Relations of the Jews in Eretz-Israel with the Nations of the Frontier and the Desert during the Hellenis-*

tic and Roman Era (332 BCE – 70 CE). Texte und Studien zum antiken Judentum 18. Tübingen: J. C. B. Mohr (Paul Siebeck).

———. 1990. *Jews and Hellenistic Cities in Eretz Israel: Relations of the Jews in Eretz-Israel with the Hellenistic Cities during the Second Temple Period (332 BCE – 70 CE)*. Texte und Studien zum antiken Judentum 21. Tübingen: J. C. B. Mohr (Paul Siebeck).

Kautsky, Karl. 1908. *Der Ursprung des Christentums, eine historische Untersuchung*. Internationale Bibliothek 45. Stuttgart: J. H. W. Dietz.

———. 1925. *Foundations of Christianity*. Trans. Henry F. Mins. New York: International Publishers.

Kayatz, Christa. 1966. *Studien zu Proverbien 1–9. Eine form- und motivgeschichtliche Untersuchung*. WMANT 22. Neukirchen-Vluyn: Neukirchener Verlag.

Kee, Howard Clark. 1970. *Jesus in History: An Approach to the Study of the Gospels*. New York: Harcourt, Brace & World.

———. 1975. "The Function of Scriptural Quotations and Allusions in Mark 11–16." In *Jesus und Paulus: Festschrift für Werner Georg Kümmel zum 70. Geburtstag*, ed. E. Earle Ellis and Erich Grässer, 165–88. Göttingen: Vandenhoeck & Ruprecht.

———. 1977. *Jesus in History: An Approach to the Study of the Gospels*. 2d ed. New York: Harcourt Brace Jovanovich.

———. 1980. *Christian Origins in Sociological Perspective: Methods and Resources*. Philadelphia: Westminster.

———. 1995. *Who Are the People of God?: Early Christian Models of Community*. New Haven: Yale Univ. Press.

———. 1996a. "Jesus: A Glutton and a Drunkard." *NTS* 42:374–93.

———. 1996b. *Jesus in History: An Approach to the Study of the Gospels*. 3d ed. Fort Worth: Harcourt Brace College Publishers

Keim, Theodor. 1867–72. *Die Geschichte Jesu von Nazara*. 3 vols. Zurich: Orell, Füssli.

———. 1873–83 <1867–72>. *The History of Jesus of Nazara*. Trans. Arthur Ransom and E. M. Geldart. 6 vols. London and Edinburgh: Williams and Norgate.

Kelber, Werner H. 1976. *The Passion in Mark: Studies on Mark 14–16*. Philadelphia: Fortress Press.

———. 1983. *The Oral and the Written Gospel: The Hermeneutics of Speaking and Writing in the Synoptic Tradition, Mark, Paul, and Q*. Philadelphia: Fortress Press.

Kertelge, Karl. 1985. "Das Doppelgebot der Liebe im Markusevanglium." In *À cause de l'évangile: études sur les Synoptiques et les Actes: offertes au P. Jacques Dupont, O.S.B. à l'occasion de son 70ᵉ anniversaire*, 303–22. Lectio divina 123. Paris: Publications de Saint-André and Les Éditions du Cerf.

Kiilunen, Jarmo. 1989. *Das Doppelgebot der Liebe in synoptischer Sicht: Ein redaktionskritischer Versuch über Mk 12, 28-34 und die Parallelen*. Annales Academiae Scientiarum Fennicae. B/250. Helsinki: Suomalainen Tiedeakatemia.

Kilpatrick, G. D. 1941. "The Disappearance of Q." *JTS* 42:182–84.

Kim, Myung-Soo. 1990. *Die Trägergruppe von Q: Sozialgeschichtliche Forschung zur Q-Überlieferung in den synoptischen Evangelien*. Wissenschaftliche Beiträge aus europäischen Hochschulen Reihe 1, Theologie 1. Hamburg: Verlag an der Lottbek [Peter Jensen].

Kirk, Alan. 1996. "The Structure of Q: Genre, Synchrony, and the Sapiential Composition in the Synoptic Sayings Source." Ph.D. diss., Centre for the Study of Religion, Univ. of Toronto.

———. 1998. *The Composition of the Sayings Source: Genre, Synchrony, and Wisdom Redaction in Q.* NovTSup 91. Leiden: E. J. Brill.

Kitchen, Kenneth A. 1979. "The Basic Literary Forms and Formulations of Ancient Instructional Writings in Egypt and Western Asia." In *Studien zu altägyptischen Lebenslehren*, ed. Erik Hornung and Othmar Keel, 235–82. OBO 28. Göttingen: Vandenhoeck & Ruprecht.

Kiwiet, John J. 1991. "Historical Introduction to the Debate Regarding the Sequence of the Synoptic Gospels." In *A History and Critique of the Origin of the Marcan Hypothesis, 1835–1866: A Contemporary Report Rediscovered*, by Hajo Uden Meijboom, ed. and trans. John J. Kiwiet, xiii–xxxiv. New Gospel Studies 8. Louvain: Peeters; Macon, Ga.: Mercer Univ. Press.

Klein, Samuel. 1909. *Die Barajta der vierundzwanzig Priesterabteilungen: Beiträge zur Geographie und Geschichte Galilaeas.* Kirchhain: Max Schmersow.

———. [1924]. "Baraita' Shel-'Arba'ah Ve-'Esrim Mismarot." In *Ma'amarim shonim le-hakirat Erets Yisra'el*, 1–29. Mehkarim Erets yisre'eliyim 2. Vinah [Wien]: Hotsa'at "Menorah."

Kleinhans, A. 1955. "De nova Enchridii Biblici editione." *Antonianum* 30:63–65.

Kloppenborg, John S. 1978. "Wisdom Christology in Q." *LTP* 34:129–47.

———. 1979. "Didache 16,6-8 and Special Matthaean Tradition." *ZNW* 70:54–67.

———. 1984a. "The Literary Genre of the Synoptic Sayings Source." Ph.D. diss., Univ. of St. Michael's College.

———. 1984b. "Tradition and Redaction in the Synoptic Sayings Source." *CBQ* 46:34–62.

———. 1986a. "Blessing and Marginality: The 'Persecution Beatitude' in Q, Thomas and Early Christianity." *Forum* 2(3):36–56.

———. 1986b. "The Formation of Q and Antique Instructional Genres." *JBL* 105:443–62.

———. 1987a. *The Formation of Q: Trajectories in Ancient Wisdom Collections.* Studies in Antiquity and Christianity. Philadelphia: Fortress Press.

———. 1987b. "Symbolic Eschatology and the Apocalypticism of Q." *HTR* 80:287–306.

———. 1988a. *Q Parallels: Synopsis, Critical Notes, and Concordance.* Foundations and Facets: New Testament. Sonoma, Calif.: Polebridge.

———. 1988b. "Redactional Strata and Social History in the Sayings Gospel Q." Paper Presented at the One Hundred and Twenty-Fourth Annual Meeting of the Society of Biblical Literature (Q Seminar), Chicago, Illinois.

———. 1989a. "The Dishonoured Master (Luke 16,1-8a)." *Bib* 70:474–95.

———. 1989b. "*The Formation of Q* Revisited: A Response to Richard Horsley." In *Society of Biblical Literature 1989 Seminar Papers*, ed. David J. Lull, 204–15. SBLSP 28. Atlanta: Scholars Press.

———. 1990a. "City and Wasteland: Narrative World and the Beginning of the Sayings Gospel (Q)." In *How Gospels Begin*, ed. Dennis E. Smith, 145–60. Semeia 52. Atlanta: Scholars Press.

———. 1990b. "'Easter Faith' and the Sayings Gospel Q." In Cameron 1990a:71–99.

———. 1990c. "Nomos and Ethos in Q." In *Gospel Origins and Christian Beginnings: In Honor of James M. Robinson*, ed. James E. Goehring et al., 35–48. Sonoma, Calif.: Polebridge.

———. 1991. "Literary Convention, Self-Evidence, and the Social History of the Q People." In Kloppenborg and Vaage 1991a:77–102.

———. 1992a. "Response to Lamar Cope et al., 'Narrative Outline of the Composition of Luke according to the Two Gospel Hypothesis.'" Paper read at the One Hundred and Twenty-Eighth Annual Meeting of the Society of Biblical Literature, San Francisco, California.

———. 1992b. "The Theological Stakes in the Synoptic Problem." In Van Segbroeck et al. 1992:93–120.

———. 1994a <1986>. "The Formation of Q and Antique Instructional Genres." In Kloppenborg 1994b:138–55.

———. 1994b. *The Shape of Q: Signal Essays on the Sayings Gospel*. Minneapolis: Fortress Press.

———. 1995a. *Conflict and Invention: Literary, Rhetorical and Social Studies on the Sayings Gospel Q*. Valley Forge, Pa.: Trinity Press International.

———. 1995b. "Jesus and the Parables of Jesus in Q." In Piper 1995a:275–319.

———. 1995c. "The Transformation of Moral Exhortation in *Didache* 1–5." In Jefford 1995:88–109.

———. 1996a. "Critical Histories and Theories of Religion: A Response to Burton Mack and Ron Cameron." *MTSR* 8:279–89.

———. 1996b. "The Sayings Gospel Q and the Quest of the Historical Jesus." *HTR* 89:307–44.

———. 1996c. "The Sayings Gospel Q: Literary and Stratigraphic Problems." In Uro 1996:1–66.

———, and Leif E. Vaage, eds. 1991a. *Early Christianity, Q and Jesus*. Semeia 55. Atlanta: Scholars Press.

———, and Leif E. Vaage. 1991b. "Early Christianity Q and Jesus: The Sayings Gospel and Method in the Study of Christian Origins." In Kloppenborg and Vaage 1991a:1–14.

Kloppenborg Verbin, John S. 1999. "A Dog among the Pigeons: The 'Cynic Hypothesis' as a Theological Problem." In *From Quest to Quelle: Festschrift James M. Robinson*, ed. Jon Asgeirsson, Kristin de Troyer, and Marvin W. Meyer, 73–117. BETL 146. Louvain: Peeters.

Knibb, Michael A. 1987. *The Qumran Community*. Cambridge and New York: Cambridge Univ. Press.

Knox, W. L. 1957. *The Sources of the Synoptic Gospels. II St. Luke and St. Matthew*. Cambridge: Cambridge Univ. Press.

Koester, Helmut. 1965. "ΓΝΩΜΑΙ ΔΙΑΦΟΡΟΙ: The Origin and Nature of Diversification in the History of Early Christianity." *HTR* 58:279–318.

———. 1968. "One Jesus and Four Primitive Gospels." *HTR* 61:203–47.

———. 1971a <1965>. "GNOMAI DIAPHOROI: The Origin and Nature of Diversification in the History of Early Christianity." In *Trajectories through Early Christianity*, by James M. Robinson and Helmut Koester, 114–57. Philadelphia: Fortress Press.

———. 1971b <1968>. "One Jesus and Four Primitive Gospels." In *Trajectories through Early Christianity*, by James M. Robinson and Helmut Koester, 158–204. Philadelphia: Fortress Press.

————. 1971c. "The Structure and Criteria of Early Christian Beliefs." In *Trajectories through Early Christianity*, by James M. Robinson and Helmut Koester, 205–31. Philadelphia: Fortress Press.

————. 1980. "Apocryphal and Canonical Gospels." *HTR* 73:105–30.

————. 1982a. *Einführung in das Neue Testament*. De Gruyter Lehrbuch. Berlin and New York: Walter de Gruyter.

————. 1982b. *Introduction to the New Testament*. Vol. 2: *History and Literature of Early Christianity*. Hermeneia: Foundations and Facets. Philadelphia: Fortress Press.

————. 1983. "History and Development of Mark's Gospel (from Mark to Secret Mark and 'Canonical Mark')." In *Colloquy on New Testament Studies: A Time for Reappraisal and Fresh Approaches*, ed. Bruce Corley, 35–57. Macon, Ga.: Mercer Univ. Press.

————. 1984. "Überlieferung und Geschichte der frühchristlichen Evangelienliteratur." *ANRW* II.25.2:1463–542.

————. 1990. *Ancient Christian Gospels: Their History and Development*. Philadelphia: Trinity Press International; London: SCM.

————. 1992. "Jesus the Victim." *JBL* 111:3–15.

————. 1997. "The Sayings of Q and Their Image of Jesus." In *The Canonical and Non-Canonical Sayings of Jesus: Collected Essays in Honour of Tjitze Baarda*, ed. W. L. Petersen, J. S. Vos, and H. J. de Jonge, 137–54. NovTSup 66. Leiden: E. J. Brill.

Koppe, Johann B. 1782. *Marcus non epitomator Matthaei*. Göttingen [Helmstadii]: Programm der Universität Göttingen [C. G. Fleckeisen].

Körtner, Ulrich. 1983. *Papias von Hierapolis: Ein Beitrag zur Geschichte des frühen Christentums*. FRLANT 131. Göttingen: Vandenhoeck & Ruprecht.

Kosch, Daniel. 1989a. *Die eschatologische Tora des Menschensohnes: Untersuchungen zur Rezeption der Stellung Jesu zur Tora in Q*. NTOA 12. Freiburg/ Sw.: Universitätsverlag; Göttingen: Vandenhoeck & Ruprecht.

————. 1989b. "Q: Rekonstruktion und Interpretation: Eine methodenkritische Hinführung mit einem Exkurs zur Q-Vorlage des Lk." *FZPT* 36:409–25.

————. 1992. "Q und Jesus." *BZ* NF 36:30–58.

Köstlin, Karl R. 1853. *Der Ursprung und die Komposition der synoptischen Evangelien*. Stuttgart: Mächen.

Kristen, Peter. 1995. *Familie, Kreuz und Leben: Nachfolge Jesu nach Q und dem Markusevangelium*. Marburger Theologische Studien 42. Marburg: N. G. Elwert Verlag.

Kuhn, Johann E. 1838. *Das Leben Jesu, wissenschaftlich bearbeitet*. Mainz: Florian Kupferberg.

Kümmel, Werner Georg. 1972. *The New Testament: The History of the Investigation and Its Problems*. Trans. S. McLean Gilmour and Howard C. Kee. Nashville: Abingdon.

————. 1973. *Einleitung in das Neue Testament*. 17. Aufl. Heidelberg: Quelle & Meyer.

————. 1975 <1973>. *Introduction to the New Testament*. Rev. ed. Trans. Howard C. Kee. Nashville: Abingdon.

Kurtz, Lester R. 1986. *The Politics of Heresy: The Modernist Crisis in Roman Catholicism*. Berkeley and Los Angeles: Univ. of California Press.

Kürzinger, Josef. 1983. *Papias von Hierapolis und die Evangelien des Neuen Testaments: Gesammelte Aufsätze. Neuangabe und Übersetzung der Fragmente. Kommentierte Bibliographie.* Eichstätter Materialien. Abteilung Philosophie und Theologie 4. Regensburg: Friedrich Pustet.

Lachmann, Karl. 1835. "De ordine narrationum in evangeliis synopticis." *TSK* 8:570–90.

Lagrange, Marie-Joseph. 1895. "Les sources du troisième évangile." *RB* 4:5–22.

————. 1896. "Les sources du troisième évangile." *RB* 5:5–38.

————. 1897. "Recension: H. J. Holtzmann, *Lehrbuch der neutestamentlichen Theologie.*" *RB* 6:468–74.

————. 1903. *La méthode historique: La critique biblique et l'Église.* EBib 1. Paris: Victor Lecoffre; édition augmentée 1904; repr. with an introduction by R. de Vaux, Paris: Les Éditions du Cerf 1966.

————. 1911. *Évangile selon saint Marc.* EBib. Paris: Victor Lecoffre.

————. 1912. "Recension: Pasquier, La solution du problème synoptique." *RB* n.s. 9:280–84.

————. 1985. *Père Lagrange: Personal Reflections and Memoirs.* Trans. Henry Wansbrough. Foreword by Pierre Benoit. New York: Paulist.

Lagrange, Marie-Joseph, and Ceslas Lavergne. 1926. *Synopsis evangelica: textum Graecum quattuor evangeliorum recensuit et iuxta ordinem chronologicum Lucae praesertim et Johannis concinnavit.* Barcelona: Editorial Alpha.

Lake, Kirsopp. 1904. "The New Sayings of Jesus and the Synoptic Problem." *HibJ* 3:332–41.

————. 1909. "The Date of Q." *Expositor* 7:494–507.

Lambrecht, Jan. 1966. "Die Logia-Quellen von Markus 13." *Bib* 47:321–60.

————. 1981. *Once More Astonished: The Parables of Jesus.* New York: Crossroad.

————. 1982. "Q-Influence on Mark 8,34-9,1." In Delobel 1982:277–304.

————. 1992. "John the Baptist and Jesus in Mark 1.1-15: Markan Redaction of Q?" *NTS* 38:357–84.

————. 1995. "The Great Commandment Pericope and Q." In Piper 1995a:73–96.

Lang, Bernhard. 1972. *Die weisheitliche Lehrrede: Eine Untersuchung von Sprüche 1–7.* SBS 54. Stuttgart: Katholisches Bibelwerk.

Lang, Marijke H. de. 1993a. "De Opkomst Van de Historische en Literaire Kritiek in de Synoptische Beschouwing Van de Evangelikn Van Calvijn (1555) Tot Griesbach (1774)." Proefschrift (diss.), Rijksuniversiteit te Leiden.

————. 1993b. "Gospel Synopses from the 16th to the 18th Centuries and the Rise of Literary Criticism of the Gospels." In *The Synoptic Gospels: Source Criticism and New Literary Criticism,* ed. Camille Focant, 599–607. BETL 110. Louvain: Louvain Univ. Press; Peeters.

————. 1993c. "Literary and Historical Criticism as Apologetics: Biblical Scholarship at the End of the Eighteenth Century." *Nederlands Archief Voor Kerkgeschiedenis/Dutch Review of Church History* 72:149–65.

————. 1993d. "The Prehistory of the Griesbach Hypothesis." *ETL* 69:134–39.

Langen, Josef. 1868. *Grundriss der Einleitung in das Neue Testament.* Freiburg: Herder.

Larfeld, Wilhelm. 1911. *Griechisch-deutsche Synopse der vier neutestamentlichen Evangelien nach literarhistorischen Gesichtspunkten und mit textkritischem Apparat.* Tübingen: J. C. B. Mohr (Paul Siebeck).

Laufen, Rudolf. 1980. *Die Doppelüberlieferungen der Logienquelle und des Markusevangeliums.* BBB 54. Königstein: Peter Hanstein.

Lenski, Gerhard Emmanuel. 1966. *Power and Privilege: A Theory of Social Stratification.* New York: McGraw-Hill.

Léon-Dufour, Xavier. 1959. "Les évangiles synoptiques." In *Introduction à la Bible, II: Nouveau Testament,* ed. André Robert and A. Feuillet, 2:143–334. Tournai: Desclée et Cie.

———. 1972. "Autour de la question synoptique." *RSR* 60:491–518.

Lessing, Gotthold Ephraim. 1784 <1778>. "Neue Hypothese über die Evangelisten als bloss menschliche Geschichtsschreiber betrachtet." In *Theologischer Nachlass,* 45–72. Berlin: Voss.

———. 1900a <1778>. "Nötige Antwort auf eine sehr unnötige Frage des Herrn Hauptpastor Goeze in Hamburg." In *Lessings Werke,* ed. Georg Witkowski, 7:326–31. Leipzig: Bibliographische Institut.

———. 1900b <1777>. "Über den Beweis des Geistes und der Kraft." In *Lessings Werke,* ed. Georg Witkowski, 7:79–89. Leipzig: Bibliographische Institut.

———. 1956a <1778>. "Necessary Answer to a Very Unnecessary Question of Herr Haupt-Pastor Goeze in Hamburg." In *Lessing's Theological Writings,* trans. Henry Chadwick, 62–64. London: A. & C. Black.

———. 1956b <1778>. "New Hypothesis concerning the Evangelists Regarded as Merely Human Historians." In *Lessing's Theological Writings,* trans. Henry Chadwick, 65–81. London: A. & C. Black.

———. 1956c. *Theological Writings: Selections in Translation.* Ed. Henry Chadwick. London: A. & C. Black.

Levie, Jean. 1954. "L'évangile araméen de S. Matthieu est-il la source de l'évangile de S. Marc?" *NRT* 76:689–715, 812–43.

———. 1958. *La Bible, parole humaine et message de Dieu.* Museum Lessianum. Section biblique 1. [Bruges]: Desclée de Brouwer.

———. 1961 <1958>. *The Bible, Word of God in Words of Men.* Trans. S. H. Treman. New York: P. J. Kennedy.

Levine, Amy-Jill. 1990. "Who's Catering the Q Affair? Feminist Observations on Q Paraenesis." In *Paraenesis: Act and Form,* ed. Leo G. Perdue and John G. Gammie, 145–61. Semeia 50. Atlanta: Scholars Press.

———. 1994. "Second Temple Judaism, Jesus and Women: Yeast of Eden." *Biblical Interpretation* 2:8–33.

———, ed. 1991. *"Women like This": New Perspectives on Jewish Women in the Greco-Roman World.* Early Judaism and Its Literature 1. Atlanta: Scholars Press.

Levine, Lee I. 1974. "R. Simeon ben Yohai and the Purification of Tiberias." *HUCA* 49:143–85.

———. 1989. *The Rabbinic Class of Roman Palestine in Late Antiquity.* New York: Jewish Theological Seminary of America.

———. 1992. *The Galilee in Late Antiquity.* New York: Jewish Theological Seminary of America.

Lewis, Naphtali. 1983. *Life in Egypt under Roman Rule.* Oxford: Clarendon.

Lichtenstein, H. 1931. "Die Fastenrolle: Eine Untersuchung zur jüdisch-hellenistischen Geschichte." *HUCA* 8/9:257–351.

Lightstone, Jack N. 1980. "Yose the Galilean in Mishnah-Tosephta and the History of Early Rabbinic Judaism." *JJS* 31:37–45.

Lindars, Barnabas. 1983. *Jesus, Son of Man: A Fresh Examination of the Son of Man Sayings in the Gospels.* London: SPCK; Grand Rapids, Mich.: Eerdmans.

Linnemann, Eta. 1992. *Is There a Synoptic Problem?: Rethinking the Literary Dependence of the First Three Gospels.* Trans. Robert W. Yarbrough. Grand Rapids, Mich.: Baker.

Lips, Hermann von. 1990. *Weisheitliche Traditionen im Neuen Testament.* WMANT 64. Neukirchen-Vluyn: Neukirchener Verlag.

Liver, J. 1963. "The Half-Shekel Offering in Biblical and Post-Biblical Literature." *HTR* 56:163–98.

Llewelyn, S. R. 1992. *New Documents Illustrating Early Christianity.* Vol. 6: *Inscriptions and Papyri First Published in 1980–81.* North Ryde, N.S.W., Australia: Macquarie Univ.

Lock, Walter, and William Sanday. 1897. *Two Lectures on the "Sayings of Jesus" Recently Discovered at Oxyrhynchus.* Oxford: Clarendon.

Loffreda, Stanislav. 1976. "La città romana de Magdala." In *Studia Hierosolymitana: In onore del P. Bellarmino Bagatti. I: Studi Archeologici,* 355–78. Studium Biblicum Franciscanum. Collectio maior 22. Jerusalem: Franciscan Printing Press.

Lohfink, Gerhard. 1971. *Die Himmelfahrt Jesu: Untersuchungen zu den Himmelfahrts- und Erhöhungstexten bei Lukas.* SANT 26. Munich: Kösel Verlag.

Loisy, Alfred Firmin. 1907–8. *Les évangiles synoptiques.* 2 vols. Ceffonds, Près Montier-en-Der: chez l'auteur.

Longstaff, Thomas R. W. 1977. *Evidence of Conflation in Mark? A Study in the Synoptic Problem.* SBLDS 28. Missoula, Mont.: Scholars Press.

———. 1987–8. "Order in the Synoptic Gospels: A Response." *SecCent* 6(2):98–107.

Lührmann, Dieter. 1969. *Die Redaktion der Logienquelle.* WMANT 33. Neukirchen-Vluyn: Neukirchener Verlag.

———. 1985. "Synopse der Q-Überlieferung." Unpublished version distributed to the SBL Q Seminar.

———. 1993. "Marinus de Jonge's Shaffer Lectures: Where Does Jesus Research Now Stand?" In *From Jesus to John: Essays on Jesus and New Testament Christology in Honour of Marinus de Jonge,* ed. Martinus C. de Boer, 51–64. JSNTSup 84. Sheffield: JSOT Press.

———. 1994. "Q in the History of Early Christianity." In Kloppenborg 1994b:59–73.

———. 1995. "Q: Sayings of Jesus or Logia?" In Piper 1995a:97–116.

Luz, Ulrich. 1983. "Sermon on the Mount/Plain: Reconstruction of Qmt and Qlk." In *Society of Biblical Literature 1983 Seminar Papers,* ed. Kent H. Richards, 473–79. SBLASP 22. Chico, Calif.: Scholars Press.

———. 1985–97. *Das Evangelium nach Matthäus.* EKKNT 1/1–3. Zurich: Benziger Verlag; Neukirchen-Vluyn: Neukirchener Verlag.

———. 1989 <1985>. *Matthew 1–7.* Trans. W. Linss. Continental Commentaries. Minneapolis: Augsburg.

MacAdam, Henry Innes. 1983. "Epigraphy and Village Life in Southern Syria during the Roman and Early Byzantine Periods." *Berytus* 31:103–15.

McArthur, Harvey K. 1966. *The Quest through the Centuries: The Search for the Historical Jesus.* Philadelphia: Fortress Press.

McCown, C. C. 1922. *The Testament of Solomon Edited from Manuscripts at Mount Athos, Bologna, Holkham Hall, Jerusalem, London, Milan, Paris and Vienna.* Ph.D. diss., Univ. of Chicago. Leipzig: J. C. Hinrichs.

―――. 1940. "The Scene of John's Ministry and Its Relation to the Purpose and Outcome of His Mission." *JBL* 59:113–31.

McKane, William. 1970. *Proverbs: A New Approach.* Old Testament Library. Philadelphia: Westminster.

McLoughlin, Swithun. 1963. "An Approach to the Synoptic Problem." S.T.L. Thesis, Katholieke Universiteit Louvain.

―――. 1967. "Les accords mineurs Mt-Lc contre Mc et le problème synoptique: Vers la théorie des deux sources." In *De Jésus aux évangiles: Tradition et rédaction dans les évangiles synoptiques. Donum Natalicium J. Coppens, II,* ed. Ignace De la Potterie, 17–40. BETL 25. Gembloux: Duculot; Paris: Lethielleux.

McNicol, Allan J. 1990. "The Composition of the Synoptic Eschatological Discourse." In Dungan 1990a:157–200.

―――. 1996. *Beyond the Q Impasse — Luke's Use of Matthew: A Demonstration by the Research Team of the International Institute for Gospel Studies.* In collaboration with David L. Dungan and David B. Peabody. Valley Forge, Pa.: Trinity Press International.

Mack, Burton L. 1985. *Wisdom and the Hebrew Epic: Ben Sira's Hymn in Praise of the Fathers.* Chicago Studies in the History of Judaism. Chicago: Univ. of Chicago Press.

―――. 1988a. "The Kingdom That Didn't Come: A Social History of the Q Tradents." In *Society of Biblical Literature 1988 Seminar Papers,* ed. David J. Lull, 608–35. SBLASP 27. Atlanta: Scholars Press.

―――. 1988b. *A Myth of Innocence: Mark and Christian Origins.* Philadelphia: Fortress Press.

―――. 1990a. "Lord of the Logia: Savior or Sage?" In *Gospel Origins and Christian Beginnings: In Honor of James M. Robinson,* ed. James E. Goehring et al., 3–18. Sonoma, Calif.: Polebridge.

―――. 1990b. *Rhetoric and the New Testament.* Guides to Biblical Scholarship. Minneapolis: Fortress Press.

―――. 1991a. "A Myth of Innocence at Sea." *Continuum* 1:140–57.

―――. 1991b. "Q and the Gospel of Mark: Revising Christian Origins." In Kloppenborg and Vaage 1991a:15–39.

―――. 1993. *The Lost Gospel: The Book of Q and Christian Origins.* San Francisco: HarperSanFrancisco.

―――. 1995. *Who Wrote the New Testament? The Making of the Christian Myth.* San Francisco: HarperSanFrancisco.

Mack, Burton L., and Edward N. O'Neil. 1986. "The Chreia Discussion of Hermogenes of Tarsus." In *The Chreia in Ancient Rhetoric.* Vol. 1. *The Progymnasmata,* ed. Ronald F. Hock and Edward N. O'Neil, 153–81. SBLTT 27; Graeco-Roman Religion Series 9. Atlanta: Scholars Press.

Mack, Burton L., and Vernon K. Robbins. 1989. *Patterns of Persuasion in the Gospels.* Sonoma, Calif.: Polebridge.

Magness, J. 1990. "Some Observations on the Roman Temple at Kedesh." *IEJ* 40:173–81.

Mahnke, Hermann. 1978. *Die Versuchungsgeschichte im Rahmen der synoptischen Evangelien.* BBET 9. Frankfurt am Main: Lang.

Maier, Adalbert. 1848. "Beiträge zur Einleitung in das Neue Testament." *Zeitschrift für Theologie* 20:3–76.

———. 1852. *Einleitung in die Schriften des Neuen Testaments*. Freiburg: Herder.

Maier, Friedrich W. 1912. "Die drei älteren Evangelien." In *Die Heilige Schrift des Neuen Testamentes*, ed. Fritz Tillmann 1:29–72. Berlin: Hermann Walter.

Malherbe, Abraham J., ed. 1977. *The Cynic Epistles: A Study Edition*. SBLSBS 12. Missoula, Mont.: Scholars Press.

———. 1978. "Pseudo Heraclitus, Epistle 4: The Divinization of the Wise Man." *JAC* 21:42–64.

———. 1982. "Self-Definition among Epicureans and Cynics." In *Jewish and Christian Self-Definition*. Volume 3: *Self-Definition in the Graeco-Roman World*, ed. Ben F. Meyer and E. P. Sanders, 46–59, 192–97. Philadelphia: Fortress Press.

Malinowski, Francis Xavier. 1973. "Galilean Judaism in the Writings of Flavius Josephus." Ph.D. diss., Duke Univ..

Maloney, Elliott C. 1981. *Semitic Interference in Marcan Syntax*. SBLDS 51. Chico, Calif.: Scholars Press.

Mangenot, Eugène. 1895–1912. "Évangiles." In *Dictionnaire de la Bible*, ed. Fulcran G. Vigouroux, 2:2058–99. Paris: Letouzey et Ané.

———. 1895–1912b. "Mark (Évangile de saint)." In *Dictionnaire de la Bible*, ed. Fulcran G. Vigouroux, 4:719–42. Paris: Letouzey et Ané.

———. 1895–1912c. "Matthieu (Évangile de saint)." In *Dictionnaire de la Bible*, ed. Fulcran G. Vigouroux, 4:876–96. Paris: Letouzey et Ané.

———. 1908. "Sur la composition des évangiles." *RCF* 53:395, 717–26.

———. 1911. *Les évangiles synoptiques: conférences apologétiques faites à l'Institut catholique de Paris*. Paris: Letouzey et Ané.

Manson, T. W. 1937. "The Sayings of Jesus." In *The Mission and Message of Jesus: An Exposition of the Gospels in the Light of Modern Research*, ed. Henry Dewsbury Alves Major, Thomas William Manson, and Charles James Wright, 299–639. London: Ivor Nicholson and Watson; New York: E. P. Dutton, 1938.

———. 1949 <1937>. *The Sayings of Jesus*. London: SCM; repr. 1971.

Marcus, Joel. 1995. "The Old Testament and the Death of Jesus: The Role of Scripture in the Gospel Passion Narratives." In *The Death of Jesus in Early Christianity*, ed. John T. Carroll and Joel B. Green, 205–33. Peabody, Mass.: Hendrickson.

Marriott, McKim. 1955. "Little Communities in an Indigenous Civilization." In *Village India: Studies in the Little Community*, ed. McKim Marriott, 171–222. Comparative studies in cultures and civilizations. Chicago: Univ. of Chicago Press.

Marrou, Henri I. 1956. *A History of Education in Antiquity*. Trans. George Lamb. Wisconsin Studies in Classics. Madison: Univ. of Wisconsin Press.

Marsh, Herbert. 1801. *A Dissertation on the Origin of Our Three Canonical Gospels*. Cambridge: John Burges and F. & C. Rivington; London: J. Deighton.

Martin, Raymond A. 1987. *Syntax Criticism of the Synoptic Gospels*. Studies in the Bible and Early Christianity 10. Lewiston: Edwin Mellen Press.

———. 1995. *Studies in the Life and Ministry of the Historical Jesus*. Lanham, Md.: Univ. Press of America.

Marxsen, Willi. 1956. *Der Evangelist Markus: Studien zur Redaktionsgeschichte des Evangeliums*. FRLANT 67. Göttingen: Vandenhoeck & Ruprecht.

———. 1969 <1959>. *Mark the Evangelist: Studies on the Redaction History of the Gospel*. Trans. Roy A. Harrisville. Nashville: Abingdon.

Massey, Marilyn Chapin. 1983. *Christ Unmasked: The Meaning of the Life of Jesus in German Politics.* Studies in religion. Chapel Hill: Univ. of North Carolina Press.

Matera, Frank J. 1982. *The Kingship of Jesus: Composition and Theology in Mark 15.* SBLDS 66. Chico, Calif.: Scholars Press.

Mathews, Shailer. 1897. *The Social Teaching of Jesus: An Essay in Christian Sociology.* New York: Hodder & Stoughton and Macmillan.

Mattila, Sharon L. 1994. "A Problem Still Clouded: Yet Again—Statistics and Q." *NovT* 36:313–29.

Mayer, Anton. 1983. *Der zensierte Jesus: Soziologie des Neuen Testaments.* Olten: Walter.

Meadors, Edward P. 1995. *Jesus the Messianic Herald of Salvation.* WUNT 2/72. Tübingen: J. C. B. Mohr (Paul Siebeck).

———. 1992. "The Orthodoxy of the 'Q' Sayings of Jesus." *TynBul* 43:233–57.

Meagher, John C. 1983. "The Implications for Theology of a Shift from the K. L. Schmidt Hypothesis of the Literary Uniqueness of the Gospels." In *Colloquy on New Testament Studies: A Time for Reappraisal and Fresh Approaches,* ed. Bruce Corley, 203–33. Macon, Ga.: Mercer Univ. Press.

Meier, John P. 1994. *A Marginal Jew: Rethinking the Historical Jesus.* Vol. 2: *Mentor, Message, and Miracles.* Anchor Bible Reference Library. New York, London, and Toronto: Doubleday.

———. 1997. "The Circle of the Twelve: Did It Exist during Jesus' Public Ministry?" *JBL* 116:635–72.

Meijboom, Hajo Uden. 1866. *Geschiedenis en critiek der Marcushypothese.* Proefschriff, Groningen. Amsterdam: Gebroeders Kraay.

———. 1991 <1866>. *A History and Critique of the Origin of the Marcan Hypothesis, 1835–1866: A Contemporary Report Rediscovered.* Ed. and trans. John J. Kiwiet. New Gospel Studies 8. Louvain: Peeters; Macon, Ga.: Mercer Univ. Press.

Meinertz, Max. 1932. *Einführung in das Neue Testament.* 4. Aufl. Paderborn: Ferdinand Schöningh.

Menoud, Philippe H. 1964. "Le sens du verbe ΠΟΡΘΕΙΝ (Gal. 1.13,23; Act. 9.21)." In *Apophoreta: Festschrift für Ernst Haenchen zu seinem siebzigsten Geburtstag,* ed. Walther Eltester and F. H. Kettler, 178–86. BZNW 30. Berlin: Alfred Töpelmann.

Merkel, Helmut. 1971. *Die Widersprüche zwischen den Evangelien: Ihre polemische und apologetische Behandlung in der Alten Kirche bis zu Augustin.* WUNT 1/13. Tübingen: J. C. B. Mohr (Paul Siebeck).

———. 1990. "Die Überlieferungen der alten Kirche über das Verhältnis der Evangelien." In Dungan 1990a:566–90.

Merklein, Helmut. 1981. *Die Gottesherrschaft als Handlungsprinzip: Untersuchung zur Ethik Jesu.* 2. Aufl. FzB 34. Würzburg: Echter.

Meshorer, Yaʿakov. 1973. כורזין בחפירות שנתגלו מטבעות חמ (Coins from the Excavations at Khorazin)." *EI* 11:158–62.

———. 1976. "A Hoard of Coins from Migdal." *ʿAtiqot* 11:54–71, plates X–XV.

———. 1982. *Ancient Jewish Coinage.* 2 vols. Dix Hills, N.Y.: Amphora Books.

Metzger, Bruce M. 1963. *Chapters in the History of New Testament Textual Criticism.* NTTS 4. Leiden: E. J. Brill.

———. 1964. *The Text of the New Testament: Its Transmission, Corruption, and Restoration.* New York: Oxford Univ. Press.

Meyer, Heinrich A. W. 1832. *Kritisch exegetisches Handbuch über das Evangelium des Matthäus.* Kritisch exegetischer Kommentar uber das Neue Testament 1/1. Göttingen: Vandenhoeck & Ruprecht.
———. 1853. *Kritisch exegetisches Handbuch über das Evangelium des Matthaus.* 3. Aufl. Kritisch exegetischer Kommentar über das Neue Testament 1/1. Göttingen: Vandenhoeck & Ruprecht; 4. Aufl. 1858; 5. 1864; 6. Aufl. 1876; 7. Aufl. 1883.
Meyer, Paul Donald. 1967. "The Community of Q." Ph.D. diss., Univ. of Iowa.
———. 1970. "The Gentile Mission in Q." *JBL* 89:405–17.
Meyers, Eric M. 1979. "The Cultural Setting of Galilee: The Case of Regionalism and Early Judaism." *ANRW* II.19.1:686–702.
———. 1985. "Galilean Regionalism: A Reappraisal." In *Approaches to Ancient Judaism: Theory and Practice, 5: Studies in Judaism and Its Greco-Roman Context,* ed. William Scott Green, 115–31. BJS 32. Missoula, Mont.: Scholars Press.
———. 1992. "Roman Sepphoris in Light of New Archaeological Evidence and Research." In L. I. Levine 1992:321–38.
———. 1995. "An Archaeological Response to a New Testament Scholar." *BASOR* 297:17–26, with a response by Horsley (27–28).
Meyers, Eric M., A. Thomas Kraabel, and James F. Strange. 1976. *Ancient Synagogue Excavations at Khirbet Shemaʿ, Upper Galilee, Israel, 1970–1972.* Meiron Excavation Project 1. Annual of the American Schools of Oriental Research 42. Durham, N.C.: Duke Univ. Press.
Meyers, Eric M., Carol L. Meyers, and James F. Strange. 1990. *Excavations at Ancient Synagogue of Gush Halav.* Meiron Excavation Project 5. Winona Lake, Ind.: ASOR/Eisenbrauns.
Meyers, Eric M., Ehud Netzer, and Carol L. Meyers. 1992. *Sepphoris.* Winona Lake, Ind.: Eisenbrauns.
Meyers, Eric M., James F. Strange, and Carol L. Meyers. 1981. *Excavations at Ancient Meiron, Upper Galilee, 1971–72, 1974–75, 1977.* Meiron Excavation Project 3. Cambridge: Harvard Univ. Press.
Meyers, Eric M., James F. Strange, and Dennis E. Groh. 1978. "The Meiron Excavation Project: Archeological Survey in Galilee and Golan, 1976." *BASOR* 230:1–24.
Michaelis, Christine. 1968. "Die π-Alliteration der Subjektsworte der ersten 4 Seligpreisungen in MT. v 3-6 und ihre Bedeutung für den Aufbau der Seligpreisungen bei MT., LK. und in Q." *NovT* 10:148–61.
Milik, Jozef T. 1976. *The Books of Enoch: Aramaic Fragments of Qumran Cave 4.* In collaboration with Matthew Black. Oxford: Clarendon.
Mill, Joannes, ed. 1707. *Novum Testamentum. cum lectionibus variantibus mss. examplarium, versionum, editionum, SS patrum & Scriptorum ecclesiasticorum.* Oxford: E Theatro Sheldoniano.
Miller, A. 1955. "Das neue biblische Handbuch." *Benediktinische Monatsschrift* 31:49–50.
Miller, Robert J. 1997. "Can the Historical Jesus Be Made Safe for Orthodoxy? A Critique of *The Jesus Quest* by Ben Witherington III." *JIIC* 4:120–37.
Miller, Stuart S. 1984. *Studies in the History and Traditions of Sepphoris.* SJLA 37. Leiden: E. J. Brill.
Mitchell, S. 1976. "Requisitioned Transport in the Roman Empire: A New Inscription from Pisidia." *JRS* 66:103–31.

Moles, John L. 1983. "*Honestius Quam Ambitiosius:* An Exploration of the Cynic's Attitude to Moral Corruption in His Fellow Men." *JHS* 103:103–23.

———. 1996. "Cynic Cosmopolitanism." In Branham and Goulet-Cazé 1996:105–20.

Momigliano, Arnaldo. 1971. *The Development of Greek Biography.* Cambridge: Harvard Univ. Press.

Moreland, Milton C., and James M. Robinson. 1993. "The International Q Project Work Sessions 31 July – 2 August, 20 November 1992." *JBL* 112:500–506.

———. 1994. "The International Q Project Work Sessions 6–8 August, 18–19 November 1993." *JBL* 113:495–99.

———. 1995. "The International Q Project Work Sessions 23–27 May, 22–26 August, 17–18 November 1994." *JBL* 114:475–85.

Morgenthaler, Robert. 1971. *Statistische Synopse.* Zürich and Stuttgart: Gotthelf.

Mosala, Itumeleng J. 1989. *Biblical Hermeneutics and Black Theology in South Africa.* Grand Rapids, Mich.: Eerdmans.

Moule, C. F. D. 1959. *An Idiom-Book of New Testament Greek.* 2d ed. Cambridge: Cambridge Univ. Press.

Müller, Georg Hermann. 1908. *Zur Synopse: Untersuchung über die Arbeitsweise des Lukas und Matthäus und ihre Quellen, namentlich die Spruchquelle.* FRLANT 11. Göttingen: Vandenhoeck & Ruprecht.

Murphy, Roland E. 1981. *Wisdom Literature: Job, Proverbs, Ruth, Canticles, Ecclesiastes, and Esther.* FOTL 13. Grand Rapids, Mich.: Eerdmans.

Murphy-O'Connor, Jerome. 1969. "La genèse littéraire de la *Règle de la Communauté.*" *RB* 76:528–49.

Myers, Ched. 1988. *Binding the Strong Man: A Political Reading of Mark's Story of Jesus.* Maryknoll, N.Y.: Orbis.

Myllykoski, Matti. 1996. "The Social History of Q and the Jewish War." In Uro 1996:143–99.

Nadeau, Raymond E., ed. and trans. 1964. "Hermogenes' On Stases: A Translation with an Introduction and Notes." *SpeechM* 31:361–424.

Neirynck, Frans. 1967. "La rédaction matthéenne et la structure du premier évangile." In *De Jésus aux évangiles: Tradition et rédaction dans les évangiles synoptiques. Donum natilicium Josepho Coppens septuagesimum annum complenti,* ed. Ignace de la Potterie, 41–73. BETL 25. Gembloux: J. Duculot.

———. 1972. *Duality in Mark: Contributions to the Study of the Markan Redaction.* BETL 31. Louvain: Louvain Univ. Press.

———. 1973. "The Argument from Order and St. Luke's Transpositions." *ETL* 49:784–815.

———. 1974a <1973>. "The Argument from Order and St. Luke's Transpositions." In *The Minor Agreements of Matthew and Luke against Mark: With a Cumulative List,* by Frans Neiynck, 291–322. BETL 37. Louvain: Louvain Univ. Press.

———. 1974b. *The Minor Agreements of Matthew and Luke against Mark: With a Cumulative List.* BETL 37. Louvain: Louvain Univ. Press.

———. 1976. "The Sermon on the Mount in the Gospel Synopsis." *ETL* 52:350–57.

———. 1978. "The Symbol Q (= Quelle)." *ETL* 54:119–25.

———. 1982a. "The Griesbach Hypothesis: The Phenomenon of Order." *ETL* 58:111–22.

————. 1982b. "Recent Developments in the Study of Q." In Delobel 1982:29–75.

————. 1982c <1976>. "The Sermon on the Mount in the Gospel Synopsis." In *Evangelica: Gospel Studies—études d'évangile*, ed. Frans Neirynck, 729–36. BETL 60. Louvain: Peeters; Louvain Univ. Press.

————. 1984. "The Matthew-Luke Agreements in Mt 14,13-14/Lk 9,10-11 (par. Mk 6,30-34): The Two-Source Theory beyond the Impasse." *ETL* 60:25–44.

————. 1985. "The Order of the Gospels and the Making of a Synopsis." *ETL* 61:161–66.

————. 1986. "Once More: The Making of a Synopsis." *ETL* 62:141–54.

————. 1988. *Q-synopsis: The Double Tradition Passages in Greek*. Studiorum Novi Testamenti auxilia 13. Louvain: Louvain Univ. Press.

————. 1990a. "QMt and QLk and the Reconstruction of Q." *ETL* 66:385–90.

————. 1990b. "Synoptic Problem." In The *New Jerome Biblical Commentary*, ed. Raymond E. Brown, Joseph A. Fitzmyer, and Roland E. Murphy, 587–95. Englewood Cliffs, N.J.: Prentice-Hall.

————. 1991a. *Evangelica II: 1982–1991 Collected Essays*. Ed. Frans Van Segbroeck. BETL 99. Louvain: Louvain Univ. Press.

————. 1991b. "Luke 14,1-6: Lukan Composition and Q Saying." In *Der Treue Gottes trauen: Beiträge zum Werk des Lukas: Für Gerhard Schneider*, ed. Claus Bussmann and Walter Radl, 243–63. Freiburg: Herder.

————. 1991c. "The Minor Agreements and the Two-Source Theory." In *Evangelica II: 1982–1991 Collected Essays*, ed. Frans Van Segbroeck, 3–42. BETL 99. Louvain: Louvain Univ. Press.

————. 1991d. *The Minor Agreements: In a Horizontal-Line Synopsis*. Studiorum Novi Testamenti auxilia 15. Louvain: Louvain Univ. Press.

————. 1991e. "A Synopsis of Q." In *Evangelica II: 1982 – 1991 Collected Essays*, ed. Frans Van Segbroeck, 465–74. BETL 99. Louvain: Louvain Univ. Press.

————. 1993. "The International Q Project." *ETL* 69:221–25.

————. 1994. "Luke 10:25-28: A Foreign Body in Luke?" In *Crossing the Boundaries: Essays in Biblical Interpretation in Honour of Michael D. Goulder*, ed. Stanley E. Porter, Paul Joyce, and David E. Orton, 149–65. Biblical Interpretation Series 8. Leiden: E. J. Brill.

————. 1995a. "Assessment." In *Mark and Q: A Study of the Overlap Texts*, by Harry T. Fleddermann, 263–307. BETL 122. Louvain: Louvain Univ. Press and Peeters.

————. 1995b. "The Minor Agreements and Q." In Piper 1995a:49–72.

————. 1995c. "Q: From Source to Gospel." *ETL* 71:421–30.

————. 1996. "The First Synoptic Pericope: The Appearance of John the Baptist in Q?" *ETL* 72:23–74.

————. 1997. "Goulder and the Minor Agreements." *ETL* 73:84–93.

Neirynck, Frans, and Frans Van Segbroeck. 1978. "The Griesbach Hypothesis: A Bibliography." In *J. J. Griesbach, Synoptic and Text Critical Studies, 1776–1976*, ed. Bernard Orchard and Thomas R. W. Longstaff, 176–81, 219. SNTSMS 34. Cambridge and New York: Cambridge Univ. Press.

————. 1982. "Q Bibliography." In Delobel 1982:561–86.

————. 1984. *New Testament Vocabulary: A Companion Volume to the Concordance*. BETL 65. Louvain: Peeters and Louvain Univ. Press.

————. 1986. "Q Bibliography: Additional List, 1981–1985." *ETL* 62:157–65.

Neirynck, Frans, J. Verheyden, and R. Corstjens. 1998. *The Gospel of Matthew and the Gospel Source Q: A Cumulative Bibliography 1950–1995*. 2 vols. BETL 140a. Louvain: Louvain Univ. Press and Peeters.

Neusner, Jacob. 1973. *From Politics to Piety: The Emergence of Pharisaic Judaism*. Engelwood Cliffs, N.J.: Prentice-Hall.

———. 1976. "'First Cleanse the Inside': The Halakic Background of a Controversy Saying." *NTS* 22:486–95.

———. 1981. *Judaism: The Evidence of the Mishnah*. Chicago: Univ. of Chicago Press.

Neville, David J. 1994. *Arguments from Order in Synoptic Source Criticism: A History and Critique*. New Gospel Studies 7. Louvain: Peeters; Macon, Ga.: Mercer Univ. Press.

New, David S. 1993. *Old Testament Quotations in the Synoptic Gospels and the Two-Document Hypothesis*. SCS 37. Atlanta: Scholars Press.

Nickelsburg, George W. E. 1972. *Resurrection, Immortality, and Eternal Life in Intertestamental Judaism*. HTS 26. Cambridge: Harvard Univ. Press.

———. 1980. "The Genre and Function of the Marcan Passion Narrative." *HTR* 73:153–84.

Niederwimmer, Kurt. 1989. *Die Didache*. Kommentar zu den apostolischen Vätern 1. Göttingen: Vandenhoeck & Ruprecht.

———. 1998. *The Didache: A Commentary*, Trans. L. M. Maloney. Hermeneia. Minneapolis: Fortress Press.

Nippel, Karl. 1876. "Das Verhältnis der Evangelien des Marcus and Lucas." *TQ* 58:551–79.

Nösgen, Karl F. 1880. "Der Ursprung und die Entstehung des dritten Evangeliums." *TSK* 53:49–137.

Nun, Mendel. 1989. *Sea of Galilee: Newly Discovered Harbours from New Testament Days*. Rev. ed. Kibbutz Ein Gev, Israel: Kinnereth Sailing Co.

O'Malley, Pat. 1979. "Social Bandits, Modern Capitalism and the Traditional Peasantry: A Critique of Hobsbawm." *JPS* 6:489–501.

O'Neil, Edward, trans. 1977. *Teles (the Cynic Teacher)*. SBLTT 11. Graeco-Roman religion series 3. Missoula, Mont.: Scholars Press.

Oakman, Douglas E. 1991. "The Countryside in Luke-Acts." In *The Social World of Luke-Acts: Models for Interpretation*, ed. Jerome H. Neyrey, 151–79. Peabody Mass.: Hendrickson.

———. 1994. "The Archaeology of First Century Galilee and the Social Interpretation of the Historical Jesus." In *Society of Biblical Literature 1994 Seminar Papers*, ed. Eugene H. Lovering, 220–51. SBLSP 33. Atlanta: Scholars Press.

———. 1997. "The Love of Money or the Curse of Mammon? Money in the Moral Universe of the New Testament." Unpublished Paper Presented at Annual Meeting of the Catholic Biblical Association, Seattle, Washington.

———. 1999. "The Lord's Prayer in Social Perpective." In *Authenticating the Words of Jesus*, ed. Bruce Chilton and Craig A. Evans, 137–186. NTTS 28/1. Leiden: E. J. Brill.

Oertel, Friedrich. 1917. *Die Liturgie: Studien zur ptolemäischen und kaiserlichen Verwaltung Ägyptens*. Leipzig: B. G. Teubner.

Orchard, Bernard. 1978. "Are All Gospel Synopses Biased?" *TZ* 34:157–61.

———. 1983. *A Synopsis of the Four Gospels in Greek: Arranged according to the Two-Gospel Hypothesis*. Edinburgh: T. & T. Clark.

————. 1986. "The 'Neutrality' of Vertical-Column Synopses." *ETL* 62:155–56.

Osiander, Andreas. 1537. *Harmoniae evangelicae libri quatuor Graece et Latine.* Basel and Geneva: Oliua Roberti Stephani.

Overman, J. Andrew. 1988. "Who Were the First Urban Christians? Urbanization in Galilee in the First Century." In *Society of Biblical Literature 1988 Seminar Papers*, ed. David J. Lull, 160–68. SBLSP 27. Atlanta: Scholars Press.

————. 1990. *Matthew's Gospel and Formative Judaism: The Social World of the Matthean Community.* Minneapolis: Fortress Press.

————. 1993. "Recent Advances in the Archaeology of the Galilee in the Roman Period." *CRBS* 1:35–57.

Owen, Henry. 1764. *Observations on the Four Gospels: Tending Chiefly to Ascertain the Times of Their Publication, and to Illustrate the Form and Manner of Their Composition.* London: T. Payne.

Pack, Roger A. 1965. *The Greek and Latin Literary Texts from Greco-Roman Egypt.* 2d. ed. Ann Arbor: Univ. of Michigan Press.

Palmer, N. Humphrey. 1966–67. "Lachmann's Argument." *NTS* 13:368–78.

Pannenberg, Wolfhart. 1990. "Religious Pluralism and Conflicting Truth Claims: The Problem of a Theology of the World Religions." In *Christian Uniqueness Reconsidered: The Myth of a Pluralistic Theology of Religions*, ed. Gavin D'Costa, 96–106. Maryknoll, N.Y.: Orbis.

Parker, Robert. 1983. *Miasma: Pollution and Purification in Early Greek Religion.* Oxford: Clarendon.

Pasquier, H. 1911. *La solution du problème synoptique.* Tours: Maison Alfred Mame et Fils.

Patterson, John R. 1991. "Settlement, City and Elite in Samnium and Lycia." In Rich and Wallace-Hadrill 1991:148–68.

Patterson, Stephen J. 1992a. "The Gospel of Thomas and the Synoptic Tradition: A Forschungsbericht and Critique." *Forum* 8(1–2):45–97.

————. 1992b. "Gospels, Apocryphal." *ABD* 2:1079–81.

Patton, Carl S. 1915. *Sources of the Synoptic Gospels.* University of Michigan Studies, Humanistic series 5. New York: Macmillan.

Peabody, David B. 1983. "Augustine and the Augustinian Hypothesis: A Reexamination of Augustine's Thought in De Consensu Evangelistarum." In *New Synoptic Studies: The Cambridge Gospel Conference and Beyond*, ed. William R. Farmer, 37–64. Macon, Ga.: Mercer Univ. Press.

————. 1987. "Chapters in the History of the Linguistic Argument for Solving the Synoptic Problem: The Nineteenth Century in Context." In *Jesus, the Gospels, and the Church: Essays in Honor of William R. Farmer*, ed. E. P. Sanders, 61–65. Macon, Ga.: Mercer Univ. Press.

————. 1995. "H. J. Holtzmann and His European Colleagues: Aspects of the Nineteenth Century European Discussion of Gospel Origins." In Reventlow and Farmer 1995:50–131.

Pearson, Birger A. 1971. "1 Thessalonians 2:13-16: A Deutero-Pauline Interpolation." *HTR* 64:79–94.

————. 1995. "The Gospel according to the Jesus Seminar." *Religion* 25:317–38.

Perdue, Leo G. 1990. "Cosmology and the Social Order in the Wisdom Tradition." In Gammie and Perdue 1990:457–78.

Perdue, Leo G., Bernard Brandon Scott, and William J. Wiseman, eds. 1993. *In*

Search of Wisdom: Essays in Memory of John G. Gammie. Louisville: Westminster John Knox.

Perelman, Chaim, and Lucie Olbrechts-Tyteca. 1969. *The New Rhetoric: A Treatise on Argumentation*. Trans. John Wilkinson and Purcell Weaver. Notre Dame, Ind.: Univ. of Notre Dame Press.

Perrin, Norman. 1968. "The Son of Man in the Synoptic Tradition." *BR* 13:3–25.

———. 1969. *What Is Redaction Criticism?* Guides to Biblical Scholarship. Philadelphia: Fortress Press.

———. 1974a. *A Modern Pilgrimage in New Testament Christology*. Philadelphia: Fortress Press.

———. 1974b. *The New Testament: An Introduction: Proclamation and Parenesis, Myth and History*. New York: Harcourt Brace Jovanovich.

Perrin, Norman, and Dennis Duling. 1982. *The New Testament: An Introduction: Proclamation and Parenesis, Myth and History*. 2d ed. New York: Harcourt Brace Jovanovich.

Petersen, Norman R. 1978. *Literary Criticism for New Testament Critics*. Guides to Biblical Scholarship: New Testament. Philadelphia: Fortress Press.

Piper, Ronald A. 1982. "Matthew 7,7-11 Par. Lk 11,9-13: Evidence of Design and Argument in the Collection of Jesus' Sayings." In Delobel 1982:411–18.

———. 1989. *Wisdom in the Q-tradition: The Aphoristic Teaching of Jesus*. SNTSMS 61. Cambridge and New York: Cambridge Univ. Press.

———. 1994. "Matthew 7:7-11 Par. Luke 11:9-13: Evidence of Design and Argument in the Collection of Jesus' Sayings." In Kloppenborg 1994b:131–37.

———. 1995a. *The Gospel behind the Gospels: Current Studies on Q*. NovTSup 75. Leiden: E. J. Brill.

———. 1995b. "The Language of Violence and the Aphoristic Sayings in Q: A Study of Q 6:27-36." In Kloppenborg 1995a:53–72.

Plaskow, Judith. 1990. *Standing Again at Sinai: Judaism from a Feminist Perspective*. San Francisco: Harper & Row.

Polag, Athanasius. 1966. "Der Umfang der Logienquelle." Lizentiatsarbeit, Univ. of Trier.

———. 1977. *Die Christologie der Logienquelle*. WMANT 45. Neukirchen-Vluyn: Neukirchener Verlag (Dr. Theol. diss., Trier, 1969).

———. 1979. *Fragmenta Q: Textheft zur Logienquelle*. Neukirchen-Vluyn: Neukirchener Verlag.

———. 1986. "The Text of Q." In *Q: The Sayings of Jesus*, ed. and trans. Ivan Havener, 109–65. Good News Studies 19. Wilmington, Del.: Michael Glazier.

———. 1991. "The Theological Center of the Sayings Source." In *The Gospel and the Gospels*, ed. Peter Stuhlmacher, 97–105. Grand Rapids, Mich.: Eerdmans.

Pölzl, Francis X., and Theodor Innitzer. 1932. *Kommentar zum Evangelium des heiligen Matthäus mit Ausschluß der Leidensgeschichte*. 4. Aufl. Kurzgefaßter Kommentar zu den vier heiligen Evangelien 1. Graz: Styria.

Pouilly, Jean. 1976. *La Règle de la communauté de Qumrân. Son évolution littéraire*. Cahiers de la Revue biblique 17. Paris: J. Gabalda et Cie.

Preisigke, Friedrich. 1903. *Städtisches Beamtenwesen im römischen Ägypten*. Halle: Max Niemeyer.

Pritchard, James B. 1969. *Ancient Near Eastern Texts Relating to the Old Testament*. 3d ed. with Supplement. Princeton, N.J.: Princeton Univ. Press.

Puech, Émile. 1979. "Recension: J. Pouilly, *La Règle de la Communauté de Qumran. Son évolution littéraire.*" *RevQ* 10(37):103–11.

———. 1992. "Une apocalypse messianique *(4Q521).*" *RevQ* 15(60):475–522, with plates.

Qimron, Elisha, and John Strugnell. 1994. *Qumran Cave 4. V: Miqsat Maase Ha-Torah.* DJD 10. Oxford: Clarendon.

Quasten, Johannes. 1966. *Patrology.* 3 vols. Utrecht: Spectrum.

Quinn, Kenneth. 1982. "The Poet and His Audience in the Augustan Age." *ANRW* II.30.1:75–180.

Rahner, Karl. 1978. *Foundations of Christian Faith: An Introduction to the Idea of Christianity.* New York: Seabury Press.

Rajak, Tessa. 1983. *Josephus: The Historian and His Society.* London: Duckworth.

Rappaport, Uriel. 1992. "How Anti-Roman Was the Galilee?" In L. I. Levine 1992:95–102.

Rast, Walter. 1987. "Bab Edh-Dhra and the Origin of the Sodom Saga." In *Archaeology and Biblical Interpretations: Essays in Memory of D. Glenn Rose,* ed. Leo G. Perdue, L. E. Tombs, and G. L. Johnson, 185–201. Atlanta: John Knox.

Raynor, Joyce Toby, and Ya'akov Meshorer. 1988. *The Coins of Ancient Meiron.* In collaboration with Richard Simon Hanson. Meiron Excavation Project 4. [Cambridge, Mass.]: ASOR; Winona Lake, Ind.: Eisenbrauns.

Redfield, Robert. 1965. *Peasant Society and Culture: An Anthropological Approach to Civilization.* Chicago: Univ. of Chicago Press.

Reed, Jonathan L. 1992a. *The Population of Capernaum.* Institute for Antiquity and Christianity, Occasional Papers 24. Claremont: Institute for Antiquity and Christianity.

———. 1992b. "The Social Map of Q." Paper Presented at the 1992 Annual Meeting of the Society of Biblical Literature, San Francisco (=Reed 1995).

———. 1994a. "Places in Early Christianity: Galilee, Archaeology, Urbanization, and Q." Ph.D. diss., Claremont Graduate School.

———. 1994b. "Populations Numbers, Urbanization, and Economics: Galilean Archaeology and the Historical Jesus." In *Society of Biblical Literature 1994 Seminar Papers,* ed. Eugene H. Lovering, 203–19. SBLSP 33. Atlanta: Scholars Press.

———. 1995 <1992b>. "The Social Map of Q." In Kloppenborg 1995a:17–36.

———. 1996. "The Sign of Jonah (Q 11:29-32) and Other Epic Traditions in Q." In Castelli and Taussig 1996:130–43.

Reich, Ronny. 1984. "A *Miqweh* at *'Isawiya near Jerusalem.*" *IEJ* 34:220–23.

———. 1990. "Miqwa'ôt (Jewish Ritual Baths) in the Second Temple Period and the Period of the Mishnah and Talmud (Hebrew)." Ph.D. diss., Hebrew Univ. of Jerusalem.

———. 1993. "The Great Mikveh Debate." *BAR* 19 (March–April):52–53.

Reicke, Bo I. 1976. "Griesbach und die synoptische Frage: Beitrag zu einem Griesbach-Symposium an der Universität Münster im Juli 1976." *TZ* 32:341–59.

———. 1978. "Griesbach's Answer to the Synoptic Question." In *J. J. Griesbach, Synoptic and Text Critical Studies,* 1776–1976, ed. Bernard Orchard and Thomas R. W. Longstaff, 50–73, 198–200. SNTSMS 34. Cambridge and New York: Cambridge Univ. Press.

———. 1986. *The Roots of the Synoptic Gospels.* Philadelphia: Fortress Press.

————. 1987. "From Strauss to Holtzmann and Meijboom: Synoptic Theories Advanced During the Consolidation of Germany, 1830–70." *NovT* 29:1–21.

————. 1990. "The History of the Synoptic Discussion." Dungan 1990a:291–316.

Reimarus, Hermann Samuel. 1774–78. *Fragmente des Wolfenbüttelschen Ungenannten.* Ed. Gotthold Ephraim Lessing. Berlin: In der Sanderschen Buchhandlung (C. M. Eichhoff).

————. 1778. "Von dem Zwecke Jesu und seiner Jünger." In *Fragmente des Wolfenbüttelschen Ungenannten,* ed. Gotthold Ephraim Lessing. Berlin: In der Sanderschen Buchhandlung (C.M. Eichhoff).

————. 1970 <1774–78>. *Fragments.* Ed. Charles H. Talbert. Trans. Ralph S. Fraser. Lives of Jesus Series. Philadelphia: Fortress Press.

————. 1972 <1760–68>. *Apologie, oder, Schutzschrift für die vernünftigen Verehrer Gottes.* Ed. Gerhard Alexander. 2 vols. Frankfurt am Main: Insel Verlag [composed in 1760–68 but not published until 1972].

Renan, Ernest. 1863a <1863>. *The Life of Jesus.* Origins of Christianity 1. London: Trübner.

————. 1863b. *Vie de Jésus.* Histoire des origines du christianisme 1. Paris: Michel Levy Frères; éd. 1–10, 1863; éd. 11–12, 1864; éd. 13, 1867; éd. 15. 1876; éd 16. 1879; éd. 17. 1882; éd. 19–24. Paris: Calmann Lévy, 1888–95 (1916, 1923, 1964); Paris: Aubry, 1945; Paris: Gallimard 1974.

Resch, Alfred. 1897. "'Τὰ λόγια Ἰησοῦ.' Ein Beitrag zur synoptischen Evangelienforschung." In *Theologische Studien Herrn. Wirkl. Oberkonsistorialrath Professor D. Bernhard Weiss zu seinem 70. Geburtstag dargebracht,* 95–128. Göttingen: Vandenhoeck & Ruprecht.

————. 1898. *Die Logia Jesu nach dem Griechischen und Hebräischen Text wiederhergestellt.* Leipzig: J. C. Hinrichs.

————. 1906. *Agrapha: Aussercanonische Schriftfragmente.* 2. Aufl. TU NF 15/3–4. Leipzig: J. C. Hinrichs.

Reventlow, Henning Graf. 1995. "Conditions and Presuppositions of Biblical Criticism in Germany in the Period of the Second Empire and Before: The Case of Heinrich Julius Holtzmann." In Reventlow and Farmer 1995:272–90.

Reventlow, Henning Graf, and William R. Farmer, eds. 1995. *Biblical Studies and the Shifting of Paradigms, 1850–1914.* JSOTSup 192. Sheffield: Sheffield Academic Press.

Rich, John, ed. 1992. *The City in Late Antiquity.* Leichester-Nottingham Studies in Ancient Society 3. London and New York: Routledge.

Rich, John, and Andrew Wallace-Hadrill, eds. 1991. *City and Country in the Ancient World.* Leichester-Nottingham Studies in Ancient Society 2. London and New York: Routledge.

Riddle, Donald Wayne. 1936. *Early Christian Life as Reflected in Its Literature.* Chicago: Willett, Clark.

Ritschl, Albrecht B. 1846. *Das Evangelium Marcions und das kanonische Evangelium des Lucas: eine kritische Untersuchung.* Tübingen: Osiander.

————. 1851. "Ueber den gegenwärtigen Stand der Kritik der synoptischen Evangelien." *ThJb(T)* 10:480–538.

Robbins, Vernon K. 1984. *Jesus the Teacher: A Socio-Rhetorical Interpretation of Mark.* Philadelphia: Fortress Press.

————. 1988. "The Chreia." In *Greco-Roman Literature and the New Testament:*

Selected Forms and Genres, ed. David E. Aune, 1–23. SBLSBS 21. Altanta: Scholars Press.

———. 1989. *Ancient Quotes and Anecdotes: From Crib to Crypt.* Sonoma, Calif.: Polebridge.

———. 1994. "Oral, Rhetorical, and Literary Cultures: A Response." In *Orality and Textuality in Early Christian Literature,* ed. Joanna Dewey, 75–91. Semeia 65. Atlanta: Society of Biblical Literature.

———. 1996a. *Exploring the Texture of Texts: A Guide to Socio-Rhetorical Interpretation.* Valley Forge, Pa.: Trinity Press International.

———. 1996b. *The Tapestry of Early Christian Discourse: Rhetoric, Society and Ideology.* London and New York: Routledge.

Robinson, J. Armitage. 1902. *The Study of the Gospels.* London: Longmans, Green.

Robinson, James M. 1962. "Basic Shifts in German Theology." *Interp* 16:76–97.

———. 1964. "ΛΟΓΟΙ ΣΟΦΩΝ: Zur Gattung der Spruchquelle Q." In *Zeit und Geschichte: Dankesgabe an Rudolf Bultmann,* ed. Erich Dinkler, 77–96. Tübingen: J. C. B. Mohr (Paul Siebeck).

———. 1970–71. "On the Gattung of Mark (and John)." In *Jesus and Man's Hope: Pittsburgh Theological Seminary Festival on the Gospels,* ed. David G. Buttrick, 1:99–129. Perspective 11/1–2. Pittsburgh: Pittsburgh Theological Seminary.

———. 1971a. "Dismantling and Reassembling the Categories of New Testament Scholarship." In *Trajectories through Early Christianity,* James M. Robinson, and Helmut Koester, 1–19. Philadelphia: Fortress Press.

———. 1971b <1964>. "LOGOI SOPHON: On the Gattung of Q." In *Trajectories through Early Christianity,* by James M. Robinson and Helmut Koester, 71–113. Philadelphia: Fortress Press.

———. 1982. "Jesus—From Easter to Valentinus (or to the Apostles' Creed)." *JBL* 101:5–37.

———. 1990. "The International Q Project Work Session 17 November 1989." *JBL* 109:499–501.

———. 1991a. "The International Q Project Work Session 16 November 1990." *JBL* 110:494–98.

———. 1991b. "The Q Trajectory: Between John and Matthew via Jesus." In *The Future of Early Christianity: Essays in Honor of Helmut Koester,* ed. Birger A. Pearson, 173–94. Minneapolis: Fortress Press.

———. 1992a. "The International Q Project Work Session 16 November 1991." *JBL* 111:500–508.

———. 1992b. "The Sayings Gospel Q." In Van Segbroeck et al. 1992:361–88.

———. 1993. "Die Logienquelle: Weisheit oder Prophetie? Anfragen an Migaku Sato, Q und Prophetie." *EvT* 53:367–89.

———. 1994a. "The History-of-Religions Taxonomy of Q: The Cynic Hypothesis." In *Gnosisforschung und Religionsgeschichte: Festschrift für Kurt Rudolph zum 65. Geburtstag,* ed. Holger Preißler and Hubert Seiwert, 247–65. Marburg: Diagonal-Verlag.

———. 1994b. "The Son of Man in the Sayings Gospel Q." In *Tradition und Translation: Zum Problem der interkulturellen Übersetzbarkeit religiöser Phänomene. Festschrift für Carsten Colpe zum 65. Geburtstag,* ed. Christoph Elsas, 315–35. Berlin and New York: Walter de Gruyter.

———. 1995. "The Incipit of the Sayings Gospel Q." *RHPR* 75:9–33.

―――. 1996. "Building Blocks in the Social History of Q." In Castelli and Taussig 1996:87–112.

―――. 1997. "Galilean Upstarts: A Sot's Cynical Disciples?" In *The Canonical and Non-Canonical Sayings of Jesus: Collected Essays in Honour of Tjitze Baarda*, ed. W. L. Petersen, J. S. Vos, and H. J. de Jonge, 223–49. NovTSup 66. Leiden: E. J. Brill.

Robinson, James M., John S. Kloppenborg, and Paul Hoffmann, gen. eds. 1996–. *Documenta Q: Reconstructions of Q through Two Centuries of Gospel Research.* Ed. Stanley D. Anderson, Sterling G. Bjorndahl, Shawn Carruth, Robert Derrenbacker, and Christoph Heil. Louvain: Peeters.

Robinson, James M., Paul Hoffmann, and John S. Kloppenborg, eds. 2000. *The Critical Edition of Q: A Synopsis, Including the Gospels of Matthew and Luke, Mark and Thomas, with English, German and French Translations of Q and Thomas.* Managing editor, Milton C. Moreland. Louvain: Peeters; Minneapolis: Fortress Press.

Rohrbaugh, Richard L. 1991. "The Pre-Industrial City in Luke-Acts." In *The Social World of Luke-Acts: Models for Interpretation*, ed. Jerome H. Neyrey, 125–49. Peabody Mass.: Hendrickson.

―――. 1993. "A Peasant Reading of the Parable of the Talents/Pounds: A Text of Terror?" *BTB* 23:32–39.

Rolland, Philippe. 1984. *Les premiers évangiles: un nouveau regard sur le problème synoptique.* Lectio divina 116. Paris: Les Éditions du Cerf.

Rollmann, Hans. 1995. "Baron Friedrich von Hügel and the Conveyance of German Protestant Biblical Criticism in Roman Catholic Modernism." In Reventlow and Farmer 1995:197–222.

Rome and the Study of Scripture: A Collection of Papal Enactments on the Study of Holy Scripture Together with the Decisions of the Biblical Commission 1962. 7th. ed., revised and enlarged. St. Meinrad: Grail Publications.

Rordorf, Willy, and A. Tuilier. 1978. *La Doctrine des douze apôtres (Didachè): introduction, texte, traduction, notes, appendice et index.* SC 248. Paris: Les Éditions du Cerf.

Rosché, Theodore R. 1960. "The Words of Jesus and the Future of the 'Q' Hypothesis." *JBL* 79:210–20.

Rosenan, Naftali. 1970. "Climate: Rainfall." In *Atlas of Israel: Cartography, Physical Geography, Human and Economic Geography, History.* 2d English ed., IV/2. Jerusalem: Survey of Israel, Ministry of Labour; Amsterdam: Elsevier.

Safrai, Zeᶜev. 1994. *The Economy of Roman Palestine.* London and New York: Routledge.

Saldarini, Anthony J. 1988a. *Pharisees, Scribes and Sadducees in Palestinian Society: A Sociological Approach.* Wilmington, Del.: Michael Glazier.

―――. 1988b. "Political and Social Roles of the Pharisees and Scribes in Galilee." In *Society of Biblical Literature 1988 Seminar Papers*, ed. David J. Lull, 200–209. SBLSP 27. Atlanta: Scholars Press.

―――. 1988c. "The Social Class of the Pharisees in Mark." In *The Social World of Formative Christianity and Judaism: Essays in Tribute to Howard Clark Kee*, ed. Jacob Neusner et al., 69–77. Philadelphia: Fortress Press.

―――. 1992. "The Gospel of Matthew and Jewish-Christian Conflict in the Galilee." In L. I. Levine 1992:23–38.

———. 1994. *Matthew's Christian-Jewish Community*. Chicago: Univ. of Chicago Press.

Sand, Alexander. 1992. "Die Logia Jesu, die vier Evangelien und der Kanon der neutestamentlichen Schriften." In *Theologie im Werden: Studien zu den theologischen Konzeptionen im Neuen Testament in Zusammenarbeit mit dem Collegium Biblicum München*, ed. Josef Hainz, 125–41. Paderborn: Ferdinand Schöningh.

Sanday, William. 1872. *The Authorship and Historical Character of the Fourth Gospel, Considered in Reference to the Contents of the Gospel Itself: A Critical Essay*. London: Macmillan.

———. 1893. "Gospels." In *Smith's Dictionary of the Bible*, ed. William Smith, 1:217–43. London: J. Murray.

———. 1899–1900. "A Plea for the Logia." *ExpT* 11:471–73.

———. 1911. *(Oxford) Studies in the Synoptic Problem*. Oxford: Clarendon.

Sanders, E. P. 1968–69. "The Argument from Order and the Relationship between Matthew and Luke." *NTS* 15:249–61.

———. 1969. *The Tendencies of the Synoptic Tradition*. SNTSMS 9. Cambridge and London: Cambridge Univ. Press.

———. 1977. *Paul and Palestinian Judaism: A Comparison of Patterns of Religion*. Philadelphia: Fortress Press.

———. 1985. *Jesus and Judaism*. London: SCM.

———. 1992. *Judaism: Practice and Belief 63 BCE–66 CE*. Philadelphia: Trinity Press International.

Sanders, E. P., and Margaret Davies. 1989. *Studying the Synoptic Gospels*. London: SCM; Philadelphia: Trinity Press International.

Sato, Migaku. 1984. "Q und Prophetie: Studien zur Gattungs- und Traditionsgeschichte der Quelle Q." Inauguraldissertation, Evangelisch-Theologische Fakultät, Bern.

———. 1988 <1984>. *Q und Prophetie: Studien zur Gattungs- und Traditionsgeschichte der Quelle Q*. WUNT 2/29. Tübingen: J. C. B. Mohr (Paul Siebeck).

———. 1994 <1988>. "The Shape of the Q-Source." In Kloppenborg 1994b:156–79.

———. 1995. "Wisdom Statements in the Sphere of Prophecy." In Piper 1995a:139–58.

Saunier, Heinrich. 1825. *Ueber die Quellen des Evangeliums des Marcus: Ein Beitrag zu den Untersuchungen über die Entstehung unserer kanonischen Evangelien*. Berlin: F. Duemmler.

Sawicki, Marianne. 1994. "Archaeology as Space Technology: Digging for Gender and Class in the Holy Land." *MTSR* 6:319–48.

———. 1997. "Spatial Management of Gender and Labor in Greco-Roman Galilee." In Edwards and McCollough 1997:7–28.

Schenk, Wolfgang. 1981. *Synopse zur Redenquelle der Evangelien: Q-Synopse und Rekonstruktion in deutscher Übersetzung*. Düsseldorf: Patmos Verlag.

———. 1993. "Die Verwünschung der Küstenorte Q 10,13-15: Zur Funktion der konkreten Ortsangaben und zur Lokalisierung von Q." In *The Synoptic Gospels: Source Criticism and New Literary Criticism*, ed. Camille Focant, 477–90. BETL 110. Louvain: Louvain Univ. Press; Peeters.

Schenkel, Daniel. 1864. *Das Charakterbild Jesu*. 3. Aufl. Wiesbaden: C. W. Kreidel.

————. 1869 <1864>. *A Sketch of the Character of Jesus: A Biblical Essay.* 3d ed. London: Longmans.

Schermann, Theodor. 1907. *Propheten- und Apostellegenden nebst Jüngerkatalogen des Dorotheus und verwandter Texte.* TU 31/3. Leipzig: J. C. Hinrichs.

Schiffman, Lawrence H. 1992. "Was There a Galilean Halakhah?" In L. I. Levine 1992:143–56.

Schillebeeckx, Edward. 1975. *Jezus: het verhaal van een levende.* Bloemendaal: Nelissen.

————. 1979 <1975>. *Jesus: An Experiment in Christology.* Trans. Hubert Hoskins. New York: Seabury Press.

Schleiermacher, Friedrich. 1832. "Über die Zeugnisse des Papias von unsern beiden ersten Evangelien." *TSK* 5:735–68.

————. 1836. "Über die Zeugnisse des Papias von unsern beiden ersten Evangelien." In *Sämmtliche Werke* 1/2, 361–92. Berlin: Georg Reimer.

————. 1864. *Sämmtliche Werke.* Vol. 1/6: *Das Leben Jesu: Vorlesungen an der Universität zu Berlin im Jahr 1832.* Ed. K. A. Rütenik. Berlin: Georg Reimer.

————. 1975 <1864>. *The Life of Jesus.* Lives of Jesus Series. Philadelphia: Fortress Press.

Schlosser, Jacques. 1983. "Lk 17,2 und die Logienquelle." SNTU/A 8:70–78.

Schmeller, Thomas. 1989. *Brechungen: Urchristliche Wandercharismatiker im Prisma soziologisch orientierter Exegese.* SBS 136. Stuttgart: Katholisches Bibelwerk.

Schmid, Josef. 1930. *Matthäus und Lukas: Eine Untersuchung des Verhältnisses ihrer Evangelien.* BibS(F) 23/2–4. Freiburg: Herder.

————. 1949. *Synopse der drei ersten Evangelien mit Beifügung der Johannes-Parallelen.* Regensburg: Friedrich Pustet.

————. 1953. "Markus und der aramäische Matthäus." In *Synoptische Studien Alfred Wikenhauser zum siebzigsten Geburtstag am 22. Februar 1953 dargebracht von Freunden, Kollegen und Schülern,* ed. Josef Schmid and Anton Vögtle, 148–83. Munich: Karl Zink.

————. 1964. "Synoptiker. I. Synoptische Frage." *LTK*[2] 9:1240–45.

Schmidt, Charles. 1885. *The Social Results of Early Christianity.* London: Wm. Isbister.

Schmidt, Daryl. 1977. "The LXX Gattung 'Prophetic Correlative,'" *JBL* 96:517–22.

Schmidt, Karl Ludwig. 1919. *Der Rahmen der Geschichte Jesu: Literarkritische Untersuchungen zur ältesten Jesus-Überlieferung.* Berlin: Trowitsch & Sohn.

————. 1923. "Die Stellung der Evangelien in der allgemeinen Literaturgeschichte." In *EYXAPIΣTHPION: Festschrift Hermann Gunkel,* ed. Hans Schmidt, 50–134. FRLANT 36. Göttingen: Vandenhoeck & Ruprecht.

————. 1929. "Jesus Christus." *RGG*[2] 3:110–51.

————. 1969 <1929>. "Jesus Christ." In *Twentieth Century Theology in the Making,* ed. Jaroslav Pelikan, trans. R. A. Wilson, 1:93–168. London: Collins; New York: Harper & Row.

Schmithals, Walter. 1980. *Das Evangelium nach Lukas.* Zürcher Bibelkommentare NT 3.1. Zürich: Theologischer Verlag.

————. 1985. *Einleitung in die drei ersten Evangelien.* De Gruyter Lehrbuch. Berlin: Walter de Gruyter.

————. 1994. *Theologiegeschichte des Urchristentums: Eine problemgeschichtliche Darstellung.* Stuttgart: Kohlhammer.

———. 1997 <1994>. *The Theology of the First Christians*. Louisville: Westminster John Knox Press.

Schnackenburg, Rudolf. 1953. "Mk 9,33-50." In *Synoptische Studien Alfred Wikenhauser zum siebzigsten Geburtstag am 22. Februar 1953 dargebracht von Freunden, Kollegen und Schülern*, ed. Josef Schmid and Anton Vögtle, 184–206. Munich: Karl Zink.

Schneider, Gerhard. 1977–78. *Das Evangelium nach Lukas*. 2 vols. ÖTKNT 3. Gütersloh: Gütersloher Verlagshaus Mohn; Würzburg: Echter-Verlag.

Scholer, David M. 1986. "Q Bibliography 1981–1986." In *Society of Biblical Literature 1986 Seminar Papers*, ed. David J. Lull, 27–36. SBLASP 25. Atlanta: Scholars Press.

———. 1988. "Q Bibliography 1981–1988." In *Society of Biblical Literature 1988 Seminar Papers*, ed. David J. Lull, 483–95. SBLASP 27. Atlanta: Scholars Press.

———. 1989. "Q Bibliography 1981–1989." In *Society of Biblical Literature 1989 Seminar Papers*, ed. David J. Lull, 23–56. SBLSP 28. Atlanta: Scholars Press.

———. 1990. "Q Bibliography Supplement I: 1990." In *Society of Biblical Literature 1990 Seminar Papers*, ed. David J. Lull, 11–13. SBLSP 29. Atlanta: Scholars Press.

———. 1991. "Q Bibliography Supplement II: 1991." In *Society of Biblical Literature 1991 Seminar Papers*, ed. Eugene H. Lovering, 1–7. SBLSP 30. Atlanta: Scholars Press.

———. 1992. "Q Bibliography Supplement III: 1992." In *Society of Biblical Literature 1992 Seminar Papers*, ed. Eugene H. Lovering, 1–4. SBLSP 31. Atlanta: Scholars Press.

———. 1993. "Q Bibliography Supplement IV: 1993." In *Society of Biblical Literature 1993 Seminar Papers*, ed. Eugene H. Lovering, 1–5. SBLSP 32. Atlanta: Scholars Press.

———. 1994. "Q Bibliography Supplement V: 1994." In *Society of Biblical Literature 1994 Seminar Papers*, ed. Eugene H. Lovering, 1–8. SBLSP 33. Atlanta: Scholars Press.

———. 1995. "Q Bibliography Supplement VI: 1995." In *Society of Biblical Literature 1995 Seminar Papers*, ed. Eugene H. Lovering, 1–5. SBLSP 34. Atlanta: Scholars Press.

———. 1996. "Q Bibliography Supplement VII: 1996." In *Society of Biblical Literature 1996 Seminar Papers*, 1–7. SBLSP 35. Atlanta: Scholars Press.

———. 1997. "Q Bibliography Supplement VIII: 1997." In *Society of Biblical Literature 1997 Seminar Papers*, 750–56. SBLSP 36. Atlanta: Scholars Press.

———. 1998. "Q Bibliography Supplement IX: 1998." In *Society of Biblical Literature 1998 Seminar Papers*, 1005–12. SBLSP 37. Atlanta: Scholars Press.

Scholten, Johann Heinrich. 1869. *Das älteste Evangelium: Kritische Untersuchung der Zusammensetzung, des wechselseitigen Verhältnisses, des geschichtlichen Werths und des Ursprungs der Evangelien nach Matthäus und Marcus*. Elberfeld: R. L. Friderichs.

Schönle, Volker. 1982. *Johannes, Jesus und die Juden: Die theologische Position des Matthäus und des Verfassers der Redenquelle im Lichte von Mt. 11*. BBET 17. Frankfurt am Main and Bern: Peter Lang.

Schottroff, Luise. 1978. "Schafe unter Wölfen: Die Wanderpropheten der Logienquelle." In *Jesus von Nazareth: Hoffnung der Armen*, by Luise Schottroff and Wolfgang Stegemann, 54–88. Stuttgart: Kohlhammer.

————. 1986 <1978>. "Sheep among Wolves: The Wandering Prophets of the Say-ings-Source." In *Jesus and the Hope of the Poor*, by Luise Schottroff and Wolf-gang Stegemann, trans. M. J. O'Connell, 38–66. Maryknoll, N.Y.: Orbis.

————. 1991a. *Itinerant Prophetesses: A Feminist Analysis of the Sayings Source Q*. Institute for Antiquity and Christianity, Occasional Papers 21. Claremont: Insti-tute for Antiquity and Christianity.

————. 1991b. "Wanderprophetinnen: Eine feministische Analyse der Logien-quelle." *EvT* 51:332–44.

————. 1992. "Feminist Observations on the Eschatology of the Sayings Source." Unpublished Paper Presented at the One Hundred and Twenty-Eighth Annual Meeting of the Society of Biblical Literature (Q Section), San Francisco.

Schottroff, Luise, and Wolfgang Stegemann. 1978. *Jesus von Nazareth: Hoffnung der Armen*. Stuttgart: Kohlhammer.

————. 1986 <1978>. *Jesus and the Hope of the Poor*. Trans. Matthew J. O'Con-nell. Maryknoll, N.Y.: Orbis.

Schubart, Wilhelm. 1918. *Einführung in die Papyruskunde*. Berlin: Weidmann.

Schüling, Joachim. 1991. *Studien zum Verhältnis von Logienquelle und Markus-evangelium*. FzB 65. Würzburg: Echter Verlag.

Schulz, Siegfried. 1964. "Die Bedeutung des Markus für die Theologiegeschichte des Urchristentums." *SE* 2 (= TU 87):135–45.

————. 1972. *Q: Die Spruchquelle der Evangelisten*. Zurich: Theologischer Verlag.

————. 1973. "Die Gottesherrschaft ist nahe herbeigekommen (Mt 10,7/Lk 10,9): Der kerygmatische Entwurf der Q-Gemeinde Syriens." In *Das Wort und die Wörter: Festschrift Gerhard Friedrich*, ed. Horst Balz, 57–67. Stuttgart: Kohlhammer.

Schürer, Emil. 1973–87. *The History of the Jewish People in the Age of Jesus Christ (175 B.C.–A.D. 135)*. New English edition. Revised by Géza Vermès, Fergus Mil-lar, Matthew Black, and Martin Goodman. Edinburgh: T. & T. Clark.

Schürmann, Heinz. 1968. "Sprachliche Reminiszenzen an abgeänderte oder ausge-lassene Bestandteile der Redequelle im Lukas- und Matthäusevangelium." In *Traditionsgeschichtliche Untersuchungen zu den synoptischen Evangelien*, by Heinz Schürmann, 111–25. Kommentare und Beiträge zum Alten und Neuen Tes-tament. Düsseldorf: Patmos Verlag.

————. 1969–84. *Das Lukasevangelium. 1: Kommentar zu Kap.1,1-9,50. 2/1: Kommentar zu Kapitel 9,51-11,54*. HTKNT 3/1–2/1. Freiburg: Herder.

————. 1975. "Beobachtungen zum Menschensohn-Titel in der Redequelle." In *Jesus und der Menschensohn: Für Anton Vögtle*, ed. Rudolf Pesch and Rudolf Schnackenburg, 124–47. Freiburg: Herder.

————. 1979. "Jesu ureigenes Todesverständnis: Bemerkungen zur 'impliziten Sote-riologie' Jesu." In *Begegnung mit dem Wort: Festschrift für Heinrich Zimmer-mann*, ed. Josef Zmijewski and Ernst Nellessen, 273–309. BBB 53. Bonn: Peter Hanstein.

————. 1982. "Das Zeugnis der Redenquelle für die Basileia-Verkündigung Jesu." In Delobel 1982:121–200.

————. 1983. *Gottes Reich, Jesu Geschick: Jesu ureigener Tod im Licht seiner Basileia-Verkündigung*. Freiburg: Herder.

————. 1986. "Die Redekomposition wider 'dieses Geschlecht' und seine Führung in der Redenquelle (vgl. Mt 23,1-39 par Lk 11,37-54): Bestand — Akoluthie — Kompositionsformen." *SNTU/A* 11:33–81.

────. 1991. "Zur Kompositionsgeschichte der Redenquelle: Beobachtungen an der lukanischen Q-Vorlage." In *Der Treue Gottes trauen: Beiträge zum Werk des Lukas: Für Gerhard Schneider*, ed. Claus Bussmann and Walter Radl, 326–42. Freiburg: Herder.

────. 1992. "QLk 11,14-36 kompositionsgeschichtlich befragt." In Van Segbroeck et al. 1992:563–86.

────. 1994 <1975>. "Observations on the Son of Man Title in the Speech Source: Its Occurrence in Closing and Introductory Expressions." In Kloppenborg 1994b:74–97.

Schüssler Fiorenza, Elisabeth. 1983. *In Memory of Her: A Feminist Theological Reconstruction of Christian Origins.* New York: Crossroad.

────. 1995. *Jesus: Miriam's Child, Sophia's Prophet: Critical Issues in Feminist Christology.* New York: Continuum.

Schutz, Alfred, and Thomas Luckmann. 1973. *The Structures of the Life-World.* Trans. Richard M. Zaner and H. Tristram Engelhardt Jr. Northwestern University Studies in Phenomenology and Existential Philosophy. Evanston, Ill.: Northwestern Univ. Press.

Schwartz, Seth. 1989. "The 'Judaism' of Samaria and Galilee in Josephus' Version of the Letter of Demetrius I to Jonathan (*Antiquities* 13.48-57)." *HTR* 82:377–91.

────. 1994. "Josephus in Galilee: Rural Patronage and Social Breakdown." In *Josephus and the History of the Greco-Roman Period: Essays in Memory of Morton Smith*, ed. Fausto Parente and Joseph Sievers, 290–306. SPB 41. Leiden: E. J. Brill.

Schwarz, Franz J. 1844. *Neue Untersuchungen über das Verwandtschafts-Verhältniss der synoptischen Evangelien, mit besonderer Berücksichtigung der Hypothese vom schöpferischen Urevangelisten.* Tübingen: H. Laupp.

Schwegler, Albert. 1846. *Das nachapostolische Zeitalter in den Hauptmomenten seiner Entwicklung.* 2 vols. Tübingen: Ludwig Friedrich Fues.

Schweitzer, Albert. 1901. *Das Messianitäts- und Leidensgeheimnis: Eine Skizze des Lebens Jesu.* Das Abendmahl im Zusammenhang mit dem Leben Jesu und der Geschichte des Urchristentums, Heft 2. Tübingen: J. C. B. Mohr (Paul Siebeck).

────. 1906. *Von Reimarus zu Wrede: Eine Geschichte der Leben Jesu Forschung.* Tübingen: J. C. B. Mohr (Paul Siebeck).

────. 1910 <1906>. *The Quest of the Historical Jesus: A Critical Study of Its Progress from Reimarus to Wrede.* Trans. William Montgomery. Preface by F. C. Burkitt. New York: Macmillan; 2d ed. 1948; 3d ed. 1956; new edition, with a new introduction by James M. Robinson, 1968.

Schweizer, Eduard. 1959. "Der Menschensohn: Zur eschatologischen Erwartung Jesu." *ZNW* 50:185–209.

────. 1963. "Der Menschensohn: Zur eschatologischen Erwartung Jesu." In *Neotestamentica: Deutsche und englische Aufsätze, 1951–1963*, 56–84. Zürich: Zwingli.

Scott, Bernard Brandon. 1990. "Jesus as Sage: An Innovating Voice in Common Wisdom." In Gammie and Perdue 1990:399–415.

────. 1993. "The Gospel of Matthew: A Sapiential Performance of an Apocalyptic Discourse." In Perdue et al. 1993:245–62.

Scott, James C. 1977a. "Patronage or Exploitation?" In *Patrons and Clients in*

Mediterranean Societies, ed. Ernest Gellner and John Waterbury, 21–39. London: Duckworth.

———. 1977b. "Protest and Profanations: Agrarian Revolt and the Little Tradition." *Theory and Society* 4:1–38, 211–46.

Scott, James C., and Benedict J. Kerkvliet. 1977 <1973>. "How Traditional Rural Patrons Lose Legitimacy." In *Friends, Followers, and Factions: A Reader in Political Clientelism*, ed. Steffen W. Schmidt et al., 147–61. Berkeley: Univ. of California Press.

Scroggs, Robin. 1975. "The Earliest Christian Communities as Sectarian Movement." In *Christianity, Judaism and Other Greco-Roman Cults: Studies for Morton Smith at Sixty*, ed. Jacob Neusner, 2:1–23. 4 vols. SJLA 12. Leiden: E. J. Brill.

———. 1986. "Sociology and the New Testament." *Listening* 21:138–47.

———. 1993. "The Earliest Christian Communities as Sectarian Movement." In *The Text and the Times: New Testament Essays for Today*, 20–45. Minneapolis: Fortress Press.

Seeley, David. 1992. "Jesus' Death in Q." *NTS* 38:222–34.

———. 1996. "Jesus and the Cynics: A Response to Hans Dieter Betz." *JHC* 3:284–90.

———. 1997. "Jesus and the Cynics Revisited." *JBL* 116:704–12.

Seligman, Jon. 1997. "Naḥal Ḥaggit." *Excavations and Surveys in Israel* 16:61–63.

Sellew, Philip. 1986. "Early Collections of Jesus' Words: The Development of Dominical Discourses." Th.D. diss., Harvard Divinity School.

———. 1990. "Argument and Design in the Q Sermon." Paper Presented at the One Hundred and Twenty-Sixth Annual Meeting of the Society of Biblical Literature (Q Section), New Orleans, Louisiana.

———. 1992. "Eusebius and the Gospels." In *Eusebius, Christianity, and Judaism*, ed. Harold W. Attridge and Gohei Hata, 110–38. Studia post-Biblica 42. Leiden: E. J. Brill.

Sevenich-Bax, Elisabeth. 1993. *Israels Konfrontation mit den letzten Boten der Weisheit: Form, Funktion und Interdependenz der Weisheitselemente in der Logienquelle*. Münsteraner theologische Abhandlungen 21. Altenberge: Oros.

Shanin, Teodor. 1971. "Peasantry as a Political Factor." In *Peasants and Peasant Societies*, ed. Teodor Shanin, 238–63. Harmondsworth: Penguin.

Shaw, Brent D. 1984. "Bandits in the Roman Empire." *P&P* 105:5–52.

———. 1993. "Tyrants, Bandits and Kings: Personal Power in Josephus." *JJS* 44:176–204.

Sheppard, Gerald T. 1980. *Wisdom as a Hermeneutical Construct: A Study in the Sapientializing of the Old Testament*. BZAW 151. Berlin and New York: Walter de Gruyter.

Sherwin-White, A. N. 1963. *Roman Society and Roman Law in the New Testament*. Oxford: Oxford Univ. Press.

Shuler, Philip L. 1982. *A Genre for the Gospels: The Biographical Character of Matthew*. Philadelphia: Fortress Press.

———. 1990. "The Genre(s) of the Gospels." In Dungan 1990a:459–83, with a response by Peter Stuhlmacher (484–94) and a "Nachtrag" by Shuler (495–96).

Sickenberger, Joseph. 1911. "Das neue Dekret der Bibelkommission über das Mt-Evangelium und die sog. Zweiquellentheorie." *BZ* 9:391–96.

———. 1916. *Kurzgefasste Einleitung in das Neue Testament*. Freiburg: Herder; 2. Aufl. 1920; 3–4. Aufl. 1925.

———. 1933. "Drei angebliche Hinweise auf die Matthäuspriorität." *BZ* 31:1–8.

Sieffert, Friedrich L. 1832. *Über den Ursprung des ersten kanonischen Evangeliums: Eine kritische Abhandlung.* Königsberg: J. H. Bon.

Simons, Eduard. 1880. *Hat der dritte Evangelist den kanonischen Matthäus benutzt?* Bonn: Carl Georgi.

Skehan, Patrick W. 1971. *Studies in Israelite Poetry and Wisdom.* CBQMS 1. Washington: Catholic Biblical Association of America.

Skladny, Udo. 1962. *Die ältesten Spruchsammlungen in Israel.* Göttingen: Vandenhoeck & Ruprecht.

Smith, Jonathan Z. 1975a. "The Social Description of Early Christianity." *RSR* 1:19–25.

———. 1975b. "Wisdom and Apocalyptic." In *Religious Syncretism in Antiquity: Essays in Conversation with Geo Widengren,* ed. Birger A. Pearson, 131–56. Missoula, Mont.: Scholars Press.

———. 1978. *Map Is Not Territory: Studies in the History of Religions.* SJLA 23. Leiden: E. J. Brill.

———. 1990. *Drudgery Divine: On the Comparison of Early Christianities and the Religions of Late Antiquity.* London: The School of Oriental and African Studies; Chicago: Univ. of Chicago Press.

Soiron, Thaddaeus. 1916. *Die Logia Jesu: Eine literarkritische und literargeschichtliche Untersuchung zum synoptischen Problem.* NTAbh 6/4. Münster: Aschendorff.

Sokoloff, Michael. 1990. *A Dictionary of Jewish Palestinian Aramaic.* Dictionaries of Talmud, Midrach and Targumim 2. Ramat-Gan: Bar Ilan Univ. Press.

Sokolowski, Franciszek. 1955. *Lois sacrées de l'Asie Mineure.* École française d'Athènes. Travaux et mémoires, fasc. 9. Paris: E. de Boccard.

———. 1962. *Lois sacrées des cités grecques: supplément.* École française d'Athènes. Travaux et mémoires, fasc. 11. Paris: E. de Boccard.

———. 1969. *Lois sacrées des cités grecques.* École française d'Athènes. Travaux et mémoires, fasc. 18. Paris: E. de Boccard.

Solages, Bruno de. 1959. *Synopse grecque des évangiles: Méthode nouvelle pour résoudre le problème synoptique.* Preface by Eugène Cardinal Tisserant. Leiden: E. J. Brill; Toulouse: Institut Catholique.

———. 1973. *La composition des évangiles: de Luc et de Matthieu et leurs sources.* Leiden: E. J. Brill.

Sparks, H. F. D. 1964. *A Synopsis of the Gospels: The Synoptic Gospels with the Johannine Parallels.* London: A. & C. Black.

Sperber, Daniel. 1971. "Mishmarot and Maʿamadot." *EncJud* 12:89–93.

Stanton, Vincent H. 1899. "Gospels." In *Hastings' Dictionary of the Bible,* ed. James Hastings, 2:234–49. Edinburgh: T. & T. Clark.

———. 1903–20. *The Gospels as Historical Documents.* 3 vols. Cambridge: Cambridge Univ. Press.

Steck, Odil H. 1967. *Israel und das gewaltsame Geschick der Propheten: Untersuchungen zur Überlieferung des deuteronomistischen Geschichtsbildes im Alten Testament, Spätjudentum und Urchristentum.* WMANT 23. Neukirchen-Vluyn: Neukirchener Verlag.

Stein, Robert H. 1969. "What Is Redaktionsgeschichte?" *JBL* 88:45–56.

———. 1970. "The 'redaktionsgeschichtlich' Investigation of a Markan Seam (Mc 1 21f.)." *ZNW* 61:70–94.

————. 1971. "The Proper Methodology for Ascertaining a Markan Redaction History." *NovT* 13:181–98.

Steinhauser, Michael G. 1992. "The Violence of Occupation: Matthew 5:40-41 and Q." In *Scriptures and Cultural Conversations: Essays for Heinz Guenther at 65.* = *Toronto Journal of Theology* 8/1, ed. John S. Kloppenborg and Leif E. Vaage, 28–37. Toronto: Univ. of Toronto Press.

Stern, Menahem. 1976. "The Reign of Herod and the Herodian Dynasty." In *The Jewish People in the First Century*, 216–307. CRINT 1/1. Philadelphia: Fortress Press.

Stinchcombe, Arthur. 1961–62. "Agricultural Enterprise and Rural Class Relations." *AJS* 67:165–76.

Stoldt, Hans-Herbert. 1980 <1977>. *History and Criticism of the Marcan Hypothesis*. Trans. Donald L. Niewyk. Macon, Ga.: Mercer Univ. Press; Edinburgh: T. & T. Clark.

Strange, James F. 1992. "Six Campaigns at Sepphoris: The University of South Florida Excavations, 1983–1989." In L. I. Levine 1992:339–55.

————. 1994. "First-Century Galilee from Archaeology and from the Texts." In *Society of Biblical Literature 1994 Seminar Papers*, ed. Eugene H. Lovering, 81–90. SBLSP 33. Atlanta: Scholars Press.

————. 1997. "First Century Galilee from Archaeology and from the Texts." In Edwards and McCollough 1997:39–48.

Strauss, David Friedrich. 1835–36. *Das Leben Jesu: Kritisch bearbeitet*. 2 vols. Tübingen: C. F. Osiander.

————. 1864. *Das Leben Jesu: für das deutsche Volk bearbeitet*. 2 vols. Leipzig: F. A. Brockhaus.

————. 1865. *Der Christus des Glaubens und der Jesus der Geschichte: Eine Kritik des Schleiermacher'schen Lebens Jesu*. Berlin: Duncker.

————. 1879 <1964>. *The Life of Jesus for the People*. 2d ed. 2 vols. London: Williams & Norgate.

————. 1972 <1935–36>. *The Life of Jesus Critically Examined*. Ed. and introd. Peter C. Hodgson. Trans. George Eliot. Lives of Jesus Series. Philadelphia: Fortress Press.

————. 1977 <1865>. *The Christ of Faith and the Jesus of History: A Critique of Schleiermacher's Life of Jesus*. Ed., trans., and introd. Leander E. Keck. Lives of Jesus Series. Philadelphia: Fortress Press.

Strecker, Georg. 1992. *Literaturgeschichte des Neuen Testaments*. Uni-Taschenbücher 1682. Göttingen: Vandenhoeck & Ruprecht.

Streeter, B. H. 1911a. "The Literary Evolution of the Gospels." In Sanday 1911:209–27.

————. 1911b. "On the Original Order of Q." In Sanday 1911:141–64.

————. 1911c. "The Original Extent of Q." In Sanday 1911:185–208.

————. 1911d. "St. Mark's Knowledge and Use of Q." In Sanday 1911:165–83.

————. 1924. *The Four Gospels: A Study of Origins, Treating of the Manuscript Tradition, Sources, Authorship, and Dates*. London: Macmillan.

Stuhlmacher, Peter. 1990. "The Genre(s) of the Gospels: Response to P. L. Shuler." In Dungan 1990a:484–94, with a "Nachtrag" by Shuler (495–96).

Sugirtharajah, Rasiah S. 1990a. "Jesus Research and Third World Christologies." *Theology* 93:387–91.

————. 1990b. "Wisdom, Q, and a Proposal for a Christology." *ExpT* 102:42–46.

————. 1991. "What Do Men Say Remains of Me? Current Jesus Research and Third World Christologies." *AsiaJourTheol* 5:331–37.

Swete, Henry Barclay. 1914. *An Introduction to the Old Testament in Greek.* Rev. ed. Revised by Richard R. Ottley. Cambridge: Cambridge Univ. Press.

Talbert, Charles H. 1977. *What Is a Gospel? The Genre of the Canonical Gospels.* Philadelphia: Fortress Press.

Tannehill, Robert C. 1986. *The Narrative Unity of Luke-Acts: A Literary Interpretation.* Vol. 1: *The Gospel according to Luke.* New Testament. Philadelphia: Fortress Press.

————. 1991. "Beginning to Study 'How Gospels Begin.'" In *How Gospels Begin,* ed. Dennis E. Smith, 185–92. *Semeia* 52. Atlanta: Scholars Press.

Taylor, R. O. P. 1946. *The Groundwork of the Gospels.* Oxford: Basil Blackwell.

Taylor, Vincent. 1953. "The Order of Q." *JTS* 4:27–31.

————. 1959. "The Original Order of Q." In *New Testament Essays: Studies in Memory of T. W. Manson,* ed. A. J. B. Higgins, 246–69. Manchester: Manchester Univ. Press.

Theissen, Gerd. 1973. "Wanderradikalismus: Literatursoziologische Aspekte der Überlieferung von Worten Jesu im Urchristentum." *ZTK* 70:245–71.

————. 1977. *Soziologie der Jesusbewegung: Ein Beitrag zur Entstehungsgeschichte des Urchristentums.* Theologische Existenz Heute 194. Munich: Chr. Kaiser.

————. 1978 <1977>. *Sociology of Early Palestinian Christianity.* Trans. John Bowden. Philadelphia: Fortress Press.

————. 1989. *Lokalkolorit und Zeitgeschichte in den Evangelien: Ein Beitrag zur Geschichte der synoptischen Tradition.* NTOA 8. Göttingen and Fribourg: Vandenhoeck & Ruprecht; Universitätsverlag.

————. 1991 <1989>. *The Gospels in Context: Social and Political History in the Synoptic Tradition.* Trans. Linda M. Maloney. Minneapolis: Fortress Press.

————. 1992 <1973>. "The Wandering Radicals: Light Shed by the Sociology of Literature on the Early Transmission of the Jesus Sayings." In *Social Reality and the Early Christians: Theology, Ethics, and the World of the New Testament,* by Gerd Theissen. Trans. Margaret Kohl, 33–59. Minneapolis: Fortress Press.

Theobald, Christoph. 1992. "Le Père Lagrange et le modernisme." In *Naissance de la méthode critique. Colloque de centenaire de l'École biblique et archéologique française de Jérusalem,* 49–64. Paris: Les Éditions du Cerf.

Tholuck, August. 1838. *Die Glaubwürdigkeit der evangelischen Geschichte: zugleich eine Kritik des Lebens Jesu von Strauss, für theologische und nicht theologische Leser dargestellt.* 2. Aufl. Hamburg: F. A. Perthes.

Throckmorton, Burton H. 1992. *Gospel Parallels: A Comparison of the Synoptic Gospels.* 5th ed., revised and updated. Nashville: Thomas Nelson.

Tischendorf, Constantin von. 1851. *Synopsis Evangelica.* Leipzig: Mendelssohn.

————, ed. 1869–72. *Novum Testamentum Graece.* 8th ed. Critica Maior. 2 vols. Leipzig: Giesecke & Devrient.

Tobin, Thomas H. 1990. "4Q185 and Jewish Wisdom Literature." In *Of Scribes and Scrolls: Studies on the Hebrew Bible, Intertestamental Judaism, and Christian Origins Presented to John Strugnell on the Occasion of His Sixtieth Birthday,* ed. Harold W. Attridge et al., 145–52. College Theology Society Resources in Religion 5. Lanham, Md: Univ. Press of America.

Tobler, J. T. 1858. "Die Evangelienfrage im allgemeinen und die Johannesfrage inbesondere." In *Eine Denkschrift zur Erinnerung an das 25jährige Bestehen der Universität Zürich*. Zurich: Orell, Füssli.

Tödt, Heinz Eduard. 1959. *Der Menschensohn in der synoptischen Überlieferung*. Dr. Theol. diss., Heidelberg, 1956. Gütersloh: Gerd Mohn.

——. 1965 <1959>. *The Son of Man in the Synoptic Tradition*. Trans. D. M. Barton. London: SCM.

Tricot, André. 1948. "La question synoptique." In *Initiation biblique: Introduction à l'étude de saintes écritures*. 2d ed. imprimatur Emmanuel Card. Suhard, Archiep. Parisiensis, ed. André Robert and André Tricot, preface by Achille Card. Liénart, 319–33. Paris: Société de Saint Jean L'Évangeliste.

——. 1954. "La question synoptique." In *Initiation biblique: Introduction à l'étude de saintes écritures*. 3d ed. imprimatur Mauritius Card. Feltin, Archiep. Parisiensis, ed. André Robert and André Tricot, preface by Achille Card. Liénart, 356–74. Paris: Desclée.

Trilling, Wolfgang. 1964. *Das wahre Israel: Studien zur Theologie des Matthäusevangeliums*. 3. Aufl. SANT 10. Munich: Kösel.

Tsafrir, Yoram, Leah Di Segni, and Judith Green. 1994. *Tabula Imperii Romani Iudaea Palaestina: Eretz Israel in the Hellenistic, Roman and Byzantine Periods. Maps and Gazetteer*. Jerusalem: Israel Academy of Sciences and Humanities.

Tuckett, Christopher M. 1979. "The Griesbach Hypothesis in the 19th Century." *JSNT* 3:29–60.

——. 1982. "Luke 4,16-30, Isaiah and Q." In Delobel 1982:343–54.

——. 1983. *The Revival of the Griesbach Hypothesis: An Analysis and Appraisal*. SNTSMS 44. Cambridge and New York: Cambridge Univ. Press.

——. 1989. "A Cynic Q?" *Bib* 70:349–76.

——. 1990. "Response to the Two-Gospel Hypothesis: I. Position Paper. II. The Eschatological Discourse." In Dungan 1990a:47–76, with a note by Neirynck (77–80).

——. 1991. "On the Stratification of Q." In Kloppenborg and Vaage 1991a:213–22.

——. 1992. "The Temptation Narrative in Q." In Van Segbroeck et al. 1992:479–507.

——. 1993. "Mark and Q." In *The Synoptic Gospels: Source Criticism and New Literary Criticism*, ed. Camille Focant, 149–75. BETL 110. Louvain: Louvain Univ. Press; Peeters.

——. 1995. "The Existence of Q." In Piper 1995a:19–47.

——. 1996. *Q and the History of Early Christianity: Studies on Q*. Edinburgh: T. & T. Clark; Peabody, Mass.: Hendrickson.

Turner, Nigel. 1968–69. "Q in Recent Thought." *ExpT* 80:324–28.

Tyson, Joseph B. 1961. "The Blindness of the Disciples in Mark." *JBL* 80:261–68.

Tzaferis, Vassilios. 1989. *Excavations at Capernaum*. Vol. 1: *1978–1982*. Winona Lake, Ind.: Eisenbrauns.

Udoh, Fabian Eugene. 1996. "Tribute and Taxes in Early Roman Palestine (63 BCE–70 CE): The Evidence from Josephus." Ph.D. diss., Duke Univ.

Uro, Risto. 1987. *Sheep among the Wolves: A Study on the Mission Instructions of Q*. Annales Academiae Scientiarum Fennicae. Dissertationes humanarum litterarum 47. Helsinki: Suomalainen Tiedeakatemia.

——. 1996. *Symbols and Strata: Essays on the Sayings Gospel Q*. Suomen

Eksegeettisen Seuran Julkaisuja. Publications of the Finnish Exegetical Society 65. Helsinki: Finnish Exegetical Society; Göttingen: Vandenhoeck & Ruprecht.

Usteri, Leonard. 1832. "Beitrag zur Erklärung der Versuchungsgeschichte." *TSK* 5:768–91.

Vaage, Leif E. 1987. "Q: The Ethos and Ethic of an Itinerant Intelligence." Ph.D. diss., Claremont Graduate School.

———. 1988. "The Woes in Q (and Matthew and Luke): Deciphering the Rhetoric of Criticism." In *Society of Biblical Literature 1988 Seminar Papers*, ed. David J. Lull, 582–607. SBLASP 27. Atlanta: Scholars Press.

———. 1991. "The Son of Man Sayings in Q: Stratigraphical Location and Significance." In Kloppenborg and Vaage 1991a:103–29.

———. 1994. *Galilean Upstarts: Jesus' First Followers according to Q*. Valley Forge, Pa.: Trinity Press International.

———. 1995. "Q and Cynicism: On Comparison and Social Identity." In Piper 1995a:199–229.

———. 1997. "The Scholar as *Engagé*." In Arnal and Desjardins 1997:181–86.

Vaganay, Léon. 1954. *Le problème synoptique: une hypothèse de travail*. Bibliothèque de théologie, série 3: Théologie biblique 1. Tournai: Desclée.

Vannutelli, Primo. 1936. *Evangelia synoptice secundum graecum textum disposita*. Turin: Società Editrice Internazionale.

Van Leeuwen, Raymond C. 1988. *Context and Meaning in Proverbs 25–27*. SBLDS 96. Atlanta: Scholars Press.

———. 1990. "The Sage in the Prophetic Literature." In Gammie and Perdue 1990:295–306.

Van Segbroeck, Frans, C. M. Tuckett, G. Van Belle, and J. Verheyden, eds. 1992. *The Four Gospels 1992: Festschrift Frans Neirynck*. 3 vols. BETL 100. Louvain: Peeters; Louvain Univ. Press.

Vassiliadis, Petros. 1978. "The Nature and Extent of the Q Document." *NovT* 20:49–73.

Vielhauer, Philipp. 1975. *Geschichte der urchristlichen Literatur*. De Gruyter Lehrbuch. Berlin: Walter de Gruyter.

Villeneuve, F. 1985. "L'économie rurale et la vie des campagnes dans le Hauran antique (Ier siècle avant J.-C.–VI^c siècle apres J.-C.): Une approche." In *Hauran I: Recherches archéologiques sur la Syrie du Sud à l'époque hellénistique et romaine*, ed. J. M. Dentzer, 63–136. Institut français d'archéologie du Proche Orient: Bibliothèque archéologique et historique 124. Paris: Paul Geuthner.

Vogels, Heinrich J. 1925. *Grundriss der Einleitung in das Neue Testament*. Lehrbücher zum Gebrauch beim theologischen und philosophischen Studium. Münster: Aschendorff.

Volkmar, Gustav. 1857. *Die Religion Jesu und ihre erste Entwicklung nach dem gegenwärtigen Stande der Wissenschaft*. Leipzig: F. U. Brockhaus.

Vosté, Jacques Marie. 1928. *De synopticorum mutua relatione et dependentia*. Opuscula biblica Pontificii Collegii Angelici. Romae: Collegio Angelico.

Walker, William O. 1987–88. "Order in the Synoptic Gospels: A Critique." *SecCent* 6:83–97.

Weder, Hans. 1978. *Die Gleichnisse Jesu als Metaphern: Traditions- und redaktionsgeschichtliche Analysen und Interpretationen*. FRLANT 120. Göttingen: Vandenhoeck & Ruprecht.

Weeden, Theodore J. 1968. "The Heresy That Necessitated Mark's Gospel." *ZNW* 59:145–58.

————. 1971. *Mark—Traditions in Conflict*. Philadelphia: Fortress Press.

Weiser, Alfons. 1993. *Theologie des Neuen Testaments. II: Die Theologie der Evangelien*. Kohlhammer Studienbücher Theologie 8. Stuttgart: W. Kohlhammer.

Weiss, Bernhard. 1861. "Zur Entstehungsgeschichte der drei synoptischen Evangelien." *TSK* 34:29–100, 646–713.

————. 1883–84. *The Life of Christ*. Trans. J. W. Hope. 3 vols. Clark's Foreign Theological Library. Edinburgh: T. & T. Clark.

————. 1884. *Das Leben Jesu*. 2. Aufl. 2 vols. Berlin: Hertz.

————. 1886. *Lehrbuch der Einleitung in das Neue Testament*. Berlin: W. Hertz.

————. 1887–88 <1986>. *A Manual of Introduction to the New Testament*. Trans. A. J. K. Davidson. 2 vols. London: Hodder & Stoughton.

————. 1907. *Die Quellen des Lukasevangeliums*. Stuttgart and Berlin: J. G. Cotta.

Weiss, Johannes. 1890. "Die Verteidigung Jesu gegen den Vorwurf des Bündnisses mit Beelzebul." *TSK* 63:555–69.

————. 1892. *Die Predigt Jesu vom Reiche Gottes*. Göttingen: Vandenhoeck & Ruprecht.

————. 1907. *Die Schriften des Neuen Testaments*. 2. Aufl. Göttingen: Vandenhoeck & Ruprecht.

Weisse, Christian Hermann. 1838. *Die evangelische Geschichte: Kritisch und philosophisch bearbeitet*. 2 vols. Leipzig: Breitkopf und Härtel.

————. 1856. *Die Evangelienfrage in ihrem gegenwärtigen Stadium*. Leipzig: Breitkopf und Härtel.

Weizsäcker, Carl. 1864. *Untersuchungen über die evangelische Geschichte, ihre Quellen, und den Gang ihrer Entwicklung*. Gotha: Rudolf Besser.

Wellhausen, Julius. 1904a. *Das Evangelium Lucae*. Berlin: Georg Reimer.

————. 1904b. *Das Evangelium Matthaei übersetzt und erklärt*. Berlin: Georg Reimer.

————. 1905. *Einleitung in die drei ersten Evangelien*. Berlin: Georg Reimer.

————. 1911. *Einleitung in die drei ersten Evangelien*. 2. Aufl. Berlin: Georg Reimer.

Wendt, Hans Hinrich. 1886. *Die Lehre Jesu*. Göttingen: Vandenhoeck & Ruprecht.

————. 1892 <1886>. *The Teaching of Jesus*. Trans. John Wilson. Edinburgh: T. & T. Clark.

Wengst, Klaus. 1984. *Didache (Apostellehre), Barnabasbrief, Zweiter Klemensbrief, Schrift an Diognet, eingeleitet, herausgegeben, übertragen und erläutert*. SUC 2. Darmstadt: Wissenschaftliche Buchgesellschaft.

Wernle, Paul. 1899. *Die synoptische Frage*. Leipzig, Freiburg im Breisgau, and Tübingen: J. C. B. Mohr (Paul Siebeck).

————. 1904. *Die Quellen des Leben Jesu*. Religionsgeschichtliche Volksbücher 1/1. Tübingen: J. C. B. Mohr (Paul Siebeck).

Wessely, C. 1902. "Neues über Diogenes den Kyniker." In *Festschrift Theodor Gomperz: dargebracht zum siebzigsten Geburtstage am 29. Marz 1902 von Schülern, Freunden, Kollegen*, 67–74. Vienna: Alfred Hölder; F. Tempsky.

Westcott, Brooke Foss, and F. J. A. Hort, eds. 1881. *The New Testament in the Original Greek*. New York: Macmillan.

Whedbee, J. William. 1971. *Isaiah and Wisdom*. Nashville: Abingdon.

White, L. Michael. 1986. "Sociological Analysis of Early Christian Groups: A Social Historian's Response." *SA* 47:249–66.

Whybray, R. N. 1965. *Wisdom in Proverbs: The Concept of Wisdom in Proverbs 1–9*. SBT 1/45. Naperville, Ill.: A. R. Allenson.

Wikenhauser, Alfred. 1931. "Zur synoptischen Frage." *Römische Quartalschrift* 39:43–61.

———. 1937. "Synoptische Frage." *LTK*[1] 9:949–54.

———. 1953. *Einleitung in das Neue Testament*. Freiburg: Herder; 2. Aufl. 1956.

———. 1958 <1956>. *New Testament Introduction*. Trans. J. Cunningham. New York: Herder & Herder.

Wikenhauser, Alfred, and Josef Schmid. 1973. *Einleitung in das Neue Testament*. 6. Aufl. Freiburg: Herder.

Wilcken, Ulrich. 1897. "Zur Ägyptisch-hellenistischen Litteratur." In *Aegyptiaca: Festschrift für Georg Ebers*, 142–52. Leipzig: Wilhelm Engelmann.

———. 1923. "Alexander der Grosse und die indischen Gymnosophisten." In *Sitzungsberichte der preussischen Akademie der Wissenschaften*, 150–83. Berlin: Verlag der Akademie der Wissenschaften.

Wilckens, Ulrich. 1967. "Tradition de Jésus et kérygma du Christ: la double histoire de la tradition au sein du christianisme primitif." *RHPR* 47:1–20.

Wilke, Christian Gottlob. 1838. *Der Urevangelist, oder, exegetisch-kritische Untersuchung über das Verwandtschaftsverhältniss der drei ersten Evangelien*. Dresden and Leipzig: Gerhard Fleischer.

Wilson, Bryan R. 1973. *Magic and the Millennium: A Sociological Study of Religious Movements of Protest among Tribal and Third-World Peoples*. London: Heinemann.

Witherington, Ben. 1990. *The Christology of Jesus*. Minneapolis: Fortress Press.

———. 1994. *Jesus the Sage: The Pilgrimage of Wisdom*. Minneapolis: Fortress Press.

———. 1995. *The Jesus Quest: The Third Search for the Jew of Nazareth*. Downers Grove, Ill.: InterVarsity.

Wittgenstein, Ludwig. 1922. *Tractatus logico-philosophicus*. Introd. Bertrand Russell. Trans. C. K. Ogden. London: Routledge & Kegan Paul; New York: Harcourt, Brace,

———. 1958. *Philosophical Investigations. Philosophische Untersuchungen*. 2d ed. Trans. G. E. M. Anscombe. Oxford: Basil Blackwell.

Woods, F. H. 1886–90. "The Origin and Mutual Relations of the Synoptic Gospels." In *Studia Biblica et Ecclesiastica: Essays Chiefly in Biblical and Patristic Criticism*, ed. S. R. Driver, T. K. Cheyne, and W. Sanday, 2:59–104. Oxford: Clarendon.

Wolff, Hans Walter. 1964. *Amos' Geistige Heimat*. WMANT 18. Neukirchen-Vluyn: Neukirchener Verlag.

———. 1973 <1964>. *Amos, the Prophet: The Man and His Background*. Trans. Foster R. McCurley. Philadelphia: Fortress Press.

World Council of Churches. 1972. *Classified Catalog of the Ecumenical Movement*. 2 vols. Boston: G. K. Hall.

Worsley, Peter. 1968. *The Trumpet Shall Sound: A Study of "Cargo" Cults in Melanesia*. 2d ed. London: MacGibbon & Kee.

Wrede, William. 1901. *Das Messiasgeheimnis in den Evangelien*. Göttingen: Vandenhoeck & Ruprecht.

———. 1971 <1901>. *The Messianic Secret*. Trans. J. C. G. Greig. Foreword by James M. Robinson. Greenwood, S.C.: Attic.

Wright, Benjamin G. 1997. "Jewish Ritual Baths—Interpreting the Digs and the Texts: Some Issues in the Social History of Second Temple Judaism." In *The*

Archaeology of Israel: Constructing the Past, Interpreting the Present, ed. Neil Asher Silberman and David B. Small, 190–214. JSOTSup 237. Sheffield: Sheffield Academic Press.

Wright, N. T. 1992. *The New Testament and the People of God*. Christian Origins and the Question of God 1. Minneapolis: Fortress Press; London: SPCK.

————. 1996. *Jesus and the Victory of God*. Christian Origins and the Question of God 2. Minneapolis: Fortress Press; London: SPCK.

Wrigley, Edward A. 1978. "Parasite or Stimulus: The Town in a Pre-industrial Economy." In *Towns in Societies: Essays in Economic History and Historical Sociology*, ed. Philip Abrams and Edward A. Wrigley, 295–309. Cambridge: Cambridge Univ. Press.

Yarbro Collins, Adela. 1987. "The Origin and Designation of Jesus as 'Son of Man.'" *HTR* 80:391–407.

Yeivin, Zeʿev. 1987. "Ancient Chorazin Comes Back to Life." *BAR* 13(5):22–36.

Youtie, Herbert C. 1975a. "Ὑπογραφεύς: The Social Impact of Illiteracy in Graeco-Roman Egypt." *ZPE* 17:201–21.

————. 1975b. "'Because They Do Not Know Letters.'" *ZPE* 19:101–8.

Zahn, Theodor. 1922. *Das Evangelium des Matthäus*. 4. Aufl. Leipzig: Deichert.

Zeller, Dieter. 1972. "Das Logion Mt 8,11f/Lk 13,28f und das Motif der Völkerwallfahrt." *BZ* NF 16:84–93.

————. 1975. "Der Zusammenhang der Eschatologie in der Logienquelle." In *Gegenwart und kommendes Reich: Schülergabe Anton Vögtle zum 65. Geburtstag*, ed. Peter Fiedler and Dieter Zeller, 67–77. Stuttgart: Katholisches Bibelwerk.

————. 1977. *Die weisheitlichen Mahnsprüche bei den Synoptikern*. FzB 17. Würzburg: Echter.

————. 1980. "Die Versuchungen Jesu in der Logienquelle." *TTZ* 89:61–73.

————. 1982. "Redaktionsprozesse und wechselnder 'Sitz im Leben' beim Q-Material." In Delobel 1982:395–409.

————. 1984. *Kommentar zur Logienquelle*. Stuttgarter kleiner Kommentar, Neues Testament 21. Stuttgart: Katholisches Bibelwerk.

————. 1985. "Entrückung zur Ankunft als Menschensohn (Lk 13,34f.; 11:29f.)." In *À cause de l'évangile: études sur les Synoptiques et les Actes: offertes au P. Jacques Dupont, O.S.B. à l'occasion de son 70ᵉ anniversaire*, 513–30. Lectio divina 123. Paris: Publications de Saint-André; Les Éditions du Cerf.

————. 1992. "Eine weisheitliche Grundschrift in der Logienquelle?" In Van Segbroeck et al. 1992:389–401.

————. 1994 <1982>. "Redactional Processes and Changing Settings in the Q Material." In Kloppenborg 1994b:116–30.

Zeller, Eduard. 1843a. "Studien zur neutestamentlichen Theologie 4: Vergleichende Uebersicht über den Wörtervorrath der neutestamentlichen Schriftsteller." *ThJb(T)* 2:443–543.

————. 1843b. "Über den dogmatischen Charakter des dritten Evangeliums, mit besonderer Rücksicht auf sein Verhältniss zur Apostelgeschichte und zum Johannesevangelium." *ThJb(T)* 2:59–90.

————. 1864. "Strauss und Renan." *Historische Zeitschrift* 12:70–133.

————. 1865. "Zum Markusevangelium." *ZWT* 8:308–28, 385–408.

Zimmermann, Heinrich. 1974. *Neutestamentliche Methodenlehre: Darstellung der historisch-kritischen Methode*. 4. Aufl. Stuttgart: Katholisches Bibelwerk.

Index of Authors

Abel, F. M., 222
Adam, A. K. M., 220
Adan-Bayewitz, D., 212, 215, 219, 231, 240, 427
Aland, K., 14, 46, 342
Alfaric, P., 410
Allen, W. C., 338, 339
Allison, D., 73, 81, 84, 116–17, 133, 146
Allison, H., 278
Anonymous, 284
Applebaum, S., 214, 239
Arav, R., 173, 215
Argyle, A. W., 152
Arnal, W. E., 93, 97, 172, *239–42*, 260, 412, 421, 428, 434, 437
Attridge, H. W., 109, 118, 337, 424
Audet, J. P., 134
Aune, D. E., 400–401, 406, 421, 426, 428, 431
Aviᶜam, M., 215, 220–22, 231
Avigad, N., 232
Avi-Yonah, M., 218, 222, 236, 243, 257, 426

Bacon, B. W., 332, 338–39, 343, 347
Bagnall, R., 194
Bailey, K. E., 57

Baines, J., 166
Baird, W., 285, 286
Baltzer, K., 406
Bammel, E., 61
Bar-Ilan, M., 166
Barnes, A. S., 88, 315
Barrett, C. K., 61
Barth, K., 277
Batiffol, P., 315, 321, 323, 340, 407
Batten, A. J., 97
Bauer, B., 314
Baumgarten, J. M., 230, 233
Bauer, W., 348
Baur, F. C., 282–83, *284–85*, 286–90, 304, 311, 326–27, 332, 342, 352
Bellinzoni, A. J., 27
Ben-David, A., 238
Benoit, P., 46, 320
Bergemann, T., 61–62, 64–66, 72
Bernand, E., 159
Betz, H. D., 90, 106, 381, 421, 428–30
Beyschlag, W., 310
Bigelmair, A., 410
Bigler, R. M., 286
Bilde, P., 83
Billerbeck, M., 423–24
Biran, A., 223
Bitzer, L. F., 169
Black, M., *74–80*
Blank, S. H., 82, 206

Blasi, A. J., 182
Bleek, F., 331
Blok, A., 250
Boismard, M.-E., 14, 38, 43, *46–50*, 51–53
Booth, A. D., 166
Boring, M. E., 355, 376
Bösen, D. W., 215
Bovon, F., 36, 110
Braun, W., 205
Broer, I., 153
Broshi, M., 426
Brown, R. E., 346
Brunner, H., 132
Brunt, P. A., 237
Büchler, A., 244
Bultmann, R., 97, 135, 152, 343–45, 348, 352, 364–65, 384, 399, 402, 413–14, 438
Bundy, W. E., 92
Burgess, J. A., 314
Burke, K., 122
Burkitt, F. C., 327, 331–32, 337, 339
Burney, C. F., 88
Burridge, R. A., 159, *161–62*, 400
Burton, E., 28, 46, 62, 90, 333
Bussby, F., 73
Bussmann, W., 61, 88, 343
Butler, B. C., 26–27, 38, 297, 317
Butts, J. R., 201

519

Index of Ancient Texts

Index of Subjects